BLESSED

Are The Poor In Spirit

Dr. John H. Manigo

BOOK 2

BLESSED ARE THE POOR IN SPIRIT—BOOK 2

ISBN (Paperback): 978-1-964494-27-2
ISBN (Ebook): 978-1-964494-28-9

Printed in the United States of America.

PROMINENT
BOOKS
EDGE

5830 E 2nd St, Ste 7000 #9983
Casper, WY 82609
USA

Contents

About the Author

First of all, I am hard of hearing. People do not think that I am deaf or hard of hearing or hearing impaired. They believe that I can hear. That is simple. They look at me like as if I am normal hearing person.

I am African-American. I was born in Conway, South Carolina. I went to Conway Elementary School for four and an half years. Due to my hearing problem, I stayed home for one year.

I moved to Spartanburg, South Carolina to live at the South Carolina School for the Deaf and the Blind. The campus of Cedar Spring School for the Deaf and the Blind look like a college or institution. I lodged in a dormitory for nine year. There I received my education like Math, Reading, Spelling Words and Writing. My favorite subjects are reading and writing for forty-five years.

In August 1974, I went to Tennessee Temple University in Chattanooga, Tennessee to further my studious major in Bible Theology and graduated of August in 1977.

During that time at Tennessee Temple University in Chattanooga, Tennessee, my major interesting was studying the Baptism of the Holy Spirit through Dr. John R. Rice's book called "The Power of Pentecost or The Fullness of the Spirit" in order to get an understanding of his view since it was a Fundamental Baptist Belief and I am still remaining a Pentecostal Belief.

My desire is to help deaf, hard of hearing and hearing people to come to know Jesus Christ as their personal Savior and Lord.

My desire also is to help hearing people as well and to inspire them the Word of God to apply His Word in their daily life.

Most of all, I want to remind them that I went to a deaf school. I received my education in a deaf school. I graduated from a deaf school. I went to Tennessee Temple University. I graduated from Tennessee Temple University and I am African-American, called of God to preach to the deaf, hard of hearing and hearing people.

Be Blessed!!!
Evangelist John H. Manigo
I Corinthians 6:19-20

About the Book

My main interesting is to help the deaf, hard of hearing, hearing people to understand the Word of God and to apply to their own life with God's help. It also gives us deaf, hard of hearing, hearing as well to the hearing people who need encouragement, help and inspire in the Word of God and that the Word of God is for them to receive His Word by faith.

My main reason of writing the Trinity to show the example of God, Jesus and the Holy Spirit as one and believe that God is One.

I also write Trinity for various reasons and put down Bible verses to help match the Old Testament and New Testament that speak the **Same Thing** to show them that the **Bible** in fact is **real. God's Word** is **very real**. **God's Word** Is **Reality.**

The reason that I write the major subject is because I have heard in the past about their belief, their teaching, their faith in God, and I am willing to write down what they said, what I heard and that the Bible has all the answer to our need, problem and purpose.

Whenever I hear, I would go back to study some more until I get God's answer find in the Bible. And to be ready to answer with meek and quiet interesting

I went to work for years in searching for the scriptures in God's Word.

I have studied the Bible for forty-five years seeking answers and be able to explain better from God's teaching; from God's Word. Whenever I hear people talk about their faith in God, I write down Bible verses to help inspire their life positive. I would go back to study more in the Bible for answers.

It would help all of us to grow in grace through our Lord Jesus Christ. He has the answer to all of our problem, all of our needs and all of our purpose.

My main point is to help them know that they can be saved through Jesus Christ by faith in Him. Only Him shall He save your soul.

Be Blessed!!!
Evangelist John H. Manigo
I Corinthians 6:19–20

About the Character

One day in the summer of 1980 at Gallaudet University in Washington, D.C., I met John's former classmate from the South Carolina School for the Deaf and the Blind in Spartanburg, South Carolina. We had a long talk. He wished me to go to South Carolina to meet John because John's father and my father pastor the same church as the Church of God in Christ years ago.

He described that John was very serious.

He was involved in John's deaf ministry at the South Carolina School for the Deaf and the Blind in Spartanburg, South Carolina.

John H. Manigo came to see his former classmate at the Gallaudet University, the only Deaf Liberal Arts in Washington, D.C., near the capital of the White House, on October 3, 1980. It was John H. Manigo first visit to the Gallaudet University. Then his former classmate brought John H. Manigo to come to my dormitory room. We were introduced for the first time ever.

My former roommate, Susanne Davis Rivera had the most conversation concerning her testimony from the Lord about me and John. We enjoyed having conversation with John. We took John to come to Gallaudet Christian Fellowship to meet our brothers and sisters in Christ on that Friday evening.

My former roommate, Susanne Davis Rivera and I *prayed*. Suddenly, my former roommate *prophesied* to me in amazement: "I *feel* the Lord *wants you* to *marry John*! Yea!!!" I *denied* that *quickly*, *not knowing* for *sure* of my roommate's *prophecy*! But my roommate kept *on prophesying strongly in faith*:" I *feel* the Lord *wants you* to *marry John*!" Her former suite went on to say, "You *continue on* to *pray*!" I kept *denying* my former roommate's *prophecy* from which the Lord had *revealed* to get me to *believe* it.

John H. Manigo told me on October 3, 1980 that he would write a book. Years later I asked him couple of times: "When will you write a book?"

Thirty-five years later, his dream came true. His book is entitle: "Blessed Are The Poor In Spirit." He wrote it four years ago.

John Henry Manigo and I were *married* on June 26, 1982, which was Saturday in Philadelphia, Pennsylvania at my church where John *once* preached.

Then he preached a couple of times at my father's church.

John is an easygoing person because he loves to travel serving the Lord.

John looks like a normal hearing person as well as normal deaf person. John once looked up to his father's pastoral role.

John is a man of God because he is evangelist for 45 years since age 16, began at the South Carolina School for the Deaf and the Blind in Spartanburg, South Carolina.

He is a hard working of being a student of the Word of God; through many days, nights and the wee of the hours until the morning.

He still loves to preach, teach, witness, pray for the deaf, hard of hearing and hearing.

John loves to explain the tract to the deaf people about "*This Was Your Life.*" The tract helped the deaf to understand the picture of the tract about "*This Was Your Life.*" The tract was like *a movie star.*

While John was pastor a deaf church in Columbia, South Carolina for nine years (1987-1996) affiliation with the Assemblies of God, we came to a deaf community. They wanted us to come to a birthday party at a deaf friend's home. Then we came to deaf friend's home for a birthday party but our deaf community told the deaf people to put away beer, whiskey and others. They respected us because of his deaf ministry.

We have anniversary deaf worship service through God's anointing each year for 45 years.

John's former math teacher asked me: "Is John still continuing to preach?" I said to him, "Yes."

John is still faithful serving the Lord.

We established our deaf ministries call:

<u>**Introduce To Jesus Deaf Ministries**</u>
Andrew found Peter. He introduced him to Jesus.
Jesus found Philip. He introduced *Himself* to Philip.
Philip found Nathanael. He introduced him to Jesus.
Jesus found Paul. He introduced *Himself* to Paul.
John 1:35-51, Acts 13:1-2, 6-10, Mark 1:20

I *ask* for your desire to pray for us that God will forever *lead us together* as a *team* to *do* the *work* of Him that *called us*; as we, John and I, will carry on God's Word to the *deaf* that *need* to be *heard* and be *saved*, and to *live* the *Christian's life* following Jesus' example and following His Steps. Read I Peter 2:21

Please continue to *pray* for us.

Evangelist Patricia Clark Manigo

Keynotes

So the book is about the Baptism of the Holy Spirit. I have written down 376 meaning of the Baptism of the Holy Spirit according to their teaching on the Baptism of the Holy Spirit by God's people who believe difference with the Baptism of the Holy Spirit. They do not use Acts 2:4 accordingly. They use various Bible verses such as Luke 24:49, John 17:17, I John 5:14-15, respectively.

I encourage you to read for yourself.

The Book is about Bless Are The Poor In Spirit along with Bible verses to help inspire them and to apply in their life daily. It also help that salvation is a blessing from God to give you His Gift. Salvation is free by all who ask Jesus Christ to come into your heart and He promises to save you.

Finally the book is about people who were blessed by God in their life time.

Be Blessed!!!
Evangelist John H. Manigo
I Corinthians 6:19-20

Blessed Are The Poor In Spirit—December 2011 "Started Writing And Typing!!!" Habakkuk 2:2

Started writing news for two years—1966 to 1968 at age 12

Started writing long letters to my parents, but for a short period of time. My dad once said to me: "You wrote long letter, boy!!!".

Started writing letters to female friends, but stopped due to not accepting taking advantage of, or my writing was not proper in grammar, or not enough in writing.

Started typing assignment for homework requirement semesters for three years—1974 to 1977 in Chattanooga, Tennessee at Tennessee University.

Started writing my own newsletter in the 1980's and kept them for 30 years as a diary, etc through writing or typing.

Started writing reports for nine years—1987 to 1996

Started writing again in 2011 to present monthly: My wife, Patricia for 33 years, typed my newsletter 33 years ago and typed again through computer starting January 2012 to present. The Lord is good to us as a teamwork between husband and wife these 33 years.

Been reading old books again from over thirty years ago and since that time 8 years ago which was 2007 to 2015 over107 books both spiritual and education reading, from the library and buying more couples of books from the Christian Bible Books Stores and ordering my favorite books from the computer concerning the life and ministry of *Bishop William J. Seymour*, the last person of this new twenty-first century to be voiced and to be heard of him. I also wrote about him in a brief statement. I had been reading since 2007 all over again that left many old books over thirty years ago.

Keep practicing your spelling, your wording, your writing to keep your memory going!!!

Been reading for 45 years. My former and retirement schoolteacher, Mrs. Annie Posey, from the South Carolina School for the deaf and blind in Spartanburg, S.C., advised me to continue my reading.

Patricia typed like a real professional but she came in second finished like a fast rabbit. She finished typing her course with joy.

(1)

Patricia used to type at the Willis & Elizabeth Martin School in her hometown of Philadelphia, Pennsylvania when she was in her early teenager.

At Pennsylvania School For The Deaf, her schoolteacher wanted her to stay another year but she was not allowed to stay another year. Her teacher cried because she missed Patricia skillful typing. She was a good typewriter!!!

About over twenty years later, Patricia began her typing for me as her husband. Then thirty years later she began to type again for me as her husband of thirty-three years. She had been typing for four years straight in a row.

She is happy to finish her typing for me. She finished her typing for me on July 14, 2015.

She was very happy. She finished her typing with joy. She finished her course with joy in four years, December 1, 2011 through July 12, 2015

Due to her fast typing as a real professional, I had a hard time keeping up with her. I did not want to get behind my homework. I needed to catch up with her.

Patricia was sick for one month. Her paper for me was pile up. While I did my homework, I had to wait for her to get well.

After she was well, she began typing fast again.

I was a little bit behind for double-checking for error and then return to her for correction. When I finished, Patricia would finish her last typing the next day and done.

Patricia was like a rabbit moving too fast. I was like a turtle moving very slowly. Like the turtle, I finished crossing the line first. Patricia finished second. Isn't that something?

She Finished Her Course With Joy:
Bible Scripture Readings:

1. I Thessalonians 4:11-12

2. II Timothy 2:15
3. II Timothy 3:14-17

She Finished Her Course With Joy:
Bible Scripture Readings:

1. Matthew 21:28
2. Acts 20:24
3. II Timothy 4:7-8

(2)

Be blessed as you continue your reading, your writing and your typing!!!

Be Blessed!!!
Evangelist John H. Manigo
I Corinthians 6:19-20

(3)

"Experience"

Text: Romans 5:4
Romans 5:1-23

During my deaf pastoral ministry in the late 1980's, my wife and I took our deaf youth teenagers and deaf Adult to Georgia, Florida and North Carolina for the Deaf Southern Retreat (Deaf Conference).

Deaf Pastor of Introduce To Jesus Deaf Ministry for 9 years with Christian Life Assembly of God in Columbia, South Carolina.

South Carolina School For the Deaf And The Blind Campus:
To Tell Deaf Children About Jesus:
For Three Years (1971-1974)

1. Deaf Elementary Student—Kids
2. Deaf Middle Student—Teenagers
3. Deaf High Student—Teenagers

Read Mark 16:15

Entire Bible Reading:
From Genesis To Revelation
Fifth Time for forty-four years

1st in Spartanburg, South Carolina one year
2nd in Chattanooga, Tennessee as required
3rd in Conway, South Carolina
4th in Columbia, South Carolina
5th in Columbia, South Carolina

Former Deaf Student of Temple Tennessee University, Chattanooga, Tennessee First Afro American Deaf Student To Enroll At Temple Tennessee University

First Afro American Deaf Student At Temple Tennessee University To Remain Three Years Instead Of Four Years

First African American Deaf Student to graduate at Temple Tennessee University

No Other Deaf Afro American Ever Graduate At Temple Tennessee University Since I Left Due To No Longer Operate Deaf Ministry At Temple Tennessee University In Chattanooga, Tennessee

Be Blessed!!!
Evangelist John H. Manigo
I Corinthians 6:19-20

From the Sermon, *"Justification by Faith"*

The foundation must be maintained without wavering, that faith without any works, without any merit, reconciles man to God and makes him good, as Paul says to the Romans: "But now apart from the law even the righteousness of God through faith in Jesus Christ unto all them that believe." Paul at another place says: "To Abraham, his faith was reckoned for righteousness" ; so also with us. Again: "Being therefore justified by faith, we have peace with God through our Lord Jesus Christ." Again: "For with the heart man believeth unto righteousness; and with the mouth confession is made unto salvation." These, and many more similar passages, we must firmly hold and trust in them immovably, so that to faith alone without any assistance of works, is attributed the forgiveness of sins and our justification.

Therefore the powerful conclusion follows, there must be something far greater and more precious than all good works, by which a man becomes pious and good, before he does good; just as he must first be in bodily health before he can labor and do hard work. This great and precious something is the noble Word of God, which offers us in the Gospel the grace of God in Christ. He who hears and believes this, thereby becomes good and righteous. Wherefore it is called the Word of Life, a Word of Grace, a Word of Forgiveness. But he who neither hears nor believes it, can in no way become good. For St. Peter says in the Acts: "And he made no distinction between us and them, cleansing their hearts by faith." For as the Word is, so will the heart be, which believes and cleaves firmly to it. The Word is a living, righteous, truthful, pure and good Word, so also the heart which cleaves to it, must be living, just, truthful, pure and good.

But true faith, of which we speak, cannot be manufactured by our own thoughts, for it is solely a work of God is in us, without any assistance on our part. As Paul says to the Romans, it is God's gift and grace, obtained by one man, Christ. Therefore, faith is something very powerful, active, restless, effective, which at once renews a person and again regenerates him, and leads him altogether into a new manner and character of life, so that is it impossible not to do good without ceasing.

Revised Edition The Christian Hall Of Fame by Elmer L. Town

"Justification by Faith" by Martin Luther pages 38

John H. Manigo's Background Experience

Introduction:

Since 1972 to present

Year-round habitual Bible reading

I accepted Jesus Christ at age of 11 on August 1965.

Before I was asked what I wanted for Christmas present, my thought was that I wanted a Bible. I received my first Bible at the age of 14 on December 17th, 1967 by Dr. Wilson; I still have it!!!

I started out to read my Bible since 1972. This is my fifth time reading the entire Bible. I read my first entire Bible reading for two years before I entered the Tennessee Temple University in Chattanooga, Tennessee in 1974 to 1977.

Make this your Bible reading a habit. You can do it!!! Keep on reading God's Word today and everyday of your life and beyond. Be blessed!!!

"What Is The Bible Like?"

A. The Bible is my daily newspaper.
B. The Bible is my news
C. The Bible is my television program.
D. The Bible is my movie set.
E. The Bible is my source of help.
F. The Bible is my relief.
G. The Bible is my faith.
H. The Bible is my hope.
I. The Bible is my trustworthy.
J. The Bible is my salvation.
K. The Bible is my strength.
L. The Bible is talking to me.
M. The Bible is my personal need.

N. The Bible speaks to me.
O. The Bible is my pathway to Glory.
P. The Bible is my road to Heaven.
Q. The Bible is my eternal life for eternity.
R. The Bible is my Holy Spirit Baptism; being baptized in the Holy Spirit; being filled with the Holy Spirit.
S. The Bible help me see the light of glory of the Father, the Son and the Holy Spirit.
T. Final, my prayer is my Bible.

Dear Lord,

Thank you for helping me through the day.
Thank you for helping me through the night.
Thank you for helping me through the years.
Thank you Lord, for keeping me awake.

In Jesus' Precious Name. Amen.

Bible Quotation:
Philippians 4:13

I can do all things through Christ which strengtheneth me.

Evangelical Work:
1. Bible Theology Institution
2. Forty Five Years Of Serving
3. Publish Book

Read Philippians 4:13

Bible Scripture Readings:
1. Mark 13:10
2. Acts 19:9-10
3. Revelation 2:10

Evangelical Work:

1. Acts 19:9-10
2. Ephesians 4:11
3. II Timothy 4:5

Read Acts 21:8

South Carolina School For the Deaf And The Blind Campus, Spartanburg, South Carolina:
To Tell Deaf Children About Jesus:
For Three Years (1971-1974)

1. Deaf Elementary School
2. Deaf Middle School
3. Deaf High School Read Mark 16:25

What School Was It?
Deaf And Blind:

1. Deaf
2. And
3. Blind

Read Isaiah 29:18
A doctoral student at God's Inspiration Word Of God In The Biblical Studious—II Timothy 2:14-17 verse 16
For 45 years of studying. Acts 4:13

Working Faithful for 45 years as well as in deaf ministry with:

1. School homework where He made the Honor Roll in South Carolina Deaf School
2. School homework where he made the Honor Roll at Tennessee Temple University, Chattanooga, Tennessee
3. Faithful Husband to my wife, Patricia for thirty-three years
4. Faithful Father to my son for nineteen years
5. Faithful Worker for 23 years plus a total of 41 since 16 when I started working.

High School Diploma:

1. John Henry Manigo
2. South Carolina School for the Deaf and the Blind, Spartanburg, South Carolina—1974
3. Patricia Lynne Clark (Manigo)

4. Pennsylvania School for the Deaf, Philadelphia, Pennsylvania—1977
5. John Christopher Manigo
6. Irmo High School, Columbia, South Carolina—2014

Honor Students Graduate:

1. John Henry Manigo
2. Tennessee Temple University—1977
3. Patricia Lynne Clark (Manigo)
4. Gallaudet University—1982
5. John Christopher Manigo
6. University of South Carolina—2018
7. John Henry Manigo—1974-1977
8. Patricia Lynne Clark (Manigo)—1977-1982
9. John Christopher Manigo—2014-2018

Church Background:
Entered Spirit-Filled Non-Denominational Churches

Cause at birth:
Born a normal hearing; During three weeks, took sick due to meningitis.

Become a child of God:
At the age of eleven years old

Education:
Former student of Conway Whittemore Elementary School for four and ½ years, 1960 to 1964, Conway, South Carolina

What School Was It?
Deaf And Blind:

1. Deaf
2. And
3. Blind

Read Isaiah 29:18

A graduate of the South Carolina School for the Deaf and the Blind in Spartanburg, South Carolina, 1974.

Went to a Fundamental Baptist Bible School at Tennessee Temple University in Theological Doctrine and a graduate of Tennessee Temple University, Degree of Theology, major in Bible, in Chattanooga, Tennessee, 1977.

Life in History:
One of the students of the Pentecostal History who continues to study

Former Pastor of Introduce of Jesus Deaf Ministries 1986-1996 with the Christian Life Assembly of God, Columbia, South Carolina

Student Scholar Bible of God's Word for year-round study Reading and Studying the Bible for the fifth time

Bible Student of the Word—1972 to present Evangelist for the deaf and hearing—1970 to present

Was elected Vice President of the Christian Endeavor Society for the Deaf for one year, from 1971 to 1972, at the South Carolina School for the Deaf and the Blind, Spartanburg, South Carolina

Was elected Chaplain of the Christian Silent Deaf Club for one year, from 1976 to 1977, at the Tennessee Temple University in Chattanooga, Tennessee.

Received 1976 award as the Most Outstanding Deaf Student during his second year at Tennessee Temple University, Chattanooga, Tennessee on May 1976

Was pictured in the 1976 *Jet Magazine* from Chicago, Illinois at Johnson Publishing on May 1976.

Received Past Awards:
Was an Honor Roll Student for two years, from 1967 to 1969, 1970 and 1973 at the South Carolina School for the Deaf and the Blind, Spartanburg, South Carolina

Was an Honor Roll Student for two years 1975 to 1977 at Tennessee Temple University in Chattanooga, Tennessee

Deaf Ministry—from Trident Club of the Deaf—1984 from Columbia, South Carolina
South Carolina Black Alumni—Man of the Year—1985 from Columbia, South Carolina

Faithful Years of South Carolina Deaf Ministry—Introduce To Jesus Deaf Ministries—November 1990 by my Christian parents, Bishop T.O. Manigo and Evangelist Vivian H. Manigo, the House of Prayer Church of God in Christ Jesus of Georgetown, South Carolina in the section of North Santee Community, his native hometown.

On the deaf chorus:
Spartanburg, South Carolina, at the South Carolina School for the Deaf and the Blind and Chattanooga, Tennessee, at the Tennessee Temple University

Further studies:

A. Guideposts Home Bible Study
B. Voice of Prophecy Home Bible Study
C. One of the leading Fundamental Baptist Preachers in America—John R. Rice on the Power of Pentecost or the Fullness of the Spirit and doctrine of the Baptism of the Holy Spirit By Dr. John R. Rice
D. The Theology of the Holy Spirit concerning the Baptism of the Holy Spirit By Frederick Dale Bruner
E. The Holy Spirit on Pentecostal Interpretation By L. Thomas Holdcroft
F. An Handbook on Holy Spirit Baptism By Don Basham
G. Christian and Faith series manual
H. The King James Bible Version concerning the Spirit Baptism—On The Day of Pentecost in the Book of Acts
I. The Winds of God By Ethel E. Goss, wife of Howard A. Goss
J. Our Faith And Fellowship By G. Raymond Carlson
K. The New International Dictionary Pentecostal Charismatic Movement by Stanley M. Burgess and Edward M. Van Der Mass
L. Dictionary of Pentecostal And Charismatic Movements By Stanley M. Burgess, Gary B. McGee and Patrick H. Alexander
M. A.D. Bible Continues
N. Christ's Passion
O. The Ten Commandment
P. Women Of The Bible
Q. Jesus Of Nazarene
R. Crucifixion of Christ
S. The Dovekeepers

Most Interest Study of the late 1700's and 1800's past preachers:

1. John Wesley—1703-1791—88 age
2. Richard Allen—1760-1831—72 age
3. Charles Harrison Mason—1866-1961—95 age
4. William J. Seymour—1870-1922—52 age
5. John R. Rice—1895-1980—85 age
6. D. L. Moody—1837-1899—62 age
7. Billy Sunday—1862-1935—73 age
8. Charles S. Price—1887-1947—60 age

1. Founder of the Methodist Movement—John Wesley
2. Founder of the African Methodist Episcopal—Richard Allen
3. Holiness Minister and Church Leader—Charles Harrison Mason
4. Pastor at Azusa Street Revival—William J. Seymour
5. Fundamental Baptist Evangelist—John R. Rice
6. Evangelist at Congregational Church—D. L. Moody
7. Evangelist at Presbyterian Church—Billy Sunday
8. Evangelist and pastor at Congregational Church—Charles S. Price

Favorite Subjects:

a. Reading
b. English
c. Writing
d. History of the past, present and future

Born between1886 to 1899: *met or seen in Persons:*

1. Great Aunt Sally Spain Palmey—1886-1963
2. Dr. John R. Rice—1895-1980
3. Grandfather John Manigo—1896-1975
4. Great Aunt Frosty Spain Sellers—1896-1997
5. Great Uncle Charles Spain—1893-1981
6. Missionary Mary Maynard 1896-1999
7. Grandfather Samuel J. Clark, Sr 1899-1984
8. Grandmother Daisy Robinson Clark 1899-1996

Hobbies:

Studying the Bible for year-round habit since 1972 Studying and working on homework all the time Reading, Writing, Working and Studying Mediating my heart to pray daily for others Traveling—Ministry

Staying at home with family with Patricia and John Christopher "JJ"

Done Personal Yard Raking And Mowing year-round for thirty-seven years

My Personal Ministry Home Work:

Continuing Further Studies:
Reading Historical Books
Christian Books And their Testimonies
Christian Doctrine of the Bible And The Baptism Of The Holy Spirit Forced Into Glory Concerning Abraham Lincoln
I Was Born A Slave
African American Slaves History Presidents' History
African-America Heroes "Blessed Are The Poor In Spirit" "The Trinity"
The Original African Heritage Study Bible Of King James Version 1611

Favorite Presidents:

1. Abraham Lincoln—16th President—1809-1865 "Though passion may have strain, it must not break our bond of affection." 1861 President's Speech
2. Franklin D. Roosevelt—32nd President—1882-1945 "The only thing we have to fear is fear itself" 1933 President's Speech
3. John F. Kennedy—35th President—1917-1963 "Ask not what your country can do for you, ask what you can do for your country." 1961 President's Speech

Favorite African Male:

1. Frederick Douglas—American Abolitionist Leader and a former slave—1818-1895
2. W.E.B. DuBois—former slave scholar and Activist Abolitionist Leader—1868-1963
3. Martin Luther King, Jr.—Civil Right Leader and Baptist Minister—1929-1968

Favorite African Female:

1. Mary Bethune—Educator—1875-1955

2. Sojourner Truth—used to speak Dutch language; spoke major English language in America; Antislavery Activist—American Abolitionist 1797-1883
3. Harriet Truman led more than 300 slaves to freedom into North, called her "Moses" former slave, Antislavery Activist—American Abolitionist 1820-1913

John's Favorite numbers
3 or three or third or 1, 2, 3
Why?
Father, Son and Holy Ghost!!!

Favorite Bible Quotations
I can do all things through Christ that strength me.

Favorite Bible Verses
I Corinthians 6:19-20

Martin Luther King Jr.'s Speech:
"I Have A Dream"
One of the favorite Bible to read: Acts
Baptism with the Holy Spirit
Or
Continue to fill with the Holy Spirit "*after*" *the day of Pentecost*

One of the favorite American History Books to read:
Forced Into Glory concerning Abraham Lincoln

Christian Testimony:

1. Martin Luther King, Jr.: "I've been to the mountain top, and I've seen the promise land."—1929-1968
2. Sojourner Truth—"I must be about my Father's business."—1797-1883
3. George Washington Carver—Botanist—"God made the clay in the hills; they have been there for countless generations, changeless. All I do is prepare what God has made, for use to which man can put it. It is God's work-not mine."—1864-1943

Experienced Christian Worker:

1. Minister

2. Elder
3. Reverend
4. Evangelist
5. Bishop, but decline
6. Doctorate Degree is my goal to come true
7. Religious Worker through Jesus Christ
8. Religious Experience through Jesus Christ
9. Religious Education through Jesus Christ

Reading my Bible at the age of 19, on November 15, 1972. Still reading for 43 years—1972-2015

Videotape Numbers:
5 Videos on Bible Stories 11 Videos on Deaf Ministry
3 My personal life on Videos
5 Tapes Recorder to preach to the hearing congregation 5 pictures on Deaf Conference
1 tape for Patricia through interpreter

Education And Studied On The Baptism Of The Holy Spirit:
I Thessalonians 4:11-12, II Timothy 2:15, II Timothy 3:14-17

I received my education and studied on the *Baptism of the Holy Spirit* where I went to work to study under Evangelist John R. Rice's book called "**The Power Of Pentecost or The Fullness Of The Spirit** on November 28, 1975 when I was a sophomore student at Tennessee Temple University in Chattanooga, Tennessee.

Dr. John R. Rice received an Honorary Litt Doctorate Degree from Bob Jones College in 1946 in Cleveland, Tennessee.

How I loved to study Dr. John R. Rice's book over and over and over again for years!!!

However, he did not encourage his congregation to speak in tongues, but he did encourage the congregation to seek the baptism of the Holy Spirit through soul winning power according to **Proverbs 11:30** and **Acts 1:8** and **Acts 2:4 (a)** where the scripture read in **part:** "*They were all filled with the Holy Spirit*" and all that *with soul winning power to reach lost souls for Christ.*

Dr. John Rice was 27 years old when Bishop William J. Seymour passed away in1922. John Rice was 66 years when Bishop Charles H. Mason passed away in 1961.

Had he met those black ministers when he met those white Assemblies of God such as the Rev. Eudorus N. Bell who died in 1923 when Dr. John Rice was 28 years old?

I was sure that Dr. John Rice would have an open heart to have had the chance or the opportunity if he had met them. But he never wrote them in his book on **The Power Of Pentecost or The Fullness Of The Spirit**!!!

Evangelist John H. Manigo's Acknowledgments

To My Parents:
Bishop Thomas O. Manigo, Sr and Evangelist Vivian H. Manigo inspired me to become a minister when I was a child. My mother always gave an awesome testimony everywhere about me as an infant's life threaten spinal meningitis and did not eat for three weeks. He didn't make it until the nurse called his mom to come back because he breathed again. This became God's miracle. The doctor informed her that he had a hearing problem. My parents attended our deaf ministry conference faithfully.

To My Parents' Close Family Friend:
Missionary Mary Maynor attended our deaf ministry conference at South Carolina School for the Deaf and the Blind in Spartanburg, South Carolina.

To My Parents' Close Friends:
Elder Edward N. Brockington and Missionary Cynthia Brockington invited me to preach at their church revival in Conway, South Carolina for one week before entering my first enrollment at Tennessee Temple University in Chattanooga, Tennessee.

To My Spiritual Parents:
Elder Rosco Anderson and Missionary Carrie Anderson and their church members attended our deaf ministry conference at South Carolina School for the Deaf and the Blind in Spartanburg, South Carolina.

To My Sunday School Teacher Of South Carolina School for the Deaf and the Blind:
Ruth Catto became a warrior prayer for my deaf ministry. She received her faithful Sunday School Teacher Of The Year because she inspired me with God's Word where I was a student at the South Carolina School For The Deaf and Blind in Spartanburg, S.C.

To My Formerly Teacher Of South Carolina School for the Deaf and the Blind:
Mrs. Betty Reynolds attended our deaf ministry conference on deaf campus in Spartanburg, South Carolina. She said she was touch.

To My Formerly Teacher Of South Carolina School for the Deaf and the Blind:
Mrs. Phyllis Petty attended our deaf ministry conference on deaf campus in Spartanburg, South Carolina. She said she was touch.

To My Parents-In-Law:
Rev. Samuel J. Clark, Jr. and Evangelist Effie Clark invited me to preach at their church in Philadelphia, Pennsylvania before I married their daughter, Patricia who is deaf.

To Our Christian Friend:
Margene Todd attended our first deaf ministry anniversary in Myrtle Beach, South Carolina. As a result of our deaf ministry conference, she established her own deaf ministry for over thirty three years.

To My Wife's Former Classmate Of Columbia International University In Columbia, South Carolina:
Donnitta Donaldson got information from her husband, Jeff concerning sign language class because her husband, Jeff was in classroom with my wife, Patricia and saw an interpreter in the classroom and chapel. Donnitta took sign language class from my wife, Patricia. Then the Donaldson Family went to their deaf missionary.

To My Wife's Former Student Of Columbia College In Columbia, South Carolina:
Alexis Murdough Bingham listened to out special testimonies concerning our personal lives and our deaf ministry and they inspired her. She encouraged me to publish a book through agencies and we did plan to do just that. Our dreams became a reality.

To Our Friend:
Evangelist David Lee worked with us in deaf ministry in Conway, South Carolina. He interpreted for Patricia and me at Mason Temple Church of God in Christ. He also attended our deaf ministry conference in Myrtle Beach, South Carolina.

To Our Spiritual Deaf Daughter:
Minister April Jacobs spread the gospel of Jesus Christ to her friends and family about our monthly Christian report through email. She was invited to minister at our deaf ministry conference in Columbia, South Carolina.

To Our Faithful Deaf Christian Friend:
Shirley Mears attended our deaf ministry conference faithfully. She sang at our deaf ministry conference in Columbia, South Carolina. She even wrote poem for our deaf ministry as well.

To Our Beloved Christian Friend:
Mrs. Gequetta Cates attended our deaf ministry conference. She interpreted the message for my father, Bishop Thomas Oliver Manigo, Sr. at our Introduce To Jesus Deaf Ministries in Columbia, South Carolina.

Met New Christian Friends:
Mr. Dean Slade and his wife, Pamela attended our deaf ministry conference. Mr. Dean Slade, a former Payroll and Benefits Manager at Columbia International University in Columbia, South Carolina helped me and Patricia by opening up our deaf ministry conference when we moved to Columbia, South Carolina in August 1988.

A New Christian Friend Joined Us:
Edwin Dunlap interpreted our deaf ministry conference. He interpreted the message for my mother, Evangelist Vivian H. Manigo at our Introduce to Jesus Deaf Ministries. His wife, Dorrie Dunlap was a missionary in Africa. After he took interesting at seeing our deaf ministry, Mr. Dunlap was interpreting for the hearing impaired students at Richland District School I for many years.

Our Friends In Christ:
Glendia Boon and also Mrs. Christina Whitehouse-Suggs attended our deaf ministry conference respectively. They voiced interpreted the message for two of our deaf Christians, Minister April Scott in 2005 and Evangelist Patricia C. Manigo in 2010, to the hearing congregation in Columbia, South Carolina. What a blessing!!!

To Our New Friend In Christ:
Eight years ago, Kevin Wilson started to learn spiritual sign language as he interpreted the songs and message at the church. My wife Patricia helped to aid him. He has improved rapidly.

To My Faithful Wife:
Patricia C. Manigo had done lot of typing on my various topics since we married. I thanked her and much appreciation. She deserved a lot of credits She often asked me when would I write a book. She also ministered at our deaf conference in Columbia, South Carolina. She is hot in typing. She had done some typing when she was a childhood at the Willis and Elizabeth Martin School in Philadelphia, Pennsylvania. She finished typing on May 2015. She had typed my homework and re-typed for correctly for four years and five

months!!! December 1, 2011 to July 14, 2015. She is a follower of Christ because I follow Christ. I Corinthians 11:1, I Peter 2:21

To Our Only Son:
John Christopher Manigo goes with us faithfully wherever we plan on church events and activities. He goes to University of South Carolina in Columbia, South Carolina. His major is in Computer Science. He took part-time work for one month during Christmas break, hired by his young boss, a self—employed and a former student of University of South Carolina. John Christopher Manigo gave remark at our deaf ministry conference twice in Columbia, South Carolina

"Footprints Prayer"

I Peter 2:21

One night a man had a dream.
He dreamed he was walking along the beach with the Lord.
Across the sky flashed scenes from his life.
For each scene, he noticed two sets of footprints in the sand:
One belonging to him, and the other to the Lord.
When the last scene of his life flashed before him, he
looked back at the footprints in the sand.
He noticed that many times along the path of his life
there was only one set of footprints.
He also noticed that it happened at the very lowest and saddest times in his life.
This really bothered him and he questioned the Lord about it.
"Lord, you said that once I decided to follow you, you'd walk with me all the way.
But I have noticed that during the most troublesome times
in my life, there is only one set of footprints.
I don't understand why when I needed you most you would leave me."
The Lord replied, "My son, My precious child,
I love you and I would never leave you. During your times of trial and suffering,
when you see only one set of footprints, it was then that I carried you."
—Author Unknown

Part CCCXXXVI

Blessed Are The Poor In Spirit. Matthew 5:3

Blessed Means Happy

Poor means meek in spirit. Poor means humble in spirit. Poor means lowly in spirit. Poor means quiet in spirit. Read Matthew 5:3-12, Read also Mark 1:15

Jesus did not say "*rich*" in spirit. Jesus said "*poor*" in spirit.

1. Blessed are the poor in spirit to those who *believe that Jesus Christ* is the *King of the Jews. John 19:19*
2. Blessed are the poor in spirit to those who *believe* that *Jesus Christ* is the *Son of God. Hebrews 4:14*
3. Blessed are the poor in spirit to those who believe that *Jesus Christ* is the *son of Joseph. John 6:42.* See *Matthew 1:18-25*
4. Blessed are the poor in spirit to those who believe that *Jesus Christ* was the *son of Mary. Matthew 1:18-25.*
5. Blessed are the poor in spirit to those who *believe that Jesus Christ is the Word which God sent unto the children of Israel, preaching "peace" by Jesus Christ: (He is Lord of all). Acts 10:36*
6. Blessed are the poor in spirit to those who *believe that Jesus Christ* is "*That Word,*" *which we know, which was "published" throughout all Judaea,* and *began from Galilee, after the baptism which John preached. Acts 10:37*
7. Blessed are the poor in spirit to those who *believe that Jesus Christ, How God anointed Jesus of Nazareth with the Holy Ghost and with power: who (Jesus Christ) went about doing good, and healing all that were oppressed* (dominated by) *of the devil; for God was with Him (Jesus Christ). Acts 10:38*
8. Blessed are the poor in spirit to those who *believe that Jesus Christ was slew (killed, murdered) and hanged on a tree: (But) Him (Jesus Christ) God raised up the third day, and showed Him (Jesus Christ) openly (visible—alive). Acts 10:39-40*
9. Blessed are the poor in spirit to those who *believe that Jesus Christ commanded us to preach unto the people and to testify that it is He (Jesus Christ) which was ordained of God to be the Judge of quick* (living) *and dead. Acts 10:42*
10. Blessed are the poor in spirit to those who *believe that Jesus Christ is King of saints. Revelation 15:3*

11. Blessed are the poor in spirit to those who believe that *Jesus Christ is King of Glory. Psalm 24:7-10*
12. Blessed are the poor in spirit to those who believe that *Jesus Christ is the Rabbi and the King of Israel. John 1:49*

Part CCCXXXVII

Blessed Are The Poor In Spirit. Matthew 5:3

Blessed Means Happy

Poor means meek in spirit. Poor means humble in spirit. Poor means lowly in spirit. Poor means quiet in spirit. Read Matthew 5:3-12, Read also Mark 1:15

Jesus did not say "*rich*" in spirit. Jesus said "*poor*" in spirit.

1. Blessed are the poor in spirit to those who believe this Psalmist: "I have set the Lord always before me: because he is at my right hand, I shall not be moved." Psalm 16:8
2. Blessed are the poor in spirit to those who believe this Psalmist: "Therefore my heart is glad, and my glory rejoiceth: my flesh also shall rest in hope." Psalm 16:9
3. Blessed are the poor in spirit to those who believe this Psalmist: "For thou wilt not leave my soul in hell; neither wilt thou suffer thine Holy One to see corruption." Psalm 16:10
4. Blessed are the poor in spirit to those who believe this Psalmist: "Thou wilt shew me the path of life: in thy presence is fullness of joy; at thy right hand there are pleasures for evermore.: Psalm 16:11
5. Blessed are the poor in spirit to those who believe to call on the Name: JESUS. JESUS. JESUS. For He shall save us from our sins. Matthew 1:21, 25, Luke 1:31, Luke 2:21
6. Blessed are the poor in spirit to those who believe this Psalmist: "The fool hath said in his heart, There is no God. They are corrupt, they have done abominable works, there is none that doeth good." Psalm 14:1 (Roman 3:12)
7. Blessed are the poor in spirit to those who believe this Psalmist: "The Lord looked down from heaven upon the children of men, to see if there were any that did understand, and seek God." Psalm 14:2
8. Blessed are the poor in spirit to those who believe this Psalmist: "They are all gone aside, they are all together become filthy: there is none that doeth good, no, not one." Psalm 14:3 (Romans 3:12)
9. Blessed are the poor in spirit to those who believe this Psalmist: "Have all the workers of iniquity no knowledge? Who eat up my people as they eat bread, and call not upon the Lord." Psalm 14:4

10. Blessed are the poor in spirit to those who believe this Psalmist: "There were they in great fear: for God is in the generation of the righteous." Psalm 14:5
11. Blessed are the poor in spirit to those who believe this Psalmist: "Ye have shamed the counsel of the poor, because the Lord is his refuge." Psalm 14:6
12. Blessed are the poor in spirit to those who believe this Psalmist: "Oh that the salvation of Israel were come out of Zion! When the Lord bringeth back the captivity of his people, Jacob shall rejoice, and Israel shall be glad." Psalm 14:7

Part CCCXXXVIII

Blessed Are The Poor In Spirit. Matthew 5:3

Blessed Means Happy

Poor means meek in spirit. Poor means humble in spirit. Poor means lowly in spirit. Poor means quiet in spirit. Read Matthew 5:3-12, Read also Mark 1:15

Jesus did not say "*rich*" in spirit. Jesus said "*poor*" in spirit.

1. Blessed are the poor in spirit to those who *believe that Jesus Christ is the Saviour of the world. John 4:42, I John 4:14*
2. Blessed are the poor in spirit to those who *believe that Jesus Christ is the seed of David. II Timothy 2:8*
3. Blessed are the poor in spirit to those who *believe that Jesus Christ is the Servant. Isaiah 42:1, Matthew 3:17, Matthew 12:17-18, Mark 1:11, John 17:1-4*
4. Blessed are the poor in spirit to those who *believe that Jesus Christ is the Son of David. Mark 10:47-48, Luke 18:38, Matthew 9:27*
5. Blessed are the poor in spirit to those who *believe that Jesus Christ is the Blessed One. Mark 14:61-62*
6. Blessed are the poor in spirit to those who believe that *Jesus Christ is the Son of the Father. II John 1:3*
7. Blessed are the poor in spirit to those who believe that Jesus is the *Son of Man. Matthew 8:20*
8. Blessed are the poor in spirit to those who *believe that Jesus is the son of Mary. Luke 1:1-3*
9. Blessed are the poor in spirit to those who believe that *Jesus Christ is our spiritual meat. I Corinthians 10:3*
10. Blessed are the poor in spirit to those who believe that *Jesus Christ is our spiritual drink. I Corinthians 10:4*
11. Blessed are the poor in spirit to those who *believe that Jesus Christ is our Spiritual Rock. I Corinthians 10:4*
12. Blessed are the poor in spirit to those who *believe that Jesus Christ is the surety of a better testament. Hebrews 7:22*

Part CCCXXXIX

Blessed Are The Poor In Spirit. Matthew 5:3

Blessed Means Happy

Poor means meek in spirit. Poor means humble in spirit. Poor means lowly in spirit. Poor means quiet in spirit. Read Matthew 5:3-12, Read also Mark 1:15

Jesus did not say "*rich*" in spirit. Jesus said "*poor*" in spirit.

1. Blessed are the poor in spirit to those who *believe that Jesus Christ is the Saviour of the world. John 4:42, I John 4:14*
2. Blessed are the poor in spirit to those who *believe that Jesus Christ is the seed of David. II Timothy 2:8*
3. Blessed are the poor in spirit to those who *believe that Jesus Christ is the Servant. Isaiah 42:1, Matthew 3:17, Matthew 12:17-18, Mark 1:11, John 17:1-4*
4. Blessed are the poor in spirit to those who *believe that Jesus Christ is the Son of David. Mark 10:47-48, Luke 18:38, Matthew 9:27*
5. Blessed are the poor in spirit to those who *believe that Jesus Christ is the Blessed One. Mark 14:61-62*
6. Blessed are the poor in spirit to those who believe that *Jesus Christ is the Son of the Father. II John 1:3*
7. Blessed are the poor in spirit to those who believe that Jesus is the *Son of Man. Matthew 8:20*
8. Blessed are the poor in spirit to those who *believe that Jesus is the son of Mary. Luke 1:1-3*
9. Blessed are the poor in spirit to those who believe that *Jesus Christ is our Spiritual meat. I Corinthians 10:3*
10. Blessed are the poor in spirit to those who believe that *Jesus Christ is our spiritual drink. I Corinthians 10:4*
11. Blessed are the poor in spirit to those who *believe that Jesus Christ is our Spiritual Rock. I Corinthians 10:4*
12. Blessed are the poor in spirit to those who *believe that Jesus Christ is the surety of a better testament. Hebrews 7:22*

Part CCCXL

Blessed Are The Poor In Spirit. Matthew 5:3

Blessed Means Happy

Poor means meek in spirit. Poor means humble in spirit. Poor means lowly in spirit. Poor means quiet in spirit. Read Matthew 5:3-12, Read also Mark 1:15

Jesus did not say "*rich*" in spirit. Jesus said "*poor*" in spirit.

1. Blessed are the poor in spirit to those who *believe that Jesus Christ is the Lamb*, is *worthy, that was slain, to receive power*, and *riches*, and *wisdom* and *strength*, *honor* and *glory* and *blessing. Revelation 5:12*
2. Blessed are the poor in spirit to those who *believe that Jesus Christ has sent the Comforter*; which is the Spirit of truth. *John 14:16*, John 14:17
3. Blessed are the poor in spirit to those who *believe that Jesus Christ is the Eternal Spirit. Hebrews 9:14*
4. Blessed are the poor in spirit to those who believe that *Jesus Christ is the Free Spirit. Psalm 51:12*
5. Blessed are the poor in spirit to those who *believe that Jesus Christ is the Holy Spirit. Psalm 51:11*
6. Blessed are the poor in spirit to those who *believe that Jesus Christ is the Spirit of Adoption. Romans 8:15-17*
7. Blessed are the poor in spirit to those who believe that *Jesus Christ is the Spirit of Christ. I Peter 1:11*
8. Blessed are the poor in spirit to those who *believe that Jesus Christ is the Spirit of Counsel. Isaiah 11:2*
9. Blessed are the poor in spirit to those who *believe that Jesus Christ is the Spirit of Glory. I Peter 4:14*
10. Blessed are the poor in spirit to those who believe that *Jesus Christ is the Spirit of God. Genesis 1:2*
11. Blessed are the poor in spirit to those who *believe that Jesus Christ is the Spirit of Grace. Zechariah 12:10*
12. Blessed are the poor in spirit to those who *believe that Jesus Christ is the Spirit of Holiness. Romans 1:4*

Part CCCXLI

Blessed Are The Poor In Spirit. Matthew 5:3

Blessed Means Happy

Poor means meek in spirit. Poor means humble in spirit. Poor means lowly in spirit. Poor means quiet in spirit. Read Matthew 5:3-12, Read also Mark 1:15

Jesus did not say "*rich*" in spirit. Jesus said "*poor*" in spirit.

1. Blessed are the poor in spirit to those who believe that *Jesus Christ is the Spirit of Judgment. Isaiah 4:4*
2. Blessed are the poor in spirit to those who believe that *Jesus Christ is the Spirit of knowledge. Isaiah 11:2*
3. Blessed are the poor in spirit to those who believe that *Jesus Christ is the Spirit of life. Romans 8:2*
4. Blessed are the poor in spirit to those who *believe that Jesus Christ is the Spirit of the Lord God. Isaiah 61:1*
5. Blessed are the poor in spirit to those who believe that *Jesus Christ is the Spirit of Might. Isaiah 11:2*
6. Blessed are the poor in spirit to those who *believe that Jesus Christ is the Spirit of Prophecy. Revelation 19:10*
7. Blessed are the poor in spirit to those who *believe that Jesus Christ is the Spirit of the Father. Matthew 10:20*
8. Blessed are the poor in spirit to those who believe that *Jesus Christ is the Spirit of the Lord, Isaiah 11:2*
9. Blessed are the poor in spirit to those who *believe that Jesus Christ is the Spirit of the Son. Galatians 4:6*
10. Blessed are the poor in spirit to those who *believe that Jesus Christ is the Spirit of Understanding. Isaiah 11:2*
11. Blessed are the poor in spirit to those who *believe that Jesus Christ is the Spirit of Wisdom. Isaiah 11:2*
12. Blessed are the poor in spirit to those who believe that *Jesus Christ is the Deity of Eternal. Hebrews 9:14*

Part CCCXLII

Blessed Are The Poor In Spirit. Matthew 5:3

Blessed Means Happy

Poor means meek in spirit. Poor means humble in spirit. Poor means lowly in spirit. Poor means quiet in spirit. Read Matthew 5:3-12, Read also Mark 1:15

Jesus did not say "*rich*" in spirit. Jesus said "*poor*" in spirit.

1. Blessed are the poor in spirit to those who *believe that Jesus Christ is the Light of the Gentiles. Isaiah 42:6, Luke 2:32* and *John 8:12*
2. Blessed are the poor in spirit to those who *believe that Jesus Christ is the Son of Man* and He *is Lord of the Sabbath. Mark 2:28 and Luke 6:5*
3. Blessed are the poor in spirit to those who *believe that Jesus Christ is our Lord*; *our Redeemer*; the *Holy One of Israel, our King. Isaiah 43:14-15*
4. Blessed are the poor in spirit to those who *believe that Jesus Christ is the Man, Jesus of Nazareth, a man approved of God among you by miracles and wonders and signs, which God did by him (Jesus Christ) in the midst of you as ye yourselves know. Acts 2:22*
5. Blessed are the poor in spirit to those who *believe that Jesus Christ is our Mediator. I Timothy 2:5 and Hebrews 9:15*
6. Blessed are the poor in spirit to those who believe the *gospel*: "*And for this cause He (Christ) is the Mediator (Christ) of the New Testament, that by means of death for the redemption of the transgressions (sins committed) that were under the first testament, they which are called might receive the promise of eternal inheritance. Hebrews 9:15*
7. Blessed are the poor in spirit to those who *believe that Jesus Christ is the Mighty One to save sinners*; *for He said, if I be lifted up from the earth, I will draw all men into Myself.* John 12:32
8. Blessed are the poor in spirit to those who believe that *Jesus Christ is our only wise God our Saviour. Jude 25*
9. Blessed are the poor in spirit to those who believe that *Jesus Christ is the Rose of Sharon*, and *the Lily of the Valley. Song of Solomon 2:1*
10. Blessed are the poor in spirit to those who *believe that Jesus Christ is our salvation. Luke 2:30-34*

11. Blessed are the poor in spirit to those who *believe the child Jesus' spoken word*: "*And He said unto them. How is it that ye sought Me? Know ye not that I must be about My Father's business?* Luke 2:49-52
12. Blessed are the poor in spirit to those who believe that Jesus Christ is our wisdom, our "*righteousness*," "our "*sanctification*" and our "*redemption*;" and "*our Lord*; and *we may glorify in the Lord.*" *I Corinthians 1:30-31*

Part CCCXLIII

Blessed Are The Poor In Spirit. Matthew 5:3

Blessed Means Happy

Poor means meek in spirit Poor means humble in spirit Poor means lowly in spirit Poor means quiet in spirit Read Matthew 5:3-12, Read also Mark 1:15

Jesus did not say "*rich*" in spirit. Jesus said "*poor*" in spirit.

1. Blessed are the poor in spirit to those who *believe that Jesus is the Omnipotent. Romans 8:11*
2. Blessed are the poor in spirit to those who *believe that Jesus is the Omniscient. I Corinthians 2:10-11*
3. Blessed are the poor in spirit to those who *believe that Jesus is the Omnipresent. Psalm 139:11*
4. Blessed are the poor in spirit to those who *believe that Jesus Christ is the Inspirational Scriptures. II Timothy 3:16*
5. Blessed are the poor in spirit to those who *believe that Jesus Christ is the Agent in Christ's incarnation. Luke 1:35*
6. Blessed are the poor in spirit to those who *believe that Jesus Christ is to convicts the world. John 16:8, Matthew 1:18*
7. Blessed are the poor in spirit to those who *believe that Jesus Christ cannot regenerate the sinners unless or except they are born again. John 3:3, 5, 7, Luke 13:3, 5, John 14:6-9 verse 6, John 6:37, 65, John 19:11*
8. Blessed are the poor in spirit to those who *believe that Jesus sets believers free from law of sin and death.* Romans 8:2, I Thessalonians 1:10
9. Blessed are the poor in spirit to those who *believe the Gospel*: "*Then Phillip went down to the city of Samaria, and preached* "*Christ*" *unto them.*" *Acts 8:5*
10. Blessed are the poor in spirit to those who *believe that faith, hope, love* and *trust in God through Jesus Christ can never die.* John 11:25, John 14:6, I John 4:9, 18-19, 21, Philippians 1:21, Revelation 14:13, I Corinthians 15:22, 31 Romans 14:8, John 21:23, John 11:16, John 8:21, John 6:47-51, 59, Luke 20:36, I Corinthians 13:13
11. Blessed are the poor in spirit to those who *believe to a* "*saving knowledge*" *of our Lord and Saviour Jesus Christ.* I Corinthians 2:2, II Peter 3:18

12. Blessed are the poor in spirit to those who *believe the Gospel*: "*Therefore I endure all things for the elect's sakes*, that *they may also obtain the salvation which is in Christ Jesus with eternal glory.*" *II Timothy 2:10*

Part CCCXLIV

Blessed Are The Poor In Spirit. Matthew 5:3

Blessed Means Happy

Poor means meek in spirit Poor means humble in spirit Poor means lowly in spirit Poor means quiet in spirit Read Matthew 5:3-12, Read also Mark 1:15

Jesus did not say "*rich*" in spirit. Jesus said "*poor*" in spirit.

1. Blessed are the poor in spirit to those who *believe that Jesus Christ claimed to be the Savior, a suffering Messiah,* who *would "Himself" bear the sin of fallen humanity.* John 4:42, I John 4:14, I John 4:9, Matthew 1:21, Acts 22:1-30 verse 7-10, 18, 21, Matthew 26:53-54, John 10:17-18, John 18:1-40, I Peter 2:1-12, 24, Psalm 22:24, 25, 26, 27, 28, Hebrews 2:3-4, 12, Hebrews 13:20-21, Hebrews 7:25, II Peter 1:3, I Peter 3:18, John 19:34, Mark 15:34, John 19:30, Luke 22:39-46 verse 42, 44, John 19:24, Mark 15:24, Matthew 27:35, Psalm 26:1-12, 27:1-14, 28:1-9, Luke 23:32-34, Luke 22:53, Isaiah 53:5, 7-9, Luke 22:53, John 19:28, Psalm 22:12-15, Matthew 27:43, 46, Hebrews 2:18, Psalm 22:1, 6-8, Psalm 22:16-18, 22, 23, Hebrews 2:11-12
2. Blessed are the poor in spirit to those who *believe that according to hundred of eyewitnesses, Jesus did die for the world of sinners; for you and me.* Luke 1:2, II Peter 2:16
3. Blessed are the poor in spirit to those who *believe that the acknowledging the inspiration of Scripture is part of the Christian confession.* Romans 10:8-13, 17
4. Blessed are the poor in spirit to those who *believe that every Scripture is God breathed. II Timothy 3:16*
5. Blessed are the poor in spirit to those who believe that *God is not playing with man. God is activity speaking and working in history for man's salvation; for man to repent of his sin, with the great truths, and issues of good and evil, life and death* (Bible) *because God "takes" man or even sinner "seriously."* Mark 1:15, Matthew 3:2, Matthew 4:17, Acts 9:5-6, Acts 9:15-16
6. Blessed are the poor in spirit to those who *believe that the Breathing of God, the Inspiration of God is no accident of history because He comes to bring us salvation by faith through Jesus Christ.* II Timothy 3:16, Genesis 1:1, John 1:1, II Corinthians 1:6

7. Blessed are the poor in spirit to those who *believe that the inspired words are the "original words" in "Greek" and "Hebrew," not the words of the King James Version of the Bible or any other Bible of Interpretations our translation of the Bible.* Genesis 14:13, Exodus 2:11, Jeremiah 34:9, Jonah 1:9, John 19:20, John 19:13, 17, John 5:2, Luke 23:38, Acts 21:40, Acts 22:2, Acts 26:14, Philippians 3:5, Revelation 9:11, Revelation 16:16, Romans 1:16, 10:12, Galatians 2:3, 3:28, Colossians 3:11, Acts 19:17, 20:21, 28, Romans 1:14, I Corinthians 1:22, 23, 24
8. Blessed are the poor in spirit to those who *believe the Word of God*: *"So shall My word be that goeth forth out of My mouth*: it shall *not return unto me "void"* (i.e, without result), *but it shall accomplish that which I please,* and *it shall prosper in the thing whereto I sent it.* Isaiah 55:11
9. Blessed are the poor in spirit to those who *believe that God's Holy Scripture is the supreme rule of faith and practice; everything necessary to salvation is found in God's scripture; the final authority in all matters of faith and practice.* II Timothy 3:16, Hebrews 5:9, Hebrews 12:2
10. Blessed are the poor in spirit to those who *believe that God "Himself" who in all His authority speaks in and through Scripture.* Hebrews 1:1-2
11. Blessed are the poor in spirit to those who *believe that the Holy Spirit or even the Spirit is God's Spirit bearing witness to God's Word and work in Jesus Christ. The Holy Spirit even the Spirit Himself takes the Scriptural Word and makes it clear to heart, mind, will—the whole duty of man—in it's total reach and dimension. God is his own interpreter and God will make it plain.* John 4:24, John 14:17, 15:26, 16:13, Matthew 10:20, Psalm 51:11, Isaiah 63:10, 11, Ephesians 4:30, Ephesians 1:13, Ecclesiastes 12:13, II Timothy 3:14-17
12. Blessed are the poor in spirit to those who *believe that the Scripture is silent. And God say Be Still and know that I am God.* Psalm 46:10

Part CCCXLV

Blessed Are The Poor In Spirit. Matthew 5:3

Blessed Means Happy

Poor means meek in spirit Poor means humble in spirit Poor means lowly in spirit Poor means quiet in spirit Read Matthew 5:3-12, Read also Mark 1:15

Jesus did not say "*rich*" in spirit. Jesus said "*poor*" in spirit.

1. Blessed are the poor in spirit to those who *believe that God is the God of grace and glory to whom we are to fear-(respect) Him and to worship Him and to serve Him.* John 4:24, Acts 4:10, Luke 4:8, Hebrews 11:6, John 12:26, Romans 1:9, Hebrews 12:28, Revelation 7:15, 22:3, Psalm 27:8, II Chronicles 7:14, Isaiah 55:6-9 verse 6, Mark 11:22
2. Blessed are the poor in spirit to those who *believe that when we receive Jesus Christ as our personal Savior and Lord,* we are *forgiven and have life with Him forever.* **I John 1:7, 9**, Matthew 9:2, 5, 6, Mark 2:5, 9, 10, 3:28, 29, 4:12, Luke 5:20, Luke 5:23, 24, Luke 6:37, 7:47, Luke 7:48, 12:10, Acts 8:22, Romans 4:7, **Ephesians 4:32**, Colossians 2:13, **James 5:15**, **I John 2:12, John 1:12, John 5:24, I John 3:14,** Isaiah 6:10, Psalm 32:1, John 20:22, Romans 8:15-16, Galatians 4:5, Ephesians 1:5, Mark 11:22, Habakkuk 2:4, Romans 1:17, Romans 10:17, Galatians 3:11, Hebrews 10:38-39 verse 38
3. Blessed are the poor in spirit to those who *believe that the Word of God is not as merely approved for "private reading" or "secret reading," but is "approved" and "authorized" for public use in church and everywhere to men to come to the knowledge of the truth of the Gospel of Jesus Christ openly.* **I Timothy 2:4**, II Timothy 3:7, Hebrews 10:26, II Peter 2:20, **3:18, II Timothy 3:16,** Hebrews 5:9, Hebrews 2:10, **Mark 16:15**, Luke 24:40, **Isaiah 45:19, Isaiah 48:16, John 14:1-12 verse 6, 8, 9, Genesis 1:1, John 1:1-14 verse 1, Exodus 3:3-16, Philippians 2:6-11 verses 6, 10, 11, Philippians 3:10, Acts 17:27, II Timothy 2:15, I Thessalonians 4:11, Ecclesiastes 12:12-14 verse 13, Mark 11:22, John 4:24, Hebrews 11:6,** Isaiah 7:14, Isaiah 9:6, Matthew 1:21, 23, 25, Luke 1:30, 68, 76-80, Luke 2:11, 21, Luke 7:16
4. Blessed are the poor in spirit to those who *believe God's children who are reliance on the Holy Scripture, prayed this prayer:* "*O Gracious God,* and *Most Merciful*

Father, which *hast vouchsafed us the rich and precious jewels of thy Holy Word, assist us with Thy Spirit, that it may be written in our hearts to our everlasting comfort*, to *reform us*, to *renew us, according to thine own image*; to *build us up*, and to *edify us into the perfect increasing of thy Christ, sanctifying and increasing in us all heavenly virtues. Grant us, O heavenly Father, for Jesus Christ's sake.* "Amen." John 17:17, 19, Ephesians 5:26, I Thessalonians 5:23, Hebrews 13:12, I Peter 3:15, I Peter 1:19, 2:4-5, II Peter 1:1, II Corinthians 6:18, I Corinthians 1:30, John 1:29, 36

5. Blessed are the poor in spirit to those who *believe the Gospel*: "Saying, Where is *He* that is *born King of the Jews*? for *we* have *seen His Star* in the east, and are *come* to *worship Him*. Matthew 2:2, Numbers 24:17, Jeremiah 23:5
6. Blessed are the poor in spirit to those who believe that *That Star is the Lord Jesus Christ.* Numbers 23:17, Matthew 2:2
7. Blessed are the poor in spirit to those who believe that *a Righteousness Brand and a King is the Lord Jesus Christ.* Jeremiah 23:5, Matthew 2:2, Isaiah 11:1, Revelation 22:16
8. Blessed are the poor in spirit to those who believe that the *King of the Jews and His Star is the Lord Jesus Christ.* Matthew 2:2, Numbers 24:17, Jeremiah 23:5
9. Blessed are the poor in spirit to those who believe the Power of Pentecost in the early day of the church. The book of Acts 1 to 28 chapters; Acts 11:26 *The Power of Pentecost through The Acts.* Acts 2:1, Acts 20:16, I Corinthians 16:8
10. Blessed are the poor in spirit to those who *believe in "publicly showing"* by the *scriptures* that *Jesus was Christ.* Acts 18:28
11. Blessed are the poor in spirit to those who believe in the Gift of Peace through Jesus Christ. Ephesians 2:5, 8, Romans 6:23, Ephesians 3:7, James 1:17, Romans 5:16, Romans 5:15, John 3:16
12. Blessed are the poor in spirit to those who believe that the New Testament is the Words of *Christ is "printed in red."* (*Thou say The Lord*) **Matthew** 3:15, 4:4, 7, 10, 17, 19, 5:3-48, 6:1-34, 7:1-27, 8:3-4, 7, 10-13, 20, 22, 26, 9:2, 4-6, 9, 12-13, 15-17, 22, 24, 28, 29-30, 37-38, 10:5-42, 11:4-19, 21-30, 12:3-8, 25-37, 39-45, 48-50, 13:3-9, 11-33, 37-52, 57, 14:16-17, 27, 29, 31, 15:3-11, 13-14, 16-20, 24, 26, 28, 32, 34, 16:2-4, 6, 8-11, 13, 15, 17-19, 23-28, 17:7, 9, 11-12, 17, 20-23, 25-27, 18:3-20, 22-35, 19:4-6, 8-9, 11-12, 14, 17-19, 21, 23-24, 26, 28-30, 20:1-16, 18-19, 21, 22-23, 25-28, 32, 21:2-3, 13, 16, 19, 21-22, 24-25, 27-40, 42-44, 22:2-14, 18-21, 29-32, 37-40, 42-45, 23:2-39, 24:2, 4-51, 25:1-46, 26:2, 10-13, 18, 21, 23, 29, 31-32, 34, 36, 38-42, 45,

50, 52-56, 64, 28:9-10, 18-20, **Mark** 1:15, 17, 25, 38, 44, 2:5, 8-11, 14, 17, 19-22, 25-28, 3:3-5, 23-29, 33-35, 4:3-9, 11-32, 35, 39-40, 5:8-9, 19, 30, 34, 36, 39, 41, 6:4, 10-11, 31, 37-38, 50, 7:6-16, 18-23, 27, 29, 34, 8:2-3, 5, 12, 15, 17-21, 26, 27, 29, 33-38, 9:1, 12-13, 16, 19, 21, 23, 25, 29, 31, 33, 35, 37, 39-50, 10:3, 5-12, 14-15, 18-19, 21, 23-25, 27, 29-31, 33-34, 36, 38-40, 42-45, 51-52, 11:2-3, 14, 17, 22-26, 29-30, 33, 12:1-11, 15-17, 24-27, 29-31, 34-40, 43-44, 13:2, 5-37, 14:6-9, 13-15, 18, 20-21, 24-25, 27-28, 30-32, 34, 36-38, 41-42, 48-49, 62, 15:2, 34, 16:15-18, **Luke** 2:49, 4:4, 8, 12, 18-19, 21, 23-27, 35, 43, 5:4, 10, 13-14, 20, 22-24, 27, 31-32, 34-39, 6:3-5, 8-10, 20-49, 7:9, 13-14, 22-28, 31-35, 40-48, 50, 8:5-8, 10-18, 21-22, 25, 30, 45-46, 48, 50, 52, 54, 9:3-5, 13-14, 18, 20, 22-27, 41, 44, 48, 50, 55-56, 58, 60, 62, 10:2-16, 18-24, 26, 28, 30-37, 41-42, 11:2-13, 17-26, 28-36, 39-44, 46-52, 12:1-12, 14-40, 42-59, 13:2-9, 12, 15-16, 18-21, 24-30, 32-35, 14:3, 5, 8-14, 16-24, 26-35, 15:4-32, 16:1-13, 15-31, 17:1-4, 6-10, 14, 17-37, 18:2-8, 10-14, 16-17, 19-20, 22, 24-25, 27, 29-33, 41-42, 19:5, 9, 12-27, 30-31, 40-44, 46, 20:3-4, 8-18, 24-25, 34-38, 41-44, 46-47, 21:3-4, 6, 8-36, 22:8, 10-12, 15-22, 25-32, 34-38, 40, 42, 46, 48, 51-53, 61, 67-70, 23:3, 28-31, 34, 43, 46, 24:17, 19, 25-26, 36, 38-39, 41, 44-49, **John** 1:38-39, 42-43, 47-48, 50-51, 2:4, 7-8, 16, 19, 3:3, 5-21, 4:7, 10, 13-14, 16-18, 21-24, 26, 32, 34-38, 48, 50, 53, 5:6, 8, 14, 17, 19-47, 6:5, 10, 12, 20, 26-27, 29, 32-40, 43-51, 53-58, 62-65, 67, 70, 7:6-8, 16-19, 21-24, 28-29, 33-34, 37-38, 8:7, 10-12, 14-19, 21, 23-26, 28-29, 31-32, 34-47, 49-51, 54-56, 58, 9:3-5, 7, 35, 37, 39-41, 10:1-5, 7-18, 25-30, 32, 34-38, 11:4, 7, 9-11, 14-15, 23, 25-26, 34`, 39-44, 12:7-8, 23-28, 30-32, 35-36, 44-50, 13:7-8, 10-21, 26-27, 31-36, 38, 14:1-4, 6-7, 9-21, 23-31, 15:1-27, 16:1-16, 19-28, 31-33, 17:1-26, 18:4-5, 7-8, 11, 20-21, 23, 34, 36-37, 19:11, 26-28, 30, 20:15, 16, 17, 19, 21-23, 26-27, 29, 21:5-6, 10, 12, 15-19, 22, **Acts** 1:4-5, 7-8, 9:4-6, 11-12, 15-16, 11:16, 18:9-10, 20:35, 22:7-8, 10, 18, 21, 23:11, 26:14-18, **I Corinthians** 11:24-25 (Mark 14:22-24, Luke 22:19-20), **II Corinthians** 12:9, **Revelation** 1:8, 11, 17-20, Revelation 2:1-29, Revelation 3:1-22, Revelation 16:15, Revelation 22:7, 12-13, 16, 20

Part CCCXLVI

Blessed Are The Poor In Spirit. Matthew 5:3

Blessed Means Happy

Poor means meek in spirit Poor means humble in spirit Poor means lowly in spirit Poor means quiet in spirit Read Matthew 5:3-12, Read also Mark 1:15

Jesus did not say "*rich*" in spirit. Jesus said "*poor*" in spirit.

1. Blessed are the poor in spirit to those who believe the Word of the Lord: "*Sing unto the Lord a new song,* and *his praise from the end of the earth, ye that go down to the sea,* and *all that is therein; the isles,* and *the inhabitants thereof.*" Isaiah 42:10
2. Blessed are the poor in spirit to those who believe the Word of the Lord: "*Let the wilderness and the cities thereof lift up their voice, the villages that Kedar doth inhabit: let the inhabitants of the rock sing, let them shout from the top of the mountains.*" Isaiah 42:11
3. Blessed are the poor in spirit to those who believe the Word of the Lord: "*Let them give glory unto the Lord,* and *declare his praise in the islands.*" Isaiah 42:12
4. Blessed are the poor in spirit to those who *believe that Paul was truly called of Jesus Christ and was appointed a preacher, an apostle and a teacher of the Gentiles.* II Timothy 1:11, See Acts 9:15-16
5. Blessed are the poor in spirit to those who *believe "this holy calling:" "Who hath saved us,* and *called us with an holy calling, not according to our works, but according to His own purpose and grace, which was given us in Christ Jesus before the world began.*" II Timothy 1:9
6. Blessed are the poor in spirit to those who *believe like Paul, that Christ's vision is that the Lord call us to preach the gospel to His people.* Acts 16:10
7. Blessed are the poor in spirit to those who *believed liked the Samaritans that many more believed because of "Jesus' own word;"* And *said unto the woman, Now we believe, not because of thy saying:* for *we have heard Him "ourselves,"* and "*know*" *that this is indeed the "Christ,"* the *Saviour of the world.* John 4:41-42, I John 4:9, 14
8. Blessed are the poor in spirit to those who believe in sound doctrine, sound ministry, sound teaching, sound principal of the Word of God where the gospel is preached. II Timothy 3:14-17, II Timothy 4:1-5, Titus 1:9, Titus 2:1, II Timothy 1:7

9. Blessed are the poor in spirit to those who believe that "*since*" God's children *believe in the singular form for Oneness*; that *is they believe God as One. Since we as children of God, believe in the singular form of God who is as One, we believe in the plural form of finding Triune God as the Father, the Son and the Holy Spirit.* **II Corinthians 13:14**, Acts 17:29, Romans 1:20, Colossians 2:9, Matthew 28:18-20, verse 19 Genesis 1:26, I John 5:20, **Hebrews 13:8**, Matthew 3:17, 12:18, Matthew 17:5, Mark 1:11, 9:7, Luke 3:22, 9:35, Isaiah 52:6, John 4:26, John 5:18, John 9:37, John 10:30, 33, John 4:26, John 5:18, John 10:30, 33, John 19:7, Luke 32:2, John 8:55-59 verse 58, John 5:22-29 verse 27, Matthew 6:13, 9:6, 8, 10:1, Matthew 22:29, Mark 2:10, Luke 4:32, 5:24, 9:1, 10:19, John 10:18, 17:2, 19:11, 1:8, Acts 26:18, **Acts 9:1-5** verse 5, Revelation 1:7-8, 11, 17-18, Revelation 2:8, Revelation 16:15, Revelation 22:7, 12-13, 16, 20, Revelation 3:11, John 14:6-12 verse 6, 7-9, Acts 2:36, **Acts 10:36, Philippians 3:10,** I Timothy 3:16, Ephesians 4:30, Psalm 51:11, Isaiah 63:10-11, II Peter 3:4, II Peter 3:10, I Thessalonians 5:2-4 verse 2, Matthew 24:32-44, Revelation 3:3, **Amos 4:12,** II Peter 3:10, I Thessalonians 5:2-4 verse 2, Matthew 24:32-44, Revelation 3:3, Isaiah 55:6-9 verse 6, John 8:32, 36
10. Blessed are the poor in spirit to those who *kept back nothing*, or *held back nothing*, but to *show us to teach us publicly* (*openly*) *from house to house testifying both to the Jews*, and also to the *Greeks*, *repentance toward God*, and *faith toward our Lord Jesus Christ. Acts 20:20-21*
11. Blessed are the poor in spirit to those who *believe The Bible is alive*; **The Bible** *speak to me*; Then *opened He their understanding*, that *they might understand the scriptures. Luke 24:45*
12. Blessed are the poor in spirit to those who *might understand the scriptures*; it is *written*, and thus it *behoved* (*to be necessary for*) *Christ to suffer*, and to *rise from the dead the third day*: And that *repentance and remission of sins should be preached in His Name among all nations, beginning at Jerusalem.* And ye *are witnesses of these things*. And, *behold*, *I—(Jesus) send the promise of my Father upon you*: "*but*" *tarry* (*stay, wait*) ye *in the city of Jerusalem, until ye be endued* (clothed) *with power from on high*; *that Christ led them out as far as to Bethany*; and *Christ lifted up His Hands and blessed them*; and *Christ parted* (*left*) *from them*, and *carried up* (*went back*) into heaven. And they worshipped **Him**, and *returned to Jerusalem with great joy*: *continuing in the temple praising and blessing God. Amen. Luke 24:46-53.* See *Hosea 6:1-3, Luke 24:46*, I *Corinthians 15:4, Matthew 20:22*

Part CCCXLVII

Blessed Are The Poor In Spirit. Matthew 5:3

Blessed Means Happy

Poor means meek in spirit Poor means humble in spirit Poor means lowly in spirit Poor means quiet in spirit Read Matthew 5:3-12, Read also Mark 1:15

Jesus did not say "*rich*" in spirit. Jesus said "*poor*" in spirit.

1. Blessed are the poor in spirit to those who *believe that God is our builder and our Maker.* Hebrews 11:10
2. Blessed are the poor in spirit to those who *believe*: "*are looking for a builder and Maker, whose name is God.*" *Hebrews 11:10*
3. Blessed are the poor in spirit to those who *believe*: "For he *looked for a city which hath foundations, whose builder and maker is God. Hebrews 11:10*
4. Blessed are the poor in spirit to those who *give our very best to the Master, the Lord Jesus Christ, through faithfulness until death or until He comes to take us home to glory.* Revelation 2:10, I Thessalonians 4:16-17, Colossians 3:4, Matthew 25:31
5. Blessed are the poor in spirit to those who *believe to keep the "flame burning" for Jesus Christ.* Luke 24:49, Acts 1:8, Acts 2:1-4, Acts 1:4-5, Luke 3:16, Acts 7:31, Exodus 3:1-15
6. Blessed are the poor in spirit to those who *believe the Word of God*: "The *grass withereth, the flower fadeth: because the Spirit of the Lord bloweth upon it: surely the people is grass. Isaiah 40:6-7, I Peter 1:24*
7. Blessed are the poor in spirit to those who *believe the Word of God*: "The *grass withereth, the flower fadeth: but the word of our God shall stand for ever.*" *Isaiah 40:8, Psalm 100:5, Psalm 111:7-8, Psalm 117:2, Ezekiel 24:14, Matthew 24:35*
8. Blessed are the poor in spirit to those who believe that "*the words of Holy Scripture*" "*as originally*" *penned in* "*the Hebrew*" *and* "*Greek*" *were inspired by God. II Timothy 3:16, Genesis 1:1, John 1:1-18 verse 1, 14, John 14:1-12 verses 7, 8, 9, Philippians 2:6-11 verses 10, 11, Philippians 3:10, Hebrews 13:8*
9. Blessed are the poor in spirit to those who *believe that the Bible, God's Word,* the *Eternal Word of God, speak* "*with fresh power,*" to *give knowledge that leads to salvation that men and women may serve Christ to the glory of God.* Luke 1:77,

Matthew 25:46, Acts 1:8, John 10:28, John 3:15, John 6:54, 68, John 12:25, 17:2-3, Acts 13:48, Romans 5:21, 6:23, I Timothy 6:12, 19, II Timothy 2:10, Titus 1:2, 3:7, Hebrews 5:9, Hebrews 6:2-4 verse 4, Hebrews 9:12, 14, 15, I Peter 5:10, I John 1:2, I John 2:25, I John 5:11, 13, 5:20, Mark 11:22, John 20:22, Isaiah 28:12

10. Blessed are the poor in spirit to those who believe that the *Words of Christ in red is spoken by the mouth of Jesus.* **Matthew** 3:15, 4:4, 7, 10, 17, 19, 5:3-48, 6:1-34, 7:1-27, 8:3-4, 7, 10-13, 20, 22, 26, 9:2, 4-6, 9, 12-13, 15-17, 22, 24, 28, 29-30, 37-38, 10:5-42, 11:4-19, 21-29, 12:3-8, 25-37, 39-45, 48-50, 13:3-9, 11-33, 37-52, 57, 14:16-17, 27, 29, 31, 15:3-11, 13-14, 16-20, 24, 26, 28, 32, 34, 16:2-4, 6, 8-11, 13, 15, 17-19, 23-28, 17:7, 9, 11-12, 17, 20-23, 25-27, 18:3-20, 22-35, 19:4-6, 8-9, 11-12, 14, 17-19, 21, 23-24, 26, 28-30, 20:1-16, 18-19, 21, 22-23, 25-28, 32, 21:2-3, 13, 16, 19, 21-22, 24-25, 27-40, 42-44, 22:2-214, 18-21, 29-32, 37-40, 42-45, 23:2-39, 24:2, 4-51, 25:1-46, 26:2, 10-13, 18, 21, 23, 29, 31-32, 34, 36, 38-42, 45, 50, 52-56, 64, 28:9-10, 18-20, **Mark** 1:15, 17, 25, 38, 44, 2:5, 8-11, 14, 17, 19-22, 25-28, 3:3-5, 23-29, 33-35, 4:3-9, 11-32, 35, 39-40, 5:8-9, 19, 30, 34, 36, 39, 41, 6:4, 10-11, 31, 37-38, 50, 7:6-16, 18-23, 27, 29, 34, 8:2-3, 5, 12, 15, 17-21, 26, 27, 29, 33-38, 9:1, 12-13, 16, 19, 21, 23, 25, 29, 31, 33, 35, 37, 39-50, 10:3, 5-12, 14-15, 18-19, 21, 23-25, 27, 29-31, 33-34, 36, 38-40, 42-45, 51-52, 11:2-3, 14, 17, 22-26, 29-30, 33, 12:1-11, 15-17, 24-27, 29-31, 34-40, 43-44, 13:2, 5-37, 14:6-9, 13-15, 18, 20-21, 24-25, 27-28, 30-32, 34, 36-38, 41-42, 48-49, 62, 15:2, 34, 16:15-18, **Luke** 2:49, 4:4, 8, 12, 18-19, 21, 23-27, 35, 43, 5:4, 10, 13-14, 20, 22-24, 27, 31-32, 34-39, 6:3-5, 8-10, 20-49, 7:9, 13-14, 22-28, 31-35, 40-48, 50, 8:5-8, 10-18, 21-22, 25, 30, 45-46, 48, 50, 52, 54, 9:3-5, 13-14, 18, 20, 22-27, 41, 44, 48, 50, 55-56, 58, 60, 62, 10:2-16, 18-24, 26, 28, 30-37, 41-42, 11:2-13, 17-26, 28-36, 39-44, 46-52, 12:1-12, 14-40, 42-59, 13:2-9, 12, 15-16, 18-21, 24-30, 32-35, 14:3, 5, 8-14, 16-24, 26-35, 15:4-32, 16:1-13, 15-31, 17:1-4, 6-10, 14, 17-37, 18:2-8, 10-14, 16-17, 19-20, 22, 24-25, 27, 29-33, 41-42, 19:5, 9, 12-27, 30-31, 40-44, 46, 20:3-4, 8-18, 24-25, 34-38, 41-44, 46-47, 21:3-4, 6, 8-36, 22:8, 10-12, 15-22, 25-32, 34-38, 40, 42, 46, 48, 51-53, 61, 67-70, 23:3, 28-31, 34, 43, 46, 24:17, 19, 25-26, 36, 38-39, 41, 44-49, **John** 1:38-39, 42-43, 47-48, 50-51, 2:4, 7-8, 16, 19, 3:3, 5-21, 4:7, 10, 13-14, 16-18, 21-24, 26, 32, 34-38, 48, 50, 53, 5:6, 8, 14, 17, 19-47, 6:5, 10, 12, 20, 26-27, 29, 32-40, 43-51, 53-58, 62-65, 67, 70, 7:6-8, 16-19, 21-24,

28-29, 33-34, 37-38, 8:7, 10-12, 14-19, 21, 23-26, 28-29, 31-32, 34-47, 49-51, 54-56, 58, 9:3-5, 7, 35, 37, 39-41, 10:1-5, 7-18, 25-30, 32, 34-38, 11:4, 7, 9-11, 14-15, 23, 25-26, 35, 39-44, 12:7-8, 23-28, 30-32, 35-36, 44-50, 13:7-8, 10-21, 26-27, 31-36, 38, 14:1-4, 6-7, 9-21, 23-31, 15:1-27, 16:1-16, 19-28, 31-33, 17:1-26, 18:4-5, 7-8, 11, 20-21, 23, 34, 36-37, 19:11, 26-28, 30, 20:15, 16, 17, 19, 21-23, 26-27, 29, 21:5-6, 10, 12, 15-19, 22, **Acts** 1:4-5, 7-8, 9:4-6, 11-12, 15-16, 11:16, 18:9-10, 20:35, 22:7-8, 10, 18, 21, 23:11, 26:14-18, **I Corinthians** 11:24-25 (Mark 14:22-24, Luke 22:19-20), **II Corinthians** 12:9, **Revelation** 1:8, 11, 17-20, Revelation 2:1-29, Revelation 3:1-22, Revelation 16:15, Revelation 22:7, 12-13, 16, 20

11. Blessed are the poor in spirit to those who *believe in Jesus*: "And He said unto them, *I must preach the kingdom of God to other cities also*: for *therefore* (*for this reason*) *am I sent.*" *Luke 4:43*
12. Blessed are the poor in spirit to those who *believe that the Word of the Lord is God*; that the *Word of the Lord is Jesus*, is "*the One*" *and* "*the Same Lord.*" *John 6:34, Acts 9:5, John 6:33, 34, 35, 36, 37, 38, 39, 40, 41, 42, 43, 44* (*See John 14:6-9, See Jeremiah 31:3*), *45*, (*See Isaiah 54:13*), *46, 47, 48*, (*See verse 33, 50, 51*), *49, 50, 51, 52, 53, 54, 55, 56, 57, 58, 59, 60* (*See John 8:13-19, John 6:60, II Peter 3:16*), Acts 10:26, Philippians 2:6-11, verse 10, 11, Philippians 3:10, Hebrews 13:8, Revelation 1:7-8, 17-18, Revelation 2:8, Revelation 3:7, 11, Revelation 4:8, Revelation 16:15, Revelation 22:7, 12-23, 16, 20

PART CCCXLVIII

Blessed Are The Poor In Spirit. Matthew 5:3

Blessed Means Happy

Poor means meek in spirit. Poor means humble in spirit. Poor means lowly in spirit. Poor means quiet in spirit. Read Matthew 5:3-12, Read also Mark 1:15

Jesus did not say "*rich*" in spirit. Jesus said "*poor*" in spirit.

1. Blessed are the poor in spirit to those who believe this Psalmist: "*But God will redeem my soul from the power of the grave*: for *he shall receive me*." Psalm 49:15
2. Blessed are the poor in spirit to those who believe this Psalmist: "*For thou wilt not leave my soul in hell; neither wilt thou suffer thine Holy One to see corruption*." Psalm 16:10
3. Blessed are the poor in spirit to those who believe: "*Wherefore he saith also in another psalm, Thou shalt not suffer thine Holy One to see corruption*." Acts 13:35
4. Blessed are the poor in spirit to those who believe: "*I have seen his ways*, and *will heal him*: *I will lead him also*, and restore comforts unto him and to his mourners." Isaiah 57:18
5. Blessed are the poor in spirit to those who believe: "*I create the fruit of the lips; Peace, peace to him that is far off*, and *to him that is near*, saith the Lord; *and I will heal him*." Isaiah 57:19
6. Blessed are the poor in spirit to those who believe: "*For the promise is unto you, and to your children, and to all that afar off, even as many as the Lord our God shall call*." Acts 2:39
7. Blessed are the poor in spirit to those who believe: "*Now therefore ye are no more strangers and foreigners, but fellowcitizens with the saints, and of the household of God*;" Ephesians 2:19
8. Blessed are the poor in spirit to those who *believe that the bread of God is He which cometh down from heaven*, and *giveth life unto the world. John 6:33*
9. Blessed are the poor in spirit to those who *believe*: "Then said they unto *Him, Lord, evermore (forever) give us this bread. John 6:34*
10. Blessed are the poor in spirit to those who *hear the mouth of Jesus' spoken word*: "*I am the bread of life*: *he that cometh to Me shall never hunger*; and *he that believeth on Me shall never thirst*." John 6:35

11. Blessed are the poor in spirit to those who believe the mouth of Jesus' spoken *word*: "*But I said unto you*, That *ye also have seen Me*, and *believe not*." *John 6:36*
12. Blessed are the poor in spirit to those who *believe the mouth of Jesus' spoken word*: "*All that the Father giveth Me shall come to Me*; and *him that cometh to me I will in no wise cast out*." *John 6:37*

Part CCCXLIX

Blessed Are The Poor In Spirit. Matthew 5:3

Blessed Means Happy

Poor means meek in spirit. Poor means humble in spirit. Poor means lowly in spirit. Poor means quiet in spirit. Read Matthew 5:3-12, Read also Mark 1:15

Jesus did not say "*rich*" in spirit. Jesus said "*poor*" in spirit.

1. Blessed are the poor in spirit to those who *believe the mouth of Jesus' spoken word*: "For I *came down from heaven, not to do mine own will*, but the *will of Him that sent Me*." *John 6:38*
2. Blessed are the poor in spirit to those who *believe the mouth of Jesus' spoken word*: "And *this is the Father's will which hath sent Me*, that of *all which He hath given Me I should lose nothing*, but should *raise it up again at the last day*." *John 6:39*
3. Blessed are the poor in spirit to those who *believe the mouth of Jesus' spoken word*: "And *this is the will of Him* (*God the Father*) that *sent Me* (Jesus), that every one which *seeth the Son* (*Jesus*) and *believeth on him*(Jesus), *may have everlasting life*: and I (Jesus) will *raise him up at the last day. John 6:40*
4. Blessed are the poor in spirit to those who have *heard and have believed that Jesus is the bread, "but" the Jews then murmured* (*grumbled*) *at Him, because He said, I am the bread which came down from heaven. John 6:41*
5. Blessed are the poor in spirit to those who had *heard and had believed that Jesus is the bread, "But"* the *Jews said, "how is it then that He saith, I came down from heaven?" John 6:42*
6. Blessed are the poor in spirit to those who *believe the mouth of Jesus' spoken word*: "*No man can come to Me* (Jesus), *except the Father* (God) *which hath sent Me*(Jesus) *draw him*: and I (Jesus) *will raise him up at the last day*." *John 6:44, See Jeremiah 31:3, John 14:6*
7. Blessed are the poor in spirit to those who *believe the mouth of Jesus' spoken word*: "It is *written in the prophets*, And they shall *be all taught of God. Every man therefore that hath heard*, and *hath learned of the Father, cometh unto Me*." *John 6:45. See Isaiah 54:13*

8. Blessed are the poor in spirit to those who *believe the mouth of Jesus' spoken word*: "*Not that any men hath seen the Father, save* (*except*) *He which is of God, He hath seen the Father.*" *John 6:46*
9. Blessed are the poor in spirit to those who *believe the mouth of Jesus' spoken word*: "Verily, verily, *I say unto you, He that believe on Me* (Jesus) *hath everlasting life.*" *John 6:47*
10. Blessed are the poor in spirit to those who *believe the mouth of Jesus' spoken word*: "*I am that bread of life; Jesus is that bread of life.*" *John 6:48*
11. Blessed are the poor in spirit to those who had *heard and had believed that Jesus* "*admitted*" *from His mouth, the spoken word*: "*Your fathers did eat* "*manna*" *in the wilderness*, and *are dead. John 6:49. See John 6:31, 32.*
12. Blessed are the poor in spirit to those who *believe the mouth of Jesus' spoken word*: "*This is the bread* (*manna*) *which cometh down from heaven, that a man may eat thereof, and not die.*" *John 6:50*

Part CCCL

Blessed Are The Poor In Spirit. Matthew 5:3

Blessed Means Happy

Poor means meek in spirit. Poor means humble in spirit. Poor means lowly in spirit. Poor means quiet in spirit. Read Matthew 5:3-12, Read also Mark 1:15

Jesus did not say "*rich*" in spirit. Jesus said "*poor*" in spirit.

1. Blessed are the poor in spirit to those who *believe the mouth of Jesus' spoken word*: "*I am the living bread (Jesus) which came down from heaven*: "*if*" *any man eat of this bread (Jesus, living bread)*, he shall *live for ever*: and the *bread (flesh of Jesus)* that I (Jesus) *will give is my flesh*, which *I will give for the life (free to) of the world.*" *John 6:51*
2. Blessed are the poor in spirit to those who believe that Jesus is *all presence*. Romans 8:11
3. Blessed are the poor in spirit to those who believe that Jesus is *all knowledge*. I Corinthians 2:10-11
4. Blessed are the poor in spirit to those who believe that Jesus is *everywhere*. Psalm 139:11
5. Blessed are the poor in spirit to those who *believe what Jesus has to say*: "*Enter ye in at the strait* (narrow) *gate*: for *wide is the gate*, and *broad is the way, that leadeth to destruction*, and *many there be which go in thereat*. Matthew 7:13
6. Blessed are the poor in spirit to those who *believe why Jesus has to say*: "*Because strait is the gate*, and *narrow* is the *way*, whihch *leadeth unto life*, and *few there be that find it* (the gate of Heaven). Matthew 7:14
7. Blessed are the poor in spirit to those who *know, believe, understand and realize that we do not want to die and be burnt in hell because that is not God's plan for us but to live with Him in Glory unto Heaven to those who have accept Jesus Christ as Personal Lord and Saviour and believe in His Second Coming*. Revelation 22:7, 12, 20
8. Blessed are the poor in spirit to those who *believe that Jesus is the bread from heaven*; that *Jesus is the true bread from heaven*; that *Jesus is the bread of God which is He what come down from heaven*, to *give life unto the world*; that *Jesus is Lord of*

that bread from which He come down; that *Jesus is the bread of life*; *that Jesus is the everlasting life*; *that Jesus is the living bread to give life of the world. John 6:32, 33, 34, 35, 40, 47, 48, 50, 51.*

9. Blessed are the poor in spirit to those who *believe that Jesus is that Flesh,* to *give for the light of the world*; *sinners to see the light which is Jesus Christ*, our *Saviour, in the flesh. John 6:51*
10. Blessed are the poor in spirit to those who *believe that Jesus is the flesh of the Son of Man and He is that Blood. John 6:53*
11. Blessed are the poor in spirit to those who *believe that whoever eat Christ's flesh and drink Christ's blood has eternal life because Christ will raise us up at the last day. John 6:54*
12. Blessed are the poor in spirit to those who *believe that Christ's flesh is meat*; *indeed that Christ's flesh is food indeed*; and *that Christ's blood is drink indeed. John 6:55*

Part CCCLI

Blessed Are The Poor In Spirit. Matthew 5:3

Blessed Means Happy

Poor means meek in spirit. Poor means humble in spirit. Poor means lowly in spirit. Poor means quiet in spirit. Read Matthew 5:3-12, Read also Mark 1:15

Jesus did not say "*rich*" in spirit. Jesus said "*poor*" in spirit.

1. Blessed are the poor in spirit to those who *believe the mouth of Jesus' spoken word*: "*He that eateth my flesh*, and *drinketh my blood, dwell* (*abide*) *in me, and I in him.*" *John 6:56*
2. Blessed are the poor in spirit to those who *believe the mouth of Jesus's spoken word*: "*As the living Father hath sent Me, and I live by the Father: so he that eateth Me, even he shall live by* (*because of*) *Me.*" *John 6:57*
3. Blessed are the poor in spirit to those who *believe the mouth of Jesus' spoken word*: "*This is that bread which came down from heaven: not as your fathers did eat manna*, and *are dead: he that eateth of this bread shall live for ever.*" *John 6:58*
4. Blessed are the poor in spirit to those who *believe and have some hard time, understand Christ's teaching, are difficult to be heard and to be understaood because when Christ's disciples heard this said*; "*This is an hard* (*difficult*) *saying; who can hear* (*understand*) *it* (*this*). *John 6:60, see John 8:13-19, II Peters 3:16*
5. Blessed are the poor in spirit to those who *believe the mouth of Jesus' spoken word*: "*Therefore said I unto you, that no man can come unto me, except it were given unto him of my Father. John 6:65*
6. Blessed are the poor in spirit to those who *believe that Jesus is Lord*; that *Jesus has the words of eternal life*; that *Jesus is* "*that Christ*;" that *Jesus is the Son of the living God. John 6:68-69*
7. Blessed are the poor in spirit to those who *believe the mouth of Jesus' spoken word*: "*Very very, I say unto you, If a man keep* (obey) *My saying, he shall* "*never see*" (never taste, never experience, never believe in) death. John 8:51, Luke 2:26, Matthew 16:28, Mark 9:1
8. Blessed are the poor in spirit to those who *believe that the Red Bold Mark is spoken from the mouth of Jesus Christ in Acts 1:4-5, Acts 1:7-8, Acts 9:4-6, Acts 9:10-12,*

15, Acts 11:16, Acts 18:9-10, Acts 20:35, Acts 22:7-8, Acts 22:10, Acts 22:18, 21, Acts 23:11, Acts 26:14-18, I Corinthians 11:24-25, II Corinthians 12:9, Revelation 1:8, 11, 17-20, Revelation 2:1-29, Revelation 3:1-27, Revelation 22:7, Revelation 22:12-13, 16, 20.

9. Blessed are the poor in spirit to those who *believe the mouth of Jesus' spoken word*: "*Behold, I come quickly,...behold, I come quickly,... Surely I come quickly. Revelation 22:7, 12, 20*
10. Blessed are the poor in spirit to those who *believe the mouth of Jesus' spoken word*: "*In Big Red Bold Mark*:" Matthew 3:15, Matthew 4:4, 7, 10, 17, 19, Matthew 5:3-48, Matthew 6:1-34, Matthew 7:27, Matthew 8:3-4, 7, 10-13, 20, 22, 26, Matthew 9:2, 4-6, 9, 12-13, 15-17, 22, 24, 28-30, 37-38, Matthew 10:5-42, Matthew 11:4-19, 21-30, Matthew 12:3-8, 11-13, 25-37, 39-45, 48-50, Matthew 13:3-9, 11-33, 37-52, 57, Matthew 14:16-17, 27, 29, Matthew 14:31, Matthew 15:3-11, 13-14, 16-20, 24, 26, 28, 32, 34, Matthew 16:2-4, 6, 8-11, 13, 15, 17-19, 23-28, Matthew 17:7, 9, 11-12, 17, 20-23, 25-27, Matthew 18:3-20, 22-25, Matthew 19:4-6, 8-9, 11-12, 14, 17-19, 21, 23-24, 26, 28-30, Matthew 20:1-16, 18-19, 21-23, 25-28, 32, Matthew 21:2-3, 13, Matthew 21:16-19, 21-22, 24-25, 27-40, 42-44, Matthew 22:2-14, Matthew 22:18-21, 29-32, 37-45, Matthew 23:2-39, Matthew 24:2, 4-51, Matthew 25:1-46, Matthew 26:2, 10-13, 18, 21, 23-29, 31-32, 34, 36, 38-42, 45-46, 50, 52-56, 64, Matthew 27:11, 46, Matthew 28:9-10, Matthew 28:18-20
11. Blessed are the poor in spirit to those who *believe the mouth of Jesus' spoken word*: "*In Red With Bold Mark in Mark*:" Mark 1:15, 17, 25, 38, 44, Mark 2:8-11, 14, 17, 19-22, 25-28, Mark 3:4-5, 23-29, Mark 3:33-35, Mark 4:3-9, 11-32, 35, 39-40, Mark 5:8-9, Mark 5:19, 30, 34, 36, 39, 41, Mark 6:4, 10-11, 31, 37-38, Mark 6:50, Mark 7:6-16, 18-23, 27, 29, 34, Mark 8:2-3, 5, 12, 15, 17-21, 26, 27, 29, 33-38, Mark 9:1, 12-13, 16, 19, 21, 23, 25, 29, 31, 33, 35, 37, 39-50, Mark 10:3, 5-9, 11-12, 14-15, 18-19, 21, 23-25, 27, 29-31, 33-34, 36, 38-40, 42-45, 51-52, Mark 11:2-3, 14, 17, 22-26, 29-30, 33, Mark 12:1-11, 15-17, 24-27, 29-31, 34-40, 43-44, Mark 13:2, 5-37, Mark 14:6-9, 13-15, 18, 20-22, 24-25, 27-28, 30, 32, 34, 36-38, 41-42, 48-49, 62, Mark 15:2, 34, Mark 16:15-18
12. Blessed are the poor in spirit to those who *believe the mouth of Jesus' spoken word*: "*In Red With Bold Mark*:" Luke 2:49, Luke 4:4, 8, 12, 18-19, 21, 23-27, 35, Luke 5:4, 10, 13-14, 20, 22-24, 27, 31-32, 34-39, Luke 6:3-5, 8-10, 20-49,

Luke 7:9, 13-14, 24-28, 31-35, 40-48, 50, Luke 8:5-8, 10-18, 21-22, 30, 45-46, 48, 50, 52, 54, Mark 9:3-5, 13-14, 18, 20, 22-27, 41, 44, 48, 50, 55-56, Mark 10:2-16, 18-24, 26, 28, 30-37, 41-42, Mark 11:2-13, 17-26, 28-36, 39-44, 46-52, Luke 12:1-12, 14-40, 42-59, Luke 13:2-9, 12, 15-16, 18-21, 24-30, 32-35, Luke 14:3, 5, 8-14, 16-24, 26-35, Luke 15:4-32, Luke 16:1-13, 15-31, Luke 17:1-4, 6-10, 14, 17-36, Luke 18:2-8, 10-14, 16-17, 19-20, 22-24, 25, 27, 29-33, 41-42, Luke 19:5, 9-10, 12-27, 30-31, 40-44, 46, Luke 20:3-4, 8-18, 23-25, 34-38, 41-47, Luke 21:3-4, 6, 8-36, Luke 22:8, 10-12, 15-22, 25-32, 34-36, 40, 42, 46, 48, 51-53, 61, 67-70, Luke 23:3, Luke 23:28-31, 34, 43, 46, Luke 24:17, 19, 25-26, 36, 38-39, 41, 44, 46-49.

Part CCCLII

Blessed Are The Poor In Spirit. Matthew 5:3

Blessed Means Happy

Poor means meek in spirit. Poor means humble in spirit. Poor means lowly in spirit. Poor means quiet in spirit. Read Matthew 5:3-12, Read also Mark 1:15

Jesus did not say "*rich*" in spirit. Jesus said "*poor*" in spirit.

1. Blessed are the poor in spirit to those who *believe the Word of the Lord*: "*Saying, Touch not mine anointed, and do my prophets no harm.*" *I Chronicles 16:22, Psalm 105:15*
2. Blessed are the poor in spirit to those who *believe in asking God for forgiveness through prayer like David prayed*: *I have sinned greatly, because I have done this thing*: *but now, I beseech* (beg) *thee do* (take) *away the iniquity of Thy Servant*; *Read I Chronicles 21:8-30*
3. Blessed are the poor in spirit to those who *believe the mouth of Jesus' spoken word*: "*In Red Bold Mark*:" John 1:38-39, 42, 47-48, 50-51, John 2:4, 7-8, 16, 19, John 3:3, 5-8, 10-21, John 4:7, 10, 13-14, 16-18, 21-24, 26, 32, 34-38, 48, 50, 53, John 5:6, 8, 14, 17, 19-47, John 6:5, 10, 12, 20, 26-27, 29, 32-33, 35-40, 43-51, 53-58, 61-65, 67, 70, John 7:6-8, 16-19, 21-24, 28-29, 33-34, 37-38, John 8:7, 10-12, 14-19, 21, 23-26, 28-29, 31-32, 34-47, 49-51, 54-56, 58, John 9:3-5, 7, 35, 37, 39, 41, John 10:1-5, 7-18, 25-30, 32, 34-38, John 11:4-7, 9-11, 14-15, 23, 25-26, 34, 39-44, John 12:7-8, 23-28, 30-32, 35-36, 44-50, John 13:7-8, 10-21, 26-27, 31-36, 38, John 14:1-4, 6-7, 9-21, 23-31, John 15:1-27, John 16:1-16, 19-28, 31-33, John 17:1-26, John 18:4-5, 7-8, 11, 20-21, 23, 34, 36-37, John 19:11, 26, 28, 30, John 20:15-17, 19, 21-23, 26-27, 29, John 21:5-6, 10, 12, 15-19, 22
4. Blessed are the poor in spirit to those who *believe and want to be saved* "*Now*:" *Behold, I stand at the door and knock*: *If anyone hear my voice, and open the door, I will come in to him, and will sup* (abide, live, stay, remain) *with him, and he with me. Revelation 3:20*
5. Blessed are the poor in spirit to those who *believe in searching for Jesus through*: *Love, Joy, Peace, Longsuffering, Gentleness, Goodness, Faith, Meekness, Temperance*

(self-control), *Hope, Smile, Happiness, Cheerful, Care* and *Commitment.* Galatians 5:22-23, I Peter 5:7, Psalm 37:3-5, Proverbs 15:13, Ephesians 6:7-17,

6. Blessed are the poor in spirit to those who *believe the testimony of one of God's children, named Apostle Peter*: "*And the Spirit bade* (was told what to do, commanded) *me go with them, nothing doubting.*" *Acts 11:12. See Acts 10:20, Acts 10:17*
7. Blessed are the poor in spirit to those who *believe the Word of the Lord God*: "*Be not afraid nor dismayed by reason of this great multitude*; "*for the battle*" is "*not yours,*" *but* "*God's. II Chronicles 20:15*
8. Blessed are the poor in spirit to those who *believe the Word of the Lord God*: "Ye *shall not need to fight in this battle*: *set yourselves, stand ye still,* and *see the salvation of the Lord with you,* O *Judah and Jerusalem* (*people of God, people of Israel, men and women of faith in God, in the Lord*): *fear not, nor be dismayed*; *to morrow go out against them*; *for the Lord will be with you.*" *II Chronicles 20:17*
9. Blessed are the poor in spirit to those who *believe from the Word of the Lord God that every man shall die for his own sin. II Chronicles 25:4*
10. Blessed are the poor in spirit to those who *believe that the Name of the Lord will be for ever. II Chronicles 33:4, 7-8*
11. Blessed are the poor in spirit to those who *believe that upon an human being, this story of a person*; stay *reverently*; *humble relying upon the Spirit of God through Jesus Christ to teach him, he will find truths that will satisfy the mind and edify the soul*; Job 6:24, Psalm 25:4-5, 8, Psalm 86:11, Exodus 24:12, Exodus 4:12, 15, John 14:26, Luke 12:12, Psalm 90:12, Psalm 119:33, Psalm 132:10-18, Psalm 143:10, Psalm 40:8, Hebrews 10:7, Psalm 81:10
12. Blessed are the poor in spirit to those who *believe and hear the Word of the Lord God*: "*And unto man He said,* "*Behold, the fear of the Lord, that is wisdom*; *and to depart from evil is understanding. Job 28:28*

Part CCCLIII

Blessed Are The Poor In Spirit. Matthew 5:3

Blessed Means Happy

Poor means meek in spirit Poor means humble in spirit Poor means lowly in spirit Poor means quiet in spirit Read Matthew 5:3-12, Read also Mark 1:15

Jesus did not say "*rich*" in spirit. Jesus said "*poor*" in spirit.

1. Blessed are the poor in spirit to those who *believe in salvation of the Lord in this Psalmist: "Hear, O Lord, when I cry with my voice: have mercy also upon (be gracious to) me, and answer me." Psalm 27:7*
2. Blessed are the poor in spirit to those who *believe in salvation of the Lord in this Psalmist: "When Thou saidst, "Seek ye My face;" my heart said, unto Thee, "Thy face, Lord, will I seek." Psalm 27:8*
3. Blessed are the poor in spirit to those who *believe in salvation of the Lord in this Psalmist: "Hide not Thy face far from me; put not Thy servant away in anger: Thou hast been my help; leave me not, neither forsake me, O God of my salvation." Psalm 27:9*
4. Blessed are the poor in spirit to those who *believe in salvation of the Lord in this psalmist: "I will instruct thee and teach thee in the way which thou shall go: I will guide Thee with Mine eye." Psalm 32:8*
5. Blessed are the poor in spirit to those who *believe the Word of the Lord: "Be ye not as the horse, or as the mule, which have no understanding: whose mouth must be held in with bit and bridle, lest they come near unto thee. Psalm 32:9*
6. Blessed are the poor in spirit to those who *believe the Word of the Lord: "Many sorrows shall be to the wicked: but he that trusteth in the Lord, Mercy shall compass him about." Psalm 32:10*
7. Blessed are the poor in spirit to those who *believe the Word of the Lord: "Be glad in the Lord, and rejoice, ye righteous: and shout for joy, all ye that are upright in heart. Psalm 32:11*
8. Blessed are the poor in spirit to those who *believe and heard the Word of the Lord God: "Therefore the Lord "Himself" shall give you a sign; Behold, a virgin shall conceive and bear a son, and shall call His name Immanuel (God with us)." Isaiah 7:14. See Matthew 1:23*

9. Blessed are the poor in spirit to those who *believe and hear the Word of the Lord*: "*Seek ye out of the book of the Lord, and* "*read*:" *no one of these shall fail, none shall want it's mate*: *for My mouth it hath commanded*, and *His Spirit it hath gathered them.*" *Isaiah 34:16*
10. Blessed are the poor in spirit to those who *believe and hear the Word of the Lord*: "*Before I formed thee in the belly I knew thee*; *and before thou camest forth out of the womb I sanctified* (*consecrated*) *thee*, *and I ordained thee a prophet unto the nations.*" *Jeremiah 1:5. See Galatians 1:15*
11. Blessed are the poor in spirit to those who *believe the testimony of Apostle Paul, one of God's children*: "*But when it pleased God, who separated me from my mother's womb, and called me by His grace, to reveal His Son in me, that I might preach Him among the heathen* (*Gentiles*); *immediately I conferred not with flesh and blood.*" *Galatians 1:15-16. See Acts 9:1-31*
12. Blessed are the poor in spirit to those who *believe in turning back to God or return to God in faith*; *for the Lord our God is salvation. Jeremiah 3:22*

Part CCCLIV

Blessed Are The Poor In Spirit. Matthew 5:3

Blessed Means Happy

Poor means meek in spirit. Poor means humble in spirit. Poor means lowly in spirit. Poor means quiet in spirit. Read Matthew 5:3-12, Read also Mark 1:15

Jesus did not say "*rich*" in spirit. Jesus said "*poor*" in spirit.

1. Blessed are the poor in spirit to those who *are able to say to the Word of the Lord God*: "*Behold, we come unto Thee; Thou art the Lord our God. Jeremiah 3:22*
2. Blessed are the poor in spirit to those who *believe the Word of the Lord*: "*Truly in vain is salvation hoped for from the hills, and from the multitude of mountains: truly in the Lord our God is the salvation of Israel. Jeremiah 3:23*
3. Blessed are the poor in spirit to those who "*purpose*" *in his heart to obey the will of the Lord by faith in Jesus Christ. Be like the Daniel. Daniel 1:8*
4. Blessed are the poor in spirit to those who *believe the Word of the Lord God*: "*Therefore also now, saith the Lord, turn ye even to Me with* "*all*" *your heart, and* "*with fasting,*" *and* "*with weeping,*" *and* "*with mourning*:" And *rend* (tear) *your heart, and not your garments*, and *turn unto the Lord your God*: *for He is* "*gracious*" and "*merciful,*" "*slow to anger*" and "*of great kindness,*" and *repenteth Him of the evil. Joel 2:12-13*
5. Blessed are the poor in spirit to those who *believe that the Lord* "*bid*" *His children to* "*preach*" *the truth gospel. Be like the Jonah. Jonah 3:1-2*
6. Blessed are the poor in spirit to those who *believe that salvation is of the Lord. Jonah 2:10*
7. Blessed are the poor in spirit to those who *believe one of God's children, Moses that spoke*: "*But if ye will not do so, behold, ye have sinned against the Lord*: *and be sure your sin will find you out.*" *Numbers 32:23*
8. Blessed are the poor in spirit to those who *believe the Word of God spoke in Bold Red Mark by God*: "*Genesis*" 1:3, 6, 9, 11, 14-15, 20, 22, 24, 26, 28-30; Genesis 2:16-18; Genesis 3:3, 9, 11, 13, 14-19, 22; (*God indeed spoke to Adam, Eve and the serpent whose name was Lucifer*; see Isaiah 14:12); Genesis 4:6-7, 9-12, 15; Genesis 6:3, 7, 13-21; Genesis 7:1-4 (To Noah); Genesis 8:16-17, 21-22; Genesis

9:1-7, 9-17; Genesis 11:6-7; Genesis 12:1-3, 7; Genesis 13:14-17; Genesis 15:1, 4-5, 7, 9, 13-16, 18-21; Genesis 16:8-12; Genesis 17:1-16 (*God indeed spoke to Abraham*); 19-21; Genesis 18:10, 13-15, 17-21, 26, 28-32, Genesis 19:17, 21-22 (*God spoke to Lot*); Genesis 20:3, 6-7 (*God indeed spoke to Abimelech*); Genesis 21:12-13, 17-18; Genesis 22:1-2, 11-12; 16-18; Genesis 24:7; Genesis 25:23 (*God spoke to Isaac's wife, Rebekah*, see verse 20); Genesis 26:2-5, 24 (*God indeed spoke to Isaac*); Genesis 28:13-15 (*God spoke to Jacob*); Genesis 31:3, 11-13, 24 (*God indeed spoke to Laban* verse 24, 29); Genesis 32:9, 12, 26-29 (*Jacob become Israel*; Genesis 35:10-12); Genesis 35:1, 10-12, Genesis 46:2-4, Genesis 48:4.

9. Blessed are the poor in spirit to those who *believe the Word of God spoke in Bold Red Mark by God*: "*Exodus*" *God indeed spoke to Moses*: Exodus 3:4-10, 12, 14-22; Exodus 4:2-9, 11-12, 14-17, 19, 21-23, 27; God spoke to Aaron—Genesis 4:27, Exodus 5:1 (*God spoke to Pharaoh through Moses and Aaron*); Exodus 6:1-8, 11, *26, 29* (*God spoke to Aaron and Moses verse 26*); Exodus 7:1-5, 9, 14-19; Exodus 8:1-5, 16, 20-23; Exodus 9:1-5, 8-9, 13-19, 22; Exodus 10:1-6, 12, 21, Exodus 11:1-2, 4-7, 9; Exodus 12:2-20; Exodus 12:43-49; Exodus 13:2, 17, Exodus 14:2-4, 15-18, 26; Exodus 16:4-5, 12, 16, 23, 28-29, 32; Exodus 17:5-6, 14, Exodus 19:3-6, 9-13, 21-24; Exodus 20:2-17, 22-26; Exodus 21:1-36; Exodus 22:1-31; Exodus 23:1-33; Exodus 24:1-2, 12; Exodus 25:2-40; Exodus 26:1-37; Exodus 27:1-21; Exodus 28:1-43; Exodus 29:1-46; Exodus 30:1-38; Exodus 31:1-18; Exodus 32:7-10, 13, 27, 33-34; Exodus 33:1-3, 5, 12, 14, 17, 19-23; Exodus 34:1-3, 6-7, 10-27; Exodus 35:2-3, 5-19; Exodus 40:2-15
10. Blessed are the poor in spirit to those who *believe the Word of God spoke in Bold Red Mark by God*: "*Leviticus*" 1:2-17; 2:1-6; 3:1-17; 4:2-35; 5:1-19; 6:2-7, 9-18, 20-23, 25-30; 7:1-27, 29-34; 8: 2; 10:3, 9-11; 11:2-47; 12:2-8; 13:1-59; 14:2-32, 34-57; 15:2-33; 16:2-34; 17:2-16; 18:2-30; 19:2-37; 20:2-27; 21:1-23; 22:2-16, 18-25, 27-33; 23:1-8, 10-32, 34-43; 24:2-9, 14-22; 25:2-55; 26:1-45; 27:2-33
11. Blessed are the poor in spirit to those who *believe the Word of the Lord spoke in Bold Red Mark by God*: "*Numbers*" 1:2-15, 49-53; 2:2-3, 5, 7, 10, 12, 14, 17-18, 20, 22, 25, 27, 29; 3:6-10, 12-15, 40-41, 45-48; 4:2-16, 18-20, 22-33; 5:2-3, 6-10, 12-31; 6:2-21, 23-27; 7:5, 11; 8:2, 5-19, 24-26; 9:2-3, 10-14; 10:2-10, 29; 11:12, 16-21, 23; 12:4, 6-8, 14; 13:2; 14:11-12, 18, 20-25, 27-35; 15:2-16, 18-31, 35, 38-41; 16:21, 24, 37-38, 45; 17:2-5, 10; 18:1-32 (*God spoke to Aaron verse 1, 8, 20*); 19:1 (*God spoke to Moses and Aaron* verse 1); 19:2-22;

20:8, 12, 24-26 (*God spoke to Moses and Aaron verse 12*); 21:8, 16, 34; 22:9, 14, 20, 32-33, 35 (*God spoke to Balaam verse 9, 12, 20, 32-33, 35*); 23:5, 16; 25:4, 11-13, 17-18, ; 26:2, 53-56, 65; 27:7-14, 19, 21; 28:1-31; 29:1-39; 31:2, 26-30; 32:11-12; 33:51-56; 34:2-12; 17-28; 35:2-8, 10-34; 36:6-9

12. Blessed are the poor in spirit to those who *believe the Word of God spoke in Bold Red Mark by God in*: "*Deuteronomy*" 1:6-8, 35-40; 2:3-7, 0, 18-19, 24-25, 31; 3:2, 21-28; 4:10; 5:6-21, 28-31; 7:4; 9:12-14, 23; 10:1-2, 11; 17:16; 18:17-22; 31:2, 14, 16-21; 32:20-27, 34-35, 37-42, 49-52; 33:27; 34:4

Part CCCLV

Blessed Are The Poor In Spirit. Matthew 5:3

Blessed Means Happy

Poor means meek in spirit. Poor means humble in spirit. Poor means lowly in spirit. Poor means quiet in spirit. Read Matthew 5:3-12, Read also Mark 1:15

Jesus did not say "*rich*" in spirit. Jesus said "*poor*" in spirit.

1. Blessed are the poor in spirit to those who *believe the Word of God that spoke in Bold Red Mark by God in: "Joshua;" God indeed spoke to Joshua*: 1:1-9; 2:1-9; 3:7-8; 4:2, 16; 5:2, 9; 6:2-5; 7:10-15; 8:1-2, 18; 10:8; 11:6; 13:1-7; 20:2-6; 24:2-
2. Blessed are the poor in spirit to those who *believe the Word of God that spoke in Bold Red Mark by God Himself*: "*God spoke to Judah—Judge 1:2*; Judge 1:2; 2:1-3, 20-22; 4:6-7; 6:8-10, 14, 16, 18, 23, 25-26 (God spoke to Gideon—verse 14, 16, 18, 23, 25-26); 7:2-5, 7, 9-11; 10:11-14; 20:18, 23.
3. Blessed are the poor in spirit to those who *believe the Word of God that spoke in Bold Red Mark by God in "I Samuel"* 2:27-36; 3:4 (God called Samuel 3:4, 6, 8, 10-14); 8:7-9, 22; 9:22, 9:15-17; 10:18-19, 22; 15:2-3, 11, 18; 16:1-3, 12; 23:2, 4 (God spoke to David); 11, 12; 30:8
4. Blessed are the poor in spirit to those who *believe the Word of God that spoke in Bold Red Mark by God in "II Samuel"* 2:1, 5:2, 19, 23-24 (*God spoke to David in verse 2, 19, 23-24*), 7:5-16 (*God spoke to Nathan*); 12:7-11; 21:1; 23:3-4; 24:12.
5. Blessed are the poor in spirit to those who *believe the Word of the Lord God*: "*Return ye backsliding children. And I will heal your backslidings*. Jeremiah 3:22
6. Blessed are the poor in spirit to those who believe *on the Day of Pentecost or on the Day of Pentecostal Service or and when the day of Pentecost was fully come, they were all with one accord in one place*. Acts 1:1
7. Blessed are the poor in spirit to those who believe the *power of Pentecostal message of Stephen's preaching*: Acts 7:1-55
8. Blessed are the poor in spirit to those who believe the *Pentecostal message of Peter's preaching*. Acts 2:13-47
9. Blessed are the poor in spirit to those who believe that *Peter remembered the word of the Lord how that He said, "John indeed baptized with water*: but *ye shall*

be baptized with the Holy Ghost." Acts 11:16. See Acts 1:4-5 as a reminder or remember Jesus said that.

10. Blessed are the poor in spirit to those who believe that the *Word of God is my Diet Food and my Diet Drink* because we are *hungry and thirsty in the Word of God.* Our *spiritual diet food and our spiritual diet drink are delicious for healthy and healing.* Job 23:12, Acts 2:42, John 6:55-59, Psalm 34:8, I Corinthians 6:19-20, Matthew 22:37, Ecclesiastes 9:7
11. Blessed are the poor in spirit to those who believe that the *original disciples of Jesus did not know what Jesus meant when He say,* "Ye have heard of Me, For John "*truly*" *baptized with* "*water;*" "*but*" ye shall be *baptized with the* "*Holy Ghost*" not many days hence. Acts 1:4-5
12. Blessed are the poor in spirit to those who are *bold* and are *able to say* even so come Lord Jesus. Revelation 22:20

Part CCCLVI

Blessed Are The Poor In Spirit. Matthew 5:3

Blessed Means Happy

Poor means meek in spirit Poor means humble in spirit Poor means lowly in spirit Poor means quiet in spirit Read Matthew 5:3-12, Read also Mark 1:15

Jesus did not say "*rich*" in spirit. Jesus said "*poor*" in spirit.

1. Blessed are the poor in spirit to those who believe that the *original disciples did not know or did not understand or did not realize 6 times "repeatedly"* when they "*heard*" *the words,* "I indeed *baptize with water and baptize with the Holy Ghost.*" Matthew 3:11, Mark 1:8, Luke 3:16, John 1:33, Acts 1:5, Acts 11:16
2. Blessed are the poor in spirit to those who *believe in preaching holiness and righteousness because God say so in His Word.* Luke 1:75, Ephesians 4:24-30
3. Blessed are the poor in spirit to those who *believe in Jesus Christ through the Bible at His Word.* John 14:6, Mark 11:22, Genesis 1:1, John 1:1-18, II Timothy 3:16
4. Blessed are the poor in spirit to those who *believe in giving our hearts and live completely to Lord at salvation.* Acts 16:31, Romans 10:8-13, 17, I Thessalonians 5:23-24
5. Blessed are the poor in spirit to those who *believe that the Holy Spirit's blessing is on God's Word*: "*Sanctify them through thy truth: thy word is truth.*" John 17:17
6. Blessed are the poor in spirit to those who *believe in listening to the Holy Spirit*: "*Howbeit when he, the Spirit of truth, is come, he will guide you into all truth: for he shall not speak of himself; but whatsoever he shall hear, that shall he speak: and he will shew you things to come.*" John 16:13; I John 2:27-29
7. Blessed are the poor in spirit to those who *believe the gospel ministry*: "*I charge thee therefore before God,* and the *Lord Jesus Christ, who shall judge the quick and the dead at His Appearing and His Kingdom.*" II Timothy 4:1
8. Blessed are the poor in spirit to those who *believe the gospel ministry*: "*Preach The Word; be instant in season, out of season; reprove, rebuke, exhort with all longsuffering and doctrine.*" II Timothy 4:2
9. Blessed are the poor in spirit to those who *believe in sound doctrine of God through Jesus Christ and the Holy Spirit*: "*For the time will come when they will not endure*

sound doctrine; but after their own lusts shall they heap to themselves teachers, having itching ears." II Timothy 4:3

10. Blessed are the poor in spirit to those who *believe The Foundation of Jesus Christ*: "*For other foundation can no man lay than that is laid, which is Jesus Christ.*" I Corinthians 3:11
11. Blessed are the poor in spirit to those who *believe The Foundation of Jesus Christ*: "*Now if any man build upon this foundation gold, silver, precious stones, wood, hay, stubble; Every man's work shall be made manifest: for the day shall declare it,* because *it shall be revealed by fire*; and *the fire shall try every man's work of what sort it is*" I Corinthians 3:12-13
12. Blessed are the poor in spirit to those who believe that *salvation is grace through our Lord and Savior Jesus Christ.* Acts 15:11, II Corinthian 8:9, Ephesians 2:5, Ephesians 2:8, Ephesians 4:7, I Peter 5:10, II Peter 1:2, II Peter 3:18, II Timothy 1:9, II Timothy 2:1 Titus 2:11, Titus 3:7, James 4:6

Part CCCLVII

Blessed Are The Poor In Spirit. Matthew 5:3

Blessed Means Happy

Poor means meek in spirit Poor means humble in spirit Poor means lowly in spirit Poor means quiet in spirit Read Matthew 5:3-12, Read also Mark 1:15

Jesus did not say "*rich*" in spirit. Jesus said "*poor*" in spirit.

1. Blessed are the poor in spirit to those who *believe the foundation of Jesus Christ*: "*If any man's work abide which he hath built thereupon, he shall receive a reward.*" I Corinthians 3:14
2. Blessed are the poor in spirit to those who *believe God's repentance toward faith through Jesus Christ*: "*If any man's work shall be burned, he shall suffer loss*: but he himself shall be saved; yet so as by fire." I Corinthians 3:15
3. Blessed are the poor in spirit to those who believe that the Psalm will put our *conversion*: "*And he hath put a new song in my mouth, even praise unto our God*: *many shall see it*, and fear, *and shall trust in the Lord.*" Psalm 40:3
4. Blessed are the poor in spirit to those who *believe that only the Holy Spirit convicts hearts and draws lost sinners unto repentance.* John 16:8-11, II Timothy 2:25, II Corinthians 7:9-10, John 12:32
5. Blessed are the poor in spirit to those who *believe the Word of the Lord*: "Thus saith the Lord, *Stand ye in the ways, and see, and ask for the old paths, where is the good way, and walk therein, and ye shall find rest for your souls.*" Jeremiah 6:16, Matthew 11:28-30, verese 28, 29, Acts 2:1-2, 26, John 20:22, II Corinthians 12:9, Isaiah 11:2, Isaiah 61:1,
6. Blessed are the poor in spirit to those who *believe the old paths of the Word of God through the gospel of Jesus Christ in order to find rest for our souls.* Jeremiah 6:16, Isaiah 11:2, Isaiah 61:1, Matthew 11:28-30, verses 28, 29, John 20:22, Acts 2:1-2, 26, II Corinthians 12:9
7. Blessed are the poor in spirit to those who *believe the Gospel*: "*Ye adulterers and adulteresses, know ye not that the friendship of the world is enmity with God*: *whosoever therefore will be a friend of the world is the enemy of God?*" James 4:4
8. Blessed are the poor in spirit to those who *believe that Jesus Christ was tortured*; *that Jesus Christ was bled*; *that Jesus Christ was crucified*; *but three days later He rose*

from the dead to victory over death, sin, world and Satan and sit at the right hand of the Father in Heaven. Romans 6:4-5, I Corinthians 15:1-4, Hebrews 12:2, Revelation 3:21, Romans 9:34, Acts 2:36

9. Blessed are the poor in spirit to those who *believe that the sharp, two-edged sword of God's scripture is doing the convicting.* Hebrews 4:12, Revelation 1:16, Revelation 2:12, 16, Revelation 19:15
10. Blessed are the poor in spirit to those who believe in *reading* and *obeying* God's Word and *confessing* and *forsaking* our sin and *studying* to prove ourselves sincerely to God. Matthew 4:4, I Timothy 4:13, II Timothy 2:7, II Timothy 2:15-17, I Peter 2:2, II Peter 1:5, I John 1:9, Psalm 1:2, Psalm 119:18
11. Blessed are the poor in spirit to those who *believe that God does not play game in religion to those who want to come unto repentance toward faith in Jesus Christ.* Acts 20:21, Acts 26:20, Acts 5:31, I Corinthians 7:9-10, II Timothy 2:25, Hebrews 6:6, II Peter 3:9
12. Blessed are the poor in spirit to those who *believe and listen to Godly music to bring us closer to our Lord and Savior Jesus Christ: "Let the word of Christ dwell in you richly in all wisdom; teaching and admonishing one another in psalms and hymns and spiritual songs, singing with grace in your hearts to the Lord."* Colossians 3:16

Part CCCLVIII

Blessed Are The Poor In Spirit. Matthew 5:3

Blessed Means Happy

Poor means meek in spirit Poor means humble in spirit Poor means lowly in spirit Poor means quiet in spirit Read Matthew 5:3-12, Read also Mark 1:15

Jesus did not say "*rich*" in spirit. Jesus said "*poor*" in spirit.

1. Blessed are the poor in spirit to those who believe that the Bible tells us how to be saved from death, hell and eternal separation from God. Romans 3:23, Romans 6:23, Luke 13:5, Romans 10:9, 10, 13, II Corinthians 5:17
2. Blessed are the poor in spirit to those who believe for salvation in Jesus Christ; and was shed in the blood of Jesus Christ. Matthew 25:34-40, Ephesians 1:5-7, verse 7, Hebrews 9:14, Acts 20:28, Acts 26:18, Romans 5:9, Colossians 1:14, Hebrews 9:12, Revelation 5:9, Hebrews13:20, I John 1:7, Revelation 1:5, Revelation 12:11, I Corinthians 11:23-26 verse 25, Matthew 26:28, Hebrews 9:22, Hebrews 10:4-5, Psalm 40:6
3. Blessed are the poor in spirit to those who believe that *Heaven for Real is an eternal home with God forever more.* John 14:1-6, Revelation 21:1-7 verse 1-2, I Peter 1:4
4. Blessed are the poor in spirit to those who believe this *old spiritual hymn of the African*: "*Kumbaya*" *meaning* "*Come By Here*:
   Kum bay ya, my Lord, kum bay ya;
   Kum bay ya, my Lord, kum bay ya;
   Kum bay ya, my Lord, kum bay ya,
   O Lord, kum bay ya."
   Kumbaya, my Lord" was first recored by an out-of-work English professor, Robert Winslow Gordon, in 1927. Gordon went on a search for black spirituals and recorded a song "Come by Here, My Lord", sung by H. Wylie. The song was sung in Gullah on the islands of South Carolina between Charleston and Beaufort. Gullah is the creole language featured in the Uncle Remus series of Joel Chandler Harris and the Walt Disney production of "Song of the South." "Kum by here, my Lord" in Gullah is "Kum by (h)yuh, my lawd"-(Lord) Mark 16:15, Luke 24:47

5. Blessed are the poor in spirit to those who believe that *Heaven for Real as a dwelling place for God.* John 14:1-6, I Peter 1:4, Revelation 21:1-7 verse 1-2, Matthew 25:34-40
6. Blessed are the poor in spirit to those who believe that Heaven for Real is an eternal dwelling place. John 14:2, Luke 23:43
7. Blessed are the poor in spirit to those who believe that *Heaven for Real is the city of our God.* Psalm 48:8, Revelation 21:1-3, John 14:2, Hebrews 11:16,
8. Blessed are the poor in spirit to those who believe that *Heaven for Real is the Home of our Almighty God.* John 14:1-6, I Peter 1:4, Revelation 21:1-7 verse 1-2, Matthew 25:34-40
9. Blessed are the poor in spirit to those who *believe the Gospel of Acts*: "And when he (Jesus) had spoken these things, while they beheld, he (Jesus) was taken up; and a cloud received him (Jesus) out of their sight." Acts 1:9
10. Blessed are the poor in spirit to those who *believe the Gospel of Acts*: "*And while they looked steadfastly toward heaven as he went up, behold, two men stood by them in white apparel.*" Acts 1:10
11. Blessed are the poor in spirit to those who *believe the Gospel of Acts*: "*Which also said, Ye men of Galilee, why stand ye gazing up into heaven? This same Jesus, which is taken up from you into heaven, shall so come in like manner as ye have seen him go into heaven.*" Acts 1:11
12. Blessed are the poor in spirit to those who believe that the *Real Bible is not just for children's Bible or children's Book, but for men and women who are in need of a Savior who died on the cross for them.* Luke 23:33, Genesis 1:1, John 1:1-24, Romans 5:8-11, II Timothy 3:14-17, II Timothy 2:15, I Thessalonians 4:11, Ecclesiastes 12:13, Luke 18:13, Luke 7:37-39, 15:7, 10, John 9:16, James 5:20, I Peter 4:18, Matthew 9:10-11, 13, 11:19, Matthew 26:45, Mark 2:15-17, Luke 5:30, 32, 33, 34, Luke 7:34, 13:2, 4, 15:1-2, I Timothy 1:15, James 4:8, Hebrews 7:26-28

Part CCCLIX

Blessed Are The Poor In Spirit. Matthew 5:3

Blessed Means Happy

Poor means meek in spirit Poor means humble in spirit Poor means lowly in spirit Poor means quiet in spirit Read Matthew 5:3-12, Read also Mark 1:15

Jesus did not say "*rich*" in spirit. Jesus said "*poor*" in spirit.

1. Blessed are the poor in spirit to those who believe that *Heaven is indeed for Real.* John 14:2-3
2. Blessed are the poor in spirit to those who believe that *Heaven for Real is in the Kingdom of God*: "*Verily I say unto you, Whosoever shall not receive the Kingdom of God as a little child, he shall not enter therein.*" Mark 10:15
3. Blessed are the poor in spirit to those who *believe that Heaven or Kingdom of God belong to the little children.* Men and Women must act like little children or they will not enter the Kingdom of God. Mark 10:15
4. Blessed are the poor in spirit to those who believe that Heaven is for Real to those who belong to the Kingdom of God. Mark 10:15
5. Blessed are the poor in spirit to those who believe that David was never a top dancer in the world. He was a gospel musician. He came to glorify the Lord thy God. **II Samuel 6:14,** Amos 6:5, Psalm 92:3, I Chronicles 15:16, I Chronicles 15:28, I Chronicles 25:6, II Chronicles 5:13, Revelation 18:22, Psalm 68:25
6. Blessed are the poor in spirit to those who believe that the wicked lost sinners in desperate need of a Savior. Matthew 9:13 Matthew 18:11, Mark 2:17, Luke 5:32, Luke 19:10, John 3:17, John 12:47, I Timothy 1:12-16, verse 15
7. Blessed are the poor in spirit to those who believe in Michael Pierre's testimony, one of God's children: "My call is to win souls for Jesus." Proverbs 11:30, Matthew 6:33
8. Blessed are the poor in spirit to those who believe in the saving knowledge by the blood of the Lord Jesus Christ. Hebrews 10:39, II Peter 1:1-3 verse 3, 5, 2:20, 3:18, Hebrews 10:26, I Timothy 2:4
9. Blessed are the poor in spirit to those who believe in asking sinners in the name of Jesus Christ to repent and to come to the knowledge of God's truth word. II Timothy 2:4, Luke 13:3, 5, Mark 1:15, 6:12, Matthew 3:2, 4:17

10. Blessed are the poor in spirit to those who *believe and are seeking the truth of the heart.*" Jeremiah 29:13
11. Blessed are the poor in spirit to those who believe that the only real expert is the Word of God; straight to the Truth with all the answers in the Bible from Genesis to Revelation. Genesis 1:1, John 1:1-18, verse 1, II Timothy 3:16, I John 5:20, Revelation 22:20
12. Blessed are the poor in spirit to those who believe that sinners may get genuinely converted by repenting of their sins and come to Jesus as Lord and Savior. Psalm 51:13, Isaiah 6:10, James 5:19, Matthew 13:15, 18:3, Mark 4:12, Luke 22:32, John 12:40, Acts 3:19, Acts 28:27, II Chronicles 7:14

Part CCCLX

Blessed Are The Poor In Spirit. Matthew 5:3

Blessed Means Happy

Poor means meek in spirit Poor means humble in spirit Poor means lowly in spirit Poor means quiet in spirit Read Matthew 5:3-12, Read also Mark 1:15

Jesus did not say "*rich*" in spirit. Jesus said "*poor*" in spirit.

1. Blessed are the poor in spirit to those who *believe that our God can do anything, even the impossible things.* Luke 1:37
2. Blessed are the poor in spirit to those who *believe the true Bible—believing, God—honoring, soul—winning,* and living the *Christian life. He that win soul is wise.* Proverbs 11:30, I Peter 2:21
3. Blessed are the poor in spirit to those who *believe that real Christians already have the answer. His name is Jesus Christ.* Revelation 3:20
4. Blessed are the poor in spirit to those who *believe that what the world realize* and *needs is Jesus Christ.* John 3:16
5. Blessed are the poor in spirit to those who *believe that God's love cannot be separate from righteousness and holiness*: "*Follow peace with all men, and holiness, without which no man shall see the Lord.*" Hebrews 12:14, See Matthew 5:20
6. Blessed are the poor in spirit to those who *believe that we came from original the dust of the earth*: *But thank be to God, we become saved through Jesus Christ.* Acts 11:14, 15:1, 11, 16:30-31, Romans 5:9-10, 10:1, 9, 13, Acts 4:12, Acts 2:21, 47, Romans 5:1-21, Genesis 13:16, 18:27, Genesis 2:7, 3:14, 19, Romans 11:26, I Corinthians 1:18, Genesis 28:14, Exodus 8:17, Job 10:9, 14:19, 30:19, 34:15, 38:38, Psalm 30:9, 44:25, 103:14, 104:29, Ecclesiastes 3:20, Ephesians 2:5, 8, I Thessalonians 2:16, II Thessalonians 2:10, I Timothy 2:4, II Timothy 1:9, Titus 3:5, Revelation 21:24
7. Blessed are the poor in spirit to those who *believe The Gospel*: "*For they that are after the flesh do mind the things of the flesh*; *but they that are after the Spirit, the things of the Spirit.*" Romans 8:5
8. Blessed are the poor in spirit to those who *believe The Gospel*: "*For to be carnally minded is death*: *but to be spiritually minded is life and peace.*" Romans 8:6

9. Blessed are the poor in spirit to those who *believe The Gospel*: "*Because the carnal mind is enmity against God: for it is not subject to the law of God, neither indeed can be.*" Romans 8:7
10. Blessed are the poor in spirit to those who *believe The Gospel*: "*So then they that are in the flesh cannot please God.*" Romans 8:8
11. Blessed are the poor in spirit to those who *believe the scriptures*: "*And one of them, named Caiaphas, being the high priest that same year, said unto them, Ye know nothing at all.*" John 11:49
12. Blessed are the poor in spirit to those who *believe the scriptures*: "Nor consider that it is expedient for us, *that one man should die for the people, and that the whole nation perish not*; **That One Man** should die *is Jesus Christ.*" John 11:50

Part CCCLXI

Blessed Are The Poor In Spirit. Matthew 5:3

Blessed Means Happy

Poor means meek in spirit Poor means humble in spirit Poor means lowly in spirit Poor means quiet in spirit Read Matthew 5:3-12, Read also Mark 1:15

Jesus did not say "*rich*" in spirit. Jesus said "*poor*" in spirit.

1. Blessed are the poor in spirit to those who *believe the scriptures*: "*And this spake he not of himself: but being high priest that year, he prophesied that Jesus should die for that nation.*" John 11:50-51, see John 18:14
2. Blessed are the poor in spirit to those who believe the scriptures: "*Now Caiaphas was he, which gave counsel to the Jews, that it was expedient that one man should die for the people.*" John 18:14, see John 11:50-51
3. Blessed are the poor in spirit to those who *believe that this is not God's plan*; *this is not God's will that we should die and go to hell*; for God has kept His promise and is longsuffering to us-ward, not willing that any should perish, *but that all should come to repentance*. II Peter 3:9
4. Blessed are the poor in spirit to those who are abled to say, "*Thank you God. Thank you Jesus, for letting us know about God, about Satan, about Heaven and about Hell before I die tonight.* I have come to accept Jesus Christ as my personal Savior as my Lord. *In Christ's name. Amen.*" Genesis 1:1, John 1:1-18, verse 12, John 14:6, Philippians 3:10, Hebrews 13:8, Revelation 2:24, Revelation 21:8, Revelation 21:1-7, Matthew 25:46, Acts 17:27-30, verse 27, Psalm 104:33, Romans 10:8-13, 17, Acts 4:12, Acts 16:30-31, Romans 8:15-16 verse 16, Romans 1:17, Habakkuk 2:4, Galatians 3:11, Hebrews 10:38-39 verse 38, Galatians 4:5, Ephesians 1:5, Ephesians 2:2, 8
5. Blessed are the poor in spirit to those who *believe that if sinners should die tonight, they will go to hell. Pray without ceasing before it's too late.* I Thessalonians 5:17, II Peter 3:9, Romans 5:7-21, Amos 9:10-12, Ezekiel 18:4, 20-32, Jeremiah 11:22, Jeremiah 27:9-18, Romans 6:23, Hebrews 10:38-39 verse 39
6. Blessed are the poor in spirit to those who *believe The Gospel*: "*Not by works of righteousness which we have done, but according to His Mercy He saved us, by the washing of regeneration, and renewing of the Holy Ghost.*" Titus 3:5

7. Blessed are the poor in spirit to those who *believe The Gospel*: "*Knowing that a man is not justified by the works of the law, but by the faith of Jesus Christ, even we have believed in Jesus Christ, that we might be justified by the faith of Christ, and not by the works of the law*: for by the works of the law shall no flesh be justified." Galatians 2:16
8. Blessed are the poor in spirit to those who *believe The Gospel*: "For whosoever shall keep the whole law, and yet offend in one point, he is *guilty of all*." James 2:10
9. Blessed are the poor in spirit to those who *believe The Gospel*: "*Seek ye the Lord while he may be found, call ye upon him while he is near: Let the wicked forsake his way, and the unrighteous man his thoughts: and let him return unto the Lord, and he will have mercy upon him*; *and to our God, for he will abundantly pardon*." Isaiah 55:6-7
10. Blessed are the poor in spirit to those who *believe in making a decision for Christ*: "*By confessing to God that I am a sinner, and believing that the Lord Jesus Christ died for my sins on the cross and was raised for my justification, I do now receive and confess Him as my personal Savior*. Romans 10:8-13, I Corinthians 15:4, Romans 4:25, Romans 5:16, 18, II Timothy 3:15, Luke 23:33, Luke 18:13
11. Blessed are the poor in spirit to those who *believe that the Bible shows us how to be saved*: *Isaiah 55:6-7, John 3:16, Romans 10:9*
12. Blessed are the poor in spirit to those who *believe that the Bible shows us how God's Son died to minister to us and to give us redemption*; to give us His Life a ransom for many *Romans 5:8, I Corinthians 15:3, Ephesians 1:7, Matthews 20:28*, Luke 21:28, I Corinthians 1:30, Ephesians 4:30, Colossians 1:14, Hebrews 9:12, 15

Part CCCLXII

Blessed Are The Poor In Spirit. Matthew 5:3

Blessed Means Happy

Poor means meek in spirit Poor means humble in spirit Poor means lowly in spirit Poor means quiet in spirit Read Matthew 5:3-12, Read also Mark 1:15

Jesus did not say "*rich*" in spirit. Jesus said "*poor*" in spirit.

1. Blessed are the poor in spirit to those who *believe that the Bible shows us how God gives the Christian grace to live the Christian life*; *I Corinthians 10:13, I John 1:9, Philippians 4:13, I Peter 2:21*
2. Blessed are the poor in spirit to those who *believe that the Bible show us how the Christians should be working for our Lord*: *Acts 1:8*, Ephesians 2:10, *Matthew 28:18-20, I Peter 2:21*
3. Blessed are the poor in spirit to those who *believe that the Bible show us how we need to be saved*: *Romans 5:12, Romans 3:10, Romans 3:23, Romans 6:23, John 3:3*
4. Blessed are the poor in spirit to those who *believe that the Bible show us that we cannot save all by ourselves*: Titus 3:5, Galatians 2:16, *James 2:10*
5. Blessed are the poor in spirit to those who *believe that from Genesis to Revelation, God lays everything out in blacks and whites*: *Blessing/Cursing, Life/Death, Heaven/Hell, God/Satan, Christ/the World*; in public; in the wide opening for us all in the world to see Genesis 1:1, John 1:1-18, Hebrews 13:8, II Timothy 3:16, I John 5:20, Philippians 3:10, Revelation 21:8, John 14:6-12, verse 6, 7, 8, 9, Revelation 21:1-7, Malachi 2:2, Deuteronomy 30:19-20
6. Blessed are the poor in spirit to those who *believe this true statement*: "*Man, I got THE DEVIL in me*: *If I didn't have, I'd be a Christian…Cause I'm dragging the audience to hell with me. How am I gonna get 'em to heaven with whole lotta shakin' Going On*"? *You can't serve two masters, you'll hate one an' love the other*." Matthew 6:24, Luke 16:13 and Matthew 16:26, Mark 8:36, Luke 9:25
   —Jerry Lee Lewis (1935-present)—
7. Blessed are the poor in spirit to those who *believe*, *understand*, *know*, *realize*, and *recognize* the difference between Holy Dance and Worldly Dance. II Samuel 6:14, Matthew 11:17, Luke 7:32, Exodus 15:20 (Holy), Psalm 150:4, (Worldly)—Exodus 32:14-35 verse 26, Mark 6:22, Matthew 14:6

8. Blessed are the poor in spirit to those who *are able to say "for instance:"* I was born on December 1995. *I was born again*; *born of the Spirit* on September 2005. John 3:6, Romans 8:9, I Corinthian 15:50, I John 5:1, I John 5:4, John 1:13, I John 4:7, II Corinthians 5:17, Romans 10:17, Romans 8:14, 16, John 3:7
9. Blessed are the poor in spirit to those who *believe the testimony of one of God's children may lead a sinner to Jesus Christ.* Psalm 51:13, Luke 22:32, James 5:19
10. Blessed are the poor in spirit to those who *believe that Christian music about Jesus Christ may lead a sinner to Jesus Christ.* I Chronicles 16:42, Nehemiah 12:36, I Samuel 18:6, I Chronicles 15:16, Luke 15:21-25, II Chronicles 5:13-14
11. Blessed are the poor in spirit to those who *believe that the Christian ministry of Jesus Christ may lead a sinner to Jesus Christ.* Mark 16:15
12. Blessed are the poor in spirit to those who *listen to the gospel in radio about Jesus Christ may lead a sinner to Jesus Christ.* Mark 16:15, Mark 10:13

Part CCCLXIII

Blessed Are The Poor In Spirit. Matthew 5:3

Blessed Means Happy

Poor means meek in spirit Poor means humble in spirit Poor means lowly in spirit Poor means quiet in spirit Read Matthew 5:3-12, Read also Mark 1:15

Jesus did not say "*rich*" in spirit. Jesus said "*poor*" in spirit.

1. Blessed are the poor in spirit to those who *believe that the Christian singing about Jesus Christ may lead a sinner to Jesus Christ.* II Samuel 19:35, I Chronicles 6:32, 13:8, II Chronicles 23:18, Ephesians 5:19, Colossians 3:16, II Chronicles 30:21, 35:25, Ezra 2:65, Nehemiah 7:67, 12:27, Psalm 100:2, 126:2
2. Blessed are the poor in spirit to those who *believe that The Gospel of Jesus Christ on the television ministry may lead a sinner to Jesus Christ in order to receive the Holy Spirit into their homes as well as our homes everywhere.* John 20:22, Mark 13:10, Mark 16:15, Luke 24:49, Acts 1:8, Matthew 28:18-20, I Peter 2:21
3. Blessed are the poor in spirit to those who *believe the preaching of the gospel may lead a sinner to Jesus Christ.* Mark 13:10, Mark 16:15, Proverbs 11:30, Romans 1:16, I Corinthians 1:18, II Corinthians 6:18
4. Blessed are the poor in spirit to those who *believe that Christian music is about Jesus Christ.* II Samuel 19:35, I Chronicles 6:32, 13:8, II Chronicles 23:18, Ephesians 5:19, Colossians 3:16, II Chronicles 30:21, 35:25, Ezra 2:65, Nehemiah 7:67, 12:27, Psalm 100:2, 126:2
5. Blessed are the poor in spirit to those who *believe that the word of salvation was sent by God the Father.* Acts 13:26
6. Blessed are the poor in spirit to those who *believe that The Gospel was preached the forgiveness of sins.* Acts 5:31, Acts 13:38, Acts 26:18, Ephesians 1:7, Colossians 1:14
7. Blessed are the poor in spirit to those who *believe that the Gentiles wanted Paul to preach The Gospel the next Sabbath.* Acts 13:42-44
8. Blessed are the poor in spirit to those who *believe The Gospel*: "*That the residue of men might seek after the Lord, and all the Gentiles, upon whom My Name is called,* saith the Lord, *who doeth all these things.*" Acts 15:17
9. Blessed are the poor in spirit to those who *believe The Gospel*: "*Known unto God are all this works from the beginning of the world.*" Acts 15:18

10. Blessed are the poor in spirit to those who *believe The Gospel*: "*The same followed Paul and us, and cried, saying, These men are the servants of the most high God,* which shew unto us the way of salvation." Acts 16:17
11. Blessed are the poor in spirit to those who *believe the old hymn*: "*If you're saved and you know it, clap your hands*!!! If *you're saved and you know it, stomp your feet*!!! If *you're saved and you know it, wave your hands. If you're saved and you know it, leap for joy*!!! *If you're saved and you know it, shout for joy.* I'm saved and *I know it because the Bible tell me so!!!* I John 5:13, Psalm 47:1-9 verse 1, 98:1-9 verse 8, Lamentations 2:15, Isaiah 55:12, **Romans 8:15-16 verse 15**
12. Blessed are the poor in spirit to those who *believe, understand, know, realize* and *recognize the difference between Christian music and worldly music.* Exodus 32:14-35, Exodus 12:20-21

Part CCCLXIV

Blessed Are The Poor In Spirit. Matthew 5:3

Blessed Means Happy

Poor means meek in spirit. Poor means humble in spirit. Poor means lowly in spirit. Poor means quiet in spirit. Read Matthew 5:3-12, Read also Mark 1:15

Jesus did not say "*rich*" in spirit. Jesus said "*poor*" in spirit.

1. Blessed are the poor in spirit to those who believe in "*the Justice*" "*the Equality*;" "*the Freedom and Liberty*" and all *because of freedom in Christ.* John 3:16, Galatians 5:1-26, Galatians 5:1, Galatians 5:13-14, I Corinthians 7:22, II Corinthians 3:17, John 8:32, John 8:36, Romans 8:1-4, Romans 8:21
2. Blessed are the poor in spirit to those who *believe in*: *One God*; *One Nation*; *One people through God's grace*; *through Jesus Christ as a family*; *as a family of God, bless is the nation whose God is the Lord.* Psalm 33:12
3. Blessed are the poor in spirit to those who believe Christ's Word: "*Then we which are alive and remain shall be caught up together with them in the clouds, to meet the Lord in the air*: and *so shall we ever be with the Lord.*" I Thessalonians 4:17-18
4. Blessed are the poor in spirit to those who believe *that Jesus Christ is coming*; *as* "*an imminent*;" *there is to say, it may take place at* "*any moment.*" Revelation 22:7, 12, 20
5. Blessed are the poor in spirit to those who *believe that the word* "*Rapture*" that is *not mention in the Gospel of Christ does apply to the Second Coming of Christ in Matthew 24:33-44*, Mark 13:31-37 and Luke 21:33-36, II Timothy 3:16
6. Blessed are the poor in spirit to those who believe that Jesus Christ is at the door *near your heart today. Accept Christ today.* Matthew 24:33, Revelation 3:20-22, Isaiah 49:8, I Corinthians 6:2
7. Blessed are the poor in spirit to those who *believe that the* "*Rapture*" *mean the catching up of the saved to meet the Lord in the air*; *the day of the coming of Christ, the Second Coming of Christ to the earth*; *the Coming of the Lord for His people*; *the saved one that are taken up and the saved ones that are at the graves that rest from their labors to rewards in glory.* I Thessalonians 4:13-18, Revelation 22:12, Isaiah 40:10

8. Blessed are the poor in spirit to those who *believe that the Coming of the Lord, will take us unto Himself.* I Thessalonians 4:17
9. Blessed are the poor in spirit to those who *believe, know, understand,* and *realize*: "*One will be taken, the other will be left; One will be gone away out of sight; the other will be staying here; will be left out alone because of without Christ's unexpecting of His returning very soon to bring His children; Ones that are taken home to glory.* Luke 17:34-37, Matthew 24:40-42
10. Blessed are the poor in spirit to those who believe in the *mystery, the hidden of the gospel, the Revelation of God, the mystery of Christ, revealed unto Christ's holy apostles and prophets by the Spirit.* Read Ephesians 3:1-7 by Paul, one of God's children.
11. Blessed are the poor in spirit to those who believe that *those who die in the Lord are "immediately" in Heaven, "being absent from the body and present with the Lord."* II Corinthians 5:8 *and Bless are the saints that die in the Lord. Psalm 116:15,* I Thessalonians 4:13-18, Revelation 14:13, II Timothy 4:6-8, Luke 23:43, II Corinthians 12:2-4, John 11:25-27, I Corinthians 15:51-58.
12. Blessed are the poor in spirit to those who *have believed unto salvation will never come unto judgment of sins.* John 5:24, II Corinthians 5:19-21, Galatians 3:13

Part CCCLXV

Blessed Are The Poor In Spirit. Matthew 5:3

Blessed Means Happy

Poor means meek in spirit. Poor means humble in spirit. Poor means lowly in spirit. Poor means quiet in spirit. Read Matthew 5:3-12, Read also Mark 1:15

Jesus did not say "*rich*" in spirit. Jesus said "*poor*" in spirit.

1. Blessed are the poor in spirit to those who *believe, understand* and *realize* that "*Millennium*" *mean thousand years.* Revelation 20:4-7
2. Blessed are the poor in spirit to those who *believe that some doctors and some nurses in the hospital believe in healing by faith through Christ Jesus.*
   James 5:13, 15-16
3. Blessed are the poor in spirit to those who *believe that hymn*: *The Power of the Lord, rise among us.*
   The Power of the Lord, rise among us.
   The Power of the Lord, rise among us.
   Oh, Oh, Oh, let us rise.
   The Power of our King, rise among us.
   The Power of our King, rise among us.
   The Power of our King, rise among us. Isaiah 60:1
4. Blessed are the poor in spirit to those who *have redemption through Christ's blood,* the *forgiveness of sins* according to the *riches of His grace.* Ephesians 1:7
5. Blessed are the poor in spirit to those who believe the gospel: "*Neither by the blood of goats and calves, but by his own blood he entered in once into the holy place, having obtained eternal redemption for us.*" Hebrews 9:12
6. Blessed are the poor in spirit to those who believe the gospel: "*These shall make war with the Lamb,* and the Lamb shall overcome them: for he is Lord of lords, and *King of kings*: and *they that are with him are called,* and *chosen,* and *faithful.*" Revelation 17:14
7. Blessed are the poor in spirit to those who believe the gospel: "*The Lord knoweth how to deliver the godly out of temptations,* and *to reserve the unjust unto the day of judgment to be punished*:" II Peter 2:9

8. Blessed are the poor in spirit to those who believe the gospel: "*For the earth is the Lord's*, and *the fulness thereof*." I Corinthians 10:26
9. Blessed are the poor in spirit to those who believe the gospel: "The *earth is the Lord's*, and the *fulness therof*; the world, and *they that dwell therein*." Psalm 24:1
10. Blessed are the poor in spirit to those who believe the gospel: "*Blessed is the man that endureth temptation*: for when he is tried, he shall receive the crown of life, *which the Lord hath promised to them that love him*." James 1:12
11. Blessed are the poor in spirit to those who believe the gospel: "*For we must all appear before the judgment seat of Christ*; *that every one may receive the things done in his body, according to that he hath done, whether it be good or bad.*
    II Corinthians 5:10
12. Blessed are the poor in spirit to those who believe the gospel: "*But why dost thou judge thy brother*? Or *why dost thou set at nought thy brother*? *For we shall all stand before the judgment seat of Christ*." Romans 14:10

Part CCCLXVI

Blessed Are The Poor In Spirit. Matthew 5:3

Blessed Means Happy

Poor means meek in spirit. Poor means humble in spirit. Poor means lowly in spirit. Poor means quiet in spirit. Read Matthew 5:3-12, Read also Mark 1:15

Jesus did not say "*rich*" in spirit. Jesus said "*poor*" in spirit.

1. Blessed are the poor in spirit to those who believe the gospel: "*For if God spared not the angels that sinned, but cast them down to hell,* and *delivered them into chains of darkness, to be reserved unto judgment*;" II Peter 2:4
2. Blessed are the poor in spirit to those who believe the gospel: "And *spared not the old world, but saved Noah the eighth person, a preacher of righteousness,* bringing in the flood upon the world of the ungodly;" II Peter 2:5
3. Blessed are the poor in spirit to those who believe the gospel: "And *turning the cities of Sodom and Gomorrha into ashes condemned them with an overthrow, making them an ensample unto those that after should live ungodly*;" II Peter 2:6
4. Blessed are the poor in spirit to those who believe the gospel: "And *delivered just Lot, vexed with the filthy conversation of the wicked*:" II Peter 2:7
5. Blessed are the poor in spirit to those who believe the gospel: "(*For that righteous man dwelling among them, in seeing and hearing, vexed his righteous soul from day to day with their unlawful deeds*:)" II Peter 2:8
6. Blessed are the poor in spirit to those who believe the gospel: "*The Lord knoweth how to deliver the godly out of temptations,* and to reserve the unjust unto the day of judgment to be punished:" II Peter 2:9
7. Blessed are the poor in spirit to those who believe the gospel: "*But chiefly them that walk after the flesh in the lust of uncleanness,* and despise government. *Presumptuous are they, selfwilled, they are not afraid to speak evil of dignities.*" II Peter 2:10
8. Blessed are the poor in spirit to those who believe the gospel: "*And no man hath ascended up to heaven, but he that came down from heaven, even the Son of man which is in heaven.*" John 3:13, See Proverbs 30:4
9. Blessed are the poor in spirit to those who believe the gospel: "*And as Moses lifted up the serpent in the wilderness, even so must the Son of man be lifted up*:" John 3:14, See Number 21:9

10. Blessed are the poor in spirit to those who believe the gospel: "*That whosoever believeth in him should not perish, but have eternal life,*" John 3:15
11. Blessed are the poor in spirit to those who believe the gospel: "*For God so loved the world, that he gave his only begotten Son, that whosoever believeth in him should not perish, but have everlasting life.*" John 3:16, See Acts 16:31
12. Blessed are the poor in spirit to those who believe the gospel: "For God sent not his Son into the world to condemn (judge) the world; *but that the world through him might be saved.*" John 3:17

Part CCCLXVII

Blessed Are The Poor In Spirit. Matthew 5:3

Blessed Means Happy

Poor means meek in spirit. Poor means humble in spirit. Poor means lowly in spirit. Poor means quiet in spirit. Read Matthew 5:3-12, Read also Mark 1:15

Jesus did not say "*rich*" in spirit. Jesus said "*poor*" in spirit.

1. Blessed are the poor in spirit to those who *believe that Jesus Christ is our Prophet from the Lord our God*. We found Him!!! Deuteronomy 18:15, 18, Isaiah 10:3, Malachi 3:1, Matthew 3:3, Mark 1:3, John 1:23, John 1:45, Acts 2:22, Acts 3:22, Acts 7:37, John 1:21, John 6:14, John 4:25—Messiah Christ
2. Blessed are the poor in spirit to those who believe that *Jesus took over the ministry after John, the Baptist was in prison*. Mark 1:14
3. Blessed are the poor in spirit to those who *believe Jesus' message*: "And *saying, The time is fulfilled*, and *the kingdom of God is at hand*: *repent ye and believe the gospel*." Mark 1:15
4. Blessed are the poor in spirit to those who *believe the word of the Lord*: "*And I will make an everlasting covenant with them, that I will not turn away from them, to do them good; but I will put my fear in their hearts, that they shall not depart from me*." Jeremiah 32:40
5. Blessed are the poor in spirit to those who believe this statement: Real Men, Real Issues, Serving a Real God: "And the Lord called unto Adam, and said unto him, *Where Art Thou?*" Genesis 3:9
6. Blessed are the poor in spirit to those who *believe*: *According to Deuteronomy 18:15-18*; *Isaiah 40:3, Malachi 3:1.*
   We found Him!!! John 1:45
   We found the Messiah!!! John 4:25 *We found Christ*!!! John 4:25
   We found the Child!!! Luke 1:75, 80
   We found the Prophet!!! Luke 7:27, John 6:14, Acts 2:22, Acts 3:22, Acts 7:37 *We found the Lord*!!! Luke 1:76
   We found Jesus, of Nazareth a man approved of God!!! Acts 2:22 We found *our true brother among us alike*—Acts 3:22

We found Him, Jesus of Nazareth!!! John 1:45
We *heard Him ourselves when He said*, "*I that speak unto thee*; other words, *He said*, "*I am He that speak to you*!!! Matthew 11:10, Luke 7:27, John 4:25
Read Isaiah 7:14, Matthew 1:23, 25. God is with us, God is among. God is with us in the person of Jesus Christ.

7. Blessed are the poor in spirit to those who believe that "*being revived*" *is through prayer, healing and blessing for being alive in the presence of the Lord.* our God.
8. Blessed are the poor in spirit to those who *believe that a person may convert and shall save a soul from death*, and *shall hide a multitude of sins*. James 5:19-20
9. Blessed are the poor in spirit to those who *believe the word of the Lord that says*, "*Seek ye my face Psalms 27:8*
10. Blessed are the poor in spirit to those who believe that "Prepare to meet the Lord thy God is a term of "the Day of Judgment". Amos 4:12, Matthew 12:36-37, Revelation 20:14
11. Blessed are the poor in spirit to those who believe in the *invisible God or the eternal God*. Romans 1:20, I Timothy 1:17, Colossians 1:15
12. Blessed are the poor in spirit to those who *believe in evangelical foundational principle*: *justification by faith*. Romans 1:17, Romans 3:24-25, Romans 3:28, Romans 4:3, Romans 4:5, Romans 5:1, Ephesians 2:8-10, Galatians 2:16, Galatians 3:8, Philippians 3:9

Part CCCLXVIII

Blessed Are The Poor In Spirit. Matthew 5:3

Blessed Means Happy

Poor means meek in spirit. Poor means humble in spirit. Poor means lowly in spirit. Poor means quiet in spirit. Read Matthew 5:3-12, Read also Mark 1:15

Jesus did not say "*rich*" in spirit. Jesus said "*poor*" in spirit.

1. Blessed are the poor in spirit to those who believe in the *evangelical foundational principle*: *Grace—salvation as an unearned gift or mercy gift from God.* John 1:16 Romans 3:24, I Corinthians 15:10, Ephesians 2:8-9, II Timothy 4:22, James 4:6
2. Blessed are the poor in spirit to those who believe that *we cannot control the authority of the Bible because the Bible itself is written by God than our own thinking*, than *our own belief*, than our *own knowledge*, than *our own power*, than our *own author and rule and conduct* than our *own law—abiding citizens than our religion rule or religion teaching, than our own faith.* II Timothy 3:16, John 3:3, 36, Acts 4:12, Hebrews 5:9, John 8:31-47, 56-58, I John 2:24-25, Romans 8:33-39, I John 5:11, I John 3:2, Romans 10:13, Acts 17:30, II Peter 3:18
3. Blessed are the poor in spirit to those who believe as an *expression of the joy of salvation through faith in Christ Jesus by our reaction.* Luke 2:10
4. Blessed are the poor in spirit to those who believe the Word of the Lord: "*For the eyes of the Lord run to and fro throughout the whole earth, to shew himself strong in the behalf of them whose heart is perfect toward him. Herein thou hast done foolishly: therefore from henceforth thou shalt have wars.*" II Chronicles 16:9
5. Blessed are the poor in spirit to those who believe that in Christ's human capacity Jesus was born a Jew. Luke 1:31-33
6. Blessed are the poor in spirit to those who believe *in the fundamental truth of the gospel of Jesus Christ and the early history of the Christian church*; *in which an heresy is used in the Bible to denote a sect or party and implies no judgment concerning the truth or error of the apostle doctrines. Acts 24:14-27*
7. Blessed are the poor in spirit to those who *believe that an Inspiration is the Holy Bible that come from the Almighty Authority of God.* Job 32:6-8, II Peter 1:19-21, II Timothy 3:14-17

8. Blessed are the poor in spirit to those who *were survival of slavery's, once slavery's in American have one master whose name is Jesus Christ in heaven.*
9. Blessed are the poor in spirit to those who believe that the *Holy Book, the sacrament book, except the translation of the scriptures is the same teaching of God's Word that never change more than thousand centuries ago from Genesis to Revelation.*
10. Blessed are the poor in spirit to those who *believe that on the day of Pentecost the Holy Spirit was poured on the Christian church.* Acts 2:1-41
11. Blessed are the poor in spirit to those who believe that *the Bible said that Jesus Christ had a cousin who baptized Him was John the Baptist*
12. Blessed are the poor in spirit to those who believe *in true history of Bible story.* Genesis 1:1-31, II Timothy 3:16, Romans 10:9-13, Acts 5:1-11, John 14:15, John 8:44, John 3:16-17, Jeremiah 29:11, Job 38:4, Exodus 20:11, Genesis 3:14, Genesis 2:1-28

Part CCCLXIX

Blessed Are The Poor In Spirit. Matthew 5:3

Blessed Means Happy

Poor means meek in spirit Poor means humble in spirit Poor means lowly in spirit Poor means quiet in spirit Read Matthew 5:3-12, Read also Mark 1:15

Jesus did not say "*rich*" in spirit. Jesus said "*poor*" in spirit.

1. Blessed are the poor in spirit to those who believe that the *Power of Pentecost came to an humble location of Los Angel, California in 1906 on 312 Azusa Street Revival 1906-1909* since the day of *Pentecostal Era in the Pattern of the Book of Acts 2:1-26:2-47 in order to spread the Good News of the Gospel of Jesus Christ., Matthew 20:18-20, verse 20, Mark 13:10, Mark16:15-17, verse 15, 17-(c), Luke 24:49, John 20:22, Acts 1:5-8, Acts 2:1, 4*
2. Blessed are the poor in spirit to those who *believe The Gospel*: "*When I therefore was thus minded, did I use lightness? Or the things that I purpose, do I purpose according to the flesh, that with me there should be yea yea, and nay nay?*" II Corinthians 1:17
3. Blessed are the poor in spirit to those who *believe the gospel*: "*But as God is true, our word toward you was not yea and nay.*" II Corinthians 1:18
4. Blessed are the poor in spirit to those who believe that *Christ is Lord.* He is the *Savior.* He is our *Redeemer.* He is the *Mighty One of Jacob.* Isaiah 60:16
5. Blessed are the poor in spirit to those who *believe in a local church, a congregation of Christian believers; the whole body of believers in Christ.* Matthew 16:18, Galatians 1:13, Ephesians 1:22-23, 5:27
6. Blessed are the poor in spirit to those who believe that the *city of Nazareth*, the *city of Bethlehem* are the *names given in honor of King David, call the city of David, is born this day, a Savior which is Christ the Lord.* Luke 2:4, 11, Isaiah 9:6
7. Blessed are the poor in spirit to those who *wonder if that person does have Christ in his heart.* Romans 5:7
8. Blessed are the poor in spirit to those who *believe that a person can't go to heaven if he does not have Christ in his heart, because that person has to get to know Christ "first" Psalm 27:8, Isaiah 55:6, Isaiah 58:1-14, verse 2, 8, Matthew 6:33, Luke 21:28, Acts 17:27, Romans 8:9, Romans 13:11, Philippians 3:10.*

9. Blessed are the poor in spirit to those who *believe that a stranger*, a *pilgrim land, sojourner can be saved and have Christ in his heart if he can search the scriptures and to testify of Christ in his heart to get to know Him better.* John 5:39, Philippians 3:10, Acts 17:27
10. Blessed are the poor in spirit to those who believe the *testimony of the eye witness to Heaven*. Joel 2:28-29 and Acts 2:39, Ephesians 2:19-22, verse 19
11. Blessed are the poor in spirit to those who *believe that the Scripture say that God indeed answer ur prayers*: Exodus 3:1-22; 4:1-31, Exodus 6:1-11, See Acts 13:17, 26, 29, 7:1-5, 9, 14-19, See Acts 7:36, Revelation 16:3, 8:1-5, 16, 20-23, Acts 9:1-5, 8-9, 13-19, 22, See Romans 9:17, 10:1-6, 12, 21, 11:1-2, 4-7, 9, 12:1-20, 43-49, 13:1-2, 17, 14:1-4, 14-18, 26, 15:26
12. Blessed are the poor in spirit to those who *believe that a person has to have Christ in his heart to know Him or he could not go to heaven*. Philippians 3:10, Acts 17:27, Isaiah 55:6, Isaiah 58:1-14, verse 2, 8, Matthew 6:33, Romans 13:11, Romans 8:9, Psalm 27:8, Luke 21:28

PART CCCLXX

Blessed Are The Poor In Spirit. Matthew 5:3

Blessed Means Happy

Poor means meek in spirit Poor means humble in spirit Poor means lowly in spirit Poor means quiet in spirit Read Matthew 5:3-12, Read also Mark 1:15

Jesus did not say "*rich*" in spirit. Jesus said "*poor*" in spirit.

1. Blessed are the poor in spirit to those who *believe and ask ourselves: Do that person have Christ in his heart?* Matthew 7:16, 20, Philippians 2:12
2. Blessed are the poor in spirit to those who *believe, know, understand and realize by saying, "I know He is the Saviour of the world" is not enough.* John 5:37-40
3. Blessed are the poor in spirit to those who *believe in preaching faith and repentance according to the Gospel of Jesus Christ.* Matthew 4:17, Mark 1:15, Mark 6:12
4. Blessed are the poor in spirit to those who *believe the assurance of God's forgiveness through Jesus Christ.* Acts 5:31, Acts 13:28, Acts 26:18, Ephesians 1:7, Colossians 1:14
5. Blessed are the poor in spirit to those who *believe in thanking God for His gift of repentance because of His unspeakable gift to us.* II Corinthians 9:15
6. Blessed are the poor in spirit to those who believe that *justification by faith is saving one's soul just by accepting God's offer of forgiveness by faith in Jesus Christ in our heart.* Romans 1:17, Romans 4:25, Romans 5:16, 18
7. Blessed are the poor in spirit to those who *believe by convincing the people of nominal Christians by the need to be born again and to live out a personal faith in Jesus Christ.* John 3:3, 6-7, I Peter 1:23, Mark 11:22
8. Blessed are the poor in spirit to those who *believe that the Bible offer us in repentance toward God and faith toward Jesus Christ.* Acts 20:21, Acts 26:20
9. Blessed are the poor in spirit to those who *know, understand, realize* and *discover the need of the new birth which is in Christ Jesus.* II Corinthians 5:17-21, John 3:3-7
10. Blessed are the poor in spirit to those who *believe that sinners need to be saved through Jesus Christ, the Savior of the world.* I John 4:14-15, John 4:42, I Timothy 1:15, John 12:32, John 8:24, John 3:17, Hebrews 11:7, Romans 10:9, Romans 5:8, Romans 1:16, Acts 4:12, John 14:6, John 1:29, Luke 19:10, Luke 13:3,

Matthew 11:28, Revelation 3:20, II Peter 3:9, II Timothy 2:6, I Timothy 2:4, Philippians 2:11, John 20:31, Luke 5:32, Luke 2:11, Matthew 1:20

11. Blessed are the poor in spirit to those who *believe* that the *kingdom of heaven is for righteousness of peace and joy in the Holy Spirit*. Romans 14:17
12. Blessed are the poor in spirit to those who *know and believe the love of God in our hearts*. Romans 5:5

PART CCCLXXI

Blessed Are The Poor In Spirit. Matthew 5:3

Blessed Means Happy

Poor means meek in spirit. Poor means humble in spirit. Poor means lowly in spirit. Poor means quiet in spirit. Read Matthew 5:3-12, Read also Mark 1:15

Jesus did not say "*rich*" in spirit. Jesus said "*poor*" in spirit.

1. Blessed are the poor in spirit to those who we believe in *singing praises unto our God our Savior.* Psalm 33:2, 3, Psalm 40:3, Psalm 144:9-10, Psalm 146:1-10
2. Blessed are the poor in spirit to those who *believe in the invisible reality of God.* Colossians 1:15, Colossians 2:9, John 1:18, John 1:10., Deuteronomy 6:4, II Timothy 3:16, I Timothy 6:15-16, John 1:1-51, Matthew 1:23, Daniel 7:13, Isaiah 9:6, Isaiah 7:14, Genesis 1:26
3. Blessed are the poor in spirit to those who *believe that God offer us salvation through Jesus Christ.* Hebrews 9:28
4. Blessed are the poor in spirit to those who *believe that God offer us justification by faith in Jesus Christ.* Romans 1:17
5. Blessed are the poor in spirit to those who *believe that the Spirit of God convincing the soul of sinners.* James 5:20, Revelation 21:8, John 8:44, John 6:44, John 3:3, Matthew 25:46, Matthew 25:41, Daniel 12:2, Exodus 33:20, Revelation 21:1-27, Revelation 20:14, Revelation 20:11-15, Revelation 20:10, Revelation 20:6, Revelation 19:20, Revelation 14:1-20, Revelation 2:11, I John 5:20, I John 5:4, I John 4:16, II Peter 3:9, I Peter 2:1, Hebrews 9:12, II Timothy 3:16-17, II Timothy 4:2, I Timothy 6:16, I Timothy 2:3-4, Galatians 6:7, II Corinthians 4:6, II Corinthians 5:17, I Corinthians 15:33, I Corinthians 15:22, I Corinthians 15:3, Romans 10:13, Romans 10:9, John 16:8, John 10:10, Romans 6:23, Revelation 5:12, Romans 5:8, Romans 3:23, John 6:40, John 5:24, John 3:36, Luke 23:43, Luke 12:1-59, Matthew 10:28, John 3:15-16, Acts 16:31, II Peter 2:15, II Peter 2:4-10
6. Blessed are the poor in spirit to those who *believe the authority*: "*By the authority of Jesus Christ.* Matthew 21:23-27, Mark 11:28-33, Colossians 3:15-17, Hebrews 12:2, Matthew 28:18

7. Blessed are the poor in spirit to those who believe to *take the authority of Jesus Christ and to preach the gospel.* Hebrews 12:2, I Timothy 3:16, Mark 13:10, Luke 24:47, Galatians 2:2, Ephesians 3:8, Matthew 28:18, Mark 15:16
8. Blessed are the poor in spirit to those who *hear and believe the glad tidings of salvation*, the *Good News of Christ*, the *Savior of the world.* Isaiah 40:9, Isaiah 52:7, Luke 2:10
9. Blessed are the poor in spirit to those who *believe that perfect assurance is brought by the gift of the living faith of God through Jesus Christ.* Mark 11:22, Ephesians 2:8-9, I John 5:1, John 1:12, Titus 2:11, I Timothy 2:5
10. Blessed are the poor in spirit to those who believe in the *perfect assurance of salvation is through Jesus Christ.* Mark 11:22, Ephesians 2:8-9, I John 5:1, John 1:12, Titus 2:11, I Timothy 2:5
11. Blessed are the poor in spirit to those who believe in *declaring the glad tidings of salvation of Jesus Christ.* Luke 2:10
12. Blessed are the poor in spirit to those who believe that the *Jews had their Pentecostal Festival or Passover Festival in the Old Testament day.* Exodus 34:22, Leviticus 23:15-16, Numbers 28:26

Part CCCLXXII

Blessed Are The Poor In Spirit. Matthew 5:3

Blessed Means Happy

Poor means meek in spirit Poor means humble in spirit Poor means lowly in spirit Poor means quiet in spirit Read Matthew 5:3-12, Read also Mark 1:15

Jesus did not say "*rich*" in spirit. Jesus said "*poor*" in spirit.

1. Blessed are the poor in spirit to those who *believe that Pentecost was the outpouring of the Holy Spirit according to Joel 2:28-29, 32, Acts 2:4* and *Acts 2:38*, Acts 10:45-44, verse 45, *God's approval to all believers and unbeliever sinners who come to Jesus Christ in faith.* Joel 2:32, Romans 10:13, Acts 2:21, Acts 15:11, Acts 16:30-31, Romans 5:9-11
2. Blessed are the poor in spirit to those who *believe that Pentecost means fiftieth* (50th), Leviticus 23:16, Pentecost 2:1, Acts 20:16, I Corinthians 16:8
3. Blessed are the poor in spirit to those who believe that *Pentecost mean the Baptism of the Holy Spirit or filled with the Spirit or baptized with the Holy Spirit or winning as many souls to Christ.* Proverbs 11:30, Acts 1:8, Acts 2:41, I John 5:13-14.
4. Blessed are the poor in spirit to those who *cannot see the Acts of the moving of the Holy Spirit working in the life of many people who desperate need Christ and His performance in our daily lives. Faith is the faith that move mountain. Matthew 21:21-22, Luke 11:13, Hebrews 11:6, John 4:24, Mark11:22*
5. Blessed are the poor in spirit to those who *believe that Baptism of the Holy Spirit is speaking with tongues as the Holy Spirit gave them utterance.* Acts 2:4
6. Blessed are the poor in spirit to those who believe in the fundamental faith of the resurrection of the just is our Christian faith in Jesus Christ.
   II Peter 3:18-22,
7. Blessed are the poor in spirit to those who believe that Jesus Christ is the Son of Righteousness. Malachi 4:2, Luke 1:78
8. Blessed are the poor in spirit to those who believe in the Apostles' Creed or Confession of faith as follow: "I believe in God, the Father Almighty, Maker of heaven and earth. And in Jesus Christ, His only Son, our Lord; who was conceived by the Holy Ghost, born of the Virgin Mary; suffered under Pontius

Pilate, was crucified, dead, and buried; he descended into hell [or hades]; the third day he rose from the dead; he ascended into heaven, and sitteth on the right hand of God the Father Almighty; from thence He shall come to judge the quick and the dead. I believe in the Holy Ghost; the Holy Catholic Church; the communion of Saints; the forgiveness of sins; the resurrection of the body; and the life everlasting. Amen." Genesis 15:6, Romans 4:3, James 2:23, Genesis 1:1, 26-27, John 1:18, Acts 10:36, Philippians 2:11, Luke 1:26-35 verse 31, 35, Luke 23:33, Acts 2:36, I Corinthians 15:4, I Timothy 3:16, Acts 1:11, Matthew 2:1-23 verse 16-18 (Jeremiah 31:15), John 19:30, Matthew 27:50-54, Mark 15:37-39, Luke 23:34-48, John 19:30-37, Acts 10:40, Hosea 6:2, Colossians 3:1, I Peter 4:5, II Timothy 4:1, Acts 10:42, II Corinthians 13:14, Matthew 16:13-21 verse 18, Acts 5:31, 13:38, 26:18, Ephesians 1:7, Colossians 1:14, John 11:25, John 3:16, 36, John 4:14, John 5:24, 6:27, 40, 47, II Thessalonians 2:16, I Timothy 1:16, Hebrews 13:20, II Peter 1:11, Revelation 14:6, Galatians 6:6, Romans 6:22, 16:26, John 12:50, Matthew 27:53, Luke 20:36, Acts 1:22, 2:31, Acts 4:2, 33, 17:18, 32, 23:6, 24:15, 21, Romans 1:4, 6:5, I Corinthians 15:21-23, 15:35-58, Philippians 3:10, I Peter 1:3, 3:21, Revelation 20:5-6, Genesis 17:1, Job 37:23, II Corinthians 6:18, Revelation 1:8, Revelation 4:8, Revelation 11:17, Revelation 15:3, Revelation 16:7, 14, Revelation 19:15, Revelation 21:22

9. Blessed are the poor in spirit to those who believe in *supporting the healing of our bodies from sickness, death and physical injury because God answer prayer.* James 5:13-16
10. Blessed are the poor in spirit to those who believe the scriptures: "*Verily I say unto you, All sins shall be forgiven unto the sons of men*, and *blasphemies wherewith soever they shall blaspheme*: But he that shall blaspheme against the Holy Ghost hath never forgiveness, but is in danger of eternal damnation:" Mark 3:28-29
11. Blessed are the poor in spirit to those who believe that the *Feast of Harvest means Pentecost Feast or Harvest of Pentecost mean to gather lost souls for Christ or to win lost souls for Christ. Those who win souls for Christ are wise.* See Proverbs 11:30, Matthew 9:37-38, Luke 10:2, John 4:32, 34-44, Acts 2:14-47, Acts 2:36-38
12. Blessed are the poor in spirit to those who "*believed*" and "*heard*" that after *Christ's death and Christ's suffer for sins* for the *just* and the *unjust. He went and preached unto the spirits in prisons* (shoel, hades, hell, unseen underworld, pit, grave, realm of the dead) and Christ had left to go back to heaven and is on the right hand of God; angels and authorities and powers being made subject unto Him. I Peter 3:18-19, I Peter 3:20-22

Part CCCLXXIII

Blessed Are The Poor In Spirit. Matthew 5:3

Blessed Means Happy

Poor means meek in spirit Poor means humble in spirit Poor means lowly in spirit Poor means quiet in spirit Read Matthew 5:3-12, Read also Mark 1:15

Jesus did not say "*rich*" in spirit. Jesus said "*poor*" in spirit.

1. Blessed are the poor in spirit to those who *believe in ancient times that handkerchiefs, were used as the sick handkerchiefs or aprons,* and the *diseases departed from them,* and *the evil spirits went out of them.* Acts 19:12
2. Blessed are the poor in spirit to those who believe the *harmony of the Gospels with Matthew, Mark, John* and *Luke* because *they were children of God and Christ used them to write The Gospels for the Jews,* for *the Romans,* for the *Greeks* and for the advanced *Christians of all nationalities.* II Timothy 2:15, I Thessalonians 4:11, II Timothy 3:16, Deuteronomy 29:29, Genesis 1:1, John 1:1, Ecclesiastes 12:13, Psalm 62:11, Romans 1:12-17, verse 16, Romans 10:1, I Corinthians 1:18, I Corinthians 2:4, John 1:12, John 10:18, John 19:11, Acts 1:7-8, Acts 26:18, Luke 23:38, John 19:20, Acts 21:40, Acts 22:2, Acts 26:14, Philippians 3:5, John 1:12, Romans 8:15-17, Galatians 4:5, Ephesians 1:5, Acts 21:37, Romans 10:12, Galatians 3:28, Colossians 3:11, Revelation 9:11
3. Blessed are the poor in spirit to those who *believe in* "*Al-le-lu'ia*" as "*Hallelujah*" or "*Praise the Lord;*" *for Salvation,* and *Glory and Honor and Power unto the Lord our God, for the Lord God omnipotent* (all powerful) *reigneth.* Revelation 19:1, 3-4, 6
4. Blessed are the poor in spirit to those who *believe in laying on of hands through Jesus Christ "for consecration," "for healing with spiritual gifts."* Number 27:18, Acts 8:15-17, I Timothy 4:14, II Timothy 1:6
5. Blessed are the poor in spirit to those who believe that *John, one of God's children wrote the Gospel of Salvation for advanced Christians of all nationalities. Read I, II and III books of John's epistles or letters.* I John To III John 1:1-14
6. Blessed are the poor in spirit to those who believe that "*Christ*" is the "*Governor*" to *rule His people Israel.* Matthew 2:6, John 7:42, 46, Micah 5:2, Isaiah 9:6

7. Blessed are the poor in spirit to those who *believe in Hallelujah to Christ* which mean "*Praise Ye The Lord*" or "*Praise the Lord.*" Psalm 106:1, 48, Psalm 111:1, Psalm 112:1, Psalm 113:1, 9, Psalm 117:1-2, 135:1, 3, 21
8. Blessed are the poor in spirit to those who believe that *Luke, one of God's children displays Christ's personal history.* Mark 11:22, II Peter 1:19-21, II Timothy 3:16, Hebrews 1:1
9. Blessed are the poor in spirit to those who believe that *Matthew, one of God's children, wrote the Gospel of salvation for the Jews.* Mark 11:22, Romans 1:16, II Peter 1:19-21, II Timothy 3:16, Hebrews 1:1,
10. Blessed are the poor in spirit to those who believe that *Mark, one of God's children, wrote the Gospel of salvation for the Romans.* Mark 11:22, Romans 1:16, II Peter 1:19-21, II Timothy 3:16
11. Blessed are the poor in spirit to those who believe that *Luke, one of God's children, wrote the Gospel of salvation for the Greeks.* Mark 11:22, Romans 1:16, II Peter 1:19-21, II Timothy 3:16, Hebrews 1:1
12. Blessed are the poor in spirit to those who believe that they were called of God 2000 BC to 420 BC to 2000 AD in the year of our Lord and beyond the millennium. Jeremiah 33:3, Mark 16:15, I Thessalonians 5:23-25, II Thessalonians 2:13, I Thessalonians 4:3-4, I Corinthians 1:30, I Peter 1:2

Part CCCLXXIV

Blessed Are The Poor In Spirit. Matthew 5:3

Blessed Means Happy

Poor means meek in spirit. Poor means humble in spirit. Poor means lowly in spirit. Poor means quiet in spirit. Read Matthew 5:3-12, Read also Mark 1:15

Jesus did not say "*rich*" in spirit. Jesus said "*poor*" in spirit.

1. Blessed are the poor in spirit to those who *believe that Matthew, one of God's children, described Christ as the Messiah and King of the Jews.* Mark 15:2, Matthew 2:2
2. Blessed are the poor in spirit to those who believe that *John, one of God's children, described Christ as the incarnate Son of God and Redeemer.* John 1:14, John 10:30, John 1:1, Isaiah 9:6, John 14:9, John 8:58, John 1:3, Isaiah 7:14, Genesis 1:1, Genesis 1:26, I John 5:7, Titus 2:13, Colossians 1:16, II Corinthians 13:14, John 14:6, Matthew 28:19, Matthew 1:21, Luke 1:35, Luke 2:11, Matthew 1:23, Micah 5:2, Isaiah 44:6, Hebrews 9:14, I Timothy 3:16, Philippians 2:5-8, John 20:29, John 20:31, John 17:3, John 1:49, Daniel 7:13, Revelation 1:17, Revelation 1:8, I Timothy 4:10, I Timothy 2:3, 5, Colossians 1:15, Philippians 2:10-11, Psalm 110:1-7, Isaiah 44:24, Isaiah 63:16, Matthew 26:63, Matthew 16:16, Matthew 11:27, Luke 22:70, John 5:17, John 1:34, Acts 9:20, Acts 5:31, Romans 1:20, Isaiah 43:11 = Acts 9:4-6, 20, Revelation 22:13, I John 5:20, Colossians 2:9, John 20:28
3. Blessed are the poor in spirit to those who believe that *Mark, one of God's children, displays Christ's official.* Hebrews 12:2, II Timothy 3:16
4. Blessed are the poor in spirit to those who *believe that Anna,* a *prophetess and one of God's children, announced that Jesus was the Messiah. Luke 2:36-39*
5. Blessed are the poor in spirit to those who *believe* that the *disciples knew not* "*the scripture*" that "*Christ*" "*must rise again from the dead.*" *John 20:9*
6. Blessed are the poor in spirit to those who believe that *Christ* is the *king of Israel.* John 1:49
7. Blessed are the poor in spirit to those who believe that *Jesus* is the *Lamb of God.* John 1:29

8. Blessed are the poor in spirit to those who believe that *Christ* is the *Living Stone.* I Peter 2:4
9. Blessed are the poor in spirit to those who *believe that Paul,* at least the last *apostle of the Gentiles and one of God's children after Jesus temporarily blinded him; Paul converted to the Christian faith that he had previously hated Jesus' disciples.* Acts 9:3-5
10. Blessed are the poor in spirit to those who believe that *Christ is Lord of Glory.* I Corinthians 2:8
11. Blessed are the poor in spirit to those who believe that *Christ* is the *Messiah* and is *He is the Prince.* Daniel 9:25
12. Blessed are the poor in spirit to those who believe that *Christ* is our *Passover Lamb.* I Corinthians 5:7

Part CCCLXXV

Blessed Are The Poor In Spirit. Matthew 5:3

Blessed Means Happy

Poor means meek in spirit. Poor means humble in spirit. Poor means lowly in spirit. Poor means quiet in spirit. Read Matthew 5:3-12, Read also Mark 1:15

Jesus did not say "*rich*" in spirit. Jesus said "*poor*" in spirit.

1. Blessed are the poor in spirit to those who believe that *Christ* is the *Prince of Life.* Acts 3:15
2. Blessed are the poor in spirit to those who believe that *Christ* is *the Word of God.* Revelation 19:13
3. Blessed are the poor in spirit to those who believe that "*Christian*" is the *name given in honor of Christ Jesus*, "*our Lord.*" Acts 11:26
4. Blessed are the poor in spirit to those who believe that *Christ* is the *Shepherd* and *Bishop of our souls.* I Peter 2:25
5. Blessed are the poor in spirit to those who believe that *Christ* is the *Word.* John 1:1, Genesis 1:1
6. Blessed are the poor in spirit to those who believe that *Christ* is the *Prince of the kings of the earth.* Revelation 1:5
7. Blessed are the poor in spirit to those who believe that *Christ* is the *Root of David.* Revelation 5:5
8. Blessed are the poor in spirit to those who believe that *Christ* is the *Prophet.* Deuteronomy 18:15, See Acts 7:37
9. Blessed are the poor in spirit to those who believe that *Christ* is the *Ruler in Israel.* Micah 5:2
10. Blessed are the poor in spirit to those who believe that *Christ* is the *Saviour.* Luke 2:11
11. Blessed are the poor in spirit to those who believe in the "*Rapture*" *of the church*; the *saints of God*; the *people of God who are born again believers in Jesus Christ, expecting at His return*; *which will be the coming of the Lord.* I Thessalonians 4:11-18

12. Blessed are the poor in spirit to those who believe the Psalmist: "*Let the words of my mouth, and the meditation of my heart, be acceptable in thy sight, O Lord, my strength, and my redeemer and Jesus Christ is my Redeemer.*" Psalm 19:14

Part CCCLXXVI

Blessed Are The Poor In Spirit. Matthew 5:3

Blessed Means Happy

Poor means meek in spirit. Poor means humble in spirit. Poor means lowly in spirit. Poor means quiet in spirit. Read Matthew 5:3-12, Read also Mark 1:15

Jesus did not say "*rich*" in spirit. Jesus said "*poor*" in spirit.

1. Blessed are the poor in spirit to those who believe that *Jesus Christ is my Rock and my Redeemer*. Psalm 19:14
2. Blessed are the poor in spirit to those who believe the Psalmist: "*O come, let us sing unto the Lord: let us make a joyful noise to the rock of our salvation.*" Psalm 95:1
3. Blessed are the poor in spirit to those who believe that *Jesus Christ is the Rock of our salvation*. Psalm 95:1
4. Blessed are the poor in spirit to those who believe the Psalmist: "*My lips shall greatly rejoice when I sing unto thee; and my soul, which thou hast redeemed.*" Psalm 71:23
5. Blessed are the poor in spirit to those who *believe concerning about faith, love and hope and salvation*: "*But let us, who are of the day, be sober, putting on the breastplate of faith and love; and for an helmet, the hope of salvation.*" I Thessalonians 5:8
6. Blessed are the poor in spirit to those who *believe concerning about faith, love and hope and salvation*: "*For God hath not appointed us to wrath, but to obtain salvation by our Lord Jesus Christ,*" I Thessalonians 5:9
7. Blessed are the poor in spirit to those who *believe concerning about faith, love and hope and salvation*: "*Who died for us, that, whether we wake or sleep, we should live together with him.*" I Thessalonians 5:10
8. Blessed are the poor in spirit to those who *believe concerning about faith, love and hope and salvation*: "*Wherefore comfort yourselves together, and edify one another, even as also ye do.*" I Thessalonians 5:11
9. Blessed are the poor in spirit to those who believe that we are created as white as snow because God cannot look upon sinners; covering with this white as snow, God see us through His Son Jesus in His blood that washes and cleanse us

with pure and holy through sanctification. Isaiah 1:16-18, Psalm 51:7-15, John 1:29, Hebrews 10:22, I Corinthians 6:11, Ephesians 5:26, 1 John 1:7, Matthew 26:28, Ephesians 1:7, Acts 20:28, I Corinthians 6:11, John 17:17, John 15:3, Revelation 7:14, I Peter 1:19, Hebrews 9:22, Matthew 5:8, Revelation 19:13, I John 5:6, I Peter 2:2, I Peter 1:2, Hebrews 13:12, Hebrews 13:20, John 6:53-56

10. Blessed are the poor in spirit to those who believe in healing through answering prayer. James 5:13-16
11. Blessed are the poor in spirit to those who believe that God want us to be holy because He is holy. I Peter 1:16
12. Blessed are the poor in spirit to those who believe that the *120 believers went into an Upper Room for A Prayer Meeting*. Acts 1:13-20 {verse 15}

Part CCCLXXVII

Blessed Are The Poor In Spirit. Matthew 5:3

Blessed Means Happy

Poor means meek in spirit Poor means humble in spirit Poor means lowly in spirit Poor means quiet in spirit Read Matthew 5:3-12, Read also Mark 1:15

Jesus did not say "*rich*" in spirit. Jesus said "*poor*" in spirit.

1. Blessed are the poor in spirit to those who believe that *Apostle Peter made his testimony clear to his Jewish brothers in Christ.* Acts 11:1-18, Acts 10:5, 8, 13-20, 22, 27, 33, 38-43, 44-48
2. Blessed are the poor in spirit to those who *believe that Jesus Christ is "Lord of all."* Acts 10:36
3. Blessed are the poor in spirit to those who *believe that the Word of God sent unto the children of Israel, preaching peace by Jesus Christ: He is Lord of all.* Acts 10:36
4. Blessed are the poor in spirit to those who believe this beautiful hymn with faith and confident: II Corinthians 5:6-8, II Timothy 4:6-8, Romans 14:7-9 verse 8
   "I'll fly away
   Oh glory I'll fly away
   When I die, hall-e-lu-jah by and by
   I'll fly away."
5. Blessed are the poor in spirit to those who *believe that God "Himself" in mercy, does not send His Son into the world to condemn* (judge) *the world, but that the world through Him might be saved.* John 3:17
6. Blessed are the poor in spirit to those who *believe the message of the whole Bible telling the story of salvation.* John 3:16
7. Blessed are the poor in spirit to those who *believe in the Bible is a divinely given message, at the center of which is our Savior, Jesus Christ our Lord.* II Peter 1:3, 4
8. Blessed are the poor in spirit to those who *believe that every human being stands in need of God's grace because we cannot possibly save ourselves.* Hebrews 4:16
9. Blessed are the poor in spirit to those who believe *when we say "the Bible" says so; the Word of God says so; Jesus says so; the Word of God had spoken.* Hebrews 1:1-14, Hebrews 2:1-18

10. Blessed are the poor in spirit to those who believe *that one man should die for the people as Jesus who should die for the nation. And Jesus indeed died for the whole nation. John 11:50-51*
11. Blessed are the poor in spirit to those who *believe that one or any of God's children or children of God to scatter abroad. John 11:52*
12. Blessed are the poor in spirit to those who believe that *Caiaphas* "*prophesied*" that *Jesus should die for the people; for the nation.* John 11:51, John 11:49-52, See John 18:14

Part CCCLXXVIII

Blessed Are The Poor In Spirit. Matthew 5:3

Blessed Means Happy

Poor means meek in spirit. Poor means humble in spirit. Poor means lowly in spirit. Poor means quiet in spirit. Read Matthew 5:3-12, Read also Mark 1:15

Jesus did not say "*rich*" in spirit. Jesus said "*poor*" in spirit.

1. Blessed are the poor in spirit to those who believe *this spiritually song*: "*Trust and Obey*, for *there's no other way to be happy in Jesus, but to trust and obey*." Romans 16:26
2. Blessed are the poor in spirit to those who believe *this spiritual song*: "*Then sing my soul, my Savior God, to Thee*: *How great Thou art, how great Thou art*!" Psalm 48:1
3. Blessed are the poor in spirit to those who believe *this spiritual song*: "*To God be the glory*, To God be the glory, To God be the glory *for the things He has done. With His blood He has saved me*: With His *power* He has *raised me*." Psalm 115:1, Psalm 126:3
4. Blessed are the poor in spirit to those who *believe the Psalmist*: "*For his anger endureth but a moment*; in his favour is life: *weeping may endure for a night, but joy cometh in the morning*." Psalm 30:5
5. Blessed are the poor in spirit to those who believe that *Christ's blood shed for many for the remission of sins*. Matthew 26:28, Mark 14:24
6. Blessed are the poor in spirit to those who *believe that many of the Israel shall turn to the Lord for salvation*. Luke 1:16, John 6:60, 66
7. Blessed are the poor in spirit to those who *believe the Word of the Lord in the book of Psalm*: "*When thou saidst, Seek ye My face*; *my heart said unto Thee, Thy face, Lord, will I seek*." Psalm 27:8
8. Blessed are the poor in spirit to those who *believe the Word of the Lord in the book of Psalm*: "*Hear, O Lord*, when I cry with my voice: *have mercy also upon me, and answer me*." Psalm 27:7
9. Blessed are the poor in spirit to those who *believe the Word of the Lord in the book of Psalm*: "*Hide not thy face far from me*; put not thy servant away in anger:

thou hast been my help; leave me not, neither forsake me, O God of my salvation." Psalm 27:9

10. Blessed are the poor in spirit to those who *believe the Word of the Lord in the book of Psalm*: "*When my father and my mother forsake me, then the Lord will take me up.*" Psalm 27:10
11. Blessed are the poor in spirit to those who *believe the Word of the Lord in the book of Psalm*: "*Teach me thy way, O Lord, and lead me in a plain path, because of mine enemies.*" Psalm 27:11
12. Blessed are the poor in spirit to those who believe that Jesus Christ is indeed Jesus of Nazareth. He says, "I am He." John 18:5

Part CCCLXXIX

Blessed Are The Poor In Spirit. Matthew 5:3

Blessed Means Happy

Poor means meek in spirit. Poor means humble in spirit. Poor means lowly in spirit. Poor means quiet in spirit. Read Matthew 5:3-12, Read also Mark 1:15

Jesus did not say "*rich*" in spirit. Jesus said "*poor*" in spirit.

1. Blessed are the poor in spirit to those who believe that Jesus Christ is the King of the Jews. John 19:19
2. Blessed are the poor in spirit to those who believe that Jesus Christ is a Man approved of God. Acts 2:22
3. Blessed are the poor in spirit to those who believe and heard the Apostle Peter say, "...In the name of Jesus Christ, of Nazareth, rise up and walk." Acts 3:6
4. Blessed are the poor in spirit to those who believe that Jesus Christ is the Holy One of God. Mark 1:24
5. Blessed are the poor in spirit to those who believe that Jesus Christ is the Son of David. Mark 10:47, See Matthew 1:1
6. Blessed are the poor in spirit to those who believe that Jesus Christ is a Prophet. Luke 24:19, Acts 3:22, Acts 7:37, See Deuteronomy 18:15
7. Blessed are the poor in spirit to those who believe when Jesus Christ of Nazareth say, "I am He." John 18:5
8. Blessed are the poor in spirit to those who *read the Bible as our Guiding Light*; to *show us the way to mandates us, to teach us, to live right from wrong, to act proper with respect, honor, love, faith, grace, salvation, Holy Spirit, prayer, know our history and where we come from, who our history ancestors* were, *who are those people in our world, where we are going and what happen next, and death, and life, being alive through breath, church, work, school, government, to follow the rule, the commandment, the law, how to survive, family, friends, relatives, enemies*, for *better, for worse, the help, problem solve, unseen God, Satan, rain, sun, moon, cold, hot, warm, stars, heat, lightning, thunderstorm.* Genesis 1:1-2
9. Blessed are the poor in spirit to those who *believe that Jesus was "still" alive through Paul even though many knew that Jesus was already dead. Acts 25:19*

10. Blessed are the poor in spirit to those who *believe that salvation is of the Jews as well.* John 4:22
11. Blessed are the poor in spirit to those who *believe the gospel*: "*Simeon hath declared how God at the first did visit the Gentiles, to take out of them a people for his name.*" Acts 15:14
12. Blessed are the poor in spirit to those who believe that "*God know the hearts,*" *bare them* (*Gentiles*), *giving them the Holy Ghost even as He did unto us* (*Jews*). *Acts 15:8*, See Romans 8:16-18, Acts 2:4, 21-38, 39, 47

PART CCCLXXX

Blessed Are The Poor In Spirit. Matthew 5:3

Blessed Means Happy

Poor means meek in spirit. Poor means humble in spirit. Poor means lowly in spirit. Poor means quiet in spirit. Read Matthew 5:3-12, Read also Mark 1:15

Jesus did not say "*rich*" in spirit. Jesus said "*poor*" in spirit.

1. Blessed are the poor in spirit to those who *believe that being a prophet was Jesus the resurrection of Christ.* Acts 2:31-32, 36, 13:35, See Psalm 49:15, Psalm 16:10
2. Blessed are the poor in spirit to those who *believe in spreading, telling, witnessing, preaching* "*the same gospel*" or "*the same things by mouth*" *of the gospel of Jesus Christ.* Acts 15:1-41
3. Blessed are the poor in spirit to those who *believe* "*the same gospel by mouth*: "*And the apostles and elders came together for to consider of this matter.*" Acts 15:6
4. Blessed are the poor in spirit to those who *believe* "*the same gospel by mouth*:" "*And when there had been much disputing, Peter rose up*, and *said unto them, Men and brethren, ye know how that a good while ago God made choice among us, that the Gentiles by my mouth should hear the word of the gospel*, and *believe.*" Acts 15:7
5. Blessed are the poor in spirit to those who *believe* "*the same gospel by mouth*:" "*And God, which knoweth the hearts, bare them witness, giving them the Holy Ghost, even as he did unto us; And put no difference between us and them, purifying their heats by faith.*" Acts 15:8-9
6. Blessed are the poor in spirit to those who *believe* "*the same gospel by mouth*:" "*But we believe that through the grace of the Lord Jesus Christ we shall be saved, even as they.*" Acts 15:11
7. Blessed are the poor in spirit to those who *believe* "*the same gospel by mouth*:" "*Simeon hath declared how God at the first did visit the Gentiles, to take out of them a people for his name.*" Acts 15:14
8. Blessed are the poor in spirit to those who *believe* "*the same gospel by mouth*:" "*And to this agree the words of the prophets; as it is written,*" Acts 15:15
9. Blessed are the poor in spirit to those who *believe* "*the same gospel by mouth*:" "*That the residue of men might seek after the Lord, and all the Gentiles, upon whom my name is called, saith the Lord, who doeth all these things.*" Acts 15:17

10. Blessed are the poor in spirit to those who *believe* "*the same gospel by mouth*:" *Known unto God are all his works from the beginning of the world.*" Acts 15:18
11. Blessed are the poor in spirit to those who *believe* "*the same gospel by mouth*:" "*Wherefore my sentence is, that we trouble not them, which from among the Gentiles are turned to God*:" Acts 15:19
12. Blessed are the poor in spirit to those who *believe that God had sought Him* (Himself) *a man after His own heart*. I Samuel 13:14

Part CCCLXXXI

Blessed Are The Poor In Spirit. Matthew 5:3

Blessed Means Happy

Poor means meek in spirit Poor means humble in spirit Poor means lowly in spirit Poor means quiet in spirit Read Matthew 5:3-12, Read also Mark 1:15

Jesus did not say "*rich*" in spirit. Jesus said "*poor*" in spirit.

1. Blessed are the poor in spirit to those who believe that *God sought* (search, seek) *Himself a man after His own heart.* I Samuel 13:14, Acts 13:22
2. Blessed are the poor in spirit to those who believe The Gospel: "*Him hath God exalted with his right hand to be a Prince and a Saviour,* for *to give repentance to Israel,* and *forgiveness of sins.*" Acts 5:31, Acts 15:22, 27, Acts 16:30-31
3. Blessed are the poor in spirit to those who believe the Word of the Lord: "*But now thy kingdom shall not continue*: the *Lord hath sough Him a man after His own heart, and the Lord hath commanded him to be captain over His people, because thou hast not kept* (*obeyed*) *that which the Lord commanded thee.* (*See Acts 13:22*) I Samuel 13:14
4. Blessed are the poor in spirit to those who believe The Gospel: "The *God* of our father *raised up Jesus,* whom *ye slew and hanged on a tree.* Acts 5:30, Revelation 1:5, Hebrews 9:14
5. Blessed are the poor in spirit to those who believe that when we read the Bible, God will speak to us. God still speak to us. Exodus 20:19, Hebrews 12:25, Joel 2:28, Romans 1:16, Acts 21:10, Acts 1:1, John 15:26, John 14:10, John 10:10, John 8:28, Isaiah 9:6, John 4:26, John 6:63
6. Blessed are the poor in spirit to those who believe that *a merciful God* and a kindness and gracious God give us "His *Perfect Doctrine,*" "*Jesus Christ*" is our "*Perfect Doctrine*" that we *may abide well with Him everyday through His "justification," "sanctification," "grace," "love," "mercy," "hope," "joy," "faith," "power," "promise," "unseen,"* "our *Heavenly Home," the city of our God, His Word abide in us, the kingdom of God become ours, salvation prayer.* John 18:19, Luke 4:32, Matthew 7:28, Matthew 22:23, Mark 1:22, 27, Mark 4:2, 11:18, Mark 12:38, John 4:29, Hebrews 11:6, Acts 1:8, II Timothy 1:1, Ephesians 1:13, Acts 1:4, Luke 24:49,

John 16:22, Titus 3:4-8 verse 4, Psalm 57:1, Psalm 34:8, I Peter 2:3, Jonah 4:2, Ephesians 6:18, Mark 11:22, Matthew 5:7, John 14:16, I Corinthians 13:13, John 1:1, Genesis 1:1, Revelation 21:1-2, Ephesians 3:15, Acts 4:12, Romans 4:25, Romans 5:16, 18, I Corinthians 1:30, I Thessalonians 4:3, 4, II Thessalonians 2:13, I Peter 1:2, Ephesians 2:8, John 3:16, Romans 10:17, Revelation 3:12, Revelation 22:14

7. Blessed are the poor in spirit to those who *believe that our God, is very Real Mighty Real So Real.* Genesis 1:1, John 1:1
8. Blessed are the poor in spirit to those who believe God's Word: "*God anointed Jesus of Nazareth with the Holy Ghost and with power: who went about doing good,* and *healing all that were oppressed* (dominated by or control by superior power or by influence)." Acts 10:38
9. Blessed are the poor in spirit to those who believe what Jesus Christ say, "I am Jesus of Nazareth." Acts 22:8
10. Blessed are the poor in spirit to those who believe that Jesus Christ come from Nazarene. Matthew 2:23, 21:11, Mark 1:24, 10:47, 16:6, 14:67, Luke 4:34, 18:37, 24:19, John 1:45, 46, 18:5, 7, 19:19, Acts 2:22, 3:6, 4:10, 6:14, 10:38, 22:8, 26:9, Acts 3:22, Acts 7:37, See Deuteronomy 18:15, 18, John 6:14, John 4:25, Acts 3:6, Acts 4:10
11. Blessed are the poor in spirit to those who believe He is a Man approved of God; that He is Jesus Christ; that God anointed Jesus; that Jesus said, I am Jesus of Nazareth. Acts 2:22, Acts 3:6, Acts 4:10, Acts 10:38
12. Blessed are the poor in spirit to those who believe Christ's Word: "*But pray ye that your flight be not in the winter, neither on the Sabbath day:*" Matthew 24:20

Part CCCLXXXII

Blessed Are The Poor In Spirit. Matthew 5:3

Blessed Means Happy

Poor means meek in spirit Poor means humble in spirit Poor means lowly in spirit Poor means quiet in spirit Read Matthew 5:3-12, Read also Mark 1:15

Jesus did not say "*rich*" in spirit. Jesus said "*poor*" in spirit.

1. Blessed are the poor in spirit to those who believe Christ's Word: "*Then we which are alive and remain shall be caught up together with them in the clouds, to meet the Lord in the air: and so shall we ever be with the Lord.*" I Thessalonians 4:17
2. Blessed are the poor in spirit to those who believe that believe that the *longsuffering of our Lord is salvation.* II Peter 3:15
3. Blessed are the poor in spirit to those who *believe in "Repentance:" Toward God-(Jesus) and faith toward our Lord Jesus Christ. God spoke through men telling others to use The Same Word: "Repent"* All men spoke **The Same Message Of Faith** that **God required** and that **God demand.** *John the Baptist said, "Repent." Jesus-(God) said, "Repent." Jesus' disciples went out and preached that men should repent. Peter said, "Repent." Paul said, "Repent."* Matthew 9:13, Mark 2:17, Luke 5:32, Luke 15:7, Luke 24:47, Acts 5:31, Acts 11:18, **II Corinthians 7:10**, Hebrews 6:6, II Peter 3:9, **Acts 20:21, Acts 26:20,** Mark 11:22, Matthew 3:2, **Matthew 4:17**, **Mark 1:15,** Mark 6:12, **Luke 13:3, 5,** Acts 2:38, Acts 3:19, Acts 8:22, Acts 17:30, -(I Timothy 2:1-6, verse 4), see Romans 1:12-17, verse 16, Romans 10:1, **Revelation 2:5, 16, 21, 22, Revelation 3:3, 19,** Acts 15:3, Isaiah 6:10, James 5:19, Psalm 51:1-15, verse 13, **Matthew 13:14-15, verse 15**, **Matthew 18:3**, **Mark 4:12-**(Isaiah 6:10), **Luke 22:32,** John 12:40, Acts 28:26-27, II Chronicles 7:12-22, verse 14, Hebrews 1:1-2, II Peter 1:18-21, verse 21, John 6:1-71, verse 66-69, verse 68 **Repentance** toward **God** and **faith** toward our **Lord Jesus Christ. Acts 20:21 God spoke** through men. II Peter 3:9, Acts 5:31, Romans 2:4, Acts 11:18 John said, "**Repent.**" John 3:2, Mark 1:4, Luke 3:3, Acts 13:24, Acts 19:4 **Jesus said**, "**Repent.**" John 4:17, Mark 1:15, Mark 2:17, Mark 6:12, Luke 5:32, Luke 13:3, 5, Luke 15:7, Luke 24:47, Revelation 2:5, 16 Jesus' disciple went out and preached Repent. Mark 6:12 Peter said,

"**Repent.**" Acts 2:38, 3:19, 20, 8:22 Paul "*commanded*" *all men everywhere to*: **Repent**. Acts 17:30, Acts 26:20

4. Blessed are the poor in spirit to those who *believe, understand, know, realize* and *being aware of that "Repentance" means to turn around from sin and to turn toward God and faith toward Jesus Christ with a "true"* and *"godly sorry"* and *"sincerely heart." "Repentance" means to change your mind, your thinking, your way and your own belief and believe God toward faith in Jesus Christ in your heat by faith.* Isaiah 55:8-9, Matthew 9:13, Mark 1:14, 2:17, Luke 3:8, 5:32, Luke 15:7, 24:47, Acts 5:31, 11:18, Acts 19:4, 20:21, Acts 26:20, II Corinthians 7:9-10, Hebrews 6:6, II Peter 3:9
5. Blessed are the poor in spirit to those who *believe the Word of God, the great doctrine of the Bible, God -Breathed Book, written by men who were inspired by God to set forth the truth without any error and to accept as it's face value without question.* Genesis 1:1, John 1:1, II Timothy 3:16
6. Blessed are the poor in spirit to those who believe one of God's children, John Wesley's testimony: "About a quarter before nine, while he was describing the change which God works in the heart through faith in Christ, I felt my heart strangely warmed. I felt I did trust in Christ, Christ alone, for salvation; and an assurance was given me that He had taken away my sins, even mine, and saved me from the law of sin and death. John Wesley (1703-1791) Romans 8:2, I Thessalonians 1:10, Ephesians 2:5, 8, Romans 6:23, Acts 4:12, Habakkuk 2:4, Romans 1:17, Galatians 3:11, Hebrews 10:38
7. Blessed are the poor in spirit to those who believe *Jesus Christ "Himself" is God "Himself."* I John 5:20, Genesis 1:1, John 1:1, John 1:1-51, John 10:30, 33, 38, Colossians 2:9, **John 14:1-12, verse 7, 8, 9, Philippians 2:6-11, verse 6, 10, 11, Acts 10:36, Hebrews 13:8, Revelation 1:7-8, 11 17-18, Revelation 2:8, Revelation 3:7, 11, Revelation 16:15, Revelation 22:7, 12-13, 16, 21, I Thessalonians 4:13**
8. Blessed are the poor in spirit to those who believe The Gospel: "It is the spirit that quickeneth; the flesh profiteth nothing: the words that I speak unto you, they are spirit, and they are life." John 6:63
9. Blessed are the poor in spirit to those who *believe and how to bow to the authority of the scripture; God's Word; the Word of God; the Word of Christ; the Word of Jesus.* Hebrews 5:9, Hebrews 12:2, Genesis 1:1, John 1:1-18, II Timothy 3:16

10. Blessed are the poor in spirit to those who believe *there is not just yea, yea and nay, nay, but in Christ Jesus, is yea. Yea mean yes. Nay mean no.* II Corinthians 1:17-27
11. Blessed are the poor in spirit to those who believe that *Elijah, one of God's children, went up to heaven in a whirlwind. II Kings 2:11, Mark 16:19, Acts 1:9, 11*
12. Blessed are the poor in spirit to those who believe *one of God's children*: *Heaven is the House where God dwells with His family.* Jonathan Edwards, 1703-1758 Ephesians 3:15

Part CCCLXXXIII

Blessed Are The Poor In Spirit. Matthew 5:3

Blessed Means Happy

Poor means meek in spirit. Poor means humble in spirit. Poor means lowly in spirit. Poor means quiet in spirit. Read Matthew 5:3-12, Read also Mark 1:15

Jesus did not say "*rich*" in spirit. Jesus said "*poor*" in spirit.

1. Blessed are the poor in spirit to those who believe the gospel: "*Paul, a servant of God,* and *an apostle of Jesus Christ, according to the faith of God's elect,* and *the acknowledging of the truth which is after godliness;*" Titus 1:1
2. Blessed are the poor in spirit to those who believe the gospel: "*In hope of eternal life, which God, that cannot lie, promised before the world began;*" Titus 1:2
3. Blessed are the poor in spirit to those who believe the gospel: "*But hath in due times manifested his word through preaching, which is committed unto me according to the commandment of God our Saviour;* Titus 1:3
4. Blessed are the poor in spirit to those who believe the gospel: "*So then after the Lord had spoken unto them, he was received up into heaven,* and *sat on the right hand of God.*" Mark 16:19
5. Blessed are the poor in spirit to those who believe *one of God's children, and one of our founding fathers, Jacob*: Surely *the Lord is in this place.* Genesis 28:12-13, 16-17
6. Blessed are the poor in spirit to those who believe the gospel: "*For we have not followed cunningly devised fables, when we made known unto you the power and coming of our Lord Jesus Christ, but were eyewitnesses of his majesty.*" II Peter 1:16
7. Blessed are the poor in spirit to those who believe the gospel: "*For he received from God the Father honour and glory, when there came such a voice to him from the excellent glory, This is my beloved Son,* in whom I am well pleased." II Peter 1:17
8. Blessed are the poor in spirit to those who believe the gospel: "*And this voice which came from heaven we heard, when we were with him in the holy mount.*" II Peter 1:18
9. Blessed are the poor in spirit to those who believe the gospel: "*Knowing this first, that no prophecy of the scripture is of any private interpretation.*" II Peter 1:20

10. Blessed are the poor in spirit to those who believe the gospel: "*For the prophecy came not in old time by the will of man*: *but holy men of God spake as they were moved by the Holy Ghost.*" II Peter 1:21
11. Blessed are the poor in spirit to those who *believe the gospel*: "*But as it is written, Eye hath not seen, nor ear heard, neither have entered into the heart of man, the things which God hath prepared for them that love him.*" I Corinthians 2:9
12. Blessed are the poor in spirit to those who *believe the Psalmist*: "*My flesh and my heart faileth*: *but God is the strength of my heart*, and *my portion for ever.*" Psalm 73:26

PART CCCLXXXIV

Blessed Are The Poor In Spirit. Matthew 5:3

Blessed Means Happy

Poor means meek in spirit Poor means humble in spirit Poor means lowly in spirit Poor means quiet in spirit Read Matthew 5:3-12, Read also Mark 1:15

Jesus did not say "*rich*" in spirit. Jesus said "*poor*" in spirit.

1. Blessed are the poor in spirit to those who *believe The Gospel*: "*And after these things I heard a great voice of much people in heaven, saying, Alleluia*; *Salvation*, and *Glory*, and *Honour*, and *Power*, *unto the Lord our God*:" Revelation 19:1
2. Blessed are the poor in spirit to those who *believe The Gospel*: "*And one of the elders answered, saying unto me, What are these which are arrayed in white robes?* And *whence came they*?" Revelation 7:13
3. Blessed are the poor in spirit to those who *believe The Gospel*: "*And I said unto him, Sir, thou knowest. And he said to me, These are they which came out of great tribulation, and have washed their robes, and made them white in the blood of the Lamb.*" Revelation 7:14
4. Blessed are the poor in spirit to those who *believe The Gospel*: "*Therefore are they before the throne of God, and serve him day and night in his temple: and he that sitteth on the throne shall dwell among them.*" Revelation 7:15
5. Blessed are the poor in spirit to those who *believe The Gospel*: "*They shall hunger no more, neither thirst any more*; neither shall the sun light on them, *nor any heat.*" Revelation 7:16
6. Blessed are the poor in spirit to those who *believe The Gospel*: "*For the Lamb which is in the midst of the throne shall feed them, and shall lead them unto living fountains of waters*: and *God shall wipe away all tears from their eyes.*" Revelation 7:17
7. Blessed are the poor in spirit to those who *believe the gospel*: "*He that overcometh shall inherit all things*; and *I will be his God*, and he shall be My son." Revelation 21:7
8. Blessed are the poor in spirit to those who *believe The Gospel*: "*And I say unto you, That many shall come from the east and west*, and shall sit down with Abraham, and Isaac, and Jacob, *in the kingdom of heaven.*" Matthew 8:11

9. Blessed are the poor in spirit to those who believe the *Bible to be "correct:" for the tree of life. Someone wrote and put the book of life is "incorrect."* Revelation 22:18-19
10. Blessed are the poor in spirit to those who *believe that the original Hebrew language and the original Greek followed because they were employed for the original manuscripts of the Bible and Hebrew and Greek language were "already" finished; "already"* done. Luke 23:38, John 19:20, Romans 1:16, 10:12, Colossians 3:11, Galatians 3:28
11. Blessed are the poor in spirit to those who believe that *every doctrine of scripture is where the Spirit of God give us full information about every particular doctrine.* II Timothy 3:16, Genesis 1:1, John 1:1-18 verse 1, I John 5:20, Hebrews 13:8
12. Blessed are the poor in spirit to those who believe that *I Corinthians 15* is the *doctrine of resurrection.* I Corinthians 15:1-58, Isaiah 53:3-12, Hosea 6:2, Luke 24:16, Psalm 110:1, Psalm 8:6, Isaiah 22:13, Genesis 2:7, I Timothy 2:13, Hosea 13:14, Genesis 48:14, Exodus 2:2, Acts 7:20, Exodus 12:21, Exodus 14:26

Part CCCLXXXV

Blessed Are The Poor In Spirit. Matthew 5:3

Blessed Means Happy

Poor means meek in spirit Poor means humble in spirit Poor means lowly in spirit Poor means quiet in spirit Read Matthew 5:3-12, Read also Mark 1:15

Jesus did not say "*rich*" in spirit. Jesus said "*poor*" in spirit.

1. Blessed are the poor in spirit to those who believe that *Hebrews 11* is the *action of faith*. It is called Hall of Fame Faith. **Hebrews 11:1-40**, **verse 6,** Genesis 4:4, Genesis 6:13-22, Genesis 12:14, Genesis 17:12, Genesis 15:5, Psalm 39:12**,** Genesis 5:24, Genesis 22:1-10, Genesis 21:12, Romans 8:24, Romans 9:7, Genesis 27:29, Joshua 6:4-8, Joshua 2:20
2. Blessed are the poor in spirit to those who believe that *I Corinthians 13* is the *doctrine of love*. I Corinthians 13:1-13
3. Blessed are the poor in spirit to those who believe that *I Thessalonians* is the *doctrine of the Rapture or the catching away of the saved to meet the Lord in the air*. I Thessalonians 5:2-11, I Thessalonians 4:13-18, Isaiah 35:4
4. Blessed are the poor in spirit to those who believe that *Matthew 24* is the *doctrine of The Glorious Second Coming of Christ*. Matthew 24:3-51, Luke 21:7-9, 27-28
5. Blessed are the poor in spirit to those who believe that the Bible Itself has The Best Interpretation and is inspired by God. II Timothy 3:16
6. Blessed are the poor in spirit to those who believe in the *doctrine of The Inspiration of the Scripture*: "*The things which God hath prepared for them that love Him*." I Corinthians 2:9
7. Blessed are the poor in spirit to those who believe in the *doctrine of The Inspiration of the Scripture*: "*By the Spirit of God who search all things, yea the deep things of God*. I Corinthians 2:10
8. Blessed are the poor in spirit to those who believe in the *doctrine of The Inspiration of the Scripture*: "*Not in the words which man's wisdom teach, but which The Holy Spirit teacheth*; *interpreting spiritual things to spiritual men*. I Corinthians 2:13
9. Blessed are the poor in spirit to those who believe that the *Bible, the Holy Word of God, the Gospel of Christ, may or allow or permit men and women or unbelievers should read to lead them to salvation*. John 20:30-31

10. Blessed are the poor in spirit to those who believe in *the literal of the Bible*; *and as a whole, the Word of God is True and is established by God Himself.* II Timothy 3:16
11. Blessed are the poor in spirit to those who *believe that God is a Spirit. God is manifested in a body. God is manifested in Jesus.* John 4:24, Hebrews 11:6, I Timothy 3:16, Hebrews 13:8, Genesis 1:1, John 1:1-18, verse 1, **14, John 14:1-12, verses 7, 8, 9**
12. Blessed are the poor in spirit to those who believe in *the doctrine that Jesus was born of a virgin is part of the Christian faith.* Isaiah 7:14, Matthew 1:18-25, Luke 1:26-35 verse 31, 35, Matthew 1:21, 25, Luke 2:11, 21, Matthew 2:1-2

Part CCCLXXXVI

Blessed Are The Poor In Spirit. Matthew 5:3

Blessed Means Happy

Poor means meek in spirit Poor means humble in spirit Poor means lowly in spirit Poor means quiet in spirit Read Matthew 5:3-12, Read also Mark 1:15

Jesus did not say "*rich*" in spirit. Jesus said "*poor*" in spirit.

1. Blessed are the poor in spirit to those who believe *this statement by Dr James H Brookes*: "*It is a foolish objection often urged against the statement of the Bible upon this subject* (the *Inspiration of the Scripture*), *that it permits the witness to testify for himself.*" Genesis 1:1, John 1:1, II Timothy 3:16, I John 5:20, Hebrews 13:8
2. Blessed are the poor in spirit to those who believe in the *Bible as a whole.* II Timothy 3:16, Revelation 22:19
3. Blessed are the poor in spirit to those who believe the *six attributes in Psalms 19:7 to 9*:
   i. The law of Jehovah
   ii. The testimony of Jehovah
   iii. The statues of Jehovah
   iv. The commandment of Jehovah
   v. The fear (that is, the reverence) of Jehovah
   vi. The judgments of Jehovah.
4. Blessed are the poor in spirit to those who believe in *the ten such titles for the Word of God* in Psalm 119:
   i. The way
   ii. The testimony
   iii. The precept
   iv. The commandment
   v. The saying
   vi. The law
   vii. The judgment
   viii. The righteousness
   ix. The statute

x. The word

xi. **Thou Say The Lord—(The Word/God/Jesus)**

5. Blessed are the poor in spirit to those who physical and normal can hear and see by natural, however they are "*spiritual deaf*" and *spiritual blind indeed as well*: "*Eye hath not seen, nor ear heard…God revealed the prophets unto us by His Spirit.* Romans 10:17-18
6. Blessed are the poor in spirit to those who believe that God has *revealed His holy apostles, His holy prophets, His servants even His holy servant, John, in the book of Revelation of Jesus Christ,* which *God gave unto him to show unto His servants, the things which must shortly come to pass.* Revelation 1:1
7. Blessed are the poor in spirit to those who believe the complete of the Bible as a whole. II Timothy 3:16, Revelation 22:19
8. Blessed are the poor in spirit to those who believe that *Matthew represented the Lord Jesus Christ as the Lion of the tribe of Judah, the King of Israel.* Revelation 5:5
9. Blessed are the poor in spirit to those who believe that *Mark represent the Lord Jesus Christ as the devoted servant as like an ox or a cattle always ready for service.* I Corinthians 9:9, I Timothy 5:18, Deuteronomy 25:4
10. Blessed are the poor in spirit to those who believe that *Luke represent the Lord Jesus Christ as the Son of Man, representing a lost race and bearing it's sin.* Philippians 2:6-7, Romans 8:3
11. Blessed are the poor in spirit to those who believe that *John represent the Lord Jesus Christ as the Son of God as like of a flying eagles, like a dove came from Heaven and return to Heaven, the eternal God incarnate.* Matthew 3:16, Mark 1:10, Luke 3:22, Mark 11:22, **John 14:1-`2, verses 7, 8, 9, Luke 1:35, I John 5:1-21, verse 5, 10, 11-13, verse 13**
12. Blessed are the poor in spirit to those who believe for the Gospel of Jesus Christ that wrote about Him; they are *Matthew, Mark, Luke* and *John.* John 20:30, 31

PART CCCLXXXVII

Blessed Are The Poor In Spirit. Matthew 5:3

Blessed Means Happy

Poor means meek in spirit. Poor means humble in spirit. Poor means lowly in spirit. Poor means quiet in spirit. Read Matthew 5:3-12, Read also Mark 1:15

Jesus did not say "*rich*" in spirit. Jesus said "*poor*" in spirit.

1. Blessed are the poor in spirit to those who *agree and believe that the Bible is said to be the best seller of all books.*
2. Blessed are the poor in spirit to those who believe that *Jesus is the Christ, the Son of God.* John 20:30, 31
3. Blessed are the poor in spirit to those who believe the gospel: "*And then shall appear the sign of the Son of man in heaven: and then shall all the tribes of the earth mourn, and they shall see the Son of man coming in the clouds of heaven with power and great glory.*" Matthew 24:30
4. Blessed are the poor in spirit to those who believe one of God's children, Jacob: Surely the Lord is in this place I knew not. Genesis 28:16
5. Blessed are the poor in spirit to those who believe that *God's people; whose bodies laid in the graves for centuries, God's saints, which slept arose and came out of the graves after His resurrection and went into the holy city and appeared unto many* Matthew 27:52-53
6. Blessed are the poor in spirit to those who believe *the witnessed of the testimony of Jesus when they saw Christ on the cross and saw the earthquake, saying, Truly this is the Son of God.* Matthew 7:54
7. Blessed are the poor in spirit to those who *believe that God is "here"* because God is *near us than we could ever believe God draws nigh to us. He is very close to us as a door.* Deuteronomy 4:7, Deuteronomy 30:14, Romans 8:10, Psalm 34:18, Psalm 85:9, Psalm 145:18, Joel 2:1, Matthew 24:32-44, Mark 13:28-37, Luke 21:27-36 (verse 28), Ephesians 2:13-22 (verse 13), Revelation 3:20
8. Blessed are the poor in spirit to those who *believe and are able to say with confession by faith in the heart: "I know I am saved because of the testimony of the Word of God. I have confessed with my mouth, Jesus as Lord, and I have believe with my heart that*

God hath raised Him from the dead, and *His Word says that whosever does those two things shall be saved.* Romans 10:9-10

9. Blessed are the poor in spirit to those who *believe that the Bible speaks to us to our hearts and we hear the voice of God the Father as the Bible speak to us by reading His Word.*
10. Blessed are the poor in spirit to those who believe that the *president of the United States of America is chosen, or is voted* or is *selected by this nation under God, the government of the people, by the people and for the people with liberty and justice for all, that they pick her or him to run the office of the White House in Washington, DC and to lead the nation in harmony and may God help the president of the United States of America.* Psalm 33:12-13, Psalm 57:9-11, Psalm 108:3, Psalm 67:4-5, Psalm 86:9-10, Psalm 117:1, Psalm 82:8, Psalm 22:28
11. Blessed are the poor in spirit to those who *believe, know, realize, understand* and *being aware of that "original sin" deserved God's wrath and damnation and because of that "original sin," Jesus Christ came from Heaven to die for our sin to escape the wrath of God.* Romans 2:5-6, Romans 5:9, Ephesians 2:1-10, I Thessalonians 1:10, I Thessalonians 5:9, Hebrews 2:3-18, Romans 1:18, Hosea 5:1-5, Hosea 6:1-11, John 3:36, Romans 5:6, Romans 2:8, Romans 2:1-29, Revelation 19:15 Colossians 3:6, Romans 12:19, Romans 3:5, Revelation 20:15, Revelation 6:17, II Peter 3:9, II Peter 2:9, Hebrews 9:27
12. Blessed are the poor in spirit to those who *believe one of God's children, Martin Luther insisted "that the Just shall live by faith. Romans 1:7 regarded as the true meaning of the gospel."* (*Martin Luther*, 1483-1546)

Part CCCLXXXVIII

Blessed Are The Poor In Spirit. Matthew 5:3

Blessed Means Happy

Poor means meek in spirit. Poor means humble in spirit. Poor means lowly in spirit. Poor means quiet in spirit. Read Matthew 5:3-12, Read also Mark 1:15

Jesus did not say "*rich*" in spirit. Jesus said "*poor*" in spirit.

1. Blessed are the poor in spirit to those who *believe one of God's children, John Wesley insisted: "That our justification is by grace through faith." Ephesians 2:8-10 (John Wesley*, 1703-1791)
2. Blessed are the poor in spirit to those who *believe that the Gospel is what saves our souls, is what deliver our souls, is what heal our soul.* We sing: "It is well. It is well with my soul. Isaiah 53:5, Romans 10:17, Romans 10:9, 10
3. Blessed are the poor in spirit to those who *believe that "to know Christ" is "not enough," "to know the gospel" is "not enough" the gospel must believed and should be obeyed.* II Peter 2:20-22. Jesus *says*: "*The gospel must be preached and should obey God's Word.*" Matthew 4:17, Luke 24:47, Mark 16:15, I Peter 1:23, Romans 1:16, I Peter 2:2, Romans 10:9, Acts 2:38, James 1:22, Hebrews 4:22, II Timothy 3:17, II Timothy 3:16-17, II Timothy 3:16, II Timothy 2:15, Acts 4:12, John 14:15, John 5:24, John 4:24, Matthew 28:20, Psalm 119:1-176, Psalm 19:7, Deuteronomy 4:2, Revelation 22:18, I John 3:23, II Peter 3:9, Hebrews 11:6, Hebrews 10:25, Hebrews 4:2, Titus 1:2, II Timothy 4:2, II Timothy 3:15, II Thessalonians 1:8, Colossians 3:17, Ephesians 6:17, Galatians 6:7, Galatians 3:26-27, Galatians 1:6-11, Romans 12:2, Romans 10:17, Romans 10:10, Romans 8:1, Romans 6:23, Romans 6:4, Romans 4:5, Romans 3:10, Acts 20:32, Acts 17:30, Acts 10:34, I John 5:5, I John 5:3, I John 3:22, I John 2:14, I John 2:3, I John 2:2, I John 1:9, I John 1:8, II Peter 3:18, II Peter 1:21, I Peter 2:1-25, I Peter 3:21, I Peter 2:1, I Peter 1:22, I Peter 1:21, James 5:14, James 1:21, James 1:17-18, Hebrews 13:8, Hebrews 6:18-20, Hebrews 2:3, Titus 2:11, II Timothy 1:10, I Timothy 3:16, I Timothy 2:1-15, I Thessalonians 1:5, Colossians 1:15, Philippians 4:6, Ephesians 5:26, Ephesians 5:18, Ephesians 2:8-10, Galatians 3:8, II Corinthians 5:21, II Corinthians 4:4, II Corinthians 15:1-4, I Corinthi-

ans 5:7, I Corinthians 1:21, Romans 1:1-32, Romans 12:1-2, Romans 6:1-23, Romans 5:15, Romans 5:1, Romans 4:16, Romans 4:3, Romans 3:23, Romans 3:10, Romans 1:17-18, Acts 18:8, Acts 15:7, Acts 11:23, Acts 10:48, Acts 10:43, Acts 10:1-48, Acts 8:38, Acts 2:42, Acts 2:1-47, John 17:3, John 5:10, John 14:23-24, John 13:34, John 10:9, John 8:31, John 8:24, John 6:44-45, John 3:3, John 3:5, Mark 13:1 0 Mark 12:24, Mark 10:45, Mark 6:11, Acts 8:35-39, Acts 8:12, Acts 5:29, Acts 2:41, John 17:17, John 15:3, John 14:26, John 14:6, John 10:35-36, John 3:16, John 3:1-36, John 1:29, John 1:14, John 1:12, John 1:10, Luke 24:45, Luke 11:28, Matthew 28:19, Matthew 28:18-20, Matthew 4:4, Isaiah 55:11, Psalm 119:11, Psalm 1:1-3, Joshua 1:8, Revelation 22:17, Revelation 22:1-21, Revelation 12:1-17, III John 1:2, I John 5:20, I John 5:12

4. Blessed are the poor in spirit to those who *believe that receiving Christ is what the New Testament means by believing on Christ. John 1:11-13*
5. Blessed are the poor in spirit to those who *believe that* "*the New Testament*" means "*the Will of Jesus Christ;*" "*the Will of the Bible;*" "the *Will of God's Word; Grace for Grace.* John 1:1-17
6. Blessed are the poor in spirit to those who *believe that the Church is the Body of Christ* and also His bride. Ephesians 2:10
7. Blessed are the poor in spirit to those who believe that the *church is the member of the Body of Christ, the Risen Lord's ministry gift. Ephesians 4:12*
8. Blessed are the poor in spirit to those who believe that the *Passover Lamb in Exodus 12:1-28,* is a type of the *Lamb of God* which *take away the sin of the world.* John 1:29
9. Blessed are the poor in spirit to those who believe that the *church* is the *Bride of Christ.* Ephesians 5:25-33
10. Blessed are the poor in spirit to those who believe the gospel: "*But rise, and stand upon thy feet: for I have appeared unto thee for this purpose, to make thee a minister and a witness both of these things which thou hast seen, and of those things in the which I will appear unto thee;*" Acts 26:16
11. Blessed are the poor in spirit to those who believe the gospel: "*Delivering thee from the people, and from the Gentiles, unto whom now I send thee,*" Acts 26:17
12. Blessed are the poor in spirit to those who believe the gospel: "*To open their eyes, and to turn them from darkness to light, and from the power of Satan unto God, that they may receive forgiveness of sins, and inheritance among them which are sanctified by faith that is in me.*" Acts 26:18

Part CCCLXXXIX

Blessed Are The Poor In Spirit. Matthew 5:3

Blessed Means Happy

Poor means meek in spirit. Poor means humble in spirit. Poor means lowly in spirit. Poor means quiet in spirit. Read Matthew 5:3-12, Read also Mark 1:15

Jesus did not say "*rich*" in spirit. Jesus said "*poor*" in spirit.

1. Blessed are the poor in spirit to those who believe that the *New Testament Church* is the *People of God*; the *family of God*; *redeemed by the blood of Christ*, the *people of God*, the *family of God who are not forsaking the assembling of themselves together, where the Word of God is preached and to support the ministry of the Word through tithing, through giving ministry as God had prospered and every man according as he purpose in his heart to giving ministry for God love a cheerful giver*. Hebrews 10:25, Acts 2:42, I Corinthians 16:2, II Corinthians 8:8-11, II Corinthians 9:6-7, 15
2. Blessed are the poor in spirit to those who are *overcomers which are the believer in Christ Jesus who are truly born again*; *by the blood of the Lamb and by the Word of their testimony*. I John 5:4-5, Revelation 12:11, Revelation 2:7, 11, 17, 25-26, Revelation 3:5, 8, 10, 11-12, 21
3. Blessed are the poor in spirit to those who believe that *the church of the living God is one*, and *it's unity will be manifested in the age to come*. Ephesians 5:27
4. Blessed are the poor in spirit to those who believe the Psalmist: "*Holy*" and "*Reverend*" is "*His name*." Psalm 111:9
5. Blessed are the poor in spirit to those who *believe, know, realize, understand and are being aware that to be brother in Christ or sister in Christ, he or she* "*must be born again*." John 3:7
6. Blessed are the poor in spirit to those who believe *that salvation is always by grace through faith plus nothing. Ephesians 2:8-10*
7. Blessed are the poor in spirit to those who believe that *our salvation is* "*by grace through faith*," and that not of ourselves: *it is* "*the gift of God*" not of works, lest any man should boast. Ephesians 2:8-10
8. Blessed are the poor in spirit to those who believe that we are *saved by faith and by grace through faith because of the shed* (covered) *blood of Jesus Christ*. Ephesians 2:8-20 and Acts 16:31, John 3:16

9. Blessed are the poor in spirit to those who believe that *there is a victory because of the resurrection of Jesus Christ.* John 21:1-25, Matthew 28:5-10, Mark 16:5-20, Luke 24:3-12, 33-34, John 20:9-31
10. Blessed are the poor in spirit to those who believe that the *Gospel is of God.* Romans 1:1
11. Blessed are the poor in spirit to those who believe that the *New Testament Bible had not been written during the historical Event but only the Holy Spirit was present and today the Holy Spirit is still here with us and the Bible is so to speak special of His Return.* John 21:24-25
12. Blessed are the poor in spirit to those who believe that *Jesus claim to be Christ, the Son of God because He said, "I am"* and shall *see the Son of Man sitting on the right hand of power and coming on the cloud of heaven.* Mark 14:61-62, Daniel 7:13

Part CCCXC

Blessed Are The Poor In Spirit. Matthew 5:3

Blessed Means Happy

Poor means meek in spirit. Poor means humble in spirit. Poor means lowly in spirit. Poor means quiet in spirit. Read Matthew 5:3-12, Read also Mark 1:15

Jesus did not say "*rich*" in spirit. Jesus said "*poor*" in spirit.

1. Blessed are the poor in spirit to those who believe and are *able to say* with faith *in Christ Jesus* by heart, "*I am justified*." Romans 8:16, Acts 13:38, 39
2. Blessed are the poor in spirit to those who *believe that we are able to say*, "*God say so, that we are His children*. Romans 8:16
3. Blessed are the poor in spirit to those who *believe that the "church" in the New Testament is first of all that we are of the whole body of believers in Jesus Christ.* Matthew 16:18, Acts 20:28, Acts 2:47, Ephesians 5:24, 25, Colossians 1:18, 24
4. Blessed are the poor in spirit to those who *believe, know, understand and realize* that we have the *full assurance of faith*, the *full assurance of understanding* and the *full assurance of hope through Christ Jesus in our heart.* Hebrews 10:22
5. Blessed are the poor in spirit to those who believe that *Justification is without work*. Romans 3:26, Romans 4:2, Genesis 15:6, Genesis 22:12
6. Blessed are the poor in spirit to those who believe that *Abraham was "a Friend of God*." Isaiah 41:8, II Chronicles 20:7, Genesis 22:12, Genesis 15:6
7. Blessed are the poor in spirit to those who *believe that the Bible teaches that no one can be saved without personal acceptance of Jesus Christ.* John 14:6
8. Blessed are the poor in spirit to those who *believe that all men shall be raised from the dead*. The *righteous unto the resurrection of life and those that have done evil unto the resurrection of judgment*. John 8:28-29
9. Blessed are the poor in spirit to those who believe that *only just one thing is need to do to get to heaven*: "*Accept Jesus Christ as personal Savior*." John 14:6
10. Blessed are the poor in spirit to those who *believe the Word of God that speak in Bold Red Mark by God in I Kings* 2:4, 3:5, 11-14 (God spoke to Solomon, verse 5, 11-14), 5:5, 6:12-13, 8-16, 18-19, 25 (God appeared to Solomon 9:2-9), 9:3-9 (God spoke to the children of Israel), 11:2, 11:11-13, 31-39, 12:23-24,

13:2-3, 9, 17, 21-22; 14:5; 16:1-4 (God spoke to Jehu); 17:3-4, 9, 14 (God spoke to Elijah verse 1); 18:1, 31, 19:9, 11, 13, 15-18; 20:13-14, 28, 42; 21:18-19, 21-24, 29; 22:17, 20, 22

11. Blessed are the poor in spirit to those who *believe the Word of God in Bold Red Mark by God***:** *II Kings* 1:4, 6, 16; 2:21; 3:16-19; 4:43; 7:1, 9:3, 6-10, 12, 26, 36-37; 10:30, 14:6; 15:12; 17:12-13, 35-39; 18:25, 19:6-7, 20-34; 20:1, 5-6, 17-18; 21:4, 7-8, 11-15, 22:15-20, 23:27
12. Blessed are the poor in spirit to those who believe the *Word of God that speak in Bold Red Mark by God Himself: I Chronicles* 11:2, 14:10, 14-15, 16:18-19, 22; 17:4-14, 21:10-12, 15, 22:8-10; 28:3, 6-7

Part CCCXCI

Blessed Are The Poor In Spirit. Matthew 5:3

Blessed Means Happy

Poor means meek in spirit. Poor means humble in spirit. Poor means lowly in spirit. Poor means quiet in spirit. Read Matthew 5:3-12, Read also Mark 1:15

Jesus did not say "*rich*" in spirit. Jesus said "*poor*" in spirit.

1. Blessed are the poor in spirit to those who *believe the Word of God that speak in Bold Red Mark by God in II Chronicles* 1:11-12; 6:5-6, 8-9, 16, 7:12-22; 11:3-4, 12:5, 7-8, 18:16, 19-21; 20:15-17, 21:12-15, 24:20, 25:4, 33:4, 7-8, 34:23-28
2. Blessed are the poor in spirit to those who believe the *Word of God that speak in Bold Red Mark by God in Nehemiah* 1:8-9
3. Blessed are the poor in spirit to those who *believe the Word of God that speak in Bold Red Mark by God in "Job"*1:7-8, 12; 2:2-3, 6; 33:24, 37:6; 38:2-41, 39:1-30, 40:2 (*The Lord spoke to Satan) Job 1:7, 8, 12, 2:2-36* (God spoke to Job 38:1); 41:1-34; 42:7-8
4. Blessed are the poor in spirit to those who believe the *Word of God that speak in Bold Red Mark by God in "Psalm"* 2:6-9; 32:8-9; 46:10; 50:5-23; 68:22-23; 75:2-5, 10; 87:4, 7; 89:3-4; 19-37, 90:3, 91:14-16; 95:8-11; 101:4-8, 105:11, 15, 108:7-9, 110:1-4
5. Blessed are the poor in spirit to those who *believe the Word of God that speak in Bold Red Mark by God in "Isaiah"* 1:2-3, 11-31; 3:4-5, 10-12, 14-26; 5:1-7, 9-10, 6:8-13, 7:3-9, 11, 14 (The Lord Spoke to Isaiah 7:3), 8:1, 3-4, 6-8, 12-16, 10:1-14, 24-34, 11:9, 13:1-22, 14:1-27, 29-32, 15:1-9, 16:1-12, 14; 17:1-6, 18:4, 19:2-4, 25, 20:2-6, 21:2, 6, 11-17, 22:14-25, 23:12, 24:1-3, 27:2-5, 28:12, 16-21, 29:1-8, 13-24, 30:1-13, 15, 31:4-9, 33:10-13, 34:1-17, 37:6-7, 21-35, 38:1, 4-8, 39:6-7, 40:1-2, 25, 41:1-29; 42:1-20, 43:1-28, 44:1-22, 24-28, 45:1-25, 46:1-13, 47:1-3, 5-15, 48:1-19, 22; 49:1-26; 50:1-3, 11, 51:1-8, 12-23, 52:1-6, 13-15, 53:11-12, 54:1-17, 55:1-5, 8-13; 56:1-12, 57:1-21, 58:1-14, 59:20-21, 60:1-22; 61:8-9, 62:1-12, 63:1-6, 8, 15:1-25, 66:1-24
6. Blessed are the poor in spirit to those who *believe the Word of God that speak in Bold Red Mark by God in "Jeremiah"* 1:5, 7-19, 2:1-3, 5-37 (God spoke to

Jeremiah 1:1, 2:1), 3:1-20, 22, 4:1-7, 9, 11-12, 14-25, 5:1-2, 7-11, 14-31, 6:1-30, 7:2-34, 8:1-17, 19, 9:3-11, 13-26, 10:2-5, 18, 11:2-17, 22-23, 12:5-17, 13:1, 4, 6, 9-14, 24-27, 14:2-6, 10-12, 14-18, 15:1-9, 11-14, 19-21, 16:2-18, 20-21, 17:1-11, 19-27, 18:2, 6-17, 19:1-13, 15, 20:4-6, 21:4-14, 22:1-30, 23:1-8, 11-40, 24:3, 5-10, 25:5-16, 27-38, 26:2-6, 18, 27:2-11, 15-20, 22, 28:13-14, 16, 29:4-32, 30:2-3, 5-24, 3`:1-34, 36-40, 32:3-7, 14-15, 25, 27-44, 33:2-18, 20-22, 24-26, 34:2-5, 13-22, 35:2, 13-19, 36:2-3, 36:2-3, 28-31, 37:7-10, 17, 38:2-3, 17-18, 22-23, 39:16-18, 42:10-12, 15-18, 19, 43:9-13, 44:2-14, 25-30, 45:3-5; 46:3-12, 14-28, 47:2-7, 48:1-47, 49:1-39, 50:2-44, 51:1-9, 14-58, 64

7. Blessed are the poor in spirit to those who *believe the Word of God that speak in Bold Red Mark by God in* "*Ezekiel*" (God spoke to Ezekiel 2:1), 2:1, 3-8, (God spoke to Ezekiel 3:1) 3:1, 3-12, 17-22, 24-27, 4:1-13, 15-17, 5:1-17, 6:2-14, 7:2-27, 8:5-6, 8-9, 12-13, 15, 17-18, 9:1, 4-7, 9-10, 10:2, 11:2-12, 15-21, 12:2-6, 9-16, 18-28, 13:2-23, 14:3-23, 15:2-8, 16:2-63, 17:24; 18:2-32, 19:1-14, 20:3-48, 21:2-17, 19-32, 22:2-22, 24-31, 23:2-49, 24:2-17, 21-27, 25:2-17, 26:2-21, 27:2-36, 28:2-19, 21-26, 29:2-16, 18-21, 30:2-19, 21-26, 31:2-18, 32:2-16, 18-32, 33:2-20, 24-33, 34:2-31, 35:2-15, 36:1-15, 17-38, 37:3-6, 9, 11-14, 16-28, 38:2-23, 39:1-29, 43:7-21, 44:2-31, 45:1-25, 46:1-18, 20, 24, 47:6, 8-23, 48:1-35 /**Daniel 4:31-32* God spoke to Daniel* 4:31-32
8. Blessed are the poor in spirit to those who *believe the Word of God that speak in Bold Red Mark by God in* "*Hosea*" 1:2, 4-11, 2:1-23, 3:1, 4:1-19, 5:1-15, 6:4-11, 7:1-16, 8:1-14, 9:10-17, 10:1-15, 11:1-12, 12:1-14, 13:1-16, 14:1-8
9. Blessed are the poor in spirit to those who *believe the Word of God that speak in Bold Red Mark by God Himself: in* "*Joel*" (God spoke to Joel 1:1), Joel 1:2-12, 2:12-13, 19-21, 25-32, 3:1-15, 17-21
10. Blessed are the poor in spirit to those who *believe the Word of God that speak in Bold Red Mark by God* "*Himself*" *in* "*Amos*" 1:3-15, 2:1-16, 3:1-2, 9-15, 4:1-13, 5:1-27, 6:1-14, 7:3, 6, 8-9, 15, 17, 8:2-3, 7-14, 9:1-15
11. Blessed are the poor in spirit to those who *believe the Word of God that speak in Bold Red Mark by God in* "*Obadiah*" 1:2-18
12. Blessed are the poor in spirit to those who *believe the Word of God that speak in Bold Red Mark by God in* "*Jonah*" 1:2, 3:2, 4:4, 9-11

Part CCCXCII

Blessed Are The Poor In Spirit. Matthew 5:3

Blessed Means Happy

Poor means meek in spirit. Poor means humble in spirit. Poor means lowly in spirit. Poor means quiet in spirit. Read Matthew 5:3-12, Read also Mark 1:15

Jesus did not say "*rich*" in spirit. Jesus said "*poor*" in spirit.

1. Blessed are the poor in spirit to those who *believe the Word of God that speak in Bold Red Mark by God in "Micah"* 1:6, 15, 2:3-13, 3:1-3, 6-7, 4:6-13, 5:1-2, 10-15, 6:1-5, 10-16
2. Blessed are the poor in spirit to those who *believe the Word of God that speak in Bold Red Mark by God in "Nahum"* 1:12-14, 2:13, 3:5-17
3. Blessed are the poor in spirit to those who *believe the Word of God that speak in Bold Red Mark by God to "Habakkuk"* 1:5-11, 2:2-20, 3:5-15
4. Blessed are the poor in spirit to those who *believe the Word of God that speak in Bold Red Mark by God in Zephaniah* (God spoke to Zephaniah 1:1), 1:2-18, 2:1-15, 3:1-20
5. Blessed are the poor in spirit to those who *believe the Word of God that speak in Bold Red Mark by God in "Haggai"* 1:2-11, 13, 2:2-12, 14-19, 21-23
6. Blessed are the poor in spirit to those who *believe the Word of God that speak in Bold Red Mark by God "Himself" in "Zechariah"* (*God spoke to Zechariah*); 1:2-6, 8, 14-17, 21, 2:4-13, 3:2-4, 7-10, 4:6-7, 9-10, 5:4, 6:10-15, 7:5-14, 8:2-23, 9:1-17, 10:1-12, 11:1-17, 12:2-14, 13:1-9, 14:1-21
7. Blessed are the poor in spirit to those who *believe the Word of God that speak in Bold Red Mark by God in "Malachi"* 1:2-14, 2:1-17, 3:1-18, 4:1-6 ("The End of The Old Testament")
8. Blessed are the poor in spirit to those who *believe the gospel of the prophecy of Revelation*: "And *the smoke of their torment ascendeth up for ever and ever*: and *they have* "*no rest day nor night*" *who worship the beast* (*anti-Christ*) and *his image and whosoever receiveth the mark of his name.*" Revelation 14:11
9. Blessed are the poor in spirit to those who *believe the gospel of the prophecy of Revelation*: "Here is *the patience of the saints*: here are *they that keep* (*obey*) *the commandment's of God*, and *the faith of Jesus.*" Revelation 14:12

10. Blessed are the poor in spirit to those who *believe the spiritual songs*: "And *they sing the song of Moses the servant of God*, and the *song of the Lamb*, saying *Great and marvellous* are Thy *works, Lord God Almighty*; *just and true are Thy ways, Thou King of saints*. Revelation 15:3, See Exodus 15:1
11. Blessed are the poor in spirit to those who *believe that Christ will lay hold on the dragon, that old serpent*, which is the *Devil*, and *Satan*, and *bound him a thousand years*; and *cast him into the bottomless pit*, and *shut* (lock) *him up and get a seal upon him*, that *he should deceive the nations no more, till the thousand years should be fulfilled*: and *after that he must be loosed* (released) *a little season* (while). Revelation 20:2-3
12. Blessed are the poor in spirit to those who believe the gospel of Christ's prophecy: And the beast was taken, and with him the false prophet that brought miracles before him, with which he deceived them that had received the mark of the beast, and them that worshipped his image. These both were cast *alive* into a lake of fire burning with brimstone. Revelation 19:20, Revelation 12:7-10. See Revelation 18:8-9, Revelation 20:10, Revelation 21:8

Part CCCXCIII

Blessed Are The Poor In Spirit. Matthew 5:3

Blessed Means Happy

Poor means meek in spirit. Poor means humble in spirit. Poor means lowly in spirit. Poor means quiet in spirit. Read Matthew 5:3-12, Read also Mark 1:15

Jesus did not say "*rich*" in spirit. Jesus said "*poor*" in spirit.

1. Blessed are the poor in spirit to those who are having the everlasting gospel to preach unto them that dwell on the earth, that dwell to every nation, and every kindred, and every tongue, and people; saying, with a loud voice, Fear (Reverence) and give along to Him; for the hour of His judgment is come: and worship Him that made heaven and earth, and the sea and the fountains of waters. Psalm 146:6, Revelation 14:6-7
2. Blessed are the poor in spirit to those who *believe the gospel of the prophecy of Revelation*: "*Behold, I come as a thief. Blessed is he that watcheth*, and *keepeth his garments, lest he walk naked*, and *they see his shame*." Revelation 16:15
3. Blessed are the poor in spirit to those who *believe that Jesus Christ is called "the Word of God*." Revelation 19:13
4. Blessed are the poor in spirit to those who *believe the gospel*: "And *he said unto me, These sayings are faithful and true*: and the *Lord God of the holy prophets sent His angel to show unto His servants the things which must shortly be done*." Revelation 22:6
5. Blessed are the poor in spirit to those who *believe the gospel*: "*Behold, I come quickly*: *blessed is he that keepeth the sayings of the prophecy of this book*." Revelation 22:7
6. Blessed are the poor in spirit to those who *believe the gospel*: "Then *saith he unto me, See thou do it not*: for *I am thy fellowservant*, and of thy *brethren the prophets*, and *of them which keep the sayings of this book*: "*worship God*." Revelation 2:9
7. Blessed are the poor in spirit to those who *believe the prophecy of the book of Revelation*; for *Jesus Christ is at hand. He is near soon to come. Be Ready. Get Ready. Prepare your heart to come like a mighty soldier you stand up for Christ's sake, God Almighty*. Amos 4:12
8. Blessed are the poor in spirit to those who believe this spiritual hymn: "Glorify Thy name in all the earth. Glorify Thy name in all the earth. Glorify thy name in all the earth." John 12:28

9. Blessed are the poor in spirit to those who believe this spiritual hymn: "Surely good-ness and mer-cy shall fol-low me All the days, all the days of my life; Surely good-ness and mer-cy shall fol-low me. All the days, all the days of my life. And I will dwell in the house of the Lord for ev-er." Psalm 23:6
10. Blessed are the poor in spirit to those who believe this spiritual hymn: "I love You, Lord, and I lift my voice to worship You, O my soul, re-joice! Take joy, my King, in what You hear: may it be a sweet, sweet sound in your ear." Psalm 31:23
11. Blessed are the poor in spirit to those who believe the spiritual hymn: "O come, let us a-dore Him, O come, let us a-dore Him, O come let us Him, Christ the Lord." Matthew 2:2
12. Blessed are the poor in spirit to those who believe this spiritual hymn: Glo-rious is Thy name, O Lord! Glo-rious is Thy name, O lord! Glo-rious is Thy name, O Lord! name, O Lord! A-men I Chronicles 29:13

Part CCCXCIV

Blessed Are The Poor In Spirit. Matthew 5:3

Blessed Means Happy

Poor means meek in spirit. Poor means humble in spirit. Poor means lowly in spirit. Poor means quiet in spirit. Read Matthew 5:3-12, Read also Mark 1:15

Jesus did not say "*rich*" in spirit. Jesus said "*poor*" in spirit.

1. Blessed are the poor in spirit to those who believe this spiritual hymn: "Praise the name of Jesus, Praise the name of Je-sus. He's my Rock, He's my For-tress, He's my Deliver, in Him will I trust, Praise the name of Je-sus." Psalm 18:2
2. Blessed are the poor in spirit to those who believe the spiritual hymn: "Jesus is the sweet-est name I know, And He's just the same as His lovely name, And that's the rea-son why I love Him so; Oh, Je-sus is the sweet-est name I know." Hebrews 13:8
3. Blessed are the poor in spirit to those who believe this spiritual hymn: "All hail the power of Je-sus' name! Let an-gels pros-trate fall; Bring forth the roy-al di-a-dem, And crown Him Lord of all; Crown Him, crown Him, al-le-lu-ia! Crown Him, crown Him, crown Him, And crown Him Lord of all." A-men. Philippians 2:9-11
4. Blessed are the poor in spirit to those who believe this spiritual hymn: "Jesus, we just want to thank you, Je-sus
   Jesus, we just want to praise you, Je-sus
   Jesus, we just want to tell you, Je-sus
   Jesus, we just want to serve you, Sav-ior
   For being so good.
   Jesus, we know you are coming, Jesus;
   Jesus, we know you are coming,
   Take us to live in your home." II Corinthians 9:15
5. Blessed are the poor in spirit to those who believe this spiritual hymn: "His Name is Wonderful. His name is Won-der-ful, His name is Wonderful, Jesus, my Lord; He is the mighty King, Master of every-thing, His name is Wonderful, Jesus, my Lord. He's the great shepherd, the Rock of all ages, Al-mighty God is

He. Bow down before Him, Love and adore, Him, His name is Won-der-ful, Jesus, my Lord." I Corinthians 12:3

6. Blessed are the poor in spirit to those who believe this spiritual hymn: "Blessed be the name, blessed be the name, Blessed be the name of the Lord, Blessed be the name, Blessed the name, Blessed the name of the Lord. Hebrews 1:4
7. Blessed are the poor in spirit to those who believe this spiritual hymn: "He is Lord! He is Lord. He is ris-en from the dead and He is Lord! Ev-'ry knee shall bow, ev-'ry tongue shall confess that Je-sus Christ is Lord." Romans 10:9
8. Blessed are the poor in spirit to those who believe this spiritual hymn: "Je-sus, name above all names, beautiful Savior, glo-rious Lord. Em-man-u-el, God is with us, bless-ed Re-deem-er, Liv-ing Word." II Thessalonians 1:12, Matthew 1:23, Isaiah 7:14
9. Blessed are the poor in spirit to those who believe this spiritual hymn:
    1. "I just came to praise the Lord, I just came to praise the Lord. I just came to praise His Ho-ly name, I just came to praise the Lord.
    2. I just came to thank the Lord, I just came to thank the Lord. I just came to praise His Ho-ly name, I just came to thank the Lord.
    3. I just came to love the Lord, I just came to love the Lord. I just came to praise His Ho-ly name, I just came to love the Lord." Psalms 146:2
10. Blessed are the poor in spirit to those who believe this spiritual hymn: "His Name is *life*; His name is *Mas-ter, Sav-ior, Li-on of Ju-dah,* Bless-ed *Prince of Peace, Shep-herd, For-tress, Rock of Sal-va-tion, Lamb of God* is He. *Son of Dav-id, King of the Ag-es, E-ter-nal Life, Ho-ly Lord of Glo-ry, His name is Life.* John 14:6, Matthew 1:1
11. Blessed are the poor in spirit to those who believe this spiritual hymn: "The Word made has dwelt a-mong us, full of grace and full of truth. We beheld His wondrous, glory of the only Son of God.
    The Word made flesh has dwelt among us, from His full-ness. We re-ceived grace on grace and last-ing mercy, truth and wis-dom, hope and peace. We have be-held His glo-ry, and we have seen the light. A-noint-ed Prince of glo-ry, we mar-vel at Thy sight." John 1:16
12. Blessed are the poor in spirit to those who believe this spiritual hymn: "Joy to the world! the Lord is come; Let earth re-ceive her King; Let ev-'ry heart pre-pare Him room. And heav'n and na-ture sing, And heav'n and na-ture sing. Micah 5:2

Part CCCXCV

Blessed Are The Poor In Spirit. Matthew 5:3

Blessed Means Happy

Poor means meek in spirit. Poor means humble in spirit. Poor means lowly in spirit. Poor means quiet in spirit. Read Matthew 5:3-12, Read also Mark 1:15

Jesus did not say "*rich*" in spirit. Jesus said "*poor*" in spirit.

1. Blessed are the poor in spirit to those who believe this spiritual hymn: "Hark! The her-ald an-gels sing, "Glo-ry to the new-born King; Peace on earth, and mer-cy mild, God and sin-ners rec-on-ciled!" Joy-ful, all ye na-tions, rise, Join the tri- umph of the skies; With the an-gel-ic host pro-claim "Christ is born in Beth-le- hem!" Hark! the her-ald an-gels sing, "Glory to the New-born King." Luke 2:14
2. Blessed are the poor in spirit to those who believe this spiritual hymn: "Em-man-u-el, Em-man-u-el, His name is called Em-man-u-el; God with us, re-vealed in us; His name is called Em-man-u-el." Matthew 1:23
3. Blessed are the poor in spirit to those who believe this spiritual hymn: "No-el, No-el, No-el, No-el, Born is the King of Is-ra-el." Luke 2:8
4. Blessed are the poor in spirit to those who believe this spiritual hymn: "Go tell it on the moun-tain, O-ver the hills and ev-'ry-where; Go tell it on the moun-tain That Je-sus Christ is born." Isaiah 42:11-12
5. Blessed are the poor in spirit to those who believe this spiritual hymn: "I won-der as I wan-der, out un-der the sky, How Je-sus the Sav-ior did come for to die For poor, orn-'ry peo-ple like you and like I; I won-der as I wan-der, out under the sky. Out un-der the sky." Luke 2:18
6. Blessed are the poor in spirit to those who believe this spiritual hymn: "O come, all ye faith-ful, joy-ful and tri-um-phant, O come ye, O come ye to Beth-le-hem! Come and be-hold Him, born the King of an-gels! O come, let us a-dore Him, O come, let us a-dore Him, O come, let us a-dore, Christ the Lord!" Luke 2:15
7. Blessed are the poor in spirit to those who believe the spiritual hymn: "For un-to us a Child is born, un-to us a Son is giv-en, un-to us a Son is giv-en: and His name shall be call-ed Won-der-ful, Coun-se-lor, The Might-y God, The Ev-er-

last-ing Fa-ther, The Prince of Peace, The Ev-er-last-ing Fa-ther, The Prince of Peace." Isaiah 9:6

8. Blessed are the poor in spirit to those who believe this spiritual hymn: "Si-lent night, ho-ly night, All is calm, all is bright Round yon vir-gin moth-er and Child. Ho-ly In-fant so ten-der and mild, Sleep in heav-en-ly peace, Sleep in heav-en-ly peace." Luke 2:16
9. Blessed are the poor in spirit to those who believe this spiritual hymn: "A-way in a man-ger, no crib for a bed, The lit-tle Lord Je-sus laid down His sweet head; The stars in the sky looked down where He lay, The lit-tle Lord Jesus, a-sleep on the hay. Luke 2:7
10. Blessed are the poor in spirit to those who believe this spiritual hymn: "Tell me the sto-ry of Je-sus, Write on my heart ev-ery word; Tell me the sto-ry most pre- cious, Sweet-est that ev-er was heard. Tell how the an-gels in cho-rus Sang as they wel-comed His birth. Glo-ry to God in the high-est! Peace and good ti-dings to earth." Acts 8:35
11. Blessed are the poor in spirit to those who believe this spiritual hymn: "Wor-thy is the Lamb that was slain, Wor-thy is the Lamb that was slain, Wor-thy is the Lamb that was slain, to re-ceive: Pow-er and rich-es and wis-dom and strength, Hon-or and glo-ry and bless-ing! Wor-thy is the Lamb, Wor-thy is the Lamb, Wor-thy is the Lamb that was slain, Wor-thy is the Lamb! Revelation 5:12
12. Blessed are the poor in spirit to those who believe this spiritual hymn:
"Were You there when they cru-ci-fied my Lord?
Were You there when they nailed Him to the tree?
Were You there when they laid Him in the tomb?
Were You there when He rose up from the dead?
O! Sometimes it caus-es me to trem-ble, trem-ble!
O! Sometimes I feel like shout-ing glo-ry, glo-ry, glo-ry!" Mark 15:25

Part CCCXCVI

Blessed Are The Poor In Spirit. Matthew 5:3

Blessed Means Happy

Poor means meek in spirit. Poor means humble in spirit. Poor means lowly in spirit. Poor means quiet in spirit. Read Matthew 5:3-12, Read also Mark 1:15

Jesus did not say "*rich*" in spirit. Jesus said "*poor*" in spirit.

1. Blessed are the poor in spirit to those who believe this spiritual hymn: "On a hill far a-way stood an old rug-ged cross, The em-blem of suf-fering and shame; And I love that old cross where the dear-est and best For a world of sin-ners was slain. So I'll cher-ish the old rug-ged cross, Till my trophies at last I lay down; I will cling to the old rug-ged cross, And ex-change it some day for a crown." Philippians 2:8
2. Blessed are the poor in spirit to those who believe this spiritual hymn: "In the cross of Christ I glo-ry; There for all was grace made free. None de-serv-ing, yet re-ceiv-ing Life through death at Cal-va-ry. For the sake of Je-sus' name. For the sake of Je-sus' name." Romans 3:24
3. Blessed are the poor in spirit to those who believe this spiritual hymn: "A-las! And did my Sav-ior bleed? And did my Sov-'reign die? Would He de-vote that sa-cred head For sin-ners such as I!
   At the cross, at the cross where I first saw the light And the bur-den of my heart rolled a-way- It was there by faith I re-ceived my sight, And now I am hap-py all the day!" I Corinthians 1:18
4. Blessed are the poor in spirit to those who believe this spiritual hymn: "Have you been to Je-sus for the cleans-ing power? Are you washed in the blood of the Lamb? Are you ful-ly trust-ing in His grace this hour? Are you washed in the blood of the Lamb? Are you washed in the blood,
   In the soul-cleans-ing blood of the Lamb?
   Are your gar-ments spot-less? Are they white as snow? Are you washed in the blood of the Lamb?" Revelation 7:14
5. Blessed are the poor in spirit to those who believe this spiritual hymn: "Would you be free from the bur-den of sin? There's pow'r in the blood, pow'r in the

blood; Would you o'er e-vil a vic-to-ry win? There's won-der-ful pow'r in the blood. There is pow'r, pow'r, won-der-work-ing pow'r
In the blood of the Lamb; There is pow'r, pow'r, won-der-work-ing pow'r in
In the pre-cious blood of the Lamb." Revelation 12:11

6. Blessed are the poor in spirit to those who believe this spiritual hymn: "Won-der-ful grace of Je-sus, Great-er than all of my sin; How shall my tongue de-scribe it, Where shall its praise be-gin? Tak-ing a-way bur-den, Set-ting my spir-it free, For the won-der-ful grace of Je-sus reach-es me
   Won-der-ful the match-less grace of Je-sus, Deep-er than the might-y roll-ing sea; Won-der-ful grace, all-suf-fi-cient for me, for e-ven me;
   Broad-er than the scope of my trans-gres-sions
   Great-er far then all my sin and shame.
   O mag-ni-fy the pre-cious name of Je-sus, Praise His name!" II Corinthians 8:9
7. Blessed are the poor in spirit to those who believe this spiritual hymn: "Mar-vel-ous grace of our lov-ing Lord, Grace that ex-ceeds our sin and our guilt! Yon-der on Cal-va-ry's mount out-poured- There where the blood of the Lamb was split. Grace, Grace, God's Grace, Grace that will par-don and cleanse with-in Grace, Grace, God's Grace, Grace that is great-er than all our sin!" Romans 5:20
8. Blessed are the poor in spirit to those who believe this spiritual hymn: "A-maz-ing Grace! How sweet the sound-That saved a wretch like me! I once was lost but now am found, Was blind but now I see." John 9:25
9. Blessed are the poor in spirit to those who believe this spiritual hymn: "Rock of A-ges, cleft for me, Let me hide my-self in Thee; Let the wa-ter and the blood, From Thy ri-ver side which flowed, Be of sin the dou-ble cure, Cleanse me from its guilt and pow'r." I Corinthians 10:4
10. Blessed are the poor in spirit to those who believe this spiritual hymn: "For God so loved the world That He gave His Son to die; And who-so-ev-er be-lieves in Him shall have ev-er-last-ing life." John 3:15
11. Blessed are the poor in spirit to those who believe this spiritual hymn: "God so loved the world, God so loved the world, that He gave His on-ly be-got-ten Son, that who-so be-live-eth, be-live-eth in Him should not per-ish, should not per-ish but have ev-er-last-ing life. For God sent not His Son in-to the world to con-demn the world, God sent not His Son in-to the world to con-demn the world; But that the world through Him might be sav-ed. life, ev-er-last-ing, ev-er-last-ing life, ev- er-last-ing, ev-er-last-ing life. God so loved the world, God so loved the world, God so loved the world." John 3:16

12. Blessed are the poor in spirit to those who believe this spiritual hymn: "We are the rea-son that He gave His life, We are the rea-son that He suf-fered and died. To a world that was lost He gave all He could give, to show us the rea-son to live. Romans 5:8

Part CCCXCVII

Blessed Are The Poor In Spirit. Matthew 5:3

Blessed Means Happy

Poor means meek in spirit. Poor means humble in spirit. Poor means lowly in spirit. Poor means quiet in spirit. Read Matthew 5:3-12, Read also Mark 1:15

Jesus did not say "*rich*" in spirit. Jesus said "*poor*" in spirit.

1. Blessed are the poor in spirit to those who believe this spiritual hymn: "I hear the Savior say, "Thy strength in-deed is small! Child of weak-ness, watch and pray, Find in Me thine all in all." Jesus paid it all. All to Him I owe; Sin had left a crim-son stain—He washed it white as snow. I Corinthians 6:19-20
2. Blessed are the poor in spirit to those who believe this spiritual hymn: "God sent His Son, they called Him Je-sus, He came to love, heal, and for-give; He lived and died to buy my par-don, An emp-ty grave is there to prove my Sav-ior lives. Be-cause He lives I can face to-mor-row, Be-cause He lives all fear is gone; Be- cause I know He holds the future. And life is worth the liv-ing just b-ecause He lives." John 14:19
3. Blessed are the poor in spirit to those who believe this spiritual hymn: "I know, I know that Je-sus liv-eth, And on the earth a-gain shall stand. I know, I know that life He giv—eth, That grace and pow'r are in His hand. John 11:25
4. Blessed are the poor in spirit to those who believe this spiritual hymn: "I serve a ris-en Sav—ior, He's in the world to-day; I know that He is liv-ing what-ev-er men may say; I see His hand of mer-cy, I hear His voice of cheer, And just the time I need Him He's al-ways near. He lives, He lives, Christ Je-sus lives to-day! He walks with me and talks with me a-long life's nar-row way. He lives, He lives, sal-va-tion to im-part! You ask me how I know He lives? He lives with-in my heart." Revelation 1:18
5. Blessed are the poor in spirit to those who believe this spiritual hymn:
   "Je-sus is King, Je-sus is King, Je-sus is King of all kings.
   Je-sus the name, Je-sus the name, Je-sus the name a-bove all names
   Je-sus is Lord, Je-sus is Lord, Je-sus is Lord of my life." John 18:37

6. Blessed are the poor in spirit to those who believe this spiritual hymn: "At the name of Jesus Ev-'ry knee shall bow,
   Ev-'ry tongue con-fess Him King of glo-ry now;
   Tis the Fa-ther's pleasure We should call Him Lord,
   Who from the be-gin-ing Was the might-y Word." Matthew 10:32
7. Blessed are the poor in spirit to those who believe this spiritual hymn: "Je-sus may come to—day. Glad day! Glad day! And I would see my Friend; Dan—gers and trou-bles would end If Jesus should come to—day Glad day! Glad Day! Is it the crown—ing day? I'll live for to—day, nor anx—ious be, Je—sus my Lord I soon shall see; Glad day! Glad day! Is it the crown—ing day? Hebrews 9:28
8. Blessed are the poor in spirit to those who believe this spiritual hymn: "Mar-vel- ous mes-sage we bring, Glo-ri-ous car-ol we sing, Won-der-ful word of the King- Je-sus is com-ing a-gain. Coming again! (a-gain!) Com-ing again, Com-ing a- gain; May-be morn-ing, may-be noon, May-be evening and may-be soon! Com- ing a-gain, Com-ing a-gain O what a wonder-ful day it will be- Je-sus is com-ing a-gain!" John 14:3, See Revelation 22:20
9. Blessed are the poor in spirit to those who believe this spiritual hymn: "While we are wait-ing, come; While we are wait-ing, come.
   Je-sus, our Lord, Em-man-u-el, While we are wait-ing, come.
   With pow'r and glo-ry, come; With pow'r and glo-ry, come.
   Je-sus, our Lord, Em-man-u-el, While we are wait-ing, come.
   Come, Sav-ior, quick-ly come; Come, Sav-ior, quick-ly come.
   Je-sus, our Lord, Em-man-u-el, While we are wait-ing, come." Revelation 22:12
10. Blessed are the poor in spirit to those who believe this spiritual hymn: "You shall go out with joy and be led forth with peace; The moun-tains and the hills will break forth be-fore you. There'll be shouts of joy, and all the trees of the field Will clap, will clap their hands. And all the trees of the field will clap their hands, The trees of the field will clap their hands, The trees of the field will clap their hands While you go out with joy." Isaiah 55:12
11. Blessed are the poor in spirit to those who believe this spiritual hymn: "Jesus is coming to earth a-gain—What if it were to-day? Com-ing in pow-er and love to reign- What if it were to-day? Com-ing to claim His cho-sen Bride, All the re- deemed and pu-ri-fied, O-ver this whole earth scat-tered wide- What if it were to- day? Glo-ry, glo-ry! Joy to my heart 'twill bring; Glo-ry, glo-ry! When we shall crown Him King; Glo-ry! glo-ry! Haste to pre-pare the way; Glo-ry, glo-ry! Glo- ry, glo-ry! Je-sus will come some-day." Luke 21:28

12. Blessed are the poor in spirit to those who believe this spiritual hymn: "Oh,
    Je-sus my Sav-ior, He is com-ing a-gain
    Oh, Je-sus my Sav-ior, He is com-ing a-gain
    Com-ing, com-ing, com-ing a-gain
    In clouds of great glo-ry, He is com-ing a-gain.
    In clouds of great glo-ry, He is com-ing a-gain.
    Com-ing, Com-ing, Com-ing a-gain.
    And we shall be like Him, He is com-ing a-gain.
    And we shall be like Him, He is com-ing a-gain.
    Com-ing, com-ing, com-ing a-gain." Revelation 1:7

Part CCCXCVIII

Blessed Are The Poor In Spirit. Matthew 5:3

Blessed Means Happy

Poor means meek in spirit. Poor means humble in spirit. Poor means lowly in spirit. Poor means quiet in spirit. Read Matthew 5:3-12, Read also Mark 1:15

Jesus did not say "*rich*" in spirit. Jesus said "*poor*" in spirit.

1. Blessed are the poor in spirit to those who believe this spiritual hymn:
   "Spi-rit of the Liv-ing God, fall fresh on me.
   Spirit of the Liv-ing God, fall fresh on me. Melt me, mold me, fill me, use me.
   Spir-it of the Living God, fall fresh on me. Galatians 5:16
2. Blessed are the poor in spirit to those who believe this spiritual hymn:
   "Come Holy Spirit, Come Holy Spirit, Come now save my soul.
   Come Holy Spirit, Come Holy Spirit, Come now fill my soul.
   Come Holy Spirit, Come Holy Spirit, Come now baptize me.
   Come Holy Spirit, Come Holy Spirit, Come now use me for your Glory
   Ephesians 5:18
3. Blessed are the poor in spirit to those who belive this spiritual hymn:
   "Where the Spir-it of the Lord is, there is peace; Where the Spir-it of the Lord is, there is love. There is com-fort in life's dark-est hour, there is light and life; There is help and pow-er in the Spir-it, in the Spir-it of the Lord." II Corinthians 3:17
4. Blessed are the poor in spirit to those who believe this spiritual hymn: "Ho-ly, Ho-ly, Ho-ly, Ho-ly! Lord God Al-mighty! All Thy works shall praise Thy name in earth and sky; Ear-ly in the morn-ing our song shall rise to Thee; Ho-ly, Ho-ly, Ho-ly mer-ci-ful and might-y! God in three Per-sons, bless-ed Trin-I-ty. A-men Revelation 4:8
5. Blessed are the poor in spirit to those who believe this spiritual hymn: "Sing praise to the Fa-ther, praise to the Son; Sing praise, sing praise. Sing praise to the Spir-it. Three in One; Sing praise, sing praise." Psalm 68:32

6.

Blessed are the poor in spirit to those who believe this spiritual hymn:

1. "Sing them o-ver a-gain to me, Won-der-ful words of Life. Let me more of their beau-ty see, Won-der-ful words of Life. Words of life and beau-ty, Teach me faith and du-ty; Beau-ti-ful words, won-der-ful words, Won-der-ful words of Life. Beau-ti-ful words, won-der-ful words, Won-der-ful words of Life.
2. Christ, the bless-ed One, give to all Wonderful words of Life; Sin-ner, list to the lov-ing call, Won-der-ful words of Life. All so free-ly giv-en, Woo-ing us to Heav-en: Won-der-ful words of Life. Beau-ti-ful words, won-der-ful words,
   Won-der-ful words of Life.
3. Sweet-ly ech-o the gos-pel call, Won-der-ful words of Life; Of-fer par-don and peace to all, Won-der-ful words of Life. Je-sus, on-ly Sav-ior, Sanc-ti-fy for- ev-er: Won-der-ful words of Life. Beau-ti-ful words, won-der-ful words, Won- der-ful words of Life." John 6:63

7.

Blessed are the poor in spirit to those who believe this spiritual hymn: "Stand-ing on the prom-is-es of Christ my King, Sanctify Thro' e-ter-nal a-ges. let His prais-es ring; Glo-ry in the high-est, I will shout and sing, Stand-ing on the Prom-is-es of God. Stand-ing, stand-ing, Stand-ing on the prom-is-es of God my Sav-ior; Stand-ing, stand-ing, I'm stand-ing on the prom-is-es of God." II Peter 1:4

8. Blessed are the poor in spirit to those who believe this spiritual hymn:" Blest Be The Tie That Bind. Galatians 3:28
9. Blessed are the poor in spirit to those who believe the bond of love. I John 3:14
10. Blessed are the poor in spirit to those who believe the Family of God. Ephesians 3:15

11.

Blessed are the poor in spirit to those who believe that there shall be showers of blessings. Ezekiel 34:26

12.

Blessed are the poor in spirit to those who believe that we are not ashamed to tell the gospel of Jesus Christ. Romans 1:16

Part CCCXCIX

Blessed Are The Poor In Spirit. Matthew 5:3

Blessed Means Happy

Poor means meek in spirit. Poor means humble in spirit. Poor means lowly in spirit. Poor means quiet in spirit. Read Matthew 5:3-12, Read also Mark 1:15

Jesus did not say "*rich*" in spirit. Jesus said "*poor*" in spirit.

1. Blessed are the poor in spirit to those who believe this spiritual hymn: "Je-sus, Je- sus, how I trust Him! How I've proved Him over and over! Je-sus, Je-sus, pre- cious Je-sus! O for grace to trust Him more!" John 14:1
2. Blessed are the poor in spirit to those who believe this spiritual hymn: "I'm a child of the King, A child of the King: With Je-sus my Sav-ior, I'm a child of the King." Romans 8:17
3. Blessed are the poor in spirit to those who believe that we are God's people. I Peter 2:9
4. Blessed are the poor in spirit to those who believe that they'll know we are Christians by our love. John 13:35
5. Blessed are the poor in spirit to those who believe in Christ that there is no east or west. Acts 10:34-35
6. Blessed are the poor in spirit to those who believe that I tell the world that I'm a Christian. Romans 1:16
7. Blessed are the poor in spirit to those who believe this spiritual hymn: "Thy Word is a lamp un-to my feet and a light un-to my path. Thy word is a lamp un-to my feet and a light un-to my path. Thy Word is a lamp un-to my feet and a light un-to my path." Psalm 119:105
8. Blessed are the poor in spirit to those who believe this spiritual hymn: "Faith of our fathers! liv-ing still In spite of dun-geon, fire and sword: O how our hearts beat high with joy. Faith of our fathers, when-ever we hear that glo-rious word! Faith of our fathers, ho-ly, faith! We will be true to thee till death! ho-ly faith! We will be true to thee till death! We will be true, We will be true, We will be true to thee till death." A-men. Jude 3

9. Blessed are the poor in spirit to those who believe this spiritual hymn: "I'm so glad I'm a part of the fam-ily of God- I've been washed in the fountain, cleansed by His blood! Joint heirs with Je-sus as we trav-el this sod, For I'm part of the fam-ily, the fam-ily of God." Ephesians 3:15
10. Blessed are the poor in spirit to those who believe this spiritual hymn: "Our God has made us one- In Him our hearts u-nite. When we His child-ren share His love, Our joy is His de-light." Amen. Ephesians 4:3
11. Blessed are the poor in spirit to those who believe this spiritual hymn: "I love to tell the sto-ry of un-seen things a-bove, Of Je-sus and His glo-ry, of Je-sus and His love; I love to tell the sto-ry be-cause I know 'tis true, It sat-is-fies my long- ings as noth-ing else can do. I love to tell the sto-ry! 'Twill be my theme in glo-ry—To tell the old, old sto-ry of Je-sus and His love." Acts 8:4
12. Blessed are the poor in spirit to those who believe this spiritual hymn: "I'll tell the world that I'm a Christian- I'm not a-shamed His name to bear; I'll tell the world that I'm a Christian- I'll take Him with me an-y—where. I'll tell the world how Je-sus saved me, And how He gave me a life brand new; And I know that if you trust Him That all He gave me He'll give to you. I'll tell the world that He's my Sav-ior, No oth-er one could love me so; My Life, my all is His for-ev-er, And where He leads me I will go. I'll tell the world that He is com-ing- It may be near or far a-way; But we must live as if His com-ing Would be to-mo-r-row or to-day. For when He comes and life is o-ver, For those who love Him there's more to be; Eyes have nev-er seen the won-ders That He's pre-par-ing for you and me. O tell the world that you're a Christian, Be not a-shamed His name to bear; O tell the world that you're a Christian, And take Him with you ev-ery—where." Romans 1:16

Part CD

Blessed Are The Poor In Spirit. Matthew 5:3

Blessed Means Happy

Poor means meek in spirit. Poor means humble in spirit. Poor means lowly in spirit. Poor means quiet in spirit. Read Matthew 5:3-12, Read also Mark 1:15

Jesus did not say "*rich*" in spirit. Jesus said "*poor*" in spirit.

1. Blessed are the poor in spirit to those who believe this spiritual hymn: "All power is giv-en un-to Me, All power is giv-en un-to me, Go ye in-to all the world and preach the gos-pel. And lo, I am with you al-way." Matthew 28:18
2. Blessed are the poor in spirit to those who believe this spiritual hymn:
    1. "Peo-ple need the Lord; Peo-ple need the Lord; At the end of bro-ken dreams, He's the o-pen door. Peo-ple need the Lord.
    2. Peo-ple need the Lord, peo-ple need the Lord; When will we re-al-ize He's the o-pen door. Peo-ple need the Lord." Psalm 40:17
3. Blessed are the poor in spirit to those who believe in "Passing the Gospel On" by loving one another. I John 4:11
4. Blessed are the poor in spirit to those who believe and remember Jesus at the Lord's table. Luke 22:19
5. Blessed are the poor in spirit to those who believe in coming to celebrate Jesus. I Corinthians 11:25
6. Blessed are the poor in spirit to those who believe that there is still room for sinners at the cross. Luke 14:22
7. Blessed are the poor in spirit to those who believe and confess: "I lay my sins on Jesus. Isaiah 53:6
8. Blessed are the poor in spirit to those who believe the Word of the Lord: Be still and know that I am God. Psalm 46:10
9. Blessed are the poor in spirit to those who believe that Jesus is Lord of all; that Jesus is Christ. Acts 2:36
10. Blessed are the poor in spirit to those who believe and are able to commit: I will love Thee, O Lord, my strength: Psalm 18:1

11. Blessed are the poor in spirit to those who would like to be like Jesus. Romans 8:29
12. Blessed are the poor in spirit to those who believe and put their hope in God and my Savior with praise. Psalm 42:11

Part CDI

Blessed Are The Poor In Spirit. Matthew 5:3

Blessed Means Happy

Poor means meek in spirit. Poor means humble in spirit. Poor means lowly in spirit. Poor means quiet in spirit. Read Matthew 5:3-12, Read also Mark 1:15

Jesus did not say "*rich*" in spirit. Jesus said "*poor*" in spirit.

1. Blessed are the poor in spirit to those who believe that our hope is in the Lord. Colossians 1:27
2. Blessed are the poor in spirit to those who believe: "Have Faith in God." Mark 11:22
3. Blessed are the poor in spirit to those who believe that the disciples were glad when they saw the Lord. John 20:20
4. Blessed are the poor in spirit to those who believe this spiritual hymn: "We have heard the joy-ful sound—Je-sus saves! Jesus saves!!! Spread the ti-dings all a- round- Je-sus saves!!! Je-sus saves!!! Bear the news to every land, Climb the steeps and cross the waves; On-ward!!! 'tis our Lord's com-mand—Je-sus saves!!! Je-sus saves!!! I Timothy 1:15
5. Blessed are the poor in spirit to those who believe this spiritual hymn:
    1. "There's a call comes ring-ing o'er the rest-less wave, "Send the light! Send the light!" There are souls to res-cue, there are souls to save, Send the light! Send the light! Send the light! Send the light, the bless-ed gos-pel light; Let it shine from shore to shore! Shine from shore to shore!
    2. We have heard the Mac-e-do-nian call to-day, "Send the light! Send the light!" And a gold-en of-fering at the cross we lay, Send the light! Send the light! Send the light, the bless-ed gos-pel light; Let it shine from shore to shore! Shine from shore to shore!
    3. Let us pray that grace may ev-ery—where a—bound, Send the light! Send the light! And a Christ-like spir-it ev-ery-where be found, Send the light! Send the light! Send the light! Send the light, the bless-ed gos-pel light; Let it shine from shore to shore! Shine from shore to shore!

4. Let us not grow wea-ry in the work of love, Send the light! Send the light! Let us gath-er jew-els for a crown a-bove, Send the light! Send the light! Send the light, the bless-ed gos-pel light; Let it shine from shore to shore! Shine from shore to shore!" II Corinthians 4:4

6.

Blessed are the poor in spirit to those who believe this spiritual hymn:

1. "Go ye there-fore and teach all na-tions, go, go, go. Go ye there-fore and teach all na-tions, go, go, go. Bap-tiz-ing them in the name of the Fa-ther and Son, and Ho-ly Ghost. Go, go, go.
2. If you love Me, real-ly love Me, feed My sheep. If you love Me, real-ly love Me, feed My sheep. Lo, I'll be with you for-ev-er and ev-er, un-til the end of the world. Go, go go.
3. Go ye there-fore and teach all na-tions, go, go, go. Go ye there-fore and teach all na-tions, go, go, go. Bap-tiz-ing them in the name of the Fa-ther and Son, and Ho-ly Ghost. Go, go, go." Matthew 28:20

7.

Blessed are the poor in spirit to those who believe that the *Bible is God's Word.* Genesis 1:1, John 1:1, II Timothy 3:16

8. Blessed are the poor in spirit to those who *believe, know, understand and realize* that we have the *full assurance of forgiveness,* the *full assurance of understanding* and the *full assurance of hope through Christ Jesus in our heart.* I John 5:11-12, Colossians 2:13-15, Proverbs 3:5-6, I John 1:9, Genesis 50:15-21, Psalm 130:7-8
9. Blessed are the poor in spirit to those who *believe, know, understand and realize* that we have the *full assurance of pardon,* the *full assurance of understanding* and the *full assurance of hope through Christ Jesus in our heart.* Psalm 103:8-12
10. Blessed are the poor in spirit to those who *believe, know, understand and realize* that we have the *full assurance of salvation,* the *full assurance of understanding* and the *full assurance of hope through Christ Jesus in our heart.* Romans 8:32-39
11. Blessed are the poor in spirit to those who believe that "*Jesus Christ*" is "*the Fountain of living water.*" Jeremiah 2:13

12.

Blessed are the poor in spirit to those who *believe in prayer without ceasing and without faint.* Luke 18:1

Part CDII

Blessed Are The Poor In Spirit. Matthew 5:3

Blessed Means Happy

Poor means meek in spirit. Poor means humble in spirit. Poor means lowly in spirit. Poor means quiet in spirit. Read Matthew 5:3-12, Read also Mark 1:15

Jesus did not say "*rich*" in spirit. Jesus said "*poor*" in spirit.

1. Blessed are the poor in spirit to those who believe this spiritual hymn: "Lord, lay some soul up-on my heart, And love that the soul through me; And may I no-bly do my part To win that soul for Thee. I Corinthians 9:19
2. Blessed are the poor in spirit to those who believe this spiritual hymn:
    1. "Reach out and touch a soul that is hun-gry; Reach out and touch a spir-it in de-spair; Reach out and touch a life torn and dirt-y, A man who is lone-ly- If you care! Reach out and touch that neigh-bor who hates you; Reach out and touch that stran-ger who meets you; Reach out and touch the brother-er who needs you; Reach out and let the smile of God touch thro' you. you.
    2. Reach out and touch a friend who is wea-ry; Reach out and touch a seek-er un- a-ware; Reach out and touch tho' touch-ing means los-ing A part of your own self- If you dare! Reach out and give your love to the love-less; Reach out and make a home for the home-less; Reach out and shed God's light in the dark- ness; Reach out and let the smile of God touch thro' you. you." I John 3:18
3.

    Blessed are the poor in spirit to those who believe this spiritual hymn:
    1. "The vi-sion of a dy-ing world Is vast be-fore our eyes; We feel the heart-beat of its need, We hear its fee-ble cries: Lord Je-sus Christ, re-vive Thy church In this, her cru-cial hour! Lord Je-sus Christ, a-wake Thy church With Spir-it—giv-en pow'r.
    2. The sav-age hugs his god of stone And fears de-scent of night; The cit-y dwell-er cring-es lone A-mid the gar-ish light: Lord Je-sus Christ, a-rouse

Thy church To see their mute dis-tress! Lord Je-sus Christ, e-quip Thy church With love and ten-der-ness.

3. To-day, as un-der-stand-ing's bounds Are stretch'd on ev-ery hand, O clothe Thy Word in bright, new sounds, And speed it o'er the land; Lord Je-sus Christ, em-pow-er us To preach by ev-ery means! Lord Je-sus Christ, em-bold-en us In near and dis-tant scenes.
4. The warn-ing bell of judg-ments tolls, A-bove us looms the cross; A-round are ev-er—dy-ing souls-How great, how great the loss! O Lord, con-strain and move Thy church The glad news to im-part! And Lord, as Thou dost stir Thy church, Be-gin with-in my heart. A-men." Acts 16:9

4. Blessed are the poor in spirit to those who believe this spiritual hymn:
    1. "This child we ded-I-cate to Thee, O God of grace and pu-ri-ty! In Thy great love its life pro-long, Shield it, we pray, from sin and wrong.
    2. O may Thy Spir-it gen-tly draw Its will-ing soul to keep Thy law; May vir- tue, pi-e-ty, and truth, Dawn e-ven with its dawn-ing youth. A-men." Ephesians 6:4
5. Blessed are the poor in spirit to those who believe this spiritual hymn:
    1. "Good Shep-herd, take this lit-tle child in-to Your lov-ing hands; And in the days that lie a-head pro-tect this lit-tle lamb.
    2. Good Shep-herd, we com-mit our-selves in ev-'ry-thing we do To be Your fam-'ly here on earth and love this child for You.
    3. Good Shep-herd, now we place this child in-to Your gen-tle trust; This pre-cious gift we give to You is one You've giv-en us." Mark 10:16
6.

    Blessed are the poor in spirit to those who believe this spiritual hymn:
    1. "Let us break bread to-gether-er on our knees: (on our knees;) Let us break bread to-geth-er on our knees; (on our knees;) When I fall on my knees with my face to the ris-ing sun, O Lord, have mer-cy on me. (on me.)
    2. Let us drink the cup to-geth-er on our knees; (on our knees;) Let us drink the cup to-geth-er on our knees: (on our knees;) When I fall on my knees with my face to the ris-ing sun, O Lord, have mer-cy on me, (on me.)
    3. Let us praise God to-geth-er on our knees; (on our knees;) Let us praise God to-geth-er on our knees; (on our knees;) When I fall on my knees with my face to the ris-ing sun, O Lord, have mer-cy on me. (on me.)" Acts 2:42

7.

Blessed are the poor in spirit to those who believe this spiritual hymn:

1. "Soft-ly and ten-der-ly Je-sus is call-ing, Call-ing for you and for me; See, on the por-tals He's wait-ing and watch-ing, Watch-ing for you and for me. Come home, come home, Ye who are wea-ry, come home; Ear-nest-ly, ten-der-ly, Je-sus is call-ing, Call-ing, O sin-ner, come home!
2. Why should we tar-ry when Je-sus is plead-ing, Plead-ing for you and for me? Why should we lin- ger and heed not His mer-cies, Mer-cies for you and for me? Come home, come home, Ye who are wea-ry, come home; Ear-nest-ly, ten-der-ly, Je-sus is call-ing, Call-ing, O sin-ner, come home!
3. Time is now fleet-ing, the mo-ments are pass-ing, Pass-ing from you and from me; Shad-ows are gath-er-ing, death's night is com-ing, Com-ing for you and for me. Come home, come home, Ye who are wea-ry, come home; Ear-nest-ly, ten-der-ly, Je-sus is call-ing, Call-ing, O sin-ner, come home!
4. O for the won-der-ful love He has prom-ised, Prom-ised for you and for me! Though we have sinned, He has mer-cy and par-don, Par-don for you and for me. Come home, come home, Ye who are wea-ry, come home; Ear- nest-ly, ten-der-ly, Je-sus is call-ing, Call-ing, O sin-ner, come home!" Matthew 11:28

8.

Blessed are the poor in spirit to those who believe this spiritual hymn:

1. "Je-sus is ten-der-ly call-ing you home, Call-ing to-day, call-ing to-day, Why from the sun-shine of love will you roam Far-ther and far-ther a-way? Call-ing to-day, Call-ing to-day, Je-sus is call-ing, Is ten-der-ly call-ing to- day.
2. Je-sus is call-ing the wea-ry to rest, Call-ing to-day, call-ing to-day, Bring Him your bur-den and you shall be blest; He will not turn you a-way Call-ing to-day, Call-ing to-day, Je-sus is call-ing, Is ten-der-ly call-ing to-day
3. Je-sus is wait-ing, O come to Him now, Wait-ing to-day, wait-ing to-day, Come with your sins, at His feet low-ly bow; Come, and no long-er de-lay. Call-ing to-day, Call-ing to-day, Je-sus is call-ing, Is ten-der-ly call-ing to- day.
4. Je-sus is plead-ing, O list to His voice: Hear Him to-day, hear Him to-day, They who be-lieve on His name shall re-joice; Quick-ly a-rise and a-way. Call-ing to-day, Call-ing to-day, Je-sus is call-ing, Is ten-der-ly call-ing to-day." Hebrews 4:7

9. Blessed are the poor in spirit to those who believe this spiritual hymn:
    1. "Have you an-y room for Je-sus, He who bore your load of sin? As He knocks and asks ad-mis-sion, Sin-ner, will you let Him in? Room for Je-sus, King of glo-ry! Has-ten now, His Word o-bey; Swing the heart's door wide-ly o-pen, Bid Him en-ter while you may.
    2. Room for pleas-ure, room for busi-ness- But, for Christ the Cru-ci-fied, Not a place that He can en-ter In the heart for which He died? Room for Je- sus, King of glo-ry! Has-ten now, His Word o-bey; Swing the heart's door wide-ly o-pen, Bid Him en-ter while you may.
    3. Have you an-y room for Je-sus, As in grace He calls a-gain? O to-day is time ac-cept-ed, Lat-er you may call in vain. Room for Je-sus, King of glo- ry! Has—ten now, His Word o-bey; Swing the heart's door wide-ly o-pen, Bid Him en-ter while you may.
    4. Room and time now give to Je-sus, Soon will pass God's day of grace; Soon your heart left cold and si-lent, And your Sav-ior's plead-ing cease. Room for Je-sus, King of glo-ry! Has—ten now, His Word o-bey; Swing the heart's door wide-ly o-pen, Bid Him en-ter while you may."
    II Corinthians 6:2
10. Blessed are the poor in spirit to those who believe this spiritual hymn:
    1. "With-out Him I could do noth-ing, With-out Him I'd sure-ly fail; With-out Him I would be drift-ing Like a ship with-out a sail. Je-sus, O Je-sus! Do you know Him to-day? Do not turn Him a-way. O Je-sus, O Je-sus, With-out Him, how lost I would be.
    2. With-out Him I would be dy-ing, With-out Him I'd be en-slaved; With-out Him life would be hope-less, But with Je-sus, thank God, I'm saved. Je- sus, O Je-sus! Do you know Him to-day? Do not turn Him a-way. O Je- sus, O Je-sus, With-out Him, how lost I would be." John 15:5
11.

    Blessed are the poor in spirit to those who believe this spiritual hymn:
    1. "Come, ye sin-ners, poor and need-y, Weak and wound-ed, sick and sore; Je-sus read-y stands to save you, Full of pit-y, love, and pow'r.
    2. Come, ye thirst-y, come, and wel-come, God's free boun-ty glo-ri-fy; true be-lief and true re-pent-ance, Ev-ery grace that brings you nigh.
    3. Let not con-science make yo lin-ger, Nor of fit-ness fond-ly dream; All the fit-ness He re-quir-eth Is to feel your need of Him.

4. Come, ye wea-ry, heav-y la-den, Lost and ru-ined by the fall; If you tar-ry till you're bet-ter, You will nev-er come at all." Revelation 22:17

12.

Blessed are the poor in spirit to those who believe this spiritual hymn: "Turn your eyes up-on Je-sus, Look full in His won-der-ful face, And the things of earth will grow strange-ly dim In the light of His glo-ry and grace." II Corinthians 3:18

Part CDIII

Blessed Are The Poor In Spirit. Matthew 5:3

Blessed Means Happy

Poor means meek in spirit. Poor means humble in spirit. Poor means lowly in spirit. Poor means quiet in spirit. Read Matthew 5:3-12, Read also Mark 1:15

Jesus did not say "*rich*" in spirit. Jesus said "*poor*" in spirit.

1. Blessed are the poor in spirit to those who believe this spiritual hymn:
    1. "Out of my bond-age, sor-row and night, Je-sus, I come, Je-sus, I come; In-to Thy free-dom, glad-ness and light, Je-sus, I come to Thee. Out of my sick- ness in-to Thy health, Out of my want and in-to Thy wealth, Out of my sin and in-to Thy-self, Je-sus, I come to Thee.
    2. Out of my shame-ful fail-ure and loss, Je-sus, I come, Je-sus, I come; In-to the glo-rious gain of Thy cross, Je-sus, I come to Thee. Out of earth's sor-rows in-to Thy balm, Out of life's storms and in-to Thy calm, Out of dis-tress to ju-bi-lant psalm, Je-sus, I come to Thee.
    3. Out of un-rest and ar-ro-gant pride, Je-sus, I come, Je-sus, I come; In-to Thy bless-ed will to a-bide, Je-sus, I come to Thee. Out of my-self to dwell in Thy love, Out of de-spair in-to rap-tures a-bove, Up-ward for aye on wings like a dove, Je-sus, I come to Thee.
    4. Out of the fear and dread of the tomb, Je-sus, I come, Je-sus, I come; In-to the joy and light of Thy home, Je-sus, I come to Thee. Out of the depths of ru-in un-told, In-to the peace of Thy shel-ter-ing fold, Ev-er Thy glo-rious face to be-hold, Je-sus, I come to Thee." Isaiah 61:1
2.

   Blessed are the poor in spirit to those who believe this spiritual hymn: "Pass me not, O gen-tle Savior—Hear my hum-ble cry! While on oth-ers Thou art call-ing, Do not pass me by. Sav-ior, Sav-ior, Hear my hum-ble cry! While on oth-ers Thou art call-ing, Do not pass me by." II Peter 3:9
3. Blessed are the poor in spirit to those who believe this spiritual hymn:
    1. "Years I spent in van -i-ty and pride, Car-ing not my Lord was cru-ci-fied, Know-ing not it was for me He died On Cal-va-ry. Mer-cy there was great

and grace was free, Par-don there was mul-ti-plied to me, There my burdened soul found lib-er-ty-At Cal-va-ry.

2. By God's Word at last my sin I learned- Then I trem-bled at the law I'd spurned, Till my guilt-y soul im-plor-ing turned To Cal-va-ry. Mer-cy there was great and grace was free, Par-don there was mul-ti-plied to me, There my bur-dened soul found lib-er-ty-At Cal-va-ry.
3. Now I've giv'n to Je-sus ev-'ry-thing, Now I glad-ly own Him as my King, Now my rap-tured soul can on-ly sing Of Cal-va-ry. Mer-cy there was great and grace was free, Par-don there was mul-ti-plied to me, There my burdened soul found lib-er-ty-At Cal-va-ry.
4. O the love that drew sal-va-tion's plan! O the grace that bro't it down to man! O the might-y gulf that God did span At Cal-va-ry. Mer-cy there was great and grace was free, Par-don there was mul-ti-plied to me, There my bur-dened soul found lib-er-ty-At Cal-va-ry." Luke 23:33

4. Blessed are the poor in spirit to those who believe this spiritual hymn:
    1. "I have a song I love to sing, Since I have been re-deemed, Of my Re-deemer, Sav-ior, King, Since I have been re-deemed. Since I have been re- deemed, Since I have been re-deemed, I will glo-ry in His name; Since I have been re-deemed, I will glo-ry in my Sav-ior's name.
    2. I have a Christ who sat-is-fies, Since I have been re-deemed, To do His will my high-est prize, Since I have been re-deemed. Since I have been re-deemed, Since I have been re-deemed, I will glo-ry in His name; Since I have been re-deemed, I will glo-ry in my Sav-ior's name.
    3. I have a wit-ness bright and clear, Since I have been re-deemed, Dis-pel-ling ev-ery doubt and fear, Since I have been re-deemed. Since I have been re-deemed, Since I have been re-deemed, I will glo-ry in His name; Since I have been re-deemed, I will glo-ry in my Sav-ior's name.
    4. I have a home pre-pared for me, Since I have been re-deemed, Where I shall dwell e-ter-nal-ly, Since I have been re-deemed. Since I have been re- deemed, Since I have been re-deemed, I will glo-ry in His name; Since I have been re-deemed, I will glo-ry in my Sav-ior's name." Galatians 3:13
5. Blessed are the poor in spirit to those who believe this spiritual hymn:
    1. "Just as I am, with-out one plea But that Thy blood was shed for me, And that Thou bidd'st me come to Thee, O Lamb of God, I come! I come!
    2. Just as I am, and wait-ing not To rid my soul of one dark blot, To thee whose blood can cleanse each spot, O Lamb of God, I come! I come!

   3. Just as I am, tho tossed a-bout With man-ya con-flict, man-y a doubt, Fight-ings and fears with-in, with-out, O Lamb of God, I come! I come!
   4. Just as I am, poor, wretched, blind-Sight, rich-es, heal-ing of the mind, Yea, all I need in Thee to find- O Lamb of God, I come! I come!
   5. Just as I am, Thou wilt re-ceive, Wilt wel-come, par-don, cleanse, relieve; Be-cause Thy prom-ise I be-lieve, O Lamb of God, I come! I come!" John 6:37
6. Blessed are the poor in spirit to those who believe this spiritual hymn:
   1. "Be still and know that I am God. Be still and know that I am God. Be still and know that I am God.
   2. I am the Lord that heal-eth thee. I am the Lord that heal-eth thee. I am the Lord that heal-eth thee." Exodus 15:26
7. Blessed are the poor in spirit to those who believe this spiritual hymn:
   1. "He's got the whole world in His hands, He's got the whole world in His hands, He's got the whole world in His hands, He's got the whole world in His hands.
   2. He's got the wind and the rain in His hands, He's got the wind and the rain in His hands, He's got the wind and the rain in His hands, He's got the whole world in His hands.
   3. He's got the ti-ny lit-tle ba-by in His hands, He's got the ti-ny lit-tle ba-by in His hands, He's got the ti-ny lit-tle ba-by in His hands, He's got the whole world in His hands.
   4. He's got you and me, brothe-er, in His hands, He's got you and me, sis-ter, in His hands, He's got you and me, brother, in His hands, He's got the whole world in His hands." Job 12:10
8. Blessed are the poor in spirit to those who believe this spiritual hymn:
   1. "Bless-ed as-sur-ance, Je-sus is mine! O what a fore-taste of glo-ry di- vine! Heir of sal-va-tion, pur-chase of God, Born of His Spirit, washed in His blood. This is my sto-ry, this is my song, Prais-ing my Sav-ior all the day long; This is my story, this is my song, Prais-ing my Sav-ior all the day long.
   2. Per-fect sub-mis-sion, per-fet de-light! Vi-sions of rap-ture now burst on my sight; An-gels de-scend-ing bring from a-bove Ech-oes of mer-cy, whis-pers of love. This is my sto-ry, this is my song, Prais-ing my Sav- ior all the day long; This is my sto-ry, this is my song, Prais-ing my Sav- ior all the day long.

   3. Per-fect sub-mis-sion-all is at rest, I in my Sav-ior am hap-py and blest; Watch-ing and wait-ing, look-ing a-bove, Filled with His good-ness, lost in His love. This is my sto-ry, this is my song, Prais-ing my Sav-ior all the day long; This is my sto-ry, this is my song, Prais-ing my Sav-ior all the day long." James 5:13
9. Blessed are the poor in spirit to those who believe this spiritual hymn:
   1. "I am trust-ing Thee, Lord Je-sus-Trust-ing on-ly Thee; Turst-ing Thee for full sal-va-tion, Great and free.
   2. I am trust-ing Thee to guide me-Thou a-lone shalt lead, Ev-'ry day and hour sup-ply-ing All my need.
   3. I am trust-ing Thee for pow-er-Thine can nev-er fail; Words which Thou Thy-self shalt give me Must pre-vail.
   4. I am trust-ing Thee, Lord Je-sus-Nev-er let me fall; I am trust-ing Thee for-ev-er, And for all. A-men." Acts 14:23
10. Blessed are the poor in spirit to those who believe this spiritual hymn:
    1. "Take the world, but give me Je-sus, All its joys are but a name; But His love a-bid-eth ev-er, Thru e-ter-nal years the same. O the height and depth of mer-cy! O the length and breadth of love! O the full-ness of re-demp-tion, Pledge of end-less life a-bove!
    2. Take the world, but give me Je-sus, Sweet-est com-fort of my soul; With my Sav-ior watch-ing o'er me, I can sing tho bil-lows roll. O the height and depth of mer-cy! O the length and breadth of love! O the full-ness of re-demp-tion, Pledge of end-less life a-bove!
    3. Take the world, but give me Je-sus, Let me view His con-stant smile; Then thru-out my pil-grim jour-ney Light will cheer me all the while. O the height and depth of mer-cy! O the length and breadth of love! O the full-ness of re-demp-tion, Pledge of end-less life a-bove!
    4. Take the world, but give me Je-sus, In His cross my trust shall be; Till, with clear-er, bright-er vi-sion, Face to face my Lord I see. O the height and depth of mer-cy! O the length and breadth of love! O the full-ness of re-demp-tion, Pledge of end-less life a-bove!" Mark 8:36
11. Blessed are the poor in spirit to those who believe that the Battle Belongs to the Lord. II Chronicle 20:15
12. Blessed are the poor in spirit to those who believe that Faith is the victory. I John 5:4

Part CDIV

Blessed Are The Poor In Spirit. Matthew 5:3

Blessed Means Happy

Poor means meek in spirit. Poor means humble in spirit. Poor means lowly in spirit. Poor means quiet in spirit. Read Matthew 5:3-12, Read also Mark 1:15

Jesus did not say "*rich*" in spirit. Jesus said "*poor*" in spirit.

1. Blessed are the poor in spirit to those who believe this song: "Faith is the victory. Faith is the victory. O, glorious victory, that over come the world." I John 5:4
2. Blessed are the poor in spirit to those who believe this spiritual song: "Je-sus, Je- sus Je-sus, sweetest name I know Je-sus, Je-sus, Je-sus, sweetest name I know. Fill my eve'ry long-ing. Keep me sing-ing as I go.
3. Blessed are the poor in spirit to those who believe this: "Take the whole world, but give me Jesus."
4. Blessed are the poor in spirit to those who believe and are able to sing: "I will sing of my Redeemer." Ephesians 1:7
5. Blessed are the poor in spirit to those who believe this spiritual hymn:
    1. "When we walk with the Lord in the light of His Word, What a glo-ry He sheds on our way! While we do His good will He a-bides with us still, And with all who will trust and o-bey. Trust and o-bey, for there's no oth-er way To be hap-py in Je-sus, But to trust and o-bey.
    2. Not a shad-ow can rise, not a cloud in the skies, But His smile quick-ly drives it a-way; Not a doubt nor a fear, not a sigh nor a tear, Can a-bide while we trust and o-bey. Trust and o-bey, for there's no oth-er way To be hap-py in Je-sus, But to turst and o-bey.
    3. Not a bur-den we bear, not a sor-row we share, But our toil He doth rich-ly re-pay; Not a grief nor a loss, not a frown nor a cross, But is blest if we trust and o-bey. Turst and o-bey, for there's no oth-er way To be hap-py in Je- sus, But to trust and o-bey.
    4. But we nev-er can prove the de-lights of His love Un-til all on the al-tar we lay; For the fa-vor He shows and the joy He be-stows Are for them who will trust and o-bey. Trust and o-bey, for there's no oth-er way To be hap- py in Je-sus, But to trust and o-bey.

5. Then in fel-low-ship sweet we will sit at His feet, Or we'll walk by His side in the way; What He says we will do, where He sends we will go- Nev-er fear, on-ly trust and o-bey. Trust and o-bey, for there's no oth-er way To be hap-py in Je-sus, But to trust and o-bey." Romans 16:26
   {John H. Manigo's favorite song}

6. Blessed are the poor in spirit to those who believe this spiritual hymn:
   1. "'Tis so sweet to trust in Je-sus, Just to take Him at His word, Jus to rest up-on His prom-ise, Just to know "Thus saith the Lord." Je-sus, Je-sus, how I trust him! How I've proved Him o'er and o'er! Je-sus, Je-sus, pre-cious Je-sus! O for grace to trust Him more!
   2. O how sweet to trust in Je-sus, Just to trust His cleans-ing blood, Just in sim-ple faith to plunge me 'Neath the heal-ing, cleans-ing flood! Je-sus, Je-sus, how I trust Him! How I;ve proved Him o'er and o'er! Je-sus, Je- sus, pre-cious Je-sus! O for grace to trust Him more!
   3. Yes, 'tis sweet to trust in Je-sus, Just from sin and self to cease. Just from Je-sus sim-ply tak-ing Life and rest and joy and peace. Je-sus, Je-sus, how I trust Him! How I've proved Him o'er and o'er! Je-sus, Je-sus, pre-cious Je-sus! O for grace to trust Him more!
   4. I'm so glad I learned to trust Him, Pre-cious Je-sus, Sav-ior, Friend; And I know that He is with me, Will be with me to the end. Je-sus, Je-sus, how I trust Him! How I've proved Him o'er and o'er! Je-sus, Je-sus, pre-cious Je-sus! O for grace to trust Him more!" John 14:1

7. Blessed are the poor in spirit to those who believe this spiritual hymn: "What a fel-low-ship, what a joy di-vine, Lean-ing on the ev-er-last-ing arms; What a bless-de-ness, what a peace is mine, Lean-ing on the ev-er- last-ing arms. Lean-ing, lean-ing, Safe and se-cure from all a-larms; Lean- ing, lean-ing, Lean-ing on the ev-er-last-ing arms." Deuteronomy 33:27

8. Blessed are the poor in spirit to those who believe this spiritual hymn:
   1. "Sim-ply trust-ing ev-ry day, Trust-ing through a storm-y way; E-ven when my faith is small, Trust-ing Je-sus- that is all. Trust-ing as the mo-ments fly, Trust-ing as the days go by; Trust-ing Him what-e'er be-fall, Trust- ing Je-sus- that is all.
   2. Bright-ly doth His Spir-it shine In-to this poor heart of mine. While He leads I can-not fall, Trust-ing Je-sus- that is all. Trust-ing as the mo- ments fly, Trust-ing as the days go by; Trust-ing Him what-e'er be-fall, Trust-ing Je-sus- that is all.

3. Sing-ing if my way is clear, Pray-ing if the path be drear; If in dan-ger, for Him call, Trust-ing Je-sus- that is all. Trust-ing as the mo-ments fly, Trust-ing as the days go by; Trust-ing Him what-e'er be-fall, Trust-ing Je-sus-that is all.
4. Trust-ing Him while life shall last, Trust-ing Him till earth be past; Till with-in the jas-per wall, Trust-ing Je-sus- that is all. Trust-ing as the mo-ments fly, Trust-ing as the days go by; Trust-in Him what-e'er be-fall, Trust-ing Je-sus- that is all." Colossians 2:5

9. Blessed are the poor in spirit to those who believe this spiritual hymn:
    1. "I am so glad that our Fa-ther in heav'n Tells of His love in the Book He has giv'n: Won-der-ful things in the Bi-ble I see- This is the dear-est, that Je-sus loves me. I am so glad that Je-sus loves me. Je-sus loves me. Je- sus loves me; I am so glad that Je-sus loves me, Je-sus loves e-ven me.
    2. Tho I for-got Him and wan-der a-way, Still He doth love me wher-ev-er I stray; Back to His dear lov-ing arms would I flee When I re-mem-ber that Je-sus loves me. I am so glad that Je-sus loves me, Je-sus loves me, Je-sus loves me; I am so glad that Je-sus loves me, Je-sus loves e-ven me.
    3. O if there's on-ly one song I can sing When in His beau-ty I see the great King, This shall my song in e-ter-ni-ty be: "O what a won-der, that Je-sus loves me!" I am so glad that Je-sus loves me, Je-sus loves me, Je-sus loves me; I am so glad that Je-sus loves me, Je-sus loves e-ven me." Ephesians 5:25
10. Blessed are the poor in spirit to those who believe this spiritual hymn:
    1. "My Je-sus, I love Thee, I know Thou art mine-For Thee all the fol-lies of sin I re-sign; My gra-cious Re-deem-er, my Sav-ior art Thou: If ev-er I loved Thee, my Je-sus, "tis now. I love Thee, I love Thee, I love Thee, my Lord.
    2. I love Thee be-cause Thou hast first lov-ed me And pur-chased my par-don on Cal-va-ry's tree; I love Thee for wear-ing the thorns on Thy brow: If ev-er I loved Thee, my Je-sus, 'tis now.
    3. I'll love Thee in life, I will love Thee in death, And praise Thee as long as Thou lend-est me breath; And say when the death-dew lies cold on my brow, "If ev-er I loved Thee, my Je-sus, 'tis now."
    4. In man-sions of glo-ry and end-less de-light, I'll ev-er a-dore Thee in heav-en, so bright; I'll sing with the glit-ter-ing crown on my brow, "If ev-er I loved Thee, my Je-sus, 'tis now." I love Thee, I love Thee, I love Thee, my Lord." Psalm 116:1

11. Blessed are the poor in spirit to those who believe this spiritual hymn:
    1. "All to Je-sus I sur-ren-der, All to Him I free-ly give; I will ev-er love and trust Him, In His pres-ence dai-ly live. I sur-ren-der all, I sur-ren- der all. All to Thee, my bless-ed Sav-ior, I sur-ren-der all.
    2. All to Je-sus I sur-ren-der, Hum-bly at His feet I bow, World-ly pleas- ures all for-sak-en, Take me, Je-sus, take me now. I sur-ren-der all, I sur-ren-der all. All to Thee, my bless-ed Sav-ior, I sur-ren-der all.
    3. All to Jesus I sur-ren-der, Make me, Sav-ior, whol-ly Thine; May Thy Ho-ly Spir-it fill me, May I know Thy pow'r di-vine. I sur-ren-der all, I sur-ren-der all. All to Thee, my bless-ed Sav-ior, I sur-ren-der all.
    4. All to Je-sus I sur-ren-der, Lord, I give my—self to Thee; Fill me with Thy love and pow-er, Let Thy bless-ing fall on me. I sur-ren-der all, I sur-ren-der all. All to Thee, my bless-ed Sav-ior, I sur-ren-der all." Romans 6:13
12. Blessed are the poor in spirit to those who believe this spiritual hymn:
    1. "Take up thy cross and fol-low Me." I heard my Mas-ter say: "I gave My life to ran-som thee, Sur-ren-der your all to-day." Wher-ev-er He leads I'll go, Wher-ev-er He leads I'll go, I'll fol-low my Christ who loves me so, Wher-ev-er He leads I'll go.
    2. He drew me clos-er to His side. I sought His will to know, And in that will I now a-bide, Wher-ev-er He leads I'll go. Where-ev-er He leads I'll go, Wher-ev-er He leads I'll go, I'll fol-low my Christ who loves me so, Wher-ev-er He leads I'll go.
    3. It may be thro'the shad-ows dim, Or o'er the storm-y sea, I take the cross and fol-low Him, Wher-ev-er He lead-eth me. Where-ev-er He leads I'll go, Wher-ev-er He leads I'll go, I'll fol-low my Christ who loves me so, Wher-ev-er He leads I'll go.
    4. My heart, my life, my all I bring To Christ who loves me so; He is my Mas-ter, Lord, and King, Wher-ev-er He leads I'll go. Wher- ev-er He leads I'll go, Wher-ev-er He leads I'll go, I 'll fol-low my Christ who loves me so, Wher-ev-er He leads I'll go." Matthew 16:24

Part CDV

Blessed Are The Poor In Spirit. Matthew 5:3

Blessed Means Happy

Poor means meek in spirit. Poor means humble in spirit. Poor means lowly in spirit. Poor means quiet in spirit. Read Matthew 5:3-12, Read also Mark 1:15

Jesus did not say "*rich*" in spirit. Jesus said "*poor*" in spirit.

1. Blessed are the poor in spirit to those who believe this spiritual hymn:
    1. "Have Thine own way, Lord! Have Thine own way! Thou art the Pot-ter, I am the clay. Mold me and make me aft-er Thy will, While I am wait-ing, yield-ed and still.
    2. Have Thine own way, Lord! Have Thine own way! Search me and try me, Mas-ter, to-day! Whit-er than snow, Lord, wash me just now, As in Thy pres-ence hum-bly I bow.
    3. Have Thine own way, Lord! Have Thine own way! Wound-ed and wea-ry, help me, I pray! Pow-er- all pow-er- sure-ly is Thine! Touch me and heal me, Sav-ior di-vine!
    4. Have Thine own way, Lord! Have Thine own way! Hold o'er my be-ing ab-so-lute sway! Fill with Thy Spir-it till all shall see Christ on-ly, al-ways, liv-ing in me! A-men." Isaiah 64:8
2.

   Blessed are the poor in spirit to those who believe this spiritual hymn:
    1. "I can hear my Sav-ior call-ing, I can hear my Sav-ior call-ing, I can hear my Sav-ior call-ing, "Take thy cross and fol-low, fol-low Me."
    2. I'll go with Him thru the judg-ment, I'll go with Him thru the judg-ment, I'll go with Him thru the judg-ment, I'll go with Him, with Him all the way.
    3. He will give me grace and glo-ry, He will give me grace and glo-ry, He will give me grace and glo-ry, And go with me, with me all the way." John 10:27

3.

Blessed are the poor in spirit to those who believe this spiritual hymn:

1. "I have de-cid-ed to fol-low Je-sus, I have de-cid-ed to fol-low Je-sus, I have de-cid-ed to fol-low Je-sus, No turn-ing back, no turn-ing back. I have de-cid-ed to fol-low Him.
2. The world be-hind me, the cross be-fore me; The world be-hind me, the cross be-fore me; The world be-hind me, the cross be-fore me, No turn-ing back, no turn-ing back. I have de-cid-ed to fol-low Him.
3. Tho' none go with me, I still will fol-low, Tho' none go with me, I still will fol-low, Tho' none go with me, I still will fol-low, No turn-ing back, no turn-ing back. I have de-cid-ed to fol-low Him.
4. Will you de-cide now to fol-low Je-sus? Will you de-cide now to fol-low Je-sus? Will you de-cide now to fol-low Je-sus? No turn-ing back, no turn-ing back. I have de-cid-ed to fol-low Him." John 12:26

4. Blessed are the poor in spirit to those who believe this spiritual hymn:
    1. "O-pen our eyes, Lord, we want to see Je-sus, to reach out and touch Him, and say that we love Him. Lord, we want to see Je-sus.
    2. O-pen our ears, Lord, and help us to lis-ten, O-pen our eyes, and say that we love Him. Lord, we want to see Je-sus." Matthew 5:8

5.

Blessed are the poor in spirit to those who believe this spiritual hymn: "To be like Je-sus, to be like Je-sus! My de-sire- to be like Him! All thru life's jour-ney from earth to glo-ry, My de-sire- to be like Him." I Corinthians 11:1

6.

Blessed are the poor in spirit to those who believe this spiritual hymn: "Je-sus, keep me near the cross- There a pre-cious foun-tain, Free to all, a heal-ing stream, Flows from Cal-v'ry's moun-tain. In the corss, in the cross Be my glo-ry ev-er, Till my rap-tured soul shall find Rest, be-yond the riv-er." Galatians 6:14

7.

Blessed are the poor in spirit to those who believe this spiritual hymn:

1. "More a-bout Je-sus would I know, More of His grace to oth-ers show, More of His sav-ing full-ness see, More of His love who died for me. More, more a-bout Je-sus, More, more a-bout Je-sus; More of His sav-ing full-ness see, More of His love who died for me! O to be like Thee, Bless- ed Re-deem-er, I want to be like Je-sus, my Lord.

2. More a-bout Je-sus let me learn, More of His ho-ly will dis-cern; Spir-it of God, my teach-er be, Show-ing the things of Christ to me. More, more a- bout Je-sus, More, more a-bout Je-sus; More of His sav-ing full-ness see, More of His love who died for me! O to be like Thee, Bless-ed Re-deem- er, I want to be like Je-sus, my Lord.
3. More a-bout Je-sus; in His Word, Hold-ing com-mun-ion with my Lord, Hear-ing His voice in ev-'ry line, Mak-ing each faith-ful say-ing mine. More, more a-bout Je-sus, More, more a-bout Je-sus; More of His sav-ing full-ness see, More of His love who died for me! O to be like Thee, Bless- ed Re-deem-er, I want to be like Je-sus, my Lord.
4. More a-bout Je-sus on His throne, Rich-es in glo-ry all His own, More of His king-dom's sure in-crease, More of His com-ing-Prince of Peace. More, more a-bout Je-sus, More, more a-bout Je-sus; More of His sav-ing full-ness see, More of His love who died for me! O to be like Thee, Bless- ed Re-deem-er, I want to be like Je-sus, my Lord." II Peter 3:18

8. Blessed are the poor in spirit to those who believe this spiritual hymn:
   1. "May the mind of Christ my Sav-ior Live in me from day to day, By His love and pow'r con-trol-ling All I do and say.
   2. May the Word of God dwell rich-ly In my heart from hour to hour, So that all may see I tri-umph On-ly thru His pow'r.
   3. May the peace of God my Fa-ther Rule my life in ev-'ry-thing, That I may be calm to com-fort Sick and sor-row-ing.
   4. May the love of Je-sus fill me As the wa-ters fill the sea; Him ex-alt-ing, self a-bas-ing- This is vic-to-ry.
   5. May I run the race be-fore me, Strong and brave to face the foe, Look-ing on-ly un-to Je-sus As I on-ward go.
   6. May His beau-ty rest up-on me As I seek the lost to win, And may they for-get the chan-nel, See-ing on-ly Him." Philippians 2:5
9. Blessed are the poor in spirit to those who believe this spiritual hymn: "I want to be like Je-sus Christ in ev-'ry-thing I do; I want to fol-low in His ways, o-be-dient to His Word; I want to be like Je-sus Christ, my Lord, my God, my all." John 14:15
10. Blessed are the poor in spirit to those who believe this spiritual hymn:
    1. "In my life, Lord, be glo-ri-fied, be glo-ri-fied, In my life, Lord, be glo-ri-fied to-day.

2. In my song, Lord, be glo-ri-fied, be glo-ri-fied, In my song, Lord, be glo-ri-fied to-day.
3. In Your Church, Lord, be glo-ri-fied, be glo-ri-fied, In Your Church, Lord, be glo-ri-fied to-day." Philippians 1:20

11.

Blessed are the poor in spirit to those who believe this spiritual hymn:

1. "Teach me Thy way, O Lord, Teach me Thy way! Thy guid-ing grace afford Teach me Thy way! Help me to walk a-right, More by faith, less by sight; Lead me with heav'n-ly light, Teach me Thy way!
2. When I am sad at heart, Teach me Thy way! When earth-ly joys de-part, Teach me Thy way! In hours of lone-li-ness, In times of dire dis-tress, In fail-ure or suc-cess, Teach me Thy way!
3. When doubts and fears a-rise, Teach me Thy way! When storms o'er spread the skies, Teach me Thy way! Shine thro' the cloud and rain, Thro' sor-row, toil and pain; Make Thou my path-way plain, Teach me Thy way!
4. Long as my life shall last, Teach me Thy way! Wher-e'er my lot be cast, Teach me Thy way! Un-til the race is run, Un-til the jour-ney's done, Un-til the crown is won, Teach me Thy way! A-men." Psalm 27:11

12.

Blessed are the poor in spirit to those who believe this spiritual hymn: "draw nigh to God, and He will draw nigh to you. Draw nigh to God, and He will draw nigh to you. Ac-quaint thy-self with the Lord, ac-quaint they-self with the Lord, Draw nigh to God, and He will draw nigh to you." James 4:8

Part CDVI

Blessed Are The Poor In Spirit. Matthew 5:3

Blessed Means Happy

Poor means meek in spirit. Poor means humble in spirit. Poor means lowly in spirit. Poor means quiet in spirit. Read Matthew 5:3-12, Read also Mark 1:15

Jesus did not say "*rich*" in spirit. Jesus said "*poor*" in spirit.

1. Blessed are the poor in spirit to those who believe this spiritual hymn: "I'm pressing on the up-ward way, New heights I'm gain-ing ev-'ry day- Still pray-ing as I'm on-ward bound, "Lord, plant my feet on high-er ground." Lord, lift me up and let me stand By faith on heav-en's ta-ble—land; A high-er plane than I have found-Lord, plant my feet on high-er ground." Philippians 3:14
2. Blessed are the poor in spirit to those who believe this spiritual hymn:
    1. "My hope is built on noth-ing less Than Je-sus' blood and right-eous-ness; I dare not trust the sweet-est frame, But whol-ly lean on Je-sus' name. On Christ, the sol-id Rock, I stand: All oth-er ground is sink-ing sand.
    2. When dark-ness veils His love-ly face, I rest on His un-chang-ing grace; In ev-'ry high and storm-y gale, My an-chor holds with-in the veil. On Christ, the sol-id Rock, I stand: All oth-er ground is sink-ing sand.
    3. His oath, His cov-e-nant, His blood, Sup-port me in the whelm-ing flood; When all a-round my soul gives way, He then is all my hope and stay. On Christ, the sol-id Rock, I stand: All oth-er ground is sink-ing sand.
    4. When He shall come with trum-pet sound, O may I then in Him be found: Dressed in His right-eous-ness a-lone, Fault-less to stand be-fore the throne. On Christ, the sol-id Rock, I stand: All oth-er ground is sink-ing sand." Matthew 7:24
3.

    Blessed are the poor in spirit to those who believe this spiritual hymn:
    1. "My faith has found a rest-ing place-Not in de-vice or credd: I trust the Ev- er-liv-ing One- His wounds for me shall plead. I need no oth-er ar-gu-ment, I need no oth-er plea; It is e-nough that Je-sus died, And that He died for me.

2. E-nough for me that Je-sus saves-This ends my fear and doubt; A sin-ful soul I come to Him- He'll nev-er cast me out. I need no oth-er ar-gu-ment, I need no oth-er plea; It is e-nough that Je-sus died, And that He died for me.
3. My heart is lean-ing on the Word-The writ-ten Word of God: Sal-va-tion by my Sav-ior's name- Sal-va-tion thru His blood. I need no oth-er ar-gu-ment, I need no other-er plea; It is e-nough that Je-sus died, And that He died for me.
4. My great Phy-si-cian heals the sick- The lost He came to save; For me His pre-cious blood He shed- For me His life He gave. I need no oth-er ar-gu-ment, I need no oth-er plea; It is e-nough that Jesus died, And that He died for me." Hebrews 4:3

4. Blessed are the poor in spirit to those who believe this spiritual hymn:
   1. "I know not why God's won-drous grace To me He hath made known, Nor why, un-wor-thy, Christ in love Re-deemed me for His own. But "I know whom I have be-live-ed, And am per-suad-ed that He is a-ble To keep that which I've com-mit-ted Un-to Him a-gainst that day."
   2. I know not how this sav-ing faith To me He did im-part, Nor how be-live-ing in His Word Wrought peace with-in my heart. But "I know whom I hae be-live-ed, And am per-suad-ed that He is a-ble To keep that which I've com-mit-ted Un-to Him a-gainst that day."
   3. I know not how the Spir-it moves, Con-vinc-ing men of sin, Re-veal-ing Je-sus through the Word, Cre-at-ing faith in Him. But "I know whom I have be-live-ed, And am per-suad-ed that He is a-ble To keep that which I've com-mit-ted Un-to Him a-gainst that day."
   4. I know not when my Lord may come, At night or noon-day fair, Nor if I'll walk the vale with Him, Or "meet Him in the air." But "I know whom I have be-live-ed, And am per-suade-ed that He is a-ble To keep that which I've com-mit-ted Un-to Him a-gainst that day." II Timothy 1:12

5. Blessed are the poor in spirit to those who believe this spiritual hymn:
   1. "The joy of the Lord is my strength, The joy of the Lord is my strength, The joy of the Lord is my strength, The joy of the Lord is my strength.
   2. He heals the bro-ken heart-ed and they cry no more, He heals the bro-ken heart-ed and they cry no mre, He heals the bro-ken heart-ed and they cry no more, The joy of the Lord is my strength.

3. He gives me liv-ing wa-ter and I thirst no more, He gives me liv-ing wa- ter and I thirst no more, He gives me liv-ing wa-ter and I thirst no more, The joy of the lord is my strength." Nehemiah 8:10

6.

Blessed are the poor in spirit to those who believe this spiritual hymn:

1. "I heard the voice of Je-sus say, "Come un-to Me and rest; Lay down, thou wea-ry one, lay down Thy head up-on My breast." I came to Je-sus as I was, Wea-ry, and worn, and sad; I found in Him a rest-ing place, And He has made me glad.
2. I hear the voice of Je-sus say, "Be-hold, I free-ly give The liv-ing wa-ter; thirst-y one, Stoop down, and drink, and live." I came to Je-sus, and I drank Of that life-giv-ing stream; My thirst was quenched, my soul re-vived, And now I live in Him.
3. I heard the voice of Je-sus say, "I am this dark world's Light; Look un-to Me, thy morn shall rise, And all the day be bright." I looked to Je-sus, and I found In Him my Star, my Sun; And in that Light of life I'll walk, Till trav-'ling days are done." Matthew 11:29

7.

Blessed are the poor in spirit to those who believe this spiritual hymn: "On-ly be- lieve, on-ly be-lieve; All things are pos-si-ble, on-ly be-lieve; On-ly be-lieve, on- ly be-lieve; All things are pos-si-ble, on-ly be-lieve." Mark 9:23

8. Blessed are the poor in spirit to those who believe this spiritual hymn:
    1. "There is a balm in Gil-e-ad to make the wound-ed whole; There is a balm in Gil-e-ad to heal th sin-sick soul. Some-times I feel dis-cour- aged, And think my work's in vain, But then the Ho-ly Spir-it Re-vives my soul a-gain.
    2. There is a balm in Gil-e-ad to make the wound-ed whole; There is a balm in Gil-e-ad to heal the sin-sick soul. If you can-not preach like Pe- ter, If you can-not pray like Paul, You can tell the love of Je-sus, And say, "He died for all." Jeremiah 8:22
9. Blessed are the poor in spirit to those who believe this spiritual hymn:
    1. "Tell me the old, old sto-ry Of un-seen things a-bove, Of Je-sus and His glo-ry, Of Je-sus and His love. Tell me the sto-ry sim-ply, As to a lit-tle child, For I am weak and wea-ry, And help-less and de-filed. Tell me the old, old sto-ry, Tell me the old, old sto-ry, Tell me the old, old sto-ry Of Je-sus and His love.

2. Tell me the sto-ry slow-ly, That I may take it in- That won-der-ful re-demp-tion, God's rem-e-dy for sin. Tell me the sto-ry oft-en, For I for- get so soon; The ear-ly dew of morn-ing Has passed a-way at noon. Tell me the old, old sto-ry, Tell me the old, old sto-ry, Tell me the old, old sto-ry Of Je-sus and His love.
3. Tell me the same old sto-ry When you have cause to fear That this world's emp-ty glo-ry is cost-ing me too dear Tell me the sto-ry al-ways, If you would real-ly be, In an-y time of trou-ble, A com-fort-er to me. Tell me the old, old sto-ry, Tell me the old, old sto-ry, Tell me the old, old sto-ry Of Je-sus and His love." I John 4:19

10. Blessed are the poor in spirit to those who believe this spiritual hymn:
    1. "Dear Lord and Fa-ther of man-kind, For-give our fool-ish ways! Re- clothe us in our right-ful mind; In pur-er lives Thy serv-ice find, In deep- er rev-'rence, praise.
    2. In sim-ple trust like theirs who heard, Be-side the Syr-ian Sea, The gra-cious call-ing of the Lord, Let us, like them, with-out a word, Rise up and fol-low Thee.
    3. Drop Thy still dews of qui-et-ness, Till all our striv-ings cease; Take from our souls the strain and stress, And let our or-dered lives con-fess The beau-ty of Thy peace.
    4. Breathe through the heats of our de-sire Thy cool-ness and Thy balm; Let sense be dumb, let flesh re-tire; Speak through the earth-quake, wind, and fire, O still small voice of calm! A-men." Luke 11:2, 4

11\.

Blessed are the poor in spirit to those who believe this spiritual hymn:
1. "I need Thee ev-'ry hour, Most gra-cious Lord; No ten-der voice like Thine Can peace af-ford. I need Thee, O I need Thee; Ev-'ry hour I need Thee! O bless me now, my Sav-ior, I come to Thee. A-men.
2. I need Thee ev-'ry hour, Stay Thou near-by; Temp-ta-tions lose their pow'r When Thou art nigh. I need Thee, O I need Thee; Ev-'ry hour I need Thee! O bless me now, my Sav-ior, I come to Thee. A-men.
3. I need Thee ev-'ry hour, In joy or pain; Come quick-ly, and a-bide, Or life is vain. I need Thee, O I need Thee; Ev-'ry hour I need Thee! O bless me now, my Sav-ior, I come to Thee. A-men.

4. I need Thee ev-'ry hour, Teach me Thy will, And Thy rich prom-is-es In me ful-fill. I need Thee, O I need Thee; Ev-'ry hour I need Thee! O bless me now, my Sav-ior, I come to Thee. A-men." Psalm 86:1

12.

Blessed are the poor in spirit to those who believe this spiritual hymn: "Lord, listen to your chil-dren pray-ing, Lord, sent Your Spir-it in this place; Lord, lis-ten to Your chil-dren pray-ing, Send us love, send us pow'r, send us grace. Grace!" I John 5:14

PART CDVII

Blessed Are The Poor In Spirit. Matthew 5:3

Blessed Means Happy

Poor means meek in spirit. Poor means humble in spirit. Poor means lowly in spirit. Poor means quiet in spirit. Read Matthew 5:3-12, Read also Mark 1:15

Jesus did not say "*rich*" in spirit. Jesus said "*poor*" in spirit.

1. Blessed are the poor in spirit to those who believe this spiritual hymn:
    1. "I must tell Je-sus all of my tri-als, I can-not bear these bur-dens a-lone; In my dis-tress He kind-ly will help me, He ev-er loves and cares for His own. I must tell Je-sus! I must tell Je-sus! I can-not bear my bur-dens a- lone; I must tell Je-sus! I must tell Je-sus! Je-sus can help me, Je-sus a- lone.
    2. I must tell Je-sus all of my trou-bles, He is a kind, com-pas-sion-ate friend; If I but ask Him, He will de-liv-er, Make of my trou-bles quick-ly an end. I must tell Je-sus! I must tell Je-sus! I can-not bear my bur-dens a- lone; I must tell Je-sus! I must tell Je-sus! Je-sus can help me, Je-sus a- lone.
    3. O how the world to e-vil al-lures me! O how my heart is tempt-ed to sin! I must tell Je-sus, and He will help me O-ver the world the vic-t'ry to win. I must tell Je-sus! I must tell Je-sus! I can-not bear my bur-dens a-lone; I must tell Je-sus! I must tell Je-sus! Je-sus can help me, Je-sus a-lone." Hebrews 2:18
2.

    Blessed are the poor in spirit to those who believe this spiritual hymn:
    1. "I have a Sav-ior, He's plead-ing in glo-ry, A dear, lov-ing Sav-ior tho' earth-friends be few; And now He is watch-ing in ten-der-ness o'ver me, But oh, that my Sav-ior were your Sav-ior, too! For you I am pray-ing, For you I am pray-ing, For you I am pray-ing, I'm pray-ing for you.
    2. I have a Fa-ther; to me He has giv-en A hope for e-ter-ni-ty, bless-ed and true; And soon He will call me to meet Him in heav-en, But oh, that He'd let me bring you with me too! For you I am pray-ing, For you I am pray-ing, For you I am pray-ing, I'm pray-ing for you.
    3. I have a robe; 'tis re-splen-dent in white-ness, A-wait-ing in glo-ry my won-der-ing view; Oh, when I re-ceive it all shin-ing in brightness, Dear friend,

could I see you re-ceiv-ing one too! For you I am pray-ing, For you I am pray-ing, For you I am pray-ing, I'm pray-ing for you.

4. When He has found you, tell oth-ers the sto-ry, That my lov-ing Sav-ior is your Sav-ior, too; Then pray that your Savior may bring them to glo-ry, And prayer will be an-swered, 'twas an-swered for you! For you I am pray-ing, For you I am pray-ing, For you I am pray-ing, I'm pray-ing for you." I Timothy 2:3-4

3.

Blessed are the poor in spirit to those who believe this spiritual hymn: "Search me, O God, and know my heart to-day! Try me, O Fa-ther and know my thoughts I pray, See if there be some wick-ed way in me; Lead me, O Lord, in Your ev-er-last-ing way!" Psalm139:23

4. Blessed are the poor in spirit to those who believe this spiritual hymn:
    1. "What a Friend we have in Je-sus, All our sins and griefs to bear! What a priv-i-lege to car-ry Ev-ery-thing to God in prayer! O what peace we of-ten for-feit, O what need-less pain we bear, All be-cause we do not car-ry Ev-very-thing to God in prayer!
    2. Have we tri-als and temp-ta-tions? Is there trou-ble an-y-where? We should nev-er be dis-cour-aged, Take it to the Lord in prayer. Can we find a friend so faith-ful Who will all our sor-rows share? Je-sus knows our ev-ery weak-ness, Take it to the Lord in prayer.
    3. Are we weak and heav-y—la-den, Cum-bered with a load of care? Pre-cious Sav-ior, still our Ref-uge- Take it to the Lord in prayer. Do thy friends de-spise, for-sake thee? Take it to the Lord in prayer; In His arms He'll take and shield thee, Thou wilt find a sol-ace there." Philippians 4:6

5.

Blessed are the poor in spirit to those who believe this spiritual hymn:

1. "Pure and ho-ly I would be, wor-thy of your love for me. Teach me while Your light is clear, change me while my heart is near. Ho-ly, ho-ly, ho-ly Lord. ho-ly Lord. ho-ly Lord. ho-ly Lord.
2. You are great and I am small, You are King and God of all. You are wise in all You do, Lord I put my trust in You. Ho-ly, ho-ly, ho-ly Lord. ho-ly Lord. ho-ly Lord. ho-ly Lord." Leviticus 19:2

6.

Blessed are the poor in spirit to those who believe this spiritual hymn:

1. "Search me, O God, and know my heart to-day; Try me, O Sav-ior know my thoughts, I pray. See if there be some wick-ed way in me; Cleanse me from ev-'ry sin and set me free.
2. I praise Thee, Lord, for cleans-ing me from sin; Ful-fill Thy Word and make me pure with-in. Fill me with fire where once I burned with shame; Grant my de-sire to mag-ni-fy Thy name.
3. Lord, take my life and make it whol-ly Thine; Fill my poor heart with Thy great love di-vine. Take all my will, my pas-sion, self, and pride; I now sur-ren-der; Lord, in me a-bide.
4. O Ho-ly Ghost, re-viv-al comes from Thee; Send a re-viv-al, start the work in me. Thy Word de-clares Thou wilt sup-ply our need; For bless- ings now, O Lord, I hum-bly plead. A-men." Psalm 139:23

7.

Blessed are the poor in spirit to those who believe this spiritual hymn:

1. "Take time to be ho-ly, Speak of-ten with God; Find rest in Him al-ways And feed on His Word. Make friends of God's child-dren; Help those who are weak, For-get-ting in noth-ing His bless-ing to seek.
2. Take time to be ho-ly, The world rush-es on; Much time spend in se-cret With Je-sus a-lone. By look-ing to Je-sus, Like Him thou shalt be; Thy friends in thy con-duct His like-ness shall see.
3. Take time to be ho-ly, Let Him be thy guide, And run not be-fore Him, What-ev-er be-tide. In joy or in sor-row, Still fol-low thy Lord, And, look-ing to Je-sus, Still trust in His Word. Amen." Hebrews 12:14

8. Blessed are the poor in spirit to those who believe this spiritual hymn:
   1. "It may not be on the mountain's height Or o-ver the storm-y sea, It may not be at the bat-tle's front My Lord will have need of me; But if by a still, small voice He calls To paths I do not know, I'll an-swer, dear Lord, with my hand in Thine, I'll go where You want me to go. I'll go where You want me to go, dear Lord, O'er mountain or plain or sea;
   2. Per-haps to-day there are lov-ing words Which Je-sus would have me speak, There may be now, in the paths of sins, Some wand'rer whom I should seekl O Sav-ior, if Thou wilt be my Guide, Tho dark and rug-ged the way, My voice shall ech-o the mes-sage sweet, I'll say what You want me to say. I'll go where You want me to go, dear Lord, O'er mountain or plain or sea;

3. There's sure-ly somewhere a low-ly place In earth's har-vest fields so wide, Where I may la-bor thru life's short day For Je-sus the Cru-ci-fied; So, trust-ing my all un-to Thy care- I know Thou lov-est me- I'll do Thy will with a heart sin-cere, I'll be what You want me to be. I'll go where You want me to go, dear Lord, O'er mountain or plain or sea;" Jeremiah 1:7

9. Blessed are the poor in spirit to those who believe this spiritual hymn: "I will serve Thee be-cause I love Thee, You have giv-en life to me; I was noth-ing be- fore You found me, You have giv-en life to me. Heart-aches, bro-ken piec-es, Ru- ined lives are why You died on Cal-vary; Your touch was what I longed for, You have giv-en life to me." Colossians 3:24
10. Blessed are the poor in spirit to those who believe this spiritual hymn:
    1. "God for-gave my sin in Je-sus' anme, I've been born a-gain in Je-sus' name; And in Je-sus' name I come to you To share His love as He told me to: He said, "Free-ly, free-ly you have re-ceived-Free-ly, free-ly give; Go in My name and, be-cause you be-lieve, Others will know that I live."
    2. All pow'r is giv'n in Je-sus' name, In earth and heav'n in Je-sus' name; And in Je-sus' name I come to you To share His pow'r as He told me to: He said, "Free-ly, free-ly you have re-ceived-Free-ly, free-ly give; Go in My name and, be-cause you be-lieve, Others will know that I live." Matthew 10:8
11. Blessed are the poor in spirit to those who believe this spiritual hymn: "I will sing of the mer-cies of the Lord for-ev-er, I will sing, I will sing, I will sing of the mer- cies of the Lord. With my mouth will I make known Thy faith-ful-ness, Thy faith- ful-ness, With my mouth will I make known Thy faith-ful-ness to all gen-er-a- tions. I will." Psalm 89:1
12. Blessed are the poor in spirit to those who believe this spiritual hymn: "Gen-tle Shep-herd, come and lead us, For we need You to help us find our way Gen-tle Shep-herd, come and feed us, For we need Your strength from day to day. There's no oth-er we can turn to Who can help us face an-oth-er day; Gen-tle Shep-heard, come and lead us, For we need You to help us find our way." Isaiah 40:11

Part CDVIII

Blessed Are The Poor In Spirit. Matthew 5:3

Blessed Means Happy

Poor means meek in spirit. Poor means humble in spirit. Poor means lowly in spirit. Poor means quiet in spirit. Read Matthew 5:3-12, Read also Mark 1:15

Jesus did not say "*rich*" in spirit. Jesus said "*poor*" in spirit.

1. Blessed are the poor in spirit to those who believe this spiritual hymn:
    1. "Pre-cious Lord, take my hand, Lead me on, help me stand- I am tired, I am weak, I am worn; Thro' the storm, thro' the night, Lead me on to the light- Take my hand, pre-cious Lord, lead me home.
    2. When my way grows drear, Pre-cious Lord, lin-ger near- When my life is al-most gone; Hear my cry, hear my call, Hold my hand lest I fall- Take my hand, pre-cious Lord, lead me home." Isaiah 41:13
2.

   Blessed are the poor in spirit to those who believe this spiritual hymn:
    1. "In His time (in His time), in His time (in His time); He makes all things beau-ti-ful in His time (in His time). Lord, please show me ev-'ry day As You're teach-ing me Your way, That You do just what You say in Your time (in Your time).
    2. In Your time (in Your time), in Your time (in Your time); You make all things beau-ti-ful in Your time (in Your time). Lord, my life to You I bring; May each song I have to sing Be to You a love-ly thing in Your time (in Your time)." Ecclesiastes 3:11
3.

   Blessed are the poor in spirit to those who believe this spiritual hymn: "Cov-er me, Lord, with Your pres-ence, Cov-er me, Lord, with Your right-eous-ness, Cov- er me, Lord, with Your ho-li-ness, Lord Je-sus, cov-er me." Romans 13:14
4. Blessed are the poor in spirit to those who believe this spiritual hymn: "Sweet-ly, Lord, have we hard Thee call-ing, "Come, fol-low Me!" And we see where Thy foot-prints fall-ing, Lead us to Thee. Foot-prints of Je-sus that make the path-way glow; We will fol-low the steps of Je-sus wher-e'er they go." Luke 5:11

5.

Blessed are the poor in spirit to those who believe this spiritual hymn:

1. "I heard an old, old sto-ry, how a Sav-ior came from glo-ry, How He gave His life on Cal-va-ry to save a wretch like me: I heard a-bout His groan-ing, of His pre-cious blood's a-ton-ing, Then I re-pent-ed of my sins and won the vic-to-ry. O vic-to-ry in Je-sus, my Sav-ior, for-ev-er, He sought me and bo't me with His re-deem-ing blood; He loved me ere I knew Him, and all my love is due Him, He plunged me to vic-to-ry be-neath the cleans-ing flood.
2. I heard a-bout His heal-ing, of His cleans-ing pow'r re-veal-ing, How He made the lame to walk a-gain and caused the blind to see; And then I cried, "Dear Je-sus, come and heal my bro-ken spir-it," And some-how Je-sus came and bro't to me the vic-to-ry. O vic-to-ry in Je-sus, my Sav- ior, for-ev-er, He sought me and bo't me with His re-deem-ing blood, He loved me ere I knew Him, and all my love is due Him, He plunged me to vic-to-ry be-neath the cleans-ing flood.
3. I heard a-bout a man-sion He has built for me in glo-ry, And I heard a- bout the sreets of gold be-yond the crys-tal sea; A-bout the an-gels sing- ing, and the old re-demp-tion sto-ry, And some sweet day I'll sing up there the song of vic-to-ry. O vic-to-ry in Je-sus, my Sav-ior, for-ev-er, He sought me and bo't me with His re-deem-ing blood, He loved me ere I knew Him, and all my love is due Him, He plunged me to vic-to-ry be- neath the cleans-ing flood." I Corinthians 15:57

6.

Blessed are the poor in spirit to those who believe this spiritual hymn: "You're my broth-er, you're my sis-ter, so take me by the hand. To-geth-er we will work un-til He comes. There's no foe that can de-feat us when we're walk-ing side by side; As long as there is love, we will stand." Ephesians 6:14

7.

Blessed are the poor in spirit to those who believe this spiritual hymn: "Stand up, stand up for Je-sus, Ye sol-diers of the cross, Lift high His roy-al ban-ner, It must not suf-fer loss; From vic-tory un-to vic-tory His ar-my shall He lead, Till ev-ery foe is van-quished And Christ is Lord in-deed." I Corinthians 16:13

8. Blessed are the poor in spirit to those who believe this spiritual hymn: "On-ward, Chris-tian sol-diers, March-ing as to war, With the cross of Je-sus Go-ing on

be- fore! Christ, the roy-al Mas-ter, Leads a-gainst the foe; For-ward in-to bat-tle See His ban-ners go! Onward, ye sol-diers, march-ing as to war, With the cross of Je- sus go-ing on be-fore, A-men." II Corinthians 2:14

9. Blessed are the poor in spirit to those who believe this spiritual hymn: "I am a sol- dier of the cross! A fol-l'wer of the pre-cious Lamb." II Timothy 2:4
10. Blessed are the poor in spirit to those who believe this spiritual hymn: "Stand up, stand up for Je-sus, Ye sol-diers of the cross; Lift high His roy-al ban-ner, It must not suf-fer loss: From vic-t'ry un-to vic-t'ry His ar-my shall He lead, Till ev-ery foe is van-quished And Christ is Lord in-deed. Stand up for Je-sus, Ye sol-diers of the cross; Lift high His roy-al ban-ner, It must not, it must not suf-fer loss." I Corinthians 16:13
11.

    Blessed are the poor in spirit to those who believe this spiritual hymn:
    1. "In heav-en-ly ar-mor we'll en-ter the land, the battle belongs to the Lord! No wea-pon that's fashioned against us will stand, the bat-tle be-longs to the Lord! We sing glo-ry, hon-or, pow-er and strength to the Lord. We sing glo-ry, hon-or, power and strength to the Lord!
    2. When the pow-er of dark-ness comes in like a flood, the battle belongs to the Lord! He's raised up a stan-dard, the pow'r of His blood, the bat-tle be-longs to the Lord! We sing glo-ry, hon-or, power and strength to the Lord!" II Chronicle 20:15
12.

    Blessed are the poor in spirit to those who believe this spiritual hymn: "Re-joice in the Lord al-ways, a-gain I say, re-joice! Re-joice in the Lord al-ways, a-gain I say, re-joice! Re-joice, re-joice, a-gain I say, re-joice! Re-joice, re-joice, a-gain I say, re-joice!" Philippians 3:1

PART CDIX

Blessed Are The Poor In Spirit. Matthew 5:3

Blessed Means Happy

Poor means meek in spirit. Poor means humble in spirit. Poor means lowly in spirit. Poor means quiet in spirit. Read Matthew 5:3-12, Read also Mark 1:15

Jesus did not say "*rich*" in spirit. Jesus said "*poor*" in spirit.

1. Blessed are the poor in spirit to those who believe this spiritual hymn: "Thou wilt keep him in per-fect peace whose mind is stayed on Thee." When the sha-dows come and dark-ness falls, He giv-eth in-ward peace. O He is the on-ly per-fect rest-ing place, He giv-eth per-fect peace! "Thou wilt keep him in per-fect peace whose mind is stayed on Thee." Isaiah 26:3
2. Blessed are the poor in spirit to those who believe this spiritual hymn: "When peace like a riv-er at-tend-eth my way, When sor-rows like sea-bil-lows roll; What-ev-er my lot, Thou hast taught me to say, "It is well, it is well with my soul." It is well with my soul, It is well, it is well with my soul." Psalm 103:2
3. Blessed are the poor in spirit to those who believe this spiritual hymn:
    1. "O what a won-der-ful, won-der-ful day- Day I will nev-er for-get; Aft-er I'd wan-dered in dark-ness a-way, Je-sus my Sav-ior I met. O what a ten-der, com-pas-sion-ate friend- He met the need of my heart; Shad-ows dis-pel-ling, With joy I am tell-ing, He made all the dark-ness de-part! Heav-en came down and glo-ry filled my soul, When at the cross the Sav-ior made me whole; My sins were washed a-way And my night was turned to day- Heav-en came down and glo-ry filled my soul!
    2. Born of the Spir-it with life from a-bove In-to God's fam-ily di-vine, Jus-ti-fied ful-ly thro' Cal-va-ry's love, O what a stand-ing is mine! And the trans-ac-tion so quick-ly was made When as a sin-ner I came, Took of the of-fer Of grace He did prof-fer- He saved me, O praise His dear name! Heav-en came down and glo-ry filled my soul, When at the cross the Sav-ior made me whole; My sins were washed a-way And my night was turned to day- Heaven came down and glo-ry filled my soul!

3. Now I've a hope that will sure-ly en-dure Aft-er the pass-ing of time; I have a fu-ture in heav-en for sure, There in those man-sions sub-lime. And it's be-cause of that won-der-ful day When at the cross I be-lieved; Rich- es e-ter-nal And bless-ings su-per-nal From His pre-cious hand I re- ceived. Heav-en came down and glo-ry filled my soul, When at the cross the Sav-ior made me whoe; My sins were washed a-way And my night was turned to day- Heaven came down and glo-ry filled my soul!" Galatians 6:15

4. Blessed are the poor in spirit to those who believe this spiritual hymn:
   1. "I've got peace like a riv-er, I've got peace like a riv-er, I've got peace like a riv-er in my soul, I've got peace like a riv-er, I've got peace like a riv-er. I've got peace like a riv-er in my soul. (my soul.)
   2. I've got love like an o-cean, I've got love like an o-cean, I've got love like an o-cean in my soul, I've got love like an o-cean, I've got love like an o-cean, I've got love like an o-cean in my soul. (my soul.)
   3. I've got joy like a foun-tain, I've got joy like a foun-tain, I've got joy like a foun-tain in my soul, I've got joy like a foun-tain, I've got joy like a foun-tain, I've got joy like a foun-tain in my soul. (my soul.)" Philippians 4:7
5. Blessed are the poor in spirit to those who believe this spiritual hymn:
   1. "There is sun-shine in my soul to-day, More glo-ri-ous and bright Than glows in an-y earth-ly sky, For Je-sus is my light. O there's sun-shine, bless-ed sun-shine, When the peace-ful, hap-py mo-ments roll; When Je-sus shows His smil-ing face, There is sun-shine in my soul.
   2. There is mu-sic in my soul to-day, A car-ol to my King, And Je-sus, lis- ten-ing can hear The songs I can-not sing. O there's sun-shine, bless-ed sun-shine, When the peace-ful, hap-py mo-ments roll; When Je-sus shows His smil-ing face, There is sun-shine in my soul.
   3. There is spring-time in my soul to-day, For when the Lord is near The dove of peace sings in my heart, The flow'rs of grace ap-pear. O there's sun-shine, bless-ed sun-shine, When the peace-ful, hap-py mo-ments roll; When Je-sus shows His smil-ing face, There is sun-shine in my soul.
   4. There is glad-ness in my soul to-day, And hope and love and praise, For bless-ings which He gives me now, For joys in fu-ture days. O there's sun-shine, When the peace-ful, hap-py mo-ments roll; When Je-sus shows His smil-ing face, There is sun-shine in my soul."
   II Corinthians 4:6

6. Blessed are the poor in spirit to those who believe this spiritual hymn:
    1. "Shack-led by a heav-y bur-den, 'Neath a load of guilt and shame; Then the hand of Je-sus touched me, And now I am no long-er the same. He touched me, O, He touched me, And O, the joy that floods my soul; Some-thing hap-pened, and now I know, He touched me and made me whole.
    2. Since I met this bless-ed Sav-ior, Since He cleansed and made me whole; I will nev-er cease to praise Him, I'll shout it while e-ter-ni-ty rolls. He touched me, O, He touched me, And O, the joy that floods my soul; Some-thing hap-pened, and now I know, He touched me and made me whole." Matthew 8:3
7. Blessed are the poor in spirit to those who believe this spiritual hymn:
    1. "I was sink-ing deep in sin, Far from the peace-ful shore, Ver-y deep-ly stained with-in, Sink-ing to rise no mre; But the Mas-ter of the sea Heard my de-spair-ing cry, From the wa-ters lift-ed me, Now safe am I. Love lift-ed me! Love lift-ed me! When noth-ing else could help, Love lift-ed me. Love lift-ed me.
    2. All my heart to Him I give, Ev-er to Him I'll cling, In His bless-ed presence live, Ev-er His prais-es sing; Love so might-y and so true Mer-ts my soul's best songs; Faith-ful, lov-ing ser-vice, too, To Him be-longs. Love lift-ed me! Love lift-ed me! When noth-ing else could help, Love lift-ed me. Love lift-ed me.
    3. Souls in dan-ger, look a-bove, Je-sus com-plete-ly saves; He will lift you by His love Out of the an-gry waves; He's the Mas-ter of the sea, Bil-lows His will o-bey; He your Sav-ior wants to be, Be saved to-day. Love lift-ed me! Love lift-ed me! When noth-ing else could help, Love lift-ed me. Love lift-ed me." I John 4:10
8. Blessed are the poor in spirit to those who believe this spiritual hymn: "Through it all, Through it all, I've learned to trust in Je-sus, I've learned to trust in God' Through it all, Through it all, I've learned to de-pend up- on His Word." I Peter 1:6-7
9. Blessed are the poor in spirit to those who believe this spiritual hymn:
    1. "I will sing the won-drous sto-ry Of the Christ who died for me- How He left His home in glo-ry For the cross of Cal-va-ry. Yes, I'll sing the won- drous sto-ry Of the Christ who died for me, Sing it with the saints in glo-ry, Gath-ered by the crys-tal sea.

2. I was lost but Je-sus found me-Found the sheep that went a-stray, Threw His lov-ing arms a-round me, Drew me back in-to His way. Yes, I'll sing the won-drous sto-ry Of the Christ who died for me, Sing it with the saints in glo-ry, Gath-ered by the crys-tal sea.
3. Days of dark-ness still come o'ver me, Sor-row's paths I oft-en tread; But the Sav-ior still is with me-By His hand I'm safe-ly led. Yes, I'll sing the won-drous sto-ry Of the Christ who died for me, Sing it with the saints in glo-ry, Gath-ered by the crys-tal sea.
4. He will keep me till the riv-er Rolls its wa-ters at my feet; Then He'll bear me safe-ly o-ver, Where the loved ones I shall meet. Yes, I'll sing the won- drous sto-ry Of the Christ who died for me, Sing it with the saints in glo-ry, Gath-ered by the crys-tal sea." Revelation 15:2-3

10. Blessed are the poor in spirit to those who believe this spiritual hymn:
    1. "Je-sus is all the world to me, My life, my joy, my all; He is my strength from day to day, With-out Him I would fall. When I am sad to Him I go, No other-er one can cheer me so: When I am sad He makes me glad, He's my Friend.
    2. Je-sus is all the world to me, My Friend in tri-als sore; I go to Him for bless-ings, and He gives them o'er and o'er. He sends the sun-shine and the rain, He sens the har-vest's gold-en grain; Sun-shine and rain, har-vest of grain, He's my Friend.
    3. Je-sus is all the world to me, And true to Him I'll be; O, how could I this Friend de-ny, When He's so true to me? Fol-low-ing Him I know I'm right, He watch-es o'er me day and night; Fol-low-ing Him by day and night, He's my Friend.
    4. Je-sus is all the world to me, I want no bet-ter friend; I trust Him now, I'll trust Him when Life's fleet-ing days shall end. Beau-ti-ful life with such a Friend; Beau-ti-ful life that has no end; E-ter-nal life, e-ter-nal joy, He's my Friend." Philippians 1:21
11. Blessed are the poor in spirit to those who believe this spiritual hymn:
    1. "Je-sus my Lord will love me for-ev-er, From Him no pow'r of e-vil can sev-er, He gave His life to ran-som my soul, Now I be-long to Him; Now I be-long to Je-sus, Je-sus be-longs to me, Not for the years of time a-lone, But for e-ter-ni-ty.

2. Once I was lost in sin's deg-ra-da-tion, Je-sus came down to bring me sal-va-tion, Lift-ed me up from sor-row and shame, Now I be-long to Him; Now I be-long to Je-sus, Je-sus be-longs to me, Not for the years of time a- lone, But for e-ter-ni-ty.
3. Joy floods my soul for Je-sus has saved me, Freed me from sin that long had en-slaved me, His pre-cious bleed He gave to re-deem, Now I be-long to Him; Now I be-long to Je-sus, Je-sus be-longs to me, Not for the years of time a-lone, But for e-ter-ni-ty." Romans 14:8

12. Blessed are the poor in spirit to those who believe this spiritual hymn:
    1. "O, how He loves you and me. O, how he loves you and me; He gave His life, what more could He give? O, how He loves you; O, how He loves me; O, how He loves you and me! O, how He loves you; O, how He loves you and me, you and me.
    2. Je-sus to Cal-v'ry did go, His love for man-kind to show; What He did there brought hope from de-spair: O, how He loves you; O, how He loves me; O, how He loves you and me! O, how He loves me; O, how He loves you and me, you and me." John 15:9

Part CDX

Blessed Are The Poor In Spirit. Matthew 5:3

Blessed Means Happy

Poor means meek in spirit. Poor means humble in spirit. Poor means lowly in spirit. Poor means quiet in spirit. Read Matthew 5:3-12, Read also Mark 1:15

Jesus did not say "*rich*" in spirit. Jesus said "*poor*" in spirit.

1. Blessed are the poor in spirit to those who believe this spiritual hymn:
   1. "What a won-der-ful change in my life has been wrought Since Je-sus came in-to my heart! I have light in my soul for which long I have sought, Since Je-sus came in-to my heart! Since Je-sus came in-to my heart, Since Je-sus came in-to my heart, Floods of joy o'er my soul like the sea bil- lows roll, Since Je-sus came in-to my heart.
   2. I have ceased from my wan-d'ring and go-ing a-stray, Since Je-sus came in-to my heart! And my sins, which were man-y, are all washed a-way, Since Je-sus came in-to my heart! Since Je-sus came in-to my heart,
      Since Je-sus came in-to my hearts, Floods of joy o'er my soul like the sea bil-lows roll, Since Je-sus came in-to my heart.
   3. I shall go there to dwell in that Cit-y, I know, since Je-sus came in-to my heart! And I'm hap-py, so hap-py, as on-ward I go, Since Je-sus came in- to my heart! Since Je-sus came in-to my heart, Since Je-sus came in-to my hearts, Floods of joy o'er my soul like the sea bil-lows roll, Since Je- sus came in-to my heart." II Corinthians 5:17
2.

   Blessed are the poor in spirit to those who believe this spiritual hymn:
   1. "Since I start-ed for the King-dom, Since my life He con-trols, Since I gave my heart to Je-sus, The long-er I serve Him, the sweet-er He grows. The long-er I serve Him the sweet-er He grows, The more that I love Him, more love He be-stows; Each day is like heav-en, my heart o- ver-flows, The long-er I serve Him the sweet-er He grows.
   2. Ev-ery need He is sup-ply-ing, Plen-teous grace He be-stows; Ev-ery day my way gets bright-er, The long-er I serve Him, the sweet-er He grows.

The long-er I serve Him the sweet-er He grows, The more that I love Him, more love He be-stows; Each day is like heav-en, my heart o- ver-flows, The long-er I serve Him the sweet-er He grows." Romans 1:9

3.

Blessed are the poor in spirit to those who believe this spiritual hymn: "Something beau-ti-ful, some-thing good; All my con-fu-sion He un-der-stood; All I had to of-fer Him was bro-ken-ness and strife, But He made some-thing beau-ti-ful of my life." Luke 15:24

4. Blessed are the poor in spirit to those who believe this spiritual hymn: "Yes-ter- day He died for me, yes-ter-day, yes-ter-day, Yes-ter-day He died for me, yes-ter- day, Yes-ter-day He died for me, died for me- This is his-to-ry. To-day He lives for me, to-day, to-day, To-day He lives for me, to-day, To-day He lives for me, lives for me- This is vic-to-ry. To-mor-row He comes for me, He comes, He comes, To-mor-row He comes for me. He comes, Tomorrow He comes for me, comes for me-This is mys-ter-y. O friend, do you know Him? Know Him? Know Him? O friend, do you know Him? Know Him? O friend, do you know Him? Do you know Him? Je-sus Christ the Lord, Je-sus Christ the Lord, Je-sus Christ the Lord!" I Corinthians 15:3-4

5.

Blessed are the poor in spirit to those who believe this spiritual hymn:

1. "My Fa-ther is om-ni-po-tent, And that you can't de-ny; A God of might and mir-a-cles- 'Tis writ-ten in the sky. It took a mir-a-cle to put the stars in place, It took a mir-a-cle to hang the world in space; But when He saved my soul, Cleansed and made me whole, It took a mir-a-cle of love and grace.
2. Tho here His glo-ry has been shown, We still can't ful-ly see The won-ders of His might, His throne- 'Twill take e-ter-ni-ty. It took a mir-a-cle to hang the world in space; But when He saved my soul, Cleansed and made me whole, It took a mir-a-cle of love and grace.
3. The Bi-ble tells us of His pow'r And wis-dom all way thru, And ev-'ry lit-tle bird and flow'r Are tes-ti-mo-nies. It took a mir-a-cle to hang the world in space; But when He saved my soul, Cleansed and made me whole, It took a mir-a-cle of love and grace." Titus 2:11

6.

Blessed are the poor in spirit to those who believe this spiritual hymn:

1. "When I saw the cleans-ing foun-tain, O-pen wide for all my sin, I o-beyed the Spir-it's woo-ing When He said, "Wilt thou be clean?" I will praise Him! I will praise Him! Praise the Lamb for sin-ners slain; Give Him glo-ry, all ye peo-ple, For His blood can wash a-way each stain.
2. Tho' the way seems straight and nar-row, All I claimed was swept a-way; My am-bi-tions, plans and wish-es At my feet in ash-es lay. I will praise Him! I will praise Him! Praise the Lamb for sin-ners slain; Give Him glo-ry, all ye peo-ple, For His blood can wash a-way each stain.
3. Bless-ed be the name of Je-sus! I'm so glad He took me in; He's for-giv-en my trans-gres-sions, He has cleansed my heart from sin. I will praise Him! I will praise Him! Praise the Lamb for sin-ners slain; Give Him glo-ry, all ye peo-ple, For His blood can wash a-way each stain.
4. Glo-ry, glo-ry to the Fa-ther! Glo-ry, glo-ry to the Son! Glo-ry, glo-ry to the Spir-it! Glo-ry to the Three in One! I will praise Him! I will praise Him! Praise the Lamb for sin-ners slain; Give Him glo-ry, all ye peo-ple, For His blood can wash a-way each stain." Revelation 1:5

7.

Blessed are the poor in spirit to those who believe this spiritual hymn:

1. "Down at the cross where my Sav-ior died, Down where for cleans-ing from sin I cried, There to my heart was the blood ap-plied; Glo-ry to His name! Glo-ry to His name, Glo-ry to His name; There to my heart was the blood ap-plied; Glo-ry to His name!
2. I am so won-drous-ly saved from sin, Je-sus so sweet-ly a-bides with-in, There at the cross where He took me in; Glo-ry to His name! Glo-ry to His name, Glo-ry to His name; There to my heart was the blood ap-plied; Glo- ry to His name!
3. O pre-cious foun-tain that saves from sin, I am so glad I have en-tered in; There Je-sus saves me and keeps me clean; Glo-ry to His name! Glo-ry to His name, Glo-ry to His name; There to my heart was the blood ap-plied; Glo-ry to His name!
4. Come to this foun-tain so rich and sweet; Cast your poor soul at the Sav-ior's feet; Plunge in to-day and be made com-plete; Glo-ry to His name! Glo-ry to His name, Glo-ry to His name; There to my heart was the blood ap-plied; Glo-ry to His name!" Hebrews 9:22

8. Blessed are the poor in spirit to those who believe this spiritual hymn:
    1. "I would love to tell you what I think of Je-sus Since I found in Him a friend so strong and true; I would tell you how He chang'd my life com-plete-ly- He did some-thing that no other-er friend could do. No one ev-er cared for me like Je-sus, There's no oth-er friend so kind as He; No one else could take the sin and dark-ness from me- O how much He cared for me!
    2. All my life was full of sin when Je-sus found me, All my heart was full of mis-er-y and woe; Je-sus placed His strong and lov-ing arms a-round me, And He led me in the way I ought to go. No one ev-er cared for me like Je- sus, There's no oth-er friend so kind as He; No one else could take the sin and dark-ness from me- O how much He cared for me!
    3. Ev-'ry day He comes to me with new as-sur-ance, More and more I un-der-stand His words of love; But I'll nev-er know just why He came to save me, Till some day I see His bless-ed face a-bove. No one ev-er cared for me like Je-sus, There's no oth-er friend so kind as He; No one else could take the sin and dark-ness from me- O how much He cared for me!"

    Psalm 144:3
9. Blessed are the poor in spirit to those who believe this spiritual hymn:
    1. "There is a name I love to hear, I love to sing its worth; It sounds like mu-sic in my ear, The sweet-est name on earth. O, how I love Je-sus, O, how I love Je-sus, O, how I love Je-sus- Be-cause He first loved me!
    2. It tells me of a Sav-ior's love, who died to set me free; It tells me of His pre-cious blood, The sin-ner's per-fect plea. O, how I love Je-sus, O, how I love Je-sus, O, how I love Je-sus- Be-cause He first loved me!
    3. It tells me what my Fa-ther hath In store for ev-'ry day, And, tho I tread a dark-some path, Yields sun-shine all the way. O, how I love Je-sus, O, how I love Je-sus, O, how I love Je-sus- Be-cause He first loved me!
    4. It tells of One whose lov-ing heart Can fell my deep-est woe, Who in each sor-row bears a part That none can bear be-low. O, how I love Je-sus, O, how I love Je-sus, O, how I love Je-sus- Be-cause He first loved me!"

    I Peter 1:8
10. Blessed are the poor in spirit to those who believe this spiritual hymn:
    1. "I've found a Friend who is all to me, His love is ev-er true; I love to tell how He lift-ed me, And what His grace can do for you. Saved by His pow'r

di-vine, Saved to new life sub-lime! Life now is sweet and my joy is complete, For I'm saved, saved, saved!

2. He saves me from ev-ery sin and harm, Se-cures my soul each day; I'm leaning strong on His migh-y arm; I know He'll guide me all the way. Saved by His pow'r di-vine, Saved to new life sub-lime! Life now is sweet and my joy is com-plete, For I'm saved, saved, saved!
3. When poor and need-y and all a-lone, In love He said to me, "Come un-to Me and I'll lead you home, To live with Me e-ter-nal-ly." Saved by His pow'r di-vine, Saved to new life sub-lime! Life now is sweet and my joy is com-plete, For I'm saved, saved, saved!" Titus 3:5

11.

Blessed are the poor in spirit to those who believe this spiritual hymn: "O hap-py day that fixed my choice On Thee, my Sav-ior and my God! Well may this glowing heart re-joice And tell its rap-tures all a-broad. Hap-py day, hap-py day, When Je-sus washed my sins a-way! He taught me how to watch and pray And live re- joic-ing ev-ery day; Hap-py day, hap-py day, When Je-sus washed my sins a- way!" Isaiah 25:9

12.

Blessed are the poor in spirit to those who believe this spiritual hymn: "As for me and my house, we will serve the Lord; As for me and my house, we will praise His name. For un-less He builds the house we have worked in vain; As for me and my house we will serve the Lord." Psalm 127:1

Part CDXI

Blessed Are The Poor In Spirit. Matthew 5:3

Blessed Means Happy

Poor means meek in spirit. Poor means humble in spirit. Poor means lowly in spirit. Poor means quiet in spirit. Read Matthew 5:3-12, Read also Mark 1:15

Jesus did not say "*rich*" in spirit. Jesus said "*poor*" in spirit.

1. Blessed are the poor in spirit to those who believe this spiritual hymn:
    1. "When all my la-bors and tri-als are o'er, And I am safe on that beau-ti-ful shore, Just to be near the dear Lord I a-dore Will through the a-ges be glo-ry for me. O that will be glo-ry for me, Glo-ry for me, glo-ry for me; When by His grace I shall look on His face, That will be glo-ry, be glo-ry for me.
    2. When by the gift of His in-fi-nite grace, I am ac-cord-ed in heav-en a place, Just to be there and to look on His face Will through the a-ges be glo-ry for me. O that will be glo-ry for me, Glo-ry for me, glo-ry for me; When by His grace I shall look on His face, That will be glo-ry, be glo-ry for me.
    3. Friends will be there I have loved long a-go; Joy like a riv-er a-round me will flow; Yet, just a smile from my Sav-ior, I know, Will through the a- ges be glo-ry for me. O that will be glo-ry for me, Glo-ry for me, glo-ry for me; When by His grace I shall look on His face, That will be glo-ry, be glo-ry for me." Romans 8:18
2.

    Blessed are the poor in spirit to those who believe this spiritual hymn:
    1. "Sing the won-drous love of Je-sus, Sing His mer-cy and His grace; In the man-sions bright and bless-ed He'll pre-pare for us a place. When we all get to heav-en, What a day of re-joic-ing that will be! When we all see Je-sus, We'll sing and shout the vic-to-ry.
    2. While we walk the pil-grim path-way Clouds will o-ver-spread the sky; But when trav-'ling days are o-ver, Not a shad-ow, not a sigh. When we all get to heav-en, What a day of re-joic-ing that will be! When we all see Je-sus, We'll sing and shout the vic-to-ry.

3. Let us then be true and faith-ful, Trust-ing, serv-ing ev-ery day; Just one glimpse of Him in glo-ry Will the toils of life re-pay. When we all get to heav-en, What a day of re-joic-ing that will be! When we all see Je-sus, We'll sing and shout the vic-to-ry.
4. On-ward to the prize be-fore us! Soon His beau-ty we'll be-hold; Soon the pearl-y gates will o-pen, We shall tread the streets of gold. When we all get to heav-en, What a day of re-joic-ing that will be! When we all see Je-sus, We'll sing and shout the vic-to-ry." I Thessalonians 4:17

3.

Blessed are the poor in spirit to those who believe this spiritual hymn:

1. "When the trum-pet of the Lord shall sound and time shall be no more And the morn-ing breaks e-ter-nal, bright and fair- When the saved of earth shall gath-er o-ver on the oth-er shore And the roll is called up yon-der, I'll be there! When the roll is called up yon-der, When the roll is called up yon-der, When the roll is called up yon-der-When the roll is called up yon-der I'll be there! When we all see Je-sus, We'll sing and shout the vic-to-ry, the vic-to-ry.
2. On that bright and cloud-less morning when the dead in Christ shall rise And the glo-ry of His res-ur-rec-tion share- When His cho-sen ones shall gath-er to their home be-yond the skies And the roll is called up yon-er, I 'll be there! When the roll is called up yon-der, When the roll is called up yon-der, When the roll is called up yon-der-When the roll is called up yon-der I'll be there! When we all see Je-sus, We'll sing and shout the vic-to-ry, the vic-to-ry.
3. Let us la-bor for the Mas-ter from the dawn till set-ting sun, Let us talk of all His won-drous love and care; Then when all of life is o-ver and our work on earth is done And the roll is called up yon-der, I'll be there! When the roll is called up yon-der, When the roll is called up yon-der, When the roll is called up yon-der-When the roll is called up yonder I'll be there! When we all see Je-sus, We'll sing and shout the vic-to-ry, the vic-to-ry." I Thessalonians 4:16

4. Blessed are the poor in spirit to those who believe this spiritual hymn:
    1. "Tri-als dark on ev-'ry hand, And we can-not un-der-stand All the ways that God would lead us to that bless-ed Prom-ised Land; But He'll guide us with His eye, And we'll fol-low till we die; We will un-der- stand it bet-ter

by and by. By and by, when the morn-ing comes, When the saints of God are gath-ered home, We will tell the sto-ry How we've o-ver-come; We will un-der-stand it bet-ter by and by.

2. Oft our cher-ished plans have failed, Dis-ap-point-ments have pre- vailed, And we've wan-dered in the dark-ness, heav-y—heart-ed and a-lone; But we're trust-ing in the Lord, And, ac-cord-ing to His Word, We will un-der-stand it bet-ter by and by. By and by, when the morn- ing comes, When the saints of God are gath-ered home, We will tell the sto-ry How we've o-ver-come; We will un-der-stand it bet-ter by and by.
3. Temp-ta-tions, hid-den snares Of-ten take us un-a-wares, And our hearts are made to bleed for some tho't-less word or deed, And we won-der why the test When we try to do our best, But we'll un-der- stand it bet-ter by and by. By and by, when the morn-ing comes, When the saints of God are gath-ered home, We will tell the sto-ry How we've o-ver-come, We will un-der-stand it bet-ter by and by." Hebrews 11:1

5.

Blessed are the poor in spirit to those who believe this spiritual hymn:

1. "We shall see His love-ly face Some bright, gold-en morn-ing, When the clouds have rift-ed, And the shades have flown; Sor-row will be turned to joy, Heart-aches gone for-ev-er; No more night, on-ly light, When we see His face.
2. God shall wipe a-way all tears Some bright, gold-en morn-ing, When the jour-ney's end-ed, And the course is run; No more cry-ing, pain or death In that hour of glad-ness, Tri-als cease, all is peace, When we see His face.
3. We shall meet to part no more, Some bright, gold-en morn-ing, At the gates of glo-ry Where our loved ones stand; Songs of vic-t'ry fill the skies In that hour of greeet-ing, End-less days, en-less praise, When we see His face." Revelation 22:4

6.

Blessed are the poor in spirit to those who believe this spiritual hymn:

1. "John saw the heav'n and earth made new, The first had passed a-way, The Ho-ly cit-y com-ing down, The new Je-ru-sa-lem.
2. And God Him-self shall dwell with men, And wipe a-way all tears, There is no sor-row, pain or death, Through-out the com-ing years.

3. "Be-hold, I make all things a-new," These faith-ful words are true, To him who o-ver-com-eth sin, On earth with God shall rule.
4. In beau-ti-ful Je-ru-sa-lem, God's glo-ry gives it light, All kings and na-tions walk in it, "For there shall be no night." Revelation 21:1

7.

Blessed are the poor in spirit to those who believe this spiritual hymn: "And I shall see Him face to face, And tell the sto-ry-Saved by grace; And I shall see Him face to face, And tell the sto-ry-Saved by grace." Ephesians 2:8

8. Blessed are the poor in spirit to those who believe this spiritual hymn:
   1. "Soon and ver-y soon, We are going to see the King; Soon and ver-y soon, We are going to see the King; Soon and ver-y soon, We are going to see the King; Hal-le-lu-jah! Hal-le-lu-jah! We're going to see the King.
   2. No more cry-ing there, We are going to see the King; No more cry-ing there, We are going to see the King; No more cry-ing there, We are going to see the King; Hal-le-lu-jah! Hal-le-lu-jah! We're going to see the King.
   3. No more dy-ing there, We are going to see the King; No more dy-ing there, We are going to see the King; No more dy-ing there, We are going to see the King; Hal-le-lu-jah! Hal-le-lu-jah! We're going to see the King." Revelation 22:20
9. Blessed are the poor in spirit to those who believe this spiritual hymn:
   1. "There's a land that is fair-er than day, And by faith we can see it a-far, For the Fa-ther waits o-ver the way To pre-pare us a swell-ing place there. In the sweet by and by, We shall meet on that beau-ti-ful shore; In the sweet by and by, We shall meet on that beau-ti-ful shore.
   2. We shall sing on that beau-ti-ful shore The me-lo-di-ous songs of the blest; And our spir-its shall sor-row no more- Not a sigh for the bless-ing of rest. In the sweet by and by, We shall meet on that beau-ti-ful shore; In the sweet by and by, We shall meet on that beau-ti-ful shore.
   3. To our boun-ti-ful Fa-ther a-bove We will of-fer our trib-ute of praise, For the glo-ri-ous gift of His love And the bless-ings tht hal-low our days. In the sweet by and by, We shall meet on that beau-ti-ful shore; In the sweet by and by, We shall meet on that beau-ti-ful shore." Hebrews 13:14
10. Blessed are the poor in spirit to those who believe this spiritual hymn:

1. "Some glad morn-ing when this life iso'er, I'll fly a-way; To a home on God's ce-les-tial shore, I'll fly a-way. I'll fly a-way, O glo-ry, I'll fly a- way; When I die, hal-le-lu-jah, by and by, I'll fly a-way. I'll fly a-way.
2. When the shad-ows of this life have gone, I'll fly a-way; Like a bird from pris-on bars has flown, I'll fly a-way. I'll fly a-way, O glo-ry, I'll fly a-way; When I die, hal-le-lu-jah, by and by, I'll fly a-way. I'll fly a- way.
3. Just a few more wea-ry days and then I'll fly a-way; To a land where joys shall nev-er end, I'll fly a-way. I'll fly a-way, O glo-ry, I'll fly a- way; When I die, hal-le-lu-jah, by and by, I'll fly a-way. I'll fly a-way." II Corinthians 5:8

11.

Blessed are the poor in spirit to those who believe this spiritual hymn:

1. "Come, we that love the Lord, And let our joys be known, Join in a song with sweet ac-cord, Join in a song with sweet ac-cord And thus sur- round the throne, And thus sur-round the throne. We're march-ing to Zi-on, Beau-ti-ful, beau-ti-ful Zi-on; We're march-ing up-ward to Zi- on, The beau-ti-ful cit-y of God.
2. Let those re-fuse to sing Who nev-er knew our God, But chil-dren of the heav'nly King, But chil-dren of the heav'n-ly King May speak their joys a-broad, May speak their joys a-broad. We're march-ing to Zi-on, Beau-ti-ful, beau-ti-ful Zi-on; We're march-ing up-ward to Zi- on, The beau-ti-ful cit-y of God.
3. The hill of Zi-on yields A thou-sand sa-cred sweets Be-fore we reach the heav'nly fields, Be-fore we reach the heav'n-ly fields Or walk the gold-en streets, Or walk the gold-en streets. We're march-ing to Zi- on, Beau-ti-ful, beau-ti-ful Zi-on; We're march-ing up-ward to Zi-on, The beau-ti-ful cit-y of God.
4. Then let our songs a-boung And ev-ery tear be dry; We're march-ing thro' Im-manuel's ground, We're march-ing thro' Im-man-uel's ground To fair-er worlds on high, To fair-er worlds on high. We're march-ing to Zi-on, Beau-ti-ful, beau-ti-ful Zi-on; We're march-ing up-ward to Zi-on, The beau-ti-ful cit-y of God.

12.

Blessed are the poor in spirit to those who believe this spiritual hymn:

1. "From the first bright light of morn-ing, To the last warm glow of dusk; Ev-'ry breath we take is sa-cred, For it is God's gift to us. In thanks-giv-ing,

let us praise Him; In thanks-giv-ing, let us sing Songs of praise and ad-o-ra-tion To our gra-cious Lord, and King. A-men.

2. In the sea-son of our plen-ty, In the sea-son of our need; We will find His grace suf-fi-cient, We will find His love com-plete. In thanks-giv-ing, let us praise Him; In thanks-giv-ing, let us sing Songs of praise and ad-o-ra-tion To our gra-cious Lord, and King. A-men.
3. Safe with-in His hand that guides us, Hid-den in His heal-ing wings; Day by day His love pro-vides us Ev-'ry good and per- fect thing. In thanks-giv-ing, let us praise Him; In thanks-giv-ing, let us sing Songs of praise and ad-o-ra-tion To our gra-cious Lord, and King. A-men." Ezra 3:11

Part CDXII

Blessed Are The Poor In Spirit. Matthew 5:3

Blessed Means Happy

Poor means meek in spirit. Poor means humble in spirit. Poor means lowly in spirit. Poor means quiet in spirit. Read Matthew 5:3-12, Read also Mark 1:15

Jesus did not say "*rich*" in spirit. Jesus said "*poor*" in spirit.

1. Blessed are the poor in spirit to those who believe this spiritual hymn:
    1. "When up-on life's bil-lows you are tem-pest tossed, When you are dis-cour-aged, think-ing all is lost, Count your man-y bless-ings, name them one by one, And it will sur-prise you what the Lord hath done. Count your bless-ings, name them one by one; Count your bless-ings, see what God hath done; Count your bless-ings, name them one by one; Count your man-y bless-ings, see what God hath done.
    2. Are you ev-er bur-dened with a load of care? Does the corss seem heav-y you are called to bear? Count your man-y bless-ings, ev-'ry doubt will fly, And you will be sing-ing as the days go by. Count your bless-ings, name them one by one, Count your bless-ings, see what God hath done, Count your bless-ings, name them one by one; Count your man-y bless-ings, see what God hath done.
    3. When you look at oth-ers with their lands and gold, Think that Christ has prom-ised you His wealth un-told; Count your man-y bless-ings, mon-ey can-not buy Your re-ward in heav-en, nor your home on high. Count your bless-ings, name them one by one, Count your bless-ings, see what God hath done, Count your bless-ings, name them one by one; Count your man- y bless-ings, see what God hath done.
    4. So, a-mid the con-flict, wheth-er great or small, Do not be dis-cour-aged, God is o-ver all; Count your man-y bless-ings, an-gels will at-tend, Help and com-fort give you to your jour-ney's end. Count your bless-ings, name them one by one, Count your bless-ings, see what God hath done, Count your bless-ings, name them one by one, Count your man-y bless-ings, see what God hath done." Psalm 40:5

2.
   Blessed are the poor in spirit to those who believe this spiritual hymn: "We are so blessed by the gifts from Your hand, I just can't un-der-stand Why You've loved us so much. We are Lord, for Your touch. When we're emp-ty You fill us "Til we o-ver-flow, When we're hun-gry You feed us and cause us to know; We are so blessed, Take what we have to bring; Take it all, ev-'ry-thing, Lord, we love You so much." Ephesians 1:3
3. Blessed are the poor in spirit to those who believe this spiritual hymn:
   1. "We thak You for Your love, We thak You for Your care, We thank You for Your faith-ful-ness, We thak You, Lord.
   2. We thak You for Your Son, We thak You for Your Word, We thank You for e-ter-nal life, We thak You, Lord." Psalm 75:1
4. Blessed are the poor in spirit to those who believe this spiritual hymn: "For health and strength, and dai-ly food, We praise Thy Name, O Lord." I Timothy 6:17
5. Blessed are the poor in spirit to those who believe this spiritual hymn:
   1. "Mine eyes have seen the glo-ry of the com-ing of the Lord, He is tramp-ling out the vin-tage where the grapes of wrath are stored; He hath loosed the fate-ful light-ning of His ter-ri-ble swift sword- His truth is march-ing on. Glo-ry! Glo-ry, hal-le-lu-jah! Glo-ry! glo-ry, hal-le-lu-jah! Glo-ry! glo-ry, hal-le-lu-jah! His truth is march-ing on.
   2. I have seen Him in the watch-fires of a hun-dred cir-cling camps, They have build-ed Him an al-tar in the eve-ning dews and damps; I can read His right-eous sen-tence by the dim and flar-ing lamps- His day is march-ing on. Glo-ry! glo-ry, hal-le-lu-jah! Glo-ry! glo-ry, hal-le-lu-jah! His truth is march-ing on.
   3. He has sound-ed forth the trum-pet that shall nev-er sound re-treat, He is sift-ing out the hearts of men be-fore His judg-ment seat; O be swift, my soul, to an-swer Him! Be ju-bi-lant, my feet! Our God is march-ing on. Glo-ry! glo-ry, hal-le-lu-jah! Glo-ry! glo-ry, hal-le-lu-jah! His truth is march-ing on.
   4. In the beau-ty of the lil-ies Christ was born a-cross the sea, With a glo-ry in His bos-om that trans-fig-ures you and me; As He died to make men ho-ly, let us live to make men free, While God is march-ing on. Glo-ry! glo-ry, hal-le-lu-jah! Glo-ry! glo-ry, hal-le-lu-jah! His truth is march-ing on." Romans 8:37

6. Blessed are the poor in spirit to those who believe this spiritual hymn:
    1. "My coun-try 'tis of thee, Sweet land of lib-er-ty, Of thee I sing: Land where my fa-thers died, Land of the pil-grim's pride, From ev-'ry mountain side Let free-dom ring!
    2. My na-tive coun-try, thee, Land of the no-ble free, Thy name I love: I love thy rocks and rills, Thy woods and tem-pled hills; My heart with rap-ture thrills Like that a-bove.
    3. Let mu-sic swell the breeze, And ring from all the trees Sweet free-dom's song: Let mor-tal tongues a-wake, Let all that breathe par-take; Let rocks their si-lence break, The sound pro-long.
    4. Our fa-thers' God, to Thee, Au-thor of lib-er-ty, To thee we sing: Long may our land be bright With free-dom's ho-ly light; Pro-tect us by Thy might, Great God, our King!" Proverbs 14:34
7. Blessed are the poor in spirit to those who believe this spiritual hymn:
    1. "O beau-ti-ful for spa-cious skies, For am-ber waves of grain, For purple moun-tain maj-es-ties A-bove the fruit-ed plain! A-mer-i-ca! A-mer-i-ca! God shed His grace on thee, And crown thy good with broth-er-hood From sea to shin-ing sea!
    2. O beau-ti-ful for pil-grim feet, Whose stern im-pas-sioned stress A thorough-fare for free-dom beat A-cross the wil-der-ness! A-mer-i-ca! A-mer-i-ca! God mend thine ev-ery flaw, Con-firm thy soul in self-con-trol, Thy lib-er-ty in law!
    3. O beau-ti-ful for he-roes proved In lib-er-at-ing strife, Who more than self their coun-try loved, And mer-cy more than life! A-mer-i-ca! A-mer-i-ca! May God thy gold re-fine, Till all suc-cess be no-ble-ness, And ev-ery gain di-vine!
    4. O beau-ti-ful for pa-triot dream That sees be-yond the years Thine al-a-bas- ter cit-ies gleam, Un-dimmed by hu-man tears! A-mer-i-ca! A-mer-i-ca! God shed His grace on thee, And crown thy good with broth-er-hood From sea to shin-ing sea!" I Peter 2:17
8. Blessed are the poor in spirit to those who believe this spiritual hymn:
    1. "If My peo-ple's hearts are hum-bled, If they pray and seek My face; If they turn a-way from e-vil, I will not with-hold My grace. I will hear their prayers from heav-en; I will par-don ev-'ry sin. If My peo-ple's hearts are hum-bled, I will sure-ly heal their land.

  2. Then My eyes will see their sor-row, Then My ears will hear their plea. If My peo-ple's hearts are hum-bled I will set their na-tion free. If My peo-ple's hearts are hum-bled, If they pray and seek My face; If they turn a- way from e-vil, I will not with-hold My grace." II Chronicles 7:14

9. Blessed are the poor in spirit to those who believe this spiritual hymn:
   1. "O say, can you see, by the dawn's ear-ly light, What so proud-ly we hailed at the twi-light's last gleam-ing, Whose broad stripes and bright stars, thro' the per-il-ous fight, O'er the ram-parts we watched, were so gal-lant-ly stream-ing? And the rock-et's red glare, the bombs burst-ing in air, Gave proof thro' the night that our flag was still there. O say, does that star span-gled ban-ner yet wave O'ver the land of the free and the home of the brave?
   2. O thus be it ev-er, when free men shall stand Be-tween their loved homes and the war's des-o-la-tion! Blest with vic-t'ry and peace, may the heav'n-res-cued land Praise the Pow'r that hath made and pre-served us a na-tion! Then con-quer we must, when oour cause it is just; And this be our mot-to: "In God is our trust!" And the star-span-gled ban-ner in tri-umph shall wave O'er the land of the free and the home of the brave!" I Peter 2:16
10. Blessed are the poor in spirit to those who believe this spiritual hymn:
    1. "Bless-ed the na-tion whose God is the Lord; Bless-ed the land where He reigns. Bless-ed the peo-ple who trust in His Word, And wor-ship His glo-ri-ous name.
    2. He is a lov-ing and mer-ci-ful God; We are but chil-dren of dust. He is our Re-fuge, our Strength and our Shield; And He is the Lord that we trust.
    3. Bless-ed the na-tion whose God is the Lord; Bless-ed the land where He reigns. Bless-ed the peo-ple who trust in His Word, And wor-ship His glo-ri-ous name." Psalm 144:15
11. Blessed are the poor in spirit to those who believe this spiritual hymn:
    1. "Je-sus loves me! This I know, For the Bi-ble tells me so; Lit-tle ones to Him be-long, They are weak but He is strong. Yes, Je-sus loves me! Yes, Je-sus loves me! Yes, Je-sus loves me! The Bi-ble tells me so.
    2. Je-sus loves me! He who died Heav-en's gate to o-pen wide; He will wash a-way my sin, Let His lit-tle child come in. Yes, Je-sus loves me! Yes, Je-sus loves me! Yes, Je-sus loves me! The Bi-ble tells me so.

3. Je-sus loves me! He will stay Close be-side me all the way; He's pre- pared a home for me, And some day His face I'll see. Yes, Je-sus loves me! Yes, Je-sus loves me! Yes, Je-sus loves me! The Bi-ble tells me so." Ephesians 5:2

12. Blessed are the poor in spirit to those who believe this spiritual hymn: "Je-sus loves the lit-tle chil-dren, All the chil-dren of the world. Red and yel-low, black and white, They are pre-cious in His sight- Je-sus loves the lit-tle chil-dren of the world." Matthew 19:14

Part CDXIII

Blessed Are The Poor In Spirit. Matthew 5:3

Blessed Means Happy

Poor means meek in spirit. Poor means humble in spirit. Poor means lowly in spirit. Poor means quiet in spirit. Read Matthew 5:3-12, Read also Mark 1:15

Jesus did not say "*rich*" in spirit. Jesus said "*poor*" in spirit.

1. Blessed are the poor in spirit to those who believe this spiritual hymn: "com-mit thy way un-to the Lord, trust al-so in Him. Com-mit thy way un-to the Lord, and He will bring it to pass." Psalm 37:5
2. Blessed are the poor in spirit to those who believe this spiritual hymn:
    1. "The wise may bring their learn-ing, The rich may bring their wealth, And some may bring their great-ness, And some bring strength and health; We, too, would bring our treas-ures To of-fer to the King; We have no walth or learn-ing: What shall we chil-dren bring?
    2. We'll bring Him hearts that love Him; We'll bring Him thank-ful praise, And young souls meek-ly striv-ing To walk in ho-ly ways: And these shall be the treas-ures We of-fer to the King, And these are gifts that e-ven The poor-est child may brings.
    3. We'll bring the lit-tle du-ties We have to do each day; We'll try our best to please Him, At home, at school, at play: And bet-ter are these treas-ures To of-fer to our King, Than rich-est gifts with-out them; Yet thse a child may bring." Hebrews 6:10
3. Blessed are the poor in spirit to those who believe this spiritual hymn:
    1. We have come in-to His house and gath-ered in His name to wor-ship Him. We have come in-to His house and gath-ered in His name to wor-ship Him. We have come in-to His house and gath-ered in His name to wor-ship Christ the Lord. Wor-ship Him, Christ the Lord.
    2. Let's for-get a-bout our-selves and mag-ni-fy His name and wor-ship Him. Let's for-get a-bout our-selves and mag-ni-fy His name and wor-ship Him. Let's fpr-get a-bout our-selves and mag-ni-fy His name and wor-ship Christ the Lord. Wor-ship Him, Christ the Lord." Matthew 28:9

4. Blessed are the poor in spirit to those who this spiritual hymn: "This is the day, this is the day that the Lord hath made, that the Lord hath made. We will re-joice, we will re-joice and be glad in it, and be glad in it. This is the day that the Lord hath made; We will re-joice and be glad in it. This is the day, this is the day that the Lord hath made." Psalm 118:24
5. Blessed are the poor in spirit to those who believe this spiritual hymn: "Come, let us rea-son to-geth-er," that's what God says. "Come, let us rea-son to-geth-er," says the Lord. Lord. "Tho' your sins be as scar-let, they shall be as white as snow; Tho' they be read as crim-son, they shall be as wool." Isaiah 1:18
6. Blessed are the poor in spirit to those who believe this spiritual hymn: "In this qui-et mo-ment, Je-sus, speak to me. Fill my heart with Thy love di-vine, Your pow-er let me see." Isaiah 30:15
7. Blessed are the poor in spirit to those who believe this spiritual hymn: "O wor-ship the Lord in the beaut-y of ho-li-ness; Serve Him with glad-ness, all the earth. A-men." Psalm 96:9
8. Blessed are the poor in spirit to those who believe this spiritual hymn: "The Lord is in His ho-ly tem-ple, The Lord is in His ho-ly tem-ple; Let all the earth keep si- lence, Let all the earth keep si-lence be-fore Him, Keep si-lence, keep si-lence be- fore Him. A-men." Psalm 5:7
9. Blessed are the poor in spirit to those who believe this spiritual hymn: "Praise ye the name of the Lord of Hosts. Praise Him, praise Him, all ye peo-ple. Let all the na-tions praise the Lord. Praise ye the Lord! Let all the na-tions praise the Lord!" Psalm 66:2
10. Blessed are the poor in spirit to those who believe this spiritual hymn: "Cast thy bur-den up-on the Lord, and He shall sus-tain thee; He nev-er will suf-fer the right-eous to fall: He is at thy right hand. Thy mer-cy, Lord, is great and far a- bove the heav'ns: Let none be made a-sham-ed that wait up-on Thee. A-men." Psalm 55:22
11. Blessed are the poor in spirit to those who believe this spiritual hymn:
    1. "God be with you till we meet a-gain; By His coun-sels guide, up-hold you, With His sheep se-cure-ly fold you; God be with you till we meet a-gain.
    2. God be with you till we meet a-gain; 'Neath His wings protecting hide you, Dai-ly man-na still pro-vide you; God be with you till we meet a-gain." I Thessalonians 5:28

12. Blessed are the poor in spirit to those who believe this spiritual hymn: "The Lord whom we love, whom we wor-ship and a-dore, We will serve through-out this com-ing week. He it is who binds us to-gether, And He it is who sends us a-part, To be God's peo-ple, be God's peo-ple, A-men, a-men." Ephesians 4:12

PART CDXIV

Blessed Are The Poor In Spirit. Matthew 5:3

Blessed Means Happy

Poor means meek in spirit Poor means humble in spirit Poor means lowly in spirit Poor means quiet in spirit Read Matthew 5:3-12, Read also Mark 1:15

Jesus did not say "*rich*" in spirit. Jesus said "*poor*" in spirit.

1. Blessed are the poor in spirit to those who believe this spiritual hymn: "May the grace of Christ, our Sav-ior, and the love of God, our Fa-ther, and the fel-low-ship of the Spir-it be with us. May be with us for-ev-er, and ev-er, for-ev-er-more, A- men." II Corinthians 13:14
2. Blessed are the poor in spirit to those who believe this spiritual hymn: "The Lord bless you and keep you; The Lord lift His coun-te-nance up-on you, and give you peace, and give you peace; The Lord make His face to shine up-on you, and be gra-cious, and be gra-cious, The Lord be gra-cious, gra-cious un-to you. A-men." Numbers 6:24, 26
3. Blessed are the poor in spirit to those who believe this spiritual hymn: "May the grace of the Lord, may the grace of the Lord Je-sus Christ, and the love of God, and the fel-low-ship of the Ho-ly Spir-it, be with you all. A-men." II Corinthians 13:14
4. Blessed are the poor in spirit to those who believe this spiritual hymn: "Hear our prayer, O Lord, Hear our prayer, O Lord; In-cline Thine ear to us, And grant us Thy peace. A-men." Psalm 143:1
5. Blessed are the poor in spirit to those who believe this spiritual hymn: "Hear our prayer, O heav'nly Fa-ther, for the dear Re-deem-er's sake. A-men." Psalm 143:1
6. Blessed are the poor in spirit to those who believe this spiritual hymn: "Thou wilt keep him in per-fect peace Whose mind is stayed on Thee. Amen" Isaiah 26:3
7. Blessed are the poor in spirit to those who believe this spiritual hymn: "Let the words of my mouth and the med-i-tation of my heart be ac-cept-a-ble in Thy sight, O Lord, my strength and my Re-deem-er. A-men." Psalm 19:14

8. Blessed are the poor in spirit to those who believe this spiritual hymn: "Dear Fa- ther, our hearts are filled with thanks-giv-ing; We praise You and wor-ship You; We give You thanks to-day. A-men." Psalm 19:14
9. Blessed are the poor in spirit to those who believe this spiritual hymn: "We cannot give with-out re-ceiv-ing So much more than we have giv-en. God's ways are won-der-ful, God's ways are won-der-ful." II Corinthians 9:6
10. Blessed are the poor in spirit to those who believe this spiritual hymn: "Glo-ry be to the Fa-ther, and to the Son, and to the Ho-ly Ghost: as it was in the be-ginning, is now and ev-er shall be, world with-out end. A-men, A-men." Psalm 96:8
11. Blessed are the poor in spirit to those who believe this spiritual hymn:
    1. I want to be like Je-sus.
       I want to be like Je-sus.
       Oh, how I long to be like Him
       Oh how I long to be in that glory
    2. I want to walk like Je-sus
       I want to walk like Je-sus
       Oh, how I long to be like Him
       Oh how I long to be in that glory
    3. I want to talk like Je-sus
       I want to talk like Je-sus
       Oh, how I long to be like Him
       Oh how I long to be in that glory
    4. I want to think like Je-sus
       I want to think like Je-sus
       Oh, how I long to be like Him
       Oh how I long to be in that glory
    5. I want to act like Je-sus
       I want to act like Je-sus
       Oh, how I long to be like Him
       Oh how I long to be in that glory
    6. I want to live like Je-sus
       I want to live like Je-sus
       Oh, how I long to be like Him
       Oh how I long to be in that glory

Ephesians 2:10, Ephesians 4:1-7, Ephesians 5:2, 8, Philippians 3:16, Colossians 1:10, Colossians 2:6, Colossians 4:5, I Thessalonians 2:12, I Thessalonians 4:1, 12, I John 1:6, 7, I John 2:6, II John 1:6, III John 1:4, Revelation 3:4, Galatians 5:16, 25, II Corinthians 6:16, I Corinthians 7:17, II Corinthians 5:17, Romans 6:4, 8:1, 4, Revelation 2:24, Ephesians 3:20, II Thessalonians 3:13, Colossians 3:17, Mark 12:11, Ephesians 6:6, 7, Acts 10:38, Psalm 118:6, Matthew 21:42, Luke 5:27, 9:23, 5, 9, Mark 2:14, Mark 8:34, 10:21, Matthew 9:9, Matthew 16:24, Matthew 19:21, John 21:19, 22, Matthew 4:19, Colossians 3:4, Colossians 1:27, John 1:43, I Thessalonians 5:23-24, II Timothy 2:10, Luke 23:34, Luke 19:9, Revelation 3:20, I Peter 2:21, I Corinthians 11:23-26, Psalm 40:8, 143:10, Hebrews 10:7, I Thessalonians 1:6, Philippians 3:10

12.

Blessed are the poor in spirit to those who believe that I know that my redeemer lives, and that in the end he will stand at the latter day upon the earth
And after my skin has been destroyed, yet in my flesh I will see God;
I my self will see Him with my own eyes, and not another. How my heart yearns within me! Job 19:25-27

Part CDXV

Blessed Are The Poor In Spirit. Matthew 5:3

Blessed Means Happy

Poor means meek in spirit Poor means humble in spirit Poor means lowly in spirit Poor means quiet in spirit Read Matthew 5:3-12, Read also Mark 1:15

Jesus did not say "*rich*" in spirit. Jesus said "*poor*" in spirit.

1. Blessed are the poor in spirit to those who believe this quotation: "Speculations? I know nothing about speculations. I'm resting on certainties. *I know that my Redeemer lives*, and because He lives, I shall live also." Michael Faraday, English Physicist, 1791-1867. Job 19:25, John 14:19
2. Blessed are the poor in spirit to those who believe one of God's children: "We can proceed with bold assurance, thanks to the evidence of history that established with convincing clarity how Jesus not only preceded us in death but also *came back from the dead* and blazed the trail to heaven." Lee Strobel, American Christian author, journalist, pastor. Acts 1:11, Romans 10:9, John 11:25, I Corinthians 15:4
3. Blessed are the poor in spirit to those who believe this quotation: "There's nothing outside heaven *except hell.* Earth is not outside heaven; it is heaven's workshop, heaven's womb." Peter Kreeft, professor of philosophy at Boston College Revelation 20:10-15, Matthew 25:46, II Peter 2:9, II Thessalonians 1:9, Revelation 21:8, II Peter 2:4, 17, Jude 1:6, 13
4. Blessed are the poor in spirit to those who believe this quotation: "Something deep within us tell us that death is not natural. We fight against it as if it is a foreign enemy, and in a sense it is. God has placed eternity into the heart of every person, so we long for life to go on, yet we are so attached to life on earth that we resist heaven, the true home Jesus has prepared for us." Dave Dravecky, a motivational Christian speaker, author. John 14:2, Matthew 25:46, Revelation 21:1-7, I Peter 1:4, I Thessalonians 4:13-18, verse 16-17, II Timothy 4:6-8, verse 8, I John 3:2, John 14:1-4, verse 2 John 11:25
5. Blessed are the poor in spirit to those who believe one of God's children and wrote this beautiful hymn: "There's a land that is fairer than day, And *by faith*

we can see it afar: For the Father waits over the way To *prepare us a dwelling place there*. In the sweet by and by, we shall meet on that beautiful shore; In the sweet by and by, We shall meet on that beautiful shore. Sanford F. Bennett, 1868 (1836-1898). John 14:1-4, verse 2, Revelation 21:1-7, I Peter 1:4, I John 3:2

6. Blessed are the poor in spirit to those who believe that *Jacob had a dream*. [Jacob] had a dream in which he saw a stairway resting on the earth, with its top reaching to heaven, and the angels of God were ascending and descending on it. There above it stood the Lord…When Jacob awoke from his sleep, he thought, "Surely the Lord is in this place…This is none other than the house of God; this is the gate of heaven." Read *Genesis 28:12-13, 16-17, Revelation 21:1-7, Matthew 25:46, I Peter 1:4, I Thessalonians 4:13-18, verse 16-17, II Timothy 4:6-8 verse 8*
7. Blessed are the poor in spirit to those who believe one of God's children: "Earth recedes, heaven opens. I've been through the gates! Don't call me back…if this is death, it's sweet." Dwight L. Moody, 1837-1899 Psalm 116:15, Psalm 127:3, Psalm 9:13, Psalm 23:4, Psalm 56:13, Psalm 68:20, II Timothy 4:6-8, verse 8
8. Blessed are the poor in spirit to those who have believe and have heard one of God's children: "Some day you will read in the papers that D.L. Moody is dead. Don't you believe a word of it! At that moment I shall be more alive than I am now; I shall have gone up higher, that is all, out of this old clay tenement into a house that is immortal-a body that death cannot touch, that sin cannot taint; a body fashioned like unto His glorious body." Dwight L. Moody, 1837-1899 Philippians 1:20-30 verse 23, John 5:24, II Timothy 4:5-8 verse 6, Colossians 1:27, Philippians 3:10, 3:4, I Thessalonians 2:12, John 14:1-4, verse 2, Revelation 21:1-7 verse 1
9. Blessed are the poor in spirit to those who believe one of God's children: "[Death] is not the end. I thank God that I know that this is not all there is. My whole everlasting being, my entire personality-all that I have and all that I am are cast out on the promises of God that there is another chapter! At the close of every obituary of his believing children, God adds the word henceforth! After very biography, God adds the word henceforth! There will be a tomorrow and this is the reason for Christian joy." A. W. Tozer, 1897-1963 Psalm 116:15, Psalm 127:3, John 5:24, I John 5:4, I Corinthians 15:55, 57, I Corinthians 15:54, 55, Matthew 12:20, Isaiah 25:8, John 17:13, John 16:22, 24, John 15:11, Luke 15:7, 10, Psalm 9:13, 23:4, Psalm 56:13, Psalm 68:20, John 14:6, John 11:25
10. Blessed are the poor in spirit to those who rejoice in that day and leap for joy, because great is your reward in heaven. Luke 6:23

11. Blessed are the poor in spirit to those who believe one of God's children: "Will we know [our loved ones] in that land of light, liberty and fullness of joy? By all means! For if Moses and Elijah were recognized on the mount of transfiguration- if Stephen knew his Lord as they were stoning him…then there is no doubt that we will know one another in that land. We will not lose our identity in heaven and will have the same peculiarities and specific make-up in our entire moral being."
    E.M. Bounds, 1835-1913 Revelation 2:10, 11, Revelation 5:3, John 17:13, John 16:22, 24, John 15:11, Luke 15:7, 10, Psalm 116:15, Psalm 127:3, I Thessalonians 4:13-18
12. Blessed are the poor in spirit to those who *believe in prayer for sinners, for their salvation; or sinners for salvation.* I Timothy 2:1-4, John 17:9, John 4:22, Romans 1:12-17, verse 16, Romans 10:1

Part CDXVI

Blessed Are The Poor In Spirit. Matthew 5:3

Blessed Means Happy

Poor means meek in spirit Poor means humble in spirit Poor means lowly in spirit Poor means quiet in spirit Read Matthew 5:3-12, Read also Mark 1:15

Jesus did not say "*rich*" in spirit. Jesus said "*poor*" in spirit.

1. Blessed are the poor in spirit to those who believe this Psalmist: "The Lord has established his throne in heaven, and his kingdom rules over all." Psalm 103:19
2. Blessed are the poor in spirit to those who believe this statement: "In heaven, will we spend time with people whose lives are recorded in Scripture and church history? No doubt." Randy Alcorn Revelation 21:1-7, Matthew 25:31, Revelation 19:7-9, Ephesians 3:15, Psalm 118:24, John 14:1-4
3. Blessed are the poor in spirit to those who believe Jesus spoken word: "I say to you that many will come from the east and the west, and will take their places at the feast with Abraham, Isaac and Jacob in the kingdom of heaven." Matthew 8:11
4. Blessed are the poor in spirit to those who believe one of God's children: "You are made for a person and a place. Jesus is the person. Heaven is the place. They are a package-you cannot get to Heaven without Jesus." John 14:6. Randy Acorn.
5. Blessed are the poor in spirit to those who believe Jesus spoken word: "Then the king will say to those on his right, 'Come, you who are blessed by my Father; take your inheritance, the kingdom prepared for you since the creation of the world.'" Matthew 25:34
6. Blessed are the poor in spirit to those who believe that For God did not appoint us to suffer wrath but to receive salvation through our Lord Jesus Christ. He died for us so that...we may live together with him. I Thessalonians 5:9-10
7. Blessed are the poor in spirit to those who believe one of God's children: "If anyone out there is unsure of [how to get to heaven], then for the love of God get out your Bible and study for your finals! To save you time—since you may die while reaching for your Bible—I will quote God's scandalously simple answer to the most important question in the world, how to get to heaven: "Believe in the Lord Jesus, and you will be saved" (Acts 16:31). Peter Kreeft

8. Blessed are the poor in spirit to those who believe one of God's children: "Why should my heart be fixed where my home is not? Heaven is my home; God in Christ is all my happiness: and where my treasure is, there my heart should be. Matthew 6:20, Luke 12:34, John 14:1-3, II Corinthians 4:7. Margaret Charlton Baxter, 1631-1681
9. Blessed are the poor in spirit to those who believe that the *Savior is the One who saves sinners like us if they ask Him to save their souls*. John 4:14, John 7:37-38, Isaiah 44:3
10. Blessed are the poor in spirit to those who believe that *Jesus Christ* is the "*Son of God*." Mark 1:1, Luke 1:35
11. Blessed are the poor in spirit to those who believe that *Jesus Christ* is the "*Son of Man*." Matthew 8:20, Matthew 16:13, 16
12. Blessed are the poor in spirit to those who believe that *Jesus Christ* is "*the Son of David*." Matthew 15:22, Matthew 1:1

Part CDXVII

Blessed Are The Poor In Spirit. Matthew 5:3

Blessed Means Happy

Poor means meek in spirit Poor means humble in spirit. Poor means lowly in spirit Poor means quiet in spirit Read Matthew 5:3-12, Read also Mark 1:15

Jesus did not say "*rich*" in spirit. Jesus said "*poor*" in spirit.

1. Blessed are the poor in spirit to those who believe that *Jesus Christ* is "*That Word*" or "*The Word.*" John 1:1 and Genesis 1:1, See Acts 17:24
2. Blessed are the poor in spirit to those who believe that *Jesus Christ* is "*the Lamb of God.*" John 1:29, 36
3. Blessed are the poor in spirit to those who believe that Jesus Christ is "*the Sacrifice*" for all sin. John 1:29
4. Blessed are the poor in spirit to those who believe that *Jesus Christ* is "*the Son of the Living God.*" Matthew 16:16
5. Blessed are the poor in spirit to those who believe that *Jesus Christ* is "the *Rabbi*"; that *Jesus Christ* "*the Master*, that Jesus Christ is the Messiah." John 1:38, 49, John 3:2, John 6:25, John 4:25, John 1:41, Daniel 9:25, 26, Isaiah 9:6, Isaiah 7:14, Luke 2:11
6. Blessed are the poor in spirit to those who believe that *Jesus Christ* is "*Author of Eternal Life*'; the one who give life ; the *Prince of life*, which is *Jesus Christ*, the *Son of God*, whom God hath raised *Him from the dead.* Acts 3:15
7. Blessed are the poor in spirit to those who believe that *Jesus Christ* is "*the Alpha and Omega—the First and the Last*," which is that *Jesus Christ is the beginning and that Jesus Christ is the end.* **Revelation 1:8, 11, 17-18, verse 18, Revelation 2:8**—(Isaiah 44:6)**, Revelation 3:7**—(Isaiah 22:22), **11, Revelation 4:8**—(Isaiah 6:2-3), **Revelation 16:15, Revelation 22:7, 12-13**—(Isaiah 44:6, Isaiah 48:12), Isaiah 52:6, John 4:26, 29, 42, John 5:18, John 8:56, 58, John 9:36-37, verse 37, John 10:30, 33, 38, **John 14:1-12, verse 7, 8, 9,** John 19:7, Luke 23:2, Mark 14:60-64, verse 62, Acts 10:36, **Philippians 2:6-11, verse 6, 10, 11, Philippians 3:10, Hebrews 13:8, Exodus 3:3-15, verse 14, Genesis 1:1, John 1:1-18, verse 1, 14,** I John 5:20, I Timothy 3:16, **Hebrews 5:9, Hebrews 12:2, John 19:30**

8. Blessed are the poor in spirit to those who believe that *Jesus Christ* is the "*Living Judah*;" "the *Messiah*." Revelation 5:5
9. Blessed are the poor in spirit to those who believe that *Jesus Christ* is "*King of kings and Lord of lords*." "The *Rules of all people*." Revelation 19:16, Revelation 17:14, I Timothy 6:15, I Timothy 1:17, Isaiah 9:6, Micah 5:2, Matthew 2:6, John 7:42
10. Blessed are the poor in spirit to those who believe that *Jesus Christ* is "*the Bright and Morning Star*;" "*the One who give light*." And He is The Star from the east. Revelation 22:16-(Isaiah 11:1), John 1:8, 9, Gene 1:1, John 1:1-3, **Hebrews 13:8**, **Acts 10:36**, **Philippians 2:6-11**, **verse 6, 10, 11**, **John 14:7, 8, 9, John 8:12, I John 1:5**, Numbers 24:17, **Matthew 2:1-2**
11. Blessed are the poor in spirit to those who believe that *Jesus Christ* is the *Word of God*; that *Jesus Christ* is the "*Voice of God*." Revelation 19:13
12. Blessed are the poor in spirit to those who believe that *Jesus Christ is Holy and Righteous*; "*the Holy One and the Just*" Acts 3:14

Part CDXVIII

Blessed Are The Poor In Spirit. Matthew 5:3

Blessed Means Happy

Poor means meek in spirit Poor means humble in spirit Poor means lowly in spirit Poor means quiet in spirit Read Matthew 5:3-12, Read also Mark 1:15

Jesus did not say "*rich*" in spirit. Jesus said "*poor*" in spirit.

1. Blessed are the poor in spirit to those who believe that *Jesus Christ* is the *Head of the Church*; "*the Leader*' *of all Christians*. Ephesians 5:23
2. Blessed are the poor in spirit to those who *believe that we cannot argue with the Bible itself the Written Hand of God say so and therefore after all is said and done, the world even to us need to get use to the Written Word of the Bible itself. Yes Get Use To It. It is said that the Bible is silent to itself.* Psalm 46:10, Genesis 1:1, John 1:1, II Timothy 3:16, Matthew 28:19, Romans 1:20, Acts 17:29, Colossians 2:9, Ephesians 4:30, Psalm 51:11, Isaiah 63:10-11,
3. Blessed are the poor in spirit to those who believe the Gospel: "*Seeing it is a righteous thing with God to recompense tribulation to them that trouble you*;" II Thessalonians 1:6
4. Blessed are the poor in spirit to those who believe the Gospel: "*And to you who are troubled rest with us, when the Lord Jesus shall be revealed from heaven with his mighty angels*," II Thessalonians 1:7
5. Blessed are the poor in spirit to those who believe the Gospel: "*In flaming fire taking vengeance on them that know not God, and that obey no The Gospel of our Lord Jesus Christ*:" II Thessalonians 1:8
6. Blessed are the poor in spirit to those who believe the Gospel: "*Who shall be punished with everlasting destruction from the presence of the Lord, and from the glory of his power*;" II Thessalonians 1:9
7. Blessed are the poor in spirit to those who believe the Gospel: "*And with all deceivableness of unrighteousness in them that perish*; *because they received not the love of the truth, that they might be saved*." II Thessalonians 2:10
8. Blessed are the poor in spirit to those who believe that *anyone who "reject" the Gospel of Jesus Christ" before the Rapture will not have "a chance" or "second chance" to be saved "after" the Rapture*." II Thessalonians 1:6-9, II Thessalonians 2:10

9. Blessed are the poor in spirit to those who *believe in teaching, exhorting, warning* and *preaching the Word of God to the lost world: to the lost sinners and seek their salvation while the door is still open to the public is still surely open to them. Now is the accepted time and now is the day of salvation is come to thee* Colossians 1:28, II Timothy 4:1-21, verse 2, II Corinthians 6:2, Isaiah 49:8
10. Blessed are the poor in spirit to those who believe that *Jesus Christ is our peace*, who *hath made both one*, and *hath broken down the middle wall of partition between us*, (the *Jews and Gentiles*); *having abolished in the flesh the emnity*, even the *law of commandments* contained *in ordinances*; for *to make in Himself of twain one new man*, so *making peace*; and that He *might reconcile both (Jew and Gentile) unto God in one body by the cross, having slain the enmity thereby*: and *came and preached peace to you that was afar off* (the *Gentiles*), and to *them (Jews) that were nigh*. For *through Him we both have the access by one Spirit unto the Father*." Ephesians 2:14-18—See Romans 4:9-12
11. Blessed are the poor in spirit to those who believe that we are saved because Salvation is the power of God. Romans 1:16-17, I Corinthians 1:18, I Peter 1:5, II Timothy 1:8
12. Blessed are the poor in spirit to those who believe this Psalmist:"The Lord hath done great things for us; whereof we are glad." Psalm 126:3

Part CDXIX

Blessed Are The Poor In Spirit. Matthew 5:3

Blessed Means Happy

Poor means meek in spirit. Poor means humble in spirit. Poor means lowly in spirit. Poor means quiet in spirit. Read Matthew 5:3-12, Read also Mark 1:15

Jesus did not say "*rich*" in spirit. Jesus said "*poor*" in spirit.

1. Blessed are the poor in spirit to those who believe that Apostle Peter one of God's children, preached his very first sermon under the power of the Holy Spirit on the day of Pentecost. His sermon was "*Power Of Penteost Is Jesus Christ.*" Peter, an apostle of Jesus Christ to the strangers (i.e. strangers in the world) scattered throughout Pontus, Galatia, Cappadocie, Asia and Bothynia, elected according to the *foreknowledge of God the Father through sanctification of the Spirit unto obedience and sprinkle of the blood of Jesus Christ*: *Grace* unto you, and *peace*, be multiplied. I Peter 1:1-2, and Apostle Peter had *been with Jesus for three years*. See Acts 4:13, Read Acts 4:12-20. See also Exodus 12:48-49, Isaiah 56:6-7. So Apostle Peter began to preach concerning Acts 2:11, 41; Acts 2:17—(Isaiah 44:3, Joel 2:28, John 7:37-38, 39, Deuteronomy 18:15-19, John 17:8, Acts 3:23, Isaiah 12:3, Jeremiah 2:13, Psalm 36:9, Zechariah 13:1, I Corinthians 6:11, Hebrews 9:14, Revelation 7:17, Isaiah 25:8, Hebrews 2:14), II Timothy 1:10, John 14:6, II John 1:9, Revelation 5:8-9, Ephesians 5:2, John 13:34), Acts 2:18 (I Corinthians 12:10-14, I John 4:1, Jeremiah 14:14, II Thessalonians 2:9-11, Deuteronomy 13:1-4, I Corinthians 11:19, I John 1:7, Revelation 2:16, Isaiah 11:4), Acts 2:19 (Joel 2:30, Mark 13:12), Acts 2:22—(Hebrews 2:4), Acts 2:23 - (Luke 24:44, Luke 24:44-49, Matthew 16:21, II Corinthians 1:6, Psalm 27:1, Isaiah 2:5, Acts 26:23, Daniel 9:24, Galatians 3:14, Acts 1:22, Ephesians 1:20) Acts 2:25 (Psalm 16:8) Acts 2:27, Acts 8:37, Romans 1:44, Luke 1:35, Acts 2:31—(Psalm 16:11), Acts 2:32—(Luke 24:44-48), Acts 2:33—(Philippians 2:9-13, Hebrews 10:12, Colossians 1:3, Ephesians 2:6), Acts 2:36—(II Thessalonians 2:7-11), Acts 2:38—(II Corinthians 7:10), Acts 2:39—(Romans 9:8, Ephesians 2:13, Acts 2:47, Galatians 3:28, Romans 10:1-3, Joel 2:32, Acts 2:21, Psalm 50:15), Acts 2:42—(Hebrews 10:25, II Peter 3:9, Acts 2:47), Acts 4:32-33, Mark 16:20,

I Thessalonians 1:5-7, Hebrews 2:4-5, I Corinthians 2:4-5, II Peter 1:16-17, I Peter 1:5, John 10:28-30). Read Acts 2:11-47

2. Blessed are the poor in spirit to those who believe that one of God's children, Apostle *Peter* began to *preach his second sermon*: "*The Lame Man Healed*:" Acts 3:1-11 as the beginning. Then he preached about Jesus: Acts 3:12-26, concerning; II Corinthians 3:5—(Acts 3:12), I Corinthians 15:10—(Acts 3:12), Galatians 2:8—(Acts 3:12), Acts 22:21, Colossians 1:29—(Acts 3:12), Romans 1:5—{Acts 3:12), Ephesians 3:8—(Acts 3:12), I Timothy 1:13—(Acts 3:17), Acts 8:3—(Acts 3:17), Acts 26:9—(Acts 3:17), Galatians 1:13—(Acts 3:17), Philippians 3:6—(Acts 3:17), Psalm 22:1-31—(Acts 3:18), Isaiah 30:6—(Acts 3:18), Daniel 9:26—(Acts 3:18)—(See Messiah verse 26), Hebrews 8:1—(Acts 3:18), Colossians 3:1—(Acts 3:21), Ephesians 2:6—(Acts 3:21), Matthew 17:11—(Acts 3:21)
3. Blessed are the poor in spirit to those who believe one of God's children, Apotle *Peter began to preach his third sermon*: "*Delivered From Egypt*:" Acts 5:30-33 concerning; Galatains 3:13—(Acts 5:30), Joshua 10:26, 27—(Acts 5:30), Deuteronomy 21:23—(Acts 5:30), Numbers 35:34—(Acts 5:30), Hosea 9:3—(Acts 5:30), Revelation 1:5—(Acts 5:31), Hebrews 9:14—(Acts 5:31), Ephesians 1:7—(Acts 5:31), Hebrews 9:12—(Acts 5:31), Daniel 9:24—(Acts 5:31), Proverbs 21:30—(Acts 5:38), Matthew 15:13—(Acts 5:38), John 15:2—(Acts 5:38), Hebrews 6:8—(Acts 5:38), Genesis 24:50—(Acts 5:38), Psalm 118:23—(Acts 5:38), Isaiah 28:16—(Acts 5:39), Matthew 21:42—(Acts 5:39), Romans 9:33—(Acts 5:39), Isaiah 8:14—(Acts 5:39), Psalm 118:22—(Acts 5:39), Mark 12:11—(Acts 5:39), I Corinthians 1:25—(Acts 5:39), II Corinthians 4:7—(Acts 5:39), Ephesians 1:19, 20—(Acts 5:39), Revelation 17:14—(Acts 5:39), II Peter 2:9—(Acts 5:39), Revelation 5:10—(Acts 5:39), Exodus 19:5—(Acts 5:39), I Kings 8:53—(Acts 5:39), I Corinthians 10:26—(Acts 5:39), Matthew 10:17—(Acts 5:40), Acts 5:40, Mark 13:9—(Acts 5:40), Revelation 2:10—(Acts 5:40), James 1:12—(Acts 5:40), Hebrews 12:5—(Acts 5:40), Job 5:17—(Acts 5:40), Romans 5:3—(Acts 5:41), Ephesians 2:8—(Acts 5:41), Matthew 5:12—(Acts 5:41), Hebrews 10:34—(Acts 5:41).
4. Blessed are the poor in spirit to those who believe one of God's children, Apostle *Peter began to preach his fourth sermon*: "*A Vision*:" Acts 10:34-43 concerning; Galatians 2:6—(Acts 10:34), Acts 10:34, Romans 2:11—(Acts 10:34), Deuteronomy 10:17—(Acts 10:34), I Peter 1:17—(Acts 10:34), Romans 2:13—(Acts

10:35), I Corinthians 12:13—(Acts 10:35), John 6:63—(Acts 10:35), Galatians 2:6—(Acts 10:35), Romans 2:11—(Acts 10:35), Acts 10:34—(Acts 10:35), John 1:1-51, verse 1 (Acts 10:41), John 14:17—(Acts 10: 41), I John 2:27—(Acts 10:41), Genesis 12:3—(Acts 10:41), Jeremiah 24:7—Acts 10:41), Zechariah 8:8—(Acts 10:41), Leviticus 25:17—(Acts 10:41), Jeremiah 7:6—(Acts 10:41), Jeremiah 4:2—(Acts 5:41), Galatians 3:8—(Acts 10:41), Revelation 21:3—(Acts 10:41), I Corinthians 1:31—(Acts 10:41), I Thessalonians 4:6—(Acts 10:41), John 21:13, II Corinthians 5:10—(Acts 10:4 2 }

5. Blessed are the poor in spirit to those who *believe that Apostle Peter*, one of God's children, began to *preach his fifth sermon*: "*The Name of Jesus Christ of Nazareth*:"Acts 4:10, Acts 4:7-13, { *because he took knowledge that he and his disciples had been with Jesus for three years}*, concerning, Luke 12:11-12—(Acts 4:7-8), Exodus 4:12—(Acts 4:7-8), I Peter 5:7—(Acts 4:8), Isaiah 28:16—(Acts 4:11); Romans 9:33—(Acts 4:11), Psalm 118:22—(Acts 4:11), I Peter 2:4, 7, 8—(Acts 4:11), Isaiah 8:14—(Acts 4:11), Romans 9:33—(Acts 4:11), Matthew 21:42—(Acts 4:11), Isaiah 28:16—(Acts 4:11), Romans 3:24—(Acts 4:12), I Peter 1:18, 19—(Acts 4:12), Matthew 11:25—(Acts 4:13), Psalm 8:2—(Acts 4:13), I Corinthians 1:27—(Acts 4:13)
6. Blessed are the poor in spirit to those who believe that Apostle Peter, one of God's children, began to *preach his sixth sermon*: "*Obey God Rather Than Men*:" Acts 5:29; Acts 5:29-42; concerning; Galatians 1:10—(Acts 5:29), I John 3:19—(Acts 5:29), James 4:4—(Acts 5:29), John 15:19—(Acts 5:29), John 4:5—(Acts 5:29), Genesis 33:19—(Acts 5:29), Joshua 24:32—(Acts 5:29), Galatians 3:13—(Acts 5:30), Joshua 10:26, 27—(Acts 5:30), Deuteronomy 21:23—(Acts 5:30), Numbers 35:34—(Acts 5:30), Hosea 9:3—(Acts 5:30), Revelation 1:5—(Acts 5:31), Hebrews 9:14—(Acts 5:31), Micah 2:10—(Acts 5:31), Ephesians—(Acts 5:31), Hebrews 9:12—(Acts 5:31), Daniel 9:24—(Acts 5:31), Proverbs 21:30—(Acts 5:38), Matthew 15:13—(Acts 5:38), John 15:13—(Acts 5:38), John 15:21—(Acts 5:38), I Corinthians 3:12—(Acts 5:38), Genesis 24:50—(Acts 5:39), Psalm 118:23—(Acts 5:39), Matthew 21:42—(Acts 5:39), Isaiah 28:16—(Acts 5:39), Romans 9:33—(Acts 5:39), Mark 12:11—(Acts 5:39), Psalm 118:22 (Acts 5:39), I Peter 2:4, 7—(Acts 5:39), I Corinthians 1:25—(Acts 5:39), II Corinthians 4:7—(Acts 5:39), Ephesians 1:19-20—(Acts 5:39), Revelation 17:14 (Acts 5:39), I Peter 2:9, Revelation 5:10, Exodus 19:5-6—(Acts 5:39), I Thessalonians 5:27, I Kings 8:53—(Acts 5:39), I Corinthians 10:26—(Acts 5:39), Matthew

10:17—(Acts 5:40), Acts 5:40, Mark 13:9—(Acts 5:40), Revelation 2:10-11—(Acts 5:40), Romans 5:3—(Acts 5:41), Galatians 4:6 (Acts 5:41), Ephesians 1:13—Acts 5:41), II Corinthians 5:5—(Acts 5:41), Isaiah 29:23—(Acts 5:41), Ephesians 2:10—(Acts 5:41), Ephesians 2:8-12—(Acts 5:41), Revelation 3:10-12—(Acts 5:41), Hebrews 10:34—(Acts 5:41), Matthew 5:12—(Acts 5:41)

7. Blessed are the poor in spirit to those who believe that Apostle Peter, one of God's children, began to *preach his seventh sermon*: "*Receive the Holy Spirit*:" John 20:21-23, Acts 2:4, Acts 10:47, Acts 10:34-48
8. Blessed are the poor in spirit to those who believe the *power of Pentecostal message of Peter's preaching where 3, 000 souls were saved under the power of Jesus Christ's Pentecostal power of the Holy Spirit as the Spirit gave them* (one of them was Peter, too) *utterance*. Acts 1:1-7 Acts 1:8, Acts 2:1-4, Acts 2:4, Acts 2:1-47
9. Blessed are the poor in spirit to those who believe the *Pentecostal message of Peter's preaching*: Acts 2:13-47: concerning Joel 2:28, 2:29—(Acts 2:18), 2:30, 31—(Acts 2:20), 2:32—(Acts 2:21), Deuteronomy 18:15—Acts 2:22), Psalm 16:8 (Acts 2:25), Joel 2:30—Acts 2:19), I Chronicles 17:14—(Acts 2:30), Psalm 132:11—(Acts 2:30), Psalm 49:15—(Acts 2:31), Psalm 16:10—(Acts 2:31), Psalm 110:1—(Acts 2:34), Isaiah 57:19—(Acts 2:39), Hebrews 10:25—(Acts 2:42), See also Revelation 6:12, Romans 10:13, John 1:45, Acts 2:22, Acts 3:22, Acts 7:37, John 1:21, Acts 2:25, Acts 13:35, Matthew 22:44, Mark 12:35, Hebrews 1:3, Luke 20:43, Acts 2:34, Hebrews 10:13, I Corinthians 15:25, Ephesians 1:20, Hebrews 1:13, Ephesians 2:1
10. Blessed are the poor in spirit to those who believe the *power of Pentecostal testimony of a short life of a young man by the name of Stephen*, who was *cut off short in his ministry by the hand of Saul* (See Acts 7:58; Acts 22:20} and one of *God's most trusted and honest report, full of the Holy Ghost and wisdom*: Acts 6:5, 8, 10-15, Acts 7:1-2.
11. Blessed are the poor in spirit to those who believe the *power of Pentecostal message of Stephen's preaching*: His sermon was "*The Glory Of God*" *Acts 7:1-55* concerning, Genesis 11:31—(Acts 6:2), Genesis 12:1—(Acts 6:3), Genesis 12:7—(Acts 6:5), Genesis 15:13—(Acts 6:7), Genesis 17:19—(Acts 6:8), Genesis 41:41—(Acts 6:10), Genesis 45:3—(Acts 6:13), Deuteronomy 10:22—(Acts 6:14), Joshua 24:31—(Acts 7:16), Exodus 1:8—(Acts 7:18), Exodus 2:2—(Acts 7:20), Exodus 2:14—(Acts 7:27), Exodus 3:3—(Acts 7:31), Exodus 7:3—(Acts 7:36), Deuteronomy 18:15—(Acts 7:37), Numbers 14:4—(Acts 7:39), Exodus

32:1—(Acts 7:40), Exodus 32:6—(Acts 7:41), Amos 5:25—(Acts 7:42), Joshua 24:20—(Acts 7:43), Jeremiah 20:6—(Acts 7:43), Joshua 3:14—(Acts 7:44), Psalm 132:5—(Acts 7:46), I Kings 6:11-38—(Acts 7:48), Isaiah 66:1-2—(Acts 7:49), II Kings 17:14—(Acts 7:51), Exodus 33:3—(Acts 7:51)

12. Blessed are the poor in spirit to those who *witnessed the death of Stephen including Saul* (See Acts 7:58), Acts 7:55-60, Acts 22:20

Part CDXX

Blessed Are The Poor In Spirit. Matthew 5:3

Blessed Means Happy

Poor means meek in spirit Poor means humble in spirit Poor means lowly in spirit Poor means quiet in spirit Read Matthew 5:3-12, Read also Mark 1:15

Jesus did not say "*rich*" in spirit. Jesus said "*poor*" in spirit.

1. Blessed are the poor in spirit to those who believe that Paul, one of God's children, began to *preach his first sermon*: "*Honor God*:" Acts 13:15-41, Prophets Acts 13:17 (Exodus 6:1, 6) Acts 13:22 (I Samuel 13:14), Acts 13:22 (I Peter 1:22, I Thessalonians 4:8, John 13:20, Luke 10:16, Hosea 13:11), Acts 13:23 (II Samuel 7:12, Psalms 132:11, I Kings 8:25, Luke 1:69), Romans 11:26 (Joel 2:28, 29), Acts 13:23 (Psalm 2:7, Hebrews 5:5) Acts 13:34 (Isaiah 55:3), Acts 13:35 (Psalm 16:10, Acts 2:31, Psalm 49:15), Acts 13:47 (Isaiah 49:6) (Matthew 3:11, Acts 1:4-5, Acts 2:3, 4, Titus 3:5, John 3:3, 5, I Peter 3:21, Ephesians 5:26, John 3:15, Malachi 3:2, Revelation 6:17, Psalm 76:7, Job 41:10, I Corinthians 10:22, Ezekiel 22:14, Ezekiel 21:7, Ezekiel 28:9, Psalm 9:20, Job 9:4, Nahum 1:6, Isaiah 4:4, John 6:63, 2 verse 23, Galatians 3:28, Romans 10:12, Mark 1:8, Proverbs 1:23, John 1:33, John 7:37, 38, 39, Deuteronomy 18:15, Jeremiah 7:13, Psalm 36:9, Zechariah 13:1, Revelation 21:6, Isaiah 12:3, John 4:10, Revelation 7:17, Isaiah 25:8, II Corinthians 5:4, I Corinthians 15:53, Hebrews 2:14-18, II Timothy 2:10, II Corinthians 1:6, Philippians 2:7-13, John 14:6, II John 9, John 1:1, 2, Hebrews 12:1-2, Hebrews 5:2, Hebrews 1:4, John 13:13, Hebrews 13:21, Luke 6:46, James 1:22, I Corinthians 8:6, Hebrews 1:1, Number 12:6, 8, Matthew 1:20, Luke 1:35, Acts 8:37, Romans 1:4, Acts 13:27 (I Corinthians 2:8), Acts 13:30 (Matthew 28:6, Hebrews 13:20, Ezekiel 34:23, Jeremiah 30:9, Luke 1:69, John 10:11) Acts 13:31 (I Corinthians 15:1-11, Romans 5:2, Psalm 2:7, Acts 13:33, Isaiah 5:3, 5, Hebrews 1:5, Psalm 89:26) Acts 13:32 (Genesis 12:3, Romans 4:13, Galatians 3:16, I Corinthians 12:12, Galatians 3:29) Acts 13:33 (Psalm 2:7, Acts 13:33, Isaiah 53:6, Hebrews 1:5, Psalm 89:26) Acts 13:34 (Isaiah 53:5), Acts 13:35 (Psalm 16:10, Acts 2:27, Daniel 9:24, Luke 1:35, Acts 8:37, Romans 1:4-8, Ephesians 3:8-12, Romans 16:25-27, Ephesians 3:3, 5, Acts

10:28, Colossians 1:27-29) Acts 13:40-41 (Habakkuk 1:5), Acts 13:43 (Titus 2:11, Matthew 23:14, Ezekiel 22:25, Acts 20:29, II Peter 2:1, I Corinthians 6:20, I Peter 1:18, Ezekiel 20:18, Revelation 5:9-10, I Peter 5:12), Acts 13:45 (I Peter 4:4-5, II Timothy 4:1-4, Jude 10), Acts 13:46 (Romans 1:16), Acts 13:48 (II Timothy 2:19), Acts 13:51 (I Peter 1:7-9 verse 8, I John 4:20)

2.

Blessed are the poor in spirit to those who believed that one of the seven men, of honest report, *Philip*, one of God's children, too, preached a Pentecostal message to an *Ethiopian Eunuch* near the road: His sermon was "*Jesus Christ*:" According to Isaiah 53:7, Matthew 27:12, Acts 6:3, 5, 8:5, 26-40

3.

Blessed are the poor in spirit to those who *believe that some of the 120 went into an upper room prayer meeting*: Acts 1:13-15; they were lists as: Peter, James, John, Andrew, Philip, Thomas, Bartholomew, Matthew, James, the son of Alphae, and Simon Aielotes, Judas brother of James, and Mary, the mother of Jesus.

4.

Blessed are the poor in spirit to those who *believe that Jesus' disciples went out and preached that men should repent*. Mark 6:12

5.

Blessed are the poor in spirit to those who believe this spiritual hymn: "Spir-it Di- vine, hear our prayer, And make our hearts Your Home; De-scend with all Your Gra-cious." Acts 10:1-9 verse 1-4, Psalm 143:1, John 14:1-4, Psalm 34:8, I Peter 2:3, II Peter 1:3, 4, Hebrews 9:1, Psalm 145:8, Psalm 112:4, Psalm 111:4, Psalm 86:15, Psalm 77:9, Nehemiah 9:31, II Chronicles 30:9, Numbers 6:25, Exodus 22:27, 33:19, 34:6, Jonah 4:2, Malachi 1:9, Luke 4:22

6.

Blessed are the poor in spirit to those who believe that the Power of Pentecost is Jesus Christ. Luke 24:44, 47, Acts 28:31, Romans 1:16, I Corinthians 1:23

7. Blessed are the poor in spirit to those who believe that the Power of Pentecost is Jesus Christ. Hosea 6:2, John 14:16-21, Luke 24:44-49, Acts 1:2-5, Acts 2:1-47 I Corinthians 1:23-31, Philippians 1:10-21, I John 2:27-29

8.

Blessed are the poor in spirit to those who believe that the Messiah is Jesus of Nazareth. Matthew 2:23, Matthew 4:13, Mark 16:6, Acts 2:22, Acts 22:8

9. Blessed are the poor in spirit to these who "*listen*," "*believe*," and "*hear*" *the testimony of Simon in Acts 8:9-25.*

    i. "*Simon Himself*" *also believe the gospel.* Acts 8:13
    ii. Simon "*offered*" *Philip, Peter* and *John some money to purchase the power for a living "for himself" by laying hands on someone else so that the person may receive the power.* Acts 8:19
    iii. *Simon "truly" was not saved because of money. Peter said to Simon, "thy money "perish" with thee,"* because *thou* hast "*thought*" that the *gift of God may be purchased with money.* Acts 8:20
    iv. *Simon "thought" that the gift was purchased with money. He indeed "thought"* dead *wrong.* Acts 8:20
    v. *Simon's heart was not right with God. Simon's heart was not right in the sight of God.* Acts 8:21
    vi. *Peter said to Simon, "Repent therefore of this wickedness and pray God, if perhaps the thought of thine heart may be forgiven thee.*
    Acts 8:22
    vii. *Simon asked for prayer. He said, "Pray ye to the Lord for me, that none of these things which ye have spoken come upon me."* Acts 8:24
    viii. And they, when *they had testified and preached the word of the Lord, returned to Jerusalem,* and *preached the gospel in many villages of the Samaritans.* Acts 8:25

10. Blessed are the poor in spirit to those who believe the *necessity of knowing God* and *His power*; the *Sovereignty of God.* Genesis 1:1 and John 1:1, **John 1:12, verses 7, 8, 9, Philippians 2:2-11 verse 6, 10, 11, Philippians 3:10**
11. Blessed are the poor in spirit to those who believe *The Grace and Peace which is from God our Father and the Lord Jesus Christ.* II Corinthians 1:2, Galatians 1:3, Ephesians 1:1-3, Philippians 1:2, II Thessalonians 1:2, II Peters 1:2, Revelation 1:8
12.

    Blessed are the poor in spirit to those who believe that to *act like Apostle Paul leading others to Jesus Christ*; they were *Martin Luther, John Wesley, Richard Allen, William J. Seymour, Charles H. Mason, Charles G. Finney, Dwight L. Moody, Billy Sunday, John R. Rice* and *Billy Graham* that *opened up the World Wide ministries to God's people.* Mark 16:15, Luke 24:47-49, Acts 1:4-8, Isaiah 61:1-3, Luke 4:18-19

PART CDXXI

Blessed Are The Poor In Spirit. Matthew 5:3

Blessed Means Happy

Poor means meek in spirit. Poor means humble in spirit. Poor means lowly in spirit. Poor means quiet in spirit. Read Matthew 5:3-12, Read also Mark 1:15

Jesus did not say "*rich*" in spirit. Jesus said "*poor*" in spirit.

1. Blessed are the poor in spirit to those who believe *one of God's children*, Martin Luther spoke: "Their *miracles, Spirit,* and *sanctify*, therefore, *belong to us who preach Jesus Christ,* and *not the ability and works of men.*" Martin Luther (1483-1596). I Corinthians 2:2, Mark 15:16
2. Blessed are the poor in spirit to those who believe that the *church* is the *pillar and ground of the truth*; which is the gospel, of *Jesus Christ and His church.* Jesus said, "I will build my church". I Timothy 3:15 and Matthew 16:18
3. Blessed are the poor in spirit to those who *believe the Word of the Lord*: "*Assemble yourselves and come; draw near together, ye that are escaped of the nations: they have no knowledge that set up the wood of their graven image, and pray unto a god that cannot save.*" Isaiah 45:20, See Jeremiah 15:19-21
4. Blessed are the poor in spirit to those who *believe the Word of the Lord*: "*Tell ye, and bring them near; yea, let them take counsel together: who hath declared this from ancient time? Who hath told it from that time: have not I the Lord? and there is no God else beside Me; a just God and a Saviour; there is none beside Me.*" Isaiah 45:21
5. Blessed are the poor in spirit to those who *believe the Word of the Lord*: "*Look unto me, and be ye saved, all the ends of the earth: for I am God, and there is none else.*" Isaiah 45:22
6. Blessed are the poor in spirit to those who *believe the Word of the Lord*: "Awake, awake; put on the strength, O Zion; put on thy beautiful garments, O Jersualem, the holy city: for henceforth there shall no more come into thee the uncircumcised and the unclean." Isaiah 52:1
7. Blessed are the poor in spirit to those who *believe the Word of the Lord*: "Shake thyself from the dust; arise, and sit down, O Jersusalem: loose thyself from the bands of thy neck, O captive daughter of Zion." Isaiah 52:2

8. Blessed are the poor in spirit to those who *believe the Word of the Lord*: "Therefore thus saith the Lord, *If thou return, then will I bring thee again, and thou shalt stand before me: and if thou take forth the precious from the vile, thou shalt be as my mouth: let them return unto thee; but return not thou unto them.*" Jeremiah 15:19
9. Blessed are the poor in spirit to those who *believe in a Loving God, a Loving Lord and a Loving Christ* is the *same One*; in *the same Person*: "*Thou shalt love the Lord thy God with all thine heart is a commandment and requirement because He is a loving God, a loving Lord*, and *a loving Christ*. Deuteronomy 6:4-7, Deuteronomy 11:1-9, Matthew 22:37-40, Mark 12:29-31, Luke 10:26-28
10. Blessed are the poor in spirit to those who believe the Word of the Lord: "*Have I any pleasure at all that the wicked should die*? saith the Lord God: *and not that he should return from his ways, and live*? Ezekiel 18:23
11. Blessed are the poor in spirit to those who believe *these two Words from the Lord*: "*And in very deed for this cause have I raised thee up, for to shew in thee my power; and that my name may be declared throughout all the earth.*" Exodus 9:16 "For the scripture saith unto Pharaoh, *Even for this same purpose have I raised thee up, that I might shew my power in thee, and that my name might be declared throughout all the earth.*" Romans 9:17 See Exodus 9:16
12. Blessed are the poor in spirit to those who *believe the Bible*; *God Himself wrote the Bible, the Holy Book, the Holy Word. He has indeed spoken to us all.* Hebrews 1:1-14, II Samuel 7:14, Psalm 110:1, Psalm 104:4, Psalm 45:6, Psalm 45:7, Psalm 102:25, Psalm 102:25-27, Psalm 110:1, Genesis 1:1, John 1:1, II Timothy 3:14-17

PART CDXXII

Blessed Are The Poor In Spirit. Matthew 5:3

Blessed Means Happy

Poor means meek in spirit. Poor means humble in spirit. Poor means lowly in spirit. Poor means quiet in spirit. Read Matthew 5:3-12, Read also Mark 1:15

Jesus did not say "*rich*" in spirit. Jesus said "*poor*" in spirit.

1. Blessed are the poor in spirit to those who *believe Jesus Christ's Word*: "Many are called but *few are chosen*." Matthew 22:14 and *Jesus Christ knows whom He has chosen*: "*I know whom I have chosen*." John 13:18 "*Chosen*" *mean* "A *calling*," also *mean* "*His Will*," "His Commandment and His Work" and "His Life" *concerning* Him. See Luke 24:27, 44, Acts 2:25, Acts 2:31, Acts 28:31
2. Blessed are the poor in spirit to those who believe in "*sound speech*" *by the Word of God* "*that cannot be condemned*." Titus 2:8
3. Blessed are the poor in spirit to those who *believe that for those who are not reading the Bible*, "*has missed*" *God's greatest blessings*; *His word has all the* "*answers*" for *all mankind* to *grasp His teaching* "*on salvation*" and "*a home*" to *live for eternal call* "*Heaven*." John 14:1-4
4. Blessed are the poor in spirit to those who *believe* that the *Bible speak of the Holy Spirit carrying* on the *Gospel of Jesus Christ throughout the end of the earth* and that the *Holy Spirit speak of the Second Coming of Jesus Christ*. Acts 1:11, John 14:1-4, Romans 8:16, Revelation 22:7, 12, 22, Genesis 1:1-2, John 1:1-12, I Timothy 3:16, II Peter 1:21—men were moved by the Holy Spirit of God
5. Blessed are the poor in spirit to those who believe the Scripture of Promise:" I desire not the death of a sinner, but rather that he should be converted and live." Ezekiel 18:32
6. Blessed are the poor in spirit to those who believe the Word of the Lord:"*For I have no pleasure in the death of him that dieth*, saith the Lord God: *wherefore turn yourselves, and live ye*." Ezekiel 18:32
7. Blessed are the poor in spirit to those who believe the Word of the Lord:"*Have I any pleasure at all that the wicked should die*? saith the Lord God: *and not that he should return from his ways, and live*?" Ezekiel 18:23

8. Blessed are the poor in spirit to those who believe the Word of the Lord:"*Say unto them, As I live,* saith the Lord God, *I have no pleasure in the death of the wicked; but that the wicked turn from his way and live: turn ye, turn ye from your evil ways; for why will ye die, O house of Israel?*" Ezekiel 33:11
9. Blessed are the poor in spirit to those who believe the Word of the Lord's warning: "*Son of man, I have made thee a watchman unto the house of Israel: therefore hear the word at My mouth, and give them not warning from Me.*" Ezekiel 3:17
10. Blessed are the poor in spirit to those who believe the Word of the Lord's warning:"*When I say unto the wicked, thou shalt surely die; and thou givest him not warning, nor speakest to warn the wicked from his wicked way, to save his life; the same wicked man shall die in his iniquity*—{ sin}; but his blood will I require at thine hand." Ezekiel 3:18, See John 8:24
11. Blessed are the poor in spirit to those who believe the Word of the Lord's warning:"*Yet if thou warn the wicked, and he turn not from his wickedness, nor from his wicked way, he shall die in his iniquity*-{sin}; *but thou hast delivered thy soul.*" Ezekiel 3:19
12. Blessed are the poor in spirit to those who believe the Word of the Lord's warning:"*Again, When a righteous man doth turn from his righteousness, and commit iniquity*-{sin, *and I lay a stumblingblock before him, he shall die: because thou hast not given him warning, he shall die in his sin, and his righteousness which he hath done shall not be remembered; but his blood will I require at thine hand.*" Ezekiel 3:20

PART CDXXIII

Blessed Are The Poor In Spirit. Matthew 5:3

Blessed Means Happy

Poor means meek in spirit Poor means humble in spirit Poor means lowly in spirit Poor means quiet in spirit Read Matthew 5:3-12, Read also Mark 1:15

Jesus did not say "*rich*" in spirit. Jesus said "*poor*" in spirit.

1. Blessed are the poor in spirit to those who believe the Word of the Lord's warning: "*Nevertheless if thou warn the righteous man, that the righteous sin not, and he doth not sin, he shall surely live, because he is warned; also thou hast delivered thy soul.*" Ezekiel 3:21
2. Blessed are the poor in spirit to those who believe the Word of the Lord's warning: "And the hand of the Lord was there upon me; and he said unto me, *Arise, go forth into the plain, and I will there talk with thee.*" Ezekiel 3:22
3. Blessed are the poor in spirit to those who believe the Word of the Lord's tender heart: "And *shewing mercy unto thousands of them that love me, and keep my commandments.*" Exodus 20:6
4. Blessed are the poor in spirit to those who believe the Word of the Lord's tender heart: "*For his anger endureth but a moment; in his favour is life: weeping may endure for a night, but joy cometh in the morning.*" Psalm 30:5
5. Blessed are the poor in spirit to those who believe the Word of the Lord: "*How excellent is thy lovingkindness, O God! Therefore the children of men put their trust under the shadow of thy wings.*" Psalm 36:7
6. Blessed are the poor in spirit to those who believe the Word of the Lord's promise: "*Come unto me, all ye that labour and are heavy laden, and I will give you rest.*" Matthew 11:28
7. Blessed are the poor in spirit to those who believe that *life* which is *Jesus Christ, peace,* which is *Jesus Christ and salvation* which is *Jesus Christ* is the *Gift from a loving God.* John 3:16-17
8. Blessed are the poor in spirit to those who *believe the scripture*: "*He sent His Word and healed them.*" Psalm 107:20, Deuteronomy 30:11-14, Isaiah 58:2, Matthew 19:17, II Peter 2:10-14, Romans 2:6-7, Acts 26:17-18

9. Blessed are the poor in spirit to those who believe the *Biblical Foundation for Evangelism is found in Joel 2:28-32* and *Acts 2:16-21 as God's purpose with Acts 1:8 and Acts 2:1-47 and Luke 24:47-53*
10. Blessed are the poor in spirit to those who believe that *Christians,* the *children of God,* are *saved to serve; not saved to stay.* I Thessalonians 5:23-25, John 1:12, Romans 8:14-16 verse 15, Romans 9:4, Galatians 4:5, Ephesians 1:5
11. Blessed are the poor in spirit to those who believe the eleven statement of Evangelism Affirmation:[1] The Inspiration of the Bible [2] The Trinity [3] The Depravity Of Man [4] The Medication Of Christ [5] Justification By Faith [6] Conversion And Sanctification By The Spirit [7] The Baptism of the Holy Spirit [8] Anointing Of The Sick [9] The Return Of Christ And The Final Judgment [10] The Ministry Of the Word and [11] The Sacrament Of Water Baptism And The Lord's Super Genesis 1:1-2, John1:1-12, Matthew 28:18-20, II Timothy 3:16-17
12. Blessed are the poor in spirit to those who believe that speaking in sign language is intended to be the baptism of the Holy Spirit to spread the gospel to the deaf world so that the deaf shall hear the word of the book and be saved before the Second Coming of Jesus Christ to those who are unbelievers in the world. **Isaiah 29:18**, Luke 7:22, Acts 1:4-5, Acts 1:8, Acts 2:1-4, verse 4, Acts 2:1-47, verse 1-11, Acts 10:44

Part CDXXIV

Blessed Are The Poor In Spirit. Matthew 5:3

Blessed Means Happy

Poor means meek in spirit. Poor means humble in spirit. Poor means lowly in spirit. Poor means quiet in spirit. Read Matthew 5:3-12, Read also Mark 1:15

Jesus did not say "*rich*" in spirit. Jesus said "*poor*" in spirit.

1. Blessed are the poor in spirit to those who believe that The *Holy Interpretion of God is right, The Holy Interpretation of Christ is right,* The *Holy Interpretation of the Holy Spirit is right,* The *Holy Interpretation of Grace is right because He is The Holy Author,* The *Authour of Eternatl Salvation, Obey it, Just do it. Be satisfied.* I Corinthians 12:6, Genesis 1:1, John 1:1, II Timothy 3:16, Hebrews 5:9
2. Blessed are the poor in spirit to those who believe that *an holy interpretation does not make mistake*; does not make *an error.* It is God that make the *interpretation clear according to His Written Word...does not fall into the hand of man*, but to *help us see clearly the salvation of our Lord.* II Corinthians 12:6, Genesis 1:1, John 1:1, II Timothy 3:16
3. Blessed are the poor in spirit to those who beliece that as children of God, we worship together as one with God through Jesus Christ because we, *red, yellow, black, brown* and *white* are washed away by Jesus' Precious Blood. I Peter 2:19-25
4. Blessed are the poor in spirit to those who believe that *finding wells of salvation and drawing waters out of the well of salvation is Jesus Christ* who is "*That Well*" because *Jesus is the Living Water* and that the *Living Water is the Gift of God. John 4:6-15*
5. Blessed are the poor in spirit to those who *teach, testify* and *preach the same language*, the *same sermon*; *Jesus Christ* and *His Second Coming.* Joel 2:28, Acts 1:11, Revelation 22:20
6. Blessed are the poor in spirit to those who believe the scripture: "It is not by might nor by power but by my Spirit saith the Lord." Zechariah 4:6
7. Blessed are the poor in spirit to those who believe that our *God Almighty through Jesus Christ* is our *interrpretation to get us to understand the salvation of our souls and to be delivered from sin, death and hell so that we may get to Heaven to live with*

Him for ever more. Genesis 1:1, John 1:1, I Corinthians 14:20-33, II Timothy 3:15-17

8. Blessed are the poor in spirit to those who are *sad to see a lost and dying world "without" Jesus Christ* and *that the sinners are depravity in need of the Savior.* Matthew 1:21, 25, Luke 2:11, John 4:42, II Peter 2:20, I John 4:14
9. Blessed are the poor in spirit to those who *are ready for the marriage supper of the Lord's return* because *we are blessed to have Christ that have the call in our lives.* Revelation 19:9
10. Blessed are the poor in spirit to those who believe this scripture: "And Enoch also, the seventh from Adam, prophesied of these, saying, Behold, the Lord cometh with ten thousands of his saints." Jude 14
11. Blessed are the poor in spirit to those who believe this scripture: "Then shall the Lord go forth, and fight against those nations, as when he fought in the day of battle." Zechariah 14:3
12. Blessed are the poor in spirit to those who believe this scripture: "And his feet shall stand in that day upon the mount of Olives, which is before Jerusalem on the east, and the mount of Olives shall cleave in the midst thereof toward the east and toward the west, and there shall be a very great valley; and half of the mountain shall remove toward the north, and half of it toward the south." Zechariah 14:4

Part CDXXV

Blessed Are The Poor In Spirit. Matthew 5:3

Blessed Means Happy

Poor means meek in spirit. Poor means humble in spirit. Poor means lowly in spirit. Poor means quiet in spirit. Read Matthew 5:3-12, Read also Mark 1:15

Jesus did not say "*rich*" in spirit. Jesus said "*poor*" in spirit.

1. Blessed are the poor in spirit to those who believe this scripture: "And I heard a great voice out of heaven saying, Behold, the tabernacle of God is with men, and he will dwell with them, and they shall be his people, and God Himself shall be with them, and be their God." Revelation 3:21
2. Blessed are the poor in spirit to those who believe that *justification and sancification is through Jesus Christ in our heart by faith.* John 17:14-19, I Corinthians 6:11, Romans 1:17, Hebrews 13:12, 13, Romans 5:1, I Thessalonians 4:3, II Thessalonians 5:23
3. Blessed are the poor in spirit to those who believe this scripture pardon: "Let the wicked forsake his way, and the unrighteous man his thoughts: and let him return unto the Lord, and he will have mercy upon him; and to our God, for he will abundantly pardon." Isaiah 55:7
4. Blessed are the poor in spirit to those who believe the *Blood of Jesus Christ give life, power and fire, joy, peace, happiness and faith. Jesus is alive for ever more.* Luke 16:6, Revelation 1:18
5. Blessed are the poor in spirit to those who believe that Personal Pentecost is connected with the bapitsm of the Holy Spirit. Matthew 3:11
6. Blessed are the poor in spirit to those who believe that *Prayer will see us through* James 5:14-15.
7. Blessed are the poor in spirit to those who believe that the *Doctrine of the Bible of salvation will take us into heaven. God's salvation is so real. Accept His salvation today.* Now is the time. II Corinthians 6:2
8. Blessed are the poor in spirit to those who believe *Jesus' statement*: "*Preach ye upon the housetops.*" Matthew 10:27
9. Blessed are the poor in spirit to those who believe *the Old Testament and the New Testament*: "But it shall be one day which shall be known to the Lord, not

day, nor night: but is shall come to pass, that at evening time it shall be light." Zechariah 14:7

10. Blessed are the poor in spirit to those who believe *the Old Testament and the New Testament*: "But of that day and hour knoweth no man, no, not the angels of heaven, but my Father only." Matthew 24:36
11. Blessed are the poor in spirit to those who believe that *a sinner in need of a prayer for salvation*: "*God, I know that I am a sinner*, and that *only you can be my Savior, I am asking you to forgive the sins of my old life*, and *give me a brand new life. By faith I believe that you have saved me*, and *now give me the strength to abide in you. Amen.*" John 15:10, John 1:12, Romans 3:23, John 3:6, Acts 4:12, I John 1:9, Luke 18:23
12. Blessed are the poor in spirit to those who believe that on *Christ's sacrifice*, on *suffering*, on opposition, as well as on "*the year of Jubilee*," the *Levitical doctrine never once actual out*, but that offered the *prospect of freedom to slaves and justice for all.* See Leviticus 25:1-25 (verse 9, 10, 11, 12, 13, 15, 28, 30, 31, 33, 40, 50, 52, 54) in Old Testament and Acts 2:1-47, See Joel 2:1-32 (verse 1, 11, 12, 13, 14, 15, 16, 19-32)

Part CDXXVI

Blessed Are The Poor In Spirit. Matthew 5:3

Blessed Means Happy

Poor means meek in spirit. Poor means humble in spirit. Poor means lowly in spirit. Poor means quiet in spirit. Read Matthew 5:3-12, Read also Mark 1:15

Jesus did not say "*rich*" in spirit. Jesus said "*poor*" in spirit.

1. Blessed are the poor in spirit to those who believe that the *gift of tongues*; the *gift of the Holy Spirit*; the *gift of the Baptism of the Holy Spirit represented for the mission field around the world; the outpouring of the Holy Spirit in this way would enable missionaries to preach to foreign heathens* (*unsaved, pagans, ungodly*) *without having to learn the language* (or *the sermon*) *called the exneoglossa, the God given gift of speaking in our writing an authentic language unknown to the speaker.* Acts 2:4-11, See I Corinthians 14:1-40
2. Blessed are the poor in spirit to those who *believe* to *look* at the *portraits* of the *great leaders*; they were *John the Baptist, St. James, St Peter, St. Paul, Martin Luther, John Wesley and William J. Seymour.* Matthew 17:4, Mark 9:5, Luke 9:33
3. Blessed are the poor in spirit to those who believe that *without Jesus Christ*; *without His Spirit, we can do nothing to save our own selfish* and *desires.* "Without Me, You can do nothing." John 15:5, See John 5:30
4. Blessed are the poor in spirit to those who *believe Christ's warning of those that are in the graves and the resurrection of damnation of those who are without Him.* John 5:28-29
5. Blessed are the poor in spirit to those who "*hear*" *Christ's voice* and *to come forth to those that are in the graves to those that are born again*; *to those that are saved*; *unto the resurrection of life.* John 5:28
6. Blessed are the poor in spirit to those who believe and are able to pray *for salvation, "Lord, be merciful to me a sinner."* Luke 18:13
7. Blessed are the poor in spirit to those who believe that *God in the Bible tell us that He bring "Love"*, that He bring "*Peace"* that *He bring "Hope"* that He bring "*salvation*" and that He bring "*healing*". Isaiah 53:5, Isaiah 57:19, Exodus 15:26, Hosea 6:1, Galatians 5:22, I Corinthians 1:18, II Thessalonians 2:16, John 3:16

8. Blessed are the poor in spirit to those who *believe that Pentecost is the "Jewish National Holiday."* Acts 2:1
9. Blessed are the poor in spirit to those who *believe the Word of the Lord*: "*Write the vision*, and *make it (His) plain upon tables*, that *he may run that readeth it*." Habakkuk 2:2
10. Blessed are the poor in spirit to those who believe *this spiritual hymn*: "*He loves us.*
    Oh, He loves us.
    Oh, He loves us
    Oh, He loves
    He loves us;" John 3:16, II Thessalonians 2:16
11. Blessed are the poor in spirit to those who *believe the Word of the Lord*:" *See now that I, am he, and there is no god with me: I kill, and I make alive; I wound, and I heal: neither is there any that can deliver out of my hand.*" Deuteronomy 32:39
12. Blessed are the poor in spirit to those who believe that the *claim of the Azusa Street Pentecost in Los Angeles, California in 1906-1909 belong to the whole body of Christ.* Isaiah 57:19, Joel 2:27-32, *Acts 2:39, 47, Romans 10:13, Ephesians 2:19*

Part CDXXVII

Blessed Are The Poor In Spirit. Matthew 5:3

Blessed Means Happy

Poor means meek in spirit Poor means humble in spirit Poor means lowly in spirit Poor means quiet in spirit Read Matthew 5:3-12, Read also Mark 1:15

Jesus did not say "*rich*" in spirit. Jesus said "*poor*" in spirit.

1. Blessed are the poor in spirit to those who believe that *Pentecostal Name was named or was given after the Jewish Feast of Pentecost* when the *Holy Spirit was first given to the church and the believers first spoke in tongues*. Acts 2:1-11, verse 4, see Mark 16:17 (c), Acts 1:4-8, Act 11:16
2. Blessed are the poor in spirit to those who are continuing *faithful servants until the end, will hear God honoring faithfully servants*; "*Well done, good and faithful servant, enter thou into the joy of the Lord*. Matthew 25:21
3. Blessed are the poor in spirit to those who believe that the *Gospel of Jesus Christ* give us "*Hope*" *through grace*. II Thessalonians 2:16
    a. All power is given unto me in heaven and in earth. Matthew 28:18
    b. God has given Jesus the authority to execute judgment; also He is the Son of Man. John 5:27
    c. Jesus gave 12 disciples the power and authority. Luke 9:1
    d. Again God the Father say, "Hear Him, Hear Jesus." that God gave Jesus permission to make decision. John 5:22, 27, Matthew 28:18-20 verse 18, Luke 3:22, 9:35, Mark 1:11, Mark 9:7, Matthew 17:5, Matthew 3:17, 12:18
4. Blessed are the poor in spirit to those who *believe and preach the Old Time Power of Pentecost*, the *latter days* and the *soon return of Christ*. Acts 1:12, Acts 2:1-4, Revelation 22:7, 12, 20
5. Blessed are the poor in spirit to those who *believe that the Power of Pentecost*, the *Power of Prayer is first to pray*; *The Power to save*; *the Power to preach. And the Power to lead sinful men and women to Jesus Christ at the foot of an old rugged cross where Jesus breathed His last word: "It Is Finished." John 19:30*
6. Blessed are the poor in spirit to those who *believe the unknown tongues or different languages according to Mark 16:17-(c), Acts 2:4*, Act 10:46, Acts 19:6 and at least

in *I Corinthians 14:2, 4, 13, 14, 19 and 27.* Read I Corinthians 14:21-23 and Isaiah 28:11

7. Blessed are the poor in spirit to those who believe that the *Only "Fallen From Grace" is from the law which we cannot be justified by the law of Moses. Quotation is from*: "Christ is become of no effect unto you, whosoever of you are justified by the law; ye are fallen from grace. Galatians 5:4
8. Blessed are the poor in spirit to those who *believe that the Bible itself* is the "*Witness of the Spirit.*" Romans 8:16, Galatians 4:6, Ephesians 1:13, I Peter 2:2-4 (verse 3), Psalm 34:8, Romans 8:1, 2, II Corinthians 1:22, I John 5:6, John 4:24
9. Blessed are the poor in spirit to those who *believe that God want to talk with you, needs to talk with you because He loves you and because you need to feel the love of God in you.* John 3:16, I John 4:19, Romans 5:5, Romans 8:39, II Corinthians 13:14, II Thessalonians 3:5, Titus 3:4, I John 2:5, I John 3:16, I John 4:6-21, Jude 2, Acts 17:27, **Philippians 3:10, Romans 8:16**
10. Blessed are the poor in spirit to those who believe that the *people of God are filled with the Holy Spirit by talking, laughing and weeping about Jesus Christ every where*; *in church, in home, in school in the neighborhood, in the street*, and the *place else where.* Luke 1:15, Luke 1:41, Luke 1:47, Luke 6:21, Acts 4:31, Acts 2:4, Acts 13:9, Acts 4:8, Acts 2:2
11. Blessed are the poor in spirit to those who believe that *all the flesh will see the salvation of God.* Luke 3:6
12. Blessed are the poor in spirit to those who *believe by being filled of the Holy Spirit through hungry through weeping and through laughing.* Luke 6:21

Part CDXXVIII

Blessed Are The Poor In Spirit. Matthew 5:3

Blessed Means Happy

Poor means meek in spirit. Poor means humble in spirit. Poor means lowly in spirit. Poor means quiet in spirit. Read Matthew 5:3-12, Read also Mark 1:15

Jesus did not say "*rich*" in spirit. Jesus said "*poor*" in spirit.

1. Blessed are the poor in spirit to those who believe *with joy by being filled of the Holy Spirit.* Acts 13:52
2. Blessed are the poor in spirit to those who believe that the *Holy Spirit witnesses in every city, testifying the gospel of the grace of God and preaching the kingdom of God, concerning the Lord Jesus Christ.* Acts 20:23-25, See Acts 20:21
3. Blessed are the poor in spirit to those who believe that *ministry* is through *being filled with the Spirit, the baptism of the Spirit.* Acts 1:8, Ephesians 5:17, Acts 20:21, 23, 24, 25, Acts 2:12, 15, 21, See Joel 2:28-32, Romans 10:8-13
4. Blessed are the poor in spirit to those who *believe in finding God's match or God's will for both couple. If both agree in my name, then I am in middle of them.* Amos 3:3, Matthew 18:19-20
5. Blessed are the poor in spirit to those who believe by saying "*Yes,*" that the *sound of the gospel went into all the earth and God's people,* the *family of God through their words and by mouth unto the end.* Romans 10:8-21, See Psalm 19:4
6. Blessed are the poor in spirit to those who *believe that Jeremiah, one of God's children, wept.* So *God wept and Jesus Christ wept* over the people in the city of Jerusalem. Luke 19:41, Jeremiah 1:1-3
7. Blessed are the poor in spirit to those who *bellieve that Anna,* a *prophetess and one of God's children, announced that Jesus was the Messiah.* Luke 2:36-39
8. Blessed are the poor in spirit to those who *believe* that the *disciples knew not* "*the scripture*" that "*Christ*" "*must rise again from the dead.*" John 20:9
9. Blessed are the poor in spirit to those who believe that God through Jesus Christ *honor us with true, honest,* and *rightly repentance.* I John 1:9
10. Blessed are the poor in spirit to those who *believe* that while the *World is being* "*insult at,*" is the *gospel of Jesus Christ still spread the Word of God getting men,* women and children saved. Mark 16:15, Mark 13:16

11. Blessed are the poor in spirit to those who *believe that our Lord is not only our Savior*, but *our Lord is our Healer*, and the *Soon Coming King, God Almighty*. Revelation 1:8, Isaiah 53:5, Exodus 15:26, I Peter 2:24, Psalm 103:3-5, Psalm 147:3, Isaiah 30:26, Matthew 8:7, Read Luke 14:3-4, Matthew 13:15, Read Matthew 10:1-8, Mark 3:14-19, Luke 9:2, 10:9, Read Isaiah 61:1-3, Luke 4:18-19, Luke 5:17, Luke 7:3, John 4:47-51, Acts 4:30, Mark 7:37
12. Blessed are the poor in spirit to those who believe that *Jesus Christ want the world to* "*repent*" or likewise "*perish*." Luke 13:3, 5, Numbers 21:7

Part CDXXIX

Blessed Are The Poor In Spirit. Matthew 5:3

Blessed Means Happy

Poor means meek in spirit Poor means humble in spirit Poor means lowly in spirit Poor means quiet in spirit Read Matthew 5:3-12, Read also Mark 1:15

Jesus did not say "*rich*" in spirit. Jesus said "*poor*" in spirit.

1. Blessed are the poor in spirit to those who believe that *Jesus Christ want the world* "*to repent*" or else *He will come quickly and will fight against them with the sword of His mouth*. Revelation 2:16
2. Blessed are the poor in spirit to those who believe in *this old spiritual hymn*: "Jesus, Jesus, how I trust Him. How I've proved Him over and over, Jesus, Jesus, blessed Jesus. Oh, for grace to trust Him more." Acts 4:12, Matthew 1:21, 25, Luke 1:30, Luke 2:11, 21, I John 4:9, 14, John 4:42
3. Blessed are the poor in spirit to those who believe the scripture:
    a. "*Pardon*"—Isaiah 55:7
    b. "*Forgiveness*"—Matthew 18:21-22, Mark 2:1-12
    c. "*Justification*"—Galatians 2:16, See Romans 5:8
4. Blessed are the poor in spirit to those who believe the scripture:
    a. Ye are washed—converted, repented, saved—I Corinthians 6:11
    b. Ye are sanctified—sanctification—John 17:17, I Corinthians 6:11
    c. Ye are justified—justification—I Corinthians 6:11, Romans 5:1, Romans 1:17
5. Blessed are the poor in spirit to those who believe, know, understand, realize that *without faith in Jesus Christ*, we are not saved; we are not born again. Matthew 18:3
6. Blessed are the poor in spirit to those who believe that the doctrine is about Jesus Christ concerning salvation, water baptism and the baptism of the Holy Spirit and His Second Coming. Matthew 28:9, Acts 1:11, Acts 2:1-4, Acts 4:12, Acts 16:30-34, 38-40, Revelation 22:7, 14:20
7. Blessed are the poor in spirit to those who *believe that God can heal the saved ones and the unsaved loved ones, however, does not mean that the unsaved ones would go to heaven without salvation. Unsaved loved ones need to be repented; need to be saved through Jesus Christ*. Matthew 4:17

8. Blessed are the poor in spirit to those who *believe that God is as true, faithfulness, promise, forgiveness, powerful and merciful God.* Isaiah 55:6-7, I John 1:9
9. Blessed are the poor in spirit to those who believe in *faith is that we must believe God.* Without fait; faith is impossible to please Him. Hebrews 11:6
10. Blessed are the poor in spirit to those who believe and read only the *Bible* to be "*blessed*" and "*inspired*" *by God through Jesus Christ.* II Timothy 3:16
11. Blessed are the poor in spirit to those who *believe The Gospel*: "And these are they likewise which are sown on stony ground; who, when they have heard the word, immediately receive it with gladness." Mark 4:16
12. Blessed are the poor in spirit to those who believe that *real men and real women must become like real children of God, may enter the kingdom of heaven* or likewise perish. Matthew 18:1-5{verse 3}, John 3:3, Luke 13:3, 5

PART CDXXX

Blessed Are The Poor In Spirit. Matthew 5:3

Blessed Means Happy

Poor means meek in spirit. Poor means humble in spirit. Poor means lowly in spirit. Poor means quiet in spirit. Read Matthew 5:3-12, Read also Mark 1:15

Jesus did not say "*rich*" in spirit. Jesus said "*poor*" in spirit.

1. Blessed are the poor in spirit to those who believe and are *sad* to *see a lost and dying world "without" Jesus Christ* and that *Jesus* may *say to the sinners* even to un-saved-loved ones; even precious souls or poor souls *may not be looking* or *not believing the return of their Lord;but Jesus said in Revelation 22:20:"He which testifieth these things saith, Surely I come quickly. Amen. Even so, come Lord Jesus.* Revelation 3:11, Revelation 22:7, 12, 20
2. Blessed are the poor in spirit to those who believe that the Baptism of the Holy Spirit with Fire is telling us that Jesus is coming soon; that Jesus will return immediately; that Jesus is the *imminent.* Revelation 3:11, Revelation 22:7, 12, 20
3. Blessed are the poor in spirit to those who believe that the Scriptures tells us to be prepared to meet the Lord thy God. Isaiah 40:3, Amos 4:12, Malachi 3:1, Matthew 3:3, Luke 3:4, John 1:23, Acts 1:11, Revelation 3:11, Revelation 22:7, 12, 20
4. Blessed are the poor in spirit to those who believe that even though the *Lord "delay" His Coming* for centuries which is good, for the best, for the better or the worse, even to those who are in the graves as well to this day and time, still the *Lord* surely *keep His Promise* that *He will come again;He will come The Second Time.* Be prepaed to meet the Lord thy God. Amos 4:12, Matthew 24:48, Luke 12:45, Acts1:11, Revelation 3:11, Revelation 22:7, 12, 20
5. Blessed are the poor in spirit to those who believe and are abled to say:"And he said unto Jesus, Lord, remember me when Thou come into thy kingdom. And Jesus said unto him, Verily, I say unto thee, Today shall thou be with Me in paradise." Luke 23:40-43, See Isaiah 49:8 and II Corithians 6:2
6. Blessed are the poor in spirit to those who believe when Jesus breathed His Statement: "It is *finished*" which means that "*Salvation* is *finished* upon the "*old rugged*

cross" John 19:30, {See Joshua 4:10 and notice the word that said: "*finished...*" Also notice the word: "*Ark*" is a type of th "*Old Rugged Cross*" wher Jesus died for all mankind.}

7. Blessed are the poor in spirit to those who believe what Jesus would want us to know: "{1}Jeus wants to save us. Matthew 1:21, 25:{2] Jesus wants to sanctify us. John 17:17: {3} Jesus wants baptize us. Acts 1:4-5, 8, Acts 2:1-47, Acts10:33-48
8. Blessed are the poor in spirit to those who believe what Jesus would want us to know: {1} Jesus saved us just as He did to His disciples. Matthew 1:21, 25 {2} Jesus sanctified us just as He did to His disciples. John 17:17 {3} Jesus baptized us with His Spirit just as He did to His disciples. Acts 1:4-5, 8, Acts 2:1-47, Acts10:33-48
9. Blessed are the poor in spirit to those who believe the Authority of Scriptures by Word of God. Genesis1:1, John 1:1, II Timothy 3:16, Isaiah 46:10-11—Foundation Stand Forever, II Timothy 2:19, My Word Stand Forever, Romans 3:4, Titus 1:2, Hebrews 11:6
10. Blessed are the poor in spirit to those who believe one of God's children, Martin Luther{1483-1546}, his own statement: "In Isaiah, he says, "My counsel shall, stand, and my will shall be done," {Isaiah 46:10}. And what schoolboy does not understand the meaning of these expressions, "counsel," "will," "shall be done," "shall stand." Isaiah 46:10
11. Blessed are the poor in spirit to those who believe in finding God's will; not our own will, but His own will will be done. Luke 22:42, Acts 13:22, Mark 3:34-35, John 1:13, Acts 13:36-37, Romans 1:10, Romans 8:27-28, Ephesian 2:8-10, Psalms 100:3, Romans 12:2, Romans 15:32-33, I Corinthians 1:1, II Corithians 1:1, Ephesians 1:1, Colossians 1:1, II Timothy 1:1, II Corinthians 8:5, Galatians 1:3-5, Ephesians 6:6-10, Colossians 4:12, I Thessalonians 4:3, I Thessalonians 5:18, Hebrews 10:36, I Peter 2:15-17, I Peter 3:17, I Peter 4:2, 19, I John 2:17
12. Blessed are the poor in spirit to those who believe Christ's Word: "HE that is not with Me is against Me:and he that gathereth not with Me scattereth." Luke11:23

Part CDXXXI

Blessed Are The Poor In Spirit. Matthew 5:3

Blessed Means Happy

Poor means meek in spirit. Poor means humble in spirit. Poor means lowly in spirit. Poor means quiet in spirit. Read Matthew 5:3-12, Read also Mark 1:15

Jesus did not say "*rich*" in spirit. Jesus said "*poor*" in spirit.

1. Blessed are the poor in spirit to those who believe by letting Christ be preached to us. Philippians 1:15-18
2. Blessed are the poor in spirit to those who *believe that Christ's Truth and Christ's doctrine which is of God are to be preached always, open to the public and firmly to be proclaimed.* Mark 16:15, Matthew 10:7, 27, Matthew 11:1, Mark1:38, Luke 4:18-19, 43, Isaiah 61:1-3, Luke 9:2, 60, Acts 5:42, Acts 17:3, Romans 10:8, I Corinthians 1:23, II Timothy 4:2, Mark 2:2, Mark 6:12, Mark 16:20, Luke 24:47, Acts 3:20, Acts 4:2, Acts 8:5, 25, 35, Acts 9:20, 27, 37-44, 46-52, Acts 17:18-19, 30
3. Blessed are the poor in spirit to those who believe that the Gospel mean *Good News, True Story, Real Story, Real Fact, Real Promise, Real Tidings to the herald of salvation through Christ, Real Blessing* because of the *Death, Burial and Resurrection of Christ and His Second Coming.* Acts 1:11, Revelation 22:20, I Corinthians 15:1-10
4. Blessed are the poor in spirit to those who believe that the *New Testament mean the New Covenant*; that is the *agreement with God and His Word,* which is the *Bible* that *revealed in fulfillment of the Old Testament and dealing with the nativity, the ministry, the life, the death, the resurrection,* the *predict Messiah, Christ's Return the inauguration of the new dispensation of the Christian Church* on the *Day of Pentecost.* Genesis 1:1, John 1:1, II Timothy 3:14-17, chapters Acts 2:1-Acts 28:1-31
5. Blessed are the poor in spirit to those who believe that *Pentecost* is the *result following the death of our Lord Jesus Christ and His Risen from the dead and the Spirit Baptism according to Mark 16:17, Acts 1:5, 8, Luke 24:49, Acts 2:1-4,* John 20:1-9, Luke 24:1-7, Mark 16:1-20, Matthew 28:1-7, 9-10, 17-20

6. Blessed are the poor in spirit to those who *believe that it is the will of God that all men should be saved*; I Timothy 2:4, I Timothy 4:10, John 5:40
7. Blessed are the poor in spirit to those who believe that an *Eternal Life* is a *gift from God*; which is in *Jesus Christ*. John 10:10, Colossians 1:27, John 3:3, John1:13, I John 15:12
8. Blessed are the poor in spirit to those who *believe in an* "*Eternity*," the *everlasting to everlasting*, which is *God*. Psalm 90:2, 102:26-28, Isaiah 44:6, 57:15, Revelation 2:8, Revelation 22:13, Isaiah 48:12, Revelation 1:4, II Peter 3:8, I Timothy 6:16
9. Blessed are the poor in spirit to those who believe that *an* "*Evangelist*" is *announcing the good news of the gospel of Christ to proclaim the mercy, grace of God*, to *preach the truth and to establish His kindom*. Ephesians 4:11, Acts 21:8, Acts 8:25, Acts 14:7, I Corinthians 1:17, I Corinthians 2:2
10. Blessed are the poor in spirit to those who *believe that God allowed Adam to name the woman* "*Eve*" who *was his wife. Eve and Adam had three sons and more else children*. Genesis 3:20, Genesis 2:18-22, Genesis 3:16, Genesis 4:1, Genesis 4:2, Genesis 5:3, Genesis 5:4
11. Blessed are the poor in spirit to those who *believe in* "*Too Blessed To Be Stressed*!!!" I Peter 5:7, Matthew 24:6, Mark 13:7, John 14:1-3, 27-31
12. Blessed are the poor in spirit to those who believe that the word "*Ghost*" means *Breath*; that the word "*Ghost*" means "*Life*;" that the word *Ghost* means "*Spirit*." Also the word "*Ghost*" mean "*Giver*." Job 11:20, Jeremiah 15:9, Matthew 27:50, John 19:30

PART CDXXXII

Blessed Are The Poor In Spirit. Matthew 5:3

Blessed Means Happy

Poor means meek in spirit. Poor means humble in spirit. Poor means lowly in spirit. Poor means quiet in spirit. Read Matthew 5:3-12, Read also Mark 1:15

Jesus did not say "*rich*" in spirit. Jesus said "*poor*" in spirit.

1. Blessed are the poor in spirit to those who believe that the word "*Ghost*" is the *same* as the "*Spirit.*" II Timothy 1:7
2. Blessed are the poor in spirit to those who believe that the Word "*Holy Ghost*" is the *same* as the *word* "*Holy Spirit*" and is the *third person* of the *trinity*: God, the *Father*, *God*, the *Son* and God the *Holy Ghost* or *Holy Spirit*: Matthew 28:19
3. Blessed are the poor in spirit to those who believe that the *gift of tongues* or the *spiritual gift* is the *gift of grace* or the *gift of divine and the Baptism of the Holy Spirit according to Acts 2:4*. I Corinthians 7:7, I Peter 4:10, See II Corinthians 11:12
4. Blessed are the poor in spirit to those who believe that the *Book of Acts stands for the Acts of the Holy Spirit*. Chapters: Acts 1:1 to Acts 28:1-31
5. Blessed are the poor in spirit to those who *believe* that *the Book of Acts* is the *Acts of the Holy Spirit who still goes on fishing to win as much souls to Christ until He comes for His children who are born again and looking for His second coming*; and *those who are in the graves first, and secondly, which we are alive will be caught up together with them in the clouds to meet the Lord in the air and so shall we ever be with the Lord. Comfort one another with these words*. I Thessalonians 4:16-18. See Genesis 50:20, Luke 9:56, Matthew 1:21
6. Blessed are the poor in spirit to those who believe that *Adam* is the *first man* because *God Almighty formed Adam of the dust of the earth, breathed into his nostril the breath of life and Adam became a living soul*. Genesis 2:7
7. Blessed are the poor in spirit to those who believe that the *very first disciple to receive Christ was Andrew. John 1:36-40*
8. Blessed are the poor in spirit to those who believe that the *Bible has 39 books of the Old Testament and 27 of the New Testament*; *a total of 66 books in the Holy Bible, the Word of God*. Genesis 1:1, John 1:1, II Timothy 3:14-17 (verse 16)

9. Blessed are the poor in spirit to those who *believe* that the *first born of the human race and as well as the first murderer was Cain, son of Adam and Eve.* Genesis 4:1-3, 5-26. See Hebrew 11:4, I John 3:12, Jude 11
10. Blessed are the poor in spirit to those who believe that a "*call*" to "*salvation*" *show the invitation to the blessings of the Gospel to offer salvation through Christ.* This *offer of salvation is a calling from God.* I Corinthians 7:20 and *a call according to His purpose and His will.* Romans 8:27, 28, 29, 30.
11. Blessed are the poor in spirit to those who *believe that the children of God are those who of the fallen race,* are *regenerated as a result of faith in Jesus Christ.* John 1:12-16, Ephesians 4:6, Galatians 4:1-6
12. Blessed are the poor in spirit to those who believe that the *Lamb of God was slain from the foundation of the world* Psalms 78:2-3, Matthew 13:35, Matthew 25:31-46{verse 34}, Luke 11:47-54{verse 50}, John 17:1-26 {verse 24}, Ephesians 1:1-23{verse 4}, Hebrews 4:3, Hebrews 9:26, Revelation 13:8

PART CDXXXIII

Blessed Are The Poor In Spirit. Matthew 5:3

Blessed Means Happy

Poor means meek in spirit. Poor means humble in spirit. Poor means lowly in spirit. Poor means quiet in spirit. Read Matthew 5:3-12, Read also Mark 1:15

Jesus did not say "*rich*" in spirit. Jesus said "*poor*" in spirit.

1. Blessed are the poor in spirit to those who believe what Jesus has to say about "*being ashamed*:" Whosoever therefore shall be ashamed of me and of my words in this adulterous and sinful generation; of him also shall the Son of man be ashamed, when he cometh in the glory of his Father with the holy angels. Mark 8:38
2. Blessed are the poor in spirit to those who believe *in knowing that the Bible is very important.* I I Timothy 3:16, Genesis 1:1, John 1:1
3. Blessed are the poor in spirit to those who believe and *have heard the testimony of God's children*; *God's people that testify*: "*If it had not been for the Lord on my side, where will I be*? Psalm 124:1-2, See Exodus 32:26
4. Blessed are the poor in spirit to those who *believe the Word of God*: *I am the Lord that heal thee. By His stripes we are healed.* Jesus says, "I will come and heal. Jesus says, "Be healed." Jesus says "Be Made Whole. Our God is the Healer today. Psalm 41:4, Psalm 6:1-4, Ecclesiastes 3:3, Jeremiah 3:22, Jeremiah 17:14, Jeremiah 30:17, Isaiah 53:5, Hosea 14:4, Matthew 8:7, Matthew 13:15, Isaiah 6:10, Acts 28:27, Luke 4:18, Acts 4:30, Luke 5:17, Luke 7:3, John 4:47, Exodus 15:26, Psalm 103:3, Psalm 147:3, Isaiah 30:26, I Peter 2:24, James 5:13-16, 19-20, Matthew 9:22, Mark 5:34, Mark 10:46-52
5. Blessed are the poor in spirit to those who believe that while the dark age was in the world; in a dark world, the gospel of *Jesus Christ still spread the word of the gospel, getting* men, women and children *saved.* Mark 13:10, Mark 16:15
6. Blessed are the poor in spirit to those who believe that while the world is getting big, the *gospel of Jesus Christ still spread, the Word of God getting* men, women and children *saved.* Mark 13:10, Mark 16:15

7. Blessed are the poor in spirit to those who believe that while the world is getting nasty, the *gospel of Jesus Christ* still spread the *Word of God getting* men, women and children *saved.* Mark 13:10, Mark 16:15
8. Blessed are the poor in spirit to those who believe that while the world is *being cursed,* the *gospel of Jesus Christ still spread the Word of God getting* men, women and children *saved.* Mark 13:10, Mark 16:15
9. Blessed are the poor in spirit to those who believe that while the world *still exist,* the *world cannot stop the gospel of Jesus Christ* that *spread the Word of God getting* men, women and children *saved.* Mark 13:10, Mark 16:15
10. Blessed are the poor in spirit to those who believe that while the world will come to an end, the gospel of Jesus Christ *still spread the Word of God, getting* men, women and children *saved.* Mark 13:10, Mark 16:15
11. Blessed are the poor in spirit to those who *believe* that while the world is *hurting,* the *gospel of Jesus Christ still spread the Word of God,* getting men, women and children *saved.* Mark 16:15, Mark 13:10
12. Blessed are the poor in spirit to those who believe that while the world is getting mighty big, the *gospel of Jesus Christ still spread the Word of God,* getting men, women and children *saved.* Mark 16:15, Mark 13:10

Part CDXXXIV

Blessed Are The Poor In Spirit. Matthew 5:3

Blessed Means Happy

Poor means meek in spirit. Poor means humble in spirit. Poor means lowly in spirit. Poor means quiet in spirit. Read Matthew 5:3-12, Read also Mark 1:15

Jesus did not say "*rich*" in spirit. Jesus said "*poor*" in spirit.

1. Blessed are the poor in spirit to those who believe that the *world is "too small"* to *box or fight or wrestle with God* because *God is mighty bigger than the whole wide world. God through Jesus Christ say, "I will spue thee out of my mouth."* Revelation 3:16
2. Blessed are the poor in spirit to those who believe that the world is going to be *destroyed* and *shall be great tribulation not since the beginning of the world* through Noah's time and the cities of Sodom and Gomorrah. Matthew 24:21-27, See Daniel 12:1
3. Blessed are the poor in spirit to those who *believe* that *we have not yet "seeing," but believing by faith in God through Jesus Christ.* Matthew 13:13, Galatians 3:1, Ecclesiastes 1:8, Romans 10:17
4. Blessed are the poor in spirit to those who *believe* that *we have not yet "hearing,"* but *believing by faith in God through Jesus Christ.* Galatians 3:2, 5, Matthew 13:13, Romans 10:17, Amos 8:11, Ecclesiastes 1:8
5. Blessed are the poor in spirit to those who *believe* that "*seeing*" and "*hearing*" are our *Bible reading*, and *our Bible Study* and "*not by feeling*," *but "by faith."* Romans 10:17, Galatians 3:1-2, 5-8, 9-12, 13-14, Acts 18:8, II Peter 2:7-9, Habakkuk 2:4, Proverbs 20:12, Ecclesiastes 1:8, Matthew 13:15, Acts 28:27
6. Blessed are the poor in spirit to those who believe that repentance *is this*: "Then said I, woe is me! For I am undone; because I am a man of unclean lips, and I dwell in the midst of a people of unclean lips: for mine eyes have seen the King, the Lord of host. Isaiah 6:5. Repentance is when a person becomes aware that he cannot justify himself or meet God's requirement by being good or performing some deed, but rather that he needs God. Repentance is the full realization of one's sin or wrong and a will to change one's way; a change of mind, with sorrow

for something done, and a wish that it was undone, also when a person sees himself as he is wretched and undone. Jesus says: "I tell you, Nay: but, except ye repent, ye shall all likewise perish. Luke 13:3

7. Blessed are the poor in spirit to those who believe Sojourner Truth's mother, Mau Mau Brett used to say to her little children: "There is a God who hears and see you." Genesis 16:13
8. Blessed are the poor in spirit to those who believe that the "*Jewish*" *Pentecostal, People of God, the family of God, spoke in tongues as the Spirit give utterance* (other languages given by the Holy Spirit). Acts 2:4
9. Blessed are the poor in spirit to those who believe that the "*Roman*" *Pentecostal, People of God, the family of God, spoke in tongues as the Spirit give utterance* (other language given by the Spirit). Acts 10:44-48
10. Blessed are the poor in spirit to those who believe that the "*Greek*" *Pentecostal, People of God, the family of God, spoke in tongues as the Spirit give utterance* (other languages given by the Holy Spirit). Acts 19:1-6
11. Blessed are the poor in spirit to those who believe that the "*Samaritan*" *Pentecostal, People of God, the family of God, spoke in tongues as the Spirit give utterance* (other languages given by the Holy Spirit). Acts 8:14-19
12. Blessed are the poor in spirit to those who believe that *Paul* (a Jewish apostle called to the Gentiles by Christ Jesus), *spoke in tongues as well.* Acts 9:17-19 and I Corinthians 14:18

Part CDXXXV

Blessed Are The Poor In Spirit. Matthew 5:3

Blessed Means Happy

Poor means meek in spirit. Poor means humble in spirit. Poor means lowly in spirit. Poor means quiet in spirit. Read Matthew 5:3-12, Read also Mark 1:15

Jesus did not say "*rich*" in spirit. Jesus said "*poor*" in spirit.

1. Blessed are the poor in spirit to those who believe that the *purpose of the Holy Spirit was given the utterance was to spread the Gospel of Jesus Christ in order for the world to come to Jesus Christ as Personal Savior and Lord.* Acts 2:4, 41, 47 (verse 37-39), Acts 2:42-47 (verse 47).
2. Blessed are the poor in spirit to those who believe that "*Roman*" *Pentecostal, People of God, the family of God,* that "*Greek*" *Pentecostal, People of God, the family of God* and that "*Samaritan*" *Pentecostal, People of God, the family of God* which are called the "*Gentiles*" *Pentecostal, People of God, the family of God.* Acts 10:44-48, Acts 19:1-6, Acts 8:14-19.
3. Blessed are the poor in spirit to those who believe that the "*Jewish*" *Pentecostal, People of God, the family of God* is *God's first choice, God's first chosen people of Israel,* th-e *nation of Israel, God's first mission to save much people alive.* Acts 2:4, Matthew 1:21, See Genesis 50:20
4. Blessed are the poor in spirit to those who *believe in getting wisdom of this Proverbs*: "To know wisdom and instruction; to perceive the words of understanding;" Proverbs 1:2
5. Blessed are the poor in spirit to those who *believe in getting wisdom of this Proverbs*: "To receive the instruction of wisdom, justice, and judgment, and equity;" Proverbs 1:3
6. Blessed are the poor in spirit to those who *believe in getting wisdom of this Proverbs*: "To give subtilty to the simple, to the young man knowledge and discretion." Proverbs 1:4
7. Blessed are the poor in spirit to those who *believe in getting wisdom of this Proverbs*: "A wise man will hear, and will increase learning; and a man of understanding shall attain unto wise counsels:" Proverbs 1:5

8. Blessed are the poor in spirit to those who *believe in getting wisdom of this Proverbs*: "To understand a proverb, and the interpretation; the words of the wise, and their dark sayings." Proverbs 1:6
9. Blessed are the poor in spirit to those who *believe in getting wisdom of this Proverbs*: "The fear of the Lord is the beginning of knowledge: but fools despise wisdom and instruction." Proverbs 1:7
10. Blessed are the poor in spirit to those who *believe in getting wisdom of this Proverbs*: "My son, hear the instruction of thy father, and forsake not the law of thy mother:" Proverbs 1:8
11. Blessed are the poor in spirit to those who *believe in getting wisdom of this Proverbs*: "Then shalt thou understand the fear-{respect} of the Lord, and find the knowledge of God." Proverbs 2:5
12. Blessed are the poor in spirit to those who *believe in getting wisdom of this Proverbs*: "For the Lord giveth wisdom: out of his mouth cometh knowledge and understanding." Proverbs 2:6

Part CDXXXVI

Blessed Are The Poor In Spirit. Matthew 5:3

Blessed Means Happy

Poor means meek in spirit. Poor means humble in spirit. Poor means lowly in spirit. Poor means quiet in spirit. Read Matthew 5:3-12, Read also Mark 1:15

Jesus did not say "*rich*" in spirit. Jesus said "*poor*" in spirit.

1. Blessed are the poor in spirit to those who *believe in getting wisdom of this Proverbs*: "When wisdom entereth into thine heart, and knowledge is pleasant unto thy soul:" Proverbs 2:10
2. Blessed are the poor in spirit to those who *believe in getting wisdom of this Proverbs*: "Discretion shall preserve thee, understanding shall keep thee:" Proverbs 2:11
3. Blessed are the poor in spirit to those who *believe in getting wisdom of this Proverbs*: "My son, forget not my law; but let thine heart keep my commandments:" Proverbs 3:1
4. Blessed are the poor in spirit to those who *believe in getting wisdom of this Proverbs*: "For length of days, and long life, and peace, shall they add to thee." Proverbs 3:2
5. Blessed are the poor in spirit to those who *believe in getting wisdom of this Proverbs*: "Let not mercy and truth forsake thee: bind them about thy neck; write them upon the table of thine heart:" Proverbs 3:3
6. Blessed are the poor in spirit to those who *believe in getting wisdom of this Proverbs*: "So shalt thou find favour and good understanding in the sight of God and man." Proverbs 3:4
7. Blessed are the poor in spirit to those who *believe in getting wisdom of this Proverbs*: "Trust in the Lord with all thine heart; and lean not unto thine own understanding." Proverbs 3:5
8. Blessed are the poor in spirit to those who *believe in getting wisdom of this Proverbs*: "In all thy ways acknowledge him, and he shall direct thy paths." Proverbs 3:6
9. Blessed are the poor in spirit to those who *believe in getting wisdom of this Proverbs*: "Be not wise in thine own eyes: fear the Lord, and depart from evil." Proverbs 3:7
10. Blessed are the poor in spirit to those who *believe in getting wisdom of this Proverbs*: "It shall be health to thy navel, and marrow to thy bones." Proverbs 3:8

11. Blessed are the poor in spirit to those who *believe in getting wisdom of this Proverbs*: "Honour the Lord with thy substance, and with the firstfruits of all thine increase:" Proverbs 3:9
12. Blessed are the poor in spirit to those who *believe in getting wisdom of this Proverbs*: "So shall thy barns be filled with plenty, and thy presse shall burst out with new wine." Proverbs 3:10

Part CDXXXVII

Blessed Are The Poor In Spirit. Matthew 5:3

Blessed Means Happy

Poor means meek in spirit. Poor means humble in spirit. Poor means lowly in spirit. Poor means quiet in spirit. Read Matthew 5:3-12, Read also Mark 1:15

Jesus did not say "*rich*" in spirit. Jesus said "*poor*" in spirit.

1. Blessed are the poor in spirit to those who *believe in getting wisdom of this Proverbs*: "My son, despise not the chastening of the Lord; neither be weary of his correction:" Proverbs 3:11
2. Blessed are the poor in spirit to those who *believe in getting wisdom of this Proverbs*: "For whom the Lord loveth he correcteth; even as a father the son in whom he delighteth." Proverbs 3:12
3. Blessed are the poor in spirit to those who *believe in getting wisdom of this Proverbs*: "Happy is the man that findeth wisdom, and the man that getteth understanding." Proverbs 3:13
4. Blessed are the poor in spirit to those who *believe in getting wisdom of this Proverbs*: "The Lord by wisdom hath founded the earth; by understanding hath he established the heavens." Proverbs 3:19
5. Blessed are the poor in spirit to those who *believe in getting wisdom of this Proverbs*: "My son, let not them depart from thine eyes: keep sound wisdom and discretion:" Proverbs 3:21
6. Blessed are the poor in spirit to those who *believe in getting wisdom of this Proverbs*: "So shall they be life unto thy soul, and grace to thy neck." Proverbs 3:22
7. Blessed are the poor in spirit to those who *believe in getting wisdom of this Proverbs*: "Then shalt thou walk in thy way safely, and thy foot shall not stumble." Proverbs 3:23
8. Blessed are the poor in spirit to those who *believe in getting wisdom of this Proverbs*: "When thou liest down, thou shalt not be afraid: yea, thou shalt lie down, and thy sleep shall be sweet." Proverbs 3:24
9. Blessed are the poor in spirit to those who *believe in getting wisdom of this Proverbs*: "Be not afraid of sudden fear-{burst, or pop or boo or frighten, or scare or terror}, neither of the desolation of the wicked, when it cometh." Proverbs 3:25

10. Blessed are the poor in spirit to those who *believe in getting wisdom of this Proverbs*: "For the Lord shall be thy confidence, and shall keep thy foot from being taken." Proverbs 3:26
11. Blessed are the poor in spirit to those who *believe in getting wisdom of this Proverbs*: "For the froward is abomination to the Lord: but his secret is with the righteous." Proverbs 3:32
12. Blessed are the poor in spirit to those who *believe in getting wisdom of this Proverbs*: "Surely he scorneth the scorners: but he giveth grace unto the lowly." Proverbs 3:34, {See James 4:6}

Part CDXXXVIII

Blessed Are The Poor In Spirit. Matthew 5:3

Blessed Means Happy

Poor means meek in spirit. Poor means humble in spirit. Poor means lowly in spirit. Poor means quiet in spirit. Read Matthew 5:3-12, Read also Mark 1:15

Jesus did not say "*rich*" in spirit. Jesus said "*poor*" in spirit.

1. Blessed are the poor in spirit to those who *believe in getting wisdom of this Proverbs*: "The wise shall inherit glory; but shame shall be the promotion of fools." Proverbs 3:35
2. Blessed are the poor in spirit to those who *believe in getting wisdom of this Proverbs*: "Hear, ye children, the instruction of a father, and attend to know understanding." Proverbs 4:1
3. Blessed are the poor in spirit to those who *believe in getting wisdom of this Proverbs*: "For I give you good doctrine, forsake ye not my law." Proverbs 4:2
4. Blessed are the poor in spirit to those who *believe in getting wisdom of this Proverbs*: "For I was my father's son, tender and only beloved in the sight of my mother." Proverbs 4:3 {Solomon's father was King David. Solomon's mother was Bathsheba II Samuel 12:24}.
5. Blessed are the poor in spirit to those who *believe in getting wisdom of this Proverbs*: "He taught me also, and said unto me, Let thine heart retain my words: keep my commandments, and live." Proverbs 4:4
6. Blessed are the poor in spirit to those who *believe in getting wisdom of this Proverbs*: "Get wisdom, get understanding: forget it not; neither decline from the words of my mouth." Proverbs 4:5
7. Blessed are the poor in spirit to those who *believe in getting wisdom of this Proverbs*: "Wisdom is the principal thing; therefore get wisdom: and with all thy getting get understanding." Proverbs 4:7
8. Blessed are the poor in spirit to those who *believe in getting wisdom of this Proverbs*: "Hear, O my son, and receive my sayings; and the years of thy life shall be many." Proverbs 4:10

9. Blessed are the poor in spirit to those who *believe in getting wisdom of this Proverbs*: "My son, attend to my words; incline thine ear unto my sayings." Proverbs 4:20
10. Blessed are the poor in spirit to those who *believe in getting wisdom of this Proverbs*: "Let them not depart from thine eyes; keep them in the midst of thine heart." Proverb 4:21
11. Blessed are the poor in spirit to those who *believe in getting wisdom of this Proverbs*: "For they are life unto those that find them, and health to all their flesh." Proverbs 4:22
12. Blessed are the poor in spirit to those who *believe in getting wisdom of this Proverbs*: "Keep thy heart with all diligence; for out of it are the issues of life." Proverbs 4:23

PART CDXXXIX

Blessed Are The Poor In Spirit. Matthew 5:3

Blessed Means Happy

Poor means meek in spirit. Poor means humble in spirit. Poor means lowly in spirit. Poor means quiet in spirit. Read Matthew 5:3-12, Read also Mark 1:15

Jesus did not say "*rich*" in spirit. Jesus said "*poor*" in spirit.

1. Blessed are the poor in spirit to those who *believe in getting wisdom of this Proverbs*: "Ponder the path of thy feet, and let all thy ways be established." Proverbs 4:26
2. Blessed are the poor in spirit to those who *believe in getting wisdom of this Proverbs*: "Turn not to the right hand nor to the left: remove thy foot from evil." Proverbs 4:27
3. Blessed are the poor in spirit to those who *believe in getting wisdom of this Proverbs*: "My son, attend unto my wisdom, and bow thine ear to my understanding:" Proverbs 5:1
4. Blessed are the poor in spirit to those who *believe in getting wisdom of this Proverbs*: "That thou mayest regard discretion, and that thy lips may keep knowledge." Proverbs 5:2
5. Blessed are the poor in spirit to those who *believe in getting wisdom of this Proverbs*: "Hear me now therefore, O ye children, and depart not from the words of my mouth." Proverbs 5:7
6. Blessed are the poor in spirit to those who *believe in getting wisdom of this Proverbs*: "My son, keep my words, and lay up my commandments with thee." Proverbs 7:1
7. Blessed are the poor in spirit to those who *believe in getting wisdom of this Proverbs*: "Keep my commandments, and live; and my law as the apple of thine eye." Proverbs 7:2
8. Blessed are the poor in spirit to those who *believe in getting wisdom of this Proverbs*: "Bind them upon thy fingers, write them upon the table of thine heart." Proverbs 7:3
9. Blessed are the poor in spirit to those who *believe in getting wisdom of this Proverbs*: "Hearken unto me now therefore, O ye children, and attend to the words of my mouth." Proverbs 7:24

10. Blessed are the poor in spirit to those who *believe in getting wisdom of this Proverbs*: "Unto you, O men, I call; and my voice is to the sons of man." Proverbs 8:4
11. Blessed are the poor in spirit to those who *believe in getting wisdom of this Proverbs*: "O ye simple, understand wisdom: and, ye fools, be ye of an understanding heart." Proverbs 8:5
12. Blessed are the poor in spirit to those who *believe in getting wisdom of this Proverbs*: "Hear; for I will speak of excellent things; and the opening of my lips shall be right things." Proverbs 8:6

Part CDXL

Blessed Are The Poor In Spirit. Matthew 5:3

Blessed Means Happy

Poor means meek in spirit. Poor means humble in spirit. Poor means lowly in spirit. Poor means quiet in spirit. Read Matthew 5:3-12, Read also Mark 1:15

Jesus did not say "*rich*" in spirit. Jesus said "*poor*" in spirit.

1. Blessed are the poor in spirit to those who *believe in getting wisdom of this Proverbs*: "They are all plain to him that understandeth, and right to them that find knowledge." Proverbs 8:9
2. Blessed are the poor in spirit to those who *believe in getting wisdom of this Proverbs*: "Receive my instruction, and not silver; and knowledge rather than choice gold." Proverbs 8:10
3. Blessed are the poor in spirit to those who *believe in getting wisdom of this Proverbs*: "For wisdom is better than rubies; and all the things that may be desired are not to be compared to it." Proverbs 8:11
4. Blessed are the poor in spirit to those who *believe in getting wisdom of this Proverbs*: "I wisdom dwell with prudence, and find out knowledge of witty inventions." Proverbs 8:12
5. Blessed are the poor in spirit to those who *believe in getting wisdom of this Proverbs*: "The fear of the Lord is to hate evil: pride, and arrogancy, and the evil way, and the froward mouth, do I hate." Proverbs 8:13
6. Blessed are the poor in spirit to those who *believe in getting wisdom of this Proverbs*: "Counsel is mine, and sound wisdom: I am understanding; I have strength." Proverbs 8:14
7. Blessed are the poor in spirit to those who *believe in getting wisdom of this Proverbs*: "I love them that love me; and those that seek me early shall find me." Proverbs 8:17
8. Blessed are the poor in spirit to those who *believe in getting wisdom of this Proverbs*: "The Lord possessed me in the beginning of his way, before his works of old." Proverbs 8:22

9. Blessed are the poor in spirit to those who *believe in getting wisdom of this Proverbs*: "Now therefore hearken unto me, O ye children: for blessed are they that keep my ways." Proverbs 8:32
10. Blessed are the poor in spirit to those who *believe in getting wisdom of this Proverbs*: "Hear instruction, and be wise, and refuse it not." Proverbs 8:33
11. Blessed are the poor in spirit to those who *believe in getting wisdom of this Proverbs*: "Blessed is the man that heareth me, watching daily at my gates, waiting at the posts of my doors." Proverbs 8:34
12. Blessed are the poor in spirit to those who *believe in getting wisdom of this Proverbs*: "For whoso findeth me findeth life, and shall obtain favour of the Lord." Proverbs 8:35

Part CDXLI

Blessed Are The Poor In Spirit. Matthew 5:3

Blessed Means Happy

Poor means meek in spirit. Poor means humble in spirit. Poor means lowly in spirit. Poor means quiet in spirit. Read Matthew 5:3-12, Read also Mark 1:15

Jesus did not say "*rich*" in spirit. Jesus said "*poor*" in spirit.

1. Blessed are the poor in spirit to those who *believe in getting wisdom of this Proverbs*: "But he that sinneth against me wrongeth his own soul: all they that hate me love death." Proverbs 8:36
2. Blessed are the poor in spirit to those who *believe in getting wisdom of this Proverbs*: "Forsake the foolish, and live; and go in the way of understanding." Proverbs 9:6
3. Blessed are the poor in spirit to those who *believe in getting wisdom of this Proverbs*: "The fear of the Lord is the beginning of wisdom: and the knowledge of the holy is understanding." Proverbs 9:10
4. Blessed are the poor in spirit to those who *believe in getting wisdom of this Proverbs*: "For by me thy days shall be multiplied, and the years of thy life shall be increased." Proverbs 9:11
5. Blessed are the poor in spirit to those who *believe in getting wisdom of this Proverbs*: "If thou be wise, thou shalt be wise for thy self: but if thou scornest, thou alone shalt bear it." Proverbs 9:12
6. Blessed are the poor in spirit to those who *believe in getting wisdom of this Proverbs*: "The memory of the just is blessed: but the name of the wicked shall rot." Proverbs 10:7
7. Blessed are the poor in spirit to those who *believe in getting wisdom of this Proverbs*: "The wise in heart will receive commandments: but a prating fool shall fall." Proverbs 10:8
8. Blessed are the poor in spirit to those who *believe in getting wisdom of this Proverbs*: "He that walketh uprightly walketh surely: but he that perverteth his ways shall be known." Proverbs 10:9
9. Blessed are the poor in spirit to those who *believe in getting wisdom of this Proverbs*: "He that winketh with the eye causeth sorrow: but a prating fool shall fall." Proverbs 10:10

10. Blessed are the poor in spirit to those who *believe in getting wisdom of this Proverbs*: "The mouth of a righteous man is a well of life: but violence covereth the mouth of the wicked." Proverbs 10:11
11. Blessed are the poor in spirit to those who *believe in getting wisdom of this Proverbs*: "Hatred stirreth up strifes: but love covereth all sins." Proverbs 10:12
12. Blessed are the poor in spirit to those who *believe in getting wisdom of this Proverbs*: "In the lips of him that hath understanding wisdom is found: but a rod is for the back of him that is void of understanding." Proverbs 10:13

Part CDXLII

Blessed Are The Poor In Spirit. Matthew 5:3

Blessed Means Happy

Poor means meek in spirit. Poor means humble in spirit. Poor means lowly in spirit. Poor means quiet in spirit. Read Matthew 5:3-12, Read also Mark 1:15

Jesus did not say "*rich*" in spirit. Jesus said "*poor*" in spirit.

1. Blessed are the poor in spirit to those who *believe in getting wisdom of this Proverbs*: "Wise men lay up knowledge: but the mouth of the foolish is near destruction." Proverbs 10:14
2. Blessed are the poor in spirit to those who *believe in getting wisdom of this Proverbs*: "He is in the way of life that keepeth instruction: but he that refuseth reproof erreth." Proverbs 10:17
3. Blessed are the poor in spirit to those who *believe in getting wisdom of this Proverbs*: "In the multitude of words there wanteth not sin: but he that refrainedth his lips is wise." Proverbs 10:19
4. Blessed are the poor in spirit to those who *believe in getting wisdom of this Proverbs*: "The lips of the righteous feed many: but fools die for want of wisdom." Proverbs 10:21
5. Blessed are the poor in spirit to those who *believe in getting wisdom of this Proverbs*: "The blessing of the Lord, it maketh rich, and he addeth no sorrow with it." Proverbs 10:22
6. Blessed are the poor in spirit to those who *believe in getting wisdom of this Proverbs*: "It is as sport to a fool to do mischief: but a man of understanding hath wisdom." Proverbs 10:23
7. Blessed are the poor in spirit to those who *believe in getting wisdom of this Proverbs*: "The fear of the wicked, it shall come upon him: but the desire of the righteous shall be granted." Proverbs 10:24
8. Blessed are the poor in spirit to those who *believe in getting wisdom of this Proverbs*: "As the whirlwind passeth, so is the wicked no more: but the righteous is an everlasting foundation." Proverbs 10:25

9. Blessed are the poor in spirit to those who *believe in getting wisdom of this Proverbs*: "The hope of the righteous shall be gladness: but the expectation of the wicked shall perish." Proverbs 10:28
10. Blessed are the poor in spirit to those who *believe in getting wisdom of this Proverbs*: "The way of the Lord is strength to the upright: but destruction shall be to the workers of iniquity." Proverbs 10:29
11. Blessed are the poor in spirit to those who *believe in getting wisdom of this Proverbs*: "The righteous shall never be removed: but the wicked shall not inhabit the earth." Proverbs 10:30
12. Blessed are the poor in spirit to those who *believe in getting wisdom of this Proverbs*: "The mouth of the just bringeth forth wisdom: but the froward tongue shall be cut out." Proverbs 10:31

Part CDXLIII

Blessed Are The Poor In Spirit. Matthew 5:3

Blessed Means Happy

Poor means meek in spirit. Poor means humble in spirit. Poor means lowly in spirit. Poor means quiet in spirit. Read Matthew 5:3-12, Read also Mark 1:15

Jesus did not say "*rich*" in spirit. Jesus said "*poor*" in spirit.

1. Blessed are the poor in spirit to those who *believe in getting wisdom of this Proverbs*: "The lips of the righteous know what is acceptable: but the mouth of the wicked speaketh frowardness." Proverbs 10:32
2. Blessed are the poor in spirit to those who *believe in getting wisdom of this Proverbs*: "A false balance is abomination to the Lord: but a just weight is his delight." Proverbs 11:1
3. Blessed are the poor in spirit to those who *believe in getting wisdom of this Proverbs*: "When pride cometh, then cometh shame: but with the lowly is wisdom." Proverbs 11:2
4. Blessed are the poor in spirit to those who *believe in getting wisdom of this Proverbs*: "An hypocrite with his mouth destroyeth his neighbour: but through knowledge shall the just be delivered." Proverbs 11:9
5. Blessed are the poor in spirit to those who *believe in getting wisdom of this Proverbs*: "He that is void of wisdom despiseth his neighbour: but a man of understanding holdeth his peace." Proverbs 11:12
6. Blessed are the poor in spirit to those who *believe in getting wisdom of this Proverbs*: "A talebearer revealeth secrets: but he that is of a faithful spirit concealeth the matter." Proverbs 11:13
7. Blessed are the poor in spirit to those who *believe in getting wisdom of this Proverbs*: "Where no counsel is, the people fall: but in the multitude of counsellors there is safety." Proverbs 11:14
8. Blessed are the poor in spirit to those who *believe in getting wisdom of this Proverbs*: "The fruit of the righteous is a tree of life; and he that winneth souls is wise." Proverbs 11:30

9. Blessed are the poor in spirit to those who *believe in getting wisdom of this Proverbs*: "Whoso loveth instruction loveth knowledge: but he that hateth reproof is brutish." Proverbs 12:1
10. Blessed are the poor in spirit to those who *believe in getting wisdom of this Proverbs*: "A good man obtaineth favour of the Lord: but a man of wicked devices will he condemn." Proverbs 12:2
11. Blessed are the poor in spirit to those who *believe in getting wisdom of this Proverbs*: "The way of a fool is right in his own eyes: but he that hearkeneth unto counsel is wise." Proverbs 12:15
12. Blessed are the poor in spirit to those who *believe in getting wisdom of this Proverbs*: "A fool's wrath is presently known: but a prudent man covereth shame." Proverbs 12:16

Part CDXLIV

Blessed Are The Poor In Spirit. Matthew 5:3

Blessed Means Happy

Poor means meek in spirit. Poor means humble in spirit. Poor means lowly in spirit. Poor means quiet in spirit. Read Matthew 5:3-12, Read also Mark 1:15

Jesus did not say "*rich*" in spirit. Jesus said "*poor*" in spirit.

1. Blessed are the poor in spirit to those who *believe in getting wisdom of this Proverbs*: "He that speaketh truth sheweth forth righteousness: but a false witness deceit." Proverbs 12:17
2. Blessed are the poor in spirit to those who *believe in getting wisdom of this Proverbs*: "There is that speaketh like the piercings of a sword: but the tongue of the wise is health." Proverbs 12:18
3. Blessed are the poor in spirit to those who *believe in getting wisdom of this Proverbs*: "The lip of truth shall be established for ever: but a lying tongue is but for a moment." Proverbs 12:19
4. Blessed are the poor in spirit to those who *believe in getting wisdom of this Proverbs*: "Deceit is in the heart of them that imagine evil: but to the counsellors of peace is joy." Proverbs 12:20
5. Blessed are the poor in spirit to those who *believe in getting wisdom of this Proverbs*: "There shall no evil happen to the just: but the wicked shall be filled with mischief." Proverbs 12:21
6. Blessed are the poor in spirit to those who *believe in getting wisdom of this Proverbs*: "Lying lips are abomination to the Lord: but they that deal truly are his delight." Proverbs 12:22
7. Blessed are the poor in spirit to those who *believe in getting wisdom of this Proverbs*: "A prudent man concealeth knowledge: but the heart of fools proclaimeth foolishness." Proverbs 12:23
8. Blessed are the poor in spirit to those who *believe in getting wisdom of this Proverbs*: "In the way of righteousness is life; and in the pathway thereof there is no death." Proverbs 12:28

9. Blessed are the poor in spirit to those who *believe in getting wisdom of this Proverbs*: “A wise son heareth his father’s instruction: but a scorner heareth not rebuke.” Proverbs 13:1
10. Blessed are the poor in spirit to those who *believe in getting wisdom of this Proverbs*: “A man shall eat good by the fruit of his mouth: but the soul of the transgressors shall eat violence.” Proverbs 13:2
11. Blessed are the poor in spirit to those who *believe in getting wisdom of this Proverbs*: “He that keepeth his mouth keepeth his life: but he that openeth wide his lips shall have destruction.” Proverbs 13:3
12. Blessed are the poor in spirit to those who *believe in getting wisdom of this Proverbs*: “Whoso despiseth the word shall be destroyed: but he that feareth the commandment shall be rewarded.” Proverbs 13:13

Part CDXLV

Blessed Are The Poor In Spirit. Matthew 5:3

Blessed Means Happy

Poor means meek in spirit. Poor means humble in spirit. Poor means lowly in spirit. Poor means quiet in spirit. Read Matthew 5:3-12, Read also Mark 1:15

Jesus did not say "*rich*" in spirit. Jesus said "*poor*" in spirit.

1. Blessed are the poor in spirit to those who *believe in getting wisdom of this Proverbs*: "The law of the wise is a fountain of life, to depart from the snares of death." Proverbs 13:14
2. Blessed are the poor in spirit to those who *believe in getting wisdom of this Proverbs*: "Good understanding giveth favour: but the way of transgressors is hard." Proverbs 13:15
3. Blessed are the poor in spirit to those who *believe in getting wisdom of this Proverbs*: "Every prudent man dealeth with knowledge: but a fool layeth open his folly." Proverbs 13:16
4. Blessed are the poor in spirit to those who *believe in getting wisdom of this Proverbs*: "A wicked messenger falleth into mischief: but a faithful ambassador is health." Proverbs 13:17
5. Blessed are the poor in spirit to those who *believe in getting wisdom of this Proverbs*: "Poverty and shame shall be to him that refuseth instruction: but he that regardeth reproof shall be honoured." Proverbs 13:18
6. Blessed are the poor in spirit to those who *believe in getting wisdom of this Proverbs*: "The desire accomplished is sweet to the soul: but it is abomination to fools to depart from evil." Proverbs 13:19
7. Blessed are the poor in spirit to those who *believe in getting wisdom of this Proverbs*: "He that walketh with wise men shall be wise: but a companion of fools shall be destroyed." Proverbs 13:20
8. Blessed are the poor in spirit to those who *believe in getting wisdom of this Proverbs*: "Evil pursueth sinners: but to the righteous good shall be repaid." Proverbs 13:21
9. Blessed are the poor in spirit to those who *believe in getting wisdom of this Proverbs*: "A faithful witness will not lie: but a false witness will utter lies." Proverbs 14:5

10. Blessed are the poor in spirit to those who *believe in getting wisdom of this Proverbs*: "A scorner seeketh wisdom, and findeth it not: but knowledge is easy unto him that understandeth." Proverbs 14:6
11. Blessed are the poor in spirit to those who *believe in getting wisdom of this Proverbs*: "Go from the presence of a foolish man, when thou perceivest not in him the lips of knowledge." Proverbs 14:7
12. Blessed are the poor in spirit to those who *believe in getting wisdom of this Proverbs*: "The wisdom of the prudent is to understand his way: but the folly of fools is deceit." Proverbs 14:8

PART CDXLVI

Blessed Are The Poor In Spirit. Matthew 5:3

Blessed Means Happy

Poor means meek in spirit. Poor means humble in spirit. Poor means lowly in spirit. Poor means quiet in spirit. Read Matthew 5:3-12, Read also Mark 1:15

Jesus did not say "*rich*" in spirit. Jesus said "*poor*" in spirit.

1. Blessed are the poor in spirit to those who *believe in getting wisdom of this Proverbs*: "Fools make a mock at sin: but among the righteous there is favour." Proverbs 14:9
2. Blessed are the poor in spirit to those who *believe in getting wisdom of this Proverbs*: "The simple inherit folly: but the prudent are crowned with knowledge." Proverbs 14:18
3. Blessed are the poor in spirit to those who *believe in getting wisdom of this Proverbs*: "The fear of the Lord is a fountain of life, to depart from the snares of death." Proverbs 14:27
4. Blessed are the poor in spirit to those who *believe in getting wisdom of this Proverbs*: "He that is slow to wrath is of great understanding: but he that is hasty of spirit exalteth folly." Proverbs 14:29, James 1:19
5. Blessed are the poor in spirit to those who *believe in getting wisdom of this Proverbs*: "A sound heart is the life of the flesh: but envy the rottenness of the bones." Proverbs 14:30
6. Blessed are the poor in spirit to those who *believe in getting wisdom of this Proverbs*: "He that oppresseth the poor reproacheth his Maker: but he that honoureth him hath mercy on the poor." Proverbs 14:31
7. Blessed are the poor in spirit to those who *believe in getting wisdom of this Proverbs*: "The wicked is driven away in his wickedenss: but the righteous hath hope in his death." Proverbs 14:32
8. Blessed are the poor in spirit to those who *believe in getting wisdom of this Proverbs*: "Wisdom resteth in the heart of him that hath understanding: but that which is in the midst of fools is made known." Proverbs 14:33

9. Blessed are the poor in spirit to those who *believe in getting wisdom of this Proverbs*: “The king’s favour is toward a wise servant: but his wrath is against him that causeth shame.” Proverbs 14:35
10. Blessed are the poor in spirit to those who *believe in getting wisdom of this Proverbs*: “A soft answer turneth away wrath: but grievous words stir up anger.” Proverbs 15:1
11. Blessed are the poor in spirit to those who *believe in getting wisdom of this Proverbs*: “The tongue of the wise useth knowledge aright: but the mouth of fools poureth out foolishness.” Proverbs 15:2
12. Blessed are the poor in spirit to those who *believe in getting wisdom of this Proverbs*: “The eyes of the Lord are in every place, beholding the evil and the good.” Proverbs 15:3

Part CDXLVII

Blessed Are The Poor In Spirit. Matthew 5:3

Blessed Means Happy

Poor means meek in spirit. Poor means humble in spirit. Poor means lowly in spirit. Poor means quiet in spirit. Read Matthew 5:3-12, Read also Mark 1:15

Jesus did not say "*rich*" in spirit. Jesus said "*poor*" in spirit.

1. Blessed are the poor in spirit to those who *believe in getting wisdom of this Proverbs*: "A wholesome tongue is a tree of life: but perverseness therein is a breach in the spirit." Proverbs 15:4
2. Blessed are the poor in spirit to those who *believe in getting wisdom of this Proverbs*: "A fool despiseth his father's instruction: but he that regardeth reproof is prudent." Proverbs 15:5
3. Blessed are the poor in spirit to those who *believe in getting wisdom of this Proverbs*: "The lips of the wise disperse knowledge: but the heart of the foolish doeth not so." Proverbs 15:7
4. Blessed are the poor in spirit to those who *believe in getting wisdom of this Proverbs*: "The sacrifice of the wicked is an abomination to the Lord: but the prayer of the upright is his delight." Proverbs 15:8
5. Blessed are the poor in spirit to those who *believe in getting wisdom of this Proverbs*: "The way of the wicked is an abomination unto the Lord: but he loveth him that followeth after righteousness." Proverbs 15:9
6. Blessed are the poor in spirit to those who *believe in getting wisdom of this Proverbs*: "Correction is grievous unto him that forsaketh the way: and he that hateth reproof shall die." Proverbs 15:10
7. Blessed are the poor in spirit to those who *believe in getting wisdom of this Proverbs*: "A scorner loveth not one that reproveth him: neither will he go unto the wise." Proverbs 15:12
8. Blessed are the poor in spirit to those who *believe in getting wisdom of this Proverbs*: "A merry heart maketh a cheerful countenance: but by sorrow of the heart the spirit is broken." Proverbs 15:13

9. Blessed are the poor in spirit to those who *believe in getting wisdom of this Proverbs*: "The heart of him that hath understanding seeketh knowledge: but the mouth of fools feedeth on foolishness." Proverbs 15:14
10. Blessed are the poor in spirit to those who *believe in getting wisdom of this Proverbs*: "All the days of the afflicted are evil: but he that is of a merry heart hath a continual feast." Proverbs 15:15
11. Blessed are the poor in spirit to those who *believe in getting wisdom of this Proverbs*: "Better is little with the fear of the Lord than great treasure and trouble therewith." Proverbs 15:16
12. Blessed are the poor in spirit to those who *believe in getting wisdom of this Proverbs*: "Better is a dinner of herbs where love is, than a stalled ox and hatred therewith." Proverbs 15:17

Part CDXLVIII

Blessed Are The Poor In Spirit. Matthew 5:3

Blessed Means Happy

Poor means meek in spirit. Poor means humble in spirit. Poor means lowly in spirit. Poor means quiet in spirit. Read Matthew 5:3-12, Read also Mark 1:15

Jesus did not say "*rich*" in spirit. Jesus said "*poor*" in spirit.

1. Blessed are the poor in spirit to those who *believe in getting wisdom of this Proverbs*: "A wise son maketh a glad father: but a foolish man despiseth his mother." Proverbs 15:20
2. Blessed are the poor in spirit to those who *believe in getting wisdom of this Proverbs*: "Folly is joy to him that is destitute of wisdom: but a man of understanding walketh uprightly." Proverbs 15:21, Ephesians 5:15
3. Blessed are the poor in spirit to those who *believe in getting wisdom of this Proverbs*: "A man hath joy by the answer of his mouth: and a word spoken in due season, how good is it!" Proverbs 15:23
4. Blessed are the poor in spirit to those who *believe in getting wisdom of this Proverbs*: "The way of life is above to the wise, that he may depart from hell beneath." Proverbs 15:24
5. Blessed are the poor in spirit to those who *believe in getting wisdom of this Proverbs*: "The Lord is far from the wicked: but he heareth the prayer of the righteous." Proverbs 15:29
6. Blessed are the poor in spirit to those who *believe in getting wisdom of this Proverbs*: "The light of the eyes rejoiceth the heart: and a good report maketh the bones fat." Proverbs 15:30
7. Blessed are the poor in spirit to those who *believe in getting wisdom of this Proverbs*: "The ear that heareth the reproof of life abideth among the wise." Proverbs 15:31
8. Blessed are the poor in spirit to those who *believe in getting wisdom of this Proverbs*: "He that refuseth instruction despiseth his own soul: but he that heareth reproof getteth understanding." Proverbs 15:32
9. Blessed are the poor in spirit to those who *believe in getting wisdom of this Proverbs*: "The fear of the Lord is the instruction of wisdom; and before honour is humility." Proverbs 15:33

10. Blessed are the poor in spirit to those who *believe in getting wisdom of this Proverbs*: "The preparations of the heart in man, and the answer of the tongue, is from the Lord." Proverbs 16:1
11. Blessed are the poor in spirit to those who *believe in getting wisdom of this Proverbs*: "All the ways of a man are clean in his own eyes; but the Lord weigheth the spirits." Proverbs 16:2
12. Blessed are the poor in spirit to those who *believe in getting wisdom of this Proverbs*: "Commit thy works unto the Lord, and thy thoughts shall be established." Proverbs 16:3

Part CDXLIX

Blessed Are The Poor In Spirit. Matthew 5:3

Blessed Means Happy

Poor means meek in spirit. Poor means humble in spirit. Poor means lowly in spirit. Poor means quiet in spirit. Read Matthew 5:3-12, Read also Mark 1:15

Jesus did not say "*rich*" in spirit. Jesus said "*poor*" in spirit.

1. Blessed are the poor in spirit to those who *believe in getting wisdom of this Proverbs*: "By mercy and truth iniquity is purged: and by the fear of the Lord men depart from evil." Proverbs 16:6
2. Blessed are the poor in spirit to those who *believe in getting wisdom of this Proverbs*: "When a man's ways please the Lord, he maketh even his enemies to be at peace with him." Proverbs 16:7
3. Blessed are the poor in spirit to those who *believe in getting wisdom of this Proverbs*: "A man's heart deviseth his way: but the Lord directeth his steps." Proverbs 16:9
4. Blessed are the poor in spirit to those who *believe in getting wisdom of this Proverbs*: "A divine sentence is in the lips of the king: his mouth transgresseth not in judgment." Proverbs 16:10
5. Blessed are the poor in spirit to those who *believe in getting wisdom of this Proverbs*: "A just weight and balance are the Lord's all the wights of the bag are his work." Proverbs 16:11
6. Blessed are the poor in spirit to those who *believe in getting wisdom of this Proverbs*: "How much better is it to get wisdom than gold! And to get understanding rather to be chosen than silver!" Proverbs 16:16
7. Blessed are the poor in spirit to those who *believe in getting wisdom of this Proverbs*: "The highway of the upright is to depart from evil: he that keepeth his way preserveth his soul." Proverbs 16:17
8. Blessed are the poor in spirit to those who *believe in getting wisdom of this Proverbs*: "Pride goeth before destruction, and an haughty spirit before a fall." Proverbs 16:18
9. Blessed are the poor in spirit to those who *believe in getting wisdom of this Proverbs*: "Better it is to be of an humble spirit with the lowly, than to divide the spoil with the proud." Proverbs 16:19

10. Blessed are the poor in spirit to those who *believe in getting wisdom of this Proverbs*: "He that handleth a matter wisely shall find good: and whoso trusteth in the Lord, happy is he." Proverbs 16:20
11. Blessed are the poor in spirit to those who *believe in getting wisdom of this Proverbs*: "The wise in heart shall be called prudent: and the sweetness of the lips increaseth learning." Proverbs 16:21
12. Blessed are the poor in spirit to those who *believe in getting wisdom of this Proverbs*: "Understanding is a wellspring of life unto him that hath it: but the instruction of fools is folly." Proverbs 16:22

Part CDL

Blessed Are The Poor In Spirit. Matthew 5:3

Blessed Means Happy

Poor means meek in spirit. Poor means humble in spirit. Poor means lowly in spirit. Poor means quiet in spirit. Read Matthew 5:3-12, Read also Mark 1:15

Jesus did not say "*rich*" in spirit. Jesus said "*poor*" in spirit.

1. Blessed are the poor in spirit to those who *believe in getting wisdom of this Proverbs*: "The heart of the wise teacheth his mouth, and addeth learning to his lips." Proverbs 16:23
2. Blessed are the poor in spirit to those who *believe in getting wisdom of this Proverbs*: "Pleasant words are as an honeycomb, sweet to the soul, and health to the bones." Proverbs 16:24
3. Blessed are the poor in spirit to those who *believe in getting wisdom of this Proverbs*: "The hoary head is a crown of glory, if it be found in the way of righteousness." Proverbs 16:31
4. Blessed are the poor in spirit to those who *believe in getting wisdom of this Proverbs*: "He that is slow to anger is better than the mighty; and he that ruleth his spirit than he that taketh a city." Proverbs 16:32
5. Blessed are the poor in spirit to those who *believe in getting wisdom of this Proverbs*: "The lot is cast into the lap; but the whole disposing thereof is of the Lord." Proverbs 16:33
6. Blessed are the poor in spirit to those who *believe in getting wisdom of this Proverbs*: "A friend loveth at all times, and a brother is born for adversity." Proverbs 17:17
7. Blessed are the poor in spirit to those who *believe in getting wisdom of this Proverbs*: "A man void of understanding striketh hands, and becometh surety in the presence of his friend." Proverbs 17:18
8. Blessed are the poor in spirit to those who *believe in getting wisdom of this Proverbs*: "A merry heart doeth good like a medicine: but a broken spirit drieth the bones." Proverbs 17:22
9. Blessed are the poor in spirit to those who *believe in getting wisdom of this Proverbs*: "Wisdom is before him that hath understanding; but the eyes of a fool are in the ends of the earth." Proverbs 17:24

10. Blessed are the poor in spirit to those who *believe in getting wisdom of this Proverbs*: "He that hath knowledge spareth his words: and a man of understanding is of an excellent spirit." Proverbs 17:27
11. Blessed are the poor in spirit to those who *believe in getting wisdom of this Proverbs*: "Even a fool, when he holdeth his peace, is counted wise: and he that shutteth his lips is esteemed a man of understanding." Proverbs 17:28
12. Blessed are the poor in spirit to those who *believe in getting wisdom of this Proverbs*: "The words of a man's mouth are as deep waters, and the wellspring of wisdom as a flowing brook." Proverbs 18:4

Part CDLI

Blessed Are The Poor In Spirit. Matthew 5:3

Blessed Means Happy

Poor means meek in spirit. Poor means humble in spirit. Poor means lowly in spirit. Poor means quiet in spirit. Read Matthew 5:3-12, Read also Mark 1:15

Jesus did not say "*rich*" in spirit. Jesus said "*poor*" in spirit.

1. Blessed are the poor in spirit to those who *believe in getting wisdom of this Proverbs*: "A fool's mouth is his destruction, and his lips are the snare of his soul." Proverbs 18:7
2. Blessed are the poor in spirit to those who *believe in getting wisdom of this Proverbs*: "The name of the Lord is a strong tower: the righteous runneth into it, and is safe." Proverbs 18:10
3. Blessed are the poor in spirit to those who *believe in getting wisdom of this Proverbs*: "The heart of the prudent getteth knowledge; and the ear of the wise seeketh knowledge." Proverbs 18:15
4. Blessed are the poor in spirit to those who *believe in getting wisdom of this Proverbs*: "He that is first in his own cause seemeth just; but his neighbour cometh and searcheth him." Proverbs 18:17
5. Blessed are the poor in spirit to those who *believe in getting wisdom of this Proverbs*: "A man's belly shall be satisfied with the fruit of his mouth; and with the increase of his lips shall he be filled." Proverbs 18:20
6. Blessed are the poor in spirit to those who *believe in getting wisdom of this Proverbs*: "Death and life are in the power of the tongue: and they that love it shall eat the fruit thereof." Proverbs 18:21
7. Blessed are the poor in spirit to those who *believe in getting wisdom of this Proverbs*: "Whoso findeth a wife findeth a good thing, and obtaineth favour of the Lord." Proverbs 18:22
8. Blessed are the poor in spirit to those who *believe in getting wisdom of this Proverbs*: "A man that hath friends must shew himself friendly: and there is a friend that sticketh closer than a brother." Proverbs 18:24

9. Blessed are the poor in spirit to those who *believe in getting wisdom of this Proverbs*: "Better is the poor that walketh in his integrity, than he that is perverse in his lips, and is a fool." Proverbs 19:1
10. Blessed are the poor in spirit to those who *believe in getting wisdom of this Proverbs*: "Also, that the soul be without knowledge, it is not good; and he that hasteth with his feet sinneth." Proverbs 19:2
11. Blessed are the poor in spirit to those who *believe in getting wisdom of this Proverbs*: "The foolishness of man perverteth his way: and his heart fretteth against the Lord." Proverbs 19:3
12. Blessed are the poor in spirit to those who *believe in getting wisdom of this Proverbs*: "Wealth maketh many friends; but the poor is separated from his neighbour." Proverbs 19:4

Part CDLII

Blessed Are The Poor In Spirit. Matthew 5:3

Blessed Means Happy

Poor means meek in spirit. Poor means humble in spirit. Poor means lowly in spirit. Poor means quiet in spirit. Read Matthew 5:3-12, Read also Mark 1:15

Jesus did not say "*rich*" in spirit. Jesus said "*poor*" in spirit.

1. Blessed are the poor in spirit to those who *believe in getting wisdom of this Proverbs*: "A false witness shall not be unpunished, and he that speaketh lies shall not escape." Proverbs 19:5
2. Blessed are the poor in spirit to those who *believe in getting wisdom of this Proverbs*: "He that getteth wisdom loveth his own soul: he that keepeth understanding shall find good." Proverbs 19:8
3. Blessed are the poor in spirit to those who *believe in getting wisdom of this Proverbs*: "A false witness shall not be unpunished, and he that speaketh lies shall perish." Proverbs 19:9
4. Blessed are the poor in spirit to those who *believe in getting wisdom of this Proverbs*: "Hear counsel, and receive instruction, that thou mayest be wise in thy latter end." Proverbs 19:20
5. Blessed are the poor in spirit to those who *believe in getting wisdom of this Proverbs*: "The fear of the Lord tendeth to life: and he that hath it shall abide satisfied; he shall not be visited with evil." Proverbs 19:23
6. Blessed are the poor in spirit to those who *believe in getting wisdom of this Proverbs*: "Smite a scorner, and the simple will beware: and reprove one that hath understanding, and he will understand knowledge." Proverbs 19:25
7. Blessed are the poor in spirit to those who *believe in getting wisdom of this Proverbs*: "Cease, my son, to hear the instruction that causeth to err from the words of knowledge." Proverbs 19:27
8. Blessed are the poor in spirit to those who *believe in getting wisdom of this Proverbs*: "Wine is a mocker, strong drink is raging: and whosoever is deceived thereby is not wise." Proverbs 20:1

9. Blessed are the poor in spirit to those who *believe in getting wisdom of this Proverbs*: "Counsel in the heart of man is like deep water; but a man of understanding will draw it out." Proverbs 20:5
10. Blessed are the poor in spirit to those who *believe in getting wisdom of this Proverbs*: "Most men will proclaim every one his own goodness: but a faithful man who can find?" Proverbs 20:6
11. Blessed are the poor in spirit to those who *believe in getting wisdom of this Proverbs*: "The just man walketh in his integrity: his children are blessed after him." Proverbs 20:7
12. Blessed are the poor in spirit to those who *believe in getting wisdom of this Proverbs*: "Who can say, I have made my heart clean, I am pure from my sin?" Proverbs 20:9

Part CDLIII

Blessed Are The Poor In Spirit. Matthew 5:3

Blessed Means Happy

Poor means meek in spirit. Poor means humble in spirit. Poor means lowly in spirit. Poor means quiet in spirit. Read Matthew 5:3-12, Read also Mark 1:15

Jesus did not say "*rich*" in spirit. Jesus said "*poor*" in spirit.

1. Blessed are the poor in spirit to those who *believe in getting wisdom of this Proverbs*: "Even a child is known by his doings, whether his work be pure, and whether it be right." Proverbs 20:11
2. Blessed are the poor in spirit to those who *believe in getting wisdom of this Proverbs*: "The hearing ear, and the seeing eye, the Lord hath made even both of them." Proverbs 20:12
3. Blessed are the poor in spirit to those who *believe in getting wisdom of this Proverbs*: "Love not sleep, lest thou come to poverty; open thine eyes, and thou shalt be satisfied with bread." Proverbs 20:13
4. Blessed are the poor in spirit to those who *believe in getting wisdom of this Proverbs*: "Whoso curseth his father or his mother, his lamp shall be put out in obscure darkness." Proverbs 20:20
5. Blessed are the poor in spirit to those who *believe in getting wisdom of this Proverbs*: "Say not thou, I will recompense evil; but wait on the Lord, and he shall save thee." Proverbs 20:22, Romans 12:17
6. Blessed are the poor in spirit to those who *believe in getting wisdom of this Proverbs*: "Man's goings are of the Lord; how can a man then understand his own way?" Proverbs 20:24
7. Blessed are the poor in spirit to those who *believe in getting wisdom of this Proverbs*: "The spirit of man is the candle of the Lord, searching all the inward parts of the belly." Proverbs 20:27
8. Blessed are the poor in spirit to those who *believe in getting wisdom of this Proverbs*: "The glory of young men is their strength: and the beauty of old men is the grey head." Proverbs 20:29

9. Blessed are the poor in spirit to those who *believe in getting wisdom of this Proverbs*: "The blueness of a wound cleanseth away evil: so do stripes the inward parts of the belly." Proverbs 20:30
10. Blessed are the poor in spirit to those who *believe in getting wisdom of this Proverbs*: "The king's heart is in the hand of the Lord, as the rivers of water: he turneth it whithersoever he will." Proverbs 21:1
11. Blessed are the poor in spirit to those who *believe in getting wisdom of this Proverbs*: "Every way of a man is right in his own eyes: but the Lord pondereth the hearts." Proverbs 21:2
12. Blessed are the poor in spirit to those who *believe in getting wisdom of this Proverbs*: "To do justice and judgment is more acceptable to the Lord than sacrifice." Proverbs 21:3

Part CDLIV

Blessed Are The Poor In Spirit. Matthew 5:3

Blessed Means Happy

Poor means meek in spirit. Poor means humble in spirit. Poor means lowly in spirit. Poor means quiet in spirit. Read Matthew 5:3-12, Read also Mark 1:15

Jesus did not say "*rich*" in spirit. Jesus said "*poor*" in spirit.

1. Blessed are the poor in spirit to those who *believe in getting wisdom of this Proverbs*: "An high look, and a proud heart, and the plowing of the wicked, is sin." Proverbs 21:4
2. Blessed are the poor in spirit to those who *believe in getting wisdom of this Proverbs*: "The getting of treaures by a lying tongue is a vanity tossed to and fro of them that seek death." Proverbs 21:6
3. Blessed are the poor in spirit to those who *believe in getting wisdom of this Proverbs*: "The soul of the wicked desireth evil: his neighbour findeth no favour in his eyes." Proverbs 21:10
4. Blessed are the poor in spirit to those who *believe in getting wisdom of this Proverbs*: "When the scorner is punished, the simple is made wise: and when the wise is instructed, he receiveth knowledge." Proverbs 21:11
5. Blessed are the poor in spirit to those who *believe in getting wisdom of this Proverbs*: "Whoso stoppeth his ears at the cry of the poor, he also shall cry himself, but shall not be heard." Proverbs 21:13
6. Blessed are the poor in spirit to those who *believe in getting wisdom of this Proverbs*: "It is joy to the just to do judgment: but destruction shall be to the workers of iniquity." Proverbs 21:15
7. Blessed are the poor in spirit to those who *believe in getting wisdom of this Proverbs*: "The wicked shall be a ransom for the righteous, and the transgressor for the upright." Proverbs 21:18
8. Blessed are the poor in spirit to those who *believe in getting wisdom of this Proverbs*: "He that followeth after righteousness and mercy findeth life, righteousness, and honour." Proverbs 21:21

9. Blessed are the poor in spirit to those who *believe in getting wisdom of this Proverbs*: "Whoso keepeth his mouth and his tongue keepeth his soul from troubles." Proverbs 21:23
10. Blessed are the poor in spirit to those who *believe in getting wisdom of this Proverbs*: "A good name is rather to be chosen than great riches, and loving favour rather than silver and gold." Proverbs 22:1
11. Blessed are the poor in spirit to those who *believe in getting wisdom of this Proverbs*: "The rich and poor meet together: the Lord is the maker of them all." Proverbs 22:2
12. Blessed are the poor in spirit to those who *believe in getting wisdom of this Proverbs*: "By humility and the fear of the Lord are riches, and hoour, and life." Proverbs 22:4

Part CDLV

Blessed Are The Poor In Spirit. Matthew 5:3

Blessed Means Happy

Poor means meek in spirit. Poor means humble in spirit. Poor means lowly in spirit. Poor means quiet in spirit. Read Matthew 5:3-12, Read also Mark 1:15

Jesus did not say "*rich*" in spirit. Jesus said "*poor*" in spirit.

1. Blessed are the poor in spirit to those who *believe in getting wisdom of this Proverbs*: "Train up a child in the way he should go: and when he is old, he will not depart from it." Proverbs 22:6, Ephesians 6:4
2. Blessed are the poor in spirit to those who *believe in getting wisdom of this Proverbs*: "He that hath a bountiful eye shall be blessed; for he giveth of his bread to the poor." Proverbs 22:9
3. Blessed are the poor in spirit to those who *believe in getting wisdom of this Proverbs*: "The eyes of the Lord preserve knowledge, and he overthroweth the words of the transgressor." Proverbs 22:12
4. Blessed are the poor in spirit to those who *believe in getting wisdom of this Proverbs*: "Bow down thine ear, and hear the words of the wise, and apply thine heart unto my knowledge." Proverbs 22:17
5. Blessed are the poor in spirit to those who *believe in getting wisdom of this Proverbs*: "That thy trust may be in the Lord, I have made known to thee this day, even to thee." Proverbs 22:19
6. Blessed are the poor in spirit to those who *believe in getting wisdom of this Proverbs*: "Have not I written to thee excellent things in counsels and knowledge," Proverbs 22:20
7. Blessed are the poor in spirit to those who *believe in getting wisdom of this Proverbs*: "That I might make thee know the certainty of the words of truth; that thou mightest answer the words of truth to them that send unto thee?" Proverbs 22:21
8. Blessed are the poor in spirit to those who *believe in getting wisdom of this Proverbs*: "Rob not the poor, because he is poor: neither oppress the afflicted in the gate:" Proverbs 22:22

9. Blessed are the poor in spirit to those who *believe in getting wisdom of this Proverbs*: "For the Lord will plead their cause, and spoil the soul of those that spoiled them." Proverbs 22:23
10. Blessed are the poor in spirit to those who *believe in getting wisdom of this Proverbs*: "Make no friendship with an angry man; and with a furious man thou shalt not go:" Proverbs 22:24
11. Blessed are the poor in spirit to those who *believe in getting wisdom of this Proverbs*: "Lest thou learn his ways, and get a snare to thy soul." Proverbs 22:25
12. Blessed are the poor in spirit to those who *believe in getting wisdom of this Proverbs*: "Remove not the ancient landmark, which thy fathers have set." Proverbs 22:28

Part CDLVI

Blessed Are The Poor In Spirit. Matthew 5:3

Blessed Means Happy

Poor means meek in spirit. Poor means humble in spirit. Poor means lowly in spirit. Poor means quiet in spirit. Read Matthew 5:3-12, Read also Mark 1:15

Jesus did not say "*rich*" in spirit. Jesus said "*poor*" in spirit.

1. Blessed are the poor in spirit to those who *believe in getting wisdom of this Proverbs*: "Remove not the old landmark; and enter not into the fields of the fatherless:" Proverbs 23:10
2. Blessed are the poor in spirit to those who *believe in getting wisdom of this Proverbs*: "For their redeemer is mighty; he shall plead their cause with thee." Proverbs 23:11
3. Blessed are the poor in spirit to those who *believe in getting wisdom of this Proverbs*: "Apply thine heart unto instruction, and thine ears to the words of knowledge." Proverbs 23:12
4. Blessed are the poor in spirit to those who *believe in getting wisdom of this Proverbs*: "My son, if thine heart be wise, my heart shall rejoice, even mine." Proverbs 23:15
5. Blessed are the poor in spirit to those who *believe in getting wisdom of this Proverbs*: "Yea, my reins shall rejoice, when thy lips speak right things." Proverbs 23:16
6. Blessed are the poor in spirit to those who *believe in getting wisdom of this Proverbs*: "Let not thine heart envy sinners: but be thou in the fear of the Lord all the day long." Proverbs 23:17
7. Blessed are the poor in spirit to those who *believe in getting wisdom of this Proverbs*: "For surely there is an end; and thine expectation shall not be cut off." Proverbs 23:18
8. Blessed are the poor in spirit to those who *believe in getting wisdom of this Proverbs*: "Hear thou, my son, and be wise, and guide thine heart in the way." Proverbs 23:19
9. Blessed are the poor in spirit to those who *believe in getting wisdom of this Proverbs*: "Hearken unto thy father that begat thee, and despise not thy mother when she is old." Proverbs 23:22

10. Blessed are the poor in spirit to those who *believe in getting wisdom of this Proverbs*: "Buy the truth, and sell it not; also wisdom, and instruction, and understanding." Proverbs 23:23
11. Blessed are the poor in spirit to those who *believe in getting wisdom of this Proverbs*: "The father of the righteous shall greatly rejoice: and he that begetteth a wise child shall have joy of him." Proverbs 23:24
12. Blessed are the poor in spirit to those who *believe in getting wisdom of this Proverbs*: "Thy father and thy mother shall be glad, and she that bare thee shall rejoice." Proverbs 23:25

Part CDLVII

Blessed Are The Poor In Spirit. Matthew 5:3

Blessed Means Happy

Poor means meek in spirit. Poor means humble in spirit. Poor means lowly in spirit. Poor means quiet in spirit. Read Matthew 5:3-12, Read also Mark 1:15

Jesus did not say "*rich*" in spirit. Jesus said "*poor*" in spirit.

1. Blessed are the poor in spirit to those who *believe in getting wisdom of this Proverbs*: "My son, give me thine heart, and let thine eyes observe my ways." Proverbs 23:26
2. Blessed are the poor in spirit to those who *believe in getting wisdom of this Proverbs*: "My son, eat thou honey, because it is good; and the honeycomb, which is sweet to thy taste:" Proverbs 24:13
3. Blessed are the poor in spirit to those who *believe in getting wisdom of this Proverbs*: "So shall the knowledge of wisdom be unto thy soul: when thou hast found it, then there shall be a reward, and thy expectation shall not be cut off." Proverbs 24:14
4. Blessed are the poor in spirit to those who *believe in getting wisdom of this Proverbs*: "Then I saw, and considered it well: I looked upon it, and received instruction." Proverbs 24:32
5. Blessed are the poor in spirit to those who *believe in getting wisdom of this Proverbs*: "As cold waters to a thirsty soul, so is good news from a far country." Proverbs 25:25
6. Blessed are the poor in spirit to those who *believe in getting wisdom of this Proverbs*: "Boast not thyself of to morrow; for thou knowest not what a day may bring forth." Proverbs 27:1
7. Blessed are the poor in spirit to those who *believe in getting wisdom of this Proverbs*: "Let another man praise thee, and not thine own mouth; a stranger, and not thine own lips." Proverbs 27:2
8. Blessed are the poor in spirit to those who *believe in getting wisdom of this Proverbs*: "Open rebuke is better than secret love." Proverbs 27:5

9. Blessed are the poor in spirit to those who *believe in getting wisdom of this Proverbs*: "Faithful are the wounds of a friend; but the kisses of an enemy are deceitful." Proverbs 27:6
10. Blessed are the poor in spirit to those who *believe in getting wisdom of this Proverbs*: "The full soul loatheth an honeycomb; but to the hungry soul every bitter thing is sweet." Proverbs 27:7
11. Blessed are the poor in spirit to those who *believe in getting wisdom of this Proverbs*: "As a bird that wandereth from her nest, so is a man that wandereth from his place." Proverbs 27:8
12. Blessed are the poor in spirit to those who *believe in getting wisdom of this Proverbs*: "Ointment and perfume rejoice the heart: so doth the sweetness of a man's friend by hearty counsel." Proverbs 27:9

Part CDLVIII

Blessed Are The Poor In Spirit. Matthew 5:3

Blessed Means Happy

Poor means meek in spirit. Poor means humble in spirit. Poor means lowly in spirit. Poor means quiet in spirit. Read Matthew 5:3-12, Read also Mark 1:15

Jesus did not say "*rich*" in spirit. Jesus said "*poor*" in spirit.

1. Blessed are the poor in spirit to those who *believe in getting wisdom of this Proverbs*: "Thine own friend, and thy father's friend, forsake not; neither go into thy brother's house in the day of thy calamity: for better is a neighbour that is near than a brother far off." Proverbs 27:10
2. Blessed are the poor in spirit to those who *believe in getting wisdom of this Proverbs*: "My son, be wise, and make my heart glad, that I may answer him that reproacheth me." Proverbs 27:11
3. Blessed are the poor in spirit to those who *believe in getting wisdom of this Proverbs*: "Evil men understand not judgment: but they that seek the Lord understand all things." Proverbs 28:5
4. Blessed are the poor in spirit to those who *believe in getting wisdom of this Proverbs*: "Better is the poor that walketh in his uprightness, than he that is perverse in his ways, though he be rich." Proverbs 28:6
5. Blessed are the poor in spirit to those who *believe in getting wisdom of this Proverbs*: "Whoso keepeth the law is a wise son: but he that is a companion of riotous men shameth his father." Proverbs 28:7
6. Blessed are the poor in spirit to those who *believe in getting wisdom of this Proverbs*: "He that turneth away his ear from hearing the law, even his prayer shall be abomination." Proverbs 28:9
7. Blessed are the poor in spirit to those who *believe in getting wisdom of this Proverbs*: "The rich man is wise in his own conceit; but the poor that hath understanding searcheth him out." Proverbs 28:11
8. Blessed are the poor in spirit to those who *believe in getting wisdom of this Proverbs*: "He that covereth his sins shall not prosper: but whoso confesseth and forsaketh them shall have mercy." Proverbs 28:13

9. Blessed are the poor in spirit to those who *believe in getting wisdom of this Proverbs*: "Happy is the man that feareth always: but he that hardeneth his heart shall fall into mischief." Proverbs 28:14
10. Blessed are the poor in spirit to those who *believe in getting wisdom of this Proverbs*: "Whoso walketh uprightly shall be saved: but he that is perverse in his ways shall fall at once." Proverbs 28:18
11. Blessed are the poor in spirit to those who *believe in getting wisdom of this Proverbs*: "Whoso robbeth his father or his mother, and saith, It is not transgression; the same is the companion of a destroyer." Proverbs 28:24
12. Blessed are the poor in spirit to those who *believe in getting wisdom of this Proverbs*: "He that is of a proud heart stirreth up strife: but he that putteth his trust in the Lord shall be made fat." Proverbs 28:25

Part CDLIX

Blessed Are The Poor In Spirit. Matthew 5:3

Blessed Means Happy

Poor means meek in spirit. Poor means humble in spirit. Poor means lowly in spirit. Poor means quiet in spirit. Read Matthew 5:3-12, Read also Mark 1:15

Jesus did not say "*rich*" in spirit. Jesus said "*poor*" in spirit.

1. Blessed are the poor in spirit to those who *believe in getting wisdom of this Proverbs*: "He that trusteth in his own heart is a fool: but whoso walketh wisely, he shall be delivered." Proverbs 28:26
2. Blessed are the poor in spirit to those who *believe in getting wisdom of this Proverbs*: "Correct thy son, and he shall give thee rest; yea, he shall give delight unto thy soul." Proverbs 29:17
3. Blessed are the poor in spirit to those who *believe in getting wisdom of this Proverbs*: "Where there is no vision, the people perish: but he that keepeth the law, happy is he." Proverbs 29:18
4. Blessed are the poor in spirit to those who *believe in getting wisdom of this Proverbs*: "A servant will not be corrected by words: for though he understand he will not answer." Proverbs 29:19
5. Blessed are the poor in spirit to those who *believe in getting wisdom of this Proverbs*: "A man's pride shall bring him low: but honour shall uphold the humble in spirit." Proverbs 29:23
6. Blessed are the poor in spirit to those who *believe in getting wisdom of this Proverbs*: "Many seek the ruler's favour; but every man's judgment cometh from the Lord." Proverbs 29:26
7. Blessed are the poor in spirit to those who *believe in getting wisdom of this Proverbs*: "I neither learned wisdom, nor have the knowledge of the holy." Proverbs 30:3
8. Blessed are the poor in spirit to those who *believe in getting wisdom of this Proverbs*: "Who hath ascended up into heaven, or descended? Who hath gathered the wind in his fists? Who hath bound the waters in a garment? Who hath established all the ends of the earth? What is his name, and what is his son's name, if thou canst tell?" Proverbs 30:4, John 3:13

9. Blessed are the poor in spirit to those who *believe in getting wisdom of this Proverbs*: "Every word of God is pure: he is a shield unto them that put their trust in him." Proverbs 30:5
10. Blessed are the poor in spirit to those who *believe in getting wisdom of this Proverbs*: "Lest I be full, and deny thee, and say, Who is the Lord? or lest I be poor, and steal, and take the name of my God in vain." Proverbs 30:9
11. Blessed are the poor in spirit to those who *believe in getting wisdom of this Proverbs*: "There is a generation that curseth their father, and doth not bless their mother." Proverbs 30:11
12. Blessed are the poor in spirit to those who *believe in getting wisdom of this Proverbs*: "There is a generation that are pure in their own eyes, and yet is not washed from their filthiness." Proverbs 30:12

Part CDLX

Blessed Are The Poor In Spirit. Matthew 5:3

Blessed Means Happy

Poor means meek in spirit. Poor means humble in spirit. Poor means lowly in spirit. Poor means quiet in spirit. Read Matthew 5:3-12, Read also Mark 1:15

Jesus did not say "*rich*" in spirit. Jesus said "*poor*" in spirit.

1. Blessed are the poor in spirit to those who *believe in getting wisdom of this Proverbs*: "The ants are a people not strong, yet they prepare their meat in the summer;" Proverbs 30:25
2. Blessed are the poor in spirit to those who *believe in getting wisdom of this Proverbs*: "Open thy moth, judge righteously, and plead the cause of the poor and needy." Proverbs 31:9
3. Blessed are the poor in spirit to those who *believe in getting wisdom of this Proverbs*: "Who can find a virtuous woman? For her price is far above rubies." Proverbs 31:10
4. Blessed are the poor in spirit to those who *believe in getting wisdom of this Proverbs*: "The heart of her husband doth safely trust in her, so that he shall have no need of spoil." Proverbs 31:11
5. Blessed are the poor in spirit to those who *believe in getting wisdom of this Proverbs*: "She will do him good and not evil all the days of her life." Proverbs 31:12
6. Blessed are the poor in spirit to those who *believe in getting wisdom of this Proverbs*: "She riseth also while it is yet night, and giveth meat to her household, and a portion to her maidens." Proverbs 31:15
7. Blessed are the poor in spirit to those who *believe in getting wisdom of this Proverbs*: "She stretcheth out her hand to the poor; yea, she reacheth forth her hands to the needy." Proverbs 31:20
8. Blessed are the poor in spirit to those who *believe in getting wisdom of this Proverbs*: "She is not afraid of the snow for her household: for all her household are clothed with scarlet." Proverbs 31:21
9. Blessed are the poor in spirit to those who *believe in getting wisdom of this Proverbs*: "Her husband is known in the gates, when he sitteth among the elders of the land." Proverbs 31:23

10. Blessed are the poor in spirit to those who *believe in getting wisdom of this Proverbs*: "Her children arise up, and call her blessed; her husband also, and he praiseth her." Proverbs 31:28
11. Blessed are the poor in spirit to those who *believe in getting wisdom of this Proverbs*: "Many daughters have done virtuously, but thou excellest them all." Proverbs 31:29
12. Blessed are the poor in spirit to those who *believe in getting wisdom of this Proverbs*: "Favour is deceitful, and beauty is vain: but a woman that feareth the Lord, she shall be praised." Proverbs 31:30

Part CDLXI

Blessed Are The Poor In Spirit. Matthew 5:3

Blessed Means Happy

Poor means meek in spirit. Poor means humble in spirit. Poor means lowly in spirit. Poor means quiet in spirit. Read Matthew 5:3-12, Read also Mark 1:15

Jesus did not say "*rich*" in spirit. Jesus said "*poor*" in spirit.

1. Blessed are the poor in spirit to those who believe that *repentance and forgiven are the same as receiving salvation*. Acts 8:22
2. Blessed are the poor in spirit to those who believed the *prophetic message of Joel*: Joel 2:28-32, Acts 2:16-21, Acts 2:21 and Joel 2:32.
3. Bless are the poor in spirit to those who believe that the *Bible is not about*: "the Baptist, the Irivingites, the Pentecost, the Catholic, the Lutheran, the Methodist, the Presbyterian, the Holiness, the Non-denomination, the Church of God, the Church of God in Christ, the Church of Christ, the Assembly of God, the Pentecostal Holiness, the Southern Baptist, the Independent Fundamental Baptist, the Free Will Baptist, the Missionary Baptist, the Independent Church, the Individual Person, the church member, the Evangelical Church, our own belief, the Jewish Church, the Greek Orthodox, the Gnostic Church, the Fire Baptized Holiness, personal belief of the Bible, our own belief of the Bible, the Bible Way Church, the Congregational Church, the Monk, the Mennonite, the African Methodist Episcopal, the Christian Methodist Episcopal, the United Methodist Episcopal, the Methodist Episcopal Church, the Faith Bible Church, the Faith Church, the Church of Prophecy, the Four Square Gospel Church, the Gospel Church, the Church of God of Prophecy, the Christ's Church, the Self Claim Baptism of the Spirit, the Faith Doctrine of the Bible, The Oneness, the Orthodox Trinity Church, the Community Church, the Seventh Day Adventist, the Church of the Nazarene, the Covenant Church, the Disciples of Christ, the Fellowship Church, the Christ Church, the Church of God In Christ Jesus, the International Church of God In Christ, the Open Bible Standard Church, the Evening Light Saint Church, the Trinity Church or the Non member of the church; however, the Bible is about **Jesus Christ and Him crucified**. Although

they are good and nice to name these churches, where Jesus say, I will build my church and the gates of hell will not prevail against it. Nevertheless, I decide not to know anything, **except Jesus Christ and Him crucified**. I Corinthians 2:2

4. Blessed are the poor in spirit to those who believe that Church is my college, Heaven is my Unversity; Jesus is my Principal; The Holy Spirit is my Teacher; Angels are my Class Mates; The Bible is my Study Book, ;Trial and Temptation are my Exams; Winning Souls are my Assignments; Prayer is my Attendance; Crown of Life is my Degree; and Praise and Worship is my Motto; Enroll today! There is room for all and tuition is Free!!! Genesis 1:1, John1:1, II Timothy 3:14-17
5. Blessed are the poor in spirit to those who believe that the *Bible* is *translated by God* to *give* to those who would "*speak*" the "*same language*," "*preach*" the "*same language*," "*exhort*" the "*same language*," "*encourage*" the "*same language*" with the "*same teaching*," the "*same doctrine*," the "*same commendment*," the "*same truth*" of *His Word* that is "*written*" *by* "*the Holy Spirit of God*" *to man* everywhere because one day there will be "*one language*" amd of "*one speech*" in heaven *since God* left "*one language*" and "*one speech*" before He "*confound*" (confused) *their language* so that they *could not understand* "*one another's speech*." Therefore the name was *called* "*Babel*," which is called "*confusion*" there *confound* (confused) the language. Genesis 11:1-9 (verse 1, 6, 7, 9), Genesis 1:1, John 1:1, II Timothy 3:14-17
6. Blessed are the poor in spirit to those who believe, realize and understand that the church is "*about*" Jesus Christ Coming; Jesus' Second Coming; Jesus Christ Return. Be Prepared To Meet The Lord Thy God. Are you ready to prepare to meet the Lord thy God? See Amos 4:12 Jesus say, "Behold, I come quickly." Are you ready to meet Jesus Christ when He come? Revelation 3:11, Revelation 22:7, 2, 20. See I Thessalonians 4:14-18. See also Acts 1:11.
7. Blessed are the poor in spirit to those who believe that the church mean the Second Coming of Christ. Be thou faithful until He come. Acts 1:11, I Corinthians 4:2, I Corinthians 11:26, Revelation 2:10, Revelation 3:11, Revelation 22:7, 12, 20
8. Blessed are the poor in spirit to those who believe that God through Jesus Christ truly loved the people of the whole human entire race; the Jewish, the Gentiles, the pagan, the heathen, the slavery, the African American, black, the caucasian, white, the Hispanic, the Native American, the Asian American, Pacific Islander, The Japanese American, the Chinese American, the Russian American, the German American, males and females, or race/ethnicity. John 3:16, Accept Jesus

Christ today!!! II Corinthians 6:2, Galatians 3:8, 28-29, Acts 16:31, Genesis 1:26-27, Matthew 19:4, Colossians 3:10, Genesis 3:22, Jeremiah 33:3, Psalm 22:9-10, Psalm 51:1-17, Jeremiah 31:3, Malachi 1:2, John 13:34, John 15:9, 12, Revelation 3:9, Leviticus 19:18

9. Blessed are the poor in spirit to those who believe in God's healing of forgiveness. Exodus 15:26, Psalm 103:1-3, Isaiah 53:5, Matthew 8:7, John 3:16, Philippians 4:13, James 5:16, I Peter 2:24
10. Blessed are the poor in spirit to those who believe that the Pentecost is about the birth of Jesus, the death of Jesus, the Resurrection of Jesus and His Second Coming. Acts 1:6-11, Acts 2:1-47, Revelation 3:11, Revelation 22:7, 12, 20
11. Blessed are the poor in spirit to those who believe that believers were multitudes both of men and women who were added to (by) the Lord. Acts 5:14. See also Acts 2:47
12. Blessed are the poor in spirit to those who believe that God bless our nation; our America; God bless America. Psalm 33:12, Psalm 67:1, 6, 7

Part CDLXII

Blessed Are The Poor In Spirit. Matthew 5:3

Blessed Means Happy

Poor means meek in spirit Poor means humble in spirit Poor means lowly in spirit Poor means quiet in spirit Read Matthew 5:3-12, Read also Mark 1:15

Jesus did not say "*rich*" in spirit. Jesus said "*poor*" in spirit.

1. Blessed are the poor in spirit to those who believe that "*fish*" mean people. Matthew 4:19
2. Blessed are the poor in spirit to those who believe that "*world*" mean people. John 1:10-11, John 3:10, Genesis 1:1, 26-27, Genesis 2:7, 17-25, Genesis 5:2, Matthew 19:4, Colossians 3:10, Genesis 3:4, II Corinthians 11:13, Hebrews 4:13, Genesis 12:1-6, Genesis 8:1-22, Genesis 9:1-29
3. Blessed are the poor in spirit to those who believe that "*ants*" mean people. Proverb 6:6, Proverbs 30:25, John 4:1-6
4. Blessed are the poor in spirit to those who believe that the "*Color of Rainbow*" or "*the promise of Rainbow*" mean people of *culture*; people of *race*; or people of *red, yellow, black* and *white*. Genesis 9:13, 17, Genesis 11:1-32, verse 1-10
5. Blessed are the poor in spirit to those who believe in giving praise and giving thanks to God through Jesus Christ for the appearance of Pentecost on the day of Pentecost in Acts 2:1, with salvation and faith in Jesus Christ, who *came* to *deliver*, to *save*, to *heal* and to *set us free* from the wrath of God, from hell and His Second Coming to bring us, Home To Glory to spend eternal with Him forever more. Acts 2:1-28, verse 1-31, I Thessalonians 4:13-18, Revelation 3:11, Revelation 22:7, 12, 20, Acts 1:9-11, Act2:1, Acts 20:16, I Corinthians 16:8,
6. Blessed are the poor in spirit to those who believe in this spiritual hymn: "When I see the blood; when I see the blood; when I see the blood, I will pass, I will pass over you. Exodus 12:13
7. Blessed are the poor in spirit to those who believe that the Blood of Jesus Christ is for peace of mind and rest of heart. Isaiah 26:3, Matthew 11:28. Read I John 5:8-15, John 19:34-35.

8. Blessed are the poor in spirit to those who are faithful children of God are on the Blood of Jesus. I Peter 1:2-5, Hebrews 13:20.
9. Blessed are the poor in spirit to those who believe that the Blood sprinkling, the Word of God speaketh for better things and purpose through Jesus Christ. Hebrews 12:24
10. Blessed are the poor in spirit to those who believe that we are not to think of how we get here on earth by chance but by God's choosing, He called us. II Thessalonians 2:13-16, I Peter 1:9-10, 24-25
11. Blessed are the poor in spirit to those who believe that God has faithfully and duty kept His promise, His covenant, His agreement and His Word as He did with Noah. Isaiah 54:4-10, 13. See also Jeremiah 31:3, Genesis 12:1-7, Genesis 13:14-17, Genesis 15:1-21, Hebrews 11:12, Romans 4:3, James 2:23, Isaiah 41:8, Acts 7:7, Galatians 3:7, Exodus 2:22-:25, James 5:4, Exodus 3:3-15, Revelation 1:8, Galatians 3:14, 18-19 verse 18, II Peter 3:4, 9, 13, I John 2:25, Hebrews 4:1, Hebrews 6:13, 15, 17, Hebrews 9:25, Hebrews 10:36, Hebrews 11:9, 39, Romans 4:13, 20-25, Romans 9:8-9,
12. Blessed are the poor in spirit to those who believe Exodus 15:26: "I am the Lord that healeth thee. Exodus 15:26

Part CDLXIII

Blessed Are The Poor In Spirit. Matthew 5:3

Blessed Means Happy

Poor means meek in spirit. Poor means humble in spirit. Poor means lowly in spirit. Poor means quiet in spirit. Read Matthew 5:3-12, Read also Mark 1:15

Jesus did not say "*rich*" in spirit. Jesus said "*poor*" in spirit.

1. Blessed are the poor in spirit to those who believe Psalm 103:3: "Who forgiveth all thine iniquities; who healeth all thy diseases. Psalm 103:3
2. Blessed are the poor in spirit to those who believe Isaiah 53:5: "With His stripes we are healed." Isaiah 53:5
3. Blessed are the poor in spirit to those who believe Matthew 8:7: "I will come and heal him." Matthew 8:7
4. Blessed are the poor in spirit to those who believe Philippians 4:13: "I can do all things through Christ which strengtheneth me." Philippians 4:13
5. Blessed are the poor in spirit to those who believe I Peter 2:24: "By whose stripes we were healed." I Peter 2:24
6. Blessed are the poor in spirit to those who believe James 5:16: "That ye may be healed." James 5:16
7. Blessed are the poor in spirit to those who believe in the name of Jesus. Behold. I am what the word of God say I am. I am more than conquered. I am more than victory. And I can do what the Word of God say I can do. Thank You Lord. Thank You Jesus for healing my body. Psalm 103:3, Romans 8:37-39
8. Blessed are the poor in spirit to those who believe that God love American Indian or Native Alaskan, Asian, Black or African American, Hispanic/Latino, Native Hawaiian or other Pacific Island, White or Caucasian, or more than one race even to those who refuse to decline to answer their race origin John 3:16, Jeremiah 33:3
9. Blessed are the poor in spirit to those who believe that God through Jesus Christ is number one in the world because He loves us indeed. John 3:16
10. Blessed are the poor in spirit to those who believe that Beloved mean Christ. Romans 5:8, Ephesians 1:6 or Beloved mean David as well which is in Christ Jesus.

11. Blessed are the poor in spirit to those who believe that Gracious mean John. John 1:16. Gracious also mean Christ Jesus.
12. Blessed are the poor in spirit to those who believe that Stone or Rock mean Peter. Matthew 16:17-18, John 1:42. Rock also mean Christ who is That Rock. I Corinthians 10:4

Part CDLXIV

Blessed Are The Poor In Spirit. Matthew 5:3

Blessed Means Happy

Poor means meek in spirit. Poor means humble in spirit. Poor means lowly in spirit. Poor means quiet in spirit. Read Matthew 5:3-12, Read also Mark 1:15

Jesus did not say "*rich*" in spirit. Jesus said "*poor*" in spirit.

1. Blessed are the poor in spirit to those who believe that the *good seed* is the *Son of Man*; which is *Jesus Christ.* Matthew 13:37
2. Blessed are the poor in spirit to those who believe the Scripture: "Ye are washed (converted, repented, saved) in the name of the Lord Jesus, and by the Spirit of our God." I Corinthians 6:11a
3. Blessed are the poor in spirit to those who believe the Scripture: "Ye are sanctified (santification) (set apart or setting apart) in the name of the Lord Jesus, and by the Spirit of our God." I Corinthians 6:11b
4. Blessed are the poor in spirit to those who believe the Scripture: "Ye are justified (justification) in the name of the Lord Jesus, and by the Spirit of our God." I Corinthians 6:11c
5. Blessed are the poor in spirit to those who believe to find these words in the scriptures:

   a. The Apostles of our Lord Jesus Christ—Jude 17
   b. The Baptist—Matthew 3:1
   c. The Calvary (The Cross)—Matthew 27:50-53, John 19:31, Luke 23:33, John 19:18-22, Acts 2:36
   d. The Church—I Timothy 3:15, Acts 2:47, Matthew 16:18, Acts 20:28
   e. The Church of God—I Timothy 3:15a, Acts 20:28
   f. The Church of God in Christ Jesus—I Corinthians 1:2, I Thessalonians 2:14
   g. The Church of the Living God—I Timothy 3:15b
   h. The Churches of the Saints—I Corinthians 14:33
   i. The Covenant—Exodus 31:16, Genesis 19:13, 17, Malachi 3:1
   j. The Disciples of Christ—Luke 5:10-11, Luke 9:1-6, Acts 11:26

k. The Harvest—Luke 10:2, Matthew 9:37
l. The Holiness—Hebrews 8:5, Hebrews 9:2, Hebrews 12:14, Exodus 28:36, Exodus 39:30, Zechariah 14:20
m. The House of Prayer—Matthew 21:13, Isaiah 56:7, Luke 19:46
n. The House of Prayer For All People—Isaiah 56:7
o. The Macedonia—Acts 16:9-12, Acts 18:5, Acts 19:21, 22, Acts 20:1, I Thessalonians 4:10
p. The Narzene—Mathew 2:23, 4:13, 21:11, 26:71, Mark 1:9, 24, 10:47, 14:67, 16:6, Luke 1:26, 2:4, 39, 51, 4:16, 34, John 1:45-46, 18:5, 7, 19:19, Acts 2:22, 3:6, 4:10, 6:14, 10:38, 22:8, 24:5, 26:9
q. The Pentecost—Acts 2:1
r. The Pillar and Ground of the Truth—I Timothy 3:15c
s. The Potter's House of the Lord—Zechariah 11:13, Jeremiah 18:1-17 (verse 2-3), Matthew 27:10
t. The Sabbath; The Lord's Day—Revelation 1:10-11. Read Revelation 1:7-11
u. The Tabernacle of God which is the holy place—Exodus 26:33, Hebrews 8:5, Hebrews 9:2, Revelation 21:3, Leviticus 26:11
v. The Temple of God—I Corinthians 6:19, Matthew 21:12, Ephesians 2:21, Luke 24:53
w. The Spirit of Christ—I Peter 1:11,
x. The Way of the Lord Jesus Christ—John 14:6, Romans 13:14, II Corinthians 13:14, Isaiah 40:3, Matthew 3:3, Acts 16:31

6. Blessed are the poor in spirit to those who believe the spiritual hymn: "Be-hold He come Be-hold He come And every eye shall see Him. Friends, will you be read-y when He come??? Revelation 3:11, Revelation 22:7, 12, 20. See Amos 3:12, See Revelation1:7, Daniel 7:13, Zechariah 12:10, John 19:37
7. Blessed are the poor in spirit to those who preach Jesus Christ and Him crucified and His Second Coming. Matthew 24:4-14, Mark 16:15, I Corinthians 2:2, Acts 1:11
8. Blessed are the poor in spirit to those who believe that our Heavenly Home is with God because He has already prepared each a place for us when we die someday when He call us home to be with Him in Glory for eternal. John 14:1-4
9. Blessed are the poor in spirit to those who minister to the sinners, and teach God's children to grow in the grace of our Lord and Savior Jesus Christ. II Peter 3:18, Psalm 51:12-13

10. Blessed are the poor in spirit to those who believe this spiritual hymn: "Give your best to the Master. Give Him your best that you have "Give Jesus Christ your best that you have." Romans 14:12, I Chronicles 29:3, 13
11. Blessed are the poor in spirit to those who believe and know that we do not want to die without our Lord and Savior Jesus Christ. II Timothy 1:12-14. Read I Timothy 1:7-14 and II Timothy 2:10-15
12. Blessed are the poor in spirit to those who believe and have discovered in the old prophecy Biblical Interpretation of Tongues that there was one language of one speech, one tongue, many kind of voices and one lip, that tongues were spoken as the Spirit give utterance. Acts 2:4-11, Acts 17:18-21, 22-34, Genesis 1:1-9, Psalm 63:1-6, Isaiah 28:11-12, I Corinthians 14:21-33, Hebrews 13:15, Acts 2:3 (verse 10), I Corinthians 12:1-11, 14:1-12 (verse 2), 14:1-40, Genesis 10:5, Acts 2:8-9, 10-41, Joel 2:28, 29, 30, 31, 32, Revelation 14:6-7, Mark 16:17, Acts 2:11, Acts 10:46, Acts 19:6, I Corinthians 13:8, 13, Revelation 7:9-17, Revelation 10:11-17, Revelation 13:7-9, I Corinthians 12:30, I Corinthians 14:5, 13, 27, I Corinthians 12:10, II Peter 1:20-21, II Peter 1:16-21, Matthew 1:23, John 1:41, I Corinthians 14:28

PART CDLXV

Blessed Are The Poor In Spirit. Matthew 5:3

Blessed Means Happy

Poor means meek in spirit. Poor means humble in spirit. Poor means lowly in spirit. Poor means quiet in spirit. Read Matthew 5:3-12, Read also Mark 1:15

Jesus did not say "*rich*" in spirit. Jesus said "*poor*" in spirit.

1. Blessed are the poor in spirit to those who believe in *fasting, praying* and *believing.* Matthew 17:14-21 (verse 21), Mark 9:27-29 (verse 29), Acts 10:30, Acts 14:23, Acts 27:33-38 (verse 33), I Corinthians 7:5, Luke 2:36-39 (verse 37), Esther 4:1-3 (verse 3), Psalm 35:13, 69:10, 109:24, Jeremiah 36:4-6 (verse 6), Joel 2:12-21, 24-32, II Chronicle 7:14-16 (verse 14), Matthew 21:22, Mark 9:23, I Corinthians 13:7
2. Blessed are the poor in spirit to those who believe the Word of the Lord in the book of Psalm: "*When thou saidst, seek ye My face; my heart said unto thee, Thy face, Lord, will I seek.*" Psalm 27:8
3. Blessed are the poor in spirit to those who believe the Word of the Lord in book of Psalm: "*Hear, O Lord, when I cry with my voice: have mercy also upon me,* and *answer me.*" Psalm 27:7
4. Blessed are the poor in spirit to those who believe the Word of the Lord in the book of Psalm: "*Hide not thy face far from me; put not thy servant away in anger: thou hast been my help; leave me not, neither forsake me, O God of my salvation.*" Psalm 27:9
5. Blessed are the poor in spirit to those who believe the Word of the Lord in the book of Psalm: "*When my father and my mother forsake me, then the Lord will take me up.*" Psalm 27:10
6. Blessed are the poor in spirit to those who believe the Word of the Lord in book as Psalm: "*Teach me thy way, O Lord,* and *lead me in a plain path, because of mine enemies.*" Psalm 27:11
7. Blessed are the poor in spirit to those who believe the Psalmist: "*For his anger endureth but a moment; in his favour is life: weeping may endure for a night, but joy cometh in the morning.*" Psalm 30:5

8. Blessed are the poor in spirit to those who believe that the Baptism in the Holy Spirit make you feel good, joyful or joy, glad or gladness in the Lord. Acts 2:28, Acts 13:52, Acts 20:24, Acts 26:2, Acts 11:20-26 (verse 23), Acts 2:46-47, Acts 8:4-8 (verse 8), Acts 15:3-4, 7-9, 11, 36
9. Blessed are the poor in spirit to those who believe: "He is a man approved of God". Jesus was that man. Acts 2:22
10. Blessed are the poor in spirit to those who believe:"He is Jesus Christ". Acts 3:6, Acts 4:10
11. Blessed are the poor in spirit to those who believe that God anointed Jesus of Nazareth with the Holy Ghost and with power: who went about doing good, and healing all that were oppressed of the devil: for God was with him. Acts 10:38
12. Blessed are the poor in spirit to those who believe that Jesus said, I am Jesus of Nazareth. Acts 22:8, See also Acts 9:5, Acts 26:15

PART CDLXVI

Blessed Are The Poor In Spirit. Matthew 5:3

Blessed Means Happy

Poor means meek in spirit. Poor means humble in spirit. Poor means lowly in spirit. Poor means quiet in spirit. Read Matthew 5:3-12, Read also Mark 1:15

Jesus did not say "*rich*" in spirit. Jesus said "*poor*" in spirit.

1. Blessed are the poor in spirit to those who *believe* and *know* and are *being aware* of that we have a *matter* of *choice*: "Our *home* is *in Heaven with Jesus or* we *land ourselves* in *hell with Satan* and *his angels for ever: Right Hand for the sheep-(meaning saved-loved ones) or Left Hand for the goats-(meaning unsaved-loved ones).* See right-hand for the sheep Matthew 25:33 and or see left-hand for the goats Matthew 25:41
2. Blessed are the poor in spirit to those who believe when God says that there is life and there is death. He says that he who believes in Him shall live. Deuteronomy 30:15-16, Jeremiah 21:8, John 8:51, Romans 6:23, Romans 8:38-39
3. Blessed are the poor in spirit to those who believe that babies are precious in the sight of God because God created them in their mother's wombs. Psalm 51:5, Proverbs 22:6, Mark 9:36-37, I Corinthians 13:11, II Timothy 3:15, Matthew 18:2-5, Mark 10:13-16, Luke 18:15-17, Luke 2:17, 21, 22-23, 34, 41-52, Matthew 2:13-14
4. Blessed are the poor in spirit to those who believe that they urge their loved ones to accept Jesus Christ or they would land in hell gnashing of teeth day and night with brimstone fire where there is no rest day and night. Luke 13:23-28, Matthew 8:12, Matthew 13:42, 50, Matthew 25:33, Matthew 25:41, Revelation 14:10-11
5. Blessed are the poor in spirit to those who believe that God is our Saviour; that the Lord Jesus Christ is our Savior. He is the One and the Same. Titus 1:3-4
6. Blessed are the poor in spirit to those who believe and sing this spiritual hymn: "Jesus promise never to leave me alone, No Never Alone, because Jesus say," I am with you always. Matthew 28:20

7. Blessed are the poor in spirit to those who believe that the Bible itself appear on the Pentecost into the Word of God because God say so: "And when the day of "*Pentecost*" was "*fully come*," they were all with *one accord in one place*." Acts 2:1, Read Acts 2:1-47, Joel 2:28-29, 32, Isaiah 28:11, 12, Romans 3:10, Acts 16:31
8. Blessed are the poor in spirit to those who believe in the anointing and blessing; and the consecrated and blessed oil in the name of Jesus Christ; anointing with oil in the name of the Lord. James 5:13-15
9. Blessed are the poor in spirit to those who believe and preach Jesus Christ and His Resurrection. Revelation 1:4-8, I Peter 1:1-25, Revelation 20:6
10. Blessed are the poor in spirit to those who believe that we are saved through Jesus Christ by faith alone. Romans 1:17, Romans 5:1, Ephesians 2:8-9, Acts 16:31, Acts 20:21, Acts 24:24, Romans 10:17, Romans 16:24-27, II Corinthians 4:13-14, Galatians 5:6, Ephesians 6:23-24, I Thessalonians 1:1-10 (verse 10), I Thessalonians 5:8-10, 16-28, I Timothy 1:14, Titus 1:1-4 (verse 4), Galatians 5:5-6, Ephesians 3:17-21, Philippians 3:9, Philemon 5, Hebrews 12:2, Galatians 3:11, Acts 15:9, Romans 3:22-26, Galatians 2:20, Galatians 3:22, 26
11. Blessed are the poor in spirit to those who believe in the anointing and blessing in the name of The Father and of The Son and of The Holy Spirit. James 5:13-15
12. Blessed are the poor in spirit to those who believe in the anointing and blessing with faith or by faith or through faith in the Lord that healing and blessing can or may or will happen. James 5:13-15

PART CDLXVII

Blessed Are The Poor In Spirit. Matthew 5:3

Blessed Means Happy

Poor means meek in spirit. Poor means humble in spirit. Poor means lowly in spirit. Poor means quiet in spirit. Read Matthew 5:3-12, Read also Mark 1:15

Jesus did not say "*rich*" in spirit. Jesus said "*poor*" in spirit.

1. Blessed are the poor in spirit to those who believe the sealing, the anointing and blessing in the name of the Lord. James 5:13-15
2. Blessed are the poor in spirit to those who believe in healing of the body with the anointing oil or the blessing oil through the balm of our hands. James 5:13-15
3. Blessed are the poor in spirit to those who believe that the anointing oil or the blessing oil is use for the purpose of laying on hands, consecrating, or dedicating or a special set apart or use of the Lord in His service in the ministry of the Gospel of Jesus Christ in the name of the Lord Jesus Christ. James 5:13-15
4. Blessed are the poor in spirit to those who believe in the anointing or blessing that the authority or the power is given to us as children of God for it is found in the book of John 1:11-13, for we are the children of God that believe in His name. For we are called Brothers and Sisters in God's family. John 1:11-13
5. Blessed are the poor in spirit to those who believe that Pentecost is about Jesus Christ, Power of the Resurrection, Salvation, Water Baptism, Spirit Baptism, Healing, getting people saved and His second Coming and Home to Glory to Eternal Home with Jesus for ever more. Matthew 3:2, Isaiah 40:3, Matthew 3:11, Matthew 4:17, Mark 1:8, 15, Mark 16:15, 17, Luke 3:16, Luke 24:45-49, Luke 24:27, John 1:29-37, Acts 1:4-8, Acts 2:1-47, Joel 2:28, 29, 32, Acts 2:22 (Deuteronomy 18:15), Revelation 3:11, Revelation 22:7, 12, 20. Juke 24:27, Acts 13:22-52, Matthew 10:5-42, Mark 1:4, 38, Luke 9:1-6, Acts 17:5, II Timothy 4:2, Mark 6:10-12, Luke 4:43, Luke 4:18, 19, Acts 5:41-42, Acts 10:34-48, Acts 15:17-29, II Corinthians 1:19-24, Ephesians 2:1-22, I Timothy 3:15-16, I Peter 3:15-22, Acts 4:7-16, 17-33, Acts 8:5-8, 12, Acts 9:20, 27, Acts 10:36-48, Acts 13:5, Acts 15:36, Acts 17:18

6. Blessed are the poor in spirit to those who *believe in old time power*, and *preach* the *old time Full Gospel*, the *old time, religious gospel*, the *old time belief of the Gospel of Jesus Christ*, the *old time—Old Testament*, the *old time—New Testament*, the *old time—Holy Bible*, the *old time regeneration*, the *old time salvation*, the *old time—repentance*, the *old time—conversion*, the *old time—justification*, the *old time—sanctification*, the *old time—baptism in water*, the *old time baptism with the Holy Spirit*, the *old time teaching of the doctrine of Christ*, and the *old time gift of the Holy Spirit*, the *fillfulment of the Spirit*, and the *gift of tongues* according to Acts 2:4. See Mark 16:17, Application is Acts 1:4-5, Luke 24:39, Acts 1:8, John 1:33, Matthew 3:11, Mark 1:8, Luke 3:16, Acts :16, Acts 10:45-47, Acts 19:1-7, Genesis 1:1, John 1:1, I Timothy 3:16-17, I Corinthians 14:33 (not the author of confusion, but of peace)
7. Blessed are the poor in spirit to those who *believe the Pentecostal doctrine* because *they, too can receive their personal Pentecost through the Spirit of Christ*. Just Ask Him 1 John 5:14-15, Matthew 7:7-11, Mark 11:24, Luke 11:13
8. Blessed are the poor in spirit to those who believe that *Jesus believe in hell; like Jesus says, we also believe in hell*. Read Psalm 9:17, Matthew 13:41-42, Matthew 13:49-50, Luke 16:25, Revelation 21:8, and Revelation 20:10, Luke 16:19, Matthew 18:8, Jude 7, Revelation 14:9, 11, Matthew 16:26, Matthew 10:28, Luke 12:20, John 3:5-6
9. Blessed are the poor in spirit to those who believe this scripture: "And the Spirit bade me go." Acts 11:12
10. Blessed are the poor in spirit to those who believe that the *baptism* of the *Holy Spirit* is the *gift of power for service*. Acts 1:8
11. Blessed are the poor in spirit to those who believe that *white, black, brown, red* and *yellow cultural people who belong to God's children are washed enter One Blood; That One Blood is Jesus Christ whose blood cleansed us from all sin; We are washed in the Blood of Jesus Christ*. I John 1:9
12. Blessed are the poor in spirit to those who *believe* and are *able to say*; "*My name is "I Am." That is My Name*." Isaiah 42:8

Part CDLXVIII

Blessed Are The Poor In Spirit. Matthew 5:3

Blessed Means Happy

Poor means meek in spirit. Poor means humble in spirit. Poor means lowly in spirit. Poor means quiet in spirit. Read Matthew 5:3-12, Read also Mark 1:15

Jesus did not say "*rich*" in spirit. Jesus said "*poor*" in spirit.

1. Blessed are the poor in spirit to those who believe *that human blood is under the Blood of Jesus; Christ's Blood; the Sacrifice Lamb's Blood that washed*; that *died for us on the cross for our sin.* I John 1:9
2. Blessed are the poor in spirit to those who believe that *Jesus still saves even today*, right now: O *sinner, give your heart to Jesus and be saved. Jesus hung, Jesus bled*, and *Jesus died on Calvary's cross to redeem your soul from sin and from hell.* O, *Jesus loves you*, and *Jesus is calling you to come home*, come back home. *Come home*, O, *poor sinner, come home. Come back Home to Jesus.* Luke 19:10, Matthew 1:21, Matthew 18:11, I Corithians 2:2, II Corinthians 6:2, See Isaiah 49:8
3. Blessed are the poor in spirit to those who *believe in spreading the eternal gospel of Jesus Christ and His Second Coming* Mark 16:15, Luke 24:47, Matthew 12:21, John 20:31, Acts 1:11, Revelation 3:11, Revelation 22:7, 12, 20
4. Blessed are the poor in spirit to those who believe that there is *only one race—the children of Adam and Eve.* Genesis 9:18, 19, Genesis 10:6, 7, Isaiah 43:3, Acts 17:26
5. Blessed are the poor in spirit to those who *believe* that *our highest place* is *low at the feet of Jesus; Every knee shall bow.* That Jesus Christ is Lord. Romans 14:11, Philippians 2:10
6. Blessed are the poor in spirit to those who believe this Wise or Wisdom of Proverbs: "When a man's ways please the Lord, he maketh even his enemies to be at peace with him." Proverbs 16:7
7. Blessed are the poor in spirit to those who *believe* that the *coming of Jesus Christ* is the *Christian's hope.* I Thessalonians 4:17, Titus 2:13
8. Blessed are the poor in spirit to those who *believe the Old Scripture*, the *Word of God*: "*Where there is no vision*, the *people perish*: but *he that keep the law, happy is he.*" Proverb 29:18

9. Blessed are the poor in spirit to those who believe the Scripture, the Word of God: "*My people are destroyed for lack of knowledge: because thou hast rejected knowledge, I will also reject thee, that thou shalt be no priest to me: seeing thou hast forgotten the law of thy God, I will also forget the children.*" Hosea 4:6
10. Blessed are the poor in spirit to those who *believe* that Jesus came to *love*; that *Jesus* came to *heal*; that Jesus came to *save*; that Jesus came to *deliver*; that Jesus came to *set us free. John 3:16, Exodus 15:26*, Psalm 103:3, Psalm 147:3, Isaiah 30:26, *Isaiah 53:5, I Peter 2:24, James 5:16, Matthew 1:21, Romans 4:25*
11. Blessed are the poor in spirit to those who *believe* that *Pentecost mean* "*the Latter Rain.*" Acts 2:1
12. Blessed are the poor in spirit to those who *believe* that the *Baptism of the Holy Spirit is about Jesus Christ is coming soon.* Get Excited!!! Get Ready!!! Be Prepared!!! Amos 4:12, Revelation 3:11, Revelation 22:7, 12, 20.

Part CDLXIX

Blessed Are The Poor In Spirit. Matthew 5:3

Blessed Means Happy

Poor means meek in spirit. Poor means humble in spirit. Poor means lowly in spirit. Poor means quiet in spirit. Read Matthew 5:3-12, Read also Mark 1:15

Jesus did not say "*rich*" in spirit. Jesus said "*poor*" in spirit.

1. Blessed are the poor in spirit to those who *believe in* "*love, faith* and *unity in the Body of Christ.*" Colossians 3:14, I Corinthians 12:12, I Corinthians 12:27, Ephesians 4:1-6, Philippains 2:3
2. Blessed are the poor in spirit to those who believe *the Messenger of Christ*—Malachi 3:1, Malachi 2:7, *the preaching of salvation*—I Corinthians 1:18, Acts 2:38, Hebrews 6:4-6, *the justification*—Mark 1:5, Acts 13:38-39, Romans 5:1, John 3:3, *the sanctification*—John 15:2, 17, 17:16-17, Ephesians 5:26-27, I John 1:9, *the healing*—I Peter 2:24, Acts 10:38, Matthew 4:23, Matthew 8:16-17, Matthews 12:15, *the baptism with the Holy Ghost*—Matthew 3:11, Acts 17:11, Acts 1:5, Acts 10:23-47, and *signs following*.- Mark 16:13-29, John 4:48, Romans 15:19, Acts 17:11. Jesus was doing all thing well—Mark 7:31-37, John 21:25. So how shall we escape if we neglect so great salvation? Hebrews 2:3
3. Blessed are the poor in spirit to those who believe in *laboring* in the *Lord's vineyard.* Matthew 20:1-16
4. Blessed are the poor in spirit to those who believe that *Jesus Christ, being the Jew,* the Prophet, the *Great Shepherd,* the *King,* the *Lord,* the Author of Everlasting Life, the *Mediator,* the *Priest,* the *First,* the *Last,* the *beginning,* the *ending,* the *Great Redeemer, Alpha, Omega,* the *Second Coming of Christ,* is the *promise of true and sure.* Revelation 22:20
5. Blessed are the poor in spirit to those who have *experienced Christ;* who have *found Christ* who have *tried* (tested) *Christ* and who have *proved Christ. His promise is true and sure.* I Peter 1:7, Acts 17:11, James 1:2
6. Blessed are the poor in spirit to those who *believe in the Old—time—Power of Pentecost or Pentecostal Power.* Acts 1:8

7. Blessed are the poor in spirit to those who believe that the *Holy Spirit is Power.* Acts 1:8
8. Blessed are the poor in spirit to those who believe the *Heaven* is *our future* and *eternal home for those who are born again, born of the Spirit, children of God.* Hebrews 10:34, I Peter 1:4, 5, Colossians 1:5, II Timothy 4:18
9. Blessed are the poor in spirit to those who *believe that Heaven* is a *prepared place for God's children.* John 14:2, 3, II Corinthians 5:1
10. Blessed are the poor in spirit to those who believe the Scripture: "And that ye study to be quiet, and to do your own business, and to work with your own hands, as we commanded you." I Thessalonians 4:11
11. Blessed are the poor in spirit to those who believe what *Jesus say*: "*All power is given unto me in heaven and in earth. Go ye therefore*, and *teach all nations, baptizing them in the name of the Father*, and of *the Son*, and of *the Holy Ghost*: *Teaching* them to *observe all things* whatsoever I have *commanded you*: and, lo, I am *with you alway*, even *unto the end of the world.* Amen." Matthew 28:18-20
12. Blessed are the poor in spirit to those who *believe the Scripture*: "I *heard a voice from heaven saying unto me, Write, Blessed are the dead which die in the Lord from henceforth*: Yea, saith the Spirit, that *they rest from their labors*; and their works do follow them." Revelation 14:13

Part CDLXX

Blessed Are The Poor In Spirit. Matthew 5:3

Blessed Means Happy

Poor means meek in spirit. Poor means humble in spirit. Poor means lowly in spirit. Poor means quiet in spirit. Read Matthew 5:3-12, Read also Mark 1:15

Jesus did not say "*rich*" in spirit. Jesus said "*poor*" in spirit.

1. Blessed are the poor in spirit to those who *believe our Lord Jesus Christ, who is the resurrection and the life*; *to raise us from the death of sin unto the life of righteousness*; that when we shall depart this earthly life, *we may rest in Christ*; and *at the resurrection on the last day may be found acceptable in thy sight and receive that blessing from Him saying*, "*Come ye blessed children of my Father, receive the kingdom prepared from you from the beginning of the world.*" Romans 10:9, I Corinthians 15:20-22, I Timothy 2:3, I Peter 3:19
2. Blessed are the poor in spirit to those who *believe* that the *Lord Jesus Christ will give each of us a new body, just to be like Him.* II Corinthians 5:10, I John 3:2-3, Philippians 3:20-21, Romans 8:28-30, Psalm 17:15, II Corinthians 3:17-18, I Corinthians 35-49, 35-58, Philippians 1:21-23, II Corinthians 5:1-5
3. Blessed are the poor in spirit to those who believe that *my God, our God is an awesome God. He is our Savior, our Protector, our Healer, He is an awesome God.* Psalm 68:35, II Peter 1:17, Job 37:16
4. Blessed are the poor in spirit to those who believe in the *symbolic* of the *four ministries* of *Jesus* as "*Savior,*" *Jesus* as "*Healer*" *Jesus* as "*Baptizer*" and *Jesus* as "*Soon Coming King.*" John 4:42, I John 4:14, Matthew 4:23, Acts 1:5, Revelation 22:7, 12, 20
5. Blessed are the poor in spirit to those who believe that the *Only Creed* we have is the *Word of God*, the *Word of Christ*, the *Spirit of God*, the *Spirit of Christ*, our *Lord and Savior Jesus Christ.* II Timothy 3:14-17, I Peter 4:11
6. Blessed are the poor in spirit to those who believe that he *preach the One and Only Gospel—Jesus Christ who is Lord of all.* Romans 1:16-17, Galatians 1:6-9
7. Blessed are the poor in spirit to those who *believe* that the *Baptism of the Holy Spirit and with fire is a definition of and an outward sign of: Jesus Is Coming Again*

Soon!!! *Get Excited*!!! *Get Ready*!!! *Be Prepared for His Coming*!!! Revelation 22:7, 12, 20. See Matthew 3:11, Luke 3:16, Amos 4:12

8. Blessed are the poor in spirit to those who believe this *Scripture*: "I (Jesus) *must work* (do) the *works of Him* (God) that *sent Me* (Jesus), *while it is day*: *the night come, when no man can work*." John 9:4
9. Blessed are the poor in spirit to those who *believe* and *use to sing this very very* "*old hymn*: "Wo-rk whi-le it's day. Wo-rk whi-le it's day. When no man can work at night. Wo-rk whi-le it's day, wo-rk whi-le it's day when no man can work at night. John 9:4, Read John 9:3-5
10. Blessed are the poor in spirit to those who *believe* that *through Jesus Christ, this is* "*eternal life*" *because Christ give eternal life as many as He give to those to who believe in Jesus Christ which is the only true God*. John 17:1-26. See Psalm 41:9, *for one that is lost verse 17* and Psalm 119:142; *for them that sanctify through thy truth verse 17*.
11. Blessed are the poor in spirit to those who believe that *God is not black that God is not white*; that *God is not red*; that *God is not yellow*. *God is a spirit and they that worship Him must worship Him* "*in Spirit*" and "*in Truth*." John 4:24
12. Blessed are the poor in spirit to those who believe this statement of Faith: We believe in the "*verbal inspiration*" and "*authority of the Scripture*." We *believe* that "*the Bible*" *reveal God*, *the fall of man*, *the way of salvation*, and *God's plan and purpose in the ages*. We *believe in God the Father*, *God the Son*, and *God the Holy Spirit*. We *believe* in "the *deity*," "*virgin birth*" and "*bodily resurrection of Jesus Christ*." We *believe* that *salvation* is "*by grace*" *plus nothing* and *minus nothing*. The *condition to salvation* are "*repentance*" and "*faith*." We *believe* that *men are justified by faith alone and all accounted righteous before only through the merit of our Lord and Savior Jesus Christ*. We *believe* in the "*visible*," "*personal*" and "*premillennial*" *return of Jesus Christ*. We *believe* in "the *everlasting*" (Matthew 25:33-40) *conscious* "*blessed of the saved*" and "*everlasting* (Matthew 25:41-46) *conscious punishment of the last*." Genesis 1:1, John 1:1, II Timothy 3:16, Hebrews 5:9, Hebrews 12:2, John 14:6, Luke 24:3-9, Mark 16:5-20, Matthew 27:5-10, 16-20, Ephesians 2:8-9, John 3:16, Acts 16:31, Romans 8:28-30, Acts 20:21, Romans 1:17, Romans 3:26, Romans 4:5, Romans 8:33, Romans 5:1, Romans 3:28, Acts 13:39, Romans 3:20, 24, 25, Titus 3:7, Galatians 2:16, Galatians 3:24, Habakkuk 2:4, Galatians 3:11, Hebrews 10:38, Acts 1:9-11, Acts 1:3, I Thessalonians 4:13-18, Revelation 22:7, 12, 20, I Thessalonians 5:1-11, Matthew 24:30, Matthew 24:40-51, Matthew 25:1-13, Matthew 25:33-40, Matthew 25:41-46, Revelation 19:20, Daniel 12:2

Part CDLXXI

Blessed Are The Poor In Spirit. Matthew 5:3

Blessed Means Happy

Poor means meek in spirit. Poor means humble in spirit. Poor means lowly in spirit. Poor means quiet in spirit. Read Matthew 5:3-12, Read also Mark 1:15

Jesus did not say "*rich*" in spirit. Jesus said "*poor*" in spirit.

1. Blessed are the poor in spirit to those who *believe in Working Together according to God's plan of salvation and His purpose*. Romans 8:28, Acts 16:31, Ephesians 2:8, John 3:16
2. Blessed are the poor in spirit to those who *believe the Gospel of Jesus*: "And this *gospel of the Kingdom shall be preached in all the world for a witness unto all nation; and then shall the end come*." Matthew 24:14
3. Blessed are the poor in spirit to those who believe that the *gospel* of the *kingdom shall be preached in "all the world" "for a witness" unto "all nations*." Matthew 24:14, Acts 1:4-8, Luke 24:44-48
4. Blessed are the poor in spirit to those who believe that the "*Living One*" is *Jesus Christ who rose from the dead and now is alive forever more*. Luke 24:5-9, Romans 6:9-11, 13, Revelation 1:17-18, 19-20, Revelation 2:8, Mark 16:11, Luke 24:23, Acts 1:3
5. Blessed are the poor in spirit to those who believe that the *world* is *so evil*; that the *world* is *so bad* because of *continuing murdering*, *murdering* and *murdering* or that is *why Jesus* want men and women to *return to Him through salvation*, *repentance*, *be converted* "*as little children*" *men and women need to act "like little children" "not act like Real Men and Real Women*." No! Matthew 18:1-7 (verse 2, 3, 4, 5, 6)
6. Blessed are the poor in spirit to those who *believe* that *Jesus Christ* has *the key* or *the words of Eternal Life*. John 6:68
7. Blessed are the poor in spirit to those who believe in *Pentecostal Holiness*. "*Pentecost on the day of Pentecost*" and "*Holiness unto the Lord*" which is for "*Pentecostal Holiness standard*." Exodus 28:36, Exodus 39:30, Chronicles 31:18, Zechariah 14:20, Acts 2:1, Romans 1:4-7, II Corinthians 7:1, I Thessalonians 4:7, Hebrews 12:14
8. Blessed are the poor in spirit to those who believe that the *Words are Christ's Spirit and Christ's Life*; These *two words belong to Jesus*. John 6:63

9. Blessed are the poor in spirit to those who believe that the *Gentiles enjoyed hearing the Word of God through Apostle Paul; first sermon : "Honor God"*—Acts 13:15-41 and *wanted him to preach the next sabbath and encouraged Apostle Paul to continue in the grace of God because the Lord God commanded Apostle Paul and Barnabas saying, "I have set thee to be a light of the Gentiles, that thou should be for salvation unto the ends of the earth and after hearing, the Gentiles was glad and gloried the Word of God and as many as were ordained to eternal life."* Acts 13:42-44. See II Timothy 2:19
10. Blessed are the poor in spirit to those who *believe the Word of the Lord has to say*: "*To know wisdom and instruction; to perceive the words of understanding;*" Proverbs 1:2
11. Blessed are the poor in spirit to those who *believe* what the *Word of the Lord* has *to say*; "*There is a way which seenth right unto a man but the end thereof are the ways of death.*" Proverbs 14:12
12. Blessed are the poor in spirit to those who *believe the Word of the Lord has to say*: "*The poor hated* (despised) even of *his own neighbor*: but the *rich hath many friends.*" Proverbs 14:20

Part CDLXXII

Blessed Are The Poor In Spirit. Matthew 5:3

Blessed Means Happy

Poor means meek in spirit. Poor means humble in spirit. Poor means lowly in spirit. Poor means quiet in spirit. Read Matthew 5:3-12, Read also Mark 1:15

Jesus did not say "*rich*" in spirit. Jesus said "*poor*" in spirit.

1. Blessed are the poor in spirit to those who *believe the Word of the Lord has to say*: "He that *despiseth his neighbor sinneth*: but he not hath *mercy in the poor, happy is he.*" Proverbs 14:21
2. Blessed are the poor in spirit to those who *believe the Word of the Lord has to say*: "A true *witness deliver souls*: but a *decentful witness speak lies*. Proverbs 14:25. See aslo Isaiah 40:15 about a prophet speaking lie.
3. Blessed are the poor in spirit to those who believe in the *Imminet of Jesus Christ*, and the *Rapture of the church to those who are born again, born of the Spirit, children of God that look for His Second Coming*. Acts 1:11-12, II Thessalonians 4:17, Revelation 3:11, Revelation 22:7, 12, 20. Matthew 24:
4. Blessed are the poor in spirit to those who believe *in the premillenniumal return of Jesus Christ and will return with Christ in the millennium*. Revelation 20:1-10
5. Blessed are the poor in spirit to those who *believe that Jesus Christ loves precious infant they are precious life in the world*. Infants are precious because God has made them. Infants are precious in His sight. I Kings 17:17-23
6. Blessed are the poor in spirit to those who believe in judgment and the justice of the peace through our Lord and Savior Jesus Christ because He has made a way. John 14:6
7. Blessed are the poor in spirit to those who believe and are able to say: "You will die because the Bible say so." John 8:24, Ezekiel 3:18, Ezekiel 33:8, Psalm 13:3, John 11:25, Matthew 5:4, Revelation 1:18

8. Blessed are the poor in spirit to those who believe that we as *children of God, born of the Spirit, believe in Jesus, will live again to be with Christ in glory forever.* Job 19:25-26, Psalm 17:15, Psalm 49:15, Acts 2:31, Ezekiel 37:1-38, Revelation 11:11 (verse 5), Hosea 13:14, Psalm 16:10, Acts 2:31, Acts 13:35, Matthew 22:31-33, Luke 14:14, John 5:28-29, John 11:23-27, Acts 2:2, Romans 6:5-11, I John 3:2-3, 9, I Thessalonians 4:13-18, I Kings 17-23, II King s4:1, 14-37, II Kings 13:20-23, Matthew 9:23-25, Luke 7:12-17, John 11:33-45, Acts 9:36, Psalm 16:10-11.
9. Blessed are the poor in spirit to those who *believe in preaching through Jesus the resurrection from the dead.* Acts 4:2, Matthew 16:21, Matthew 28:5-9, Acts 2:20-47, Acts 4:1-31, II Corinthians 4:14, Philippians 3:9-21, Matthew 28:1-20, Mark 16:9-20, Luke 24:13-53 (verse 35), John 20:1-31 (verse 19, 26), I Corinthians 15:1-31 (verse 6, 8), See Acts 9:4-16, 20, Acts 18:5, Acts 27:7-10, Revelation 1:17-20 (verse 18)
10. Blessed are the poor in spirit to those who *believe* that *children are precious in God's sight* because He has made them as well as us. Psalm 100:3
11. Blessed are the poor in spirit to those who *believe and have strong knowledge of the Scriptures, the Bible.* II Timothy 3:14-17, II Peter 1:21
12. Blessed are the poor in spirit to those who *believe that an Heart stand for "I Love You,"* Declare: "*I Love Jesus.*" John 3:16

The Millennium (*Revelation 20:1-10*) is described as a period of a thousand years during which Satan is bound and the resurrected saints reign with Christ before the final judgment. There is no other clear mention of the millennium in the Bible. The nature of the millennium is a subject of great debate within Christianity, and beliefs about it fall into several categories:

- *Amillennialism* views the millennium as a symbol of the present age where the Church carries on Christ's work and the binding of Satan was accomplished by Jesus in the past.
- *Postmillennialism* views the millennium as a future period during which the gospel message will eliminate evil from the world and Christ will rule spiritually for a thousand years before before the Second Coming.
- *Premillennialism* views the millennium as a thousand year period between the Second Coming and the final judgment. Two subcategories of premillennialism can be identified:
    - *Historic premillennialism* views the millennium as the next stage in advancement of the kingdom of God, coming after the present age of the Church and before the new heaven and earth.
    - *Dispensationalism* views the millennium as a period during which the Old Testament promises to the nation of Israel will be fulfilled. In this view:
        - Establishment of the State of Israel in 1948 is evidence that the Second Coming is approaching.
        - The Rapture (see below) will occur before the Great Tribulation begins so that Christians will not have to face that time of suffering.

Part CDLXXIII

Blessed Are The Poor In Spirit. Matthew 5:3

Blessed Means Happy

Poor means meek in spirit Poor means humble in spirit Poor means lowly in spirit Poor means quiet in spirit Read Matthew 5:3-12, Read also Mark 1:15

Jesus did not say "*rich*" in spirit. Jesus said "*poor*" in spirit.

1. Blessed are the poor in spirit to those who believe that *Dying mean*, "*Good News*" because *we will live with Jesus that is the Good News*, the *Gospel News*, the *Positive News which is Eternal In Glory and Forever more*; *that dying also mean a New Beginning with God to be reunited with Him in which we believe in life after death* II Timothy 1:10, I Peter 4:6, I Corinthians 15:1-58. Read More Good News!!! Get Out And Read The Bible!!! You should be Blessed!!!
2. Blessed are the poor in spirit to those who believe in four theological doctrines: Salvation—Matthew 3:1-2, 4:17, Acts 20:21, Romans 8:16, 32 Luke 19:8-10, Acts 8:30-39 (See Isaiah 53:7)
   Healing—I Peter 2:24, Acts 10:38, Matthew 4:23, Matthew 8:16-17 (Isaiah 53:4), Matthew 12:15, I Corinthians 12:8-11 Search the scriptures. Jesus taught disciples to do the same. Matthew 10:1,
   Baptism of the Holy Spirit—II Timothy 1:6, Acts 10:44-46, Acts 15:7, 9, Acts 1:8, Acts 2:38-39, Acts 19:1-6, I Corinthians 14:2, 18, Jude 20, Romans 12:6-8, I Corinthians 12:1-11, Ephesians 4:11, I Corinthians 12:28,
   And the Second Coming of Christ—Acts 1:11, Titus 2:11-13, Matthew 16:27, Matthew 24:30, Matthew 25:31, Luke 21:27, I Thessalonians 4:13-18 (verse 16-17).
3. Blessed are the poor in spirit to those who *believe the Scripture*: "*He being dead yet he speak.*" Hebrew 11:4
4. Blessed are the poor in spirit to those who *believe in getting*: "*An instruction, a wisdom, an understanding, a knowledge*, and a sound judgment from a wise proverbs. Proverbs 1:2-3
5. Blessed are the poor in spirit to those who *believe in getting*: "*For if the word spoken by angels was stedfast*, and *every transgression and disobedience received a just recompence of reward.*" Hebrews 2:2

6. Blessed are the poor in spirit to those who *believe in getting*: "*If any of you lack wisdom, let him ask of God, that giveth to all men liberally*, and *upbraideth not*; and *it shall be given him*." James 1:5
7. Blessed are the poor in spirit to those who believe and are able to say: "*I am rich in Jesus*." Ephesians 2:4-10, Romans 10:8-13 (verse 12), Read Romans 10:1-21, Leviticus 18:5, Deuteronomy 30:12-14, Isaiah 49:23, Isaiah 5:27, Isaiah 53:1, Psalm 19:4, Isaiah 65:2
8. Blessed are the poor in spirit to those who *believe and attend faithful fellowship. Truly our fellowship* (*Holy Spirit with us*) *is with the Father and with His Son Jesus Christ until He come back for us or His children to take us home with Him to live for eternal.* Acts 2:47, I John 1:1-10 (verse 3)
9. Blessed are the poor in spirit to those who *believe Christ's promise to us, even eternal life*. I John 2:25
10. Blessed are the poor in spirit to those who *believe and divide in Christ that when He shall appear*, *we may have confidence*, and *not be ashamed before Him at His coming*. I John 2:28
11. Blessed are the poor in spirit to those who *believe that holy men of God spoke as they were moved by the Holy Spirit*. II Peter 1:21
12. Blessed are the poor in spirit to those who *believe and sing this old spiritual hymn*. "Oh, Lord, I want to be in that numb-er, when the saints go march-ing in." I Thessalonians 4:13-18

Part CDLXXIV

Blessed Are The Poor In Spirit. Matthew 5:3

Blessed Means Happy

Poor means meek in spirit. Poor means humble in spirit. Poor means lowly in spirit. Poor means quiet in spirit. Read Matthew 5:3-12, Read also Mark 1:15

Jesus did not say "*rich*" in spirit. Jesus said "*poor*" in spirit.

1. Blessed are the poor in spirit to those who believe that "*the serpent*" is "*a type of Christ*; "*lifting up the serpent*" is "*a type of Christ*" must be "*the Son of Man*" which is "*truly Christ*" *be lifted up*; that *whoever believe in Him should not perish*, but have "*eternal life*;" for *Christ say*, "*If I be lifted up from the cross*" (earth), *I will draw all men into myself*." John 3:13-22 (verse 14), Luke 13:3, 5, John 12:31-34. See Numbers 21:6-9 (verse 6-8)
2. Blessed are the poor in spirit to those who *believe this spiritual hymn*: "*If I be lifted up from cross, I will draw all men unto me*." John 12:32-33
3. Blessed are the poor in spirit to those who *believe that those who are dead and are in the graves shall hear the voice of the son of God and they that hear shall live*. John 5:25, 29, See John 5:1-47, Daniel 12:2, Matthew 25:46
4. Blessed are the poor in spirit to those who *believe that the wisdom of God make us wisely*, or *become wisely through His instruction, His knowledge, His getting us understanding, His direction, His teaching of the Word through the Bible or Bible Study and His judgment through sound doctrine and sound mind*. Proverb 1:2-3, Hebrews 2:2, II Timothy 3:15-17, Genesis 1:1, John 1:1, II Timothy 1:7, Titus 1:9, Titus 2:1
5. Blessed are the poor in spirit to those who believe that *Jesus Christ* is the *Messenger* that is He is greater thn the prophet; John the Baptist. John 7:27
6. Blessed are the poor in spirit to those who believe one of God's children, *W.J. Henry that declared*: "*There is no room for prejudice of any kind in the hearts of sanctified people. If you*, as a white man *find any of this in your heart toward the black man as an individual or toward his people, you need to go to the Lord for cleansing*; *to the black brother, I will say the same. All prejudice of every kind is outside the church of God*. Read Galatians 3:26-28 (verse 28)

7. Blessed are the poor in spirit to those who believe in the *justied—soul* or *purified—soul* or repented—soul or *sanctifed—soul* :
   a. (*justifed—soul*)—Acts 13:38-39, Romans 5:15-18, Romans 3:24, 28, Titus 3:7, Romans 5:1, Galatians 2:16, Galatians 3:24, Romans 3:26, Romans 4:5, Romans 8:33-39, Hebrews 2:4, Romans 1:17 John 17:15, John 15:3, Galatians 3:11,
   b. (*purified—soul*)—I Peter 1:22-23, Read I Peter 1:1-25, I John 3:3
   c. (*repented—soul*)—Matthew 12:41, See Jonah 3:5, Luke 11:32, Luke 15:1-7, 10, Read Luke 15:1-32,
   d. (*sanctified—soul*)—Hebrews 2:11, John 17:17-19, Read John 17:1-26, Acts 20:32, Acts 26:14-18, Romans 15:16-19, I Corinthians 1:2-10, I Corinthians 6:11, I Timothy 4:5, II Timothy 2:21-23, Hebrews 10:10, 14-23
8. Blessed are the poor in spirit to those who *believe one of God's chidren, William J. Seymour's Quotations*: "Our *colored brethren must love* our *white brethren and respect them in truth* so that the *Word of God can have it's free course*, and our *white brethren must love* their *colored brethren* and *respect them in truth*, so that the *Holy Spirit won't be grieved*. I *hope we won't have anymore trouble and division spirit*. William J. Seymour (1870-1922). Ephesians 4:30, I John 3:11, I John 4:7, 11, Galatians 3:26-28
9. Blessed are the poor in spirit to those who believe the *mission* and *mandate statement*: "*R.H.E.M.A*; "*R*" *stands* for *R*estore the Body of Christ; "*H*" *stands* for *H*ealing the emotionally and spiritual wounded; "*E*" *stands* for *E*quip the Church for purpose; "*M*" *stands* for *M*ove, men, women and children towards successful living through the Biblical principles; "*A*" *stands* for *A*dvance the Kingdom of God through the *powerful message* of *hope*, *love* and *faith*." Hebrews 5:12, Hebrews 6:1-2, I Corinthians 13:13
10. Blessed are the poor in spirit to those who believe if they ever *heard this song*: "There's pen-te-cost, pen-te-cost, in my soul; there's pen-te-cost, pen-te-cost in my soul, today. Yes there's pen-te-cost, pen-te-cost in my soul. There's pen-te-cost, pen-te-cost in my soul. Yes, there's pen-te-cost, pen-te-cost in my soul, today." Pentecost had come." Acts 2:1
11. Blessed are the poor in spirit to those who believe that they "*urge*" *their loved ones to accept Jesus Christ* or *they would be in hell gnawing of teeth day and night with brimesh-fire* where "*there is no rest*" *days nor night*. Luke 13:23-28, Matthew 8:12, Matthew 13:42, 50, *Revlation 14:10-11*. Wake-Up!!! Accept Jesus Christ Now. II Corinthians 6:2. See Isaiah 49:8

12. Blessed are the poor in spirit to those who *believe* that *there will be no black men and black women* in heaven; *there will be no white men and white women* in heaven; *there will be no red men and red women* in heaven; *there will be no yellow men and yellow women* in heaven: "*Only*" the *children of God*; "*Only*" the *born of God*, "*Only*" the *born of the Spirit of God*. "*Only*" be *like the children of God that enter the kingdom of God*; the *kingdom of heaven*. Matthew 18:3-4, Mark 9:36-37, Luke 9:46-48, John 3:1-8, 13-18, 21, Galatians 3:24-29, I John 1:1-3, I John 4:2, 4, 6-21

Part CDLXXV

Blessed Are The Poor In Spirit. Matthew 5:3

Blessed Means Happy

Poor means meek in spirit. Poor means humble in spirit. Poor means lowly in spirit. Poor means quiet in spirit. Read Matthew 5:3-12, Read also Mark 1:15

Jesus did not say "*rich*" in spirit. Jesus said "*poor*" in spirit.

1. Blessed are the poor in spirit to those who believe that *Christ's power* is the *Baptism of the Holy Spirit* to signify "*of His Imminent Return.*" Revelation 3:11, Revelation 22:7, 12, 20. Even so come Lord Jesus.
2. Blessed are the poor in spirit to those who *believe Christ's mercy and Christ's grace are upon our lives through faith in Him.* Matthew 5:7, Luke 1:50, 72, 78-80, Romans 9:23, Romans 11:30-32, Romans 15:4-13, Ephesians 2:4-10, Philippians 2:27, I Timothy 2:1-2, II Timothy 1:2, Titus 1:4, II John 3, I Timothy 1:13, 16, II Timothy 1:18, Titus 3:5, Hebrews 4:6, James 5:11, I Peter 1:3, I Peter 2:10, Jude 2, 21, John 1:14, 16, 17, Acts 20:32, I Corinthians 1:3-10, II Corinthians 1:2-5, Ephesians 1:1-23, Philippians 1:2, Colossians 1:2, II Thessalonians 1:2, Philemon 3, Romans 3:19-26, Romans 4:1-25
3. Blessed are the poor in spirit to those who *believe God's Name has been "Heard"* around the *globe*, around the *world*, *universe world*, places, cities, communities, countries, homes and families, relatives, friends, children of God, generations, books, radio, televisions, schools, colleges, universities, churches, tents, tabernacle, creatures, temples, *word of mouth*, *hearing through faith*, *things clearly seen without excuse*, holy scroll, *Holy Bible*, mighty hand movement, day and night, thunder, lightning, lights, sun, moon, star, rain, snow, floods, people, animals, *living things*, *creeping things*, *faith miracles*, *spoken word*, *touch*, feeling all over, *faith that name*, mountain, animal barking noise, strange thing happening, *real life historical events*, *eternal existence*, *be still know that{or this or who} is God*, waters, earth, heavens, *food* or *manna* or *bread*. Genesis 1:1-31, John 1:1-51, Acts 17:24, II Corinthians 4:6, II Peter 3:5, I Corinthians 15:38, Matthew 19:4, Colossians 3:10, Deuteronomy 18:15, 18, Isaiah 40:3, Daniel 9:25, Genesis 28:12, Romans 8:1-39, Ecclesiastes 1:1-18, John 3:18, Psalm 139:1-39, Ephesians 2:8-9, John

3:11-36, Jeremiah 32:37-42, Ezekiel 36:19-28, Proverbs 30:1-14, Numbers 21:5-9, Psalm 118:1-29(verse 6), Romans 8:31 II Kings 6:16, Psalm 118:24, Revelation 19:17, Matthew 21:9, Matthew 23:39, Mark 11:9, Luke 13:35, Hebrews 11:1, Psalm 44:22, Romans 1:6-8, Romans 1:15-32, II Timothy 3:16, Isaiah 45:23, Romans 14:11

4. Blessed are the poor in spirit to those who *believe and read this Scripture*: "*Nevertheless I* (Jesus) *must walk today*, and *to morrow*, and *the day following* (next day): for it (this) *cannot be that a prophet perish out of Jerusalem. Jesus Christ out of Jerusalem is that "Prophet."* Luke 13:33
5. Blessed are the poor in spirit to those who believe that *God our Father from Heaven is not a Racist. He is a Spirit and He is the Christ and He is the Savior of the world.* John 3:16, Acts 2:1-47 (verse 5-12), Galatians 3:26-29, John 4:23-26, 29, 39-42 (verse 24, 25-42)
6. Blessed are the poor in spirit to those who believe that the Pentecostal Baptism restores the Promised Latter Rain continuing pouring out on God's humble people today until Jesus Christ return. Acts 2:1-42
7. Blessed are the poor in spirit to those who believe that the *need to be saved is so great that the experience of salvation is through being born again*: *so that we can be ready to meet the Lord when He come.* Revelation 3:11, Revelation 22:7, 12, 20. See I Thessalonians 4:16-18 (verse 17). See Amos 4:12

   A moment of thought: *Become a child of God so that you can be "ready"* to *meet the Lord when He come, will you*? See I Thessalonians 4:16-18, Revelation 3:11, 22:7, 12, 22 Amos 4:12
8. Blessed are the poor in spirit to those who in *honoring the Spirit of Christ in all of these manifestations, graces, the Spirit Baptism and power for service and the imminent return.* Philippians 3:30, Matthew 5:6, Luke 24:49, Acts 1:8, Acts 2:1-12, I Thessalonians 4:16-18, Revelation 3:11, 22:7, 12, 20
9. Blessed are the poor in spirit to those who *believe* on the *basic doctrines of the Bible as salvation*; through the *atoning blood of Jesus Christ who was born of a virgin*; *the Holy Ghost or Holy Spirit Baptism according to Acts 2:4*; the *Second Coming of Christ; diving healing*; and the *gifts of the Spirit.* Genesis 1:1, John 1:1, I Timothy 3:16, Acts 16:31, Romans 5:11, I Peter 1:19-25, I John 1:7, Matthew 1:21, 23, 25, Luke 1:35, Luke 2:21, Matthew 3:11, Acts 1:4-5, Acts 2:4, James 5:16, I Corinthians 14:1, 12, Ephesians 1:3, Ephesians 5:19, I Thessalonians 4:14-18, Revelation 3:11, 22:7, 12, 20

10. Blessed are the poor in spirit to those who *believe* that *we are not baptized with the Holy Spirit in order to be saved*, but that we are "already" saved. John 3:5, Acts 19:1-6
11. Blessed are the poor in spirit to those who believe that *we do not believe that water baptism "alone" is a means of salvation, but is an outward demonstration that one has "already"* had a *conversion experience and has accepted Christ as his personal Savior*. Romans 6:3-11, Colossians 2:12, Matthew 28:19
12. Blessed are the poor in spirit to those who *believe the Scripture*: "*Truly my soul waiteth upon God's from Him cometh my salvation. He only is my rock and my salvation*; *He is my defence* (defense, stronghold) I *shall not be greatly moved.* Psalm 62:1-2

PART CDLXXVI

Blessed Are The Poor In Spirit. Matthew 5:3

Blessed Means Happy

Poor means meek in spirit. Poor means humble in spirit. Poor means lowly in spirit. Poor means quiet in spirit. Read Matthew 5:3-12, Read also Mark 1:15

Jesus did not say "*rich*" in spirit. Jesus said "*poor*" in spirit.

1. Blessed are the poor in spirit to those who believe in "*JESUS*" Matthew 1:21, 23, 25, Acts 1:21, Acts 2:21 (John 2:22), Acts 2:36, Acts 7:59, Acts 8:16, Acts 11:20, Acts 16:31 (John 3:16, Ephesians 2:8-9), Acts 19:10, 17 Acts 20:35, I Corinthians 11:23-34, I Corinthians 12:1-14, 26-31 (verse 3), II Corinthians 1:14, II Corinthians 4:4-6, 10-18 (verse 5, 10), Galatians 6:14-15, 17-18, I Thessalonians 2:14-15, 19 (verse 5), I Thessalonians 4:1-2, II Thessalonians 1:1-12 (verse 7, 12), Hebrews 13:8, 12, 20, 21, II Peter 1:1-2, 8, 11, 14, 16, 17, II Peter 3:18, Revelation 3:11, Revelation 22:7, 12, 21, Mark 14:72, John 2:22, John 4:53, John 13:21, John 21:23, Matthew 17:8, Mark 9:8, Matthew 21:11, Matthew 26:19-25, Matthew 26:75, Matthew 27:37, 46, Mark 15:37, Matthew 28:5-10, Matthew 28:17-20, Mark 9:1, 4-5, 8, John 6:26-71, John 11:11-13, John 11:35, John 12:21, John 19:28 (See Psalm 69:21), John 19:30, John 20:14-31, John 21:1-25, Acts 1:1-11, 16, 21-26, Acts 2:32, Acts 3:26, Acts 5:30, Acts 4:2, 13, 18-20, 27, 30, Acts 6:14, Acts 7:55, 59, Acts 8:35, Acts 9:5, Acts 22:8, Acts 26:15-18, Acts 9:17, 27, Acts 10:38, Acts 13:23, Acts 17:7, 18, Acts 19:10-13, 15, 17, Acts 19:4-5, Acts 25:19, Acts 28:23, Romans 3:26, Romans 8:11, I Corinthians 12:3, II Corinthians 4:5, 10-11, Ephesians 4:21, Philippians 2:10-11, I Thessalonians 1:10, I Thessalonians 4:13-18 (verse 14), I Thessalonians 4:1-2, Hebrews 2:9, Hebrews 4:14-16 (verse 14), Hebrews 6:20, Hebrews 7:22, Hebrews 10:19-25, Hebrews 12:1-2, 24, Hebrews 13:12-16, 20-21, I John 4:2, 3, 15, I John 4:1-21, I John 5:5-6, 20, Revelation 1:1, 5, 17, Revelation 14:12, Revelation 17:6, Revelation 20:4, Revelation 20:16, Revelation 3:11, Revelation 20:1, 7, 12, 22, I John 5:1-21
2. Blessed are the poor in spirit to those who believe that slavery in 1619 to 1865 was not the first issues because it was God's Hebrew people who were God's

Israel, had been slavery for over 430 years. Genesis 15:13, Exodus 12:41, Acts 7:6, Galatians 3:16-17

3. Blessed are the poor in spirit to those who believe in the *Spirit of God who is call Jesus*. I Corinthians 12:3
4. Blessed are the poor in spirit to those who *believe* or *preach* or *teach* "*not*" *another* (different) *doctrine*, "*not*" *another* (different) *Jesus*, "*not*" *another* (different) *gospel*, "*not*" *another* (different) *spirit*. II Corinthians 11:4
5. Blessed are the poor in spirit to those who *believe God's healing power through Jesus Christ bring restoration*, and *forgiveness*. Exodus 15:26, Isaiah 3:5, James 5:16, Matthew 8:7, I Peter 2:24, Psalms !03:1-3, Philippians 4:13
6. Blessed are the poor in spirit to those who *believe this Scriptures*: "Brethren, *if* any of you *do err from the truth*, and *one convert him*; *Let him know*, that he *which convert* (turns) *the sinner from error of his way* (sin) *shall* (will) *save a soul*—(real person, lively—person) *from death*, and *shall* (will) *hide* (cover) *a multitude* (many) *of sins*. James 5:19-20
7. Blessed are the poor in spirit to those who believe that we are not "**Anybody**;" that we are not "**Nobody**" that we are not "**Anybody**," that we are not "**No Good Person**;" but that we are "**Somebody**;" that we know "**Someone**" that loved us even; **Jesus** who are loved us and gave *Himself* for us. Galatians 2:20 Romans 5:8, I John 3:16, Ephesians 5:25, Ephesians 5:2, John 3:16, Ephesians 2:14-15. Read Ephesians 2:4-19, Isaiah 43:4, Isaiah 63:9, Jeremiah 31:3, John 6:44-65, {key-verse—44}. There is Love!!!. Believe God!!! Believe Jesus Christ!!!
8. Blessed are the poor in spirit to those who believe that we have work to do: "Jesus says: "Therefore, *go* and *make disciples* of all nations, *baptizing* them in the *name* of the *Father* and of the *Son* and of the *Holy Spirit*. Matthew 28:19. See Jesus' example in Matthew 3:13-17.
    i. One of the first books I enjoyed *reading* was between President Abraham Lincoln, President John F. Kennedy and Barrack Obama before he became President.
    ii. The last known books to read between Frederick Douglass, Harriet Tubman, Sojourner Truth and Or Essie Mae Washington, daughter of the Senator Strom Thurmond, of Aiken, South Carolina
    iii. One of the Christian books ever read was between John Wesley, John Rice and the last known book, William J. Seymour.

9. Blessed are the poor in spirit to those who are able to say with strength; "Our profession of faith." "I am what the Word of God says I am I am more than a conqueror. I am more than victorious; and I can do what the Word of God says I can do." Romans 8:1-39 (verse 35-39), Philippians 4:13, Exodus 3:13-14 (verse 14), Revelation 1:8
10. Blessed are the poor in spirit to those who believe in letting them *live*; letting them *work*, letting them *rest*. John 6:28-29, John 9:4, John 5:17, Genesis 2:2, Hebrews 4:10
11. Blessed are the poor in spirit to those who believe when God's children *welcome us into the Lord's House*: "I was *glad* when *they say unto me, let us go into the house of the Lord*. Psalm 122:1
12. Blessed are the poor in spirit to those who believe that *Jesus* was *preaching* and *showing* the *glad tidings of the Kingdom of God*. Luke 8:1

Part CDLXXVII

Blessed Are The Poor In Spirit. Matthew 5:3

Blessed Means Happy

Poor means meek in spirit. Poor means humble in spirit. Poor means lowly in spirit. Poor means quiet in spirit. Read Matthew 5:3-12, Read also Mark 1:15

Jesus did not say "*rich*" in spirit. Jesus said "*poor*" in spirit.

1. Blessed are the poor in spirit to those who believe that *the Seed Is The Word Of God.* Luke 8:11
2. Blessed are the poor in spirit to those who believe that Death is not an end. Death is a new beginning over the other side of the Jordon River because of living with God in Glory. Joshua 3:1-5:12, Isaiah 9:1
3. Blessed are the poor in spirit to those who believe in putting God first; secondly, others and thirdly, ourselves. Matthew 6:33, Exodus 20:1-3, Deuteronomy 6:4-5, Mark 12:28-33, I John 3:11-23, John 14:15, Mark 12:31, John 15:12, Matthew 22:36-40, Mark 12:31,
4. Blessed are the poor in spirit to those who believe that tithes belong to God. Malachi 3:7-10 (verse 8, 10). All is mine. John 17:10, John 16:15, Psalm 50:10, Isaiah 43:1, Ezekiel 18:4,
5. Blessed are the poor in spirit to those who believe tht communion of bread and water represent the Body of the Lord Jesus Christ. I Corinthians 11:25, 27, Matthew 26:26, Mark 26:26, Mark 14:22, Luke 22:19
6. Blessed are the poor in spirit to those who believe that drinking of the cup represent the blood of the Lord Jesus Christ. I Corinthians 11:26-27, Matthew 26:27-29, Mark 26:27, Mark 14:23-25, Luke 22:17-18, 20
7. Blessed are the poor in spirit to those who *believe* that "*the field is the world,*" which is "*all kind of different cultural people.*" It is a *parable explanation by Jesus Christ to His own people that received Him not as Lord and Personal Savior.* Matthew 13:37-53. See John 1:10-11
8. Blessed are the poor in spirit to those who *believe* that "*the good seed*" are "*the children of the kingdom,*" which is the *children of God,* who "*become the children of God in His kingdom.*" Matthew 13:37-53. See John 1:12-13. It is a *parable explanation by Jesus Christ.*

9. Blessed are the poor in spirit to those who *believe, realize* and *understand* that "*the tares of the field*" which are "*the weeds of the field*" are "*the children of the wicked one*;" which are *the children of the devil*, which are *Satan's children*. The *parable explanation by Jesus Christ to His own people that receive Him not as Lord and Personal Savior*. Matthew 13:28, 53. See John 1:10-11
10. Blessed are the poor in spirit to those who *believe, realize* and *understand* that "*the enemy*" which is "*Satan*" called "*Lucifer*" (See Isaiah 14:12) that sowed them (*tares are children of the wicked one*) is the devil, which is "*Satan*;" which is "*Lucifer*;" *the harvest is the end of the world*;" *which is to come*; and "*the reapers*." (God's angels) are "*the angels*" (God's angels, God's messengers). It is the *parable explanation by Jesus Christ to His own people that receive Him not as Lord and Personal Savior*. Matthew 13:39, Matthew 13:53
11. Blessed are the poor in spirit to those who believe that *The Seed* is *the Word of God*. The parable of the sower *explanation by Jesus Christ to His own people that receive Him not as Lord and Personal Savior*. John 1:10-11 *but those who as many as received Him* (Jesus Christ) to them (those who receive Jesus Christ as Lord and Personal Savior) *gave He (Jesus Christ) power to because the sons of God give to them that believe or His (Christ) name*. John 1:12, 13, Luke 8:11
12. Blessed are the poor in spirit to those who *believe* that *the preaching of the cross is the power of God to save us*. I Corinthians 1:18

Part CDLXXVIII

Blessed Are The Poor In Spirit. Matthew 5:3

Blessed Means Happy

Poor means meek in spirit. Poor means humble in spirit. Poor means lowly in spirit. Poor means quiet in spirit. Read Matthew 5:3-12, Read also Mark 1:15

Jesus did not say "*rich*" in spirit. Jesus said "*poor*" in spirit.

1. Blessed are the poor in spirit to those who believe the History of the Bible stories from Genesis to Revelation that endeavors to stay true to the Spirit of the body which is the Bible, that is of God, which is of the Spirit of God, which is God our Father that say, I am the Lord that healeth thee. Exodus 15:26, See Genesis 1:1-2, John 1:1, II Timothy 3:16, Hebrews 1:1-4, II Peter 1:21. **Noah told story about God's creation** to his family: Genesis 1:1-31, Genesis 2:1-6, **Story of Adam and Eve**: Genesis 2:7-25, Story of Cain and Abel: Genesis 4:1-8, **Story of Noah**: Genesis 6:1-22, Genesis 7:1-24, Genesis 8:1-22, Genesis 9:1-17, **Story of Abram**: Genesis 12:1-9, Genesis 13:10-18 (One year later): Genesis 15:1-21, Genesis 16:1-6 (14 years later), Genesis 17:1-27, Genesis 18:1-33, **Life of Sodom**, Genesis 19:1-26, 27-30, Genesis 21:1-14 (**Ten years later**) Genesis 22:1-19, Genesis 25:20, 26, Genesis 32:26-30, See Genesis 15:12-16, Acts 7:6-7 **(410 years later) Story of Moses**—Exodus 1:1-22, Exodus 2:1-25, (**40 years later**) Genesis 3:1-22, Genesis 4:1-31, Genesis 5:1-23, Genesis 6:1-30, Genesis 7:1-25, Genesis 8:1-32, Genesis 9:1-35, Genesis 10:1-29, Genesis 11:1-10, Genesis 12:1-51, Genesis 13:1-22, Red Sea, Genesis 14:1-31, (**After 430 years, Israelites were free from Egypts's land**, **Egypt's property**) (**Red Sea**) (**Freedom from slavery**), Genesis 15:1-13, Genesis 19:16-25, Genesis 20:1-26, (**40 years later**)
2. Blessed are the poor in spirit to those who believe the story of the Bible that told about God's creation by Noah to his family. **The story of the Bible story of Adam**, **Eve**, and **the serpent called Satan or Lucifer**. (40 years later). **The story of Joshua**—Joshua 1:1-18, Joshua 2:1-24, Joshua 3:1-17, Joshua 4:1-24, Joshua 5:6, Joshua 6:1-27, An hundred years later, the story of Samson; Judges 13:1-25, Judges 14:1-20, Judges 15:1-20, Judges 16:1-31, Stories of Samuel, Saul and David; I Samuel 1-28, I Samuel 2:1-36, I Samuel 3:1-21, I Samuel

7:1-17, I Samuel 8:1-22, The story of King Saul—I Samuel 9:1-27, I Samuel 10:1-27, I Samuel 11:1-15, Back into the story of Samuel: I Samuel 12:1-25, I Samuel 13:1-16, 22, Back into the life of Saul—I Samuel 14:1-52, I Samuel 15:1-35, I Samuel 16:1-23, Story of Goliath—I Samuel 17:1-5, 8, The story of David, I Samuel 16:1-23, I Samuel 18:1-30, I Samuel 19:1-24, I Samuel 20:1-34, I Samuel 21:1-15, I Samuel 22:1-23, I Samuel 23:1-29, I Samuel 24:1-22, I Samuel 26:1-25, I Samuel 27:1-12, I Samuel 31:1-13, II Samuel 1:1-27, II Samuel 5:1-25, II Samuel 6:1-23, II Samuel 7:1-29, II Samuel 11:1-27, II Samuel 12:1-31, The Story of Daniel; Daniel 1:1-21, Daniel 2:1-49, Daniel 3:1-30, Daniel 4:1-37, Daniel 5:1-31, Daniel 6:1-28, Daniel 7:1-28, 500 years later…Luke 1:26

3. Blessed are the poor in spirit to those who believe **the Bible story in Nazareth, Galilee in the capital of Jerusalem…the story of Mary and Joseph**; Matthew 1:1-25, **Life of Mary**—Luke 1:27-38, 67-80, **the story of Mary and Joseph; in Bethlehem, Life of Joseph**—Matthew 1:18-20, 21-25, Luke 2:1-7, Matthew 2:13-23. **The Wise Men**, **the king Herod**, **Baby Jesus**, **Mary and Joseph**, **The Shepherd**—Luke 2:8-20, (**25 years later**) **The life and story of Jesus**, **His resurrection** ; **His Second Coming**, and **features with Satan**, **John the Baptist**, **Peter**, and **the rest of the disciples and the story of John the Baptist**—Matthew 3:1-17, Mark 6:27, Luke 3:6, 9
4. Blessed are the poor in spirit to those who believe **the Bible story in Capernaum**; Mark 2:1-18. **Jesus said**, "Son, thy sins be forgiven thee, Arise and take up thy bed, and walk?…**hath power on earth to forgiven sins**. Read Mark 2:1-28. **Mustard of Seed**: Mark 4:30-32, and Luke 5:16-26, **The Pharisee and the Publican—went up to pray to God**. Luke 18:9-14. **Jesus said**: "**Bless are the poor**," Matthew 5:1-48, **Jesus taught His disciples how to pray**. Luke 11:1-4, Matthew 6:9-13; **A woman taken in adultery**: **Hear Jesus's speech**: John 8:1-11, **Jesus Feed Five thousand men**, **women**, **boys and girls**: Matthew 14:13-21, Luke 9:11-17, Mark 6:31-44, John 6:1-15, **Jesus asked questions to disciples who Jesus was**. Luke 9:18-20, John 13:1-17, Matthew 24:3; **Peter tried to come Jesus on the water**: Mark 6:47-51, Matthew 4:24-33; **Triumphal Entry**—Matthew 21:1-11, Luke 19:28-40, John 12:11-50; **Jesus read** from Isaiah 61:1-3, Luke 4:16-21, **Jesus heard of John's passing, the forerunner or the Baptist**. Mark 6:22-30, John 3:29, Matthew 11:13, 25, Malachi 3:1, Luke 1:17; **Jesus advisement**. Matthew 5:38-39, **In the village of Bethany**:

John 11:1-57, **The week before Passover In Nazareth, Jesus**—Mark 11:1-11, **Jesus Over turned the thief thing in the Temple of God**—Matthew 21:12-13, Luke 16:13, Mark 11:15-18. See Isaiah 56:7, Matthew 23:10-29, Matthew 19:23-25, Matthew 22:37-39, Mark 12:28-35, Luke 10:25-28. **Paying Taxes**. Luke 20:21-26, **The Temple** Mark 14:58, John 2:19, Acts 6:14. **Nicodemus and Jesus**—John 3:1-21, **Satan entered the heart of Judas to destroy Jesus**—Matthew 26:14-30, John 18:1-9, Mark 14:10-26, Luke 22:1-23, John 13:1-30, **Jesus showed the way**—John 14:1-31, **Jesus' Predict Peter's deny**—Matthew 26:33-35, Mark 14:29-31, Luke 22:31-34, John 18:15-27

5. Blessed are the poor in spirit to those who believe the **Bible story in the Garden of Gethsemane—Jesus went for Farewell Prayer**: Matthew 26:36-56, Mark 14:32-50, Luke 22:39-54, John 17:1-26, **Jesus healed the soldier's ear**: Matthew 26:51-52, Mark 14:47, Luke 22:50-51, John 18:10-11, 26-27, **Accuser of Jesus**:
   i. He employed demons to heal.
   ii. He threatened to destroy the Temple of their Lord (their God)
   iii. Is Jesus the Chosen One?
   iv. Is Jesus the Son of God?
   v. Be coming in the colud of heaven, sitting at the right hand of God.

   Pharisees declared Death Sentence on Jesus for blasphemer.
6. Blessed are the poor in spirit to those who believe **the Bible story in the conclusion that was 50 days since passover, that was the day Jesus was crucified. Thousand of Jewish people and pilgrims came to Jerusalem for festival of Pentecost. All continued with one according in prayer and supplication**—Acts 1:12-14, **In the Upper Prayer Room**—Acts 2:1-12. **Story of short life of Stephen**. Acts 6:1-15, Acts 7:1-60 **Saul witnessed of Stephen's death**. Acts 8:1-2. **Healed of the Lame Beggar**—Acts 3:1-26, **Saul's conviction and conversion** -Acts 9:1-22, 26-29, **Paul explained about love**. See I Corinthians 13:6, 7, 13, Galatians 5:22. **The Spirit of Christ Jesus, met Peter to carry His name to Cornelius, a centurion**. Acts 10:1-48, *20 years later*: **History was said that** *Peter* **was** *killed*. **He was** *crucified* **upside down** *in Rome*. **History was said that** *Matthew* **was** *killed in Ethiopia*. **History was said that** *Thomas was killed in Southern India*. **History was said that** *Paul was beheaded*. **Before his life was over, he said in his farewell testimony**: "For I am now ready to be offered, and the time of my departure is at hand." II Timothy 4:6. "I have fought a good fight,

I have finished my course, I have kept the faith:" II Timothy 4:7. "Henceforth there is laid up for me a crown of righteousness, which the Lord, the righteous judge, shall give me at that day: and not to me only, but unto all them also that love his appearing." II Timothy 4:8.
And his words, letters and testimony still live on.

—Final conclusion—End of story of the Bible—

History was said that *John* **(not John the Baptist, but a brother of James and one of Jesus' disciples and their father's name was Zebedee**—See Matthew 4:21), **was** *poisoned in Rome*, **but was** *alive* **and** *was exiled in Greece in an island called Patmos.* **He lived out his days and wrote the last book of Revelation, where Jesus said**, **"I am Alpha and Omega, the beginning and the ending**, saith the **Lord, which is**, and **which was**, and **which is to come**, the **Almighty**." Revelation 1:8. John said: "And when I saw him, I fell at his feet as dead." **Jesus said**: "And he laid his right hand upon me, saying unto me, Fear not: **I am the first and the last**:" Revelation 1:17. **Jesus said**: **"I am he that liveth**, and **was dead**; and, behold, **I am alive for evermore**, **Amen**; and **have the keys of hell and of death**." Revelation 1:18. **Jesus said**: **"Write the things** which thou *hast* seen, and **the things which** *are*, and **the things which** *shall be* hereafter;" Revelation 1:19. Jesus said: "And God shall wipe away all tears from their eyes; and there shall be no more death, neither sorrow, nor crying, neither shall there be any more pain: for the former things are passed away." Revelation 21:4. Jesus said: "And he that sat upon the throne said, Behold, I make all things new. And he said unto me, Write: for **these words are true and faithful**." Revelation 21:5. **Jesus said**: "He which testifieth these things saith, **Surely I come quickly**, **Amen**. Even so, **come, Lord Jesus**." Revelation 22:20. **Jesus said**: "The **grace of our Lord Jesus Christ be with you all**. Amen." Revelation 22:21. And Jesus Christ's Word still live on. Read Revelation 3:11, Revelation 22:7, 12, 20

7. Blessed are the poor in spirit to those who believe in a second chance by coming to Jesus Christ for salvation. Matthew 4:17
8. Blessed are the poor in spirit to those who believe the foundation of the church of Jesus Christ. I Corinthians 3:11, I Corinthians 10:4. See Exodus 17:6
9. Blessed are the poor in spirit to those who believe that *Christianity mean the Christian religion, based upon belief in Jesus as the Christ and upon Christ's teachings.* Acts 11:26

10. Blessed are the poor in spirit to those who spent to those who believe in the freedom of Justice, Equally and Liberty for all through Jesus Christ. John 8:36, Matthew 10:5-42, Acts 2:28-47, Acts 26:22-32, Romans 3:19-31, Romans 8:1-39 (verse 32), I Corinthians 2:9-16, II Corinthians 11:1-7 (verse 7), Revelation 21:1-7 (verse 6), Revelation 22:1-21 (verse 17).
11. Blessed are the poor in spirit to those who believe in giving the gift of *hope*, *love* and *peace* through Jesus Christ, (*hope*—I Timothy 1:1, Titus 2:13, *love*—I John 4:6-10, 19, John 3:16, Jude 1-2, Revelation 2:4-5, *peace*—Acts 16:36, Romans 1:7, I Corinthians 1:3, II Corinthians 2:2-4, Galatians 1:3-5, Ephesians 1:2-23, Philippians 1:2, Romans 5:1, Romans 8:6, Romans 10:15, See Isaiah 52:7, Romans 14:17, Romans 15:13, I Corinthians 14:33, Ephesians 2:14-22, Ephesians 6:23, Philippians 4:7, Colossians 1:2-6, I Thessalonians 1:1, II Thessalonians 1:2, I Timothy 1:1, II Timothy 1:2, Titus 1:4, Philemon 3, II John 3, Colossians 3:15-17 (verse 15), II Thessalonians 3:16, 18, Hebrews 12:14, Revelation 1:4-8, (verse 4)
12. Blessed are the poor in spirit to those who believe in *peace, love, faith* and *grace* through our Lord Jesus Christ in sicerity. Amen. Ephesians 6:23-24

Part CDLXXIX

Blessed Are The Poor In Spirit. Matthew 5:3

Blessed Means Happy

Poor means meek in spirit. Poor means humble in spirit. Poor means lowly in spirit. Poor means quiet in spirit. Read Matthew 5:3-12, Read also Mark 1:15

Jesus did not say "*rich*" in spirit. Jesus said "*poor*" in spirit.

1. Blessed are the poor in spirit to those who believe the *Scripture*, the *Word of God* that "*inspires*" *the pastors*: "*And I will give you pastors* according to *mine heart*, which *shall feed you with knowledge and understanding*. Jeremiah 3:15, Ephesians 4:11. See I Corinthians 12:3-11, 28, II Timothy 4:5, Acts 21:8
2. Blessed are the poor in spirit to those who are *called* to be *evangelist* like Philip, the evangelist: Ephesians 4:11, II Timothy 4:5. See Acts 21:8
3. Blessed are the poor in spirit to those who believe that *missionaries*, *deacons*, *pastors*, *evangelists*, *prophets*, *disciples*, *workers of miracles*, *teachers*, and *apostles* are God's true calling according to His own heart, "to His Own Will. Jeremiah 3:15, I Corinthians 12:3-11, Ephesians 4:11, II Timothy 4:5, Acts 6:3-6, Matthew 10:42, Matthew 27:51, Matthew 18:15, John 19:38, John 21:23-24, Acts 9:10, 26, 36, Acts 16:1, Acts 21:16, Matthew 21:1-7, Luke 19:37-38, John 4:1-2, John 13:5, 7, John 20:18, Acts 11:26, Acts 19:1-10, Acts 20:7. See I Samuel 13:14, Acts 13:22
4. Blessed are the poor in spirit to those who believe in God's true calling to be His disciples and to do His will and purpose in the ministry. Matthew 10:42, Matthew 27:51, Matthew 18:15, John 19:38, John 21:23-24, Acts 9:10, 26, 36, Acts 16:1, Acts 21:16, Matthew 21:1-7, Luke 19:37-38, John 4:1-2, John 13:5, 7, John 20:18, Acts 11:26, Acts 19:1-10, Acts 20:7
5. Blessed are the poor in spirit to those who believe that God does not teach us to die a fool. He teaches us to live a fool. Proverbs 17:7, II Corinthians 11:16, 23, I Corinthians 1:20-23, 25, 27, I Corinthians 4:10, II Corinthians 11:19, 23, I Corinthians 1:18, Matthew 10:39, II Corinthians 11:1-4
6. Blessed are the poor in spirit to those who believe that the *title* for "*Christ*" is *either God* **the Savior**, or *Jesus*, the **Chris**t, or the **Savior** is **His name** forever, because He is "*the Same One*" And *He is Lord of all*. Acts 16:36, John 14:6-11

(verse 8-9), Philippians 3:20, I Timothy 1:1, Titus 1:3, 4, Titus 2:10, 11-15 (verse 10, 13), Titus 3:4-8 (verse 4, 6, 8, II Peter 1:1-3 (verse 1, 11, 16), 11, II Peter 2:20, II Peter 3:2, 18, I John 14:14-15, 16-17, 18-21, Jude 24-25 (verse 25), Jude 21, See Ephesians 5:23

7. Blessed are the poor in spirit to those who believe that the *wages* (*which is costly, is sin*) *of sin is death* (*which separate from God*), but the *gift of God's love* is *eternal life,* (*which is union with God),* through Jesus Christ, the *Savior of the world. Romans 6:23*, Matthew 1:21, 25, John 3:15-17, John 4:42, *Acts 16:31*, Ephesians 2:8-9, I John 4:14
8. Blessed are the poor in spirit to those who *believe Christ's power to save, Christ's power to heal, Christ's power to deliver, Christ's power to set us free, Christ's power to deliver us from pain, sin and death,* Christ's power to execute judgment, *Christ's power to take, Christ's power to take it again, Christ's power to take us Home in Glory to live with Him for ever more.* Matthew 3:17, Matthew 17:5, Matthew 12:17, Mark 1:11, John 17:14 (Read John 17:1-26), See Isaiah 42:1-25, Acts 26:18, Luke 2:32, John 5:27 (Read John 5:1-47 (verse 13-15, 22-24, 26, 27, 28, 29, 30, See Daniel 12:1-3, John 5:34, 39, 40, 41-47 (verse 47)—Moses wrote from Genesis to Deuteronomy), See Numbers 18:25 (John 5:30), Matthew 24:21 (Daniel 12:1), Matthew 25:46, John 5:29, John 11:23-27 (Daniel 12:2), Jude 15, See Revelation—the Second Coming of Christ—Revelation 3:11, Revelation 22:7, 12, 20—Even so come Lord Jesus.
9. Blessed are the poor in spirit to those who *believe this spiritual hymn; that Christ's power came to love, Christ's power came to live, to abide* (stay), *to heal and to forgive, to buy my pardon, an empty grave is there to prove my Savior lives because He lives, I can face tomorrow, because He lives, all fear is gone, because I know He holds the future.* And *life is worth the living just because He lives.* John 14:16-21
10. Blessed are the poor in spirit to those who believe that Jesus is the Messiah; that Jesus is the Christ; that Jesus is the Son of the Living God; that Jesus is God Himself that Jesus is the Second Coming of Christ, that Jesus is the Son of Man; that Jesus is coming soon. Amos 4:12, Acts 1:11, I Thessalonians 4:12-18, (verse 17), Revelation 3:11, 22:7, 12, 20, See Daniel 7:13, Matthew 24:30, Mark 14:62, Luke 21:27
11. Blessed are the poor in spirit to those who believe and see the different between sancification in John 17:17 as a second grace of blessing and the Baptism of the Holy Spirit with speaking in tongues in Acts 2:4 as a third grace of blessing.

12. Blessed are the poor in spirit to those who believe the Lord, send as a revival. II Chronicle 7:14, Habakkuk 3:2, II Peter 3:9, Isaiah 38:16, Isaiah 50:1-11, I Kings 19:5-18

Part CDLXXX

Blessed Are The Poor In Spirit. Matthew 5:3

Blessed Means Happy

Poor means meek in spirit. Poor means humble in spirit. Poor means lowly in spirit. Poor means quiet in spirit. Read Matthew 5:3-12, Read also Mark 1:15

Jesus did not say "*rich*" in spirit. Jesus said "*poor*" in spirit.

1. Blessed are the poor in spirit to those who believe this spiritual hymn: "Lord, send us a revival, send as a revival. Let is begin in me. II Chronicle 7:14, Habakkuk 3, Micah 6:8, II Chronicle 26:16, James 4:6b, I Peter 5:5b-7, Philippians 2:8, Psalm 80:19, Psalm 85:6, Isaiah 57:15, James 4:8
2. Blessed are the poor in spirit to those who believe: "If you are to die tonight, Heaven or Hell. John 3:13, Revelation 21:1, II Peter 3:10-13, Psalms 5:5, Hebrews 9:27, Revelation 21:1-27, Matthew 25:41, Revelation 20:14, Revelation 21:8, John 14:2, Johm 13:36, Revelation 20:6, I John 5:16-17, Romans 6:23, John 4:24, John 3:5, Luke 23:43, Philippians 3:20
3. Blessed are the poor in spirit to those who believe and know when we die. Psalm 116:15
4. Blessed are the poor in spirit to those who believe that the Holy Spirit, which is honor, can change life of many of God's people and as well sinners. Romans 8:9, John 3:19-21
5. Blessed are the poor in spirit to those who believe that the Bible is no myth. Romans 3:1-31 verses:9, 10, 11, 18, 22, 23, 26, 27, 29, 30, 31
6. Blessed are the poor in spirit to those who believe that the voice of God speak as like toPaul in Acts 9:4-7, Acts 17:11, Acts 20:22-24, I Corinthians 14:29, Proverbs 12:15, Acts 22:6, Acts 18:9, 10
7. Blessed are the poor in spirit to those who believe that every conversion is planned in Heaven. John 14:6, John 10:11, Romans 8:35-39, I John 4:9, Ecclesiastes 3:11, Romans 6:23, I Corinthians 2:9, Ephesians 2:10, Philippians 4:7, I Peter 1:8-9, John 8:36, Romans 8:2
8. Blessed are the poor in spirit to those who believe the fullness of God because of His filling with His presence in the Spirit to His people, His children, the

children of the Kingdom. I Timothy 2:4, Hebrews 6:2, 4-6, 10:26-29, I Thessalonians 4:16, I Corinthians 15:52, Acts 4:12, Matthew 11:20-24, 12:41-42, Luke 10: 12-15

9. Blessed are the poor in spirit to those who believe the *Full* Gospel, the *Whole* Gospel, the *Whole* Bible that take us to heaven to be with Christ forever more. Acts 17:11, John 14:6, John 3:16, II Corinthians 4:4
10. Blessed are the poor in spirit to those who believe the call of God in heart: "When the Lord say, go, I must go." Lucy Farrow (1851-1911) Acts 11:12
11. Blessed are the poor in spirit to those who believe the flaming revival is about the baptism of the Holy Spirit; that is Jesus is coming soon. Get Ready. See Amos 4:12, Acts 1:11, Acts 2:4, I Thessalonians 4:13-18, Revelation 3:11, 22:7, 12, 20
12. Blessed are the poor in spirit to those who believe that the Comforter, which is the Holy Spirit already has come; that Jesus is coming soon. Get Ready. Amos 4:12, Acts 1:11, I Thessalonians 4:13-17, Revelation 3:11, Revelation 22:7, 12, 20

PART CDLXXXI

Blessed Are The Poor In Spirit. Matthew 5:3

Blessed Means Happy

Poor means meek in spirit. Poor means humble in spirit. Poor means lowly in spirit. Poor means quiet in spirit. Read Matthew 5:3-12, Read also Mark 1:15

Jesus did not say "*rich*" in spirit. Jesus said "*poor*" in spirit.

1. Blessed are the poor in spirit to those who believe that one of the interpretations as we receive the Baptism of the Holy Spirit is that Jesus is coming soon. Get Ready. Revelation 3:11, Revelation 22:7, 12, 20
2. Blessed are the poor in spirit to those who believe *three things*: *Open mind*, *open heart* and *open arm* because of *Jesus' example* to *follow His step*: Do unto others as you would have them do unto you. I Peter 2:21, John 13:37, I Corinthians 14:1, Hebrews 12:14, Psalm 23, Matthew 4:19, Matthew 8:22, Matthew 9:9, Mark2:14, Luke 5:27, Matthew 16:24, Mark 8:34, Mark 10:21, Luke 9:23, Luke 18:22, Luke 9:59, John 1:43, John 21:22, John 12:26
3. Blessed are the poor in spirit to those who believe that God can put new hope in our hearts. Psalm 37:4, Psalm 9:10, Psalm 13:5, Psalm 31:24, Job 11:18, Psalm 25:2-6, Psalm 33:20, 22, Psalm 39:7, Psalm 42:11, Psalm 62:5, Psalm 65:5, Psalm 119:114, 116, Proverbs 23:18, Isaiah 40:30-31, Jeremiah 29:11, Lamentations 3:21-22, Romans 5:1-5, Romans 8:24, Romans 12:12, Romans 15:13, II Corinthians 1:10-11, Galatians 5:5, Ephesians 1:17-19, Ephesians 4:3-6, Philippians 1:20, Colossians 1:27, I Thessalonians 1:3, II Thessalonians 2:16-17, I Timothy 6:17, Titus 2:12-14, Hebrews 6:11, Hebrews 10:23, Hebrews 11:1, I Peter 1:13, I Peter 1:3-5
4. Blessed are the poor in spirit to those who believe in a deeper walk with God just liked Abraham and Noah walked with God. Genesis 17:1-2, Hebrews 11:8, Genesis 6:5-13, Hebrews 11:7, Walking—Ephesians 2:10, 4:1, 4:17, 5:2, 5:15, Perfect—Matthew 19:21, Luke 6:40, II Corinthians 13:11, II Timothy 3:17, Hebrews 10:1, I John 4:17-18, Revelation 3:2, Obey—Romans 6:15-18
5. Blessed are the poor in spirit to those who believe in a hungry of the Word of God. Psalm 19, I Peter 2:1-3, John 6:35, Exodus 20:1-26, Psalm 17:14

6. Blessed are the poor in spirit to those who believe that the church world does not understand the full proof of Christ's ministry and His Imminent Return, the Second Coming of the Lord Jesus Christ and ready to meet the Lord when He comes. Amos 4:12, Acts 1:11, I Thessalonians 4:13-18, Revelation 3:11, Revelation 20:7, 12, 22.
7. Blessed are the poor in spirit to those who believe in coming on Home to Jesus Christ to those who are backslidden for sometimes in the past years. John 1:22, Hebrews 6:6, Matthew 7:21-23, Jeremiah 29:11-14, I John 1:9, Romans 8:9, Hebrews 6:4, Hebrews 5:9, Galatians 6:1, Psalm 66:18, I Samuel 30:6, Hebrews 6:5, Romans 10:6, Romans 5:17, Acts 16:31, James 5:16, II Peter 1:5-9, Hebrews 10:26, Titus 1:2, Philippians 2:12, Ephesians 2:8-9, Galatians 5:1,
8. Blessed are the poor in spirit to those who believe not to come by the set of little book or big book of rules, but by the Holy Bible; the Inspired of the Holy Bible that sent by God on outpouring of the Holy Spirit upon His people who were already saved; already born-again; or already regeneration, already experience of salvation. Acts 17:30-31, Luke 13:3, II Corinthians 7:9-10, Psalm 51, Matthew 3:8, Acts 26:20, Acts 9:6, Matthew 19:28, Isaiah 11:6-9, Romans 8:21-23
9. Blessed are the poor in spirit to those who believe that the Virgin Birth is the New Testament Salvation; of our Lord Jesus Christ. Luke 1:31-45, Matthew 1:21-25, Isaiah 7:14
10. Blessed are the poor in spirit to those who believe that God want us to be "zeal" for the Christ's service. II Corinthians 9:2, Titus 2:14, Revelation 3:19, Acts 1:8, Romans 1:16, Mark 8:38, Romans 10:11
11. Blessed are the poor in spirit to those who receive Pentecost in our souls. Acts 2:1-47
12. Blessed are the poor in spirit to those who believe that the power of the Lord truly indeed has sent down from Heaven. I Peter 1:12

Part CDLXXXII

Blessed Are The Poor In Spirit. Matthew 5:3

Blessed Means Happy

Poor means meek in spirit. Poor means humble in spirit. Poor means lowly in spirit. Poor means quiet in spirit. Read Matthew 5:3-12, Read also Mark 1:15

Jesus did not say "*rich*" in spirit. Jesus said "*poor*" in spirit.

1. Blessed are the poor in spirit to those who believe in the salvation of Jesus.
2. Blessed are the poor in spirit to those who believe and read God's true beloved letters or epistles because He loves us and for sinners to repent of their sins or sin; be prepare to meet the Lord thy God. Amos 4:12, John 3:16, Acts 1:11, Acts 16:31, I Thessalonians 4:17-18, Revelation 3:11, Revelation 22:7, 12, 20.
3. Blessed are the poor in spirit to those who believe that the saved souls are at rest. Job 3:17, Luke 23:43, Luke 16:22, Philippians 1:21-24, II Corinthians 5:19, Genesis 50:1-13, Revelation 14:13, Job 3:17, Luke 16:25, I Thessalonians 5:10, Revelation 6:9-10, Luke 16:22, 25, 26
4. Blessed are the poor in spirit to those who believe in Christ's doctrine of the resurrection of the dead. Revelation 1:5, 7, 18-19, John 11:25, Acts 2:31, Acts 4:2, 33, Acts 17:18, Philippians 3:10-12, I Peter 1:3, Philippians 3:21, Revelation 20:6, Matthew 20:19, Mark 9:31, Mark 10:34, Luke 18:33, Luke 24:7, Luke 9:9, Matthew 17:9, Matthew 26:32, Mark 14:28, Matthew 28:6, Mark 16:6, 9, 14, John 21:14, Luke 24:34, John 2:22, I Corinthians 15:20, Acts 17:3
5. Blessed are the poor in spirit to those who believe and are able to say to a dying world: "Come on home to Jesus. He will give you rest: You will find rest to your souls through Jesus Christ. Matthew 11:28-29
6. Blessed are the poor in spirit to those who believe: Let Be Reasonable. Let us reason together say the Lord. Isaiah 1:18
7. Blessed are the poor in spirit to those who believe that our eyes are fixed (ready) for heaven to live with God/ to live with Jesus forever more. II Corinthians 5:1-10, Philippians 1:6, Hebrews 12:2-3
8. Blessed are the poor in spirit to those who believe the Golden Rule: Do unto others as they would do unto you: Treat them right; as they would treat us right. Matthew 7:12, Luke 6:31

9. Blessed are the poor in spirit to those who believe the Bible salavation and the Pentecost as recorded in the Book of Acts. Acts chapters 1:1-26 to Acts 28:1-31, Acts 2:1-47, verse 1-4. Read Genesis 1:1, John 1:1, II Timothy 3:14-17, verse 16, Acts 16:31, Acts 2:21
10. Blessed are the poor in spirit to those who believe upon the examination of repentance, conversion, consercration, sanctification, healing and the soon coming of the Lord Jesus Christ. Matthew 3:2, John 4:17, Acts 2:38, Acts 3:19-20, Acts 8:22, Acts 17:30, John 17:17, James 15:16, Revelation 3:11, Revelation 22:7, 12, 20
11. Blessed are the poor in spirit to those who believe the basic doctrines of the Bible such as salvation, through the atoning blood of Jesus Christ who was born of a virgin; the Holy Ghost Baptism according to Acts 2:4; the second coming of Christ; divine healing; and the gifts of the Spirit. Luke 1:30, 35, Matthew 1:21, 23, 15, James 5:16, Revelation 3:11, Revelation 22:7, 12, 20,
12. Blessed are the poor in spirit to those who believe that Pentecostal movement since the day of Pentecost and since the revival of John Wesley in the sixteenth century was in meetings out in the open air, in school buildings, under brush arbors, under the bushes hidden which Moses who saw the burning bush, in vacant, or abandoned buildings like the stable where Jesus was born in Bethlehem or like the old barn stable that once used as a Methodist Church and Azusa Street Mission or Azusa Street Revival in Los Angeles, California, Stoney's Top Folly out pour Topeka Revial, Bible School, Bible home, T.V. Broadcasting Network, the first Bethel Bible College and Faith Healing home, Famous Azusa Street Revival, Brae Bonnie Street Home, Stone front building, often on the wrong side of the railroad tracks. Read Exodus 3:1-22, verse 2-3, See Acts 7:30-31, 38, 44-46, 47-50, Mark 16:15, Luke 24:47, Acts 1:8

Part CDLXXXIII

Blessed Are The Poor In Spirit. Matthew 5:3

Blessed Means Happy

Poor means meek in spirit. Poor means humble in spirit. Poor means lowly in spirit. Poor means quiet in spirit. Read Matthew 5:3-12, Read also Mark 1:15

Jesus did not say "*rich*" in spirit. Jesus said "*poor*" in spirit.

1. Blessed are the poor in spirit to those who does not understand the full potential of a truly Spirit filled life ministry. II Timothy 4:5, Ephesians 5:18.
2. Blessed are the poor in spirit to those who believe in Christ's Coming: Acts 1:11, Revelation 11:3, Revelation 22:7, 12, 20.
3. Blessed are the poor in spirit to those who believe that Pentecost or fiftieth (50th) is the feast of the fiftieth day. Acts 2:1
4. Blessed are the poor in spirit to those who believe God's regeneration; not generation, God's born again; not being born, God's saving grace; not being safety or God's commandment; not mandate, God's faith; not sight, God's touch of the Spirit; not feeling, God's Word; not man's word, God's own belief of His truth; not man's belief. Matthew 19:28, John 3:3-8 verse 3, 8, Romans 10:8-21, Romans 5:1, Ephesians 2:8-9, Matthew 3:2, Matthew 4:17, II Timothy 3:15-17.
5. Blessed are the poor in spirit to those who believe that Jesus saved us just as He did to His disciples. Matthew 1:21, 25, Acts 16:31, Romans 10:13
6. Blessed are the poor in spirit to those who believe that Jesus sanctified us just as He did to His disciples. John 17:17
7. Blessed are the poor in spirit to those who believe that Jesus baptized us just as He did to His disciples. Acts 1:4-5
8. Blessed are the poor in spirit to those who believe what Jesus want us to know: that "Jesus want to save us." Matthew 1:25
9. Blessed are the poor in spirit to those who believe what Jesus want us to know: "Jesus want to sanctify us." John 17:17
10. Blessed are the poor in spirit to those who believe what Jesus want us to know: "Jesus want to baptize us." Acts 1:4-5, 8, Acts 2:4-47, Acts 10:33-48

11. Blessed are the poor in spirit to those who believe this statement of faith: "Jesus to save us." Matthew 1:25
12. Blessed are the poor in spirit to those who believe this statement of faith: "Jesus to sanctify us with His Spirit." John 17:17

Part CDLXXXIV

Blessed Are The Poor In Spirit. Matthew 5:3

Blessed Means Happy

Poor means meek in spirit. Poor means humble in spirit. Poor means lowly in spirit. Poor means quiet in spirit. Read Matthew 5:3-12, Read also Mark 1:15

Jesus did not say "*rich*" in spirit. Jesus said "*poor*" in spirit.

1. Blessed are the poor in spirit to those who believe this statement of faith: "Jesus to baptize us with His Spirit." Acts 1:4-5, 8, Acts 2:4, Acts 10:44
2. Blessed are the poor in spirit to those who believe in living well through Jesus Christ because it is well with our soul by singing, "It is well. It is well. It is well with my soul." Philippians 4:6-7
3. Blessed are the poor in spirit to those who believe that we are born from our mother's womb and we are born in sin; Job 31:14-15, Psalm 22:8-11 verse 10, Psalm 139:12-17 verse 13, Psalm 51:1-17 verse 5, Isaiah 44:2, 24, Isaiah 49:1, 5, 15-16, Isaiah 46:3, Isaiah 66:7-14 verse 9, Jeremiah 1:5, Jeremiah 20:17-18, Ezekiel 20:26, Hosea 12:3-6, Luke 1:31, 41-42, 44-47, Luke 2:21-23; "*but*" we *must born again*; born of the Spirit of God; John 1:12-13, John 3:3-8 verse 7, I John 3:9, 4:7-10 verse 7, 5-7, verse 4, 18-21
4. Blessed are the poor in spirit to those who do not want to miss heaven when God call us home some day because He has already prepared us each a place. John 14:1-2
5. Blessed are the poor in spirit to those who believe that Jesus is Lord and that Jesus is God Himself. John 9:36-37, John 14:8-9, 14:9-11
6. Blessed are the poor in spirit to those who *we* are *also the offspring of God.* Acts 17:27-28 verse 28
7. Blessed are the poor in spirit to those who believe in "*National Day Of Prayer.*" II Chronicles 7:14
8. Blessed are the poor in spirit to those who want to *find our way back to God and His holiness.* The *only way to find our way back to God is through Jesus Christ.* John 14:6, Acts 16:31, Romans 10:13, Romans 5:1, Ephesians 2:8-9, Romans 1:17, John 3:16.

9. Blessed are the poor in spirit to those who believe: *Jesus saves*!!! *Jesus saves*!!! *Jesus saves*!!! Matthew 1:21, 23, 25, Matthew 18:11, Luke 19:10, Luke 9:56, John 12:47, I Timothy 1:15, Hebrews 7:25
10. Blessed are the poor in spirit to those who believe that "*education*" and "*philosophy*" do not get us to *meet God in heaven through Jesus Christ*; and those who *believe in church do not get us to heaven*; "*only*" "*if*" we *believe Jesus Christ* as our Personal *Savior and Lord*. Amos 4:12, Psalm1:4-6, Acts 16:31, Romans 10:13, Ephesians 2:8-10. Consider: *Moses* received *high education* through *Pharaoh*; *Daniel* received *high education* through *government power*, *Paul* received *high religious education* through "*Gamaliel*." And they received the Lord in their hearts by doing the Lord's will. God is "*first*" *of business*. Read about Paul. Acts 7:58, 8:1, 9:1-22, 21:36-40, Acts 22:1-30 verse 3, Acts 24:1-27 verse 14-16, Acts 26:1-32 verse 12-18, 28:4-31
11. Blessed are the poor in spirit to those who believe *God's* "*Ten Commandments*" that are *still* in use, *in good* "*standard*," "in *good rule*," in *good mandatory*, in *good authoritative order*, or in *good trust* as it is *required* by the "*law of God*" *today*. Exodus 20:1-17
12. Blessed are the poor in spirit to those who believe that the power is to save, the power is to heal, the power is to deliver and the power is to set us free. II Chronicles 25:8, Psalm 62:11, Matthew 9:6, Mark 2:10-11, Luke 5:24, Matthew 28:18-20, John 1:12-13, John 10:18, John 19:11, Romans 1:16, I Corinthians 5:4-5, I Corinthians 1:18, Matthew 1:21, Matthew 18:11, Luke 19:10, Luke 9:56, John 12:47, I Timothy 1:15, Hebrews 7:25, James 5:15, 20, Exodus 15:20, Psalm 103:3, Psalm 147:3, Isaiah 30:26, Isaih 53:5, Matthew 8:7, 10:1, Mark 3:18, Matthew 10:8, Luke 9:2, 10:9, Galatians 5:1, Romans 8:2-4, Romans 6:18, 22-23, Romans 5:15-21, John 8:32, 36, Isaiah 49:6, Acts 13:47, 49, Romans 3:22-31, Matthew 25:33, Matthews 10:35, II Timothy 4:18, Romans 7:24, II Peter 2:9, Acts 4:30, John 4:47, Luke 5:17, Luke 4:18-19. Luke 6:7-10, Matthew 12:10-13, Luke 14:3, Matthew 13:15, John 12:40, Mark 3:2-5

Part CDLXXXV

Blessed Are The Poor In Spirit. Matthew 5:3

Blessed Means Happy

Poor means meek in spirit Poor means humble in spirit Poor means lowly in spirit Poor means quiet in spirit Read Matthew 5:3-12, Read also Mark 1:15

Jesus did not say "*rich*" in spirit. Jesus said "*poor*" in spirit.

1. Blessed are the poor in spirit to those who believe God's Ten Commandments that are still in good standard and rules today. Deuteronomy 10:16, 30:6, Jeremiah 4:4, Romans 2:29, Colossians 2:10, 11, Deuteronomy 30:11-14, Romans 10:6-8, James 2:10, Romans 14:5, Galatians 4:10-12, 3:19, 23-25, Colossians 2:16-17, Hebrews 10:1, 8:13, John 13:34, I Corinthians 9:20-21, Romans 3:31
2. Blessed are the poor in spirit to those who believe that Pentecost mean the Second Coming Christ. Jesus is coming again. See Acts 1:11, Revelation 3:11, Revelation 22:7, 12, 20. For the Jewish people's celebration of the feast meant for the slavery being freed from bondage after 400 years. Colossians 2:16-17, Leviticus 23:5-6. For us as Christian meant Jesus will come again to take us home to glory!!!
   I Thessalonians 4:13-18, Genesis 15:13, Acts 7:6
3.

   Blessed are the poor in spirit to those who believe this:
   Thank God for being our Heavenly Father. James 1:27, Ephesians 5:20 Thank God for Jesus. I Corinthians 15:57, I Thessalonians 5:18
   Thank God for the Holy Spirit. Ephesians 4:30
   Thank God for salvation. Psalm 68:19, Psalm 118:1, 29, II Thessalonians 2:13
   Thank God for the lover of my soul. Isaiah 61:10, Psalm 103:1, Psalm 139:14
   Thank God for our parents. Ephesians 6:1-4, Zephaniah 3:17
   Thank God for friends. Ecclesiastes 4:9-12, Proverbs 18:24, Proverbs 17:17, Romans 12:15, Proverbs 12:26, II Corinthians 1:4, Proverbs 20:6, Proverbs 22:11, Psalm 119:63, John 15:12-15, Luke 5:20, II Corinthians 7:1, II Peter 3:14
   Two are better than one, because they have a good return for their work: If one falls down, his friend can help him up." (NIV) Ecclesiastes 4:9-10

"I went out to find a friend,
But could not find one there.
I went out to **be** a friend,
And friends were everywhere!" (*Unknown*)

Thank God for family.

a. Acts 16:52, Genesis 2:24, Exodus 20:12,
b. Psalm 103:17, Psalm 127:3-5, Proverbs 1:8,
c. Romans 9:4, Ephesians 1:5, Ephesians 2:19,
d. Ephesians 3:14-15, Ephesians 6:1-2, Ephesians 6:4
e. Colossians 3:20, Ruth 1:14-22

4. Blessed are the poor in spirit to those who believe that "*education*" and "*philosophy*" send us *to hell*; "*but*" those who believe that "*church*" *send us to heaven* "*only*" "*if*" we *know Jesus as our Personal Lord and Savior Jesus Christ*. Read about Paul. Acts 9:1-20
5. Blessed are the poor in spirit to those who believe in the freedom of Justice, Equality and Liberty for all through Jesus Christ. John 8:36, Matthew 10:5-42, Acts 2:28-47, Acts 26:22-32, Romans 3:19-31, Romans 8:1-39 verse 32, I Corinthians 2:9-16, II Corinthians 11:1-7 verse 7, Revelation 21:1-7 verse 6, Revelation 22:1-21 verse 17
6. Blessed are the poor in spirit to those who believe that all people should know God. Psalm 46:10-11, Isaiah 19:21, Isaiah 52:6-7, Romans 10:15, Jeremiah 31:34, Hebrews 8:11, Ezekiel 34:30, Ezekiel 37:28, 39:23, Daniel 11:32, Hosea 2:20.
7. Blessed are the poor in spirit to those who believe: "*Changed*" by the Word; I Corinthians 15:44-58, "*Transformed*" by the Word; Romans 12:1-8 verse 2, "*Delivered*" by the Word, His Word, Christ's Word, God's Word through the Holy Spirit I Thessalonians 1:5-10, Colossians 1:1-20 verse 13-14, 19, His Word, Christ's Word; God's Word through the Holy Spirit.
8. Blessed are the poor in spirit to those who believe that "*Time*" and "*Chance*" happen to **all**." Ecclesiastes 9:11b
9. Blessed are the poor in spirit to those who believe that *home going* or *gone home* to be with the Lord or went home be with the Lord is *precious* in the *sight* of

the *Lord* is the *death of His saints.* Psalm 116:15, Psalm 49:8-9, John 14:1-4, I Thessalonians 4:13-17, Genesis 31:49, II Corinthians 5:5-8, II Timothy 4:6-8

10. Blessed are the poor in spirit to those who believe the Scripture: "*Thou hast The Word of Eternal Life.* And we believe (confirm) and are (being or begin aware of sure (trust) that *Thou are that Christ*, the *Son of the Living God.* John 6:68-69
11. Blessed are the poor in spirit to those who believe that where there is three, there is three in the Word of God namely; the Father, the Son (The Word) and the Holy Spirit; and those who are born of God; born of the Spirit; children of God. Genesis 1:1, John 1:1, John 1:12-14, John 3:3-8, I John 5:6-15
12. Blessed are the poor in spirit to those who believe The True Gospel, The Truth Gospel and The Real Living Gospel of Jesus Christ. I Corinthians 15:1-4

Part CDLXXXVI

Blessed Are The Poor In Spirit. Matthew 5:3

Blessed Means Happy

Poor means meek in spirit. Poor means humble in spirit. Poor means lowly in spirit. Poor means quiet in spirit. Read Matthew 5:3-12, Read also Mark 1:15

Jesus did not say "*rich*" in spirit. Jesus said "*poor*" in spirit.

1. Blessed are the poor in spirit to those who believe that the world need to stop their mouths and listen to God 's spoken word. Hebrews 11:3, Proverbs 12:6, Ephesians 4:29, James 2:5, Acts 17:11
2. Blessed are the poor in spirit to those who believe that when we see the cross, we see Jesus died for our sins, took our places and justified us through fiath. Acts 5:30, Acts 10:39, See Deuteronomy 21:23, Mark 15:42, Galatians 3:13, Acts 13:39, Romans 2:13, Romans 3:26, Romans 4:5, Read Acts 4:1-9 verse 2, 3, 5, 7 (Psalm 32:1), Romans 8:26-39 verse 33, 34, Galatians 3:8 (Genesis 12:3), the love of God which is in Christ Jesus our Lord. Romans 1:17, Habakkuk 2:4, Galatians 3:11, Hebrews 10:38, Romans 5:8-9
3. Blessed are the poor in spirit to those who believe Christ's coming: "The coming of the Lord draw night (near, coming to a close); Let us watch and be sober. I Peter 4:7, Romans 13:12, I Thessalonians 5:5-7, Zephaniah 1:14-16, Ephesians 5:16, Colossians 4:5
4. Blessed are the poor in spirit to those who this spiritual hymn: "Jesus, Jesus, *Jesus* How I *Trust Him*. How I've *proved Him ov'er*, and *ov'er*. *Jesus*, *Jesus*, *Precious Jesus*. Oh, *For Grace To Trust In Him More*." Ephesians 2:8-9
5. Blessed are the poor in spirit to those who *believe* and are *able to say*: "*Can I get a witness*? "*Can I have a witness*?" "*Do I have a witness*?" "*Do I get a witness*?" Genesis 4:4 (Hebrews 11:4), Genesis 31:44, 50, 52, Exodus 23:1, Leviticus 5:1, Numbers 5:11-22 verse 13, Number 35:29-30 verse 30, Deuteronomy 17:6-13 verse 6, Deuteronomy 19:15-21, Deuteronomy 31:19-21, 26, Joshua 22:27-28, 33-34, Joshua 24:26-27, Ruth 4:9-11, I Samuel 12:5-6, Job 16:19-21 verse 19, Job 29:8-16 verse 11, Psalm 89:33-37 verse 37, Proverbs 14:5, 25, Proverbs 24:28, Isaiah 8:1-4 verse 2, Isaiah 19:20-22 verse 20, Isaiah 43:1-28 verse

8-12, Isaiah 44:1-28 verse 8, 9, Isaiah 55:1-9 verse 4, Jeremiah 29:23, Jeremiah 31:33, Jeremiah 32:10-12, 25-44 verse 25, 44, Jeremiah 42:1-6 verse5, Hosea 2:6, Micah 1:1-7 verse 2, Malachi 2:14-17 verse 14, Malachi 3:5-18 verse 5, Matthew 18:15-20 verse 16, Matthew 24:14, Matthew 26:60-66 verse 60, 65, Mark 14:55-64 verse 55-56, 59, Luke 22:65-71 verse 71, Luke 24:46-53 verse 48, John 1:7, John 3:1-21 verse 11, John 5:30-40, Acts 1:8, Acts 2:28-47 verse 32, Acts 3:13-26 verse 15, Acts 4:33, Acts 5:29-42 verse 32, Acts 7:44-60 verse 44, 58, Acts 10:25-48 verse 39, 41, 43, Acts 13:29-52 verse 31, Acts 14:17, Acts 26:16, Romans 1:9, Romans 9:1-5 verse 1, II Corinthians 13:1-14 verse 1, I Thessalonians 2:1-20 verse 10, I Timothy 5:19-21 verse 19, I Timothy 6:11-21 verse 12-13, II Timothy 2:1-3 verse 2, Hebrews 2:1-18 verse 14, Hebrews 10:15-27 verse 15-16, Hebrews 10:28-31, Hebrews 11:4 (Genesis 4:4), Hebrews 12:1-8, I Peter 5:1-14 verse 1, I John 5:9-16 verse 9-10, Revelation 1:5-11, 18-20 verse 5, Revelation 3:11-14 verse 14, Revelation 20:1-15 verse 4

6. Blessed are the poor in spirit to those who believe that the Lord Jesus Christ is the Great I Am. God, who is the Great, **is that Great I Am**. Exodus 3:13
7. Blessed are the poor in spirit to those who believe that God has given *Jesus all things into His hands. Jesus' hands.* See Matthew 3:17, John 3:35-36, I John 2:20-25, I John 5:1-15 verse 12, John 5:27, I John 5:18-21
8. Blessed are the poor in spirit to those who believe that God is:" I AM." Exodus 3:13-15
9. Blessed are the poor in spirit to those who believe that Jesus is that "Bread Of Life". John 6:35
10. Blessed are the poor in spirit to those who believe that Jesus is the "Light of the world." John 8:12
11. Blessed are the poor in spirit to those who believe that Jesus is the "Door of the Sheep." John 10:7
12. Blessed are the poor in spirit to those who believe that Jesus is the "Good Shepherd." John 10:11

Part CDLXXXVII

Blessed Are The Poor In Spirit. Matthew 5:3

Blessed Means Happy

Poor means meek in spirit. Poor means humble in spirit. Poor means lowly in spirit. Poor means quiet in spirit. Read Matthew 5:3-12, Read also Mark 1:15

Jesus did not say "*rich*" in spirit. Jesus said "*poor*" in spirit.

1. Blessed are the poor in spirit to those who believe that Jesus is the "Resurrection" John 11:5
2. Blessed are the poor in spirit to those who believe that Jesus is the "Way." John 14:6
3. Blessed are the poor in spirit to those who believe that Jesus is the "Truth" John 14:6
4. Blessed are the poor in spirit to those who believe that Jesus is the "Life". John 14:6
5. Blessed are the poor in spirit to those who believe that Jesus is the "True Vine." John 15:1
6. Blessed are the poor in spirit to those who believe that Jesu is the "First and the Last". Revelation 1:17
7. Blessed are the poor in spirit to those who believe that the Lord Jesus Christ is "the eternal". John 8:56-58
8. Blessed are the poor in spirit to those who believe the Scripture: "Verily, verily I say unto you, "Before Abraham was, I am!" John 8:56-58
9. Blessed are the poor in spirit to those who believe that Christ is very near than we ever believe. Revelation 3:11, Revelation 16:15, Revelation 22:7, 12, 20
10. Blessed are the poor in spirit to those who believe the scripture: "Thy testimonies are very sure: holiness becometh thine house, O Lord, for ever." Psalm 93:5
11. Blessed are the poor in spirit to those who believe in this scripture: "And her merchandise and her hire shall be holiness to the Lord: it shall not be treasured nor laid up; for her merchandise shall be for them that dwell before the Lord, to eat sufficiently, and for durable clothing." Isaiah 23:18

12. Blessed are the poor in spirit to those who believe that when the Jews eat the Passover, they remember God bringing them out of Egypt and to point to His coming. Matthew 3:13-17, Mark 1:9-11, luke 2:68-80, John 1:35-51

Part CDLXXXVIII

Blessed Are The Poor In Spirit. Matthew 5:3

Blessed Means Happy

Poor means meek in spirit Poor means humble in spirit Poor means lowly in spirit Poor means quiet in spirit Read Matthew 5:3-12, Read also Mark 1:15

Jesus did not say "*rich*" in spirit. Jesus said "*poor*" in spirit.

1. Blessed are the poor in spirit to those who believe that we as Christian Passover and remember Calvary, how Jesus died and saved us, and we look forward to His coming again. Acts 1:11, I Thessalonians 4:13-18, Revelation 3:11, Revelation 16:15, Revelation 22:7, 12, 20, Amos 4:12
2. Blessed are the poor in spirit to those who believe that Jesus did *appear* as *His first Coming* to the nation of Israel, the Jewish People. John 1:35-51, Luke 2:68-80, Mark 1:9-11, Matthew 3:13-17
3. Blessed are the poor in spirit to those who believe; *never to forget* that "*the day of Pentecost* was fully *come*; that the *sound of Pentecost can be heard*;" that "*the wind of Pentecost is blowing*" and that "*the fire of Pentecost falling until Christ's Return.* Acts 2:2a, Acts 2: 2b, Acts 2: 3, Revelation 3:11, Revelation 22:7, 12, 20
4. Blessed are the poor in spirit to those who believe and view the *apparent imminent coming of our Blessed Redeemer.* Revelation 3:11, Revelation 16:15, Revelation 22:7, 12, 22.
5. Blessed are the poor in spirit to those who believe that *the Power of the Blood of Jesus came to save.* Romans 1:16, John 1:13, Romans 5:9
6. Blessed are the poor in spirit to those who believe in the *Everlasting Gospel of Jesus Christ.* Revelation 1:1, John 3:16, John 20:31, John 1:14
7. Blessed are the poor in spirit to those who believe *for the laboreres for the harvest field for the fields are now white unto the harvest.* John 4:35, John 14:1-3, I Corinthians 3:5-9, Exodus 23:16
8. Blessed are the poor in spirit to those who believe that we do not want to die a fool, but prosperity and wise and favor in God's Kingdom to Heaven to live with Him for ever. Romans 10:1-21

9. Blessed are the poor in spirit to those who believe in the gifts of God's salvation, God's Healing, God's sanctification, God's Second Coming of Christ, God's Baptism of the Holy Spirit, the kingdom of God's children, God's family, God's righteousness, God's faith, God's power to deliver us from sin and God's power to heal us from sickness or even from death and hell. Romans 6:23, Ephesians 4:5, 8, Exodus 15:26, Psalm 135:14, Hebrews 10:29-39, Hebrews 2:11, 10:10, 14, II Timothy 2:21, Acts 26:18, John 10:36, 17:19, Romans 15:16, I Corinthians 1:2, 6:11, I Timothy 4:5, Matthew 8:7, Philippians 4:13, James 5:13-15, Isaiah 53:5, I Peter 2:24, Psalm 103:1-5, I Corinthians 1:30, I Thessalonians 4:3, II Thessalonians 2:13, I Peter 1:2, Revelation 22:20, Luke 24:39, Acts 1:4-8, Acts 2:1-4, Acts 11:16, John 14:1-6, Ephesians 3:15, Romans 8:2, I Thessalonians 1:10, Romans 4:25, Romans 5:16, 18, Galatians 3:11, Hebrews 10:38, Romans 1:17, Habakkuk 2:4, Romans 3:26, Romans 8:33, Titus 3:7
10. Blessed are the poor in spirit to those who believe that the recipient of the Baptism of the Spirit according to Acts 2:4 is speaking in tongues. Acts 2:4
11. Blessed are the poor in spirit to those who search for the evidence of Spirit Baptism as seen in Acts scriptural. Acts 2:4
12. Blessed are the poor in spirit to those who believe in carrying out the message of the Holy Spirit Baptism, God's Holy Spirit Baptism to His born-again children of God to a lost and dying world. Matthew 3:2-12, John 3:5, John 3:16, Psalm 58:3, Romans 8:13, II Corinthians 4:10, Luke 9:23. Romans 6:11-13, Philippians 2:5

Part CDLXXXIX

Blessed Are The Poor In Spirit. Matthew 5:3

Blessed Means Happy

Poor means meek in spirit. Poor means humble in spirit. Poor means lowly in spirit. Poor means quiet in spirit. Read Matthew 5:3-12, Read also Mark 1:15

Jesus did not say "*rich*" in spirit. Jesus said "*poor*" in spirit.

1. Blessed are the poor in spirit to those who believe that Pentecostal fire that never burn out get us ready for the Imminent Return of Christ. Amos 4:12, I Thessalonians 4:13-5:22, Revelation 3:11, Revelation 22:7, 12, 20
2. Blessed are the poor in spirit to those who believe that without Pentecost mentioning in the Bible, there would be no true identification of color, race, creed amd background and cultural people. Acts 2:1-12 verse 4
3. Blessed are the poor in spirit to those who believe that without Pentecost, there would be no mention of the Holy Spirit, or Holy Spirit Baptism or Spirit Baptism in the Bible, but to remain the same in the old root of these churches with each Bible in God's name call tabernacle a place of worship to God, the Father who created us in His image made us male and female in His likeness. Acts 2:1-12 verse 4, and Genesis 1:26-28.
4. Blessed are the poor in spirit to those who believe that with God's Help, God's Holy Spirit, the Pentecostal Spirit Baptism drive out the desire of the Jim Crow Law, the Ku Klux Klan the slavery law and the beliefs call "liars" like as of the Pharaoh's land that drove God's people, Israel out of the land of Egypt, out of bondage, out of slavery into the Promised Land for all pople with justice, equally and the prosperity of happiness to find Jesus Christ as Savior and Lord and the Imminent Return of Christ. Revelation 3:11, Revelation 22:7, 12, 20, Amos 4:12
5. Blessed are the poor in spirit to those who believe that the same God has never change; only we have changed; we have to change to allow the Holy Spirit to take control of our daily life in Christ Jesus. Galatians 5:22-23, I Corinthians 2:15, Acts 16:7, Hebrews 13:8

6. Blessed are the poor in spirit to those who believe that the presence of the Lord seem so real to us in our lives.I Thessalonians 2:19-20, Hebrews 9:24-28
7. Blessed are the poor in spirit to those who believe in one whole body in Christ Jesus as one that others may believe. Isaiah 59:19b
8. Blessed are the poor in spirit to those who believe that the color line was broken at Azusa Street Mission with God's Holy Spirit Baptism against the Ku Klux Klan, the Jim Crow law and the slavery law. Galatians 3:28 (no Jews, no Gentiles, bond a free, melt of the race, the breaking down of racial prejudice, with the blood of Jesus washed away the human races or the color line of cultural people. With Christ cleaning blood. I John 1:7, Titus 3:4-7, Ephesians 2:12-22
9. Blessed are the poor in spirit to those who believe that God through the Holy Spirit speak all the languages of the world through God's children. Genesis 11:1-9, Acts 2:4, Romans 8:14, John 1:12, Galatians 3:26, Romans 8:16 even though deaf mute language, See Moses' mouth where God say: "Who made the deaf to speak?" Exodus 4:11
10. Blessed are the poor in spirit to those who believe that Pentecostal Movement is not any denomination or sect because Pentecostal Movement by the power of God through Jesus Christ works outside, drawing all together in one body of love, one church and one body of Christ. Colossians 2:2, Romans 8:16 draw all men to Himself, no Jews, no Gentiles, bond or free, one body, one Spirit, one baptism. Ephesians 4:4-6, 11-13, I Corinthians 12:13, Galatians 3:28
11. Blessed are the poor in spirit to those who believe in honor the Holy Spirit because Christ sent the Holy Spirit to the earth. I Corinthians 12:3
12. Blessed are the poor in spirit to those who believe that the gift of languages is given with the commission, "Go ye into all the world and preach the gospel to every creature. Mark 15:16

Part CDXC

Blessed Are The Poor In Spirit. Matthew 5:3

Blessed Means Happy

Poor means meek in spirit. Poor means humble in spirit. Poor means lowly in spirit. Poor means quiet in spirit. Read Matthew 5:3-12, Read also Mark 1:15

Jesus did not say "*rich*" in spirit. Jesus said "*poor*" in spirit.

1. Blessed are the poor in spirit to those who believe that every mouth may be stopped and that all the world (and sad people who are not born again, born of the Spirit of God) may become guilty (accountability) before God. Romans 3:19
2. Blessed are the poor in spirit to those who *believe in the covenant of the children through Jesus Christ.* Exodus 24:5, Hebrews 9:14, 18-20, Matthew 5:17, John 7:37
3. Blessed are the poor in spirit to those who believe that a man or a husband in adultery or a woman or wife in adultery, cannot enter Christ's Kindom "*without confessing*" and "*forsaking*" his/her sin; "*without repenting*" his/her sin. See Isaiah 55:7 and Galatians 5:19-21
4. Blessed are the poor in spirit to those whose *feet shed with the preparation of the gospel of peace.* Ephesians 6:15, Isaiah 52:7, Romans 10:15
5. Blessed are the poor in spirit to those who believe the scriptures concerning the dead body: "We brought nothing into the world, and it is certain we can carry nothing out." The Lord gave and the Lord hath taken away; blessed be the name of the Lord. I Timothy 6:7 and Job 1:21
6. Blessed are the poor in spirit those who believe that the Pentecostal Revival is to give all an opportunity to be saved. Acts 16:31
7. Blessed are the poor in spirit to those who believe this scripture of Psalm 39:1-13 is for unsaved loved ones who know nothing that thy might find salvation: "I said, I will take heed to my ways, that I sin not with my tongue: I will keep my mouth with a bridle, while the wicked is before me." Psalm 39:1
8. Blessed are the poor in spirit to those who believe this scripture of Psalm 39:1-13 is for unsaved loved ones who know nothing that thy might find salvation: "I

was dumb with silence, I held my peace, even from good; and my sorrow was stirred." Psalm 39:2

9. Blessed are the poor in spirit to those who believe this scripture of Psalm 39:1-13 is for unsaved loved ones who know nothing that thy might find salvation: "My heart was hot within me, while I was musing the fire burned: then spake I with my tongue," Psalm 39:3
10. Blessed are the poor in spirit to those who believe this scripture of Psalm 39:1-13 is for unsaved loved ones who know nothing that thy might find salvation: "Lord, make me to know mine end, and the measure of my days, what it is: that I may know how frail I am." Psalm 39:4
11. Blessed are the poor in spirit to those who believe this scripture of Psalm 39:1-13 is for unsaved loved ones who know nothing that thy might find salvation: "Behold, thou hast made my days as an hand breadth; and mine age is as nothing before thee: verily every man at his best state is altogether vanity. Selah." Psalm 39:5
12. Blessed are the poor in spirit to those who believe this scripture of Psalm 39:1-13 is for unsaved loved ones who know nothing that thy might find salvation: "Surely every man walketh in a vain shew: surely they are disquieted in vain: he heapeth up riches, and knoweth not who shall gather them." Psalm 39:6

PART CDXCI

Blessed Are The Poor In Spirit. Matthew 5:3

Blessed Means Happy

Poor means meek in spirit. Poor means humble in spirit. Poor means lowly in spirit. Poor means quiet in spirit. Read Matthew 5:3-12, Read also Mark 1:15

Jesus did not say "*rich*" in spirit. Jesus said "*poor*" in spirit.

1. Blessed are the poor in spirit to those who believe this scripture of Psalm 39:1-13 is for unsaved loved ones who know nothing that thy might find salvation: "And now, Lord, what wait I for? My hope is in thee." Psalm 39:7
2. Blessed are the poor in spirit to those who believe this scripture of Psalm 39:1-13 is for unsaved loved ones who know nothing that thy might find salvation: "Deliver me from all my transgressions: make me not the reproach of the foolish." Psalm 39:8
3. Blessed are the poor in spirit to those who believe this scripture of Psalm 39:1-13 is for unsaved loved ones who know nothing that thy might find salvation: "I was dumb, I opened not my mouth; because thou didst it." Psalm 39:9
4. Blessed are the poor in spirit to those who believe this scripture of Psalm 39:1-13 is for unsaved loved ones who know nothing that thy might find salvation: "Remove thy stroke away from me: I am consumed by the blow of thine hand." Psalm 39:10
5. Blessed are the poor in spirit to those who believe this scripture of Psalm 39:1-13 is for unsaved loved ones who know nothing that thy might find salvation: "When thou with rebukes dost correct man for iniquity, thou makest his beauty to consume away like a moth: surely every man is vanity. Selah." Psalm 39:11
6. Blessed are the poor in spirit to those who believe this scripture of Psalm 39:1-13 is for unsaved loved ones who know nothing that thy might find salvation: "Hear my prayer, O Lord, and give ear unto my cry; hold not thy peace at my tears: for I am a stranger with thee, and a sojourner, as all my fathers were." Psalm 39:12
7. Blessed are the poor in spirit to those who believe this scripture of Psalm 39:1-13 is for unsaved loved ones who know nothing that thy might find salvation: "O

spare me, that I may recover strength, before I go hence, and be no more.: Psalm 39:13

8. Blessed are the poor in spirit to those who believe *in the wake up call of hearing of the Pentecostal Power of the Baptism in the Holy Spirit or Spirit Baptism Acts 2:1-12 verse 4*
9. Blessed are the poor in spirit to those who believe, understand, and realize in recognizing as sinners, *in need of salvation and unable to save ourselves and by faith had then seen Calvary and to trust the finished work of Christ,* John 19:30 Ephesians 2:4-7, James 2:19-26, Ephesians 2:2, *to experience the new birth. John 3:6-7 and to enter into newness of life.* Romans 6:4, I Peter 1:23
10. Blessed are the poor in spirit to those who believe that the message of Christ become one of salvation by grace—Ephesians 2:8 and the experience of conversion. Acts 9:1, Acts 22:3-16, Acts 26:2-18, Matthew 7:21-23, Romans 3:23, Romans 6:23, John 16:17
11. Blessed are the poor in spirit to those who believe and are able to say: "The Lord bless thee (you) and keep thee (you). Numbers 6:22-27
12. Blessed are the poor in spirit to those who believe that men and women are converted, sin's power broken and lives transformed by grace Romans 5:20 and Ephesians 2:5, 8-9, James 5:16

Part CDXCII

Blessed Are The Poor In Spirit. Matthew 5:3

Blessed Means Happy

Poor means meek in spirit. Poor means humble in spirit. Poor means lowly in spirit. Poor means quiet in spirit. Read Matthew 5:3-12, Read also Mark 1:15

Jesus did not say "*rich*" in spirit. Jesus said "*poor*" in spirit.

1. Blessed are the poor in spirit to those who believe in teaching and preaching and exhorting the doctrine of the messenger of the cross, the gospel of Jesus Christ. II Timothy 4:2, I Corinthians 1:18, 21-23, Acts 4:12, I Corinthians 2:2, I Timothy 6:3
2. Blessed are the poor in spirit to those who believe that *the Christian foundation is this "Christ died for our sins."* Romans 4:25, I Peter 3:18, I Corinthians 15:1-4, Isaiah 53:5, I Peter 2:24, Romans 14:9
3. Blessed are the poor in spirit to those who believe that the charismatic gifts of the Holy Spirit mean the soon coming of the Savior. Acts 1:11, Revelation 3:11, Revelation 16:15, Revelation 22:7, 12, 13, 22
4. Blessed are the poor in spirit to those who believe the Baptism of the Holy Spirit mean: "The Lord will speak to His people." Psalm 85:8, Isaiah 55:11, II Timothy 3:16-17
5. Blessed are the poor in spirit to those who believe that the Baptism of the Holy Spirit mean: "God will pour out His Spirit upon all flesh." Joel 2:28-29, Acts 2:16, 18, Joel 2:32, Romans 10:13
6. Blessed are the poor in spirit to those who believe that the Christianity messages mean the Baptism of the Holy Spirit to a dying world as well as for the children of God and the return of Christ. Acts 1:4, 5, 8, 11, Acts 2:1-47, I Thessalonians 4:13-18, Revelation 3:11, Revelation 16:15, Revelation 22:7, 12, 13, 22
7. Blessed are the poor in spirit to those who believe that the baptism in the Holy Spirit is through prayer for nightly revival that men, women and children should be saved; be filled with the Holy Spirit, called to the mission field; and the call of God in the ministry. Acts 2:39, Acts 4:12, Acts 16:30, Acts 2:38, Acts 2:4, Ephesians 5:18, Romans 11:29, Compare to I Samuel 3:!-11

8. Blessed are the poor in spirit to those who believe that Baptism in the Holy Spirit is speaking with sign language to get deaf people around the world to be saved or accept Jesus Christ as personal Savior and Lord. Acts 1:4, 5, 8, Acts 2:1-47 verse 11, 17-18, 37-39, Exodus 4:11-12, Isaiah 29:18
9. Blessed are the poor in spirit to those who believe and are able to say: "Because of the love of God is shed abroad in our hearts by the Holy Ghost which is given unto us. Romans 5:5 Romans 8:16
10. Blessed are the poor in spirit to those who believe that Pentecostal Spirit Baptism serve as an evidence of the Spirit's Presence. Acts 2:1-47
11. Blessed are the poor in spirit to those who believe that a religious experience or religious conviction would cause us to become a conversion or causes us to get repentance or cause us to become regeneration or even to get saved or to accept Christ as Savior through salvation; it is called a religious experience or sincerely believing in heart by faith. Habakkuk 2:4, Romans 1:17, Galatians 3:11, Hebrews 10:38
12. Blessed are the poor in spirit to those who believe that the modern outpouring as on the Day of Pentecost recorded in Acts 2 indicated the soon return of Jesus Christ. Acts 1:11, I Thessalonians 4:13-18, Revelation 3:11, Revelation 16:15, Revelation 22:7, 12, 13, 16, 20. See Amos 4:12, Revelation 1:7

PART CDXCIII

Blessed Are The Poor In Spirit. Matthew 5:3

Blessed Means Happy

Poor means meek in spirit. Poor means humble in spirit. Poor means lowly in spirit. Poor means quiet in spirit. Read Matthew 5:3-12, Read also Mark 1:15

Jesus did not say "*rich*" in spirit. Jesus said "*poor*" in spirit.

1. Blessed are the poor in spirit to those who believe that *salvation by faith*—Romans, Ephesians 2:8, *healing by faith, laying on of hands and prayer*—Mark 16:18, Mark 5:23, James 5:14-16 *sactification by faith John17:17*; *coming* (pre-millennium) *of Christ*—I Thessalonians 4:16-17, Revelation 1:7, Revelation 3:11, Revelation 16:15, Revelation 22:7, 12, 13, 16, 20; (and) the *baptism of the Holy Spirit, Acts 1:4, 5, 8*
2. Blessed are the poor in spirit to those who believe *in preaching the Restoration of the Birthplace to It's Rightful Heirs, which is the Bible evidence of baptism with the Holy Ghost.* Acts 2:4, Read Acts 2:1-47
3. Blessed are the poor in spirit to those who believe that the *speaking in tongues was the Bible Evidence of the baptism with the Spirit and the gift of tongues.* Acts 2:4, Acts 2:1-47, Acts 10:44-46, Acts 19:1-7, I Corinthians 14:21, Hebrews 1:5, I Corinthians 12:8-10
4. Blessed are the poor in spirit to those who believe that the Presence of the Holy Spirit is integral a part of the regeneration. Titus 3:5
5. Blessed are the poor in spirit to those who believe that the presence of the Holy Spirit is integral, part of being born of the Spirit of God. John 3:5, Isaiah 7:14, Matthew 1:18-25
6. Blessed are the poor in spirit to those who believe that the presence of the Holy Spirit is integral part of being born again; a child of God. I Peter 1:3, 23, I John 3:9, James 1:18
7. Blessed are the poor in spirit to those who believe that the presence of the Holy Spirit is integral part of indwelling by the Spirit of God. Romans 8:9, I Corinthians 3:16, Judges 3:10

8. Blessed are the poor in spirit to those who believe that the presence of the Holy Spirit is an integral part of being filled with the Holy Spirit. Ephesians 5:18, Acts 10:38, Acts 7:55, Acts 2:3-4
9. Blessed are the poor in spirit to those who believe that the presence of the Holy Spirit is an integral part of daily growing in grace and in the knowledge of our Lord and Savior, Jesus Christ. II Peter 3:17-18
10. Blessed are the poor in spirit to those who believe that the presence of the Holy Spirit is similar being converted. Acts 3:19
11. Blessed are the poor in spirit to those who believe that every mouth may be stopped and all the world (unsaved—people, who are not born again) may become guilty (accountability) before God. Romans 3:19
12. Blessed are the poor in spirit to those who believe that while Peter was preaching to the Corenilus and his host companion, there was an interruption in the service; Let the Holy Spirit have His way as they spoke in tongues. What can Peter do to stop the interruption in the service? Nothing!!! See Acts 11:17 in Peter's statement. Let the Holy Spirit have His way as they spoke in tongues. Holy Spirit fell on all who heard the word (not Peter's best sermon, but God's own word: Let the Holy Spirit have His way as they spoke in tongue. Acts 10:34-43, and 44. See also Acts 11:15

Part CDXCIV

Blessed Are The Poor In Spirit. Matthew 5:3

Blessed Means Happy

Poor means meek in spirit. Poor means humble in spirit. Poor means lowly in spirit. Poor means quiet in spirit. Read Matthew 5:3-12, Read also Mark 1:15

Jesus did not say "*rich*" in spirit. Jesus said "*poor*" in spirit.

1. Blessed are the poor in spirit to those who believe that the evidence is not the most least of the tongues, but the evidence is about the Holy Spirit Gift or the Spirit was coming toward them as the Spirit gave them utterance Acts 2:4 and the gift of the Holy Spirit. Acts 2:38.
2. Blessed are the poor in spirit to those who believe that the Spirit Himself need no evidence to indicate initial evidence, but rather we confess Jesus Christ as our personal Lord and Savior by our witness with our Spirit that we are the children of God. Romans 8:16
3. Blessed are the poor in spirit to those who believe and accept that embraced the message of the Famous Azusa Street Mission and it's revival according to the pattern of the Book of Acts; that original happened on the breakout event history in 1908; there are tiding the Fire Baptized Holiness Church, the Church of God In Christ, the Church of God (Cleveland, Tennessee) and the Pentecostal Holiness Church. Six years later in 1914, the Assemblies of God was formed after the fellowship and with the Church of God In Christ being credible and final along side was the Pentecostal Free Will Baptist Church that came into existence a few years later. Pattern of the Book of Acrs and Acts 2:4
4. Blessed are the poor in spirit to those who believe that the Great Whte Throne Judgment is for unpardonable sin to those who have rejected Jesus Christ as personal Savior and Lord as a result of the Holy Spirit would not be forgiven when sinners die who have never received Jesus Christ as personal Savior and Lord, who have never received forgiveness of sin and go on the way to hell judgment, however, we do not have the scriptural authority for telling them that God will never forgive them. Only God know when they cross the line. Proverbs 1:23-33, Isaiah 55:6-7, John 12:37-43. Please accept Christ today before it is too late. II Corinthians 6:1-2 verse 2

5. Blessed are the poor in spirit to those who believe that salvation free; no costly. Acts 16:31, Romans 10:13, Ephesians 2:8-10, Romans 1:17, Romans 5:1
6. Blessed are the poor in spirit to those who believe in going back to the Bible; the old landmark of God's teaching and Holiness. II Peter 1:20
7. Blessed are the poor in spirit to those who believe Pentecost mean speak with tongues according to Acts 2:4, Mark 16:18, 10:44-46, Acts 19:6-7
8. Blessed are the poor in spirit to those who believe the apostolic lines or pattern signs, wonders and mighty deeds, to empower those working toward world evangelism nation, the need to have the restoration of New Testament power as the restoration of the gift of tongues, the recovery of an ability to speak languages of the world without prior knowledge or study, under the direct inspiration of the Holy Spirit and for the ultimate evangeliztion of the world. Acts 2:1-47, Acts 1:4, 5, 8, Mark 16:18
9. Blessed are the poor in spirit to those who believe in the Restoration of Religion's Birthplace to Its Rightful Heirs." Mark 16:18, Acts 2:4
10. Blessed are the poor in spirit to those who believe would expect to live up to what the Bible teaches on God's Holiness include the pattern of the Book of Acts with the inspiration of the Baptism of the Holy Spirit with speaking in tongues. Zechariah 14:20, Matthew 28:18-20, Mark 16:18, Matthew 3:11, Mark 1:8, Luke 3:33, John 1:33, Luke 24:49, Acts 1:4, 5, 8, Acts 2:1-4, Acts 2:1-47, Acts 10:44-48, Acts 19:1-6, Joel 2:28-32
11. Blessed are the poor in spirit to those who believe that none of us as human beings can match the Holy Spirit as a person and human being. *No man know the Spirit except the Holy Spirit.* I Corinthians 12:3, I Corinthians 2:11, I Peter 1:20-21, Luke 11:13
12. Blessed are the poor in spirit to those who believe that Acts in the Bible is a wake up call because of the mighty baptism of the Holy Spirit or the day of Pentecost. Acts 2:1-42, 2:1-47, Acts 8:4-24, Acts 10:44-48, Acts 11:15-18, Acts 19:1-7

Part CDXCV

Blessed Are The Poor In Spirit. Matthew 5:3

Blessed Means Happy

Poor means meek in spirit. Poor means humble in spirit. Poor means lowly in spirit. Poor means quiet in spirit. Read Matthew 5:3-12, Read also Mark 1:15

Jesus did not say "*rich*" in spirit. Jesus said "*poor*" in spirit.

1. Blessed are the poor in spirit to those who believe, understand and realize that a conversion is a relationship with God toward Jesus Christ in faith and that being baptized in the Holy Spirit is a powerful for the purpose for service through mighty powerful ministry. Matthew 3:2, Acts 2: Matthew 4:17, Acts 1:4, 5, 8, and See Acts 2:1-12, and namely Acts 2:4, Acts 10:45-47, Acts 19:1-7
2. Blessed are the poor in spirit to those who believe that the Baptism of the Holy Spirit is to give empower for service in ministry. Luke 24:49
3. Blessed are the poor in spirit to those who believe and are able to say: "*If there is "no manifestation of the Spirit" with tongues before Acts 2:4* then there is *no baptism of the Holy Spirit or Spirit Baptism* "*except*" *Mark 16:17 which we do not understand what Jesus meant when He said: "They will speak with new tongues."* Also Acts 1:4, 5, 8 when the twelve disciples did not know; did not understand; or did not know or did not understand *what Jesus meant* "*until*" it *reached Acts 2:4*. "And they were all filled with the Holy Ghost and began to *speak with tongues as the Spirit gave them utterance*. I once to my professor: If it is not for tongues, how will I get the baptism of the Holy Spirit?"
4. Blessed are the poor in spirit to those who believe and saw that God's people were *called Christians; Pentecostal Christians; Jerusalem Christians; Gentiles Christians; Jewish Christians; Samaria Christians; Ephesus Chrisitians; Galatians Christians; Corinthians Christians; Romans Christians; Philippians Christians; Hebrews Christians; Thessalonians Christians; Colossians Christians; The Acts of the Christians;* and the *Christians Believers, Charismatic Christians; Christian Spirituality in Asia Minor as new community of Christians.* Acts 2:1-47, Acts 8:14-19, Acts 10:44-48, Acts 19:1-7, Romans 1:, I Corinthians 1:1, Galatians 1:1

5. Blessed are the poor in spirit to those who believe that God's children who are called Christians may understand the wisdom of God, but the listeners may not understand unless it is made by the interpretation by the manifestation of the Spirit. I Corinthians 14:5, 12-13
6. Blessed are the poor in spirit to those who believe that outsiders as well as unbelievers thought that God's children were mad at them, they (God's children) were not. I Corinthians 14:23
7. Blessed are the poor in spirit to those who believe that the *Bible stand for the restoration of the faith "once delivered unto the saints."* Jude 3
8. Blessed are the poor in spirit to those who believe that one of God's children, Enoch, the seventh of Adam's generation, prophesied; was right and correct saying that: "Behold, the Lord cometh with ten thousand of his saints to excute judgment, to convince all that are ungodly (unbelievers, had not been born again, not children of God) that had spoken against the Lord. Jude 14-15. Read Amos 4:12, I Thessalonians 4:13-18, Revelation 3:11, Revelation 16:15, Revelation 22:7, 12, 13, 16, 20, Acts 1:11
9. Blessed are the poor in spirit to those who believe "*the manifestation of the Spirit" in Jerusalem at Pentecost.* Acts 2:1-47 verse 4
10. Blessed are the poor in spirit to those who believe "*the manifestation of the Spirit" in Samaria.* Acts 8:14-19 verse 15, 17 {does not mention speaking with tongues, however does mention might receive and laid hands on}
11. Blessed are the poor in spirit to those who believe "*the manifestation of the Spirit" in the conversion of the Gentile Cornelius.* Acts 10:44-48 verse 46
12. Blessed are the poor in spirit to those who believe "*the manifestation of the Spirit" in Ephesus.* Acts 19:1-7 *verse 6*

Part CDXCVI

Blessed Are The Poor In Spirit. Matthew 5:3

Blessed Means Happy

Poor means meek in spirit Poor means humble in spirit Poor means lowly in spirit Poor means quiet in spirit Read Matthew 5:3-12, Read also Mark 1:15

Jesus did not say "*rich*" in spirit. Jesus said "*poor*" in spirit.

1. Blessed are the poor in spirit to those who believe that the gift with the Spirit mean "being filled," being baptized with the Spirit, included with power from on high, receiving the Holy Spirit, receiving the gift of the Holy Spirit, filled with the Spirit. Luke 24:49, Acts 1:5, Acts 1:8, Acts 2:4, Acts 2:38, Ephesians 5:18
2. Blessed are the poor in spirit to those who believe Christ's statement: "I came not to bring peace, but a sward. Matthew 10:34
3. Blessed are the poor in spirit to those who believe that God hates sin but God is love. I John 4:8, John 3:16. Read I John 4:8-21. Read more on I John 4:1-21, I John 1:1-10, I John 2:1-29, I John 3:1-24, I John 5:1-21
4. Blessed are the poor in spirit to those who believe that salvation is by grace and not by our own works. Ephesians 2:5, 8-10
5. Blessed are the poor in spirit to those who believe that the just shall live by faith and not by works of the law: Romans 1:17, Ephesians 2:5, 8-9
6. Blessed are the poor in spirit to those who believe that the Holy Spirit of God as the Baptism of the Holy Spirit brought the world the genuine faith in Jesus. John 20:30-31, John 2:11, John 4:54, John 6:26
7. Blessed are the poor in spirit to those who believe how amazement God can do, can perform, can heal, can help us out, can handle for us against the power of the enemy and can keep His promise of faith because He first promise faithfully and love us and ought to love Him back. We need to know what God's Love is; Not by what Love itself has to do with it!!! Jeremiah 31:3, John 3:16, Galatians 2:20, I John 4:19

8. Blessed are the poor in spirit to those who believe that the Bible itself is very inspiration because it is very positive; it is very good news; it is very real because the finger of God wrote the written Word Himself because He first love us indeed. John 3:16, II Timothy 3:16, Genesis 1:1, John 1:1, I John 4:10, 19, Jeremiah 31:3, Revelation 3:9, Romans 9:13-15, Exodus 33:19, Malachi 1:2, John 13:34-35, John 15:12, Jeremiah 2:25, Isaiah 43:4, Acts 18:10, Exodus 20:6-7, Deuteronomy 5:10, John 8:42, John 10:14-18, John 14:15, 23, Galatians 2:20
9. Blessed are the poor in spirit to those who are able to say: "*God is a Good God. God is Good all the time.*" His mercy endured forever. Psalm 86:56, Psalm 100:5, I Peter 2:3, Psalm 34:8, Psalm 106:1, 107:1, Psalm 118:1, 29, Psalm 135:3, 136:1, Psalm 145:9, Psalm 136:15, 16, 26, Psalm 138:8, Jeremiah 33:11, John 6:27
10. Blessed are the poor in spirit to those who believe that God has indeed spoken through many signs include earthquake. Geneses 6: 11-22, Genesis 7:1-24, Matthew 24:37-39
11. Blessed are the poor in spirit to those who believe that the manifestation of the Holy Spirit is as a clear sign that Jesus would about to return to the earth; He is coming soon. Revelation 22:20
12. Blessed are the poor in spirit to those who believe we are in the center of God's will because He has called us. I Thessalonians 1:23-25, Jeremiah 33:3, I Thessalonians 4:3-4, II Thessalonians 2:13, I Peter 1:2

Part CDXCVII

Blessed Are The Poor In Spirit. Matthew 5:3

Blessed Means Happy

Poor means meek in spirit. Poor means humble in spirit. Poor means lowly in spirit. Poor means quiet in spirit. Read Matthew 5:3-12, Read also Mark 1:15

Jesus did not say "*rich*" in spirit. Jesus said "*poor*" in spirit.

1. Blessed are the poor in spirit to those who believe and have heard and are ready for His return by singing this beautiful spiritual hymn: "Go ye out to meet Him. Go ye out to meet Him. Go ye out to meet Him when He come. Are you ready? Are you ready? Are you ready, when He come? Matthew 25:6
2. Blessed are the poor in spirit to those who do not believe in the doctrine of the annihilation that is not taught in the Old Testament except the flood in Noah's Day. But we believe the flood in Noah's Day. Matthew 24:38, Genesis 7:1-24, Genesis 8:1-22, Genesis 9:1-17 verse 13. See Genesis 7:7
3. Blessed are the poor in spirit to those who believe that the world even the people on earth need to get ready for the imminent return of Jesus Christ. Amos 4:12, Acts 1:11, I Thessalonians 4:13-17, Revelation 3:5, Revelation 16:15, Revelation 22:7, 12, 13, 16, 20
4. Blessed are the poor in spirit to those who believe that a true revival is the true sign of the imminent return of the Lord Jesus Christ. Jesus made a promise to the world: "Behold, I come quickly, Amen." Revelation 22:20
5. Blessed are the poor in spirit to those who believe on the doctrine of the atonement based on the death, burial and resurrection of Jesus Christ and the shedding of His blood on the cross. Leviticus 17:11, Hebrews 9:12, 24-26, Exodus 12:23, Hebrews 10:29, John 20:17
6. Blessed are the poor in spirit to those who believe in the Rapture at Christ Coming. I Thessalonians 4:16-17

7. Blessed are the poor in spirit to those who believe this old spiritual hymn: "Oh, the blood, oh the blood, oh the blood that sign my name" Matthew 26:28, Revelation 1:5
8. Blessed are the poor in spirit to those who believe and are able to confess Jesus for salvation by heart and by mouth of confession is made into salvation: "Behold, Lord, the half of my goods I give to the pour, and if I have taken anything from any man by false accusation, I restore him fourfold. Luke 19:8. Read Luke 19:1-8, See Romans 10:10
9. Blessed are the poor in spirit to those who believe that the Pentecostal latter rain, was being poured out in the last days before the imminent return of Christ; that Jesus is coming. Joel 2:28-29, Acts 1:4, 5, 8, 11. Acts 2:1-47, I Thessalonians 4:13-18, Revelation 1:1, 3, 7, Revelation 3:11, Revelation 16:15, Revelation 22:7, 12, 13, 20
10. Blessed are the poor in spirit to those who believe that Pentecostal Spirit Baptism is power than any of us as human being whose flesh is weak because the Spirit is willing but Holy Spirit continues to carry, continue to pour out upon the unsaved world and believe until Jesus Christ imminent return. Philippians 1:6, John 14:15-17, Matthew 26:41
11. Blessed are the poor in spirit to those who believe that the Pentecostal Fire Baptism came to fall fresh on each hungry church who are hungry for God. Matthew 3:11-12, Luke 3:16, 17, Acts 1:4-5, Acts 2:2-4, Mark 1:8, Jude 23, Hebrews 10:27, II Thessalonians 1:8
12. Blessed are the poor in spirit to those who believe that the color line can be washed away by Jesus' precious blood. I Peter 1:18-19, I Corinthians 15:3, Romans 3:19, Revelation 1:5

Part CDXCVIII

Blessed Are The Poor In Spirit. Matthew 5:3

Blessed Means Happy

Poor means meek in spirit. Poor means humble in spirit. Poor means lowly in spirit. Poor means quiet in spirit. Read Matthew 5:3-12, Read also Mark 1:15

Jesus did not say "*rich*" in spirit. Jesus said "*poor*" in spirit.

1. Blessed are the poor in spirit to those who believe that the Lord Himself add daily through the Holy Spirit such as those who should be saved. Acts 2:47, Acts 16:31, Joel 2:31, Acts 2:19 or 28…and plants them in the body to suit Himself and all to work together in harmony under the power of the Holy Spirit.
2. Blessed are the poor in spirit to those who are children of God knowing only to Jesus and Him crucified. I Corinthians 6:2
3. Blessed are the poor in spirit to those who believe in old time repentance. Luke 13:3, 5, Acts 11:21, Acts 3:19, Matthew 4:17
4. Blessed are the poor in spirit to those who believe in old time conversion. Acts 9:1, Acts 22:3-16, Acts 26:2-18, Matthew 7:21-23, Romans 3:23, Romans 6:23, John 16:17
5. Blessed are the poor in spirit to those who believe in old time sanctification. Matthew 6:12, Matthew 5:27-28
6. Blessed are the poor in spirit to those who believe in healing of our bodies. Mark 9:23, Mark 16:17, I Peter 2:24, James 5:15-16
7. Blessed are the poor in spirit to those who believe in the baptism with the Holy Spirit. Acts 19:2, Acts 2:38, Acts 1:5, Acts 2:1-47, Matthew 3:11
8. Blessed are the poor in spirit to those who believe that God made Adam in His own image. Genesis 5:1, Psalm 8:4, and Matthew 19:4
9. Blessed are the poor in spirit to those who believe that after God had made all the creation in the world in seventh days He rested. Genesis 2:2
10. Blessed are the poor in spirit to those who believe the Holy Bible to be the truth of God as the authority and finish of our faith in Christ Jesus upon the cross and without compromise and honor Jesus Christ as our Personal Savior and Lord and His Second Coming to take us home to live with Him for ever more. Matthew 24:30, John 1:14, Luke 4:8

11. Blessed are the poor in spirit to those who believe in bringing back that old time power of Pentecost. Acts 1:8, Acts 2:1-47 verse 1-4
12. Blessed are the poor in spirit to those who believe that God did visit His people so many times in the past such as in the city of Jerusalem with His presence and power to give them hope, to receive their Pentecost, so God did visit His new generation of people in Los Angeles at 312 Azusa Street with His presence and power to give us hope to receive our Pentecost as well as today until Jesus come to take us home with Him forever more. Joel 2:28, Acts 1:8, Acts 2:1-47 through Acts 28:1-31, Acts 2:1-4, Amos 4:12, Revelation 3:11, Revelation 16:15, Revelation 22:7, 12, 20

Part CDXCIX

Blessed Are The Poor In Spirit. Matthew 5:3

Blessed Means Happy

Poor means meek in spirit. Poor means humble in spirit. Poor means lowly in spirit. Poor means quiet in spirit. Read Matthew 5:3-12, Read also Mark 1:15

Jesus did not say "*rich*" in spirit. Jesus said "*poor*" in spirit.

1. Blessed are the poor in spirit to those who believe that the Baptism of the Holy Spirit from Jesus is the Holy Spirit power to save, the Holy Spirit power to deliver, the Holy Spirit power to heal and the Holy Spirit power to serve. Acts 1:4, 5, 8
2. Blessed are the poor in spirit to those who believe that the "*Real Outsider,*" of course was and is the *Holy Spirit is the speaker.* Colossians 4:5-6, I Thessalonians 4:12, I Corinthians 5:12-13, Matthew 18:15-20, Matthew 10:20, Mark 13:11, Acts 2:4, 9, 11, Acts 10:23-44
3. Blessed are the poor in spirit to those who believe in the restoration of apostolic pattern of worship. Philippians 3:17, Colossians 3:17, Acts 20:27
4. Blessed are the poor in spirit to those who believe in the importance of a conversion experience. Acts 2:28, Joel 2:28, Matthew 3:4, Matthew 4:17, Acts 16:31, Romans 13:10
5. Blessed are the poor in spirit to those who believe in the baptism of believers in Christ- Acts 2:38, I John 1:7, Colossians 1:14, Acts 2:41
6. Blessed are the poor in spirit to those who believe in the baptism by immersion. Matthew 28:19
7. Blessed are the poor in spirit to those who believe in total separation of church and state. II Corinthians 5:20
8. Blessed are the poor in spirit to those who believe in the power to overcome sin after conversion. Romans 6:14, I Corinthians 15:57
9. Blessed are the poor in spirit to those who believe the need to live a holy life after conversion. I Peter 2:12
10. Blessed are the poor in spirit to those who believe that the belief in salvation is by faith, personal conversion as "new birth" and an intense personal devotion

to Jesus Christ and commit in believing to pray for the worldwide spread of the gospel. John 14:16-18, John 3:3, 8

11. Blessed are the poor in spirit to those who believe in an anticipation of the imminent return of the Lord. Revelation 3:11, Revelation 16:15, Revelation 22:7, 12, 20
12. Blessed are the poor in spirit to those who believe that there is no color line in the redemption of Christ. Ephesians 1:7, Romans 3:24-26, Galatians 2:20

Part D

Blessed Are The Poor In Spirit. Matthew 5:3

Blessed Means Happy

Poor means meek in spirit. Poor means humble in spirit. Poor means lowly in spirit. Poor means quiet in spirit. Read Matthew 5:3-12, Read also Mark 1:15

Jesus did not say "*rich*" in spirit. Jesus said "*poor*" in spirit.

1. Blessed are the poor in spirit to those who believe that the Spirit's outpouring would come the rapture of the church. I Thessalonians 4:14-18 verses 14, 17
2. Blessed are the poor in spirit to those who believe that God has built up the work through His loving people of God. Ephesians 4:12, I Corinthians 8:1b, Proverbs 24:3-4
3. Blessed are the poor in spirit to those who believe the Holy Spirit through the blood of Jesus that washed away the color line; melting of the races, and the breaking down of racial prejudice. Isaiah 59:19b, Galatians 3:28
4. Blessed are the poor in spirit to those who believe and are able to say: "I am a child of the King." I Corinthians 13:11
5. Blessed are the poor in spirit to those who believe and are able to say: "I am a child of God." Matthew 18:1-6, Mark 10:13-16 verse 15, Luke 18:17, Luke 9:46-48 verse 47, II Timothy 3:15-17 verse 15
6. Blessed are the poor in spirit to those who believe and are able to say: "I am one of God's children. Matthew 5:9, 16, 45, Luke 20:36, John 11:52, Romans 8:16, 21, Romans 9:8, 26, Read Romans 9:1-8, Hosea 1:10, II Corinthians 6:18, Galatians 3:26, I John 1:1-2, 10-11, I John 5:2
7. Blessed are the poor in spirit to those who believe and are able to say: "I am a child of an everlasting kingdom. Daniel 7:27, Obadiah 21, Matthew 24:14, Matthew 13:38, 43, Matthew 5:3, 10, 19, Daniel 7:14, Revelation 11:15
8. Blessed are the poor in spirit to those who believe in making a confession of christians faith. Acts 16:31, Romans 10:13, Romans 5:1, Ephesians 2:8-9, Acts 2:28, Joel 2:28
9. Blessed are the poor in spirit to those who believe that "*the outpouring of the baptism of the Holy Spirit*" *mean that* "*Jesus is coming soon.*" Amos 4:12, Acts 1:11,

I Thessalonians 4:13-18, Revelation 3:11, Revelation 16: 15, Revelation 22:7, 12, 20. *So be prepared to meet the Lord thy God. Be ready to meet Jesus when He come.* See Revelation 1:1, 7, Revelation 22:16, 17, 18-21

10. Blessed are the poor in spirit to those who believe in the Book of Acts because Jesus is coming soom. Get into Action. Get your acts together before He comes. Amos 4:12, Acts 1:11, I Thessalonians 4:13-17, Revelation 3:11, Revelation 16:15, Revelation 22:7, 12, 20
11. Blessed are the poor in spirit to those who believe that we have the witness of the Spirit that we are saved; that we are born again. Romans 8:16, John 3:3, Acts 16:31, Romans 10:13, Joel 2:28, Acts 2:18
12. Blessed are the poor in spirit to those who believe in praying with sinners for salvation or for conversion and for the converted to be sanctified or receive the baptism of the Holy Spirit. Acts 26:18, Hebrews 12:14, John 17:17, Acts 10:23-44, Acts 2:28, Acts 1:4, Matthew 3:11

Part DI

Blessed Are The Poor In Spirit. Matthew 5:3

Blessed Means Happy

Poor means meek in spirit. Poor means humble in spirit. Poor means lowly in spirit. Poor means quiet in spirit. Read Matthew 5:3-12, Read also Mark 1:15

Jesus did not say "*rich*" in spirit. Jesus said "*poor*" in spirit.

1. Blessed are the poor in spirit to those who believe and trust in faith, family and friends. Micah 7:5, Jeremiah 12:6, II Peter 2:9
2. Blessed are the poor in spirit to those who believe and have faith in family, friends and relatives. Jeremiah 12:6, I Timothy 5:8
3. Blessed are the poor in spirit to those who believe that the Revival has come. Acts 2:1-47, II Chronicles 7:14
4. Blessed are the poor in spirit to those who believe that the Revival is here beginning in our heart to the world by witnessing, teaching and preaching about Christ. II Chronicles 7:14, Psalm 19:7-10, John 7:38, Acts 1:8, Matthew 24:14, I Corinthians 15:1-4, Colossians 4:5-6
5. Blessed are the poor in spirit to those who believe that the revival mean Jesus is coming, but when??? Not to know when but to get ready for His return. Amos 4:12, Acts 1:11, I Thessalonians 4:13-17, Revelation 3:11, Revelation 22:7, 12, 20
6. Blessed are the poor in spirit to those who believe that Pentecost is knocking at our door; in our hearts. Revelation 3:20
7. Blessed are the poor in spirit to those who believe that the *Comforter*, which is the *Holy Spirit* is the Leader, which is *God* through *Jesus Christ*. John 14:8-9, 13, 16, 26, Hebrews 4:16
8. Blessed are the poor in spirit to those who believe that the *Baptism of the Holy Spirit is in a form of a gospel foregin language to warn a sinner to repent of his/her sins and to give his/her heart and life to Jesus Christ, who is to come soon.* Amen Amos4:12, Acts 1:11, Revelation 22:7, 12, 20
9. Blessed are the poor in spirit to those who believe that *God is His own interpretation*. Psalm 43:2, Romans 8:32, Genesis 1:27, Romans 5:8

10. Blessed are the poor in spirit to those who believe and professed faith in the Word of God and live our faith "everyday." Hebrews 10:23-25, Acts 16:31, I Peter 3:15, Romans 10:10, Romans 6:6
11. Blessed are the poor in spirit to those who saw the sign on Azusa Street Mission in Los Angeles, California—"*Jesus Saves.*" Acts 4:10-12, Romans 2:6-10, Luke 12:43-49, II Corinthians 5:21, Romans 10:8-15
12. Blessed are the poor in spirit to those who believe that we are hearing the end of this dispensation and the church to be restored to it's apostolic glory and spiritual power, with the gift of the Spirit before the Lord's return. Acts 1:11, Acts 2:1-47 verse 4, I Thessalonians 4:13-17, Amos 4:12, Revelation 3:11, Revelation 16:15, Revelation 22:7, 12, 20

Part DII

Blessed Are The Poor In Spirit. Matthew 5:3

Blessed Means Happy

Poor means meek in spirit. Poor means humble in spirit. Poor means lowly in spirit. Poor means quiet in spirit. Read Matthew 5:3-12, Read also Mark 1:15

Jesus did not say "*rich*" in spirit. Jesus said "*poor*" in spirit.

1. Blessed are the poor in spirit to those who believe that Pentecost is a night of prayer. Acts 2:1-4. Jesus shew us how to pray. See Matthew 6:5-8, Luke 11:1
2. Blessed are the poor in spirit to those who believe that Pentecostal Spirit Baptism is the work of God and Acts 2:1-47 should not be opposition. Read Job 14:14-15, Isaiah 28:10-14, Genesis 11:1-9
3. Blessed are the poor in spirit to those who belive this scripture: "Seek the Kingdom of God" Matthew 6:33, See Isaiah 55:6, Isaiah 45:22
4. Blessed are the poor in spirit to those who believe this psalmist: "Let them shout for joy, and be glad, that favour my righteous cause: yea, let them say continually, Let the Lord be magnified, which hath pleasure in the prosperity of his servant." Psalm 35:27
5. Blessed are the poor in spirit to those who believe this psalmist: "And my tongue shall speak of thy righteousness and of thy praise all the day long." Psalm 35:28
6. Blessed are the poor in spirit to those who believe this psalmist: "There is a river, the streams whereof shall make glad the city of God, the holy place of the tabernacles of the most High." Psalm 46:4
7. Blessed are the poor in spirit to those who believe this psalmist: "O let the nations be glad and sing for joy: for thou shalt judge the people righteously, and govern the nations upon earth. Selah." Psalm 67:4
8. Blessed are the poor in spirit to those who believe this psalmist: "Let thy work appear unto thy servants, and thy glory unto their children." Psalm 90:16
9. Blessed are the poor in spirit to those who believe this psalmist: "And let the beauty of the Lord our God be upon us: and establish thou the work of our hands upon us; yea, the work of our hands establish thou it." Psalm 90:17

10. Blessed are the poor in spirit to those who believe this psalmist: "It is a good thing to give thanks unto the Lord, and to sing praises unto thy name, O most High:" Psalm 92:1
11. Blessed are the poor in spirit to those who believe this psalmist: "To shew forth thy lovingkindness in the morning, and thy faithfulness every night." Psalm 92:2
12. Blessed are the poor in spirit to those who believe this psalmist: "Upon an instrument of ten strings, and upon the psaltery; upon the harp with a solemn sound." Psalm 92:3

Part DIII

Blessed Are The Poor In Spirit. Matthew 5:3

Blessed Means Happy

Poor means meek in spirit. Poor means humble in spirit. Poor means lowly in spirit. Poor means quiet in spirit. Read Matthew 5:3-12, Read also Mark 1:15

Jesus did not say "*rich*" in spirit. Jesus said "*poor*" in spirit.

1. Blessed are the poor in spirit to those who believe this psalmist: "For thou, Lord, hast made me glad through thy work: I will triumph in the works of thy hands." Psalm 92:4
2. Blessed are the poor in spirit to those who believe this psalmist: "O Lord, how great are thy works! And thy thoughts are very deep." Psalm 92:5
3. Blessed are the poor in spirit to those who believe this psalmist: "Thou hidest thy face, they are troubled: thou takest away their breath, they die, and return to their dust." Psalm 104:29
4. Blessed are the poor in spirit to those who believe this psalmist: "Thou sendest forth thy spirit, they are created: and thou renewest the face of the earth." Psalm 104:30
5. Blessed are the poor in spirit to those who believe this psalmist: "The glory of the Lord shall endure for ever: the Lord shall rejoice in his works." Psalm 104:31
6. Blessed are the poor in spirit to those who believe this psalmist: "He looketh on the earth, and it trembleth: he toucheth the hills, and they smoke." Psalm 104:32
7. Blessed are the poor in spirit to those who believe this psalmist: "I will sing unto the Lord as long as I live: I will sing praise to my God while I have my being." Psalm 104:33
8. Blessed are the poor in spirit to those who believe this psalmist: "My meditation of him shall be sweet: I will be glad in the Lord." Psalm 104:34
9. Blessed are the poor in spirit to those who believe this psalmist: "Let the sinners be consumed out of the earth, and let the wicked be no more. Bless thou the Lord, O my soul. Praise ye the Lord." Psalm 104:35
10. Blessed are the poor in spirit to those who believe this psalmist: "Egypt was glad when they departed: for the fear of them fell upon them." Psalm 105:38

11. Blessed are the poor in spirit to those who believe this psalmist: "He spread a cloud for covering; and fire to give light in the night." Psalm 105:39
12. Blessed are the poor in spirit to those who believe one of God's children, Martin Luther—1483-1546: "Christ said we "*must*" *become* "as little children" to enter the kingdom of heaven." Matthew 18:1-5, 11, verse 3, Luke 18:15-17, verse 16 Mark 10:13-16 verse 14

Part DIV

Blessed Are The Poor In Spirit. Matthew 5:3

Blessed Means Happy

Poor means meek in spirit. Poor means humble in spirit. Poor means lowly in spirit. Poor means quiet in spirit. Read Matthew 5:3-12, Read also Mark 1:15

Jesus did not say "*rich*" in spirit. Jesus said "*poor*" in spirit.

1. Blessed are the poor in spirit to those who do not believe in the doctrine of the annihilation that is not taught in the New Testament but there are the Sadducees who do not believe in the resurrection of Christ and its immortality. Matthew 22:23, Romans 2:7, I Corinthians 15:53-54, I Timothy 6:16, II Timothy 1:10
2. Blessed are the poor in spirit to those who believe in the doctrine of justification by faith by living; that the just shall live by faith. Habakkuk 2:4, Romans 1:17, Galatians 3:11, Hebrews 10:38, Acts 15:9, Acts 26:18, Romans 1:12, Romans 3:22, 28, Romans 5:1, Galatians 2:16, 3:24, Romans 3:30, II Corinthians 5:7, Galatians 2:20, Galatians 3:22, 26, Galataians 5:5, Ephesians 3:12, 17, Philippians 3:9
3. Blessed are the poor in spirit to those who believe in the hall of faith:
    i. *Abel*—Hebrews 11:4; *Enoch*—Hebrews 11:5, *Rewarder of faith*—Hebrews 11:6; *Noah*—Hebrews 11:7; *Abraham*—Hebrews 11:8-9, *Isaac*—Hebrews 11:9; *Jacob*—Hebrews 11:9; *Rewarder of faith—Whose Buildre and Maker is God*—Hebrews 11:10; *Sarah*—Hebrews 11:11, All died in faith, not having received the promises, but having seen them afar off, were persuaded (convinced) of them, embraced them, confessed that they were strangers and pilgrims on the earth—Hebrews 11:13;
    ii. They said such things declare plainly (clearly) that they seek a country; Hebrews 11:14; Acted by faith—Abraham with Isaac—Hebrews 11:17; Acted by faith—Isaac with Jacob and Esau concerning things to come; acted by faith—Jacob blessed both sons of Jospeh; Acted by faith—Joseph made mention of (spoken of) the departing of the children of Israel; and gave commandment concerning his bones; Acted by faith—Moses was not afraid of the king's commandment; and refused

to be called the son of Pharaoh's daughter, choosing rather to suffer affliction (shame) with the people of God (children of Israel) than to enjoy the pleasure of sin. Hebrews 11:24-25

iii. Acted by faith—Moses forsook (left or exiled or exited) Egypt, not fearing the wrath of the king because God Himself who is still to this day on ward is invisible—Hebrews 11:27; through faith Moses kept the passover, kept the sprinkling of blood, lest He that destroyed the first born should touch them. Hebrews 11:28; Acted by faith—Moses and the children of Israel passed through the Red Sea as by dry land; and the Egyptians assaying (attempting, or to catch up but) were drowned (were killed). Hebrews 11:29. Acted by faith—the walls of Jericho fell down, after the children of Israel were compassed (encircled) abput seven days. Hebrews 11:30; Acted by faith—the harlot Rahab perished not (did not die) with the unbelief that believed, not, when she had received the spies with peace. Hebrews 11:31; Through faith of course, had not forgotten about Gedeon, Barak, Samson, Jephthae, David, Samuel and of the prophets:Hebrews 11:32; through faith obtained promises, stopped the mouths of lions—Hebrews 11:33

iv. And obtained a better resurrection; And there all having obtained a good report (newsletter, hall of faith, rewards) through faith, received not the promise—Hebrews 11:39; God having provided (planned) some better (the very best) thing for us, that they without us should not be made perfect (complete)—Hebrews 11:40

4. Blessed are the poor in spirit to those who believe this spiritual hymn: "If you 're saved and you know it, wave your hands. If you're saved and you know it, clap your hands. If you're saved and you know it, stomp your feet. If you're saved and you know it, shout. "Hallalujeh!!! "Amen!, Amen!, Amen!." Questions: Do You Want to Know Him? Do You Know Him? Do You Know Jesus? Have You Accepted Him? I John 5:13. That ye may know that you have eternal life. Eternal life is in His Son, Jesus Christ.
5. Blessed are the poor in spirit to those who believe that the Bible is our defense to claim it, to proclaim it so that we can be saved; so that we are indeed free and that free shall make us free indeed. Jesus Christ indeed make us free. John 8:32, 36, Galatians 5:1 Not willing that any should perish—II Peter 3:9, I Timothy 2:4. Look up to me and be ye saved. Isaiah 45:22, Psalm 25:16

6. Blessed are the poor in spirit to those who have a deep respect for the Lord. Ephesians 6:5, Exodus 20:12 (Love the Lord thy God with all your heart, soul and mind…because it was a life commintment. Romans 1:21, II Peter 1:5, II Timothy 1:7
7. Blessed are the poor in spirit to those who read the Bible faithfully, will promise to feel better instead of panic, frighten, terror, failure, plague, nervous, collapse over religious problems, disorder, disturbance, horror of nightmare or the dreadful life to come to an end. There is promise of hope, trust and faith in the promise of the Bible. Read God's Word faithful that will promise you for eternal with Him:You will be glad when you feel so much better in time!!! Matthew 11:28-30, John 14:1-3, Psalms 25:16-20
8. Blessed are the poor in spirit to those who believe by fasting, and praying that sinners may transform into saints, the saints of God. James 5:16, Isaiah 55:6-8
9. Blessed are the poor in spirit to those who believe that the baptism of fire means/ or is a flame of fire to those who are not saved; not born-again and is a wak-up call {repent; be converted; be saved before it's too late}; Getting Excitmemt!!!; Good News of Christ Return!!! The Imminent Return of Christ!!! Amos 4:12, Acts 1:11, Acts 2:3, Revelation 3:11, Revelation 16:15, Revelation 22:7, 12, 13, 20
10. Blessed are the poor in spirit to those who believe that **"salvation"** is a **gift from God**. John 4:10, Romans 5:15, 16, 17, 18, 6:23, II Corinthians 9:15, Ephesians 2:5, 8, James 1:17
11. Blessed are the poor in spirit to those who are able to say: "Lord Jesus, receive my spirit—Acts 7:59, John 14:6, Acts 9:4-6
12. Blessed are the poor in spirit to those who believe and accept Jesus Christ as our personal Savior and God, because we do not want to die a pitiful fall and a shamefull fall without Him. James 5:11, Psalm 106:43-48 verse 46, Psalm 103:1-22 **verse 8-13 verse 13,** Ezekiel 24:19-27 verse 21, Matthew **18:33-35—** compassion (pity) **verse 35, James 10:1-39 verses 27, and 31, Revelation 21:8**

Part DV

Blessed Are The Poor In Spirit. Matthew 5:3

Blessed Means Happy

Poor means meek in spirit. Poor means humble in spirit. Poor means lowly in spirit. Poor means quiet in spirit. Read Matthew 5:3-12, Read also Mark 1:15

Jesus did not say "*rich*" in spirit. Jesus said "*poor*" in spirit.

1. Blessed are the poor in spirit to those who believe that Freedom is free unless accepting Christ's True Freedom. John **8:31-36 verse 36**, Romans 5:15, 16, 18, Romans 6:18, 20, 22, 23, Romans 8:1-17 verse 2, 16, 17, Galatians 3:26-29, Galatians 5:1, Ephesians 6:8-17 verse 8, 10, 15, 17, I Corinthians 7:22, Romans 3:24-32, **Hosea 14:4,** I Corinthians 2:12, II Corinthians 11:7, **Revelation 21:6**
2. Blessed are the poor in spirit to those who believe in the **Living Word** which is the **Word of God**. Matthew 4:4, Mark 7:13, Luke 3:2, 4:4, Luke 5:1, 11:28, John 1:1, Genesis 1:1, John 10:35, Acts 4:31, Acts 8:14, 10:36, 11:1, 12:24, 13:5, 13:7, 46, Acts 17:13, 18:11, 19:20, 20:32, Romans 9:6, **10:17,** I Corinthians 14:36, Ephesians 6:17, Colossians 1:25, 3:16, I Thessalonians 2:13, I Timothy 4:5, II Timothy 2:9, Titus 2:5, Hebrews 4:12, 6:5, 11:3, 13:7, I Peter 1:23, II Peter 3:5, I John 2:14, Revelation 1:2, 9, 6:9, 19:13, Revelation 20:4
3. Blessed are the poor in spirit to those who believe that "Life is Good" when we know Jesus Christ as our personal Savior and Lord. John 14:6, John 11:25-27
4. Blessed are the poor in spirit to those who believe and confess with their mouth: "I believe with **all** my heart that **Jesus Christ** is the **Son of God.** Acts 8:37, Romans 10:8-13, Joel 2:32, Acts 2:21, Acts 16:31
5. Blessed are the poor in spirit to those who **believe when Jesus spoke by the Word Only.** Acts 20:32, I Timothy 4:5. We are **sanctified by the word.** We become **"healed"**; we become **"saved;"** we become **'justified;"** we **repented of our sins;** we become **blessed of salvation;** we become **converted;** we become **forgiveness through salvation**. Isaiah 53:1-12, Romans 10:16, Romans 1:17, Hebrews 2:4, Ephesians 2:5, 8-9, Galatians 3:11 II Corinthians 6:2, Isaiah 49:8, James 5:16, 19-20, **Matthew 8:8,** Jeremiah 17:14

6. Blessed are the poor in spirit to those who are *eyewitness* and *ministers* of the *Word* of *Jesus Christ*; the *Word of God*; the *Word of Christ*. Luke 1:2
7. Blessed are the poor in spirit to those who believe that the Lord has done great things for us; whereof we are glad. Psalm 126:3
8. Blessed are the poor in spirit to those who believe that salvation mean God. II Samuel 22:47, I Chronicles 16:35, Psalm 18:46, Psalm 27:9, 50:23, 56:14, 62:1, 2, 6, 7, 65:5, 68:19, 20, 88:1, 89:26, 98:3, Isaiah 12:2, Micah 7:7, Habakkuk 3:18, Luke 3:6, Acts 16:17, Acts 28:28, Romans 1:16, Philippians 1:19, 2:12, Titus 2:11, Jeremiah 3:22, 10:10
9. Blessed are the poor in spirit to those who believe that God enjoy His people, His children, His generation with **His salvation**. He enjoy the **pleasant** with them. Ephesians 3:15, 1:5, 9, 21, Psalm 147:11, Psalm 149:1-5 verse 4, Ecclesiastes 3:4, Luke 12:31, 32, II Thessalonians 1:10-12 verse 11
10. Blessed are the poor in spirit to those who believe in publishing salvation because God still reign!!! Isaiah 52:6-7. See Luke 2:10-11 and Romans 10:15!!!
11. Blessed are the poor in spirit to those who believe not to say: "Good-Bye" or never having to say, "Good-Bye" but to say: "See you in the morning" Psalm 30:5
12. Blessed are the poor in spirit to those who believe in the Psalmist: "Restore unto me the joy of thy salvation; and uphold me with thy free (willing) spirit. Psalm 51:12

Part DVI

Blessed Are The Poor In Spirit. Matthew 5:3

Blessed Means Happy

Poor means meek in spirit. Poor means humble in spirit. Poor means lowly in spirit. Poor means quiet in spirit. Read Matthew 5:3-12, Read also Mark 1:15

Jesus did not say "*rich*" in spirit. Jesus said "*poor*" in spirit.

1. Blessed are the poor in spirit to those who believe in this Psalmist: "But let all those that put their trust in thee rejoice: let them ever shout for joy, because thou defendest them: let them also that love thy name be joyful in thee." Psalm 5:11
2. Blessed are the poor in spirit to those who believe in this Psalmist: "Be glad in the Lord, and rejoice, ye righteous: and shout for joy, all ye that are upright in heart." Psalm 32:11
3. Blessed are the poor in spirit to those who believe in this Psalmist: "Let them shout for joy, and be glad, that favour my righteous cause: yea, let them say continually, Let the Lord be magnified, which hath pleasure in the prosperity of his servant." Psalm 35:27
4. Blessed are the poor in spirit to those who believe in this Psalmist: "And my tongue shall speak of thy rightesousness and of thy praise all the day long." Psalm 35:28
5. Blessed are the poor in spirit to those who believe in this Psalmist: "When I remember these things, I pour out my soul in me: for I had gone with the multitude, I went with them to the house of God, with the voice of joy and praise, with a multitude that kept holyday." Psalm 42:4
6. Blessed are the poor in spirit to those who believe in this Psalmist: "Make me to hear joy and gladness; that the bones which thou hast broken may rejoice." Psalm 51:8
7. Blessed are the poor in spirit to those who believe in this Psalmist: "God shall bless us; and all the ends of the earth shall fear him." Psalm 67:7
8. Blessed are the poor in spirit to those who believe in this Psalmist: "And he brought forth his people with joy, and his chosen with gladness:" Psalm 105:43
9. Blessed are the poor in spirit to those who believe in this Psalmist: "When the Lord turned again the captivity of Zion, we were like them that dream." Psalm 126:1

10. Blessed are the poor in spirit to those who believe in this Psalmist: "Then was our mouth filled with laughter, and our tongue with singing: then said they among the heathen, The Lord hath done great things for them." Psalm 126:2
11. Blessed are the poor in spirit to those who believe in this Psalmist: "The Lord hath done great things for us; whereof we are glad." Psalm 126:3
12. Blessed are the poor in spirit to those who believe in this Psalmist: "Turn again our captivity, O Lord, as the streams in the south." Psalm 126:4

Part DVII

Blessed Are The Poor In Spirit. Matthew 5:3

Blessed Means Happy

Poor means meek in spirit. Poor means humble in spirit. Poor means lowly in spirit. Poor means quiet in spirit. Read Matthew 5:3-12, Read also Mark 1:15

Jesus did not say "*rich*" in spirit. Jesus said "*poor*" in spirit.

1. Blessed are the poor in spirit to those who believe in this Psalmist: "They that sow in tears shall reap in joy." Psalm 126:5
2. Blessed are the poor in spirit to those who believe in this Psalmist: "He that goeth forth and weepeth, bearing precious seed, shall doubtless come again with rejoicing, bringing his sheaves with him." Psalm 126:6
3. Blessed are the poor in spirit to those who believe in this Psalmist: "Let thy priests be clothed with righteousness; and let thy saints shout for joy." Psalm 132:9
4. Blessed are the poor in spirit to those who believe in this Psalmist: "I will abundantly bless her provision: I will satisfy her poor with bread." Psalm 132:15
5. Blessed are the poor in spirit to those who believe in this Psalmist: "I will also clothe her priests with salvation: and her saints shall shout aloud for joy." Psalm 132:16
6. Blessed are the poor in spirit to those who believe in the Gospel: "His lord said unto him, Well done, thou good and faithful servant: thou hast been faithful over a few things, I will make thee ruler over many things: enter thou into the joy of thy lord." Matthew 25:21
7. Blessed are the poor in spirit to those who believe in the Gospelt: "His lord said unto him, Well done, good and faithful servant; thou hast been faithful over a few things, I will make thee ruler over many things: enter thou into the joy of thy lord." Matthew 25:23
8. Blessed are the poor in spirit to those who believe in the Gospel: "And the angel said unto them, Fear not: for behold, I bring you good tidings of great joy, which shall be to all people." Luke 2:10
9. Blessed are the poor in spirit to those who believe in the Gospel: "For unto you is born this day in the city of David a Saviour, which is Christ the Lord." Luke 2:11

10. Blessed are the poor in spirit to those who believe in the Gospel: "And he lifted up his eyes on his deisciples, and said, Blessed be ye poor: for yours is the kingdom of God." Luke 6:20
11. Blessed are the poor in spirit to those who believe in the Gospel: "Blessed are ye that hunger now: for ye shall be filled. Bleseed are ye that weep now: for ye shall laugh." Luke 6:21
12. Blessed are the poor in spirit to those who believe in the Gospel: "Rejoice ye in that day, and leap for joy: for, behold, your reward is great in heaven: for in the like manner did their fathrs unto the prophets" Luke 6:23

Part DVIII

Blessed Are The Poor In Spirit. Matthew 5:3

Blessed Means Happy

Poor means meek in spirit. Poor means humble in spirit. Poor means lowly in spirit. Poor means quiet in spirit. Read Matthew 5:3-12, Read also Mark 1:15

Jesus did not say "*rich*" in spirit. Jesus said "*poor*" in spirit.

1. Blessed are the poor in spirit to those who believe *in the Gospel*: "Woe unto you that are full! For ye shall hunger, Woe unto you that laugh now! for ye shall mourn and weep." Luke 6:25
2. Blessed are the poor in spirit to those who believe *in the Gospel*: "For if ye love them which love you, what thank have ye? For sinners also love those that love them (too)." Luke 6:32
3. Blessed are the poor in spirit to those who believe *in the Gospel*: "And if ye do good to them which do good to you, what thank have ye? For sinners also do even the same (as well)." Luke 6:33
4. Blessed are the poor in spirit to those who believe *in the Gospel*: "Be ye therefore merciful, as your Father also is merciful." Luke 6:36
5. Blessed are the poor in spirit to those who *may have* a **personal faith in Jesus Christ**. Romans 10:10
6. Blessed are the poor in spirit to those who *may have* a clear understanding of the **gospel of Jesus Christ.** Romans 10:10
7. Blessed are the poor in spirit to those who *may have* a clear explanation of the **gospel of Jesus Christ.** Romans 1:17, Romans 5:1, Romans 10:10, Ephesians 2:5, 8
8. Blessed are the poor in spirit to those who *may believe* and *have became true believers in Christ* living near enough to tell the world of the *message of Christ* that **Jesus saves**; That **Jesus saves;** That **Jesus saves**. Mark 11:15
9. Blessed are the poor in spirit to those who believe one of the *true prophets* and *one of God's true children, Jeremiah*: "Then I said, I will not make mention of him, nor speak any more in His name. But His Word was in mine heart as a *burning fire shut up in my bones*, and I was weary with forbearing, and I could not stay. Jeremiah 20:9 of *King James Version*

***New American Standard Bible* of Jeremiah 20:9
But if I say, "I will not remember **Him**
Or speak anymore in **His name**,"
Then in my heart it becomes like a burning fire
Shut up in my bones;
And I am weary of holding it in,
And I cannot endure it.

10. Blessed are the poor in spirit to those who believe this *spiritual hymn*!
    1. "O spread the tidings 'roun, whe-ev-er man is found
    2. Wher-ev-er hu-man hearts and hu-man woes a-bound;
    3. Let ev-'ry chris-tian tongue pro-claim the joy-ful sound: The Com-fort-er has come!!! Acts 2:1-11 verse 1, John 14:26
11. Blessed are the poor in spirit to those who are *patience waiting* for **Christ**. I Corinthians 1:7-10 verse 7, II Thessalonians 3:3-5 verse 5
12. Blessed are the poor in spirit to those who believe that we do not make any such promises, but to say, **no** and **yea in Him**. Neither by crossing our heart; neither by putting our hand on the Bible and say: "I do" or say, "So help me, God" *only if* we do not meant it. Matthew 5:36-37, II Corinthians 1:17-20, II Corinthians 1:17-24

Part DIX

Blessed Are The Poor In Spirit. Matthew 5:3

Blessed Means Happy

Poor means meek in spirit. Poor means humble in spirit. Poor means lowly in spirit. Poor means quiet in spirit. Read Matthew 5:3-12, Read also Mark 1:15

Jesus did not say "*rich*" in spirit. Jesus said "*poor*" in spirit.

1. Blessed are the poor in spirit to those who are able to say as I did with *three simple words*: "Lord, save me." Then I said: "Thank you Jesus" with these three *words*. (was saved at the age of eleven). Matthew 1:21, 8:25, 18:11, Luke 19:12, John 12:47, John 3:15-17, 5:34, Acts 2:21, 47, 15:11, 11:30-31, Romans 5:8-10, 10:13, I Corinthians 1:8, 18, 2:5, I Thessalonians 2:16, II Thessalonians 2:10, I Timothy 2:4, II Timothy 1:9, Titus 3:5
2. Blessed are the poor in spirit to those who believe that our sins are forgiven. Romans 4:7, I Corinthians 15:3, Galatians 1:4, Ephesians 1:7, Colossians 1:14, Hebrews 9:28, 10:12, 17, 26, James 5:20, I Peter 2:24, I Peter 3:18, I John 1:9, 2:12, 3:5, Revelation 1:5, Matthew 1:21, Matthew 9:2, 5, 6, Matthew 26:28, Mark 2:10, 4:12, Luke 5:20, 23, 24, Luke 7:47, 48, Titus 2:11-15, II Timothy 2;11-15
3.

   Blessed are the poor in spirit to those who believe that salvation is a gift from God, for the grace of God that bring salvation has appear to '*all*' men, *by teaching* us *by denying ungodliness* and worldly lusts, we should live *soberly* (sensibly), *righteously*, and *godly* in this *present* world; (this we do believe), by looking for that blessed hope and the glorious appearing of the *great God* and our *Saviour Jesus Christ*, who gave *Himself* for us that He might (possible, maybe, willing to give our self up of all to Him) redeem us from iniquity (things we have done wrong, our own belief, our unbelief ignorantly) and purify unto Himself a peculiar (special, vip-very important persons) people zealous of good works.

   These things speak, and exhourt (urge) and rebuke (reprove) with all authority. Let no man despise thee. Titus 2:11-15

4. Blessed are the poor in spirit to those who believe that the Bible actual really inspire and excite us as we read God's Word, discover God's Word and apply God's Word to our daily life until Jesus come. II Timothy 3:15-18
5.

   Blessed are the poor in spirit to those who believe that the Gospel of Jesus Christ which is the Holy Spirit Baptism, spread to all the *tribes*, *tongues*, and *nation* the wonderful work of God. Acts 2:11-47 verses 4-11, See Acts 1:1-11 verse 4-8, Luke 24:47-53 verse 47-48, Mark 16:17
6.

   Blessed are the poor in spirit to those who believe in their spiritual hymn: "The Joy of the Lord is your strength!!! The Joy of the Lord is your strength!!! The Joy of the Lord is your strength!!!" Nehemiah 8:10
7.

   Blessed are the poor in spirit to those who believe the spiritual hymn:
   1. "O spread the ti-dings 'round, whe-ev-er man is found
   2. Wher-ev-er hu-man hearts and hu-man woes a-bound;
   3. Let ev-'ry chris-tian tongue pro-claim the joy-ful sound: The com-for-ter has come!!!" John 14:26, Acts 2:1-11 verse 1
8. Blessed are the poor in spirit to those who believe this scripture: "Thou therefore endure hardness, as a good soldier of Jesus Christ." II Timothy 2:3
9. Blessed are the poor in spirit to those who believe this scripture: "But I say unto you, That whosoever is angry with his brother without a cause shall be in danger of the judgment: and whosoever shall say to his brother, Raca, shall be in danger of the council: but whosoever shall say, Thou fool, shall be in danger of hell fire."Matthew 5:22
10. Blessed are the poor in spirit to those who believe that it is impossible to please God. We must believe God. We must believe that He is. We must believe that He is a rewarder of them that diligently seek him. Hebrews 11:6
11.

    Blessed are the poor in spirit to those who believe that God did not create the eighth day which is called the annihilation by men. Genesis 2:1-4 verse 2-3
12.

    Blessed are the poor in spirit to those who believe that the Bible does not say eighth day. Genesis 2:2-4

Part DX

Blessed Are The Poor In Spirit. Matthew 5:3

Blessed Means Happy

Poor means meek in spirit. Poor means humble in spirit. Poor means lowly in spirit. Poor means quiet in spirit. Read Matthew 5:3-12, Read also Mark 1:15

Jesus did not say "*rich*" in spirit. Jesus said "*poor*" in spirit.

1. Blessed are the poor in spirit to those who believe that the Bible teaches that God rest on the seventh day. Genesis 2:2-4
2. Blessed are the poor in spirit to those who believe that there is no eighth day in Genesis 2:2-4
3. Blessed are the poor in spirit to those who believe that there is the seventh day in Genesis 2:24 where God rest the seventh day. Genesis 2:2-4
4. Blessed are the poor in spirit to those who believe in the day that the Lord had made the earth and the heavens. Genesis 2:4, Read Genesis 1:1-31

   Day 1—**Light** verse 3-5—Evening and Morning were the **first day**

   Day 2—**Firmament (Heaven)** verse 6-8—Evening and Morning were the **second day**

   Day 3—**One place—dry land—earth** verse 9-13—Evening and Morning were the **third day**

   Day 4—**Sun and Moon**—verse 14-19—Evening and Morning were the **fourth day**

   Day 5—**Living Creatures**—verse 20-23—Evening and Morning were the **fifth day**

   Day 6—**Let the earth bring forth the Living Creatures**—verse 24-31—Evening and Morning were the **sixth day**

   Day 7—**Rest Day**—Genesis 2:2-3-**God** ended **His work**. He **rested** on the *seventh day* from all **His Work** which He had made them for **six days**. Read Genesis 1:1-31
5. Blessed are the poor in spirit to those who believe that we are *born again by the Word of God.* I Peter 1:23, John 3:1-21 verse 6, 7
6. Blessed are the poor in spirit to those who believe that the Old Testament, "Red" Print in direct to the word of **God**. Psalm 60:6-8, Psalm 62:11, Isaiah 1:20,

Isaiah 16:14, Isaiah 24:1-3, Isaiah 25:8 (Revelation 21:4), Isaiah 40:5 (Psalm 62:11), Isaiah 45:18-19, Isaiah 46:11, Isaiah 48:15-16, Jeremiah 9:12-26, Jeremiah 13:14-15, Jeremiah 23:37, Jeremiah 29:23, Jeremiah 30:1-24 verse 2, Jeremiah 36:2, 4 (Jeremiah 30:2), Ezekiel 28:10, 30:12, Ezekiel 37:13-14

7. Blessed are the poor in spirit to those who believe that the New Testament "Red" Print in direct to the word of **Jesus Christ (God).** Matthew 22:31, Matthew 24:15, Mark 13:14, Mark 14:9, Luke 12:3, Luke 24:25, John 12:48, 49, John 14:25, John 15:11, 22, John 16: 25, 33, John 17:1-26, Luke 11:22, Matthew 16:21, Matthew 17:23, Matthew 20:3, 19, Mark 9:31, Mark 10:34, Luke 9:22, Luke 12:38, Luke 13:32, Luke 18:33, Luke 20:12, 31, Luke 24:46, Acts 1:4-5, 7-8, Acts 9:4-6, 11-12, 15-16, Acts 11:16, Acts 18:9-10, Acts 20:35, Acts 22:7-8, 10, 18, 21, Acts 23:11
8. Blessed are the poor in spirit to those who believe *in the way of salvation*: John 14:6, 16, Acts 16:17, 31 and Romans 10:4, 9-13,
9. Blessed are the poor in spirit to those who believe *in Time of Loneliness*: Psalm 23:1-6, Isaiah 41:10, Hebrews 13:5, 6
10. Blessed are the poor in spirit to those who believe *in Time of Sorrow.* II Corinthians 1:3-5, Romans 8:26-28
11. Blessed are the poor in spirit to those who believe *in Relief in Time of Suffering*: I Corinthians 12:8-10, Hebrews 12:3-13
12. Blessed are the poor in spirit to those who believe *in Guidance in Time of Decision*: James 1:5, 6, Proverbs 3:5-6

Part DXI

Blessed Are The Poor In Spirit. Matthew 5:3

Blessed Means Happy

Poor means meek in spirit. Poor means humble in spirit. Poor means lowly in spirit. Poor means quiet in spirit. Read Matthew 5:3-12, Read also Mark 1:15

Jesus did not say "*rich*" in spirit. Jesus said "*poor*" in spirit.

1. Blessed are the poor in spirit to those who believe *in Protection in Time of Danger*: Psalm 91:1-16, Psalm 121:1-8
2. Blessed are the poor in spirit to those who believe *in Courage in Time of Fear*: Hebrews 13:5, 6, Ephesians 6:10-18
3. Blessed are the poor in spirit to those who believe in *Peace in Time of Turmoil*: Isaiah 26:3, 4, Philippians 4:6, 7
4. Blessed are the poor in spirit to those who believe in *Rest in Time of Weariness*: Matthew 11:28, 29, Psalm 23:1-23
5. Blessed are the poor in spirit to those who believe in *Strength in Time of Temptation*: James 1:12-16, I Corinthians 10:6-13
6. Blessed are the poor in spirit to those who believe in *Warning in Time of Indifference*: Galatians 5:19-21, Hebrews 10:26-31
7. Blessed are the poor in spirit to those who believe in *Forgiveness in Time of Conviction*: Isaiah 1:18, I John 1:7-9
8. Blessed are the poor in spirit to those who believe *in the Creation of God*: Genesis chapter:1:1-31
9. Blessed are poor in spirit to those who believe *in the Fall of Man*: Genesis Chapter 2:1-25
10. Blessed are the poor in spirit to those who believe *in the Flood of Noah*: Genesis Chapters:6:1 to 9:1-29
11. Blessed are the poor in spirit to those who believe *in the Call of Abraham*: Genesis 12:1-9
12. Blessed are the poor in spirit to those who believe in *Deliverance of Isarael from Egypt*: Chapters:Exodus 3:1 to 14:1-31

Part DXII

Blessed Are The Poor In Spirit. Matthew 5:3

Blessed Means Happy

Poor means meek in spirit. Poor means humble in spirit. Poor means lowly in spirit. Poor means quiet in spirit. Read Matthew 5:3-12, Read also Mark 1:15

Jesus did not say "*rich*" in spirit. Jesus said "*poor*" in spirit.

1. Blessed are the poor in spirit to those who believe *in Dedication of the Temple*: II Chronicles Chapters: 2:1 to 7:1-22
2. Blessed are the poor in spirit to those who believe *in the Babylonian Captivity of Israel*: II Chronicles Chapter 36:1-23
3. Blessed are the poor in spirit to those who believe *in the Revival of Israel after Captivity*: Nehemiah Chapters: 8:1 to 9:1-38
4. Blessed are the poor in spirit to those who believe *in the Promise of the Coming Messiah*:Psalms 22:1-31, Isaiah 9:2-7, Isaiah 53:1-12,
5. Blessed are the poor in spirit to those who believe *in the Birth of Christ*: Matthew 1:18-25-2:1-23, Luke 1:26-2:1-52
6. Blessed are the poor in spirit to those who believe *in the Trimphal Entry*: Luke 19:28-44
7. Blessed are the poor in spirit to those who believe *in the Last Supper*: Mark 14:12-26
8. Blessed are the poor in spirit to those who believe *in the Garden of Gethsemane*: Matthew 26:35-46
9. Blessed are the poor in spirit to those who believe *in the Betrayal of Jesus*: Matthew 26:47-56
10. Blessed are the poor in spirit to those who believe *in the Arrest and Trial of Jesus*: John 18:1 to19:1-42
11. Blessed are the poor in spirit to those who believe *in the Death of Christ*: Luke 23:26-56, John 19:16-42
12. Blessed are the poor in spirit to those who believe *in the Ressurection of Christ*: Luke 24:1-53, John 20:1- to John 21:1-25

Part DXIII

Blessed Are The Poor In Spirit. Matthew 5:3

Blessed Means Happy

Poor means meek in spirit. Poor means humble in spirit. Poor means lowly in spirit. Poor means quiet in spirit. Read Matthew 5:3-12, Read also Mark 1:15

Jesus did not say "*rich*" in spirit. Jesus said "*poor*" in spirit.

1. Blessed are the poor in spirit to those who believe *in the Ascension of Christ*: Acts 1:1-12
2. Blessed are the poor in spirit to those who believe *in the Coming of the Holy Spirit*: Acts 2:1-21
3. Blessed are the poor in spirit to those who believe *in the Conversion of Paul*: Acts 19:1-31
4. Blessed are the poor in spirit to those who believe *in the Heroes of Faith*: Hebrews 11:1-40
5. Blessed are the poor in spirit to those who believe in the Great Theme of Scripture *in the Ten Commandment*—Exodus 20:1-17
6. Blessed are the poor in spirit to those who believe the Great Theme of Scripture *in the Sermon on the Mount*—Matthew Chapters 5:1 to 7:1-29
7. Blessed are the poor in spirit to those who believe the Great Theme of Scripture *in the Golden Rule*—Matthew 7:12
8. Blessed are the poor in spirit to those who believe the Great Theme of Scripture *in the Greatest Commandment*—Matthew 22:36-40
9. Blessed are the poor in spirit to those who believe the Great Theme of Scripture *in the Righteousness of Faith*—Romans 3:19-28
10. Blessed are the poor in spirit to those who believe the Great Theme of Scripture *in the Royal Law*—James 2:8, Romans 13:8-10
11. Blessed are the poor in spirit to those who believe the Great Theme of Scripture *in the Christian Love*—I Corinthians 13:1-13
12. Blessed are the poor in spirit to those who believe *in God's Greatness And Man's Weakness* or Weariness—Isaiah 40:1-31

Part DXIV

Blessed Are The Poor In Spirit. Matthew 5:3

Blessed Means Happy

Poor means meek in spirit. Poor means humble in spirit. Poor means lowly in spirit. Poor means quiet in spirit. Read Matthew 5:3-12, Read also Mark 1:15

Jesus did not say "*rich*" in spirit. Jesus said "*poor*" in spirit.

1. Blessed are the poor in spirit to those who believe *in the Twofold Revelation of God*—Psalm 19:1-14
2. Blessed are the poor in spirit to those who believe *in Man's Universal Guilt*—Romans 1:18-2:1-16
3. Blessed are the poor in spirit to those who believe *in the Atonement*—Leviticus 16:6, 30, 32, 33, 34, Leviticus 17:11, Romans 5:11
4. Blessed are the poor in spirit to those who believe *in the New Birth*—John 3:1-8
5. Blessed are the poor in spirit to those who believe *in Justification by Faith*—Habakkuk 2:4, Romans1:17, Ephesians 2:1-10, Galatians 2:16-21, 3:11, Hebrews 10:38
6. Blessed are the poor in spirit to those who believe *in Christ, the Good Shepherd*—Psalm 23:1-6, John 10:1-18
7. Blessed are the poor in spirit to those who believe *in Christ's Intercession For His Own to save our souls before God*—John 17:9, Hebrews 7:25
8. Blessed are the poor in spirit to those who believe *in the High Priestly Work of Christ*—Hebrews 9:11-15, Hebrews 4:14-16
9. Blessed are the poor in spirit to those who believe *in Christ's Humiliation and Exaltation*—Philippians 2:5-11
10. Blessed are the poor in spirit to those who believe *in the Resurrection of the Christian* Faith—I Corinthians 15:1-58, I Thessalonians 4:13-18
11. Blessed are the poor in spirit to those who believe *in the Second Coming of Christ*—Matthew 24:1-51, Matthew 25:1-46, II Thessalonians 1:7-12, Hebrews 9:28, I John 3:2, I Thessalonians 4:13-17, Revelation 1:7, Revelation 3:11, Revelation 16:15, Revelation 22:7, 12, 13, 16, 20
12. Blessed are the poor in spirit to those who believe *in the Last Judgment Day To Come*—Revelation 20:10-15

Part DXV

Blessed Are The Poor In Spirit. Matthew 5:3

Blessed Means Happy

Poor means meek in spirit. Poor means humble in spirit. Poor means lowly in spirit. Poor means quiet in spirit. Read Matthew 5:3-12, Read also Mark 1:15

Jesus did not say "*rich*" in spirit. Jesus said "*poor*" in spirit.

1. Blessed are the poor in spirit to those who believe *in the New Heaven and New Earth*—Revelation Chapters 21:1 to 22:1-21
2. Blessed are the poor in spirit to those who believe *in Christian Home Relationship*—Ephesians 5:21 to 6:1-4, Ephesians 3:15
3. Blessed are the poor in spirit to those who believe *in Model Wife and Mother*—Proverbs 31:10-31
4. Blessed are the poor in spirit to those who believe *in Marriage and Divorce*—Matthew 19:3-9, Malachi 2:14-16
5. Blessed are the poor in spirit to those who believe *in the Sin of Adultery*—Proverbs 6:23-33
6. Blessed are the poor in spirit to those who believe *in the Prodigal Son*—Luke 15:11-30
7. Blessed are the poor in spirit to those who believe *in Employer—Employee Relationships*—Colossians 3:22-4:1
8. Blessed are the poor in spirit to those who believe *in Business and Professional*—Psalm 15:1-5
9. Blessed are the poor in spirit to those who believe *in Principles*—Proverbs 3:1-12
10. Blessed are the poor in spirit to those who believe *in Separation from Worldliness* and perfecting-(be amature) holiness in the fear of God—II Corinthians 6:14 to 7:1, I John 2:15-17
11. Blessed are the poor in spirit to those who believe *in Decisions on Doubtful Things*—Romans 14
12. Blessed are the poor in spirit to those who believe *in Christian Fruitfulness*—John 15:1-27 verse 16

Part DXVI

Blessed Are The Poor In Spirit. Matthew 5:3

Blessed Means Happy

Poor means meek in spirit. Poor means humble in spirit. Poor means lowly in spirit. Poor means quiet in spirit. Read Matthew 5:3-12, Read also Mark 1:15

Jesus did not say "*rich*" in spirit. Jesus said "*poor*" in spirit.

1. Blessed are the poor in spirit to those who believe *in Heavenly Wisdom*—James 3:14-18
2. Blessed are the poor in spirit to those who believe *in Christian Responsibilities*—Romans Chapters:13:1 to14;1-23
3. Blessed are the poor in spirit to those who believe *in Christian Stewardship*—II Corinthians 8:8-9, Luke 16:1-13
4. Blessed are the poor in spirit to those who believe *in Christian Witnessing*—Matthew 28:18-20, John 17:18-20, Luke 24:48, Acts 1:8, Proverbs 11:30
5. Blessed are the poor in spirit to those who believe *in Prevailing Prayer*—Matthew 6:5-15, Philippians 4:6, 7, I Thessalonians 5:17
6. Blessed are the poor in spirit to those who believe *in Heavenly Priorities*—Matthew 6:25-33
7. Blessed are the poor in spirit to those who believe *in Brevity of Man's Day* For Prayer-Psalm 90:1-17
8. Blessed are the poor in spirit to those who believe *in Consequences of Forgetting God*—Hosea 4:1-11
9. Blessed are the poor in spirit to those who believe *in the Causes of War*—James 4:1-4
10. Blessed are the poor in spirit to those who believe *in the Value of the Soul*—Mark 8:36, 37
11. Blessed are the poor in spirit to those who believe this scripture: "He that hath a bountiful eye shall be blessed; for he giveth of his bread to the poor." Proverbs 22:9
12. Blessed are the poor in spirit to those who believe and read these two scriptures: "Lust not after her beauty in thine heart; neither let her take thee with her eyelids…But I say unto you, that whosoever look on a woman to lust after her hath commit adultery with her already in his heart." Proverbs 6:25, Matthew 5:28

Part DXVII

Blessed Are The Poor In Spirit. Matthew 5:3

Blessed Means Happy

Poor means meek in spirit. Poor means humble in spirit. Poor means lowly in spirit. Poor means quiet in spirit. Read Matthew 5:3-12, Read also Mark 1:15

Jesus did not say "*rich*" in spirit. Jesus said "*poor*" in spirit.

1. Blessed are the poor in spirit to those who believe this scripture: "The glory of *young men* is their *strength*: and the beauty of *old men* is the gray (white, silver) head (hair)." Proverbs 20:29
2. Blessed are the poor in spirit to those who believe that our peace was upon Christ; and with Christ's stripes (wounds) we are healed. Isaiah 53:5 (Romans 4:25)
3. Blessed are the poor in spirit to those who believe that all we like sheep have gone astray (drifted; split); we have turned everyone to his own way; (gone separated); and the Lord hath laid on Christ the iniquity (sin, punishment of us all). Isaiah 53:6 (I Peter 2:25)
4. Blessed are the poor in spirit to those who for we (ye) were going astray; but are now returned unto the Shepherd (i.e (for example), Christ) and Bishop (i.e (for example), Christ) of our (your) souls. I Peter 2:25
5. Blessed are the poor in spirit to those who believe that "*Daily*" is *necessary* for Christian living while it is called "*Today*;" lest (or, unless) any of us be hardened through the deceitfulness of sin. II Timothy 4:1-5 verse 2, Luke 11:3, Hebrews 3:13, Read Hebrews 3:5-19
6. Blessed are the poor in spirit to those who believe in *watching* the "*Daily*" (Acts 5:42)—Christian Trinity of the Television Broadcasting Network. Mark 13:10, Mark 16:15, Luke 4:18 (Isaiah 61:1-3), II Timothy 4:1-5 verse 2, Luke 11:3, Matthew 4:23, Matthew 9:35, Matthew 24:14, Matthew 26:13, Mark 1:1, 14-15, Matthew 11:5-6, Mark 14:9, Luke 7:22-23, Hebrews 3:1-3, Read Hebrews 3:5-19,
7. Blessed are the poor in spirit to those who believe in *listening* to the (Daily) Acts 4:52 Gospel Radio Broadcasting Network. Mark 13:10, Mark 16:15, Luke 4:18 (Isaiah 61:1-3), II Timothy 4:1-5 verse 2, Matthew 24:14, Mark 1:1, 14-15,

Mark 14:9, Matthew 26:14, Matthew 4:23, Matthew 9:35, Matthew 11:5-6, Luke 11:3, Luke 7:22-23, Hebrews 3:13, Read Hebrews 3:5-19

8. Blessed are the poor in spirit to those who will draw near to God and God will draw near to those who believe in God through Jesus Christ. James 4:8
9. Blessed are the poor in spirit to those who believe that the Bible, God's Word, God's speaking to us to get us to work through His ministry; to work for the Lord faithfully unto He come to take us home with Him from our labors of work on the Lord's vineyard on earth; on this old planet. Matthew 21:28, Matthew 26:10, Mark 14:6, Luke 13:14, John 4:34-42, John 5:17, John 6:28-29, John 9:4, John 17:4. So get to work today in the Lord's vineyard!!! Matthew 21:28
10. Blessed are the poor in spirit to those who believe that Pentecostal festivals are the Jews, the Passover and the Tabernacle. Deuteronomy 16:1-7, John 7:2
11. Blessed are the poor in spirit to those who believe and why Pentecost has a name which fall on the fiftieth day after the Sabbath of Passover. Acts 2:1
12. Blessed are the poor in spirit to those who in equipping believers to continue to know Christ until He come the second time. Hebrews 9:28, Hebrews 13:21, Ephesians 4:1-32 verses-3-7, 12-13, 15-16, 23-24, 29-31

Part DXVIII

Blessed Are The Poor In Spirit. Matthew 5:3

Blessed Means Happy

Poor means meek in spirit. Poor means humble in spirit. Poor means lowly in spirit. Poor means quiet in spirit. Read Matthew 5:3-12, Read also Mark 1:15

Jesus did not say "*rich*" in spirit. Jesus said "*poor*" in spirit.

1. Blessed are the poor in spirit to those who believe and read the *Valley of Dry Bones*. Ezekiel 37:1-28 verse 13-14
2. Blessed are the poor in spirit to those who believe that the Prophecy Against Gog will surely come to pass. Ezekiel 38:1-23, Read Revelation 20:8
3. Blessed are the poor in spirit to those who believe that the Judgment of Gog will surely come to pass. Ezekiel 39:1-29, Read Revelation 19:17, 18
4. Blessed are the poor in spirit to those who believe that the Lord's *Marvelous Hand* is not shortened, that it cannot save; neither His ear heavy, that it cannot hear. Isaiah 59:1—See Jeremiah 23:23 and Ezekiel 22:14
5. Blessed are the poor in spirit to those who believe the spoken Word of the lord: "But your *iniquities* (sins) have separated between you and your God, and your sins have hid His face from you that He will not hear. Isaiah 59:2
6. Blessed are the poor in spirit to those who believe the spoken Word of the Lord: "For your hands are *defiled with blood* (wrongdoings), and your fingers with iniquity; your lips have spoken lies, your tongue hath muttered perverseness (wickedness). Isaiah 59:3
7. Blessed are the poor in spirit to those who believe the spoken Word of the Lord: "None calleth for justice (righteousness), nor any pleadeth for (in) truth: they trust in vanity, and speak lies; they conceive mischief, and bring forth iniquity." Isaiah 59:4
8. Blessed are the poor in spirit to those who do not want to die a pitiful fall and a shameful fall without Him because I am fearfully and wonderfully made in the image of God who created me just as I am today. Be Saved Today. Accept Jesus Christ Today. Psalm 139:14 you will be glad you did!!!

"A Gift From Above"

James 1:17, Ephesians 4:7, **Romans 6:23,** Matthew 5:24, 15:5, Mark 7:11, **John 4:10,** I Corinthians 1:7, 7:7, II Corinthians 1:11, 8:4, 9:15, Ephesians **2:8**, 3:7, **4:7**, Philippians 4:17, I Timothy 4:14, II Timothy 1:6, Hebrews 6:3, **James 1:17**, I Peter 4:10, **Matthew 7:7-11 verse 11**, Luke 11:9-13 verse 13, **I Corinthians 7:7, Ephesians 2:8, Ephesians 4:7, James 1:17, John 4:10, Romans 6:23, Philippians 4:13,** II Peter 3:18

9. Blessed are the poor in spirit to those who believe that *being well-educated* is a **gift from God**.
10. Blessed are the poor in spirit to those who *being having knowledge* is a **gift from God** to any male and females as well to each child.
11. Blessed are the poor in spirit to those who believe that *being a brilliant* is a **gift from God** to any male and females as well as each child.
12. Blessed are the poor in spirit to those who believe, have a *natural talent* **gift is from God** to any males and females as well as each child.

Part DXIX

Blessed Are The Poor In Spirit. Matthew 5:3

Blessed Means Happy

Poor means meek in spirit. Poor means humble in spirit. Poor means lowly in spirit. Poor means quiet in spirit. Read Matthew 5:3-12, Read also Mark 1:15

Jesus did not say "*rich*" in spirit. Jesus said "*poor*" in spirit.

"A Gift From Above"

James 1:17, Ephesians 4:7, **Romans 6:23,** Matthew 5:24, 15:5, Mark 7:11, **John 4:10,** I Corinthians 1:7, 7:7, II Corinthians 1:11, 8:4, 9:15, Ephesians **2:8**, 3:7, **4:7**, Philippians 4:17, I Timothy 4:14, II Timothy 1:6, Hebrews 6:3, **James 1:17**, I Peter 4:10, **Matthew 7:7-11 verse 11**, Luke 11:9-13 verse 13, **I Corinthians 7:7, Ephesians 2:8, Ephesians 4:7, James 1:17, John 4:10, Romans 6:23, Philippians 4:13,** II Peter 3:18

1. Blessed are the poor in spirit to those who believe that *being an intelligent* is a **gift from God** to any males and females as well as each child.
2. Blessed are the poor in spirit to those who believe that *being smart* is a **gift from God** to any males and females as well to each child.
3. Blessed are the poor in spirit to those who believe that *being an average* is a **gift from God** to any males and females as well as each child.
4. Blessed are the poor in spirit to those who believe that *being well to do* is a **gift from God** to any males and females as well as each child.
5. Blessed are the poor in spirit to those who believe that *being an high self esteem* and *low self esteem* are the **gift from God** to any males and females as well as each child.
6. Blessed are the poor in spirit to those who are *being ordinary* is a **gift from God** to males and females as well as each child.
7. Blessed are the poor in spirit to those who believe are *natural talent gift* is a **gift from God** to all males and females as well as each child
8. Blessed are the poor in spirit to those who have *the ability*; a **gift from God** to all males and females as well as each child.
9. Blessed are the poor in spirit to those who have *the skill is a blessing* and **the gift is from God** to all males and females as well as each child.

10. Blessed are the poor in spirit to those who have *great talent* and a *blessing* and the **gift is from God** to all males and females as well as each child.
11. Blessed are the poor in spirit to those who believe that they *have qualification* is a *blessing* and a **gift is from God** to any males and females as well as each child
12. Blessed are the poor in spirit to those who believe and are *low level* and *high level* is a *blessing* and a **gift from God** to any males and females as well as each child.

Part DXX

Blessed Are The Poor In Spirit. Matthew 5:3

Blessed Means Happy

Poor means meek in spirit. Poor means humble in spirit. Poor means lowly in spirit. Poor means quiet in spirit. Read Matthew 5:3-12, Read also Mark 1:15

Jesus did not say "*rich*" in spirit. Jesus said "*poor*" in spirit.

"A Gift From Above"

James 1:17, Ephesians 4:7, **Romans 6:23,** Matthew 5:24, 15:5, Mark 7:11, **John 4:10,** I Corinthians 1:7, 7:7, II Corinthians 1:11, 8:4, 9:15, Ephesians **2:8**, 3:7, **4:7**, Philippians 4:17, I Timothy 4:14, II Timothy 1:6, Hebrews 6:3, **James 1:17**, I Peter 4:10, **Matthew 7:7-11 verse 11**, Luke 11:9-13 verse 13, **I Corinthians 7:7, Ephesians 2:8, Ephesians 4:7, James 1:17, John 4:10, Romans 6:23, Philippians 4:13,** II Peter 3:18

1. Blessed are the poor in spirit to those who have *great a keen* and a *blessing* is a **gift from God** to any males and females as well as each child.
2. Blessed are the poor in spirit to those who have *great* and *bright future* is a *blessing* and a **gift from God** to any males and females as well as each child.
3. Blessed are the poor in spirit to those who have *great capable of doing things*, is *blessing* and a **gift from God** to any males and females as well as each child.
4. Blessed are the poor in spirit to those who are *being smart* is a *blessing* and a **gift from God** to any males and females as well as each child.
5. Blessed are the poor in spirit to those who have *great understanding* is a *blessing* and a **gift from God** to any males and females as well as each child.
6. Blessed are the poor in spirit to those who have *quick thinking* is a *blessing* and a **gift from God** to any males and females as well as each child.
7. Blessed are the poor in spirit to those who have a *quick mind* is a *blessing* and a **gift from God** to any males and females as well as each child.
8. Blessed are the poor in spirit to those whose *mind is clever* is a *blessing* and a **gift from God** to any males and females as well as each child.
9. Blessed are the poor in spirit to those who believe that *disability person* is a *blessing* and a **gift from God** to any males and females as well as each child.

10. Blessed are the poor in spirit to those who have *clever, capable of doing thing, smart, great understanding, great and wise, great thinking, keen, quick mind* are *blessings* and a **gift from God** to any males and females as well as each child.
11. Blessed are the poor in spirit to those who are **born again; born of the Spirit; children of God; the saints of God**, to those who are **alive** and **remain moment by moment**; and who **have passed from death unto life** and to those **who have ear, let him/her hear what the Spirit say unto the churches** that **overcome shall not be hurt of the second death**. Revelation 2:11, John 3:3, 5-8 verse 8, John 18:37, Matthew 5:9, 44-45, Matthew 18:1-6 verse 3, Matthew 19:14, Read Matthew 19:25-29, John 1:12, Philippians 4:21, I Corinthians 1:1-10 verse 2, I Corinthians 14:33, II Corinthians 8:4, Ephesians 1:1-23 verse 1, 15, 18, Ephesians 2:19, Ephesians 3:8, 18-21, Ephesians 4:11-13 verse 12, Ephesians 5:3-21 verse 3, Ephesians 6:18, Philippians 1:1-6 verse 1, 4:21-23, Colossians 1:1-29 verse 2, 4, 26, I Thessalonians 3:13, II Thessalonians 1:10-12 verse 10, Philippians 1:1-8 verse 5, 7, Hebrews 6:10-15 verse 10, 12, Hebrews 13:24, Jude 1:2-3, verse 3, 14, 20-21, 24, 25, Revelation 5:7-10 verse 8, 12-14, Revelation 8:3-4, Revelation 11:17-19 verse 18, Revelation 13:7, 10c, Revelation 14:12, Revelation 15:3, Revelation 16:6, Revelation 19:8, John 5:24, I Thessalonians 4:13-18 verse 15
12. Blessed are the poor in spirit to those who believe that we are *sanctified by faith* that is in **Jesus Christ** by **receiving forgiveness of sins**. Acts 26:18

Part DXXI

Blessed Are The Poor In Spirit. Matthew 5:3

Blessed Means Happy

Poor means meek in spirit. Poor means humble in spirit. Poor means lowly in spirit. Poor means quiet in spirit. Read Matthew 5:3-12, Read also Mark 1:15

Jesus did not say "*rich*" in spirit. Jesus said "*poor*" in spirit.

1. Blessed are the poor in spirit to those *whose eyes are now* **opening, knowing good and evil**. Genesis 3:5, 22, 23, 24, Hebrews 4:13
2. Blessed are the poor in spirit to those who believe that **Jesus Christ** has the **power to forgive sins**. Matthew 9:2, 6, Mark 2:5, 10, 11, Luke 5:20, 22-24
3. Blessed are the poor in spirit to those who believe this scripture: "So that *we may boldly say*, The Lord is my helper, and I will not fear what man shall do unto me." Hebrews 13:6, Psalms 27:1, Psalm 118:6, Romans 8:31, II Kings 6:16
4. Blessed are the poor in spirit to those who believe **Christ's Prophecy** in Luke 21:16 "And ye shall betrayed both by parents and brethren, and kinsfolks and friends: some of you shall they cause to be put to death.
5. Blessed are the poor in spirit to those who believe in **praising God through Jesus Christ's** *goodness, mercy, grace, peace and joy*. Galatians 5:22
6. Blessed are the poor in spirit to those who believe that *we have work to do*: "**Jesus says:** Therefore, *go* and *make disciples of* (teach) all nations, *baptizing* them in the *name* of the *Father* and of the *Son* and of the *Holy Spirit*. Matthew 28:19. See Jesus example in Matthew 3:13-17, I Peter 2:21
7. Blessed are the poor in spirit to those who are able to say with strength: "Our *profession of faith*: "*I am what* the **Word of God** says *I am*, *I am* more than a **conqueror**, I am more than **victorious**, And I will do what the **Word of God** says I can do. Romans 8:1-39 (verse 35-39), Philippians 4:13, Exodus 3:13-14 (verse 14), Revelation 1:8
8. Blessed are the poor in spirit to those who believe that we are going **up the King's Highway to Heaven**. Genesis 28:12, John 1:51, II Kings 2:1-12, Revelation 11:12
9. Blessed are the poor in spirit to those who believe that **Jesus** *teaches* us how *to pray*. Matthew 6:5-15, Luke 11:1-13

10. Blessed are the poor in spirit to those who believe that *there is no eighth day of annihilation.* **God rested on the seventh day**. Genesis 2:2-3, Hebrews 4:4
11. Blessed are the poor in spirit to those who believe in the name of Christ which is eternal. Romans 1:20
12. Blessed are the poor in spirit to those who believe that **Christ's Love** want the world for **Himself in return** because **He love them all**. **He** loved them to the end. *Drawn* all men to **Himself.** John 3:16, I John 4:19, John 12:32, John 6:44, John 13:1

Part DXXII

Blessed Are The Poor In Spirit. Matthew 5:3

Blessed Means Happy

Poor means meek in spirit. Poor means humble in spirit. Poor means lowly in spirit. Poor means quiet in spirit. Read Matthew 5:3-12, Read also Mark 1:15

Jesus did not say "*rich*" in spirit. Jesus said "*poor*" in spirit.

1. Blessed are the poor in spirit to those who believe that to be a *Christian* mean accepting **Christ** as your personal **Savior** is a *true genuine*. Romans 1:17
2. Blessed are the poor in spirit to those who believe to give up his/her will to **God** and to follow **Him** wherever **He** lead them. Genesis 12:1-4, Acts 7:3, Hebrews 11:8
3. Blessed are the poor in spirit to those who believe that **Jesus Christ** lived and died physical as a man for thirty three years and then three days later, **He rose from death unto eternal life forever**. Matthew 27:50, Mark 15:37, 39, Luke 23:46, 47, John 19:30, 33
4. Blessed are the poor in spirit to those who believe that *Pentecost* was *first* mentioned **three times** and began in the first century rather than in the 20th century!!!. Acts 2:1, Acts 20:16 and I Corinthians 16:8
5. Blessed are the poor in spirit to those **who saw the Light, the Blessed Gospel Light; which is in God through Jesus Christ**. John 1:4-5, 7-9, I John 1:4-5, 7
6. Blessed are the poor in spirit to those who believe in this spiritual hymn: "**The Blessed Gospel Light. Let it shine for ever more**." II Corinthians 4:4
7. Blessed are the poor in spirit to those who believe that *Pentecost* is still knocking at the door of the unbelievers' and the believers' hearts. Please open the door of your hearts today. **Christ** is still knocking those who are not saved and to those who are *lukewarm Christians*. Revelation 3:20, Revelation 3:16
8. Blessed are the poor in spirit to those who believe the very foretaste of the rapture; that the blessed Christ is coming soon. I Thessalonians 4:13-18, Revelation 3:11, Revelation 16:15, Revelation 22:7, 12, 20
9. Blessed are the poor in spirit to those who believe that *Pentecostal message* is for all of races; all of color lines, all of cultural people, all of God's children; all of lost sinners. Acts 2:1-47

10. Blessed are the poor in spirit to those who believe that black and white all human races are created **equal in the eyes of God**; are *created in His image*; *one body* in **Christ Jesus**: Genesis 1:26-27, Galatians 3:22-28, Romans 1:17, John 3:22-31 and that *racial prejudice* be *eradicated*; that it **must** not show *racial discrimination* in **the eye of God**. Genesis 1:26-27, Galatians 3:28
11. Blessed are the poor in spirit to those who believe and read this statement of W.J. Henry (unknown date of birth and death) one of God's children, too: "*There is no room for prejudice* of any kind in the *hearts of sanctified people*. If you, as a *white man* find any of his in your heart toward the *black man* as an individual or toward his people. *You need to go* to the **Lord** for **cleansing**; to the *black brother*, *I will say the same*. *All prejudice* of every kind is *outside the church of God*." Genesis 1:26-27, Galatians 3:22-28, Romans 1:17, John 3:22-31-(**Footnote Later** }
12. Blessed are the poor in spirit to those who believe and read the statement of Martin Wells Knopp (1853-1901) one of God's children, too: "*Barriers of race* and *color*, and *social position* have *no true place in Christ's Church*...High tonged social clubs, claiming to be churches, but *throwing stones of criticism* and *ostracism* at *saints of God* Because of *caste* or *color*, are among the most stupendous of *Satan's frauds* which *curse* the *earth* today. *Respecters* and *selectors of persons*...What a *contrast* to the *Body of Christ*." Genesis 1:26-27, Galatians 3:22-28, Romans 1:17, John 3:22-31-(**Footnote Later**}

Part DXXIII

Blessed Are The Poor In Spirit. Matthew 5:3

Blessed Means Happy

Poor means meek in spirit. Poor means humble in spirit. Poor means lowly in spirit. Poor means quiet in spirit. Read Matthew 5:3-12, Read also Mark 1:15

Jesus did not say "*rich*" in spirit. Jesus said "*poor*" in spirit.

1. Blessed are the poor in spirit to those who believe that **speaking in other tongues** are the **scriptural evidence of the Holy Spirit baptism**. Acts 2:4
2. Blessed are the poor in spirit to those who believe in *studying Christian life on marriage*. Ephesians 5:21-32
3. Blessed are the poor in spirit to those who believe and know that **God is against divorce**; that **God hate divorce**. Malachi 2:16
4. Blessed are the poor in spirit to those who believe the **Bible**; The **Word of God**; the **Written Word of God**: "*Do not argue with* the **Bible**. *Do not win over the* **Bible** for the **Bible** is *sure* and *settle. Accept* the **Bible** just as **it** is *said* and *done alone:* John 14:11-17, John 15:26, II Timothy 3:16, Genesis 1:1, John 1:1-18
5. Blessed are the poor in spirit to those who believe that a Christian is saved by giving his/her heart to Jesus Christ. Ephesians 2:8
6. Blessed are the poor in spirit to those who believe that a *Christian* is *converted* by **faith in Jesus Christ**. Acts 3:19
7. Blessed are the poor in spirit to those who believe that a *Christian* is to **repent toward God** and **faith toward our Lord Jesus Christ from** Acts 20:21
8. Blessed are the poor in spirit to those who believe that "**Holiness**" is the *right way* **in God's teaching**, **in God's standard**, **in God's mandatory** and **in God's Holiness**. Zechariah 14:20, Exodus 28:36, Exodus 39:30
9. Blessed are the poor in spirit to those who believe *in walking the walk*, and *talking the talk* **by faith**, without seeing with our natural eyes II Corinthians 1:16-18, Galatians 5:16, II Corinthians 5:7, Ephesians 2:10, Romans 6:4, Romans 8:1, 4, Ephesians 4:1, 5:2, 8, Colossians 1:10, Colossians 2:9, I Thessalonians 2:12, I Thessalonians 4:1, Revelation 21:24
10. Blessed are the poor in spirit to those who believe, have *a natural talent gift* is **from God** to any males and females as well as each child. James 1:17

11. Blessed are the poor in spirit to those who believe that *Knowledge is power*; *Without* **Christ** even though *knowledge is power*, *still we can do nothing*. John 15:4-27 **verse 5**
12. Blessed are the poor in spirit to those who believe that the **longsuffering of our Lord is salvation**. II Peter 3:15. See II Peter 3:9, Titus 2:11

Part DXXIV

Blessed Are The Poor In Spirit. Matthew 5:3

Blessed Means Happy

Poor means meek in spirit. Poor means humble in spirit. Poor means lowly in spirit. Poor means quiet in spirit. Read Matthew 5:3-12, Read also Mark 1:15

Jesus did not say "*rich*" in spirit. Jesus said "*poor*" in spirit.

1. Blessed are the poor in spirit to those who believe that *an unstable life* is not an okay to sin after we accept **Jesus Christ** as our personal **Savior and Lord.** James 1:8, II Peter 2:14, II Peter 3:16, I John 2:1, Matthew 12:31-32, John 5:14, Hebrews 12:14
2. Blessed are the poor in spirit to those who believe **Jesus spoken word** when He said: "*Go* and (*but*) *sin no more*. John 8:11
   Singing:
   "Je-sus say to sin no mo-re. Oh, Je-sus say to sin no mo-re. Je-sus say to sin no mo-re. John 8:11, John 5:14, Matthew 12:31-32, I John 2:1, James 1:8, II Peter 2:14, II Peter 3:16
3. Blessed are the poor in spirit to those who believe that **God, Jesus, Holy Spirit. Lord, Master, Christ, Angel, Prophet, Rabbi, Teacher, Father,** or **For One** is our **Father**, which is in heaven are very, very, very **complication** and **combination** but there is **one word that fix Him in all**; **There is One in "He"** or the **"I am that I Am"** involve **big word**: "**He**" in **one entire whole verse** or **passage**, or **scripture at one time from Genesis to Revelation**: **One word** is "**The Word**; In the Beginning God' In the Beginning Was "**The Word.**" **"The Word"** was with **God,** The **Word** was **God, "The Same"** was in the **Beginning** with **"God," God** said, "**Let** *Us*;" Behold **he** is **one of us**. Read **II Peter 3:16; in all epistles** (letters, scriptures, written) speaking of these things) epistles, letters, scripture, **oral written**, **Jesus' Word**, **God's Word**, **Christ's Word**, **Holy Spirit's Word**) are **hard** to be **understood** include **One Word** called "**He**" **emphasize** from Genesis to Revelation. Read also Hebrews 13:8; **The Same** as **Yesterday**, **Today** and **Forever**. Read Revelation 1:7, 8, 11, 17, 18, 19, 16:5. Read Acts 1:11, Acts 9:4-5. With these **complication** you and I **cannot outsmart God**. You and I

are very limit to the deep meaning of the Word as we study. **The Meaning of The Word Is Hidden.** There is but **One Big** two letters word; "**HE**" Just Believe **God**. Believe **Jesus**. Believe the **Holy Spirit just as The Word is that GOD Has Written**. II Timothy 3:16 There is **One** in **all** and in **all**. Ephesians 4:6. **Leave The Word Alone!!!**

4. Blessed are the poor in spirit to those who believe **what God did was right**; ending the period of sin or sins: the punishment, and death by sending **Jesus Christ to Calvary** who was **delivered for offenses**, and was **raised again** for our **justification**. Luke 23:33 and Romans 4:25
5. Blessed are the poor in spirit to those who believe in **a second chance** in whatsoever **affair** they are in. I John 1:1-9 verse 9
6. Blessed are the poor in spirit to those who believe they are not saved until they shall say, "**Blessed** is **He** that **come in the name of the Lord by faith** in their *sincerely hearts*. Matthew 23:39, Psalm 118:26
7. Blessed are the poor in spirit to those who are *free from the law of sin and death*; from the *punishment of sin* and *away from the* **wrath of God to come**. Romans 8:2, Romans 5:8-9, I Thessalonians 1:10, I Thessalonians 2:16, I Thessalonians 5:9
8. Blessed are the poor in spirit to those who believe that the **wrath of God** is upon *the sinners*; and that **He is mad** upon **the sinners** that the **wrath of God abide** (rest) upon the sinners, **waiting for sinners** to be saved because God so loved the world -(mean sinners)...John 3:15-17. Be saved today. God loves you today. Romans 5:8-9, I John 4:8-11, 19
9. Blessed are the poor in spirit to those who believe that **Jesus** *did not come to destroy people's lives* but to **come to save them**. Luke 9:24, **56**, John 12:47, Matthew 1:21, Matthew 18:11, Mark 3:4, Luke 6:9-10, Luke 19:10
10. Blessed are the poor in spirit to those who believe that **Jesus** did not come to break the law or the Sabbath Day, but to **fulfill the law**. Matthew 5:17-18, Matthew 12:1-21 verse 8, 18, verse 1 (Deuteronomy 23:25), verse 7 (Hosea 6:6), verse 17 (Isaiah 42:1-2), verse 4, 12, Mark 2:23-28 verse 23 (Deuteronomy 23:25), verse 27 (Exodus 23:12), verse 24, 26, Luke 6:1-11, verse 1 (Deuteronomy 23:25), verse 2, 4, 9, 14:1-5, John 5:1-47, **verse 9—10**, 14, **16, 17, 18**
11. Blessed are the poor in spirit to those who believe that "**claiming to know**" we are **Christians** whether by our *head knowledge* or by *our hearts within* ourselves are **not good enough to guess or to think or being ok or maybe**, Hebrews 4:1, James 1:26-27, John 5:39, Matthew 15:1-20, Isaiah 29:13, Jeremiah 12:12, Hebrews 10:31

12. Blessed are the poor in spirit to those who believe that **asking is not the question** to go to heaven, John 7:37-38, John 10:10, 12:46 but to **come to Christ** for *salvation* and **may get to know Him better each day.** The **Bible** say:" These things have I written unto you that *believe* **on the name of the Son of God**; that ye **may know** that **ye have eternal life**, and that **ye may believe on the name of the Son of God**." I John 5:13, Isaiah 45:22, Matthew 11:28, 14:29, Matthew 16:24, Matthew 25:34, Luke 19:1-10 verse 5, 9 Get to Him Daily. Be Blessed!!!

Part DXXV

Blessed Are The Poor In Spirit. Matthew 5:3

Blessed Means Happy

Poor means meek in spirit. Poor means humble in spirit. Poor means lowly in spirit. Poor means quiet in spirit. Read Matthew 5:3-12, Read also Mark 1:15

Jesus did not say "*rich*" in spirit. Jesus said "*poor*" in spirit.

1. Blessed are the poor in spirit to those who believe that there is **only** *one life to live*; then come the judgment of God. Hebrews 9:27
2. Blessed are the poor in spirit to those who believe that **salvation is free** except the decision to accept Christ. Salvation is yours, or ours or mine alone to make. And I *thank* **the Lord** that *I am* **His** and **He** is **mine**. John 17:10, Romans 10:10-13, Ephesians 2:5, 8, Acts 16:31
3. Blessed are the poor in spirit to those who believe that the **Lord** is **"Good"** Psalm 34:8, I Peter 2:3
4. Blessed are the poor in spirit to those who believe that **deaf people can find their way back to God through Jesus Christ.** Romans 10:17, John 1:18, John 5:37-47, I John 4:12, John 14:6, John 3:16, Romans 6:23, Ephesians 2:5, 8-9, Habakkuk 2:4, Galatians 3:11, Romans 1:17, John 3:1-10, Romans 3:9-20, **Romans 1:19-21,** John 7:37-38, Matthew 11:28:30, Romans 1:8
5. Blessed are the poor in spirit to those who believe that **hard of hearing people can find their way back to God through Jesus Christ.** Romans 10:17, John 1:18, John 5:37-47, I John 4:12, John 14:6, John 3:16, Romans 6:23, Ephesians 2:5, 8-9, Habakkuk 2:4, Galatians 3:11, Romans 1:17, John 3:1-10, Romans 3:9-20, **Romans 1:19-21,** John 7:37-38, Matthew 11:28:30, Romans 1:8
6. Blessed are the poor in spirit to those who believe that **hearing people can find their way back to God through Jesus Christ.** Romans 10:17, John 1:18, John 5:37-47, I John 4:12, John 14:6, John 3:16, Romans 6:23, Ephesians 2:5, 8-9, Habakkuk 2:4, Galatians 3:11, Romans 1:17, John 3:1-10, Romans 3:9-20, **Romans 1:19-21,** John 7:37-38, Matthew 11:28:30, Romans 1:8
7. Blessed are the poor in spirit to those who believe that **blind people can find their way back to God through Jesus Christ.** Romans 10:17, John 1:18, John

5:37-47, I John 4:12, John 14:6, John 3:16, Romans 6:23, Ephesians 2:5, 8-9, Habakkuk 2:4, Galatians 3:11, Romans 1:17, John 3:1-10, Romans 3:9-20, **Romans 1:19-21,** John 7:37-38, Matthew 11:28:30, Romans 1:8

8. Blessed are the poor in spirit to those who believe that **sensory multi-disabled people can find their way back to God through Jesus Christ.** Romans 10:17, John 1:18, John 5:37-47, I John 4:12, John 14:6, John 3:16, Romans 6:23, Ephesians 2:5, 8-9, Habakkuk 2:4, Galatians 3:11, Romans 1:17, John 3:1-10, Romans 3:9-20, **Romans 1:19-21,** John 7:37-38, Matthew 11:28:30, Romans 1:8
9. Blessed are the poor in spirit to those who believe that **deaf blind ladies (like famous Helen Keller) can find their way back to God through Jesus Christ.** Romans 10:17, John 1:18, John 5:37-47, I John 4:12, John 14:6, John 3:16, Romans 6:23, Ephesians 2:5, 8-9, Habakkuk 2:4, Galatians 3:11, Romans 1:17, John 3:1-10, Romans 3:9-20, **Romans 1:19-21,** John 7:37-38, Matthew 11:28:30, Romans 1:8
10. Blessed are the poor in spirit to those who believe that **deaf blind gentlemen can find their way back to God through Jesus Christ.** Romans 10:17, John 1:18, John 5:37-47, I John 4:12, John 14:6, John 3:16, Romans 6:23, Ephesians 2:5, 8-9, Habakkuk 2:4, Galatians 3:11, Romans 1:17, John 3:1-10, Romans 3:9-20, **Romans 1:19-21,** John 7:37-38, Matthew 11:28:30, Romans 1:8
11. Blessed are the poor in spirit to those who believe that **the very best ladies can find their way back to God through Jesus Christ.** Romans 10:17, John 1:18, John 5:37-47, I John 4:12, John 14:6, John 3:16, Romans 6:23, Ephesians 2:5, 8-9, Habakkuk 2:4, Galatians 3:11, Romans 1:17, John 3:1-10, Romans 3:9-20, **Romans 1:19-21,** John 7:37-38, Matthew 11:28:30, Romans 1:8
12. Blessed are the poor in spirit to those who believe that **the very best gentlemen can find their way back to God through Jesus Christ.** Romans 10:17, John 1:18, John 5:37-47, I John 4:12, John 14:6, John 3:16, Romans 6:23, Ephesians 2:5, 8-9, Habakkuk 2:4, Galatians 3:11, Romans 1:17, John 3:1-10, Romans 3:9-20, **Romans 1:19-21,** John 7:37-38, Matthew 11:28:30, Romans 1:8

Part DXXVI

Blessed Are The Poor In Spirit. Matthew 5:3

Blessed Means Happy

Poor means meek in spirit. Poor means humble in spirit. Poor means lowly in spirit. Poor means quiet in spirit. Read Matthew 5:3-12, Read also Mark 1:15

Jesus did not say "*rich*" in spirit. Jesus said "*poor*" in spirit.

1. Blessed are the poor in spirit to those who believe that **the very hard working people even deaf or blind people on the top of the world can find their way back to God through Jesus Christ.** Romans 10:17, John 1:18, John 5:37-47, I John 4:12, John 14:6, John 3:16, Romans 6:23, Ephesians 2:5, 8-9, Habakkuk 2:4, Galatians 3:11, Romans 1:17, John 3:1-10, Romans 3:9-20, **Romans 1:19-21,** John 7:37-38, Matthew 11:28:30, Romans 1:8
2. Blessed are the poor in spirit to those who believe that **the very best athlete sport man and sport woman of both the deaf and the hard of hearing and hearing people in the world of wide world sport can find their way back to God through Jesus Christ.** Romans 10:17, John 1:18, John 5:37-47, I John 4:12, John 14:6, John 3:16, Romans 6:23, Ephesians 2:5, 8-9, Habakkuk 2:4, Galatians 3:11, Romans 1:17, John 3:1-10, Romans 3:9-20, **Romans 1:19-21,** John 7:37-38, Matthew 11:28:30, Romans 1:8
3. Blessed are the poor in spirit to those who believe that **rich people can find their way back to God through Jesus Christ.** Romans 10:17, John 1:18, John 5:37-47, I John 4:12, John 14:6, John 3:16, Romans 6:23, Ephesians 2:5, 8-9, Habakkuk 2:4, Galatians 3:11, Romans 1:17, John 3:1-10, Romans 3:9-20, **Romans 1:19-21,** John 7:37-38, Matthew 11:28:30, Romans 1:8
4. Blessed are the poor in spirit to those who believe that **poor people can find their way back to God through Jesus Christ.** Romans 10:17, John 1:18, John 5:37-47, I John 4:12, John 14:6, John 3:16, Romans 6:23, Ephesians 2:5, 8-9, Habakkuk 2:4, Galatians 3:11, Romans 1:17, John 3:1-10, Romans 3:9-20, **Romans 1:19-21,** John 7:37-38, Matthew 11:28:30, Romans 1:8
5. Blessed are the poor in spirit to those who believe that **needy people can find their way back to God through Jesus Christ.** Romans 10:17, John 1:18, John

5:37-47, I John 4:12, John 14:6, John 3:16, Romans 6:23, Ephesians 2:5, 8-9, Habakkuk 2:4, Galatians 3:11, Romans 1:17, John 3:1-10, Romans 3:9-20, **Romans 1:19-21,** John 7:37-38, Matthew 11:28:30, Romans 1:8

6. Blessed are the poor in spirit to those who believe that **ladies can find their way back to God through Jesus Christ.** Romans 10:17, John 1:18, John 5:37-47, I John 4:12, John 14:6, John 3:16, Romans 6:23, Ephesians 2:5, 8-9, Habakkuk 2:4, Galatians 3:11, Romans 1:17, John 3:1-10, Romans 3:9-20, **Romans 1:19-21,** John 7:37-38, Matthew 11:28:30, Romans 1:8
7. Blessed are the poor in spirit to those who believe that **gentlemen can find their way back to God through Jesus Christ.** Romans 10:17, John 1:18, John 5:37-47, I John 4:12, John 14:6, John 3:16, Romans 6:23, Ephesians 2:5, 8-9, Habakkuk 2:4, Galatians 3:11, Romans 1:17, John 3:1-10, Romans 3:9-20, **Romans 1:19-21,** John 7:37-38, Matthew 11:28:30, Romans 1:8
8. Blessed are the poor in spirit to those who believe: what so **excuse** do we have for **not accepting Jesus Christ by faith?** See again Romans 1:19-20
9. Blessed are the poor in spirit to those who believe that **none** had ever met **God** in person **except through Jesus Christ** for 33 years that He lived upon this oldest earth and died for us all. **God** through **Jesus Christ**, **He is alive once** for ever more because **He** had **indeed spoken** throughout the world and even to this presence until we see **Him face to face** in the **soon coming days**. Hebrews 13:8, Revelation 1:8, 17-18, Revelation 16:5, Revelation 22:7, 12, 20
10. Blessed are the poor in spirit to those who believe that **which is born of the Spirit** will enter the kingdom of God and that which is born of the flesh shall not see God; will not enter the kingdom of God. John 3:6, Matthew 5:1-9, Hebrews 12:14
11. Blessed are the poor in spirit to those who believe that we have not seen **God** at any time or hear **His voice**, at any time or **Jesus** who did come upon the earth for 33 years, but did send the **Holy Spirit** to *guide us into all the truth for the* **Holy Spirit does not speak for Himself**, but **Jesus Christ** (God). John 16:13, John 14:26, John 1:3, I John 4:12, John 5:37, John 6:46, John 20:22
12. Blessed are the poor in spirit to those who believe this scripture: **"Die In Your Sin"** *mean* **"You will be killed," "Die In Your Sin"** mean **"Thou shall Surely Die."** Genesis 2:9, **16-17,** Genesis 3:3, 11, 19, Genesis 4:8, **13-15**, 16, **23,** 24, **25,** I Samuel 31:1-6

Part DXXVII

Blessed Are The Poor In Spirit. Matthew 5:3

Blessed Means Happy

Poor means meek in spirit. Poor means humble in spirit. Poor means lowly in spirit. Poor means quiet in spirit. Read Matthew 5:3-12, Read also Mark 1:15

Jesus did not say "*rich*" in spirit. Jesus said "*poor*" in spirit.

1. Blessed are the poor in spirit to those who believe that the **Bible is real; God's Word. The Bible is reality; God's Word. The Bible is sacred; God's Word. The Bible** even the **Word of God Himself** *does not play game.* **The Bible; The Word of God; God** speak of the saved loved ones **in Christ** that after we depart this earth to *be judge at the white throne of God*: "For we must **all** appear before the *judgment seat of Christ*; that everyone may receive the things done in his body, according to that he hath done, whether it be good or bad." The Bible is silent on the subject. II Corinthians 5:10, See Romans 14:10-13
2. Blessed are the poor in spirit to those who believe this Spiritual hymn:
    1. "Fa—ther, we love Thee, We wor—ship and a—dore Thee;
    Glor—ri—fy Thy name in all the earth. Glo—ri—fy Thy Name; Glo—ri—fy Thy name (Thy name);
    Glo—ri—fy Thy name in all the earth.
    2. Je—sus, we love Thee, We wor—ship and a—dore Thee; Glor—ri—fy Thy name in all the earth. Glo—ri—fy Thy Name; Glo—ri—fy Thy name (Thy name);
    Glo—ri- fy Thy name in all the earth.
    3. Spir—it, we love Thee, We wor- ship and a—dore Thee; Glor—ri—fy Thy name in all the earth. Glo—ri—fy Thy Name; Glo—ri—fy Thy name (Thy name);
    Glo—ri—fy Thy name in all the earth."
3. Blessed are the poor in spirit to those who believe that "**Holiness**" is the **right way of the Lord**'s standard and **His Commandment** is to live *a life of holiness.* Exodus 15:11, Exodus 28:36, Exodus 39:30, I Chronicles 16:29, Psalm 29:2, Psalm 30:4, Psalm 60:6, Psalm 96:9, Psalm 97:12, 108:7, Amos 4:2, Zechariah

14:20, Luke 1:75, Romans 1:4, II Corinthians 7:1, Ephesians 4:24, I Thessalonians 3:13, I Thessalonians 4:7, I Timothy 2:15, Hebrews 12:14, II Timothy 1:9, I Peter 1:15-16

4. Blessed are the poor in spirit to those who believe **Christ at His Coming**. I Corinthians 15:23, Hebrews 9:28
5. Blessed are the poor in spirit to those who believe **Jesus Christ is our King** when He spoke in a parable: "Then shall the **King** say unto them on His right hand, Come, ye blessed of my Father, inherit the kingdom prepared for you from the foundation of the world:" Matthew 25:34
6. Blessed are the poor in spirit to those who believe that **Jesus Christ is our King** when **He** spoke in a parable: "And the **King** shall answer and say unto them, Verily I say unto you, Inasmuch as ye have done it unto one of the least of these my brethren, ye have done it unto **Me**." Matthew 25:40
7. Blessed are the poor in spirit to those who read, study and believe the **Bible, God Holy Word** and we say to **Him**, "Yes, **He DID**!!!" Ecclesiastes 12:12, I Thessalonians 4:11, I Timothy 2:15, II Timothy 3:16, II Peter 3:18
8. Blessed are the poor in spirit to those who that **Jesus Christ** is **"He"** from Genesis to Revelation; that **He is God** and that **He is the Same**; and that **He is the Savio**r of *all men* that **He** is **Lord** that **He** is the **Healer**. Hebrews 13:8, Isaiah 52:6, John 4:26, John 9:37, Acts 9:5, 22, Acts 18:5, John 8:56-58, Philippians 2:11, Acts 10:36, Exodus 15:26, I Timothy 2:3, 4:10, John 4:42, Exodus 15:26
9. Blessed are the poor in spirit to those who believe that little boys and little girls even tender infants; little babies, tender babies have gone to heaven as a result of the incident or as the result of accident in a ruin world. II Samuel 12:12-23 verse 15, 18, 19, 21, Luke 9:48, 18:16-17, Matthew 18:2-5, Mark 9:36-37, 10:13-15
10. Blessed are the poor in spirit to those who believe that **God introduced "Himself"** as the "**I Am that I Am**." Exodus 3:14, John 8:48-59 verse 58 (Before Abraham came into existent at birth) **God** has always **existent.**
11. Blessed are the poor in spirit to those who believe that this is not the **Father's will** that anyone should **perish.** Matthew 18:14, Mark 4:38-41, Luke 8:24-25, Luke 13:3, 5
12. Blessed are the poor in spirit to those who are able to say **for salvation** by *heart through faith*: "You are **Christ**, the **Son of the Living God**." Matthew 16:18

Part DXXVIII

Blessed Are The Poor In Spirit. Matthew 5:3

Blessed Means Happy

Poor means meek in spirit. Poor means humble in spirit. Poor means lowly in spirit. Poor means quiet in spirit. Read Matthew 5:3-12, Read also Mark 1:15

Jesus did not say "*rich*" in spirit. Jesus said "*poor*" in spirit.

1. Blessed are the poor in spirit to those who are able to say **for salvation** by *heart through faith*: "**Jesus** is the **Christ** (God) or (Son of God). Mark 8:29
2. Blessed are the poor in spirit to those who are able to say **for salvation** by *heart through faith*: "**You** are **Christ, the Son of God**;" that **He** (God/Jesus) was **Christ**. See Hebrews 13:8—Luke 4:41
3. Blessed are the poor in spirit to those who are able to say **for salvation** by *heart through faith*: Yes, **Lord**: *I believe* that thou art the **Christ**, the **Son of God**, which should come into the world. John 11:27
4. Blessed are the poor in spirit to those who are able to say **for salvation** by *heart through faith*: "I believe that **Jesus Christ** is the **Son of God**. Acts 8:37 (Acts 8:31-32, Isaiah 53:7-10, Matthew 27:12)
5. Blessed are the poor in spirit to those who are able to say **for salvation** by *heart through faith*: "**You** are **Christ of God: Son of Man**. Luke 23:2, 35, 39, Mark 16:13
6. Blessed are the poor in spirit to those who believe that **The Word of God** is **the Holy Bible**. Genesis 1:1, John 1:1, II Timothy 3:16, I Peter 3:16
7. Blessed are the poor in spirit to those who are able to say: "*I'm blessed, not stressed.* Revelation 2:10, Ephesians 1:3, James 1:12, 25
8. Blessed are the poor in spirit to those *who are blessed*, but *are not stressed.*
9. Blessed are the poor in spirit to those who believe **Jesus' first instruction** is when you *preach*, *go* and *say*, **"The kingdom of heaven is at hand."** Matthew 10:7, Matthew 3:2, Matthew 4:17, Mark 1:15
10. Blessed are the poor in spirit to those who believe that *Christmas stand* for in **honor of Christ**, who was born; not necessary on December or in the spring but represent that **this is Christ, the Lord**; that **this is Jesus Christ, the Savior of**

the world who came **to save all mankind**. Luke 2:11, John 4:42, I John 4:14, I Timothy 4:10, I Timothy 2:4, Acts 4:12, Acts 17:30-31

11. Blessed are the poor in spirit to those who believe that the **Bible will take us to Heaven** after we **believe on Jesus Christ**. Mark 1:1, Luke 1:35, Revelation 8:16, Acts 8:37
12. Blessed are the poor in spirit to those who believe that the **Bible** will take us to **Heaven** when we believe in **Jesus Christ**. Mark 1:1, Luke 1:35, Romans 8:16, Acts 8:37

Part DXXIX

Blessed Are The Poor In Spirit. Matthew 5:3

Blessed Means Happy

Poor means meek in spirit. Poor means humble in spirit. Poor means lowly in spirit. Poor means quiet in spirit. Read Matthew 5:3-12, Read also Mark 1:15

Jesus did not say "*rich*" in spirit. Jesus said "*poor*" in spirit.

1. Blessed are the poor in spirit to those who believe that the witness of **ourselves** that believe that **Jesus** is the **Son of Man**. John 1:49, John 1:29-49 verse 29, 30, 34, 49
2. Blessed are the poor in spirit to those who believe and have the *lowly* or *lowliness* (humble, quiet) of mind of **Christ Jesus** in our hearts. Philippians 2:1-11 verse 3, 5
3. Blessed are the poor in spirit to those who believe this Gospel: "Then they also which are **fallen asleep (dead)** in **Christ** are *perished.* I Corinthians 15:18
4. Blessed are the poor in spirit to those who believe this Gospel: "If in this life only we have **hope in Christ**, we of all most **miserable** (*being without Christ* in your life). I Corinthians 15:19
5. Blessed are the poor in spirit to those who believe this Gospel: "But now is Christ risen from the dead, and become the firstfruit of them that slept (those who died in the Lord; or slept in Jesus; or rested in Jesus or went home to be with the Lord). I Corinthians 15:20
6. Blessed are the poor in spirit to those who believe this Gospel: "For since by (Because of) man (Adam) **all** (those who have not yet *accepted Christ*; believe in **Jesus**; **Have faith in God**) die, even so (them) **in Christ** shall all (those who as born again; those who are **born of the Spirit at Christ**, those who become *God's children* Be made alive. I choose to live **in Christ.** I Corinthians 15:22
7. Blessed are the poor in spirit to those who believe this Gospel: "But every man in his own order: Christ the firstfruits; afterward they (God's children; born of the Spirit of Christ; those who are born again in Christ) are **Christ's at His coming** (Going home to be with Christ in His Heavenly Home some glorious day). I Corinthians 15:23

8. Blessed are the poor in spirit to those who believe this Gospel: "The cometh the end, when he shall have delivered up the kingdom to **God**, even the **Father**; when he shall have put down all rule and all authority and power." I Corinthians 15:24
9. Blessed are the poor in spirit to those who believe this Gospel: "For **He** must reign, till **He** hath put all enemies under His Feet." I Corinthians 15:25
10. Blessed are the poor in spirit to those who believe this Gospel: "The last enemy that shall be destroyed is death." I Corinthians 15:26
11. Blessed are the poor in spirit to those who believe this Gospel: "For He hath put all things under His Feet. But when He saith all things are put under Him, it is manifest that He is excepted, which did put all things under Him."
    I Corinthians 15:27, Psalm 8:6, Ephesians 1:22, Hebrews 2:8
12. Blessed are the poor in spirit to those who believe this Gospel: "And when all things shall be subdued unto Him, then shall the Son also Himself be subject unto Him that put all things under Him, that **God** may be all **in all**."
    I Corinthians 15:28

PART DXXX

Blessed Are The Poor In Spirit. Matthew 5:3

Blessed Means Happy

Poor means meek in spirit. Poor means humble in spirit. Poor means lowly in spirit. Poor means quiet in spirit. Read Matthew 5:3-12, Read also Mark 1:15

Jesus did not say "*rich*" in spirit. Jesus said "*poor*" in spirit.

1. Blessed are the poor in spirit to those who believe this scripture: "To deliver such an one unto *Satan for the destruction of the flesh, that the spirit may be saved in the day of the Lord Jesus.* I Corinthians 5:4-13 verse 5, 6, 7, 8, 9, 10, **11, 13**
2. Blessed are the poor in spirit to those who believe that the **four words,** "Dumb and Deaf Spirit" **mean** the hidden **power of Satan command** (charge). **Satan to come out of that person inner** and enter **no more into that person's inner.** Mark 7:25
3. Blessed are the poor in spirit to those who believe that **God** is our **True** and **Available Friend** of all time. Proverbs 18:24, James 2:23, Genesis 5:6, Romans 4:3, Psalm 44:21, Numbers 32:23
4. Blessed are the poor in spirit to those who believe that **God is a jealous God**, visiting upon his people and is *grieve* and *upset* or *wrath because of iniquity*. Now is your turn *to be jealous, upset, hurt, angry* and *wrath* because of the beautiful heaven that is suppose to be made for you, *bear* you *refuse* to *accept* **Jesus Christ** as your personal **Savior and Lord**. *Be saved before it's too late.*
   I Thessalonians 5:9, Exodus 20:5, 34:14, Deuteronomy 4:24, 5:9, 6:15, Zechariah 8:1-23, verse 2, Romans 1:18, 5:9, 9:22
5. Blessed are the poor in spirit to those who are able to bear witness of the **True Light** to the world is **Jesus Christ**. John 1:7-9
6. Blessed are the poor in spirit to those who believe that we have received the **Spirit** by hearing of faith; **not by the works of the law;** not by the **law of the flesh**. Galatians 3:2
7. Blessed are the poor in spirit to those who believe that **God** give the **gift of evangelist** by making **full proof of your ministry**. II Timothy 4:5

8. Blessed are the poor in spirit to those who believe that Jesus had spoken one last and final words with Paul about bearing witness in **His Name** at Rome following in Acts 23:11 before **He** went back to Heaven. And the night following the **Lord** stood by him, and said, *Be of good cheer, Paul*: for as thou hast testified of **Me** in *Jerusalem*, so **must** thou **bear witness** also at *Rome*. Acts 23:11, See Romans 1:1-32 verse 16
9. Blessed are the poor in spirit to those who believe that **Christ** know **our names** and will call **us out of our graves**. John 5:28-29, I Peter 4:5-6
10. Blessed are the poor in spirit to those who believe that **Christ** know **our enemies** and will **call them by names out of the graves**. John 5:28-29, I Peter 4:5-6
11. Blessed are the poor in spirit to those *who come out* **to serve the True Living God** *from dead work*. Hebrews 9:14-18 verse 14, 12:23-29 verse 28, Romans 1:9, 7:6, 25, Colossians 3:22-24 verse 24
12. Blessed are the poor in spirit to those who that the *opening* **Bible knew all about Me**. Genesis 16:13, Psalm 71:6, Psalm 139:13-14, Psalm 51:15-16, Jeremiah 33:1-3, Genesis 2:7, Genesis 5:2, Matthew 19:4, Colossians 3:10, Genesis 1:26, Genesis 2:4, Genesis 2:16-17, Genesis 3:1-15, 22-24, Mark 4:22, Luke 8:17, 12:2, John 21:15, John 1:47-49, John 4:16-19, 29, Romans 11:33, Numbers 32:23, Psalm 44:21

Part DXXXI

Blessed Are The Poor In Spirit. Matthew 5:3

Blessed Means Happy

Poor means meek in spirit. Poor means humble in spirit. Poor means lowly in spirit. Poor means quiet in spirit. Read Matthew 5:3-12, Read also Mark 1:15

Jesus did not say "*rich*" in spirit. Jesus said "*poor*" in spirit.

1. Blessed are the poor in spirit to those who believe that *our job* is to **preach the gospel**. Mark 16:15, Matthew 4:17, Luke 1:15, Mark 6:12
2. Blessed are the poor in spirit to those who believe and listen to the **mouth of God** which is the **Holy Bible** that speak using **Thus say the Lord."** Exodus 3:14-15
3. Blessed are the poor in spirit to those who believe that the **Holy Bible** is the **mouth of the Word of God** which come **alive.** Ezekiel 33:22 toward us: Jeremiah 1:6, 7, 8, 9, Isaiah 52:6, John 4:26, John 9:37
4. Blessed are the poor in spirit to those who believe that the **Holy Bible** is the **mouth of God.** Isaiah 1:20, Isaiah 40:5, Jeremiah 1:1-19 verse 5, 6, 7, 8, 9
5. Blessed are the poor in spirit to those who believe that the **Holy Bible** is **It's self the mouth of the Holy Bible** because the **Holy Bible** open **it's mouth** toward us and **speak** (talk) toward us. Isaiah 6:8-13, Jeremiah 1:5, 6, 9
6. Blessed are the poor in spirit to those who believe that **"the Holy Spirit speak:" "Thus Say The Lord."** Teach you what you shall say. Exodus 4:15
7. Blessed are the poor in spirit to those who believe that the **Word of God** had **prophesied** that *God's mission*, *God's nation*, *God's people*, **Israel** would have a **new nation** which did come into existence **in 1948**. Isaiah 51:16
8. Blessed are the poor in spirit to those who believe for *uplifting* and for *supporting* **Israel that battle it's own nation until 1967** because **God's Word** seem to be clear is this! "Do not touch my anointed." I Chronicles 16:22, Psalm 105:15
9. Blessed are the poor in spirit to those who believe in **God's precious children**: male, female, and child. Psalm 49:8, Psalm 72:14, Psalm 116:15, I Peter 1:19, II Peter 1:1, 4-6, Matthew 18:1-6, Mark 9:33-37, Mark 10:13-16, Luke 9:46-48, Luke 18:13-17

10. Blessed are the poor in spirit to those who believe that **Jesus' friend** (Psalm 41:9) was Judas, *one of His disciples*, who *betrayed* **Him** and led Him to be crucified on Calvary by the Gentiles, the chief priest, the elders, the scribes, the multitudes, the soldiers of the governor even Governor Pilate whom **Jesus** called him the greater sin (John 19:11) except his wife (Matthew 27:19), Matthew 26:50
11. Blessed are the poor in spirit to those who believe in the Old Testament scripture: "Assemble yourselves and come; draw near together, ye that are escaped of the nations: they have no knowledge that set up the wood of their graven image, and *pray unto a god that cannot save*. Isaiah 45:20
12. Blessed are the poor in spirit to those who believe that **Jesus** was not giving the *world a hard time, a difficult time, a trouble time, a bad time*, but to *strengthen the matter with the law*, the *justice*, of the *misunderstanding* and *misinterpret* of the *Pharisees*, the *Sadducees*, the *chief priests* and **came not to judge the world but to save the world.** John 5:22, John 12:47, Luke 12:13-14

Part DXXXII

Blessed Are The Poor In Spirit. Matthew 5:3

Blessed Means Happy

Poor means meek in spirit. Poor means humble in spirit. Poor means lowly in spirit. Poor means quiet in spirit. Read Matthew 5:3-12, Read also Mark 1:15

Jesus did not say "*rich*" in spirit. Jesus said "*poor*" in spirit.

1. Blessed are the poor in spirit to those who believe that **Bible** is my *television* that lead us to the **true knowledge of the Gospel of Jesus Christ**. Hebrews 10:26-31 verse 26, I Timothy 2:4
2. Blessed are the poor in spirit to those who believe that the **Bible** is my *radio* that lead us to the **true knowledge of the Gospel of Jesus Christ**. Hebrews 10:26-31 verse 26, I Timothy 2:4
3. Blessed are the poor in spirit to those who believe that our **true friend** of the **Gospel of Jesus Christ** that lead us to the saving knowledge of the **Gospel of Jesus Christ.** Hebrews 10:26-31 verse 26, I Timothy 2:4
4. Blessed are the poor in spirit to those who believe that **learning, studying** and **growing** with the **Holy Bible** in **God's Word** *through faith* help us to remind ourselves everyday of our life (as a good habit and respect) not to do those things that are not **pleasing to Christ**, and to *follow His instructions by not walking in the flesh* but **by walking in the Spirit**. II Corinthians 5:7, Galatians 5:16, 25, Ephesians 2:10, 4:1, 5:2, 8, Philippians 3:16-17, Colossians 1:8-20 verse 10, 2:6-14 verse 6, 12, 14, 4:5, I Thessalonians 2:12, 4:1-18 verse 1, 4, 7, 11, 12, I John 1:6, 7, 2:6, II John 1:6, II John 1:4, Revelation 3:4, 21:24, II Peter 3:18, I Peter 2:21, Romans 4:6-25 verse 12, John 1:29, John 5:14, 8:11, Romans 6:1, 8:2, John 15:24, 16:8-9
5. Blessed are the poor in spirit to those who believe the **power of death and life**: according to the **Spirit of our God**: "Death and life are in the power of the tongue: and they that love it shall eat the fruit thereof." Proverbs 18:21
6. Blessed are the poor in spirit to those who are able to find a *good soulful wife*. Proverbs 18:22, Malachi 2:14-16

7. Blessed are the poor in spirit to those who are able to show ourselves the *friendship* of other because of **Christ's example**: "A man that hath friends must shew himself friendly: and there is *a friend* that sticketh closer than *a brother*." Proverbs 18:24
8. Blessed are the poor in spirit to those who believe this scripture: "And as it is appointed unto *men once to die*, but *after this the judgment*: Hebrews 9:27
9. Blessed are the poor in spirit to those who believe that the **Bible** is **no joke** in the **Word of God. God is Real**. There may not be a "**joke"** in the Bible, but there is a **Jot** in the Bible. See Matthew 5:18
10. Blessed are the poor in spirit to those who believe that the **Bible** is **seriousness.** There is another word for **sure**—See II Timothy 2:19, II Peter 1:19 in the Word of God. **God is Real**. There may not be a **"seriousness"** in the Word of God, but there is a **gravity** in the Word of God. Also there is a word sincerity in verse seven. I Timothy 3:4-5, Titus 2:1-15
11. Blessed are the poor in spirit to those who believe that the **Bible** is **"Real"** in the **Word of God. God is so Real**. There may not be a **real** in the **Bible** but there is a **Living God** which mean God **breath**. I Timothy 4:10, Hebrews 12:22, Revelation 7:2
12. Blessed are the poor in spirit to those who believe they are the children of Abraham. Genesis 22:18, Acts 13:26, Romans 9:7

Part DXXXIII

Blessed Are The Poor In Spirit. Matthew 5:3

Blessed Means Happy

Poor means meek in spirit Poor means humble in spirit Poor means lowly in spirit Poor means quiet in spirit Read Matthew 5:3-12, Read also Mark 1:15

Jesus did not say "*rich*" in spirit. Jesus said "*poor*" in spirit.

1. Blessed are the poor in spirit to those who believe that **God** want us to preach about **Jesus and Him Crucified**. I Corinthians 2:2, II Timothy 4:3, Mark 16:15, Mark 13:10, Luke 24:47, Luke 24:7, Matthew 26:2, **Acts 2: 23, 36,** Acts 4:10,
2. Blessed are the poor in spirit to those who believe that **following in step of the Lord Jesus Christ is a connection to Jesus Christ.** I Peter 2:21, Matthew 4:19**,** 22, Matthew 9:9, Matthew 16:24**,** Matthew 19:21, Mark 8:34**,** Mark 10:21, Mark 16:15-18 verse 17, Luke 9:23, 59, Luke 18:22, John 10:27, John 12:26, John 13:36, John 21:19, 22
3. Blessed are the poor in spirit to those who believe that **following Christ's example** is a **connection to Jesus Christ. I Peter 2:21, John 13:15**
4. Blessed are the poor in spirit to those who believe that **walking by faith** is a **connection to Jesus Christ.** II Corinthians 5:17, Mark 11:22, II John 1:4, Acts 9:31
5. Blessed are the poor in spirit to those who believe that **belonging in faith** is a **connection to Jesus Christ.** Mark 11:22, **Habakkuk 2:4,** Luke 17:5, Acts 3:16, Acts 6:5, 8, 11:24, 14:9, 22, 27, 15:9, Hebrews 10:38, Hebrews 11:1-6, 7-40, **James 1:6, 2:1,** Ephesians 2:8, Ephesians 3:17, Ephesians 4:5, 13, Ephesians 6:16, 23, Philippians 3:9, Colossians 1:4, Colossians 2:5, 12, I Thessalonians 1:8, Jude 1:3, 20, I Timothy 3:13, II Timothy 4:6, II Timothy 1:13, I Peter 1:5, 21, Revelation 14:12, Acts 16:5, **Acts 20:21,** Acts 24:24, **Acts 26:18**, **Romans 1:17, Romans 3:22-26 verse 22, Romans** 4:10-25 verse 12, 24-25, Romans 5:1-21, Romans 10:17, II Corinthians 5:7, Galatians 2:16, 20, **Galatians 3:8, 11, 14, 22-29,** Ephesians 1:15, Mark 11:22, Hebrews 2:4, Luke 17:5, Acts 3:16, Acts 6:5, 8, Acts 11:24, Acts 14:9, 22, 27, Acts 15:9, Hebrews 10:38, Hebrews 11:1-6, 7-40, James 1:6, James 2:1
6. Blessed are the poor in spirit to those who believe that **working for Christ** is a **connection to Jesus Christ.** Matthew 21:28, 26:10, Mark 14:6, Luke 13:14,

John 4:34, John 5:17, John 6:28, 29, 30, John 7:21, John 9:4, John 17:4, Acts 1:8 Acts 5:38-42, Acts 13:1-2, Acts 14:26, Romans 8:28, I Corinthians 9:1-27, I Corinthians 15:58, I Corinthians 16:10, Ephesians 4:12, Philippians 1:6, Philippians 2:12, Philippians 2:30, I Thessalonians 1:1-10 verse 3, I Thessalonians 4:11, II Thessalonians 1:11-12, I Timothy 3:1, I Timothy 5:10, II Timothy 2:21, II Timothy 4:5, Titus 3:1, Hebrews 6:10, 13:21, I Peter 1:17, I Peter 4:11, I John 2:3, 3:22, 4:14, Revelation 2:5, Revelation 22:12

7. Blessed are the poor in spirit to those who believe that **doing for Christ** is a **connection to Jesus Christ.** Matthew 9:28, Matthew 12:50, Acts 1:1, Acts 2:37-39 verse 37, Acts 9:6, Acts 15:36, Acts 16:30-34 verse 30-31, Acts 22:10, Acts 24:16, II Thessalonians 3:4, I Timothy 4:5, Hebrews 10:7, 9, Psalm 40:7-8, James 4:15, Revelation 2:5, Revelation 22:14, Acts 26:20, I Corinthians 9:23, I Corinthians 10:31, **I Corinthians 11:24, 25, 26,** Philippians 4:13, **I Peter 2:21 Colossians 3:13, 17, 23,** I Thessalonians 5:24, Psalm 9:11
8. Blessed are the poor in spirit to those who believe that **singing in spiritual hymns** are a **connection to Jesus Christ.** Ephesians 5:18, Colossians 3:16, Psalm 7:17, 9:2, 11, 13:6, Psalm 100:2, 126:2
9. Blessed are the poor in spirit to those who believe that **preaching the gospel** is a **connection to Jesus Christ.** Mark 11:15, Matthew 9:35, Mark 1:14, Luke 8:1, Luke 9:6, Acts 8:4, 12, Acts 10:36, Acts 11:19-20, Acts 15:35, Acts 20:25, Acts 28:31, Romans 16:25, I Corinthians 1:18, 21, 2:4, II Timothy 4:17-18, Titus 1:3
10. Blessed are the poor in spirit to those who believe that **sharing with faith to others are a connection to Jesus Christ.** Romans 8:28
11. Blessed are the poor in spirit to those who believe **in living for Christ daily is a connection to Jesus Christ**. Matthew 4:4, Luke 4:4, John 6:51, 57, John 11:25, John 14:19, Acts 17:28, Romans 1:17, Hebrews 2:4, Romans 6:8, 14:8, 11, II Corinthians 13:4, Acts 5:42, Acts 17:11, Acts 19:9, Acts 2:41-47, Matthew 26:55, Mark 14:49, Luke 11:3, Luke 19:47, Luke 22:53, Galatians 2:20, Galatians 3:11, Galatians 5:25, Philippians 1:21, I Thessalonians 5:10, II Timothy 2:11, 3:12
12. Blessed are the poor in spirit to those who believe that **Faith** is the **substance of things** (assurance) hoped for, the **evidence** (conviction) **not** seen is a **connection to Jesus Christ.** Hebrews 11:1, Romans 8:28, John 4:24

Part DXXXIV

Blessed Are The Poor In Spirit. Matthew 5:3

Blessed Means Happy

Poor means meek in spirit Poor means humble in spirit Poor means lowly in spirit Poor means quiet in spirit Read Matthew 5:3-12, Read also Mark 1:15

Jesus did not say "*rich*" in spirit. Jesus said "*poor*" in spirit.

1. Blessed are the poor in spirit to those who believe that **Hope** is a **connection to Jesus Christ.** Colossians 1:27, I Thessalonians 1:3, I Thessalonians 5:8, II Thessalonians 2:16, I Timothy 1:1, Titus 1:2, Titus 2:13, Titus 3:7, Hebrews 3:6, Hebrews 6:11, 18, 19, Hebrews 7:19, Hebrews 10:23, I Peter 1:3, I Peter 1:13, 21, I Peter 3:15, I John 3:3
2. Blessed are the poor in spirit to those who believe **Love** is a **connection to Jesus Christ.** I Corinthians 13:13, John 3:16, I John 3:1, I John 4:1-21, verse 7-11, 16-21, verse 19, I John 5: 1-21, verse 2, 3,
3. Blessed are the poor in spirit to those who believe that **Faith** is a **connection to Jesus Christ.** I Corinthians 13:13, Hebrews 11:1-6 verse 1, Romans 1:17, Habakkuk 2:4
4. Blessed are the poor in spirit to those who believe that the **Prophecy** is a **connection to Jesus Christ.** Matthew 13:14, II Peter 1:19, 20, 21, Revelation 1:3, 19:10, Revelation 22:7, 10, 18, 19
5. Blessed are the poor in spirit to those who believe that **Hearing By Faith** is a **connection to Jesus Christ.** Romans 10:17
6. Blessed are the poor in spirit to those who believe that **Present Your Bodies a living sacrifice, holy, acceptable unto God, which is your reasonable service** is a **connection to Jesus Christ.** Romans 12:1-2
7. Blessed are the poor in spirit to those who believe that our **praise to Christ** is a **connection to Jesus Christ.** Philippians 1:11, Revelation 19:5, Romans 2:29, Romans 15:11, Psalm 117:1
8. Blessed are the poor in spirit to those who believe that our **praise to God** is a **connection to Jesus Christ.** Philippians 1:11, Revelation 19:5, Romans 2:29, 15:11, Psalm 117:1

9. Blessed are the poor in spirit to those who believe that it take **three** people to work together as a team. Romans 8:28
10. Blessed are the poor in spirit to those who believe that **A Gift from God** is a **connection to Jesus Christ.** Romans 6:23, Ephesians 2:8, 3:7, Acts 10:45, Acts 2:38, John 4:10
11. Blessed are the poor in spirit to those who believe that **A Gift from Above (God)** is a **connection to Jesus Christ.** Acts 2:38, John 4:10, Ephesians 2:8, 3:7, Acts 10:45, James 1:17, Hebrews 6:4, I Timothy 4:14, Romans 5:18, Romans 5:16, Romans 5:15
12. Blessed are the poor in spirit to those who believe that **winning lost soul for Christ** is a **connection to Jesus Christ.** Proverbs 11:30, Acts 1:8, Acts 2:41, I Peter 2:21

Part DXXXV

Blessed Are The Poor In Spirit. Matthew 5:3

Blessed Means Happy

Poor means meek in spirit Poor means humble in spirit Poor means lowly in spirit Poor means quiet in spirit Read Matthew 5:3-12, Read also Mark 1:15

Jesus did not say "*rich*" in spirit. Jesus said "*poor*" in spirit.

1. Blessed are the poor in spirit to those who believe that **God's Voice** is speaking to us in *His Word, the Bible.* Genesis 1:1, John 1:1, II Timothy 3:16, Mark 11:22
   a. His Voice whisper in our ears—Psalm 46:10
   b. His Voice speak in our heart—Romans 5:5
   c. His Feeling is all over us—Hebrews 4:14-15 verse 15, Philippians 3:10, Acts 17:27, 28, 29, 30, Psalm 9:10, Isaiah 55:6-7, Psalm 22:26, Psalm 24:6, Psalm 27:4, 8-9
2. Blessed are the poor in spirit to those who believe that blaspheme (say evil thing, say bad thing without a reason. Has never forgiveness, but in danger of eternal damnation for not accepting or believing in the **Holy Spirit spoken by God**. Mark 3:29
3. Blessed are the poor in spirit to those who believe this scripture: "O the depth of the **riches** both of the **wisdom** and **knowledge of God**! How *unsearchable* are *His* **judgments**, and **His ways past finding out**! Romans 11:33, See Number 32:23
4. Blessed are the poor in spirit to those who believe that **God, the Father**, is the founder of this old age of the earth. I Corinthians 10:26
5. Blessed are the poor in spirit to those who believe that the *capital city of Jerusalem* is the mother of us all. Galatians 4:26
6. Blessed are the poor in spirit to those who believe that **Christ** mean **"The Savior."** Luke 2:11, John 4:25, II Timothy 1:10
7. Blessed are the poor in spirit to those who believe that **Christ** mean "**The Lord**." Luke 2:11, Acts 2:36
8. Blessed are the poor in spirit to those who believe that **Christ** mean "A (The) King." Luke 23:2

9. Blessed are the poor in spirit to those who believe that **Christ** mean **"God."** Luke 9:20
10. Blessed are the poor in spirit to those who believe that **Grace** and **Truth** mean **Jesus**. John 1:17
11. Blessed are the poor in spirit to those who believe that **Christ** mean "**The Master**." John 1:41
12. Blessed are the poor in spirit to those who believe that **Christ** mean "**The Messiah**." John 4:25, 29, 42

PART DXXXVI

Blessed Are The Poor In Spirit. Matthew 5:3

Blessed Means Happy

Poor means meek in spirit. Poor means humble in spirit. Poor means lowly in spirit. Poor means quiet in spirit. Read Matthew 5:3-12, Read also Mark 1:15

Jesus did not say "*rich*" in spirit. Jesus said "*poor*" in spirit.

1. Blessed are the poor in spirit to those who believe that **God** mean "**The Savior**." Isaiah 7:14, Acts 5:31, I Timothy 1:1, I Timothy 2:3, 4:10, Titus 1:3
2. Blessed are the poor in spirit to those who believe that the **Savior** mean **"either" or "and"** The **Father** and The **Lord Jesus Christ**. Titus 1:4
3. Blessed are the poor in spirit to those who believe that the **doctrine** mean **God** our **Savior**. Titus 2:10, Jude 1:25
4. Blessed are the poor in spirit to those who believe that **Christ** mean **Jesus**. John 6:69, 7:26
5. Blessed are the poor in spirit to those who do not know that **Christ** mean **Jesus**, The Lord in which He did come. John 7:27, 31
6. Blessed are the poor in spirit to those who believe that **Jesus** came of the seed of David, making him (David) his son. John 7:42
7. Blessed are the poor in spirit to those who believe that **Christ** mean "**The Son of Man**." John 12:34-50
8. Blessed are the poor in spirit to those who believe that **the Lord** direct our hearts into the **love of God**, and **into the patient waiting for Christ**. II Thessalonians 3:5
9. Blessed are the poor in spirit to those who believe that the **Gospel** stand for **Jesus Christ, the Son of God**. Mark 1:1
10. Blessed are the poor in spirit to those who believe that the **Bible** is **popular**, is **famous**, is **fame**, is most **sought in time of need, in time of trouble for help of all time by wanting to know who is really Jesus, who is really Christ, who is really Lord, who is really the "I Am."** I John 2:27, Hebrews 4:16, Philippians 4:19, Luke 12:30, Luke 9:11, Mark 14:63, Matthew 26:65, II Corinthians 4:8-18, Psalm 116:10, Acts 15:19

11. Blessed are the poor in spirit to those who believe that the word **"Result"** is not in the Bible but there are **three words** in the Bible. **Jesus** say: **"It is Finished."** John 19:30
12. Blessed are the poor in spirit to those who are able to confess their mouth **to Christ**: "Yes, Lord, I believe that You are the **Christ**, the **Son of God**, which should came into the world. John 11:27

PART DXXXVII

Blessed Are The Poor In Spirit. Matthew 5:3

Blessed Means Happy

Poor means meek in spirit. Poor means humble in spirit. Poor means lowly in spirit. Poor means quiet in spirit. Read Matthew 5:3-12, Read also Mark 1:15

Jesus did not say "*rich*" in spirit. Jesus said "*poor*" in spirit.

1. Blessed are the poor in spirit to those who believe that **"In One Verse," Christ** speak of both the saved and the unsaved; *The Just* and the *UnJust*, the **children of God** and the *Disobedience children*. Matthew 5:45, Acts 24:15, I Peter 3:18, John 5:29
2. Blessed are the poor in spirit to those who believe that **Christ** spoke of **"One single and simple verse** for the **just** and the **unjust;** the **saved ones** and the **unsaved ones;** the **children of God** and the **disobedient of children** (not being saved; not being born again; not being born of the Spirit; not being adoption of children of God; not being the resurrected of God's children). John 5:29
3. Blessed are the poor in spirit to those who believe that there is One Entire Verse with **One Entire Word "Him"** in **That Same Scripture, One** God: **One** Father, **One** Lord; **Jesus Christ** by **One "Him."** See Hebrews 13:8. **One Word**. See Genesis 1:1. John 1:1. One Him in John 1:**3, 4, 9, 10, 11, 12, 15, 17, 18.**
4. Blessed are the poor in spirit to those who believe that there are **nine "Him"** in the book of John 1:1-18 declaring that **Jesus Christ** is **God** as **Him,** or **He,** or **His.** See II Corinthians 1:19. **Head of Christ is God**. I Corinthians 11:3
5. Blessed are the poor in spirit to those who believe in the **power of Resurrection of Jesus Christ**. "I am the Resurrection." **John 11:25,** Acts 1:22, 4:2, 33. 17:18, 23:6, 8, 24:15, 21, Romans 1:4, 6:5, I Corinthians 15:20-32, **Philippians 3:10,** Peter 1:3, 3:21, Revelation 20:5-6, Revelation 1:8, 11, 17-18, 16:5, 15, 4:8, 22:7, 12-13, 16, 20, I Corinthians 15:1-4, Hosea 6:2, Isaiah 53:3-12, I Timothy 3:16, Acts 1:3, Matthew 27:63, Mark 16:11, Luke 24:23, Romans 6:11, 13, I Corinthians 15:22, I Thessalonians 4:15, 17, Revelation 1:18, 2:8, Matthew 16:21, 17:23, 20:19, Mark 9:31, 10:34, Luke 9:22, Luke 12:38, 13:32, 18:33, 24:7, 21, 46, John 21:14, Acts 2:15, 10:40, I Corinthians 15:4; but those are for

Satan and his angels; Revelation 19:20, 14:11, Revelation 13:8-9, 17:8, Revelation 20:12-15, Revelation 22:18, 19 (Deuteronomy 12:32)

6. Blessed are the poor in spirit to those who believe in being *excited* about the **Bible**. Genesis 1:1-2, John 1:1-18, II Timothy 3:16, John 14:6, John 11:25, Revelation 22:20, I Thessalonians 4:13-18
7. Blessed are the poor in spirit to those who believe that we have seen **God** through **Jesus Christ**. John 14:6-12 verse 7-9, John 4:26, John 9:37, I Timothy 3:16, Hebrews 13:8, Acts 9:4-5, 20, 22, Acts 18:5, 28
8. Blessed are the poor in spirit to those who believe that Christ died for the just (saved) and the unjust (not yet saved). Matthew 5:45, Acts 24:15, I Peter 3:18
9. Blessed are the poor in spirit to those who believe that the *opening* **Bible** is *worthy* to be *found* because of the **Good News of Jesus Christ**. Revelation 5:4-7, Revelation 22:16, Isaiah 11:1, Isaiah 60:1-3, Luke 4:18-21
10. Blessed are the poor in spirit to those who believe that the **Old Testament** is a **connection to Jesus Christ.** Isaiah 53:1-12
11. Blessed are the poor in spirit to those who believe that the **New Testament** is a **connection to Jesus Christ. Jesus Christ** was **among** them. He **walked** among them. John 1:26-51 verse 26, 29, 36-51
12. Blessed are the poor in spirit to those who believe that the **Whole Bible True Story** is a **connection to Jesus Christ.** Genesis 1:1-26, John 1:1-51, Matthew 1:1-25, Mark 1:7-11, Luke 2:5-15, Luke 2:25-32 verse 30

Part DXXXVIII

Blessed Are The Poor In Spirit. Matthew 5:3

Blessed Means Happy

Poor means meek in spirit. Poor means humble in spirit. Poor means lowly in spirit. Poor means quiet in spirit. Read Matthew 5:3-12, Read also Mark 1:15

Jesus did not say "*rich*" in spirit. Jesus said "*poor*" in spirit.

1. Blessed are the poor in spirit to those who believe that **Salvation** is a **connection to Jesus Christ.** Luke 19:1-10 verse 9, Acts 13:26-52, verse 26, 33, 47-48, John 14:6, Luke 1:65-80 verse 71-80, 2:3, Acts 28:28-31, Romans 1:16, Roman 10:10, Romans 11:11, 13:11, 14, II Corinthians 6:2, Isaiah 49:8, II Corinthians 7:10, Ephesians 1:13, 6:17, I Thessalonians 5:8-9, II Thessalonians 2:13, 16, Hebrews 6:6, II Pete 3:9, I Peter 1:5, 9-10, II Peter 3:15, Jude 1:3, Revelation 7:10, 12:10, 19:1, II Timothy 2:10, 3:15, Titus 2:11, Hebrews 2:3, 10, 5:9, 9:28
2. Blessed are the poor in spirit to those who believe that **Repentance** is a **connection to Jesus Christ. Acts 20:21,** 26:20, II Corinthians 7:10, Matthew 9:13, Mark 2:17, Luke 5:32, 15:7, 24:47, Acts 5:31, 11:18
3. Blessed are the poor in spirit to those who believe that **Conversion** is a **connection to Jesus Christ.** Isaiah 1:27, Acts 15:3, Isaiah 6:10, James 5:19, Psalm 51:13, Matthew 13:15, 18:3, Mark 4:12, **Luke 22:32,** John 12:40, Acts 3:19, 28:27, Psalm 19:7
4. Blessed are the poor in spirit to those who believe that **Justification** is a **connection to Jesus Christ. Romans 4:25, 5:16, 18,** Galatians 3:11, 24, Titus 3:7, Habakkuk 2:4, Romans 1:17, Romans 3:26, Galatians 3:11, Hebrews 10:38, I John 1:9, Revelation 15:1, Acts 13:39, Romans 3:24, I Corinthians 6:11, Galatians 2:16, 17
5. Blessed are the poor in spirit to those who believe that **Sanctification** is a **connection to Jesus Christ.** I Timothy 4:5, **II Timothy 2:21,** Hebrews 2:11, 10:10, 14, Jude 1:1, Acts 20:32, 26:18, Romans 15:16, I Corinthians 1:2, 6:11, **I Corinthians 1:30, I Thessalonians 4:3-4, II Thessalonians 2:13, I Peter 1:2,** John 17:19

6. Blessed are the poor in spirit to those who believe that **Pardon or Forgivenss** is a **connection to Jesus Christ.** Luke 23:34, Isaiah 55:7, Psalm 130:1-8 verse 4, Acts 5:31, Acts 13:38, 26:18, Ephesians 1:7, Colossians 1:14, Daniel 9:9, Psalm 103:3
7. Blessed are the poor in spirit to those who believe that **Water Baptism** is a **connection to Jesus Christ.** Acts 19:3, 4, Acts 16:33, 18:8, Acts 8:36-38, 10:47, 8:12, 13, 16, 10:47, Acts 11:16 (a), Matthew 3:13-17 verse 13, 20:22, 23, Mark 10:38, 39, Mark 16:15-20 verse 16, Luke 12:50, Romans 6:3, I Corinthians 12:13, Galatians 3:26-29 verse 27
8. Blessed are the poor in spirit to those who believe that **Baptism with the Spirit or the pouring out of the Spirit or the pour of out the gift of the Holy Spirit** is a **connection to Jesus Christ.** Acts 9:15-18, 22, Acts 16:16 (b), Acts 20:22-23, Acts 23:9, 11, Acts 17:15-34 verse 16, 23-32, 18:5, Romans 1:4, 9, II Corinthians 3:17, 5:5, Galatians 5:18, 22, 25, Acts 8:29, 39-40, 10:33-48 verse 38, 42, 44, 45, Joel 2:29. Luke 4:18, Isaiah 60:1-3, Acts 2:4, 17, 18, Romans 7:6, 8:1, 2, 4, 5, 9-11, 8:14, 15, 16, I Corinthians 2:4, 10, 6:11, 17, 19-20, I Corinthians 12:1-11 verse 4, 7, 8, 9, 11, John 7:37-39 verse 39, John 20:17, 22, Isaiah 28:11-12, I Corinthians 14:21
9. Blessed are the poor in spirit to those who believe that **Filled with the Spirit** is a **connection to Jesus Christ.** Ephesians 5:17, Colossians 3:16-17, Luke 6:21, Acts 2:4, 4:8, 31, 9:17, 13:9, Acts 13:52, Romans 15:14-19, Ephesians 3:19-21 verse 19-20, 5:18, Philippians 1:11, Colossians 1:1-29 verse 8, 9, 19, 25, II Timothy 1:4, Acts 8:39, Ephesians 1:13, II Timothy 1:7, 4:22, Matthew 5:6, Acts 1:4-8, 11:16, Luke 24:49, Ephesians 5:18, Colossians 3:16-17, John 14:16, 26, John 15:26-27, Mark 16:17, Acts 10:44-46
10. Blessed are the poor in spirit to those who believe that **Baptized with the Spirit** is a **connection to Jesus Christ.** Acts 1:5, 2:38, 41, 8:12, 13, 39, Acts 19:5-6
11. Blessed are the poor in spirit to those who believe that **Spirit Baptism** is a **connection to Jesus Christ.** Matthew 3:11, Luke 3:16, Mark 1:8, Luke 24:49, Mark 16:17, Isaiah 28:11-12, I Corinthians 14:21, John 1:26, 33, Acts 1:4-5, 8, Acts 2:1-4, Acts 8:15-17 verse 15-16, John 20:17 (later, verse 22), John 7:37-39 verse 39, Matthew 3:11, Mark 1:8, Luke 3:16, John 1:26, 33, Acts 1:4-5, 8, 2:1-4, Luke 24:49, Mark 16:17, Acts 8:15-17
12. Blessed are the poor in spirit to those who believe that **Prayer** is a **connection to Jesus Christ.** Acts 12:12, II Timothy 1:3, Philemon 1:4, 22, Jude 1:20, Colos-

sians 1:3, 4, I Thessalonians 1:2, I Timothy 2:1, Hebrews 5:7, I Peter 3:7, 3:12, Revelation 5:8, 8:3-4, I Corinthians 7:5, II Corinthians 1:11, 9:14, Romans 1:9, 15:30, Ephesians 6:18, Ephesians 1:16, Philippians 1:4, 19, 4:6, Acts 2:42, Mark 9:29, Luke 1:13, 6:12, 19:46, 22:45-46, Acts 1:14, Acts 3:1, Acts 6:4, Acts 10:31, 12:5, 16:16, Romans 10:1, 12:12, Luke 2:37, 5:33, Colossians 4:2, I Timothy 4:5, 5:5, James 5:15, 16, I Peter 4:7

Part DXXXIX

Blessed Are The Poor In Spirit. Matthew 5:3

Blessed Means Happy

Poor means meek in spirit Poor means humble in spirit Poor means lowly in spirit Poor means quiet in spirit Read Matthew 5:3-12, Read also Mark 1:15

Jesus did not say "*rich*" in spirit. Jesus said "*poor*" in spirit.

1. Blessed are the poor in spirit to those who believe that **Prayer and Fasting** is a **connection to Jesus Christ.** Matthew 17:21, Mark 9:29, Acts 10:30, Acts 14:23, Acts 27:33, I Corinthians 7:5, Jude 1:20, Colossians 4:3, Colossians 1:3, Acts 12:12, Acts 11:5, 11:1, Mark 11:25, 3:21, 9:18, 11:5, II Corinthians 8:4, Daniel 9:20, 6:11, I Samuel 1:12, 26, I Kings 8:54, II Chronicles 7:1
2. Blessed are the poor in spirit to those who believe in the **Bible as a Whole** (Complete), **Fullness, Faith** is a **connection to Jesus Christ**. **Genesis 1:1**, **John 1:1-18**, **II Timothy 3:16**, Exodus 25:26, Psalm 103:1-3, Isaiah 53:5, Luke 8:7, Philippians 4:13, Romans 4:25, I Corinthians 15:3, Acts 16:30-31, Romans 3:23, I Peter 2:22, Romans 4:25, Romans 5:1, Romans 5:16, 18, I Corinthians 1:30, I Thessalonians 4:3-4, **Hebrews 13:8**, **Hebrews 9:28**, I Thessalonians 4:13-17, II Timothy 4:2, I Timothy 1:7, II, Timothy 1:10, John 3:16, Ephesians 2:5, 8-9, **Revelation 1:7, 8, 17-18, 4:9, Revelation 3:11, Revelation 16:15, Revelation 22:7, 12-13, 20, II** Thessalonians 2:13, I Peter 1:2, Luke 24:47, Acts 5:31, 11:18, Acts 20:21, 26:20, II Corinthians 7:9-10, Hebrews 6:6, II Peter 3:9, Luke 2:38, 21:28, Romans 3:24, Ephesians 1:7, 14, Colossians 1:14, Hebrews 9:12, Acts 15:3, Matthew 28:18-20, Romans 6:4-6, Romans 5:11, Acts 27:29, Romans 1:20, Colossians 2:9, II Corinthians 13:14, Hebrews 2:4, Romans 1:17, Galatians 3:11, Hebrews 10:38, Amos 4:12, Luke 20:36, John 5:29, John 11:25, Acts 1:22, 2:31, Acts 4:2, 33, 17:18, 32, 23:6, 24:15, 21, Romans 1:4, 6:5, I Corinthians 15:1-4, I Corinthians 15:20-23, Philippians 3:10, I Peter 1:3, 3:21, Revelation 20:5-6, Matthew 3:11, Mark 1:8, Luke 3:16, John 1:33, Acts 1:4-5, Acts 11:16, Luke 24:47, **Acts 1:8**, Acts 2:1-4, Luke 11:13, Luke 12:12, John 7:39, 14:26, 20:22, Acts 2:38, 4:8, 31, Acts 6:5, 7:55, Acts 8:15, 17, 8:19, Acts

10:38, 44-47, Acts 11:15-16, 24, Acts 13:2, 4, 9, 52, Acts 15:8, 28, Acts 16:6, Acts 19:2-6, Romans 5:5, 14:17, Romans 15:13, 16, I Corinthians 2:13, 3:17, I Corinthians 6:19, Ephesians 1:3, 13, Matthew 16:21, 17:23, 20:19, Mark 9:31, 10:34, Luke 9:22, 13:32, 33, 24:21, John 21:14, I Corinthians 15:17, Ephesians 3:5, 4:30, Acts 2:15, I Thessalonians 1:5-6, 4:8, II Timothy 1:9, 14, II Timothy 3:15-17, Titus 3:5, Hebrews 2:4, 3:7, Hebrews 6:4, 9:8-12, 24-28, Romans 8:16, Hebrews 10:15-39, II Peter 1:12, 15, 16, I Peter 2:5, 9, II Peter 1:17-21, II Peter 3:2, I John 2:20, 5:1-15, Jude 2:20, Revelation 3:7, 4:8, 6:10, 15:4, 18:20, 20:6, 22:6-7, 22:11, 19-21

3. Blessed are the poor in spirit to those who are able to pray: **Thank you Lord** for letting me know for what I need to know **before** I die. Without you, **Lord**, I'd **die and spend eternal punishment in hell** forever with **Satan and His angels.** Matthew 25:41-46 verse 46, Jude 1:7, Romans 16:20, Genesis 3:13-15 verse 15, Revelation 12:9, See Isaiah 14:12-20
4. Blessed are the poor in spirit to those who believe that **Pentecost** stand **for fiftieth (50) day after Passover.** Acts 2:1, Acts 20:16, I Corinthians 16:8
5. Blessed are the poor in spirit to those who believe that **Pentecost** is a **Christian Festival** on the **seventh Sunday after Easter, celebrating the descent of the Holy Spirit upon the Apostles.** Acts 2:1-47 verse 1-4 verse 4, I Corinthians 15:4, **Acts 1:1-8, (Jesus being alive!!! verse 3, 4-5, 7-8), Mark 16:11, I Corinthians `5:6,** Matthew 28:5-20, **(Jesus being alive!!! verse 9-10, 18-20)** Mark 16:6-20, **(Jesus being alive !!! verse 15-18),** Luke 24:1:1-53, **(Jesus being alive!!!** verse **17, 19, 25-26, 36, 38-39, 41, 44-49),** John 20: 1-31, **(Jesus being alive !!! verse 15-17, 19, 21-23, 26-29),** John 21:1-25, **(Jesus being alive !!! verse 5-6, 10, 12, 15, 12-19, 22),** see Paul **concerning Jesus being alive** !!!- **(Jesus being alive !!! Acts 9:4-6, 11-12, 15-16, Acts 18: 9-10, Acts 20:35, Acts 22: 7-8, 10, 18, 21, Acts 23:11, Acts 14-18,**
6. Blessed are the poor in spirit to those who believe that **Pentecost stand as Whit-sunday.** Acts 2:1, Acts 20:16, I Corinthians 16:8, Mark 11:22
7. Blessed are the poor in spirit to those who believe that **Pentecost as Whitsunday represent as the first three days of that week.** Acts 2:1, 20:16, I Corinthians 16:8, Mark 11:22
8. Blessed are the poor in spirit to those who believe that **Pentecost represent as the first three days of this week.** Acts 2:1, 20:16, I Corinthians 16:8, Mark 11:22

9. Blessed are the poor in spirit to those who believe that **Pentecost was First Notice Appearing on the Both of Acts 2:1 as Notice** my own eyes witnesses; never seen **any previous Pentecost** in one of the **books of the Bible except three:** Acts 2:1, Acts 20:16 and I Corinthians 16:8, Mark 11:22
10. Blessed are the poor in spirit to those who believe in an effect to support the name **"Pentecost"** to be the **Flame** support of **preaching the Gospel of Christ** to a **dead, dry and dying** world needy to be saved **before Jesus Christ's Return**. **Amos 4:12**, Luke 24:47-49, Acts 1:4-8, Acts 2:1-47, Acts 1:11, Acts 4:12, I Thessalonians 4:13-18, Revelation 1:7-8, 11, 17-18, Revelation 2:8, **Revelation 3:11**, Revelation 4:8-10, **Revelation 16:15**, **Revelation 22**:7, **12-13,** 16, **20**, **Mark 11:22**
11. Blessed are the poor in spirit to those who believe that Christ love the church. We also ought ourselves to love the church because church belong to Christ; our body belong to Christ. Matthew 16:18, 18:17, Acts 2:47, Acts 5:11, Acts 20:28, I Corinthians 1:2, I Corinthians 4:17, I Corinthians 11:18-26, 12:28, I Corinthians 14:23, 33, I Corinthians 16:19, Galatians 1:11-20 verse 13, Ephesians 1:21-22, Acts 15:41, Ephesians 3:9-21 verse 10, 11, 12, 21, Ephesians 5:25, 27, 29, 32, Philippians 3:6, Colossians 1:18, 23-24, I Thessalonians 1:1-10 verse 1, II Thessalonians 1:1-12 verse 1, I Timothy 3:15-16, Hebrews 2:12-18 verse 12, Revelation 2:1, 8, 12, 18, Revelation 3:1, 7, 14, Revelation 2:7, 11, 17, 23, 29, 3:6, 13, 22, Revelation 22:16, Revelation 1:4, I Thessalonians 2:14, II Corinthians 11:28, II Corinthians 8:23, 24, II Corinthians 8:4, 19, I Corinthians 7:17, 14:33, Acts 16:5, Acts 9:31
12. Blessed are the poor in spirit to those who believe that when **Jesus spoke the Word;** when **Jesus** knew too much, so much; when **Jesus prophesied exactly;** when **Jesus performed some miracles;** when **Jesus** need no one else to tell **Him** what to do; what to believe; what to suggest; **we had no doubt** at all that **Jesus is, was and has always been existed in the past that He is indeed God Himself the Father, Almighty; The One True God; the One and Only, the One and the Same, JESUS** is **God always, always, always** and **there is no beginnings, no ending. He has always been existence. Some glorious day** we as God's children will **see Him as He is.** John 17:3, Romans 3:4, II Corinthians 1:18, I Thessalonians 1:9, I John 5:20, Revelation 19:9, 11, 21:5, 22:6-7, Revelation 22:20-21, **Isaiah 52:6**, **John 4:26**, **29 John 9:37**, **Acts 17:29**, Romans 1:20, Colossians 2:9, **Genesis 1:1**, **John 1:1**, John 1:1-18, **II Timothy 3:16**, John

14:6-12, **John 14:7-9**, Romans 8:21, Luke 23:8, John 6:14, **Hebrews 13:8**, John 10:41, John 12:18 **John 8:56-58, Revelation 1:7, 8, 17-18, 4:9, 16:15, Revelation 3:11,** Exodus 3:6, 14-15, Matthew 26:32, Mark 12:26-27, Luke 20:37, Mark 12:32, John 10:30, Revelation 1:11, Colossians 3:4**, Hebrews 9:28,** I Peter 5:4, I John 2:28, I John 3:2, Isaiah 53:4-5, Isaiah 7:14, Isaiah 9:6, Matthew 1:21, 23, 25, Luke 1:31, Luke 2:10-11, 21, Mark 3:21, **Luke 23:2 (Himself), John 5:18 (Himself), John 21:14 (Himself), Acts 1:3 (Himself), John 10:33 (Claim Himself They said He being a man made Himself God), John 19:7, 12 (Himself),** John 19:12, **John 21;1 (Himself),** Acts 9:4-5, 22, Acts 18:5, 25, **II Corinthians 5:18, 19 (Himself By Jesus Christ), II Corinthians 5:19 (God was in Christ—Himself), Galatians 1:2-4 verse 4 (Himself), Galatians 2:20 (Faith of the Son of God, Christ, Himself), Ephesians 1:5, 9 (Jesus Christ to Himself), Ephesians 2:20 (Himself), Ephesians 5:2, 25, 27 (Himself Christ Himself), Hebrews 2:18 (Himself), Philippians 2:18 (Himself), Philippians 3:21 (Himself), Colossians 1:20 (Himself), I Thessalonians 3:11 (Himself God), I Thessalonians 4:16 (Himself Lord) as Same as Acts 9:15 (Jesus Lord) II Thessalonians 2:16-17 (Himself), II Thessalonians 3:16 (Himself), I Timothy 2:6 (Himself), II Timothy 2:13 (Himself), Titus 2:14 (Himself), Hebrews 1:3 (Himself), Hebrews 2:14, 18 (Himself), Hebrews 5:5-14 verse 5 (Himself), Hebrews 7:27 (Himself), Hebrews 9:14, 25, 26 (Himself), Hebrews 12:1-3 (Himself), Revelation 19:12 (Himself), Revelation 21:3 (Himself God), Philippians 2:6-11, verse 6, 10, 11,—(Jesus claim Himself to be God and that He Himself is indeed God as always and always will be Him when we see Him on that Glorious Day!!! Jesus is not n imposter. He is never a robbery either. He did not come to look like God. He is really God according to Phillip not know that He had been seen Him for three years and yet did not know that Jesus was and is and will always be the Same God. Read again John 14:7, 8, 9. See verse that emphasis 9!!! Again Jesus is God. Genesis 1:1, John 1:1, 14, II Timothy 3:16**

Part DXL

Blessed Are The Poor In Spirit. Matthew 5:3

Blessed Means Happy

Poor means meek in spirit Poor means humble in spirit Poor means lowly in spirit Poor means quiet in spirit Read Matthew 5:3-12, Read also Mark 1:15

Jesus did not say "*rich*" in spirit. Jesus said "*poor*" in spirit.

1. Blessed are the poor in spirit to those who believe that **Christ Jesus** proceed from the **Father**. John 8:42
2. Blessed are the poor in spirit to those who believe that the **Holy Spirit** proceed from the **Father** and the **Son.** John 15:26
3. Blessed are the poor in spirit to those who believe that these scriptures that state: **"Who Make Thou Thyself:"** I believe that **Jesus is God** because **He knew Abraham. He knew Isaac. He knew Jacob. He also knew Moses. He knew Noah. He knew David. He knew Isaiah. He knew Jeremiah. He knew Elijah. He knew John knew John The Baptist before John the Baptist was born to prepare the way for the Lord. He knew all of them. He said**, **"Before Abraham was, I am** "Thou—(This) is the **"I Am.**" Read Exodus 3:6, 14-15, verse 14. **Jesus** is **God** the Great **I Am. John 8:55-59** verse **53; read John 14:1-12, verse 7, 8, 9, Mark 14:61-64 verse 62, Luke 23:2, John 4:26, 29, John 5:18, John 9:36-37 verse 37, John 10:30, 33, 38, John 19:7, Acts 10:36, Philippians 2:6-11 verse 6, 10, 11, Hebrews 13:8, I John 5:20, I Timothy 3: 16, Acts 9:3-6, verse 5, 22, 15-16, Acts 18:5, 9, 28, Acts 20:35, Acts 22:7-10 verse 8, 18, 21, Acts 23:11, Acts 26:13-18 verse 15, Isaiah 52:6, Revelation 1:7-8, 11, 17-18, verse 18, Revelation 2:8**—(Isaiah 44:6), **Revelation 3:7**—(Isaiah 22:22) **11, Revelation 4:8**—(Isaiah 6:3), **Revelation 16:15, Revelation 22:7, 12-13**—(Isaiah 44:6, Isaiah 48:12), **Revelation 22:16, 20;** read Matthew 17:4, Mark 9:5, Malachi 4:5, Matthew 11:14, **John 1:30**
4. Blessed are the poor in spirit to those who believe this statement: "They said I can "**be**" anything so I become **awesome**. Philippians 4:13, Psalm 139:14, Jeremiah 33:3
5. Blessed are the poor in spirit to those who believe this statement: I can "**do.**" so I become **awesome** Philippians 4:13

6. Blessed are the poor in spirit to those who believe this statement: I could **say "I believe and I accept."** Mark 11:22
7. Blessed are the poor in spirit to those who believe this spiritual hymn: "Now I be—long to Je—sus, Je—sus be—longs to me, No for the years of time a—lone, But for the e—ter—ni—ty." Romans 14:8, Matthew 28:20, Luke 23:40-43, Hebrews 13:5
8. Blessed are the poor in spirit to those who believe this scripture that state: "**Who Make Thou Thyself?"** I believe that **Jesus is God** because **He knew Abraham. He knew Isaac. He knew Jacob. He** also **knew Moses. He knew Noah. He knew David. He knew Isaiah. He knew Jeremiah. He knew Elijah. He Knew John the Baptist. He knew all of them. He said, "Before Abraham was, I Am," Jesus is the "I Am."** Read Exodus 3:6, 14-15. **"Jesus Is God The Great I Am." John 8:53-59 verse 53, John 14:1-12, verse 7, 8, 9**
9. Blessed are the poor in spirit to those who believe **"That Seed"** is **Jesus Christ.** Genesis 12:7, Galatians 3:16, 19, Acts 7:5
10. Blessed are the poor in spirit to those who believe that **Mediator** is **Jesus Christ** of a **Better Covenant** (agreement). Hebrews 8:6
11. Blessed are the poor in spirit to those who believe that **Jesus Christ** is the **Mediator of the New Covenant** (agreement), better than that of Abel. Hebrews 12:24, See Genesis 4:10
12. Blessed are the poor in spirit to those who believe that **doctors of the law mean teachers because they knew only the Old Testament Law** and **not the New Testament Law by Jesus Christ**. But **Old Testament Law** was indeed about **Christ** because **Christ Himself** was **God** from the **Scripture** that state in the **Beginning God. Christ is "He" from Genesis through Revelation.** Genesis 1:1, John 1:1-18, II Timothy 3:16, Luke 5:16,

Part DXLI

Blessed Are The Poor In Spirit. Matthew 5:3

Blessed Means Happy

Poor means meek in spirit. Poor means humble in spirit. Poor means lowly in spirit. Poor means quiet in spirit. Read Matthew 5:3-12, Read also Mark 1:15

Jesus did not say "*rich*" in spirit. Jesus said "*poor*" in spirit.

1. Blessed are the poor in spirit to those who believe that after **Jesus** rose from the dead, He visited His disciples *three times for forty days* before He went back to Heaven. John 21:14, Acts 1:3, 9—The Disciples (John) when Jesus loved—John 21:7—**Beloved Disciples: Jesus** was *clothed in white cloud*—**Acts 1:9**
2. Blessed are the poor in spirit to those who believe that the word **"Beloved"** mean "*The Children of God, Born of God*—I John 3:9, 5:4, 18, *born again, being born again*, I Peter 1:23, *Sons of God, well beloved, dearly, friends in Christ, children of God*; *born of the Spirit, adoption children, dear friends in Christ, Beloved sons, Beloved daughters, Beloved Brother* or *Brother Beloved of God, sons and daughters of God, in the saints of God*, or *the People of God*, Hosea 2:23, Acts 15:25, Romans 1:7, Romans 9:25, Romans 11:25-36 verse 28-32, verse 28, Romans 12:19, Romans 16:**8, 9, 12**, I Corinthians 4:14, **17**, 10:13-14 verse 14, 15:54-58 verse 58, II Corinthians 7:1, 12:19, Ephesians 1:6, 6:**21**, Philippians 2:5-13 verse 12, 4:1-5, 21-22, Colossians 3:12, 4:**7-18 verse 9, 14**, I Thessalonians 1:4, II Thessalonians 2:13, I Timothy 6:1-2, II Timothy 1:**2**, Philemon 1:**1-2**, 16-17, Hebrews 6:9-20 verse 9, James 1:16-27 verse 16, 19, 2:5-26 verse 5, I Peter 2:11-25 verse 11, I Peter 4:1-19 verse 12, II Peter 3:1-18, verse 1, 8, 14-15, 17, I John 3:2, 21, I John 4:1, 7-14 verse 7, 11, III John 1:**1**, 2, 5-11 verse 5, 11, Jude 1:3, 17-25 verse 17, 20, Revelation 20:4-15 verse 9 **"Winning For Christ"** Proverbs 11:30, Mark 1:1, Mark 16:15
3. Blessed are the poor in spirit to those who believe that *Christian homes* stand for **winning for Christ.**
4. Blessed are the poor in spirit to those who believe that *Christian schools* stand for **winning for Christ.**

5. Blessed are the poor in spirit to those who believe that *Christian stands* for **winning for Christ.**
6. Blessed are the poor in spirit to those who believe that *Christian colleges* stand for **winning for Christ**.
7. Blessed are the poor in spirit to those who believe that *Christian church* stand for**winning for Christ**.
8. Blessed are the poor in spirit to those who believe *doing Christian business* stand for **winning for Christ.**
9. Blessed are the poor in spirit to those who believe that *reading Christian books* stand for **winning for Christ**.
10. Blessed are the poor in spirit to those who believe that watching *Christian movie* stand for **winning for Christ.**
11. Blessed are the poor in spirit to those who believe that *reading Christian testimonies* stand for **winning for Christ.**
12. Blessed are the poor in spirit to those who believe that *reading* **the Bible**, which is the **Word of God**, the **Word of the Spirit**, the **Word of Christ**, the **Word of Jesus**, the Word of the Holy Spirit to convert sinners or to convict sinners and Christian duty stand for **winning for Christ**.

Part DXLII

Blessed Are The Poor In Spirit. Matthew 5:3

Blessed Means Happy

Poor means meek in spirit. Poor means humble in spirit. Poor means lowly in spirit. Poor means quiet in spirit. Read Matthew 5:3-12, Read also Mark 1:15

Jesus did not say "*rich*" in spirit. Jesus said "*poor*" in spirit.

"Winning For Christ" Proverbs 11:30, Mark 1:1, Mark 16:15

1. Blessed are the poor in spirit to those who believe that *Second Coming of Christ* stand for **winning for Christ.**
2. Blessed are the poor in spirit to those who believe that the *Gospel of Jesus Christ* stand for **winning for Christ**.
3. Blessed are the poor in spirit to those who believe that *Liberty University* in Lynchburg, Virginia stand for **winning for Christ**.
4. Blessed are the poor in spirit to those who believe that *Tennessee Temple University* in Chattanooga, Tennessee stand for **winning for Christ.**
5. Blessed are the poor in spirit to those who believe that *Columbia International University* in Columbia, South Carolina stand for **winning for Christ.**
6. Blessed are the poor in spirit to those who believe that *Oral Robert University* in Tulsa, Oklahoma stand for **winning for Christ**.
7. Blessed are the poor in spirit to those who believe that *Christian College* and *Seminary* stand for **winning for Christ**.
8. Blessed are the poor in spirit to those who believe that *Christian Sunday School* stand for **winning for Christ**.
9. Blessed are the poor in spirit to those who believe that *Christian vehicles* stand for **winning for Christ.**
10. Blessed are the poor in spirit to those who believe that *Christian huge truck* stand for **winning for Christ**.
11. Blessed are the poor in spirit to those who believe that *Christian school buses* stand for **winning for Christ.**
12. Blessed are the poor in spirit to those who believe that *Christian children church* stand for **winning for Christ**.

Part DXLIII

Blessed Are The Poor In Spirit. Matthew 5:3

Blessed Means Happy

Poor means meek in spirit. Poor means humble in spirit. Poor means lowly in spirit. Poor means quiet in spirit. Read Matthew 5:3-12, Read also Mark 1:15

Jesus did not say "*rich*" in spirit. Jesus said "*poor*" in spirit.

"Winning For Christ" Proverbs 11:30, Mark1:1, Mark 16:15

1. Blessed are the poor in spirit to those who believe that *Christian Universities* stand for **winning for Christ.**
2. Blessed are the poor in spirit to those who believe that *Christian Television Network* stand for **winning for Christ**.
3. Blessed are the poor in spirit to those who believe that *Christ For The Nation* stand for **winning for Christ.**
4. Blessed are the poor in spirit to those who believe that *Christian Radio Broadcasting Network* stand for **winning for Christ.**
5. Blessed are the poor in spirit to those who believe that *Christian Ministry* stand for **winning for Christ**.
6. Blessed are the poor in spirit to those who believe that *Children's Ministry* stand for **winning for Christ**.
7. Blessed are the poor in spirit to those who believe that *Christian Men's Ministry* stand for **winning for Christ.**
8. Blessed are the poor in spirit to those who believe that *Christian Women's Ministry* stand for **winning for Christ.**
9. Blessed are the poor in spirit to those who believe that *working for Christ* stand for **winning for Christ**.
10. Blessed are the poor in spirit to those who believe that *winning souls for Christ* is to win. Win souls for Christ according to Proverbs 11:30
11. Blessed are the poor in spirit to those who believe that the *fruit of the righteous*, is *a tree of life*, and he that **winneth souls** is wise according to Proverbs 11:30
12. Blessed are the poor in spirit to those who believe that *winning lost souls* stand for **winning for Christ** according to Proverbs 11:30

PART DXLIV

Blessed Are The Poor In Spirit. Matthew 5:3

Blessed Means Happy

Poor means meek in spirit. Poor means humble in spirit. Poor means lowly in spirit. Poor means quiet in spirit. Read Matthew 5:3-12, Read also Mark 1:15

Jesus did not say "*rich*" in spirit. Jesus said "*poor*" in spirit.

1. Blessed are the poor in spirit to those who *believe* that *Allen University* in Columbia, South Carolina stand for **winning for Christ**. Proverbs 11:30, Mark 1:1, Mark 16:15
2. Blessed are the poor in spirit to those who *believe* that the **Holy Spirit is a gift of God's grace.** Luke 11:13, Mark 11:22, Mark 16:17c, I John 5:14-15, I Peter 2:21, Philippians 3:10, John 20:22, Acts 2:4, Joel 2:27-29, Acts 2:16-18, Romans 6:23, Ephesians 2:5, 8, Romans 5:15, 16, 17, 18, 21, Romans 6:1-23, Luke 2:40, John 1:14, 16, 17, Acts 4:33, 11:23, Acts 13:43, 14:3, 26, 15:11, 40, 18:27, Acts 20:24, 32, Romans 1:5, 7, Romans 3:24, 4:16, Romans 5:2, 20-21, Romans 6:14, 15, 11:5-6, Romans 15:15, 16:20, 24, I Corinthians 1:3, 4, 3:10, I Corinthians 15:10, I Corinthians 16:23, II Corinthians 1:2, 12, 4:15, II Corinthians 8:9, 19, 9:8, 14, 12:9, II Corinthians 13:14, Galatians 1:3, 1:5, 2:9, 21, 5:4, 6:18, Ephesians 1:2, 6, 2:7, 3:2, 9, Ephesians 3:7, 8, 4:7, 29, 6:24, Philippians 1:2, 7, 4:23, Colossians 1:2, 6, 3:16, Ephesians 4:6, 18, I Thessalonians 1:1, 5:28, II Thessalonians 1:2, 12, 2:16, 3:18, I Timothy 1:2, 14, 6:21, II Timothy 1:2, 9, 2:1, 4:22, Titus 1:4, 2:11, Titus 3:7, 15, Philemon 1:3, 25, Hebrews 2:9, 4:16, 12:28, 13:9, 25, James 4:6-7, I Peter 1:2, 10, 13, 3:7, I Peter 4:10, 5:5, 10, 12, II Peter 1:2, 3:18, II John 1:3, Revelation 1:4, Revelation 22:21, Jonah 4:2, Malachi 1:9, Luke 4:22, I Peter 2:3, Hosea 14:2
3. Blessed are the poor in spirit to those who *believe* that **salvation** is for *sinners* who need to be saved **toward God and faith toward our Lord Jesus Christ**. Galatians 3:11, Hebrews 10:38, Romans 3:23, Romans 10:8-13, Romans 5:1, Habakkuk 2:4, Romans 1:17, Romans 6:23, Acts 4:12, Ephesians 2:5, 8, Acts 11:30-31, Romans 10:13, Acts 20:21, Joel 2:27-32, Acts 2:17-18, 37-39
4. Blessed are the poor in spirit to those who *believe* that the *Baptism in the Holy Spirit* is for the *believing saints of God*, for the *believing Christians*, that **already**

being converted, already being repented of their sins or already being regenerated by the Holy Spirit, may *have the right to believe* that they were *filled with the Holy Spirit according to Acts 2:1-4 verse 4*, when they *ask in faith* to receive it. John 20:22, Mark 11:22, Mark 16:17c, Matthew 7:7-8, 11, Luke 11:9-10, 13, I John 5:14-15, Acts 2:16-18, 38, Joel 2:27-29, Acts 1:4-5, 8, Luke 24:49, Acts 11:16, Acts 10:42-48, Acts 11:12-18, Acts 2:1-47, Acts 10:1-47, Acts 19:1-7, Isaiah 28:11-12, I Corinthians 14:21-22, John 14:14, I Corinthians 14:33, Philippians 3:10

5. Blessed are the poor in spirit to those who *believe* this **scripture** and *statement*: "If thou knew the gift (Jesus) of God and **Who** (God) It (This) Is That Saith to thee." "GIVE ME TO DRINK; thou wouldest have asked of HIM (God/Jesus), and He (God/Jesus) WOULD HAVE GIVEN thee LIVING WATER (Jesus/Holy Spirit). John 4:10, Hebrews 9:28, See Isaiah 52:6, John 4:26, John 9:37, John 10:30, 33, John 5:18, John 14:6-9, John 7:17, John 19:7, Revelation 1:7, 8, 11, 17-18, Revelation 3:11, Revelation 4:9-10, Revelation 16:15, Revelation 22:7, 12-13, 16, 20-21, Genesis 1:1, John 1:1-18 verse 1, 14, II Timothy 3:16, I John 5:20, I Timothy 3:16, Hebrews 13:8, Isaiah 44:2, 6, Revelation 2:8, Acts 1:11, John 11:25, Luke 23:2, John 6:51-63, Galatians 2:20, I Peter 4:1, I John 4:2-3, Revelation 3:7, II Corinthians 5:10, 7:12, Colossians 3:4, Hebrews 9:24, 28, I Peter 5:4, I John 2:28, 3:2, II john 1:7, I Peter 1:19-25 verse 20, II Timothy 1:7-10 verse 10, John 14:8, 9, Luke 1:78, Matthew 1:21, 25, Luke 2:21, Isaiah 7:10, 9:6, Isaiah 53:1-12, Ephesians 4:30, Exodus 3:6, 14-15, Matthew 22:32, Mark 12:26-27, Luke 20:37, Psalm 51:11, Isaiah 63:10, 11, Ephesians 1:13
6. Blessed are the poor in spirit to those who *believe* that **GIFT OF** (Jesus) **GOD WHO** (God) **IT** (This) IS **THAT SAITH** to thee, **GIVE** (Father/Jesus) **ME** (Father/Jesus) DRINK; thou WOULDEST HAVE ASKED OF **HIM** (God) AND **HE** (God) WOULDEST HAVE GIVEN THEE **LIVING** (Jesus/Holy Spirit) **WATER**, is **God's speaking in the Flesh of Jesus Christ.** John 4:10, Hebrews 9:28, See Isaiah 52:6, John 4:26, John 9:37, John 10:30, 33, John 5:18, John 14:6-9, John 7:17, John 19:7, Revelation 1:7, 8, 11, 17-18, Revelation 3:11, Revelation 4:9-10, Revelation 16:15, Revelation 22:7, 12-13, 16, 20-21, Genesis 1:1, John 1:1-18 verse 1, 14, II Timothy 3:16, I John 5:20, I Timothy 3:16, Hebrews 13:8, Isaiah 44:2, 6, Revelation 2:8, Acts 1:11, John 11:25, Luke 23:2, John 6:51-63, Galatians 2:20, I Peter 4:1, I John 4:2-3, Revelation 3:7, II Corinthians 5:10, 7:12, Colossians 3:4, Hebrews 9:24, 28, I Peter 5:4, I John

2:28, 3:2, II john 1:7, I Peter 1:19-25 verse 20, II Timothy 1:7-10 verse 10, John 14:8, 9, Luke 1:78, Matthew 1:21, 25, Luke 2:21, Isaiah 7:10, 9:6, Isaiah 53:1-12, Ephesians 4:30, Exodus 3:6, 14-15, Matthew 22:32, Mark 12:26-27, Luke 20:37, Psalm 51:11, Isaiah 63:10, 11, Ephesians 1:13

7. Blessed are the poor in spirit to those who *believe* this **scripture** that speak of *everlasting punishment*: "Then shall he say also unto them on the left hand, Depart from me, ye cursed, into everlasting fire, prepared for the devil and his angels:" Matthew 25:41
8. Blessed are the poor in spirit to those who *believe* this **scripture** that speak of *everlasting punishment*: "And these shall go away into everlasting punishment: but the righteous into life eternal." Matthew 25:46
9. Blessed are the poor in spirit to those who *believe* this **scripture** that speak of *everlasting punishment*: "Who shall be punished with everlasting destruction from the presence of the Lord, and from the glory of his power;" II Thessalonians 1:9
10. Blessed are the poor in spirit to those who *believe* this **scripture** that speak of *everlasting punishment*: "And the angels which kept not their first estate, but left their own habitation, he hath reserved in everlasting chains under darkness unto the judgment of the great day." Jude 1:6
11. Blessed are the poor in spirit to those who *believe* this **scripture** that speak of *everlasting punishment*: "Then Paul and Barnabas **waxed bold**, and said, It was necessary that the **Word of God** should **first** have been **spoken** to *you*: but seeing *ye* put it from you, and judge yourselves **unworthy** of **everlasting life**, lo, we turn *to the Gentiles*." Acts 13:46
12. Blessed are the poor in spirit to those who *believe* **Christ's promising word** of **everlasting life** to believers who put their trust in **Him** that speak of **everlasting life through eternal**: "For **God** so loved the world, that **He** gave **His Only Begotten Son**, that *whosoever believeth* in **Him** *should not perish*, but have **everlasting life**." John 3:16

Part DXLV

Blessed Are The Poor In Spirit. Matthew 5:3

Blessed Means Happy

Poor means meek in spirit. Poor means humble in spirit. Poor means lowly in spirit. Poor means quiet in spirit. Read Matthew 5:3-12, Read also Mark 1:15

Jesus did not say "*rich*" in spirit. Jesus said "*poor*" in spirit.

1. Blessed are the poor in spirit to those who *believe* **Christ's promising word of everlasting life** to those believers who put their trust in **Him** that speak of **everlasting life through eternal**: "He that believeth on the Son hath everlasting life: and he that believeth not the Son shall not see life; but the wrath of God abideth on him." John 3:36
2. Blessed are the poor in spirit to those who *believe* **Christ's promising word of everlasting life** to those believers who put their trust in **Him** that speak of **everlasting life through eternal**: "But whosoever drinketh of the water that I shall give him shall never thirst; but the water that I shall give him shall be in him a well of water springing up into everlasting life." John 4:14
3. Blessed are the poor in spirit to those who *believe* **Christ's promising word of everlasting life** to those believers who put their trust in **Him** that speak of **everlasting life through eternal**: "Verily, verily, I say unto you, He that heareth my word, and believeth on him that sent me, hath everlasting life, and shall not come into condemnation; but is passed from death unto life." John 5:24
4. Blessed are the poor in spirit to those who *believe* Christ's promising word of everlasting life to those believers who put their trust in Him that speak of everlasting life through eternal: "Labour not for the meat which endureth unto everlasting life, which the Son of man shall give unto you: for him hath God the Father sealed." John 6:27
5. Blessed are the poor in spirit to those who *believe* **Christ's promising word of everlasting life** to those believers who put their trust in **Him** that speak of **everlasting life through eternal**: "And this is the will of him that sent me, that every one which seeth the Son, and believeth on him, may have everlasting life: and I will raise him up at the last day." John 6:40

6. Blessed are the poor in spirit to those who *believe* **Christ's promising word of everlasting life** to these believers who put their trust in **Him** that speak of **everlasting life through eternal**: "Verily, verily, I say unto you, He that believeth on me hath everlasting life." John 6:47
7. Blessed are the poor in spirit to those who *believe* **Christ's promising word of everlasting life** to those believers who put their trust in **Him** that speak of **everlasting life through eternal**: "And I know that his commandment is life everlasting: whatsoever I speak therefore, even as the Father said unto me, so I speak." John 12:50
8. Blessed are the poor in spirit to those who *believe* **Christ's promising word of everlasting life** to those believers who put their trust in **Him** that speak of **everlasting life through eternal**: "For the wages of sin is death; but the gift of God is eternal life through Jesus Christ our Lord." Romans 6:23
9. Blessed are the poor in spirit to those who *believe* **Christ's promising word of everlasting life** to those believers who put their trust in **Him** that speak of **everlasting life through eternal**: "Howbeit for this cause I obtained mercy, that in me first Jesus Christ might shew forth all longsuffering, for a pattern to them which should hereafter believe on him to life everlasting." I Timothy 1:16
10. Blessed are the poor in spirit to those who *believe* **Christ's promising word of everlasting life** to those believers who put their trust in **Him** that speak of **everlasting life through eternal**: "Now the God of peace, that brought again from the dead our Lord Jesus, that great shepherd of the sheep, through the blood of the everlasting covenant." Hebrews 13:20
11. Blessed are the poor in spirit to those who *believe* **Christ's promising word of everlasting life** to those believers who put their trust in **Him** that speak of **everlasting life for eternal**: "For so an entrance shall be ministered unto you abundantly into the everlasting kingdom of our Lord and Saviour Jesus Christ." II Peter 1:11
12. Blessed are the poor in spirit to those who *believe* **Christ's promising word of everlasting life** to those believers who put their trust in **Him** that speak of **everlasting life through eternal**: "And I saw another angel fly in the midst of heaven, having the everlasting gospel to preach unto them that dwell on the earth, and to every nation, and kindred, and tongue, and people." Revelation 14:6

Part DXLVI

Blessed Are The Poor In Spirit. Matthew 5:3

Blessed Means Happy

Poor means meek in spirit. Poor means humble in spirit. Poor means lowly in spirit. Poor means quiet in spirit. Read Matthew 5:3-12, Read also Mark 1:15

Jesus did not say "*rich*" in spirit. Jesus said "*poor*" in spirit.

1. Blessed are the poor in spirit to those who believe that *Christian van* stand for **winning for Christ**. Proverbs 11:30, Mark 1:1, Mark 16:15
2. Blessed are the poor in spirit to those who believe that *Christian athletics* stand for **winning souls** for Christ. Proverbs 11:30, Mark 1:1, Mark 16:15
3. Blessed are the poor in spirit to those who believe that *Christian sport* stand for **winning for Christ**. Proverbs 11:30, Mark 1:1, Mark 16:15
4. Blessed are the poor in spirit to those who believe in the **Almighty God.** Genesis 17:1-27 verse 1-16, 19-21 verse 4
5. Blessed are the poor in spirit to those who believe in the **Everlasting God.** Genesis 21:1-34 verse 33, verse 3, 6-7, **12-13** (Red Print) (Romans 9:7, Hebrews 11:18), **17-18** (Red Print)
6. Blessed are the poor in spirit to those who believe in **The Living God.** Joshua 3:1-17 verse 10, **7-8** (Red Print)
7. Blessed are the poor in spirit to those who believe in **The Faithful God.** Deuteronomy 7:1-26 verse **4** (Red Print), 9
8. Blessed are the poor in spirit to those who believe that the United States of America dollars with **$3, 000, 000,** or **three million dollars will not get us to Heaven**!!! I Corinthians 6:9-10
9. Blessed are the poor in spirit to those who believe that **The Bible** is a **wake up call.** Amos 4:12, Matthew 5:6, Acts 2:4, Acts 4:8, 31, Acts 9:17, Acts 13:9, 52, Ephesians 5:18, Matthew 3:11b, Mark 1:8, Luke 3:16b, John 1:33, Acts 1:5b, Acts 11:16b, Luke 11:13, John 7:39, John 20:22, Acts 1:8, Acts 2:33, 38, 39, Acts 7:55, Acts 8:15, 17, 19, Acts 9:31, Acts 10:44, 45, 47, Acts 11:15, 16, 24, Acts 15:8, 28, 19:2, 6, Acts 20:23, Romans 5:5, Romans 9:1, Romans 14:17, Romans 15:13, 16, I Corinthians 2:13, 6:19-20, Acts 1:11, I Thessalonians

4:13-18, I Timothy 3:16, II Corinthians 13:14, Ephesians 1:13, Ephesians 4:30, I Thessalonians 1:5, I Thessalonians 4:8, II Timothy 1:14, Titus 3:5, Hebrews 2:4, Hebrews 3:7, Hebrews 6:4, Hebrews 10:15, I Peter 1:12, 15, 16, II Peter 1:21, Revelation 3:11, 4:8-9, I John 5:7, Jude 1:20, I Corinthians 12:3, Joel 2:26-29, Revelation 16:15, Revelation 22:7, 12-13, 20-21, Acts 2:16-18, Joel 2:32, Romans 10:13, Acts 4:12, Acts 16:30, Habakkuk 2:5, Romans 1:17, Romans 10:17, Galatians 3:11, Hebrews 10:38, Hebrews 13:8, Ephesians 2:8, Luke 24:49, Genesis 1:1, John 1:1-18, II Timothy 3:16, I John 5:10, Revelation 1:7, 8, 11, 17-18

10. Blessed are the poor in spirit to those who believe that there are **three words in one place:**
    a. There are three words in one Bible Scripture
    b. There are three words in one Bible Verse
    c. There are three words in one Bible Passage
11. Blessed are the poor in spirit to those who believe that the **Word of God** warn us that **Jesus is Coming Soon**. Amos 4:12, Revelation 22:20, Revelation 16:15, Revelation 3:11
12. Blessed are the poor in spirit to those who believe that the **Bible** warn us that **Jesus is Coming Soon**. Amos 4:12, Revelation 22:20, Revelation 16:15, Revelation 3:11

Part DXLVII

Blessed Are The Poor In Spirit. Matthew 5:3

Blessed Means Happy

Poor means meek in spirit. Poor means humble in spirit. Poor means lowly in spirit. Poor means quiet in spirit. Read Matthew 5:3-12, Read also Mark 1:15

Jesus did not say "*rich*" in spirit. Jesus said "*poor*" in spirit.

1. Blessed are the poor in spirit to those who believe **this scripture**: "**God** judgeth the righteous, and **God** is angry with the wicked every day. Psalm 7:11
2. Blessed are the poor in spirit to those who believe that the **Bible** is the sword of **the Lord**, the sword of **the Spirit**, which is **the Word of God**. Ephesians 6:17
3. Blessed are the poor in spirit to those who believe in **Faith, Family and Freedom.** Habakkuk 2:4, Romans 1:17, Galatians 3:11, Romans 10:17, Ephesians 3:15, John 8:32, 36
4. Blessed are the poor in spirit to those who believe that **God** made choice between **His** people *Israelites* and **His** people *Gentiles* that they as well as *us* to *hear* the **Word of the Gospel** and *believe*. Mark 1:15, Mark 11:22, Acts 15:1-19 verse 7
5. Blessed are the poor in spirit to those who become the man and woman that you are for His glory. Isaiah 43:7
6. Blessed are the poor in spirit to those who believe that the **Bible itself** from **Almighty God's Word**, is a **Glorious Historical Events**, to the **present until He come for His children**. Matthew 1:12, Ephesians 4:30, Revelation 1:7, 8, 11, 17-18, Revelation 2:7, 11, Revelation 16:15, Revelation 22:7, 12-13, 16, 20, Hebrews 9:28, I Thessalonians 4:13-18, Romans 8:15, 23, 9:4, Galatians 4:5, Ephesians 1:5, Luke 23:28, Acts 2:17, Acts 21:9, **II Corinthians 6:18,** I Peter 3:11, Matthew 3:9, **Matthew 19:14, I Thessalonians 5:5,** I Timothy 3:4, 12, 5:4, 10, Titus 2:4, Hebrews 2:13, Hebrews 11:23, 12:5, I Peter 1:4, I John 2:1, 12, 13, 18, 28, I John 3:7, 10, 18, 4:4, 5:2, 21, II John 1:1, 4, 13, III John 1:4, Joel 2:26-32, Acts 2:16-21, John 3:16-18, Ephesians 2:5, 8, I Timothy 6:12-21, II Timothy 4:6-8 verse 7, Romans 6:23, Mark 3:33-35 verse 33, 35, Matthew 12:46-50 verse 48, 50, Revelation 22:18, 10, Luke 8:21, Matthew 18:3, Mark

9:37, Mark 10:14, Luke 18:16, **Luke 20:36,** John 11:52, 12:36, 13:33, 21:5, Acts 2:39, Acts 10:36, 13:26, Romans 8:16, 17, 8:21, 9:7, 8, 9:26, I Corinthians 14:20, II Corinthians 12:14, 33, Galatians 3:7, 26, 4:28, Ephesians 5:1, 8, 6:1, Colossians 3:20, 21, I Thessalonians 2:11

7. Blessed are the poor in spirit to those who are able to pray *a sinner's prayer for salvation*: "*Dear Jesus, I know I am a sinner*, and I ask for *your forgiveness*. I *believe* you *died for my sins* and *rose from the dead*. I *trust* and *fellow* you as my **Lord** and **Savior**. *Guide my life* and *help me* to **do your will. In your name, Amen**." Romans 10:8-13 verse 17, Acts 16:30-31, Romans 3:6, Romans 6:1-11, I Corinthians 15:1-4, I Thessalonians 5:23-25, Ephesians 2:5, 8, Romans 8:16, Romans 6:23, Mark 11:22, Romans 5:1-21
8. Blessed are the poor in spirit to those who believe that *once-saved*-always saved mean that if that person was ever saved in the first place when he first started to believe in Christ that he was saved or not yet at all. Philippians 2:12. I believe that Judas Iscariot was not saved in the first place Christ knew it therefore Judas hang himself. Matthew 27:1-5 verse 5, John 6:64-71
9. Blessed are the poor in spirit to those who believe that *once-saved* always saved cannot be impossible saved in the first place according to Philippians 2:12 and because of Revelation 22:19, Luke 8:13, Revelation 2:4—Consider Judas Iscariot for instance: John 6:64-71, Hebrews 6:4
10. Blessed are the poor in spirit to those who believe that *once-saved*-always saved, **emphasize upon** "if" one continue in faith, growing sanctification and holiness day by day. **II Peter 3:18, II Thessalonians 2:13,** I Corinthians 1:30, I Thessalonians 4:3-4 verse 3, I Peter 1:2, **I Thessalonians 4:7,** Mark 11:12, **Colossians 1:21-23 verse 23**
11. Blessed are the poor in spirit to those who believe that **God** is not the **author of confusion**, but of peace as in *all churches* of the **saints** like as on the **Day of Pentecost** in Acts 2:1-42 verse 1-12, because **He** knew it must come to pass by **His spoken words** in Joel 2:26-32, Mark 16:17, Luke 24:46-53 verse 47-49, John 14:16-18, John 20:21, Acts 1:2-8 verse 4-8, Acts 2:1-12 verse 1-4, Acts 11:16, Acts 2:17-21, Romans 10:13 later some thing happened in Los Angeles, California in 1906 to 1909 following the pattern faith in the Book of Acts 2:1-47 verse 1-4, I Corinthians 14:33, Hebrews 5:9, Hebrews 12:2, **Ephesians 4:1-13 verse 3, 4, 5, 13, Psalm 122:1, Psalm 133:1**

12. Bless are the poor in spirit to those who believe that **"Vengeance"** is the Lord's: not ours; not yours. He will take care of the problem to those who get away with murders **on God's Judgment Day**. **Romans 12:19**, Hebrews 9:27, Psalm 10:7, **Hebrews 10:30,** I Peter 5:7, Psalm 55:22-23

Part DXLVIII

Blessed Are The Poor In Spirit. Matthew 5:3

Blessed Means Happy

Poor means meek in spirit. Poor means humble in spirit. Poor means lowly in spirit. Poor means quiet in spirit. Read Matthew 5:3-12, Read also Mark 1:15

Jesus did not say "*rich*" in spirit. Jesus said "*poor*" in spirit.

1. Bless is the poor in spirit to those who believe that the Battle is His: not ours; not yours. He will take care of the problem to those who got away with murders **on God's Judgment Day**. I Samuel 17:47, **II Chronicles 20:15**
2. Blessed are the poor in spirit to those who believe that when you accept Jesus Christ as your personal Savior and Lord, you are a change person; you are a new person; not turn over a new leaf, but by renewing of your min. II Corinthians 5:17, Romans 12:1-2
3. Blessed are the poor in spirit to those who believe that the Baptism of the Holy Spirit is **a promise** from God, the Father who shall send the Holy Spirit to baptize us, which is through Jesus Christ which He is the Holy Spirit Baptizer; not like John the Baptist because John the Baptist baptize people in water unto repentance before Jesus would come to baptize us with the Holy Spirit which is in Acts 2:4, Luke 24:49, Acts 1:4-5, Acts 1:8, Acts 2:4, Acts 11:16, See Water Baptism: Matthew 3:11, Mark 1:8, Luke 3:16, John 1:33, Acts 11:16. It has rang in my ears for years telling me that they receive the baptism in the Holy Spirit the **moment** they accept Jesus Christ as their personal Savior. I explain that it was the water baptism. See Romans 6:1-14 and Colossians 2:12, Galatians 3:26-28. This is not the baptism in the Holy Spirit. It is the water baptism identify Christ's Death, Burial and Resurrection to a new life changing. Can anybody explain to me the definition?
4. Blessed are the poor in spirit to those who are able to say: "I know that my Redeemer live. Job 19:25
5. Blessed are the poor in spirit to those who believe that there is no fun in life without Christ. John 15:5, John 5:24, 26, John 14:6, Matthew 10:39, Matthew 16:25-26 (Job 27:8), Matthew 19:16-24, John 19:18 (Exodus 20:13-16), John

19:19 (Leviticus 19:18), Matthew 25:46, Mark 8:35, Mark 10:17-25 verse 19 (Exodus 20:13-16), Mark 10:45, Luke 9:24, Luke 10:25-28, Luke 17:33, Luke 18:18-25, John 1:4, John 3:15-16, 36, John 4:14, 36, John 5:29, 40, John 6:27, 33, 35, 40, 47, 48, 51, 53, 54, 63, 68, **John 6:68**, John 8:12, John 10:10, 11, 15, 17, 28, John 11:15, John 12:25, 50, John 15:13, John 17:2-3, John 20:31, Revelation 2:7, **Revelation 2:10**

6. Blessed are the poor in spirit to those who are patient waiting at the coming of our Lord Jesus Christ. I Thessalonians 3:13, Hebrews 9:28, I John 3:2-3, Revelation 1:7, I Thessalonians 4:16-17, Revelation 3:11, Revelation 16:15, Revelation 22:7, 12-13, 16, 20
7. Blessed are the poor in spirit to those who believe to have a mind to work in the Lord's business. Jeremiah 4:6, Romans 8:28-30, Ephesians 2:8, 10, Psalm 100:3
8. Blessed are the poor in spirit to those who believe the Old Scripture: "So built we the wall; and all the wall was joined together unto the half thereof: for the people had a mind to work." Nehemiah 4:6
9. Blessed are the poor in spirit to those who believe that "**Sin**" mean **Je-sus**. John 4:11, 15, 19, 49, John 5:7, John 20:15, Revelation 7:14
10. Blessed are the poor in spirit to those who believe that God that has the power, keep as busy daily until He come.
11. Blessed are the poor in spirit to those who believe that my house is my vineyard. Matthew 21:28
12. Blessed are the poor in spirit to those who believe this scripture of Old: "The Lord watch between me and thee when (while) we are absent one from another. Genesis 31:49

Part DXLIX

Blessed Are The Poor In Spirit. Matthew 5:3

Blessed Means Happy

Poor means meek in spirit. Poor means humble in spirit. Poor means lowly in spirit. Poor means quiet in spirit. Read Matthew 5:3-12, Read also Mark 1:15

Jesus did not say "*rich*" in spirit. Jesus said "*poor*" in spirit.

1. Blessed are the poor in spirit to those who believe in wearing the cross as the symbol of their faith in Jesus Christ because of Christ's Calvary on the Cross that He died near the place of Golgotha—And when they were come unto a place called Golgotha, that is to say, a place of a skull. Matthew 27:33
2. Blessed are the poor in spirit to those who believe in wearing the cross as the symbol of their faith in Jesus Christ because of Christ's Calvary on the Cross that He died near the place of Golgotha—And they bring him unto the place Golgotha, which is, being interpreted, The place of a skull. Mark 15:22
3. Blessed are the poor in spirit to those who believe in wearing the cross as the symbol of their faith in Jesus Christ because of Christ's Calvary on the Cross that He died near the place of Golgotha—And he bearing his cross went forth into a place called the place of a skull, which is called in the Hebrew Golgotha. John 19:17
4. Blessed are the poor in spirit to those who believe that A. B. C. in classroom stand for Father, Son and Holy Spirit. Matthew 3:17, Matthew 28:19, II Corinthians 13:14, Exodus 3:6
5. Blessed are the poor in spirit to those who be that 1-2-3 in classroom stand for Father, Son and Holy Spirit. Matthew 3:17, Matthew 28:19, II Corinthians 13:14
6. Blessed are the poor in spirit to those who believe that it is well with my soul. Psalm 103:2
7. Blessed are the poor in spirit to those who believe in Faith, Family and Freedom. Habakkuk 2:4, Romans 1:17, Galatians 3:11, Romans 10:17, Ephesians 3:15, John 8:32, 36
8. Blessed are the poor in spirit to those who trust in the Lord. Psalm 33:21, Ephesians 1:12-13, II Samuel 22:3, 31, Psalm 4:5, Psalm 7:1, Psalm 9:10, Psalm 16:1,

Psalm 18:1-3, 30, Psalm 25:1-2, 20, Psalm 31:6, Psalm 37:3-5, 40, Psalm 40:1-4, Psalm 52:8, Psalm 56:3-4, 11, Psalm 62:8, Psalm 64:10, Psalm 71:1, 5, Psalm 73:28, Psalm 91:2, 4, Psalm 115:9-18, Psalm 118:1-29 verse 8-9, Psalm 119:42, Psalm 125:1, Psalm 141:8, Psalm 143:8, Psalm 144:1-2, Proverbs 3:5, Proverbs 22:19, Proverbs 30:5, Isaiah 12:2, Isaiah 26:4, Isaiah 50:10, Isaiah 51:5, Isaiah 57:13, Jeremiah 39:18, Jeremiah 49:11, Nahum1:7, Zephaniah 3:12, Matthew 12:21, Romans 15:12 (Isaiah 11:10), II Corinthians 1:9, II Corinthians 3:4, II Corinthians 10:7, Philippians 2:19, 24

9. Blessed are the poor in spirit to those who read God's Word: **To whom then will ye liken Me, or shall I be equal? saith the Holy One.** Isaiah 40:25, See Philippians 2:5-6, John 5:18, **John 10:30**, 33, John 19:7, John 9:16, John 8:56, 58, **John 4:26, John 9:35-37, John 14:7-9, Mark 14:61-62,** Isaiah 52:6, Isaiah 63:10-11, Psalm 51:11, Ephesians 4:30, Revelation 1:7, 8, 11, 17-18, Revelation 3:7, 11, Revelation 4:8, Isaiah 6:3, Revelation 16:15, Revelation 22:7, 12-13, 16, 20, 22, Isaiah 44:6, Isaiah 48:12, Isaiah 40:10, **Hebrews 13:8**
10. Blessed are the poor in spirit to those who believe that the **Bible** will take us to Heaven **after** we believe on Jesus Christ. Mark 1:1, Luke 1:35, Romans 8:16, Acts 8:37
11. Blessed are the poor in spirit to those who believe that the **Bible** will take us to Heaven *when* we believe in Jesus Christ. Mark 1:1, Luke 1:35, Romans 8:16, Acts 8:37
12. Blessed are the poor in spirit to those who believe that the witness of **ourselves** that believe that **Jesus** is the **Son of Man**. John 1:49, John 1:29-49 verse 29, 30, 34, 49

Part DL

Blessed Are The Poor In Spirit. Matthew 5:3

Blessed Means Happy

Poor means meek in spirit. Poor means humble in spirit. Poor means lowly in spirit. Poor means quiet in spirit. Read Matthew 5:3-12, Read also Mark 1:15

Jesus did not say "*rich*" in spirit. Jesus said "*poor*" in spirit.

1. Blessed are the poor in spirit to those who believe and have the lowly or lowliness (humble, quiet) of mind of Christ Jesus in our hearts. Philippians 2:1-11 verse 3, 5
2. Blessed are the poor in spirit to those who believe Jesus' **first instruction** is when you preach, go and say, "**The kingdom of heaven is at hand.**" Matthew 10:7, Matthew 3:2, Matthew 4:17, Mark 1:15
3. Blessed are the poor in spirit to those who believe that learning, studying and growing with the **Holy Bible** in God's Word through faith help us to remind ourselves everyday of our life (as a good habit and respect) not to do those things that are not pleasing to Christ, and to follow His instructions by not walking in the flesh but by walking in the Spirit. II Corinthians 5:7, Galatians 5:16, 25, Ephesians 2:10, Ephesians 4:11, Ephesians 5:2, 8, Philippians 3:16-17, Colossians 1:8-20 verse 10, Colossians 2:6-14 verse 6, 12, 14, Colossians 4:5, I Thessalonians 2:12, I Thessalonians 4:1-18 verse 1, 4, 7, 11, 12, II John 1:6, 7, II John 2:6, II John 1:6, III John 1:4, Revelation 3:4, Revelation 21:24, II Peter 3:18, I Peter 2:21, Romans 4:6-25 verse 12, John 1:29, John 5:14, John 8:11, Romans 6:8:2, John 15:24, John 16:8-9
4. Blessed are the poor in spirit to those who believe that **Christmas** stand for **in honor of Christ**, who was born, not necessary on December or in the spring but represent that this is **Christ,** the **Lord**; that this is **Jesus Christ,** the **Savior of the world** who came to save all mankind. Luke 2:11, John 4:42, I John 4:14, I Timothy 1:15, I Timothy 4:10, I Timothy 2:4, Acts 4:12, Acts 17:30-31
5. Blessed are the poor in spirit to those who *are able to boldly say*, "**I Am Saved**."
6. Blessed are the poor in spirit to those who *are able to boldly confess for salvation*: "**I confess with my mouth that Jesus is my Lord**. I believe in my heart that God raised Him (Jesus Christ) from the dead." Romans 10:9

7. Blessed are the poor in spirit to those who believe that when we accept Jesus Christ, when we accept Him as our personal Savior and Lord, we are born again; born of the Spirit; born of the Spirit of God; born of the Spirit of Christ. John 3:3, 6, 8, I Peter 1:23, John 1:12
8. Blessed are the poor in spirit to those who are able to say this old spiritually hymn: "Thank God for Jesus. Thank God for Jesus. Thank God for Jesus. Bless His Holy Name. **Hebrews 13:8, John 14:7-9, Revelation 1:8,** Revelation 1:18, Revelation 1:7, **Revelation 1:17, 18, Revelation 3:11, Revelation 16:5, Revelation 3:7,** Revelation 22:7, Revelation 22:12-13, **Revelation 22:16, Revelation 22:20-21,** John 5:18, John 8:56, 58, John 10:30, 33, I Thessalonians 4:13-18, **John 4:26, John 9:36-38, Acts 9:5, Philippians 2:6-11, Philippians 3:10, Mark 12:22, Acts 10:36, Acts 9:22,** Acts 18:5, 28, Acts 17:27-30 (Psalm 104:33)
9. Blessed are the poor in spirit to those who are able to testify: "I can't live **without Him (Lord/God/Jesus) (From Genesis to Revelation). Hebrews 13:8,** John 14:7-9, Acts 9:5, 22, Acts 18:5, 28, John 4:24, Hebrews 11:6, Mark 12:22, John 14:1-4, John 14:6-9, Acts 10:36, Philippians 2:10-11, Acts 17:27, Psalm 104:33, Psalm 27:8, Isaiah 55:1, Isaiah 58:2
10. Blessed are the poor in spirit to those who are able to testify: "Thank **God** for **Jesus** for *saving my soul.* Hebrews 10:39, I Timothy 1:15, Matthew 1:21, 25, Luke 1:31, Psalm 51:12, Psalm 23:3
11. Blessed are the poor in spirit to those who are able to testify: "Thank **God** for **Jesus** for making me whole." Matthew 9:21, 22, Matthew 12:13, Matthew 14:36, Matthew 15:28, 31, Matthew 26:13, Mark 3:5, Mark 5:28, 34, Mark 6:56, Mark 10:52, Mark 14:9, Luke 6:10, Luke 7:10, Luke 8:48, **Luke 8:50,** Luke 17:19, John 5:6, 9, John 5:11, 14, John 5:15, John 7:23, Acts 9:34, Exodus 15:25
12. Blessed are the poor in spirit to those who are able to testify: "Thank **God** for **Jesus** for **blessing** *me* **daily. Isaiah 58:2, Matthew 6:11, Luke 9:23, Luke 11:3,** Acts 2:46, Acts 17:11, **I Corinthians 15:31**

Part DLI

Blessed Are The Poor In Spirit. Matthew 5:3

Blessed Means Happy

Poor means meek in spirit. Poor means humble in spirit. Poor means lowly in spirit. Poor means quiet in spirit. Read Matthew 5:3-12, Read also Mark 1:15

Jesus did not say "*rich*" in spirit. Jesus said "*poor*" in spirit.

1. Blessed are the poor in spirit to those who are able to testify: "Thank **God** for **Jesus for healing** me. Exodus 15:26, Isaiah 53:5, I Peter 2:24, Matthew 8:7
2. Blessed are the poor in spirit to those who are able to testify: "Thank **God** for **Jesus** for **His saving grace** upon me. **II Corinthians 8:9,** Ephesians 2:5, 8-9, Romans 6:23, Luke 2:40, John 1:14, 16, 17, Acts 4:33, Acts 11:23, Acts 13:43, **Acts 14:3,** Acts 15:11, 40, Acts 18:28, **Acts 20:24, 32,** Romans 1:5, **Romans 4:16, Romans 5:2,** 15, 17, 20, Romans 6:14, Romans 12:3, Romans 15:15, Romans 16:20, 24, I Corinthians 1:3, 4, I Corinthians 3:10, **I Corinthians 15:10,** I Corinthians 16:23, II Corinthians 1:2, II Corinthians 1:12, II Corinthians 6:1, II Corinthians 8:1, 6, 7, 9, 19, II Corinthians 9:8, 14, II Corinthians 12:9, II Corinthians 13:14, Galatians 1:3, 6, **Galatians 1:15, Galatians 2:21,** Galatians 6:18, Ephesians 1:2, 6, **Ephesians 1:7, Ephesians 2:5, 8** (Romans 8:28), Ephesians 2:7, 8, Ephesians 3:2, 7, 8, Ephesians 4:7, 29, Ephesians 6:24, Philippians 1:2, 7, Philippians 4:23, Colossians 1:2, 6, Colossians 3:16, Colossians 4:6, 18, I Thessalonians 1:1, I Thessalonians 5:28, II Thessalonians 1:2, 12, **II Thessalonians 2:16,** I Timothy 1:2, 14, I Timothy 6:2, II Timothy 1:2, 9, **II Timothy 2:1,** II Timothy 4:22, Titus 1:4, 3:7, 15, Philemon 1:3, 25, Hebrews 2:9, Hebrews 4:16, Hebrews 10:29, Hebrews 12:28, Hebrews 13:9, 25, James 4:6, I Peter 1:2, 10, 13, I Peter 3:7, I Peter 4:10, I Peter 5:5, 10, II Peter 1:2, II Peter 3:18, II John 1:3, Jude 1:4, Revelation 1:4, Revelation 22:21
3. Blessed are the poor in spirit to those who **believe that Death cannot stop us because Jesus said: "In three days, I will rise again."** I Thessalonians 4:16, Matthew 17:9, Matthew 26:32, Matthew 27:64, Matthew 20:19, Matthew 27:63, Mark 8:31, Mark 9:31, Mark 10:34, Luke 18:33, Luke 24:7, Luke 24:46, John 11:23, John 20:9, Matthew 28:6, 7, Mark 9:9, Mark 14:28, Mark 16:6, 9, Mark

16:14, Luke 7:16, Luke 24:6, 34, John 2:22, John 21:14, Acts 17:3, Romans 8:34, I Corinthians 15:13-14, 20, Colossians 2:12, Colossians 3:1, Romans 8:38, I Corinthians 3:21-23, I Corinthians 15:54 (Isaiah 25:8), I Corinthians 15:55, 56, II Corinthians 1:9-10, II Corinthians 2:14-17, II Corinthians 4:10-18, Philippians 1:18-30

4. Blessed are the poor in spirit to those who believe that Death cannot hurt us because of Christ's Victory over Death, sin, and hell so that my may live with Him for eternity. I Thessalonians 4:16, Matthew 17:9, Matthew 26:32, Matthew 27:64, Matthew 20:19, Matthew 27:63, Mark 8:31, Mark 9:31, Mark 10:34, Luke 18:33, Luke 24:7, Luke 24:46, John 11:23, John 20:9, Matthew 28:6, 7, Mark 9:9, Mark 14:28, Mark 16:6, 9, Mark 16:14, Luke 7:16, Luke 24:6, 34, John 2:22, John 21:14, Acts 17:3, Romans 8:34, I Corinthians 15:13-14, 20, Colossians 2:12, Colossians 3:1, Romans 8:38, I Corinthians 3:21-23, I Corinthians 15:54 (Isaiah 25:8), I Corinthians 15:55, 56, II Corinthians 1:9-10, II Corinthians 2:14-17, II Corinthians 4:10-18, Philippians 1:18-30
5. Blessed are the poor in spirit to those who believe that Death will not hurt us because of Christ's Victory over Death, Sin, and hell so that me may live with Him for eternity. Philippians 1:20, Philippians 2:8, 27, 30, Philippians 3:10, Colossians 1:22, II Timothy 1:10, Hebrews 2:9, 14, 15, Hebrews 5:7, Hebrews 7:12-25, Hebrews 9:15, 16, James 5:20, I Peter 3:18, I John 3:14, **Revelation 1:18, Revelation 2:10-11**
6. Blessed are the poor in spirit to those who believe that God's Commandment is salvation to those who believe life everlasting. John 12:50, Romans 16:26
7. Blessed are the poor in spirit to those who believe to dare to be like Daniel. Daniel 1:8, Daniel 6:10-11, Acts 16:25-28
8. Blessed are the poor in spirit to those who are able to sing: "Dare To Be Like Dan-iel. Dare To Be Like Dan-iel Dare To Be Like Dan-iel." Daniel 1:8, Daniel 6:10-11, Acts 16:25-28
9. Blessed are the poor in spirit to those who do not believe that the Holy Spirit does not force on anyone; just an invitation to accept Christ as personal Savior and Lord. Romans 10:9, Romans 10:11, 12, 13. Revelation 3:20, John 7:37-38, Matthew 11:28-30
10. Blessed are the poor in spirit to those who believe that God Almighty is feeling angry, wrath upon those who refuse an invitation but will still abide (rest) outside until a lost soul is ready to accept Christ as personal Savior and Lord

or be done is too late for a second chance after death. But the wrath (anger) of God abide (rest) on the unsaved loved ones. John 3:36. Pray for lost souls. I Thessalonians 5:17

11. Blessed are the poor in spirit to those who believe that the 144, 000 are the tribes of the children of Israel. Revelation 7:1-17 verse 4—And I heard the number of them which were sealed: and there were sealed an hundred and forty and four thousand of all the tribes of the children of Israel. Revelation 7:1-17 verse 4
12. Blessed are the poor in spirit to those who believe that the 144, 000 are the tribes of the children of Israel. Revelation 7:1-17 verse 5—Of the tribe of Juda were sealed twelve thousand. Of the tribe of Reuben were sealed twelve thousand. Of the tribe of Gad were sealed twelve thousand. Revelation 7:1-17 verse 5

Part DLII

Blessed Are The Poor In Spirit. Matthew 5:3

Blessed Means Happy

Poor means meek in spirit. Poor means humble in spirit. Poor means lowly in spirit. Poor means quiet in spirit. Read Matthew 5:3-12, Read also Mark 1:15

Jesus did not say "*rich*" in spirit. Jesus said "*poor*" in spirit.

1. Blessed are the poor in spirit to those who who believe that the 144, 000 are the tribes of the children of Israel.—Of the tribe of Aser were sealed twelve thousand, Of the Tribe of Nepthalim were sealed twelve thousand. Of the tribe of Manasses were sealed twelve thousand. Revelation 7:1-17 verse 6
2. Blessed are the poor in spirit to those who who believe that the 144, 000 are the tribes of the children of Israel.—Of the tribe of Simeon were sealed twelve thousand. Of the tribe of Levi were sealed twelve thousand. Of the tribe of Issachar were sealed twelve thousand. Revelation 7:1-17 verse 7
3. Blessed are the poor in spirit to those who who believe that the 144, 000 are the tribes of the children of Israel.—Of the tribe of Zabulon were sealed twelve thousand. Of the tribe of Joseph were sealed twelve thousand. Of the tribe of Benjamin were sealed twelve thousand. Revelation 7:1-17 verse 8
4. Blessed are the poor in spirit to those who believe that we or they will be caught. Numbers 32:23
5. Blessed are the poor in spirit to those who believe that we or they will be manifested. Mark 4:22, Matthew 12:36, Matthew 10:26
6. Blessed are the poor in spirit to those who believe that we or they will be revealed or know. Matthew 12:36, Matthew 10:26, Mark 4:22
7. Blessed are the poor in spirit to those who believe this Holy Scripture: "Depart from me, ye cursed, into everlasting fire, prepared for the Devil and His angels. Matthew 25:41
8. Blessed are the poor in spirit to those who believe this Holy Scripture: "And these shall go away into everlasting punishment: but the righteous into life eternal." Matthew 25:46

9. Blessed are the poor in spirit to those who believe this Holy Scripture: "And whosoever was not found written in the book of life was cast into the lake of fire." Revelation 20:15
10. Blessed are the poor in spirit to those who believe this Holy Scripture: "The Lord is not slack concerning His promise, as some men count slackness; but is long- suffering to us-ward, not willing that any should perish, but that all should come to repentance." II Peter 3:9
11. Blessed are the poor in spirit to those who believe that Apostle and Missionary Paul has a name in his honor at St. Paul, Minnesota. Acts 9:11, Act 9:30, Acts 11:25, Acts 21:39, Acts 22:3
12. Blessed are the poor in spirit to those who believe that the **Lord Himself** will get them somehow. Vengeance is mine said the Lord. Deuteronomy 32:35-36, Psalm 135:14, Isaiah 35:4, Romans 12:19-21, Hebrews 10:30

Part DLIII

Blessed Are The Poor In Spirit. Matthew 5:3

Blessed Means Happy

Poor means meek in spirit. Poor means humble in spirit. Poor means lowly in spirit. Poor means quiet in spirit. Read Matthew 5:3-12, Read also Mark 1:15

Jesus did not say "*rich*" in spirit. Jesus said "*poor*" in spirit.

1. Blessed are the poor in spirit to those who believe that if you don't work, you don't eat; no work, no eat. How true is so? II Thessalonians 3:10
2. Blessed are the poor in spirit to those who believe our beloved spiritually mothers say: "The Lord will take care: to those who try to get away with murders by not indication those who claim their defensive or to avoid jail term, etc that already kills someone who did not have guns or knives to attack good citizens doing their duty. I hear the Lord say: "Vengeance is mine; I will repay. Saith the Lord. **Romans 12:19,** Acts 28:4, Romans 3:4-20, II Thessalonians 1:6-9, **Hebrews 10:27-31 verse 30, Jude 1:7, Psalm 135:14, Deuteronomy 32:35-36, Hebrews 9:27,** John 5:28, Romans 3:10, 13, 15-16, Romans 3:12, **Psalm10:7,** Psalm14:3, Psalm5:9, Isaiah 59:7-8, Mark 4:22, Matthew 12:36, Matthew 10:26, Matthew 25:41, 46, Revelation 20:15
3. Blessed are the poor in spirit to those who believe this Holy Scripture: "Come now, and let us reason together, saith the Lord: though your sins be as scarlet, they shall be as white as snow." Isaiah 1:18
4. Blessed are the poor in spirit to those who believe this Holy Scripture: "For to me to live is Christ, and to die is gain." Philippians 1:21
5. Blessed are the poor in spirit to those who believe this Holy Scripture: "Precious in the sight of the Lord is the death of His saints." Psalm 116:15
6. Blessed are the poor in spirit to those who believe this Holy Scripture: "But as it is written, Eye hath not seen, nor ear heart, neither have entered into the heart of man, the things which God hath prepared for them that love Him." I Corinthians 2:9
7. Blessed are the poor in spirit to those who believe this Holy Scripture: "Jesus said, "I am the way, the truth, and the life: no man cometh unto the Father, but by Me." John 14:6

8. Blessed are the poor in spirit to those who believe this Holy Scripture: "For there is one God, and one mediator between God and men, the man Christ Jesus." I Timothy 2:5
9. Blessed are the poor in spirit to those who believe this Holy Scripture: "For by grace are ye saved through faith; and that not of yourselves: it is the gift of God: Not of works, lest any man should boast." Ephesians 2:8-9
10. Blessed are the poor in spirit to those who believe this Holy Scripture: "**Admit** you are a sinner, and that only the Lord Jesus can save you. Romans 3:23
11. Blessed are the poor in spirit to those who believe this Holy Scripture: "**Repent:** be willing to turn away from sin and submit to God. Luke 13:5
12. Blessed are the poor in spirit to those who believe this Holy Scripture: "**Believe** that the Lord Jesus Christ died on the cross and shed His Blood to pay the price for your sins, and that He arose again. See Romans 10:9

Part DLIV

Blessed Are The Poor In Spirit. Matthew 5:3

Blessed Means Happy

Poor means meek in spirit. Poor means humble in spirit. Poor means lowly in spirit. Poor means quiet in spirit. Read Matthew 5:3-12, Read also Mark 1:15

Jesus did not say "*rich*" in spirit. Jesus said "*poor*" in spirit.

1. Blessed are the poor in spirit to those who believe this Holy Scripture: "**Ask** Christ to save you. See Romans 10:13
2. Blessed are the poor in spirit to those who believe this Holy Scripture: "**Ask** Jesus Christ to be your Lord of your life. See Romans 12:1-2
3. Blessed are the poor in spirit to those who believe this Holy Scripture: "Obey Christ's command and be baptized. See Matthew 28:19
4. Blessed are the poor in spirit to those who believe this Holy Scripture: "And I will say to my soul, Soul, thou hast much goods laid up for many years; take thine ease, eat, drink, and be merry." Luke 12:19
5. Blessed are the poor in spirit to those who believe this Holy Scripture: "But God said unto him, thou fool, this night thy soul shall be required of thee." Luke 12:20
6. Blessed are the poor in spirit to those who believe this Holy Scripture: "It is appointed unto men once to die, but after this the judgment." Hebrews 9:27
7. Blessed are the poor in spirit to those who believe this Holy Scripture: "But we are all as an unclean thing, and all our righteousness are as filthy rags; and we all do fade as a leaf; and our iniquities, like the wind, have taken us away." Isaiah 64:6
8. Blessed are the poor in spirit to those who believe this Holy Scripture: "Marvel not at this: For the hour is coming, in the which all that are in the graves shall hear His voice." John 5:28
9. Blessed are the poor in spirit to those who believe this Holy Scripture: "And shall come forth; they that have done good, unto the resurrection of life; and they that have done evil, unto the resurrection of damnation." John 5:29
10. Blessed are the poor in spirit to those who believe this Holy Scripture: "As it is written, there is none righteous, no, not one:" Romans 3:10

11. Blessed are the poor in spirit to those who believe this Holy Scripture: "And I saw the dead, small and great, stand before God: And the books were opened: and another book was opened, which is the book of life: and the dead were judged out of those things which were written in the books, according to their works." Revelation 20:12
12. Blessed are the poor in spirit to those who believe in obeying to the Holy Spirit. Colossians 1:1, Acts 11:12, Acts 8:29

Part DLV

Blessed Are The Poor In Spirit. Matthew 5:3

Blessed Means Happy

Poor means meek in spirit. Poor means humble in spirit. Poor means lowly in spirit. Poor means quiet in spirit. Read Matthew 5:3-12, Read also Mark 1:15

Jesus did not say "*rich*" in spirit. Jesus said "*poor*" in spirit.

1. Blessed are the poor in spirit to those who believe God's Wonderful Words of Life. John 6:63
2. Blessed are the poor in spirit to those who believe God's Beautiful Words of Life. John 6:63
3. Blessed are the poor in spirit to those who believe God's Word is wonderful. John 6:63
4. Blessed are the poor in spirit to those who believe God's Word is beautiful. John 6:63
5. Blessed are the poor in spirit to those who believe God's Word. John 6:63
6. Blessed are the poor in spirit to those who believe God's Life. John 6:63
7. Blessed are the poor in spirit to those who believe God's Spirit. John 6:63
8. Blessed are the poor in spirit to those who sing with me: "The Wonderful Word of Life." John 6:63
    1. Sing them o—ver a—gain to me, Won-der-ful words of Life;
Let me more of their beau—ty see, Won-der-ful words of Life.
Words of life and beau—ty, Teach me faith and du—ty;
Beau—ti—ful words, won-der-ful words, Won-der-ful words of Life.
Beau-tiful words, won-der-ful words, Won-der-ful words of Life
    2. Christ, the bless-ed One, gives to all Won-der-ful words of Life;
Sin—ner, list to the lov—ing call, Won-der-ful words of Life.
All so free—ly giv—en, Woo—ing us to Heav—en:
Beau—ti—ful words, won-der-ful words, Won-der-ful words of Life.
Beau-tiful words, won-der-ful words, Won-der-ful words of Life
    3. Sweet—ly ech—o the gos—pels call, Wn-der-ful words of Life;
Of—fer par—don and peace to all, Won-der-ful words of Life.

Je—sus, on—ly Sav—ior, Sanc—ti—fy for—ev—er:
Beau—ti—ful words, won-der-ful words, Won-der-ful words of Life.
Beau-tiful words, won-der-ful words, Won-der-ful words of Life—John 6:63

9.

Blessed are the poor in spirit to those who are able to sing this spiritual hymn: "Oh, How I Love Jesus. Oh, how I love Jesus. Oh, how I love Jesus. Because He **first** loved me. I John 4:19

10.

Blessed are the poor in spirit to those who put Jesus **First** on top of the world by saying **aloud**: "Jesus, Son of David, Have mercy on me." Matthew 9:27, Matthew 15:22, Matthew 20:30-31, Mark 10:48, Luke 18:38-39

11.

Blessed are the poor in spirit to those who believe the Word of God teaches that there is a way which **seem right** unto a man, but the end thereof are the **way of death** (See Jeremiah 17:9). Also Proverbs 16:25, Proverbs 14:12

12.

Blessed are the poor in spirit to those who believe that the Word of God teaches that the **wages of sin** is **death.** Romans 6:3, See Romans 7:1, Romans 6:22, 23

Part DLVI

Blessed Are The Poor In Spirit. Matthew 5:3

Blessed Means Happy

Poor means meek in spirit. Poor means humble in spirit. Poor means lowly in spirit. Poor means quiet in spirit. Read Matthew 5:3-12, Read also Mark 1:15

Jesus did not say "*rich*" in spirit. Jesus said "*poor*" in spirit.

1. Blessed are the poor in spirit to those who believe the Word of God teaches that the sting of death is sin. I Corinthians 15:56
2. Blessed are the poor in spirit to those who believe the Word of God teaches that living in unholy life is death. Hebrews 12:14
3. Blessed are the poor in spirit to those who believe that death is not the permanent end of our existence. Hebrews 9:27
4. Blessed are the poor in spirit to those who believe the Word Of God teaches that **death** is a **return to the dust** and that **death of the spirit will return to God** who gave it. Genesis 3:19, Ecclesiastes 12:7
5. Blessed are the poor in spirit to those who believe the Word of God teaches that the **precious in the sight** is the **death of the saints.** (did not mention sinners, but saints of God) Psalm 116:15, Revelation 2:10, Revelation 15:3, Revelation 20:4-6, Revelation 21:1-7
6. Blessed are the poor in spirit to those who believe that the Word of God teaches that the **Last Enemy** to be conquered is **Death.** I Corinthians 15:26
7. Blessed are the poor in spirit to those who believe that shall be abolished is **death**. I Corinthians 15:26
8. Blessed are the poor in spirit to those who believe to be destroyed. I Corinthians 15:26
9. Blessed are the poor in spirit to those who believe that if you need **soul save,** just call Him (Jesus) up and **He will never say, "No."** Jeremiah 33:3, Matthew 1:21, Acts 2:21, Acts 16:30-31, Romans 10:13, II Timothy 2:22, John 7:38-39
10. Blessed are the poor in spirit to those who believe the Word of God teaches that the **enemy, death,** shall be **destroyed last** (to an end) I Corinthians 15:26

11. Blessed are the poor in spirit to those who believe that the Word of God teaches that the God of peace will soon **crush Satan** under your feet. Romans 16:20
12. Blessed are the poor in spirit to those who believe the Word of God teaches that the God of peace will soon **bruise Satan** under your feet. Romans 16:20

Part DLVII

Blessed Are The Poor In Spirit. Matthew 5:3

Blessed Means Happy

Poor means meek in spirit. Poor means humble in spirit. Poor means lowly in spirit. Poor means quiet in spirit. Read Matthew 5:3-12, Read also Mark 1:15

Jesus did not say "*rich*" in spirit. Jesus said "*poor*" in spirit.

1. Blessed are the poor in spirit to those who believe the Word of God teaches that **God** will put the **Seed of the Woman,** which is **Jesus Christ to bruise** the **old serpent's head** over **His feet**. Genesis 3:15, Romans 16:20
2. Blessed are the poor in spirit to those who believe that everything rise on leadership and everything fall on leadership. Numbers 17:12, Job 34:15, Psalm 146:4, Proverbs 29:18, Zechariah 9:5, Ezekiel 25:7, Isaiah 29:14, Jeremiah 4:9, Amos 1:8
3. Blessed are the poor in spirit to those who believe that every black human being, every white human being, and every race human being need God's Spirit through salvation for healing for forgiveness, and for blessing rather than for cursing. Revelation 22:2, See Deuteronomy 30:19, James 3:10
4. Blessed are the poor in spirit to those who believe that **Cessation** does not end at the apostolic age or the canon of Revelation of the Bible, but **Cessation** will end when **Jesus** come **the Second time**. Let us **continue on until He come!!!** I Corinthians 13:8, I Thessalonians 4:13-18 verse 17, Hebrews 9:28, I John 3:2, Revelation 1:7, Revelation 22:20
5. Blessed are the poor in spirit to those who believe that God's Word need no repeating for ever because **His Word is settled once for all to accept His Salvation, His Son, Jesus Christ, His Holy Spirit. His Spirit Baptism and His Coming Again.** Be Prepared To Meet Him. **Amos 4:12, Revelation 22:20, Job 33:14, 40:5, Psalm 62:11, Psalm 89:35, John 1:29, 36, John 6:58-69, Romans 6:10,** Romans 7:9, **I Corinthians 15:6, Galatians 1:22, 23,** Ephesians 5:1-3 verse 3, Hebrews 6:4-6 verse 4, **Hebrews 7:27, Hebrews 9:12, 26, 27, 28 verse 28,** Hebrews 10:2, **Hebrews 10:10, Hebrews 12:21-29 verse 26, I Peter 3:18-22 verse 18, 20, Jude 1:3, Jude 1:5**

6. Blessed are the poor in spirit to those who believe that **Judgment "Must" Begin At The House Of God.** I Peter 4:17, II Peter 2:4, 9, II Peter 3:7, Jude 1:6, 13
7. Blessed are the poor in spirit to those who believe that God commit the keeping of their souls. I Peter 4:19
8. Blessed are the poor in spirit to those who believe in pure heart that they shall see God. Matthew 5:8
9. Blessed are the poor in spirit to those who believe that we are in danger of judgment whether it be good or bad. Matthew 5:21-22, Mark 3:29, II Corinthians 5:10, Ecclesiastes 12:14, Romans 2:16
10. Blessed are the poor in spirit to those who believe that we are **damnation** *if* we do eat and drink *to ourselves, not discerning* **the Lord's body.** I Corinthians 11:29, Romans 13:2
11. Blessed are the poor in spirit to those who believe that the Bible is a living proof for centuries. It is for us to see and to believe God. Genesis 1:1-2, John 1:1-18 verse 11, II Timothy 3:16, Habakkuk 2:4, Romans 1:17, Galatians 3:11, Hebrews 10:38-39, Mark 11:22, John 14:1-11
12. Blessed are the poor in spirit to those who serve the Lord with a smile. Psalm 100:2, Psalm 2:11

PART DLVIII

Blessed Are The Poor In Spirit. Matthew 5:3

Blessed Means Happy

Poor means meek in spirit. Poor means humble in spirit. Poor means lowly in spirit. Poor means quiet in spirit. Read Matthew 5:3-12, Read also Mark 1:15

Jesus did not say "*rich*" in spirit. Jesus said "*poor*" in spirit.

1. Blessed are the poor in spirit to those who are able to say: "I miss my mother today." Ephesians 6:1-4, Exodus 20:12, Matthew 15:4, Proverbs 31:10-31
2. Blessed are the poor in spirit to those who able to say: "I miss my father today." Ephesians 6:1-4, Exodus 20:12, Matthew 15:4
3. Blessed are the poor in spirit to those who able to say: "I miss my baby today. II Samuel 12:14-24, Proverbs 6:20, Proverbs 22:6, Psalm 127:3
4. Blessed are the poor in spirit to those who able to say: "I miss my brother today." Matthew 12:50, Mark 3:35, Revelation 1:9, I John 5:16-18, I John 2:10
5. Blessed are the poor in spirit to those who able to say: "I miss my sister today." Matthew 12:50, Mark 3:35
6. Blessed are the poor in spirit to those who able to say: "I miss my wife today." I Corinthians 7:1-4, 10, 12, 16, 34, 39, Galatians 4:27, Proverbs 31:28-31, Proverbs 31:10, 12-22, 24-27, Ephesians 5:33
7. Blessed are the poor in spirit to those who able to say: "I miss my husband today." I Corinthians 7:1-4, 11, 16, Ephesians 5:23, I Timothy 3:1-2, Titus 1:6, Proverbs 31:10-12
8. Blessed are the poor in spirit to those who able to say: "I miss my son today." Matthew 21:28-29, II Corinthians 6:18
9. Blessed are the poor in spirit to those who able to say: "I miss my daughter today." Luke 8:48, II Corinthians 6:18, Proverbs 31:29
10. Blessed are the poor in spirit to those who able to say: "I miss my aunt today." Leviticus 18:14
11. Blessed are the poor in spirit to those who able to say: "I miss my uncle today." Jeremiah 32:6-8, Please read Jeremiah 32:1-44
12. Blessed are the poor in spirit to those who able to say: "I miss my cousin today." Luke 1:36, 58

Part DLIX

Blessed Are The Poor In Spirit. Matthew 5:3

Blessed Means Happy

Poor means meek in spirit. Poor means humble in spirit. Poor means lowly in spirit. Poor means quiet in spirit. Read Matthew 5:3-12, Read also Mark 1:15

Jesus did not say "*rich*" in spirit. Jesus said "*poor*" in spirit.

1. Blessed are the poor in spirit to those who able to say: "I miss my best friend today." Proverbs 17:17, Luke 14:10
2. Blessed are the poor in spirit to those who able to say: "I miss my church today." Acts 2:42, Hebrews 10:25
3. Blessed are the poor in spirit to those who able to say: "I miss God's Word today." II Timothy 2:15, I Thessalonians 4:11, II Timothy 3:14-17
4. Blessed are the poor in spirit to those who able to say: "I miss my prayer today." I Thessalonians 5:17
5. Blessed are the poor in spirit to those who believe that the **Bible Itself Which Is The Word of God Himself** to tell us all that we are the children of God. Romans 8:16
6. Blessed are the poor in spirit to those who believe that the **Bible Itself Which Is The Word of God Himself** to tell us all that we are becoming the sons of God. John 3:12, Romans 8:14
7. Blessed are the poor in spirit to those who believe that the **Bible Itself Which Is The Word of God Himself** to tell us all that we have received the Spirit of adoption, whereby, we have the right to say, "Ab'ba, Father. Romans 8:15
8. Blessed are the poor in spirit to those who believe that the **Bible Itself Which Is The Word of God Himself** to tell us all that we **receive** (have the rights) the adoption of sons. Galatians 4:5
9. Blessed are the poor in spirit to those who believe that the **Bible Itself Which Is The Word of God Himself** to tell us all that we, having predestinated us unto the adoption of children by **Jesus Christ** to **Himself**, according to the good pleasure of **His (Own) Will.**
10. Blessed are the poor in spirit to those who believe that the **Bible Itself Which Is The Word of God Himself** to tell us all **that if** we shall *confess with our mouth*

the Lord Jesus, and shalt *believe in our hearts* that **God** has raised **Him** (The Lord Jesus) from the dead, **we shalt be saved**. Romans 10:9

11. Blessed are the poor in spirit to those who believe that the **Bible Itself Which Is The Word of God Himself** to tell us all that **with the heart** *man believe* **unto righteousness**: and with the *mouth* **confession** is made unto **salvation**. Romans 10:10
12. Blessed are the poor in spirit to those who believe that the **Bible Itself Which Is The Word of God Himself** to tell us all that *whosoever believed* **on Him** (The Lord Jesus) *shall not be ashamed*. Romans 10:11, See Isaiah 49:23

Part DLX

Blessed Are The Poor In Spirit. Matthew 5:3

Blessed Means Happy

Poor means meek in spirit. Poor means humble in spirit. Poor means lowly in spirit. Poor means quiet in spirit. Read Matthew 5:3-12, Read also Mark 1:15

Jesus did not say "*rich*" in spirit. Jesus said "*poor*" in spirit.

1. Blessed are the poor in spirit to those who believe that the **Bible Itself Which Is The Word of God Himself** to tell us all that *whosoever shall call upon* the **Name of the Lord shall be saved**. Romans 10:13
2. Blessed are the poor in spirit to those who believe that the **Bible Itself Which Is The Word of God Himself** to tell us all that **faith come by hearing** and **hearing** by the **Word of God.** Romans 10:17
3. Blessed are the poor in spirit to those who believe that the **Bible Itself Which Is The Word of God Himself** to tell us all how we **must ask:** "What **must** I do to be saved?" Acts 16:30
4. Blessed are the poor in spirit to those who believe that the **Bible Itself Which Is The Word of God Himself** to tell us all that **Believe on the Lord Jesus Christ,** and **we shalt be saved.** Acts 16:31
5. Blessed are the poor in spirit to those who believe that the **Bible Itself Which Is The Word of God Himself** to tell us all that **God so loved** *the world*, that **He** gave **His only begotten Son**, that **whosoever believeth in Him (Jesus)** should not perish, but have everlasting life. John 3:16
6. Blessed are the poor in spirit to those who believe that the **Bible Itself Which Is The Word of God Himself** to tell us all that by **grace** we are **saved**. Ephesians 2:5, 8
7. Blessed are the poor in spirit to those who believe that the **Bible Itself Which Is The Word of God Himself** to tell us all that **by grace** are we **saved through faith;** and that we cannot be saved by ourselves: **It is the Gift of God**: not of works, lest any man should boost. Ephesians 2:8-9
8. Blessed are the poor in spirit to those who believe that the **Bible Itself Which Is The Word of God Himself** to tell us all that through faith Father Abraham

believe God and it (this faith of God) was counted for righteousness. Romans 4:3, See Genesis 15:6

9. Blessed are the poor in spirit to those who believe that the **Bible Itself Which Is The Word of God Himself** to tell us all that Father Abraham believed God and it (this faith of God) was imputed (reckoned—to count, the right to have) unto him for righteousness: and he was called the **Friend of God**. James 1:23. See Isaiah 41:8
10. Blessed are the poor in spirit to those who believe that the **Bible Itself Which Is The Word of God Himself** to tell us all that *Father Abraham* believed **God** and it (this faith of God) was **accounted** (reckoned, to count on, to have the right to call on by God) and that *we are the children of Abraham*. Galatians 3:6-7
11. Blessed are the poor in spirit to those who believe that the **Bible Itself Which Is The Word of God Himself** to tell us all that faith was reckoned (accounted—count on, had the right to be called on by God) to Abraham for **righteousness.** Romans 4:9
12. Blessed are the poor in spirit to those who believe that the **Bible Itself Which Is The Word of God Himself** to tell us all that the blessedness of the man unto which God input **righteousness** "*without works*." Romans 4:6

Part DLXI

Blessed Are The Poor In Spirit. Matthew 5:3

Blessed Means Happy

Poor means meek in spirit. Poor means humble in spirit. Poor means lowly in spirit. Poor means quiet in spirit. Read Matthew 5:3-12, Read also Mark 1:15

Jesus did not say "*rich*" in spirit. Jesus said "*poor*" in spirit.

1. Blessed are the poor in spirit to those who believe that the **Bible Itself Which Is The Word of God Himself** to tell us all that **Blessed** are we whose iniquities are forgiving, and whose sins are covered. Romans 4:7. See Psalm 32:1
2. Blessed are the poor in spirit to those who believe that the **Bible Itself Which Is The Word of God Himself** to tell us all that Blessed is to us to whom the Lord will **not impute** (count) sin. Romans 4:8
3. Blessed are the poor in spirit to those who believe that the **Bible Itself Which Is The Word of God Himself** to tell us all that the **promise** was not to Father Abraham or his seed (offspring; sons or daughters) *through the law, but* **through righteousness of faith**. Romans 4:13
4. Blessed are the poor in spirit to those who believe that the **Bible Itself Which Is The Word of God Himself** to tell us all that **Noah walked with God** because **Noah** found **grace** in the eyes of the Lord. Genesis 6:8-9. See Hebrews 11:7 and Genesis 6:13-22
5. Blessed are the poor in spirit to those who believe that the **Bible Itself Which Is The Word of God Himself** to tell us all that **Enoch walked with God** and that **God** took **Enoch** with **Him to Heaven** because **Enoch pleased** (satisfied with God). Genesis 5:24. see Hebrews 11:5
6. Blessed are the poor in spirit to those who believe that the **Bible Itself Which Is The Word of God Himself** to tell us all that *without faith* **in God,** we cannot please **Him** therefore, we **must have faith in God** that **He** is and that **He** a **Rewarder** of them that **diligently seek Him.** Hebrews 11:6, See John 4:23-26 verse 23-24, Psalm 27:4, 8-9, Isaiah 55:6, Isaiah 58:1-8 verse 1-2
7. Blessed are the poor in spirit to those who believe that the **Bible Itself Which Is The Word of God Himself** to tell us all that God appeared to Abraham and

God said to Abraham, **I am The Almighty God: walk before Me (God)** and be thou perfect (blameless) at not fault of his own whatsoever before he was count for righteousness. Genesis 17:1, See Romans 4:3, 6, 9, 13, Genesis 15:6, James 1:23, Isaiah 41:8, Galatians 3:6-7

8. Blessed are the poor in spirit to those who believe that the **Bible Itself Which Is The Word of God Himself** to tell us all that we also should walk in newness of life. Romans 6:4
9. Blessed are the poor in spirit to those who believe that the **Bible Itself Which Is The Word of God Himself** to tell us all that there is therefore now no condemnation to them which are in Christ Jesus, who walk not after the flesh, but after the Spirit. Romans 8:1
10. Blessed are the poor in spirit to those who believe that the **Bible Itself Which Is The Word of God Himself** to tell us all that the **righteousness (requirement by God)** of the law *might* be fulfilled in us, who walk not after the flesh, but after the Spirit. Romans 8:4
11. Blessed are the poor in spirit to those who believe that the **Bible Itself Which Is The Word of God Himself** to tell us all that we walk by faith, not by sight: We are **confident** (of good courage through our faith in God through Jesus Christ), I (Apostle Paul) say and willing rather to be absent from the body and to be present with the Lord. II Corinthians 5:7-8 verse 7
12. Blessed are the poor in spirit to those who believe that the **Bible Itself Which Is The Word of God Himself**—And what agreement hath the temple of God with idols? For ye are the temple of the living God; as God hath said, I will dwell in them, and walk in them; and I will be their God, and they shall be my people. II Corinthians 6:16. See Leviticus 26:12, Ezekiel 37:27, Revelation 21:3, Exodus 29:45

Part DLXII

Blessed Are The Poor In Spirit. Matthew 5:3

Blessed Means Happy

Poor means meek in spirit. Poor means humble in spirit. Poor means lowly in spirit. Poor means quiet in spirit. Read Matthew 5:3-12, Read also Mark 1:15

Jesus did not say "*rich*" in spirit. Jesus said "*poor*" in spirit.

1. Blessed are the poor in spirit to those who believe that the **Bible Itself Which Is The Word of God Himself** to tell us all that if we live in the Spirit, let us also walk in the Spirit. Galatians 5:25
2. Blessed are the poor in spirit to those who believe that the **Bible Itself Which Is The Word of God Himself** to tell us all that we are His workmanship created in Christ Jesus unto good works which God had before ordained (planned, established) that we should walk in them. Ephesians 2:10, See Psalm 100:3, Romans 8:28, Ephesians 2:5, 8
3. Blessed are the poor in spirit to those who believe that the **Bible Itself Which Is The Word of God Himself** to tell us all that we walk in love, Christ also hath loved us, and hath given Himself for us an offering and a sacrifice to God for a sweetsmelling savor. Ephesians 5:2. See Exodus 20:41
4. Blessed are the poor in spirit to those who believe that the **Bible Itself Which Is The Word of God Himself** to tell us all that we were **sometime** (formerly) darkness, but **now** are we light in the Lord: walk as children of light. Ephesians 5:8, See Isaiah 2:5
5. Blessed are the poor in spirit to those who believe that the **Bible Itself Which Is The Word of God Himself** to tell us all to walk by the same rule and to let us mind the same thing. Philippians 3:16
6. Blessed are the poor in spirit to those who believe that the **Bible Itself Which Is The Word of God Himself** to tell us all that as we have therefore received Christ Jesus the Lord, so walk we in Him. Let us walk in Him. Let us walk with Him, Christ Jesus, the Lord. Colossians 2:6
7. Blessed are the poor in spirit to those who believe that the **Bible Itself Which Is The Word of God Himself** to tell us all that we are rooted and built up in

Him, and stablished in the faith, as we have been taught in the Word of God, abounding therein with thanksgiving. Colossians 2:7

8. Blessed are the poor in spirit to those who believe that the **Bible Itself Which Is The Word of God Himself** to tell us all that we walk worthy of God, who hath called you or us unto His Kingdom and glory. I Thessalonians 2:12
9. Blessed are the poor in spirit to those who believe that the **Bible Itself Which Is The Word of God Himself** to tell us all that we beseech (beg) us, brothers, and exhort you by the Lord Jesus—Furthermore then we beseech you, brethren, and exhort you by the Lord Jesus, that as ye have received of us how ye ought to walk and to please God, so ye would abound more and more. I Thessalonians 4:1
10. Blessed are the poor in spirit to those who believe that the **Bible Itself Which Is The Word of God Himself** to tell us all that this is the will of God—For ye know what commandments we gave you by the Lord Jesus. I Thessalonians 4:2
11. Blessed are the poor in spirit to those who believe that the **Bible Itself Which Is The Word of God Himself** to tell us all that everyone of you or us should know how—For this is the will of God, even your sanctification, that ye should abstain from fornication: I Thessalonians 4:3
12. Blessed are the poor in spirit to those who believe that the **Bible Itself Which Is The Word of God Himself** to tell us all that every one of you should know how to possess his vessel in sanctification and honour. I Thessalonians 4:4

Part DLXIII

Blessed Are The Poor In Spirit. Matthew 5:3

Blessed Means Happy

Poor means meek in spirit. Poor means humble in spirit. Poor means lowly in spirit. Poor means quiet in spirit. Read Matthew 5:3-12, Read also Mark 1:15

Jesus did not say "*rich*" in spirit. Jesus said "*poor*" in spirit.

1. Blessed are the poor in spirit to those who believe that the **Bible Itself Which Is The Word of God Himself** to tell us all that God hath not called us unto uncleanness, but unto holiness. I Thessalonians 4:7
2. Blessed are the poor in spirit to those who believe that the **Bible Itself Which Is The Word of God Himself** to tell us all that He therefore that despiseth, despiseth not man, but God, who hath also given unto us His Holy Spirit. I Thessalonians 4:8
3. Blessed are the poor in spirit to those who believe that the **Bible Itself Which Is The Word of God Himself** to tell us all that you study to be quiet, and to do your own business, and to work with your own hands, as we commanded you; I Thessalonians 4:11
4. Blessed are the poor in spirit to those who believe that the **Bible Itself Which Is The Word of God Himself** to tell us all about the Rapture: I Thessalonians 4:13-18
5. Blessed are the poor in spirit to those who believe that the **Bible Itself Which Is The Word of God Himself** to tell us all that if we say that we have fellowship with Him, and walk in darkness, we lie, and do not the truth. I John 1:6
6. Blessed are the poor in spirit to those who believe that the **Bible Itself Which Is The Word of God Himself** to tell us all that but if we walk in the light, as he is in the light, we have fellowship one with another, and the blood of Jesus Christ His Son cleanseth us from all sin. I John 1:7
7. Blessed are the poor in spirit to those who believe that the **Bible Itself Which Is The Word of God Himself** to tell us all that if we say that *we have no sin, we deceive ourselves*, and *the truth is not in us*. I John 1:8

8. Blessed are the poor in spirit to those who believe that the **Bible Itself Which Is The Word of God Himself** to tell us all that if we confess our sins, he is faithful and just to forgive us our sins, and to cleanse us from all unrighteousness. I John 1:9
9. Blessed are the poor in spirit to those who believe that the **Bible Itself Which Is The Word of God Himself** to tell us all that but whoso keepeth His Word, in Him verily is **the love of God** perfected: hereby know we that we are in Him. I John 2:5
10. Blessed are the poor in spirit to those who believe that the **Bible Itself Which Is The Word of God Himself** to tell us all that He that saith he abideth (live) in him ought himself also so to walk, even as He walked. I John 2:6
11. Blessed are the poor in spirit to those who believe that the **Bible Itself Which Is The Word of God Himself** to tell us all that there is no greater joy than to hear that my children walk in truth. III John 1:4
12. Blessed are the poor in spirit to those who believe that the **Bible Itself Which Is The Word of God Himself** to tell us all that to *build up ourselves* on our most *holy faith, praying in the Holy Spirit* (Holy Ghost). Jude 1:20

Part DLXIV

Blessed Are The Poor In Spirit. Matthew 5:3

Blessed Means Happy

Poor means meek in spirit. Poor means humble in spirit. Poor means lowly in spirit. Poor means quiet in spirit. Read Matthew 5:3-12, Read also Mark 1:15

Jesus did not say "*rich*" in spirit. Jesus said "*poor*" in spirit.

1. Blessed are the poor in spirit to those who believe that the **Bible Itself Which Is The Word of God Himself** to tell us all that to keep ourselves in the love of God, looking for the mercy of our Lord Jesus Christ unto eternal life. Jude 1:21
2. Blessed are the poor in spirit to those who believe that the **Bible Itself Which Is The Word of God Himself** to tell us all that now unto him that is able to keep you from falling, and to present you faultless before the presence of His Glory With Exceeding Joy. Jude 1:24
3. Blessed are the poor in spirit to those who believe that the **Bible Itself Which Is The Word of God Himself** to tell us all that to the only wise God our Saviour, be glory and majesty, dominion and power, both now and ever. Amen. Jude 1:25
4. Blessed are the poor in spirit to those who believe that the **Bible Itself Which Is The Word of God Himself** to tell us all that **Jesus** want us to walk with Him (Jesus) in white: for they are worthy. Revelation 3:4
5. Blessed are the poor in spirit to those who believe that the **Bible Itself Which Is The Word of God Himself** to tell us all that **Jesus speaking say: "Behold, I come as a thief. Blessed is he that watcheth, and keepeth his garments, lest (or) he walk naked, and they see his shame (embarrassment)." Revelation 16:15**
6. Blessed are the poor in spirit to those who believe that the **Bible Itself Which Is The Word of God Himself** to tell us all that John saw—"And I saw no temple therein: for the **Lord God Almighty** and the **Lamb** are the temple of it." Revelation 21:22
7. Blessed are the poor in spirit to those who believe that the **Bible Itself Which Is The Word of God Himself** to tell us all that John saw the city—"And the city had no need of the sun, neither of the moon, to shine in it: for the **glory of God** did *lighten it*, and the **Lamb** is the light thereof." Revelation 21:23

8. Blessed are the poor in spirit to those who believe that the **Bible Itself Which Is The Word of God Himself** to tell us all that John saw the nations—"the nations of them which are saved shall walk in the light of it: and the kings of the earth do bring their glory and honour into it." Revelation 21:24
9. Blessed are the poor in spirit to those who follow **Christ's example daily. I Peter 2:21,** Matthew 26:55, Mark 14:49, **Luke 9:23,** Luke 19:47, Luke 22:53, Acts 2:46, 47, Acts 3:1-2, Acts 5:41-42, **Acts 17:11,** Acts 19:1-10 verse 9, **I Corinthians 15:31,** Hebrews 3:9-19 verse 13
10. Blessed are the poor in spirit to those who believe and are able to say: "They are saved through grace, through faith in Jesus Christ, but they are not yet being filled with the Holy Spirit. Luke 24:48-49, John 20:22, John 7:38-39, Acts 9:1-7 verse 3, 6, **Acts 2:8, Proverbs 11:30,** Mark 11:22, **John 7:39**
11. Blessed are the poor in spirit to those who believe that the Red Robe stands for Jesus' Blood at Calvary. Luke 23:33
12. Blessed are the poor in spirit to those who believe that the White Robe stands for Jesus' Resurrection Power because He has indeed risen from the dead. Matthew 28:6-10 verse 6, 7, Luke 24:34-53 verse 34, Mark 16:6-9, 14, Mark 14:28, Mark 9:9, Luke 24:6, John 21:14, I Corinthians 15:3-5, Matthew 17:9, **Matthew 26:32, Matthew 27:64**

Part DLXV

Blessed Are The Poor In Spirit. Matthew 5:3

Blessed Means Happy

Poor means meek in spirit. Poor means humble in spirit. Poor means lowly in spirit. Poor means quiet in spirit. Read Matthew 5:3-12, Read also Mark 1:15

Jesus did not say "*rich*" in spirit. Jesus said "*poor*" in spirit.

1. Blessed are the poor in spirit to those who believe that Christ is the Only Begotten Son of the Father. Christ is Full of Grace and Truth. Christ is made **Flesh.** I Timothy 3:16. Christ is the Word. Christ is God the Father's Full of Grace and Truth. John 1:14, 16 See Genesis 1:1, John 1:1-2. Christ is God—John 1:13. Christ is the **Same.** As ever John 1:2—See **Hebrews 13:8**. Christ is the same as **"He" seven** times. Christ is the Same as **"Him" ten** times. Christ is the **Same** as **"His" four** times. See **Hebrews 13:8** again. Christ is the life. Christ is the True Light that came into the world. Christ is Full of Glory. Christ is the Beginning since Genesis 1:1
2. Blessed are the poor in spirit to those who believe that Christ was manifest the love of God toward us, and sent His Son into the world that we might live (being saved) through Him (Christ Jesus)...See Romans 5:8-9, I Thessalonians 1:10, I John 4:9. Christ is the Savior of the world. John 4:42, I John 4:14. See Luke 2:11
3. Blessed are the poor in spirit to those who believe that Christ possessed the Fullness of the Godhead—Colossians 2:9. See also Acts 17:29 and Romans 1:20. Christ is full of Grace and Truth. John 1:14, 16
4. Blessed are the poor in spirit to those who have not seen God the Father but had declared Him (Jesus) (Exodus 33:20) through Jesus in the flesh for thirty-three years upon earth before He went back to Heaven. Acts 1:11, I Timothy 3:16, **John 1:18,** I John 4:12
5. Blessed are the poor in spirit to those who believe that Christ is our Apostle. Christ is our High Priest of our profession (confession). He is Christ (God)—He is Jesus (God). He is **either** God or Jesus. **He** is the Same. Christ is the Same One. He is Christ as ever the Same as always has been. Hebrews 13:8. See Genesis 1:1 and John 1:1-18 verse 1-2, verse 2. **Read John 14:7-12 verse 7-9**, John 10:30, 38

6. Blessed are the poor in spirit to those who say like the people in Israel's time that **Christ** *claim* **to be God**, *making* **Himself equal with God**, but **Christ** is not a *robber to being in the form of* **God**, though it not *to be equal* **with God**. **Christ is still God Himself**. **Jesus Christ is Lord of all**. Acts 10:36, Philippians 2:6-11 verse 6, **Mark 3:21,** Luke 3:23, Luke 5:16, **Luke 23:2, John 5:18, John 19:7, John 10:30, 33, Mark 14:61-64 verse 62, John 8:56-57 verse 56, 58**
7. Blessed are the poor in spirit to those who believe that Christ is Jesus; that Christ is the Son of Man which is (will be) coming in the clouds of heaven. **Mark 14:55-64 verse 61-62.** See Daniel 7:13, Matthew 24:30, Matthew 26:64, **Mark 14:62, Revelation 1:7, I Thessalonians 4:16-17**
8. Blessed are the poor in spirit to those who heard that they said Jesus was saying that He was the Christ because Jesus **stated in part: "I Am."** Mark 14:61-62 verse 62. Therefore, this was not necessary or compel for Jesus to say: "in full sentence: "I Am The Christ." He just stated in part only: with two simple words: **I Am."** Mark 14:62 See Exodus 3:14-15, Hebrews 13:8. Is that the Same One of Ancient of Days that Christ use the same phrase? So I even say **Yes** that **Christ** is **God**; **Christ** is **Jesus** as the **Same One.** Psalm 102:27, Hebrews 1:12
9. Blessed are the poor in spirit to those who believe that Christ was and is still the Ancient of Time. Genesis 1:1, John 1:1-18 verse 1, Psalm 102:27, Hebrews 1:12, Daniel 7:13, Daniel 7:22, Isaiah 45:21, Jude 1:25, Philippians 3:20, I Timothy 1:1, I Timothy 2:3, I Timothy 4:10, II Timothy 1:10, Titus 1:3, **Titus 1:4,** Titus 2:10, 13, Titus 3:4, II Peter 1:1, II Peter 1:11, II Peter 2:6, II Peter 3:2, II Peter 3:18, Luke 1:47, Luke 1:69-80, John 4:42, Acts 5:31, Acts 13:23, Isaiah 52:6, John 4:25-26, 29, 42, I John 4:9, 14, I John 5:20, Philippians 2:5-11, Acts 10:36, Hebrews 9:28, Hebrews 13:8, John 1:29, 36, Hosea 4:16, Acts 8:32, I Peter 1:19, Revelation 5:6, 8, 14, Revelation 6:1, 16, Revelation 7:9, 10, 14, 17, Revelation 12:11, Revelation 13:8, Revelation 14:4, 10, Revelation 15:3, Revelation 17:14, Revelation 19:7, 9, Revelation 21:14, 22, 23, Revelation 22:1, 3
10. Blessed are the poor in spirit to those who believe that Christ will raise us who believe in Christ Jesus by faith in Him. John 5:21, John 6:40, 44, 54-58 verse 54, John 14:1-4, I Thessalonians 4:16-17, John 11:25, II Corinthians 5:7-9 verse 8, **II Corinthians 1:9-10 verse 9, I Corinthians 6:14, II Corinthians 6:14-15, Hebrews 11:9**, Mark 11:22
11. Blessed are the poor in spirit to those who believe that Christ can make us whole again; that Christ can save the sick through the prayer of faith shall raise him up. James 5:15

12. Blessed are the poor in spirit to those who believe that Christ who is still at work today is sending the Spirit that is equal with the Father; that the Truth Spirit belong to God. "**All The Earth is Mine**" **saith The Lord**—Exodus 19:5, John 14:16, John 15:26, John 4:23-26 verse 24, Hebrews 11:6, **Psalm 62:11,** Romans 1:16, I Corinthians 1:18, **Ecclesiastes 12:7,** Malachi 3:17, I John 5:6-13 verse 6, Romans 8:15, 23, Romans 9:4, Galatians 4:5, Ephesians 1:5, **John 10:17-18,** I Corinthians 11:23-26 verse 26, I Thessalonians 4:13-18, Luke 24:49, Acts 1:4-8 verse 8, Acts 2:1-47 verse 1-4, Acts 11:16, **John 20:22**

Part DLXVI

Blessed Are The Poor In Spirit. Matthew 5:3

Blessed Means Happy

Poor means meek in spirit. Poor means humble in spirit. Poor means lowly in spirit. Poor means quiet in spirit. Read Matthew 5:3-12, Read also Mark 1:15

Jesus did not say "*rich*" in spirit. Jesus said "*poor*" in spirit.

1. Blessed are the poor in spirit to those who believe that Christ's still the Son of God. Matthew 26:63-67 verse 64, Mark 14:61-64 verse 62, Daniel 7:13, Matthew 24:30, Matthew 26:64, Mark 13:36, Mark 14:62, Revelation 1:7, 8, 11, Revelation 1:17-18, Revelation 3:7, 11, Revelation 16:15, Revelation 22:7, 12-13, 16, 20, I Thessalonians 4:13-18, Hebrews 9:28
2. Blessed are the poor in spirit to those who believe that Christ is The Source, The Eternal, The Supernatural, the Finisher of our faith, The Eternal Authority, The Eternal Salvation, The Eternal Gracious and Equal With The Father. I Thessalonians 3:11, II Thessalonians 2:16-17, II Corinthians 13:14, Philemon 2:6, Philippians 2:6-11, 10-11, Acts 10:36, Philippians 3:10, Luke 23:2, John 5:18, John 4:25-26, 29, 42, I John 4:9, 14, John 8:56-58, John 10:33-38, John 19:7, John 14:6-12 verse 7-9, Ephesians 2:5, 8, John 19:30, I Corinthians 14:33, Hebrews 5:9, Hebrews 12:5, **John 19:30, Hebrews 12:2**
3. Blessed are the poor in spirit to those who believe that we have received the atonement or at one moment of Christ. Romans 5:11
4. Blessed are the poor in spirit to those who believe that church is the Supporter and Preserver of **all things.** Genesis 1:1-31, Genesis 2:1-3, Nehemiah 9:6, Colossians 1:17, Proverbs 8:22, **Acts 4:24,** Psalm 146:6, Revelation 14:7, John 1:3, Revelation 21:5, Jeremiah 10:11-13
5. Blessed are the poor in spirit to those who believe that **God** is **both Lord** and **Christ** because **Christ Himself** is **Jesus** to whom they crucifix. Acts 2:32, 36
6. Blessed are the poor in spirit to those who believe that Christ is the True God. I John 5:20, Hebrews 13:8, John 1:9, John 4:23-24, John 8:23-24 (Ezekiel 3:18), John 8:25-32, 33-59 verse 25 (Genesis 1:1, John 1:1-18), Roman 3:4, II Corinthians 1:18, I Thessalonians 1:9, I Peter 5:12, III John 1:12, **Revelation 3:7,**

14, Revelation 6:10, Revelation 15:3, Revelation 16:7, Revelation 19:2, 9, 11, Revelation 21:5, 6, Jeremiah 10:10, **John 14:7-9**

7. Blessed are the poor in spirit to those who believe that Christ is unsearchable. I Thessalonians 3:11, II Thessalonians 2:16-17
8. Blessed are the poor in spirit to those who believe that the saints of God, the children of God, the Family of God live unto Christ as He died for all, that they which live should not henceforth (hereafter) live unto (with) themselves, but unto Christ which died for us all as saints of God, children of God as well as the family of God and that Christ rose again. II Corinthians 5:15, Ephesians 3:15, I Corinthians 15:3-4, Romans 6:1-23 verse 3-11, Colossians 2:12, Galatians 3:24-29 verse 27-28
9. Blessed are the poor in spirit to those who believe that Christ by appointment hath put all things under His feet, and give Him(Jesus) to be the head over all things to the church which is Christ's Body, the Fullness of Christ that fill all in all. Ephesians 1:22, Colossians 2:9, John 1:14, 16, Philippians 2:6-11 verse 5, Ephesians 4:12, 15, Ephesians 5:23-32 verse 23
10. Blessed are the poor in spirit to those who believe that Christ is the Mystical Body, and this is about Christ's church because Christ loved the church. Ephesians 4:12, 15, Ephesians 5:23-32 verse 23
11. Blessed are the poor in spirit to those who believe that Christ's Commission to His apostles were to witness for Christ and His Second Coming. Matthew 10:1-42 verse 1, 7, Matthew 28:19-20, Mark 16:15, John 20:21-23 verse 21, Revelation 22:20, Acts 1:8, I Thessalonians 4:16-17
12. Blessed are the poor in spirit to those who believe that Christ's Himself declared against the chief priests and the Pharisees because they heard Christ's parables realizing that the parables were about them. Matthew 21:42-46 verse 42, Psalm 118:22, Isaiah 28:16, Romans 9:33, I Peter 2:6, Acts 4:11

Part DLXVII

Blessed Are The Poor In Spirit. Matthew 5:3

Blessed Means Happy

Poor means meek in spirit. Poor means humble in spirit. Poor means lowly in spirit. Poor means quiet in spirit. Read Matthew 5:3-12, Read also Mark 1:15

Jesus did not say "*rich*" in spirit. Jesus said "*poor*" in spirit.

1. Blessed are the poor in spirit to those who believe that Christ is the Head Stone of the Corner. Psalm 118:22, Matthew 21:42, Acts 4:10-12 verse 11, Isaiah 28:16, I Peter 2:1-8 verse 6, Romans 9:32-33 verse 33
2. Blessed are the poor in spirit to those who believe that Christ is the Preeminence. Colossians 1:18-20, Genesis 1:1, John 1:1, II Timothy 3:16, I John 5:20, Ephesians 4:1-32 verse 8-13 verse 8
3. Blessed are the poor in spirit to those who believe that Christ Imparts Gifts. Ephesians 4:1-13 verse 8, 11, Acts 1:4-8, Acts 2:1-47 verse 1-4, Acts 10:34-48 verse 44-47, I Corinthians 14:1-40 verse 1, I Corinthians 12:1-11 verse 1
4. Blessed are the poor in spirit to those who believe that Christ instituted the sacraments—Matthew 28:19, Luke 22:19-20, I Corinthians 11:23-26
5. Blessed are the poor in spirit to those who believe that Christ predicted concerning the priests and the Pharisees because Christ spoke of them and that they perceived but they were hurting very badly because of Christ's Predication. Matthew 21:42-46 verse 42, Acts 4:11, Isaiah 26:18, Romans 9:33, I Peter 2:6, Psalm 118:22
6. Blessed are the poor in spirit to those who believe that God will take care of the problem. Romans 16:20, Revelation 12:9, Revelation 20:2, Revelation 2:13, I Peter 5:7, Matthew 13:15-52 verse 22, II Corinthians 7:12
7. Blessed are the poor in spirit to those who believe our spiritual father was praying in the spirit: "The Lord, the Lord will git (get) ya (you). Yes, Yes, the Lord the Lord will git (get) ya (you) Yes The Lord will git (get) ya (you)!!! Romans 16:20, Revelation 12:9, Revelation 20:2, Revelation 2:13, I Peter 5:7, Matthew 13:15-52 verse 22, II Corinthians 7:12

8. Blessed are the poor in spirit to those who believe that Passover mean the lord's Supper with His Body, the New Testament in His Blood and showing His Death until He come. I Corinthians 11:23-26
9. Blessed are the poor in spirit to those who believe that Good Friday mean Christ died for all. John 19:30
10. Blessed are the poor in spirit to those who believe that Easter mean Christ indeed has risen from the dead as He had promise: "In three days I will rise again." Matthew 26:61, Matthew 27:40, Matthew 27:63, Mark 8:31, Mark 14:58, Mark 15:29, **John 2:19,** John 2:20
11. Blessed are the poor in spirit to those who believe that Another Comfort, which is the Holy Spirit that lead us to salvation in Jesus Christ. John 14:16-20 verse 16
12. Blessed are the poor in spirit to those who put their **noise** or our **noises** into the **Word of God to study** to just to **know Him.** Ecclesiastes 12:13, I Thessalonians 4:11-12, II Timothy 2:15, II Timothy 3:16, John 1:1, Genesis 1:1, John 1:1-18, II Timothy 3:14-17 verse 14, 16, Philippians 3:10, I John 5:20, Revelation 1:7-8, 11, 17-18, Revelation 2:8, Revelation 3:11, Revelation 4:8-10, Acts 9:20

Part DLXVIII

Blessed Are The Poor In Spirit. Matthew 5:3

Blessed Means Happy

Poor means meek in spirit. Poor means humble in spirit. Poor means lowly in spirit. Poor means quiet in spirit. Read Matthew 5:3-12, Read also Mark 1:15

Jesus did not say "*rich*" in spirit. Jesus said "*poor*" in spirit.

1. Blessed are the poor in spirit to those who are able to say: "Wonderful Savior." Psalm 119:129, Psalm 139:6, Isaiah 9:6, Matthew 21:14-16, Luke 2:11
2. Blessed are the poor in spirit to those who are able to say with the old saints of God: "Wonderful Savior." Psalm 119:129, Psalm 139:6, Matthew 21:14-16, Luke 2:11
3. Blessed are the poor in spirit to those who believe that strange people have done bad thing **"after" God** has done them so good at time because **God** has done good things for them. Jeremiah 20:6, John 24:20, Acts 7:43
4. Blessed are the poor in spirit to those who listen and believe. Isaiah 43:1-28
5. Blessed are the poor in spirit to those who listen. Isaiah 43:1-21
6. Blessed are the poor in spirit to those who listen and believe: "Yea, before the day was I am He; and there is none that can deliver out of my hand: I will work, and who shall let it?" Isaiah 43:13
7. Blessed are the poor in spirit to those who listen and believe: "But now thus saith the Lord that created thee, O Jacob, and he that formed thee, O Israel, *Fear not: for I have redeemed thee, I have called thee by thy name; thou art mine.*" Isaiah 43:1
8. Blessed are the poor in spirit to those who listen and believe: "*For I am the Lord thy God, the Holy One of Israel, thy Saviour: I gave Egypt for thy ransom, Ethopia and Seba for thee.*' Isaiah 43:3
9. Blessed are the poor in spirit to those who listen and believe: "*Since thou wast precious in my sight, thou hast been honourable, and I have loved thee: therefore will I give men for thee, and people for thy life.*" Isaiah 43:4
10. Blessed are the poor in spirit to those who listen and believe: "*Fear not: for I am with thee: I will bring thy seed from the east, and gather thee from the west;*" Isaiah 43:5

11. Blessed are the poor in spirit to those who listen and believe: **"Bring forth the blind people that have eyes, and the deaf that have ears." Isaiah 43:8**
12. Blessed are the poor in spirit to those who listen and believe: "Let all the nations be gathered together, and let the people be assembled: who among them can declare this, and shew us former things? Let them bring forth their witnesses, that they may be justified: or let them hear, and say, It is truth." Isaiah 43:9

Part DLXIX

Blessed Are The Poor In Spirit. Matthew 5:3

Blessed Means Happy

Poor means meek in spirit. Poor means humble in spirit. Poor means lowly in spirit. Poor means quiet in spirit. Read Matthew 5:3-12, Read also Mark 1:15

Jesus did not say "*rich*" in spirit. Jesus said "*poor*" in spirit.

1. Blessed are the poor in spirit to those who listen and believe: "*Ye are my witnesses,* saith the Lord, *and my servant whom I have chosen: that ye may know and believe me, and understand that I am He: before Me there was no God formed, neither shall there be after Me.*" Isaiah 43:10
2. Blessed are the poor in spirit to those who listen and believe: "*I, even I, am the Lord; and beside Me there is no saviour.*" Isaiah 43:11
3. Blessed are the poor in spirit to those who listen and believe: "*I have declared, and have saved, and I have shewed, when there was no strange god among you: therefore ye are my witnesses,* saith the Lord, *that I am God.*" Isaiah 43:12
4. Blessed are the poor in spirit to those who listen and believe: "*I am the Lord, your Holy One, the Creator of Israel, your King.*" Isaiah 43:15
5. Blessed are the poor in spirit to those who listen and believe: "*This people have I formed for Myself; they shall shew forth My praise.*" Isaiah 43:21
6. Blessed are the poor in spirit to those who listen and believe: "*I, even I, am He that blotteth out thy transgressions for Mine Own Sake, and (I) will not remember thy sins.*" Isaiah 43:25
7. Blessed are the poor in spirit to those who listen and believe: "*Put Me in remembrance: "Let Us" plead together: declare thou, that thou mayest be justified.*" Isaiah 43:26, Genesis 1:26
8. Blessed are the poor in spirit to those who listen: "All Flesh shall know that I the Lord am thy Savior and thy Redeemer, the Mighty One of Jacob. Isaiah 49:26
9. Blessed are the poor in spirit to those who listen and believe: "Thou shalt also suck the milk of the Gentiles, and shalt know that I the Lord am thy Savior and thy Redeemer, the Mighty One of Jacob." Isaiah 60:16

10. Blessed are the poor in spirit to those who listen and believe: "For He said, "Surely they are my people, children that will not lie (deal falsely): so He was their Savior." Isaiah 63:8
11. Blessed are the poor in spirit to those who listen and believe: "And my spirit hath rejoiced in God my Savior." Luke 1:47
12. Blessed are the poor in spirit to those who listen and believe: "For unto you is born this day in the city of David (the capital city of Jerusalem) a Savior which is Christ the Lord. Luke 2:11, See Isaiah 9:6

Part DLXX

Blessed Are The Poor In Spirit. Matthew 5:3

Blessed Means Happy

Poor means meek in spirit. Poor means humble in spirit. Poor means lowly in spirit. Poor means quiet in spirit. Read Matthew 5:3-12, Read also Mark 1:15

Jesus did not say "*rich*" in spirit. Jesus said "*poor*" in spirit.

1. Blessed are the poor in spirit to those who listen and believe: "And said unto the woman, Now we believe, not because of thy saying: for we have heard Him ourselves, and know that this is indeed the Christ, the Savior of the world." John 4:42, See I John 4:14, See Matthew 1:21, 25, Luke 1:31, Luke 2:21, Acts 9:5, 22, Acts 18:5, 28 (Isaiah 43:3, Isaiah 49:26, Isaiah 60:16, Isaiah 63:8), Acts 5:31, Acts 13:23, Philippians 3:20, I Timothy 1:1, I Timothy 2:3, I Timothy 4:10, II Timothy 1:10, Titus 1:3, 4, Titus 2:10, 13, Titus 3:4, 6, II Peter 1:1, 11, II Peter 2:20, II Peter 3:2, 18, I John 4:14, Jude 1:25
2. Blessed are the poor in spirit to those who listen and believe: "Him hath God exalted with His Right Hand to be a Prince and a Savior, for to give repentance to Israel, and forgiveness of sins." Acts 5:31, See Isaiah 9:6, Revelation 1:5
3. Blessed are the poor in spirit to those who listen and believe: "Of this man's seed (offspring) hath God according to His promise raised unto Israel a Savior, Jesus." Acts 13:23 (Isaiah 43:3)
4. Blessed are the poor in spirit to those who listen and believe: "For our conversation (citizenship) is in heaven; from whence (where) also we look for the Savior, the Lord Jesus Christ." Philippians 3:20
5. Blessed are the poor in spirit to those who listen and believe: "Paul, an Apostle of Jesus Christ by the commandment of God our Savior, and Lord Jesus Christ, which is our hope: (our Savior, our Lord, our God). I Timothy 1:1
6. Blessed are the poor in spirit to those who listen and believe: "For this is good and acceptable in the sight of God our Savior." I Timothy 2:3
7. Blessed are the poor in spirit to those who listen and believe; "For therefore we both labor and suffer reproach, because we **trust** in the living God, who is the Savior of all men, specially of those that believe." I Timothy 4:10

8. Blessed are the poor in spirit to those who listen and believe: "But is **now** made *manifest* (known) by the **appearing** (shown up in reality) of our Savior Jesus Christ, who hath abolished death, and hath brought life and immortality to light through the gospel:" II Timothy 1:10
9. Blessed are the poor in spirit to those who listen and believe: "But hath in due times manifested (made known) His Word through preaching, which is committed unto me (An Apostle Paul and to us as children of God, too) according to the commandment of God our Savior." Titus 1:3
10. Blessed are the poor in spirit to those who listen and believe: "To Titus mine (my) own son (spiritual son in the gospel) after the common faith: Grace, mercy, and peace from God the Father and the Lord Jesus Christ our Savior." Titus 1:4
11. Blessed are the poor in spirit to those who believe and listen: "Not purloining (stealing), but showing all fidelity; (faith) that they may adorn the **doctrine of God our Savior in all things.**" Titus 2:10
12. Blessed are the poor in spirit to those who listen and believe: "Looking for that Blessed Hope (our God, our Lord, our Savior, our Jesus, our Christ) and the Glorious Appearing of The Great God and Savior Jesus Christ." Titus 2:13

Part DLXXI

Blessed Are The Poor In Spirit. Matthew 5:3

Blessed Means Happy

Poor means meek in spirit. Poor means humble in spirit. Poor means lowly in spirit. Poor means quiet in spirit. Read Matthew 5:3-12, Read also Mark 1:15

Jesus did not say "*rich*" in spirit. Jesus said "*poor*" in spirit.

1. Blessed are the poor in spirit to those who listen and believe: "But after that the kindness and love of God our Savior toward man appeared." Titus 3:4
2. Blessed are the poor in spirit to those who listen and believe: "Not by works of righteousness which we have done, but according to His Mercy He saved us, by the Washing of Regeneration and Renewing of the Holy Ghost (Holy Spirit)." Titus 3:5
3. Blessed are the poor in spirit to those who listen and believe: "Which He shed on us abundantly through Jesus Christ our Savior." Titus 3:6
4. Blessed are the poor in spirit to those who listen and believe: "That being justified by His Grace, we should be made Heirs according to the Hope (our God, our Lord, our Savior, our Jesus and our Christ) of Eternal Life." Titus 3:7
5. Blessed are the poor in spirit to those who listen and believe: "This is a faithful saying, and these things I (An Apostle Paul) will that thou **affirm constantly** (speak confidently) that they which have believe in God might be careful to maintain good works. These things are good and profitable unto men. Titus 3:8
6. Blessed are the poor in spirit to those who listen and believe: "Simon Peter, a servant and an Apostle of Jesus Christ, to them that have obtained (received) like precious faith with us through the Righteousness of God and our Savior Jesus Christ. II Peter 1:1
7. Blessed are the poor in spirit to those who listen and believe: "For so entrance shall be ministered (supplied) unto you abundantly into the Everlasting Kingdom of our Lord and Savior Jesus Christ." II Peter 1:11
8. Blessed are the poor in spirit to those who listen and believe: "For if after they have escaped the pollutions (corruptions) of the world through the Knowledge of the Lord and Savior Jesus Christ, they are again entangled therein, and overcome, the latter end is worse with them than the beginning." II Peter 2:20

9. Blessed are the poor in spirit to those who listen and believe: "That ye may be mindful of the words which were spoken before by the holy prophets, and of the commandment of us the prophets of the Lord and Savior." II Peter 3:2
10. Blessed are the poor in spirit to those who listen and believe: "But Grow in Grace, and in the Knowledge of our Lord and Savior Jesus Christ To Him be glory both now and for ever." Amen. II Peter 3:18
11. Blessed are the poor in spirit to those who listen and believe: "And we have seen and do testify (speak with confidently; speak boldness) that the Father sent the Son (Christ Jesus) to be the Savior of the world." I John 4:14, See John 4:42
12. Blessed are the poor in spirit to those who listen and believe: "To The Only Wise God our Savior, be glory and majesty, dominion and power, both now and ever." Amen. Jude 1:25

Part DLXXII

Blessed Are The Poor In Spirit. Matthew 5:3

Blessed Means Happy

Poor means meek in spirit. Poor means humble in spirit. Poor means lowly in spirit. Poor means quiet in spirit. Read Matthew 5:3-12, Read also Mark 1:15

Jesus did not say "*rich*" in spirit. Jesus said "*poor*" in spirit.

1. Blessed are the poor in spirit to those who believe that Satan entered the heart of Job's wife to try to kill her husband—Job. Job 2:9
2. Blessed are the poor in spirit to those who believe that Satan entered the heart of King Herod to try to kill the newborn baby boy called the Baby Jesus. Matthew 2:8
3. Blessed are the poor in spirit to those who believe that Satan entered the heart of Judas to try to kill the man called Jesus. John 13:2, 27, Luke 22:3-6 verse 3
4. Blessed are the poor in spirit to those who believe God speaking of returning the spirit to Him who gave it (your original spirit, your original soul and your original mind). Ecclesiastes 12:7
5. Blessed are the poor in spirit to those who do not understand Christ's mystery. Mark 11:22
6. Blessed are the poor in spirit to those who come in; when we go out. Mark 11:22
7. Blessed are the poor in spirit to those who come in; when we go out. Mark 11:22
8. Blessed are the poor in spirit to those who believe that this is hard to understand Christ's blessing upon us daily. Mark 11:22, John 6:20, II Peter 3:16
9. Blessed are the poor in spirit to those who believe that this is very difficulty to understand Christ's way. Mark 11:22, I Peter 3:16, John 6:20
10. Blessed are the poor in spirit to those who believe when we are on hardship but willing to go through with Christ's strength, Christ's blessing and Christ's way of life, through Christ's faith. Mark 11:22, Philippians 4:13
11. Blessed are the poor in spirit to those who cry, mourn, wail and weep. Matthew 5:4, Luke 6:21, 25, Psalm 30:5, Joel 2:12-13, Esther 4:3, I Samuel 1:5-25 verse 12-18 verse 8, 10
12. Blessed are the poor in spirit to those who **know, understand and realize that once saved always saved is not possible to be saved "if" continue to live in**

sin or to continue living in sin which God forbid. See Romans 6:1-2, 14-15, It is call **continuous sin.** So the question is: "Would you ever saved in the first place? *Are you* **Mr. And Mrs. Judas Iscariot**? I believe that once you saved always saved is a fearful thing to fall into the hands of God. See Hebrews 10:31. I believe that once you saved always saved does not support that after you are saved, that it is okay to go on and on and do whatsoever you please. God forbid. God want your attention to be faithful to Him. No going back to sinning. Jesus said: "Go and Sin No More." Jesus say, "Go (But) sin no more or worse things can happen to you." John 5:14-15, John 8:11. I believe that once you saved is suppose to confess that Jesus save you, but you never tell a single soul of your salvation in Jesus Christ. Again *are you* **Mr. And Mrs. Judas Iscariot**? Once saved always saved is impossible for those who were once enlightened and have tasted of the heavenly gift, and were made partakers (share) of the Holy Spirit. Would you ever saved in the first place? *Are you* **Mr. and Mrs. Judas Iscariot**? Once saved always saved: Now suppose you were saved for a long period of time, then you left your faith and joined a somewhat another of religion. Then you are not possible saved which is once saved always saved. Read Hebrews 6:4, Read Luke 8:11-13 verse 13. See Revelation 22:19, **Revelation 2:5**

Part DLXXIII

Blessed Are The Poor In Spirit. Matthew 5:3

Blessed Means Happy

Poor means meek in spirit. Poor means humble in spirit. Poor means lowly in spirit. Poor means quiet in spirit. Read Matthew 5:3-12, Read also Mark 1:15

Jesus did not say "*rich*" in spirit. Jesus said "*poor*" in spirit.

1. Blessed are the poor in spirit to those who wait to get in deeper, deeper and deeper by getting to know who God really is by studying Him. Exodus 3:6-15, Matthew 22:32, Mark 12:26-27, Luke 20:37-38, **John 14:7-9**, Acts 10:36, **Philippians 2:6-11, verse 10-11, Philippians 3:10,** Acts 9:3-6, Genesis 1:1, John 1:1-18 verse 1, **Hebrews 13:8,** II Timothy 3:16, I Timothy 3:16, Luke 23:2, John 4:24-26, 29, John 5:18, John 9:36, **John 10:30,** 33, 38, John 19:7, **Isaiah 52:6,** I John 5:20, I John 5:6-8, II Corinthians 13:14, Matthew 28:19, Revelation 1:7-8, 11, 17-18, Revelation 2:8, Revelation 3:7, 11, Revelation 4:8, Revelation 16:15, Revelation 22:7, 12-13, 16, 20, Isaiah 40:10, Isaiah 44:6, Isaiah 48:12, Isaiah 6:2-3, I Thessalonians 4:13-18 verse 16-17, I John 3:1-3, Psalm 51:11, Isaiah 63:10-11, Ephesians 4:30, Acts 2:36, Daniel 9:25-26, John 1:45, Psalm 4:6 (John 1:46), Romans 1:20, Colossians 2:9, Acts 17:29, Acts 17:27
2. Blessed are the poor in spirit to those who believe that God through Jesus Christ send the Holy Spirit to convict us, to save us and to baptize us with His Spirit and to serve Him Faithful until He come to take us home with rewards. Psalm 51:11, Isaiah 28:11-12, Isaiah 63:10-11, Ephesians 4:30, Joel 2:26-32, Acts 2:16-21, Romans 10:13, Ephesians 2:5, 8, Acts 16:30-31, Matthew 3:15, Mark 16:15-17 (c), Luke 24:47-49, John 20:22, Acts 1:5-8, Acts 2:1-47 verse 1-4, Acts 11:16, John 14:16-17, 26, John 15:26, John 8:9, John 16:8-11
3. Blessed are the poor in spirit to those who believe that salvation is not of works. It is a gift from God. Salvation is by grace. Salvation is sealed by the Holy Spirit. John 3:16, **Romans 6:23, Ephesians 2:5, 8, 9,** Romans 11:6, **Ephesians 1:13-14,** Hebrews 7:25, Matthew 28:20, Hebrews 13:5
4. Blessed are the poor in spirit to those who believe that once saved always saved mean that one could lose his salvation. However, it is possible *if* you would ever

saved in the first place. *Are you* **Mr. and Mrs. Judas Iscariot**? John 6:64-71, See also Ezekiel 18:23, Ezekiel 33:11, II Peter 3:9, Isaiah 53:6, I Peter 2:25, Romans 5:8, 18, I John 2:21, also Revelation 22:19, John 3:15-18, verse 17, 18, 19 (Never have been born again in the first place) Acts 16:31

5. Blessed are the poor in spirit to those who believe that salvation is a divine work of God. **II Peter 1:1-4 verse 3,** Romans 9:16, II Timothy 1:9-10, John 3:18, I Peter 2:9-10, Hosea 2:23, Romans 9:25, Romans 9:11
6. Blessed are the poor in spirit to those who believe that Jesus Christ had talked the talk and walked the walk for three years of His ministry. Matthew 3:15, Matthew 28:18-20, I Peter 2:21, John 13:15
7. Blessed are the poor in spirit to those who believe that once saved always saved; try to justify, try to claim that Christian has a **license** to sin; continue to willingly sin, and to those who claim to continue to willingly and blatantly even blasphemy to live in sin **has not truly accepted Christ** in the **First Place even after many years.** *Are you* **Mr. And Mrs. Iscariot Judas**? Judas Iscariot had been with Jesus for three years, yet he had never been born again. He had never accepted Christ in the first place. Of course, Christ Jesus knew all about him from the beginning. John 6:63
8. Blessed are the poor in spirit to those who believe that a sinner, who has never been saved, never been born again, and is the **"fist time ever to** *receive Christ*, is willingly and humble to give up his personal life of sin, or repent of his sin and turn toward God and faith toward our Lord Jesus Christ; shall be saved. Acts 16:31, John 6:37, John 14:6, II Corinthians 5:17, John 14:26, I Thessalonians 4:8, Romans 10:8-13, 17, Ephesians 2:5, 8, **Acts 20:21,** Acts 26:20
9. Blessed are the poor in spirit to those who believe that once saved always saved stand for backslidden, **lukewarm,** continue unforgiving, plunge into sin, **brought no fruit,** disown, apostatize doctrinally, **commit suicide, atheist, license to sin or grace into a license to sin, never been saved in the first place,** unrepentant, abortion. Revelation 3:16, 17, I John 3:15, Hebrews 6:4, I Timothy 6:10. They believe that one can never go to hell once you become a Christian), never really saved to begin with drinking of alcoholic, smoking cigarette/cigar, worldly, folly of sins, dancing, **greedy of money** upon once saved always saved is impossible
10. Blessed are the poor in spirit to those who believe that once saved always saved is a dangerous teaching. Philippians 2:12, John 6:63-65, 71. Hebrews 10:31, Hebrews 10:27 *Are you* **Mr. and Mrs. Judas Iscariot**?

11. Blessed are the poor in spirit to those who believe that the Bible teaches us that we cannot live by bread alone, but by every word of God that proceed out of the mouth of God. Matthew 4:4, Luke 4:4, Deuteronomy 8:3
12. Blessed are the poor in spirit to those who believe that continuing eating **God's True Bread** will take us to Heaven to live with Him forever more. Deuteronomy 8:3, Matthew 4:4, Luke 4:4, I Corinthians 11:23-26

Part DLXXIV

Blessed Are The Poor In Spirit. Matthew 5:3

Blessed Means Happy

Poor means meek in spirit. Poor means humble in spirit. Poor means lowly in spirit. Poor means quiet in spirit. Read Matthew 5:3-12, Read also Mark 1:15

Jesus did not say "*rich*" in spirit. Jesus said "*poor*" in spirit.

1. Blessed are the poor in spirit to those who believe that the answer to the Baptism of the Holy Spirit is to fulfill God's will by serving Him, loving Him and doing His will faithfully until death and He will give us each a crown of life. Revelation 2:10.
2. Blessed are the poor in spirit to those who are **regenerated** by faith in Jesus Christ. Matthew 19:28, Titus 3:5
3. Blessed are the poor in spirit to those who are **repented** by faith in Jesus Christ. Matthew 3:2, Matthew 4:17, Mark 1:15, Mark 6:12, Luke 13:3, 5, Acts 2:38, Acts 3:19, Acts 17:30, Acts 26:20, Revelation 2:16, Revelation 3:3, 19
4. Blessed are the poor in spirit to those who are **converted** in Jesus Christ. Acts 15:3, Isaiah 6:10, James 5:19, Psalm 51:13, Matthew 13:15, Matthew 18:3, Mark 4:12, **Luke 22:32,** John 12:40, Acts 3:19, Acts 28:27
5. Blessed are the poor in spirit to those who are **saved** by faith in Jesus Christ. John 3:16, Acts 16:30-31, Romans 10:8-13, Ephesians 2:5, 8
6. Blessed are the poor in spirit to those who believe in Jesus Christ by faith. Mark 1:15, Romans 10:8-13, Acts 16:30-31, Romans 10:17, Mark 11:22, John 14:1-4
7. Blessed are the poor in spirit to those who are **justified** by Jesus Christ. Romans 1:17, Habakkuk 2:4, Galatians 3:11, Hebrews 10:38, Luke 18:10-14 verse 14, Acts 13:39, Romans 3:24, 38, Romans 5:1, 9, Romans 8:30, I Corinthians 6:11, Galatians 2:16-17, Galatians 3:11, Galatians 3:24, Titus 3:7, James 2:25, Romans 3:30, Galatians 3:8, Romans 3:26, Romans 4:5, Romans 8:33, Romans 4:25, Romans 5:16, Romans 5:18
8. Blessed are the poor in spirit to those who **receive God's Free Gift of salvation.** Romans 1:11-17 verse 11, Ephesians 2:5, 8, Romans 6:23, Romans 5:21, John 3:16, Acts 4:12, Romans 5:15, 17, 20, 21

9. Blessed are the poor in spirit to those who are **sanctified** by Jesus Christ. I Corinthians 1:30, **Acts 26:18,** I Thessalonians 4:3, 4, II Thessalonians 2:13, I Peter 1:2, John 10:36, John 17:19, **II Timothy 2:31,** Hebrews 2:11, Hebrews 10:10, 14, Hebrews 10:29-39 verse 29, Romans 15:16, I Corinthians 1:2, I Corinthians 6:11, I Timothy 4:5
10. Blessed are the poor in spirit to those who are **redeemed** by the blood of Jesus Christ. Luke 1:6, 8, Galatians 3:13, I Peter 1:18, Revelation 5:9, Psalm 34:22
11. Blessed are the poor in spirit to those who **receive Christ's Redemption.** Luke 2:38, Luke 21:28, Romans 3:24, I Corinthians 1:30, Ephesians 1:7, Ephesians 4:30, Colossians 1:14, Hebrews 9:12, Hebrews 9:15
12. Blessed are the poor in spirit to those who **receive Christ's Righteousness** which is by faith in Jesus Christ. Matthew 3:15, Matthew 5:6, Matthew 6:33, Matthew 21:32, Luke 7:75, Romans 5:21, John 16:8, John 16:10, Acts 10:35-36 verse 36, Romans 1:17, Acts 17:31, Romans 3:21-31 verse 22, 26, 28, 30, 31

Part DLXXV

Blessed Are The Poor In Spirit. Matthew 5:3

Blessed Means Happy

Poor means meek in spirit. Poor means humble in spirit. Poor means lowly in spirit. Poor means quiet in spirit. Read Matthew 5:3-12, Read also Mark 1:15

Jesus did not say "*rich*" in spirit. Jesus said "*poor*" in spirit.

1. Blessed are the poor in spirit to those who **receive Christ's Sanctification.** I Corinthians 1:30, I Thessalonians 4:3, 4, II Thessalonians 2:13, I Peter 1:2
2. Blessed are the poor in spirit to those who **receive Christ's Grace.** Luke 2:40, John 1:14, 16, 17, Acts 4:33, Acts 11:23, Acts 13:43, Acts 14:26, **Acts 15:11, Acts 18:27-28 verse 27, Acts 20:24, 32,** Romans 1:1-32 verse **5**, 6, **7**, 8, 9, 11-17, Romans 3:5, 7, Romans 3:24, Romans 4:5, **16**, Romans 5:1-2 verse, Romans 6:1-2, verse 2, Romans 15:15-17 verse 15, Romans 16:20, 24, I Corinthians 1:3-4, I Corinthians 15:10, I Corinthians 16:23-24, II Corinthians 1:2, II Corinthians 8:7-9 verse 7, 9, 19, **II Corinthians 12:9,** II Corinthians 13:14, Galatians 1:3, 15 (Jeremiah 1:5, Psalm 139:13 (Psalm 51:5), Galatians 2:20-21 verse 21, Ephesians 1:2, 6, **Ephesians 2:5, 7, 8, 9** (Romans 8:28), Ephesians 3:2, 7, 8, Ephesians 4:29, Ephesians 6:24, Philippians 1:2, 7-8, Philippians 4:23, Colossians 1:2, 6, Colossians 3:16, Colossians 4:6, 18, I Thessalonians 1:1, I Thessalonians 5:28, II Thessalonians 1:2, 12, II Thessalonians 2:16, II Thessalonians 3:18, I Timothy 1:2, 14, I Timothy 6:21, II Timothy 1:2, 9, II Timothy 2:1, II Timothy 4:22, Titus 1:4, Titus 2:11, II Timothy 3:7, 15, Philemon 1:3, 25, Hebrews 2:9, Hebrews 4:16, Hebrews 10:29-39 verse 29, Hebrews 12:28, Hebrews 13:9, 25, James 4:6 (Proverbs 3:34), I Peter 1:2, I Peter 1:10, 13, I Peter 3:7, I Peter 4:10, I Peter 5:5, 10, 12, II Peter 1:2, **I Peter 3:18,** II John 1:3, Jude 1:4, Revelation 1:4, Revelation 22:20-21 verse 21
3. Blessed are the poor in spirit to those who **believe** that **Christ** is the **Son of Man**. Matthew 8:20, Matthew 10:23, Matthew 12:8, 32, 40, Matthew 13:41, Matthew 16:13, Matthew 16:27, 28, Matthew 17:9, 12, 22, Matthew 18:11, Matthew 19:28, Matthew 20:18, 28, Matthew 24:27, 30, 37, 39, Matthew 26:45, 64, Mark 8:36, Mark 9:9, 12, 31, 33, Mark 10:45, Mark 13:26, 34, Mark

14:21, 41, 62, **Luke 5:24,** Luke 6:5, Luke 9:22, 26, Luke 26:27, Luke 24:7, John 1:51, John 3:13, 14, 16, John 5:27, John 6:27, 62, John 8:28, John 12:23, 34, John 13:31, Revelation 1:13, Revelation 14:14

4. Blessed are the poor in spirit to those who **believe** that **Christ** is the **Son of the Living God**. Matthew 16:16, John 6:69
5. Blessed are the poor in spirit to those who **believe** that **Christ** is the **Only Begotten Son**. John 3:16, 18, John 1:14
6. Blessed are the poor in spirit to those who **believe** that **Christ** is the **Son of the Blessed**. Mark 14:61
7. Blessed are the poor in spirit to those who **believe** that **Christ** is the **Son of David.** Matthew 1:1-17 verse 1, 16, Mark 12:35, Luke 20:41
8. Blessed are the poor in spirit to those who **believe** that **Jesus was born** who was **called Christ**. Matthew 1:16
9. Blessed are the poor in spirit to those who **believe** that **Christ** is **the Rabbi**. John 1:49
10. Blessed are the poor in spirit to those who **believe** that **Christ** is **the Teacher**. John 3:2, I Kings 17:24, John 3:26, John 6:25
11. Blessed are the poor in spirit to those who **believe** that **Christ** is **the Master**. Mark 9:17, John 1:38, John 4:31, John 8:4, John 9:2, John 11:8, 28, John 13:13, 14, John 20:16, **Ephesians 6:9, Colossians 4:1**
12. Blessed are the poor in spirit to those who **believe** that **Christ** is **Rabbi** or **Rabboni**. John 1:38, John 20:16, **Matthew 23:1-39 verse 8,** 9, **10, Ephesians 6:9, Colossians 4:1**

Part DLXXVI

Blessed Are The Poor In Spirit. Matthew 5:3

Blessed Means Happy

Poor means meek in spirit. Poor means humble in spirit. Poor means lowly in spirit. Poor means quiet in spirit. Read Matthew 5:3-12, Read also Mark 1:15

Jesus did not say "*rich*" in spirit. Jesus said "*poor*" in spirit.

1. Blessed are the poor in spirit to those who **believe** that **Christ** is the **Son of the Most High**. Luke 8:28, Mark 5:7
2. Blessed are the poor in spirit to those who believe that the **greater miracle** is the **regeneration of the new birth** which is in **Christ Jesus**. John 3:3, 5, 6, 7, 8, I Peter 1:21, Matthew 19:28, Titus 3:5, John 3:16
3. Blessed are the poor in spirit to those who believe that Christ was made of a woman. Galatians. 4:4, Romans 8:13, Revelation 12:5, Revelation 12:13
4. Blessed are the poor in spirit to those who believe that Christ was made in the likeness of sinful flesh. Romans 8:3
5. Blessed are the poor in spirit to those who believe that Christ was made in the likeness or as the image like us yet without sin. Genesis 1:26, **Genesis 3:22,** Isaiah 7:14, Isaiah 9:6, Isaiah 53:1-12, Matthew 1:23, Daniel 7:13, Revelation 1:7, I Timothy 3:16, Matthew 24:30, Matthew 26:64, Mark 14:61-62, Revelation 1:7, Matthew 24:30, Matthew 26:64, Mark 16:19, Acts 1:9, 11, Hebrews 9:28, Revelation 12:13, Hebrews 7:3, Hebrews 4:14-16 verse 15, Revelation 1:13, Revelation 12:5, **Matthew 2:1-23 verse 16, Luke 1:80**
6. Blessed are the poor in spirit to those who believe that Christ was in all points tempted like as we are, **yet without sin** because Christ cannot be touch with the feeling of our infirmities (weakness). He **cannot be tempted with evil (weakness),** neither tempted (by) He any man. James 1:13, Hebrews 4:15, Hebrews 9:1-28 verse 9, 11, 14-16, 24, 25, 26, 27, 28
7. Blessed are the poor in spirit to those who believe that **Christ** become our **Perfect Sacrificial Lamb. I Corinthians 5:7, Hebrews 5:1-9 verse 9,** Hebrews 8:1-13 verse 3
8. Blessed are the poor in spirit to those who believe that Christ is the Son of the Highest. Luke 1:32

9. Blessed are the poor in spirit to those who **believe** that **Christ** is **the Rock** of my salvation. Psalm 18:46, **Psalm 62:2, 6,** Psalm 89:26, Psalm 95:1, I Corinthians 10:4
10. Blessed are the poor in spirit to those who believe **that Rock is Christ.** I Corinthians 10:4
11. Blessed are the poor in spirit to those who believe that **Spiritual Rock is Christ.** I Corinthians 10:4
12. Blessed are the poor in spirit to those who believe that the Baptism of the Holy Spirit with speaking in tongues is **not yet ceased until Jesus Christ return**. **(Amos 4:12, I Thessalonians 4:13-18 verse 16-17, Hebrews 9:28, Revelation 1:7, Revelation 1:17-18, Revelation 3:11, Revelation 16:15, Revelation 22:7, 12, 16, 20)** (See Daniel 7:13—Matthew 24:30, Matthew 21:64, Mark 14:62), I Corinthians 13:8, Revelation 5:8-14, Revelation 7:9-12, Amos 4:12, Revelation 22:20, Acts 2:1-4, Acts 10:46, Acts 19:6, Luke 24:49, John 20:22, Acts 1:4-8, Acts 11:16, Mark 11:22, 24, Matthew 3:11, Mark 1:8, Luke 3:16, John 1:33, Isaiah 28:11-12, I Corinthians 14:18, 21, 22, 33, Jude 1:3, 14, Revelation 14:12, Revelation 15:13, Daniel 19:8, Psalm 116:15, Revelation 2:10, 11, 12-13, Genesis 11:1-9

Part DLXXVII

Blessed Are The Poor In Spirit. Matthew 5:3

Blessed Means Happy

Poor means meek in spirit. Poor means humble in spirit. Poor means lowly in spirit. Poor means quiet in spirit. Read Matthew 5:3-12, Read also Mark 1:15

Jesus did not say "*rich*" in spirit. Jesus said "*poor*" in spirit.

1. Blessed are the poor in spirit to those who believe in Christ's **Conversion. Acts 15:3.** Real Christ's Conversion is the same as real convert or real converted: Isaiah 6:10, James 5:19-20, **Psalm 51:13, Matthew 13:15, Matthew 18:3, Mark 4:12, Luke 22:32, Acts 3:19, Acts 28:27**
2. Blessed are the poor in spirit to those who believe that there is **Evident** in the Bible between **Old Testament Prophecy and New Testament Prophecy** to support **God's Word and Prophecy;** For instance: **Genesis 1:1 (John 1:1), Daniel 9:25** (John 1:41), **Old Testament Prophecy Isaiah 7:14** (New Testament Prophecy Matthew 1:23), **Old Testament Prophecy Habakkuk 2:4** (New Testament Prophecy Romans 1:17, Galatians 3:11, Hebrews 10:38), **Old Testament Prophecy Genesis 3:6-15** (New Testament Prophecy Matthew 22:32, Mark 12:26-27, Luke 20:37-38), **Old Testament Prophecy Isaiah 53:6** (New Testament Prophecy I Peter 2:25), **Old Testament Prophecy Isaiah 53:5** (New Testament Prophecy I Peter 2:24), **Old Testament Prophecy Isaiah 53:12** (New Testament Prophecy Luke 22:37, Luke 23:33, I Corinthians 15:3, I Peter 2:24), **Old Testament Prophecy Joel 2:28-29, 30-31, 32** (New Testament Prophecy Acts 2:16-21), **Old Testament Prophecy Psalm 49:15, Psalm 16:10** (New Testament Prophecy Acts 2:31, Acts 13:35), **Old Testament Prophecy Psalm 110:1** (New Testament Prophecy Matthew 22:44-45 verse 44, Mark 12:35-37 verse 36, Luke 24:41-44 verse 43, **Acts 2:34, Romans 16:20** (Genesis 3:15, Revelation 12:9), I Corinthians 15:25, Ephesians 1:20, Hebrews 1:3, 13, Hebrews 10:13, **Old Testament Prophecy Deuteronomy 21:22-23** (New Testament Prophecy Mark 15:42, John 19:31, **Acts 5:30-31 verse 30,** Galatians 3:13), **Old Testament Prophecy Genesis 11:31, Genesis 12:1,** 7 (New Testament Prophecy Acts

7:1-51 verse 2, 3, verse 5, verse 7 (Genesis 15:13), verse 8 (Genesis 17:10), verse 10 (Genesis 41:41), verse 13 (Genesis 45:3), verse 14 (Deuteronomy 10:22), verse 16 (Joshua 24:32), verse 18 (Exodus 1:8), verse 20 (Exodus 2:2), verse 31 (Exodus 3:3), verse 36 (Exodus 7:3), verse 37 (Deuteronomy 18:15), verse 39 (Numbers 14:4), verse 40 (Exodus 32:1), verse 41 (Exodus 32:6), verse 42 (Amos 5:25), verse 43 (Joshua 24:20, Jeremiah 20:6), verse 44 (Joshua 3:14), verse 46 (Psalm 132:5), verse 48 (I Kings 6:1-3, 11-14, 21-22, 38), verse 49 (Isaiah 66:1-2), verse 51 (II Kings 17:14, Exodus 33:3), **Old Testament Prophecy Isaiah 53:7** (New Testament Prophecy **Matthew 27:12, Acts 8:32**), **Old Testament Prophecy I Samuel 13:14** (New Testament Prophecy Acts 13:22-23 verse 22) **Old Testament Prophecy Psalm 16:10** (New Testament Prophecy Acts 13:35), **Old Testament Prophecy Habakkuk 1:5-6** (told you so) (New Testament Prophecy Acts 13:41) (though it be told you—mean I told you so) (Why—God?) (Habakkuk 1:5, Acts 13:41), **Old Testament Prophecy Isaiah 49: 1-26 verse 6** (New Testament Prophecy Acts 13:1-52 verse 47), verse 6 (Acts 13:47), verse 8 (II Corinthians 6:2, Isaiah 49:8), verse 10 (Revelation 7:16, Psalm 121:6), verse 23 (Romans 10:11), Amos 9:1-15 verse 11-12 (Acts 15:14-19, verse 16), Psalm 104:33 (Acts 17:27-34 verse 28, verse 31 (Psalm 9:8), Isaiah 43:5 (Acts 18:9-10, Joshua 1:1-18 verse 9), Isaiah 42:1-25 verse 1 (Matthew 3:17, Matthew 11:10, Mark 1:1, Luke 7:27, Luke 1:76, Matthew 12:17-18, Mark 1:11, John 17:4, Malachi 3:1), verse 5 (Acts 17:25), verse 6 (Luke 2:32), verse 7 (**Acts 26:18),** Isaiah 6:9 (Acts 28:26-31 verse 26) So Old Testament Prophecy mean New Testament Prophecy. They are *True*. They are *Real*. They are *Facts of life*. They are *Promises*. They are **so**. They are telling the truth. At least, "I told you so." **Habakkuk 1:5** and Acts 13:41 "Though It be told you mean I told you so. And they are **so!!!**

3. Blessed are the poor in spirit to those who believe that the Baptism of the Holy Spirit is winning souls to Christ. Proverbs 11:30, Acts 1:1-8, Acts 2:4, Acts 2:1-47 of various culture people, language, nations, out of every kindred, tongue, and people and nation. Revelation 5:9, Revelation 7:9-17 verse 9, Revelation 14:6, Revelation 21:24
4. Blessed are the poor in spirit to those who believe that the Bible is not a liar; that the Bible is not a lie. Romans 3:4, Proverbs 14:15, Acts 17:11, Psalm 37:23, II Timothy 3:16-17, Genesis 1:4, John 1:1-2, II Timothy 2:15, I Thessalonians 4:11, II Timothy 4:1-4, Titus 1:9, Isaiah 11:1-5, Luke 2:41-47, Luke 20:1-8,

20-47, **John 14:9,** Philippians 2:10-11, Philippians 3:10, Isaiah 52:6, John 4:24, John 9:36-37, Exodus 3:6, 14-15, **II Timothy 1:12,** Hebrews 10:38, Acts 26:28, Acts 11:26, Ecclesiastes 12:13, Galatians 3:11, Micah 6:8, Deuteronomy 10:12, Romans 1:17, Habakkuk 2:4

5. Blessed are the poor in spirit to those who believe that **without the power of Jesus,** there would be *no baptism of the Holy Spirit.* Acts 1:8, John 15:5
6. Blessed are the poor in spirit to those who believe that the **Holy Spirit** is not a force person but when **He** is come, **He** will reprove (convict) our loved-ones, our sinners, child of God to world of sin and of righteousness, and of judgment: (God's judgment) of sin, because they believe not on Jesus: of righteousness, because Jesus goes to His Father, and you see Jesus no more; of judgment, because the prince of this world (Satan) is judged. Jesus has yet many things to say unto you or us, but you or we cannot bear (understand) them (things of this world held or bound by Satan) Howbeit when He, the Spirit of truth is come, He will guide you or us as God's children into all truth: for He shall not speak of Himself (the Holy Spirit); but whatsoever **He** (the Holy Spirit) shall hear, that **He** (the Holy Spirit) shall **He** speak: and **He** (the Holy Spirit of God) will show you thing to come. (Holy Spirit is the third person of the trinity or the trinity in One I John 5:6-8) John 16:8-3, Revelation 3:19, Proverbs 3:12
7. Blessed are the poor in spirit to those who believe that the **Holy Spirit** is *not a force person,* but **He** comes to convict sinners and us a children of God of sin, of as the world (mean people) and of judgment (God's judgment, God's Judgment Day and God's punishment upon His judgment. John 16:8-11, II Peter 2:9
8. Blessed are the poor in spirit to those who believe that **Salvation** is *indeed* **free,** but **Salvation** is **require through Jesus Christ.** John 3:3-7, Matthew 11:28, Acts 4:12, Revelation 12:10, II Peter 3:15, Jude 1:3, Revelation 7:10, John 8:32, 36, Matthew 10:8, Revelation 21:6-7, John 7:37, 38, Luke 3:6, Revelation 3:20, John 14:6, Revelation 19:1, Luke 1:69, Luke 1:77, Luke 2:30, Acts 13:47, Acts 16:17, Acts 28:28, John 4:7-15, Revelation 22:17, John 10:10:24-38, Acts 13:26, Isaiah 45:22, Luke 19:9, Romans 10:10, Romans 1:16, Romans 13:11, II Corinthians 1:6, II Corinthians 6:2, II Corinthians 7:10, Ephesians 1:13, Ephesians 6:17, Philippians 1:28, I Thessalonians 5:8, 9, II Thessalonians 2:13, Titus 2:11, Hebrews 2:3, 10, Hebrews 5:9, II Timothy 2:10, Ephesians 2:5, 8, II Timothy 3:15, Hebrews 9:28, I Peter 1:5, 9, 10, Luke 1:69, Luke 1:77, Luke 2:30

9. Blessed are the poor in spirit to those who believe that the Bible itself is **not an abuse, but a warning from God to those who deny God's Word** because God's Word stand surely, solemn, sure—(sincerely, promise, certainly, real) since the Foundation of the World. II Timothy 2:19, John 6:69, John 16:30, Hebrews 6:19, II Peter 1:19, Revelation 22:20, Hebrews 7:22, Acts 12:11, Acts 10:1-48 verse 11-16, 22, 34-38, 39-47, Romans 2:1-29, Genesis 2:17, Genesis 3:4, Genesis 9:5, Genesis 20:7, Romans 16:25-27, I John 2:22-23, Luke 12:9, Acts 3:13-14, II Timothy 3:1-17 verse 5-7
10. Blessed are the poor in spirit to those who believe that Baptism of the Holy Spirit is Power of the Holy Spirit or power of the Spirit of God. Acts 1:8
11. Blessed are the poor in spirit to those who believe that the burning bush **in a flame of fire** is indicated to **be a sign of the baptism of the Holy Spirit.** Exodus 3:2, Acts 7:31
12. Blessed are the poor in spirit to those who believe in the premillennialism; a concerning of Christ's Second Return. Acts 17:30-31, II Peter 3:10, I Thessalonians 4:13-18 verse 16-17, Revelation 21:27, Revelation 22:6, Exodus 29:45, Exodus 37:27, Isaiah 66:22, Isaiah 43:19, Psalm 89:28, Isaiah 25:8, Ezekiel 48:31, Ezekiel 48:30-34, Isaiah 24:23, Isaiah 60:11, Matthew 24:27-56 verse 29-36, 30-31, 40-44, Isaiah 13:10, Joel 2:10, Daniel 7:13, Zechariah 14:7, Matthew 25:1-46, Psalm 6:8, Daniel 12:2, Revelation 16:15, Revelation 3:11, Revelation 22:7, 12-13, 20, Isaiah 40:10, II Peter 3:1-13 verse 4-6, verse 4, 10, Hebrews 9:28, Acts 1:10-11 verse 11, Genesis 8:18, Genesis 19:24, Genesis 19:16, I John 3:2, Revelation 1:7, Psalm 90:4, Genesis 6:17, Genesis 1:36, I Corinthians 2:14, Isaiah 34:4, Isaiah 65:17, Isaiah 63:10-13 verse 11, II Timothy 4:6-8, Colossians 4:3, Titus 2:13, II Timothy 1:10, Titus 3:4-8 verse 4-5, John 14:1-3 verse 3, Luke 22:34-36, Revelation 20:11-15… (Jesus Second Return)…John 6:39-40, Revelation 14:6-15, James 5:7, Revelation 1:1-20, Matthew 16:27, Luke 21:27, Mark 9:1, Revelation 17:14, I Thessalonians 5:2, Revelation 19:16, I Thessalonians 5:23, John 5:28-29, Luke 9:26, Mark 12:18-27 verse 25, Revelation 4:1-2, Luke 24:44-45, Daniel 9:24-27, Psalm 96:13, II Thessalonians 1:5-10, Revelation 16:17-21, Acts 10:42, II Corinthians 5:10, II Corinthians 7:12, I Peter 4:18, I Peter 5:4, I John 2:28, I Timothy 6:14, II Timothy 4:1-8 verse 1, 6, 7, 8, Hebrews 9:26, Revelation 12:1-3, I Peter 3:18, Mark 14:62, Luke 21:28, John 18:36, John 12:48, Luke 17:33-35, Revelation 11:11-12, I Thessalonians 3:13, I Corinthians 15:47-54, I Corinthians 13:8-10, I Corinthians 6:9-20,

Romans 14:11, John 19:37, I John 5:6, John 17:5, Matthew 26:64, Matthew 17:1-12 verse 9, Philippians 2:12, I Corinthians 8:6, (Once saved always saved: Bible verse to prove against it I John 3:14, **II Corinthians 5:17,** Romans 6:3-4, John 5:24), **Eternal Life** (Matthew 25:46, John 3:15-16, Romans 6:23, **Titus 1:2, John 4:13-14—(Never Thirst Again), "should lose nothing"** (John 6:39-40) Once saved always saved: will that mean Jesus a liar? Read Romans 3:4—Let God Be True. Once saved always saved. Jude 1:24 Once saved always saved **mean Eternal Security.** Everlasting Life—Cannot be lost; cannot be call "Once saved always saved"—John 3:16, John 5:24, Ephesians 1:13-14 We are adopted into the family of God a permanent relationship against once always saved. Romans 8:14-17 verse 16, 23, Galatians 4:5, Ephesians 1:5 Once saved always saved is when a person left his or her salvation by going to another false teaching such as Jehovah Witness, Latter Day Saint, Catholic, Buddhist, or have not accept Christ in the first place. **Against** once saved always saved because of **John 10:27-29, Philippians 4:3, Revelation 21:27, Revelation 3:5-6,** Revelation 3:4 Once always saved is a threaten and misinterpreting and dangerous teaching that contrary to the Word of God. Lay hold on the eternal life. I Timothy 6:12, I Timothy 6:19 Hebrews 10:31—It is a fearful things to fall into the Hand of God. Once always saved—Lucifer may have once been saved in Heaven, but when Lucifer was kicked out of heaven, he never return. He wrote the words "I" five times. Lucifer took on himself to leave and God had no choice but to let him go. Acts 2:28, Acts 22:16, I Peter 3:21, I John 1:5-22

Part DLXXVIII

Blessed Are The Poor In Spirit. Matthew 5:3

Blessed Means Happy

Poor means meek in spirit. Poor means humble in spirit. Poor means lowly in spirit. Poor means quiet in spirit. Read Matthew 5:3-12, Read also Mark 1:15

Jesus did not say "*rich*" in spirit. Jesus said "*poor*" in spirit.

1. Blessed are the poor in spirit to those who believe that meat, manna, bread, flesh and food mean **Jesus Christ** because He is that **Spiritual Rock**. Exodus 16:4, Exodus 16:15, John 6:31, I Corinthians 10:1-4, Psalm 78:27, Numbers 11:16-20 verse 21
2. Blessed are the poor in spirit to those who believe that **salvation** is spoken by **Jesus Christ in Luke 10:28**
3. Blessed are the poor in spirit to those who believe that there is a separation between the new birth in Jesus Christ and the Spirit Baptism or baptism of the Holy Spirit. John 3:3, 7, I Peter 1:23, Mark 16:17, Luke 24:49, Acts 1:4-8, Acts 2:1-4, Acts 11:16
4. Blessed are the poor in spirit to those who believe that our living for Christ is not in vain. I Corinthians 15:58
5. Blessed are the poor in spirit to those who believe that our praise to Christ is not in vain. I Corinthians 15:58, Psalm 150:1-6
6. Blessed are the poor in spirit to those who believe that our testimony in Jesus is not in vain. I Corinthians 15:58
7. Blessed are the poor in spirit to those who believe that our life for Christ is not in vain. I Corinthians 15:58
8. Blessed are the poor in spirit to those who believe that our dance in the Lord is not in vain. II Samuel 6:14, I Corinthians 15:58
9. Blessed are the poor in spirit to those who believe that the Gospel of Jesus Christ Second Coming is not in vain. Amos 4:12, Revelation 3:11, Revelation 16:15, Revelation 22:7, 12, 20, I Corinthians 15:58
10. Blessed are the poor in spirit to those who believe that our faith in Jesus Christ is not in vain. I Corinthians 15:58, II Corinthians 5:6-9

11. Blessed are the poor in spirit to those who believe that we are saved through Christ's Flesh and Bone, and His Body by a new and living way which He had already prepared for us. Hebrews 10:19-23 **verse 20,** John 6:30-63 verse 51, 53, 54, 55, 56, 57, I Corinthians 11:22-26 verse 23, 24
12. Blessed are the poor in spirit to those who believe this old spiritual hymn: "Saved by His power divine, Saved to new life sublime! Life now is sweet and my joy is com-plete, For I'm saved, saved, saved! Titus 3:5

Part DLXXIX

Blessed Are The Poor In Spirit. Matthew 5:3

Blessed Means Happy

Poor means meek in spirit. Poor means humble in spirit. Poor means lowly in spirit. Poor means quiet in spirit. Read Matthew 5:3-12, Read also Mark 1:15

Jesus did not say "*rich*" in spirit. Jesus said "*poor*" in spirit.

1. Blessed are the poor in spirit to those who believe that our church is our college, God's place. Acts 11:26
2. Blessed are the poor in spirit to those who believe that our heaven is our university, our home in New Jerusalem. Revelation 21:1-7 verse 1-2, Ephesians 3:15
3. Blessed are the poor in spirit to those who believe that Jesus is our principal, our school principal. Galatians 3:24-29
4. Blessed are the poor in spirit to those who believe that the Holy Spirit is our Teacher, our schoolmaster. Galatians 3:24-29
5. Blessed are the poor in spirit to those who believe that our angels are our classmate in classroom at our university which is in New Jerusalem, the city of our God. Revelation 21:1-7 verse 1-2
6. Blessed are the poor in spirit to those who believe that the Bible is our study book, for our homework. Ecclesiastes 12:13-14, I Thessalonians 4:11-12, II Timothy 2:15, II Timothy 3:14-17
7. Blessed are the poor in spirit to those who believe that *trial* and *temptation* are our examinations. James 1:2, 12, Acts 20:19, Luke 22:28, Psalm 95:8, Matthew 6:13, Matthew 26:41, Mark 14:38, Luke 4:13, Luke 8:13, Luke 11:4, Luke 22:40, 46, I Timothy 6:9, I Corinthians 10:13, Galatians 4:14,
8. Blessed are the poor in spirit to those who believe that winning souls are our daily assignments. Proverbs 11:30
9. Blessed are the poor in spirit to those who believe that prayer is our attendance. I Thessalonians 5:17, II Timothy 4:8
10. Blessed are the poor in spirit to those who believe that crown of life is our degree; our certification, our diploma. Revelation 2:10, Revelation 3:11, I Peter 5:4, James 1:12

11. Blessed are the poor in spirit to those who believe that praise and worship is our motto. John 4:23-24, Hebrews 6:11, Psalm 9:1, Psalm 34:1, Psalm 40:3, Romans 15:11, Philippians 1:11, II Corinthians 8:18
12. Blessed are the poor in spirit to those who believe to those who want to enroll now because there is room enough for all and tuition is indeed free!!! John 8:32, 36

Part DLXXX

Blessed Are The Poor In Spirit. Matthew 5:3

Blessed Means Happy

Poor means meek in spirit. Poor means humble in spirit. Poor means lowly in spirit. Poor means quiet in spirit. Read Matthew 5:3-12, Read also Mark 1:15

Jesus did not say "*rich*" in spirit. Jesus said "*poor*" in spirit.

1. Blessed are the poor in spirit to those who receive Christ's **Faith**. Habakkuk 2:4, Romans 1:17, Titus 2:2, James 1:3, Hebrews 6:12, Galatians 3:11, Galatians 5:5-6, I Thessalonians 5:8, II Thessalonians 2:4, Hebrews 10:38, Romans 10:17, Romans 10:8-13 verse 8, Philemon 1:5-6, Ephesians 1:4, 15, 23, II Timothy 3:10, Ephesians 6:23-24, Colossians 1:4, I Timothy 6:11, II Timothy 1:13
2. Blessed are the poor in spirit to those who receive Christ's **Hope.** I Corinthians 13:7, Acts 2:26, Psalm 130:7, Acts 23:6, Acts 24:15, Acts 26:6, 7, Romans 5:1-21, verse 2, **4,** 5, Romans 8:9-30 verse 25-28 verse 25, Colossians 1:5, Romans 12:12, Romans 15:4, 13, I Corinthians 13:13, I Thessalonians 5:8, I Corinthians 15:19, II Corinthians 3:12-18 verse 12, 17, 18, II Corinthians 15:15-16, Galatians 5:5, Ephesians 1:18, Ephesians 2:12-22 verse 12-14, Ephesians 4:1-32 verse 4, 7, 11, 12, I Thessalonians 1:3, Colossians 1:23, 27, I Thessalonians 4:7-18 verse 13, 14-18, II Thessalonians 2:16, **I Timothy 1:1, 2, Titus 2:13, Titus 3:1-8 verse 7, Hebrews 3:6, Hebrews 6:11, 18, 19,** Hebrews 7:19, Hebrews 10:23, I Peter 1:4, 13, 21, I John 3:3, Titus 1:2
3. Blessed are the poor in spirit to those who believe in Christ's **Love.** John 3:16, Galatians 5:5-6, I Thessalonians 5:13, II Corinthians 8:7, I John 4:1-21 verse 7, 8, 9, 10, 11, 16, 17, 18, **19**, Romans 5:8, I John 4:1-21, I John 3:1-24, I John 1:1-10, I John 2:1-29, I John 5:1-21, II John 1:1-13, III John 1:1-14, John 5:42, John 8:42, John 10:17, John 13:34, John 13:35, John 14:15, 21, 23, 31, John 15:9, 10, 12, 13, 17, 19, John 17:26, John 21:15-17, Romans 5:5, Romans 8:28, 35, 39, Romans 12:9-10, Romans 13:9 (Exodus 20:13-14), Romans 15:30-33 verse 30, I Corinthians 2:9, I Corinthians 8:3, I Corinthians 16:22-24, II Corinthians 5:14, II Corinthians 8:8-9, II Corinthians 13:11, 14, Galatians 5:6, 13-14, 22, Ephesians 1:4, 15, **Ephesians 2:4, Ephesians 3:17,**

19-21 **verse 19,** Ephesians 4:1-32 verse 2, 15-16, 32, Ephesians 5:2, 25, 28, 33, Philippians 2:1, 2-11 verse 2, Colossians 1:1-5 verse 4, 8, Colossians 2:2, **Colossians 3:19,** I Thessalonians 3:12-13 verse 12, **I Thessalonians 4:9,** I Thessalonians 5:8, II Thessalonians 3:5, I Timothy 6:11, II Timothy 1:7, 13, **Titus 2:4,** Titus 3:4, Philemon 1:5, 7, **Hebrews 6:10,** Hebrews 10:24, James 1:12, James 2:5, 8 (Leviticus 19:18), I Peter 1:5-25 **verse 8,** 11, **15, 16, 17,** 19, 21, **22, 23, 25,** I Peter 2:17, I Peter 3:8, 10, I John 2:5, verse 15, I John 3:1, 11, **14, 16,** 17, 23, I John 4:7, 8, 9, 10, 11, 12, 16, 17, 18, 19, 20, 21, I John 5:2, 3, II John 1:1, 3, 5, Ephesians 3:12, III John 1:1, Jude 1:2, **Revelation 2:4, Revelation 3:19** (Proverbs 13:10), II Corinthians 13:11

4. Blessed are the poor in spirit to those who believe in Christ's **Peace. Mark 4:39,** Mark 5:34, Mark 9:50, **Luke 1:79, Luke 2:14, Luke 4:35, Luke 7:50, Luke 8:48,** Luke 10:5, 6, Luke 14:32, Luke 18:39, Luke 19:38, Luke 19:40, 42, Luke 20:26, Luke 24:36, **John 14:21, John 16:33, John 20:19, 21, 26,** Acts 10:36 **(Philippians 2:6-11 verse 10-11),** Acts 11:18, Acts 12:17, **Acts 18:9,** Romans 1:7, Romans 2:10, **Romans 5:1, Romans 8:6, Romans 10:15,** Romans 14:17, 19, **Romans 15:13, 33, Romans 16:20,** I Corinthians 1:3, **I Corinthians 7:15,** I Corinthians 14:30, **I Corinthians 14:33,** I Corinthians 16:11, II Corinthians 1:2, II Corinthians 13:11, Galatians 1:3, **Galatians 5:22,** Galatians 6:16, Ephesians 1:2, Ephesians 2:13-14, 15, 17, Ephesians 4:3, Ephesians 6:15(Isaiah 52:6, Romans 10:15), Ephesians 6:23, Philippians 1:2, **Philippians 4:7, 9,** Colossians 1:2, **20,** Colossians 3:15, I Thessalonians 1:1, I Thessalonians 5:13, **I Thessalonians 5:23**, II Thessalonians 1:2, II Thessalonians 3:16, I Timothy 1:2, II Timothy 1:2, II Timothy 2:22, Titus 1:4, Philemon 1:3, **Hebrews 7:2, Hebrews 11:31, Hebrews 17:14,** Hebrews 13:20, James 2:16, James 3:18, I Peter 1:2, I Peter 3:11, I Peter 5:14, II Peter 1:2, II Peter 3:14, II John 1:3, III John 1:4, Jude 1:4, Revelation 1:14, Revelation 6:4
5. Blessed are the poor in spirit to those who believe in Christ's **Patience.** II Thessalonians 3:5, I Timothy 6:11, **Luke 8:15,** Romans 5:1-4, **Romans 8:25-28 verse 25,** Romans 15:4, 5, II Corinthians 6:4, II Corinthians 12:12, Colossians 1:11, I Thessalonians 1:3, II Thessalonians 1:4, I Timothy 6:11, II Timothy 3:10, Titus 2:2, Hebrews 6:12, Hebrews 10:36, **Hebrews 12:1, James 1:3, 4,** James 5:7, 10, 11 (Job 1:22, Job 2:1-13, Job 37:1-24, Job 38:1-41, Job 39:1-30, Job 40:24, Job 41:1-34, Job 42:1-17), II Peter 1:6, **Revelation 1:9, Revelation 2:2, 3, 19,**

Revelation 3:10, Revelation 13:10, Revelation 14:12 Do you have patience to wait for Christ? Or Are we acting like Job?

6. Blessed are the poor in spirit to those who believe in Christ's **Grace. II Corinthians 12:9,** Luke 2:40, **John 1:14, 16, 17, Acts 4:33, Acts 11:23,** Acts 13:43, Acts 14:3, 26, **Acts 14:11,** Acts 15:40, **Acts 18:27-28, Acts 20:24, 32, Acts 20:35, Romans 3:2, 15-21,** Romans 6:1, **14,** 15, Romans 15:15, Romans 16:20, 24, I Corinthians 1:3-10 verse 3, 4, I Corinthians 15:10, I Corinthians 16:23, II Corinthians 1:2, 12, II Corinthians 6:1-2 (Isaiah 49:8), II Corinthians 8:1, 6, 7, 9, 19, II Corinthians 9:8, 14, II Corinthians 13:14, Galatians 1:3, 15, Galatians 6:18, Ephesians 1:2, **Ephesians 1:7, Ephesians 2:5, 7, 8,** Ephesians 3:6-12, Ephesians 4:7, **29,** Ephesians 6:24, Philippians 1:2, 7, Philippians 4:23, Colossians 1:2, **Colossians 3:16, Colossians 4:6, 18,** I Thessalonians 1:1, I Thessalonians 5:28, II Thessalonians 1:2, 12, **II Thessalonians 2:16,** II Thessalonians 3:18, I Timothy 1:2, 13-14, I Timothy 6:21, II Timothy 1:2, 9, II Timothy 2:1, II Timothy 4:22 Titus 1:4, **Titus 2:11-15 verse 11,** Titus 3:7, 15, Philemon 1:3, 25, **Hebrews 2:9,** Hebrews 4:16, **Hebrews 10:29, Hebrews 12:15,** Hebrews 12:28, Hebrews 13:9, 25, **James 4:6,** I Peter 1:2, 10, 13, I Peter 3:7, I Peter 4:10, **I Peter 5:5, 10, 12,** II Peter 1:2, II Peter 3:18, II John 1:3, Revelation 1:4, Jude 1:4, Revelation 22:21
7. Blessed are the poor in spirit to those who believe in Christ's **Mercy. Matthew 5:7, Matthew 9:13,** Matthew 9:27, **Matthew 12:7,** Matthew 15:22, Matthew 17:15, Matthew 20:30, 31, **Matthew 23:23,** Mark 10:47, Mark 10:48, Luke 1:50, **58, 72, 78,** Luke 10:37, Luke 16:24, Luke 17:13, Luke 18:38, Romans 9:15, **16,** 18, **Romans 11:31, 32, Romans 12:8,** Romans 15:9 (Psalm 18:49, Psalm 117:1), I Corinthians 7:25, II Corinthians 4:1, Galatians 6:16, **Ephesians 2:4,** Philippians 2:1, **Philippians 1:27** (God Is Still Good!!!), I Timothy 1:2, 13, 16, II Timothy 1:2, 16, 18, Titus 1:4, **Titus 3:5, Hebrews 4:16,** Hebrews 9:5, James 3:17, **I Peter 2:10,** II John 1:3, Jude 1:2, 21, I John 3:17
8. Blessed are the poor in spirit to those who believe that Christ is **Eternal Life. Jude 1:21,** Hebrews 9:12, Romans 5:21, Titus 3:6-8 verse 7, Deuteronomy 33:27, **Matthew 25:46, Mark 10:30, John 3:15, John 4:36, John 5:39, John 6:54, John 6:8,** John 10:28, John 12:25, John 17:2, 3, Acts 13:15-52 **verse 48, Romans 1:20,** Romans 2:7, **Romans 5:21, Romans 6:23,** Ephesians 3:11-21 verse 11, 15, I Timothy 1:17, **I Timothy 6:12, 19,** II Thessalonians 2:10, Titus 1:2, **Hebrews 5:9,** Hebrews 6:2, **Hebrews 9:12, Hebrews 9:14,** 15, I Peter 5:10, I John 1:2, **I John 2:25, I John 3:15, I John 5:11-13, I John 5:20**

9. Blessed are the poor in spirit to those who believe in Christ's **Truth.** John 1:14-18, Colossians 1:6, Luke 4:25, **Luke 9:27,** Luke 12:44, Luke 21:3, Luke 22:59, **John 1:14, 17,** John 3:21, **John 4:23-24,** John 5:33, **John 6:14,** John 7:40, **John 8:32,** 40, **44, 45, 46, John 14:16,** John 14:17, **John 15:26,** John 16:7, **John 16:13, John 17:17, 19, John 18:37, Acts 4:27, Acts 10:34,** Acts 26:25, **Romans 1:25,** Romans 9:1, Romans 15:8, **I Corinthians 14:25,** II Corinthians 4:2, **II Corinthians 6:7,** II Corinthians 11:10, **II Corinthians 13:8, Galatians 2:5,** Galatians 2:14, **Ephesians 1:13,** Ephesians 4:15, **Ephesians 4:21,** 25, Ephesians 6:14, **Philippians 1:18, Colossians 1:5, 6, I Thessalonians 2:13, II Thessalonians 2:13, I Timothy 2:4, I Timothy 2:7, I Timothy 3:15,** I Timothy 4:3, **II Timothy 2:15, II Timothy 3:7, 8,** II John 1:3, 4
10. Blessed are the poor in spirit to those who believe in Christ's **Forgiveness. Mark 3:29, Acts 5:31, Acts 13:38, Acts 26:18, Ephesians 1:7, Colossians 1:14, Daniel 9:9,** II Timothy 2:25-26 verse 25
11. Blessed are the poor in spirit to those who believe in Christ's **Redemption.** Psalm 49:8, Psalm 111:9, Jeremiah 32:7, 8, **Luke 2:38, Luke 21:28, Romans 3:24,** Romans 8:23, **I Corinthians 1:30, Ephesians 1:7, 14, Ephesians 4:30, Colossians 1:14, Hebrews 9:12,** Hebrews 9:15
12. Blessed are the poor in spirit to those who believe in Christ's **Repentance.** Matthew 3:8, **Matthew 9:13,** Mark 1:4, **Mark 2:17,** Luke 3:3, 8, **Luke 5:32, Luke 15:7,** Luke 24:47, Acts 5:31, **Acts 11:18, Acts 20:21, Acts 26:20,** II Corinthians 7:9-10, II Timothy 2:25, Hebrews 6:6, **II Peter 3:9**

Part DLXXXI

Blessed Are The Poor In Spirit. Matthew 5:3

Blessed Means Happy

Poor means meek in spirit. Poor means humble in spirit. Poor means lowly in spirit. Poor means quiet in spirit. Read Matthew 5:3-12, Read also Mark 1:15

Jesus did not say "*rich*" in spirit. Jesus said "*poor*" in spirit.

1. Blessed are the poor in spirit to those who believe that Once saved always saved mean man made doctrine rather than Jesus Christ whose promise is truth and faithful. John 14:6, Luke 18:9-14 verse 13; and he was justified (saved). Deuteronomy 18:15, John 1:45, Galatians 5:5, Titus 2:13
2. Blessed are the poor in spirit to those who believe that the Old Testament was promise to look **ahead** to Christ Jesus, The Blessed Hope, The Return of Christ
3. Blessed are the poor in spirit to those who believe that the New Testament is to look back or recall to Christ First Coming to earth which He did live for thirty-three years of His life on earth and to His First Coming back to earth again the second time or His Return. Hebrews 9:28, Revelation 22:20
4. Blessed are the poor in spirit to those who believe that God the Father Almighty through Jesus Christ and the Holy Spirit in all is it's assertions, in this we believe the Word of God, the Holy Scripture, which is the Holy Bible that is written by God only. II Timothy 3:16, Genesis 1:1, John 1:1-2, 17 verse 1-2, 14
5. Blessed are the poor in spirit to those who believe this scripture: He that hath an ear, let him hear what the Spirit (Christ) saith unto the churches; He that overcome (saved) shall not be hurt of the second death. Revelation 2:11
6. Blessed are the poor in spirit to those who believe that Jehovah mean the Lord. Psalm 83:18, Ezekiel 6:3, Isaiah 12:2, Isaiah 26:4, Judges 6:24, Exodus 6:3, Psalm 83:18, Isaiah 12:2, Isaiah 26:4, Judges 6:24
7. Blessed are the poor in spirit to those who believe that Jehovah mean God.
8. Blessed are the poor in spirit to those who believe God when He state that our bodies which came from the Christ, will return the spirit to Him who gave us our bodies and our spirit because they belong to Him who created us. Ecclesiastes 12:7, Genesis 1:26, 27, Genesis 5:2, Matthew 19:4, I Corinthians 11:9, Colossians 3:10

9. Blessed are the poor in spirit to those who able to call on His Name: "Jesus. Jesus. Jesus" for He shall save His people from their sins. Matthew 1:21, 25, Luke 1:31, Luke 2:21
10. Blessed are the poor in spirit to those who are able to call out His Name for salvation. Matthew 1:21, 25, Luke 1:31, Luke 2:21, See Joel 2:32, Acts 2:21, Romans 10:13, Romans 10:9, Romans 10:10, Acts 16:31, Ephesians 2:5, Ephesians 2:8, II Corinthians 6:2, Isaiah 49:8, Isaiah 55:6, Isaiah 45:22, Numbers 21:8-9, John 3:14-17 verse 14
11. Blessed are the poor in spirit to those who are able to call out His name for salvation: "Jesus Save Me!!!" Matthew 1:21, 25, Luke 1:31, Luke 2:21, See Joel 2:32, Acts 2:21, Romans 10:13, Romans 10:9, Romans 10:10, Acts 16:31, Ephesians 2:5, Ephesians 2:8, II Corinthians 6:2, Isaiah 49:8, Isaiah 55:6, Isaiah 45:22, Numbers 21:8-9, John 3:14-17 verse 14
12. Blessed are the poor in spirit to those who believe that salvation is for "S-I-N-N-E-R-S" Only; not for believers in Christ!!! See **Luke 18:13-14 verse 13.** Read these: Matthew 9:13, Mark 2:17, Luke 5:32, **Luke 15:7,** Luke 24:47, So Mr. And Mrs. Sinners, be saved today before it is too late. II Corinthians 6:2, Isaiah 49:8, Isaiah 45:22, II Chronicles 7:14

Part DLXXXII

Blessed Are The Poor In Spirit. Matthew 5:3

Blessed Means Happy

Poor means meek in spirit. Poor means humble in spirit. Poor means lowly in spirit. Poor means quiet in spirit. Read Matthew 5:3-12, Read also Mark 1:15

Jesus did not say "*rich*" in spirit. Jesus said "*poor*" in spirit.

1. Blessed are the poor in spirit to those who are able to sing: "We will lift up our hands. We will lift up our hearts. We will lift up our eyes. [Beyond the hill to where our help come from] Psalm 121:1-2, Psalm 124:8, Isaiah 41:13
2. Blessed are the poor in spirit to those who are able to sing: "[Our help come from you] We will lift up our hands. We will lift up our hearts. We will lift up our eyes. [Beyond the hill to where our help come from] Psalm 121:1-2, Psalm 124:8, Isaiah 41:13
3. Blessed are the poor in spirit to those who are able to sing: [We realize where our help come from. We will lift up our hands. We will lift up our hearts. We will lift up our eyes. [Beyond the hill to where our help come from] Psalm 121:1-2, Isaiah 41:13
4. Blessed are the poor in spirit to those who believe that there is no racial segregation in the Bible; Romans 5:8, Galatians 3:22-29 verse 28, John 3:16, I John 4:1
5. Blessed are the poor in spirit to those who believe that there is no segregation in the Bible. Romans 5:8, Galatians 3:22-29 verse 28, John 3:16, I John 4:1
6. Blessed are the poor in spirit to those who believe that **Noah** found **"Grace"** in the sight of God. **Genesis 6:8, 22,** Habakkuk 2:4, Romans 1:17, Galatians 3:11, Hebrews 10:38-39 verse 38
7. Blessed are the poor in spirit to those who believe that Faith mean upside down. Habakkuk 2:4, Romans 1:17, Galatians 3:11, Hebrews 10:38, II Corinthians 5:7, Romans 10:17
8. Blessed are the poor in spirit to those who believe that dying is not a game to play with and that death is a serious threaten beyond our future control because once to die, there is judgment come at the Hand of God on Judgment Day. I Corinthians 15:54-57, Isaiah 25:28, Romans 14:10, II Corinthians 5:10, **Hebrews**

9:27, 28, I Peter 4:17-19, II Peter 2:4, 9, II Peter 2:1-9 verse 3, 4, 9, Ecclesiastes 3:2, Matthew 5:21, 22, Matthew 10:15, Matthew 11:22, 24, Matthew 12:36, Luke 10:14, John 5:22, 27, 30

9. Blessed are the poor in spirit to those who believe in wearing the cross as the symbol of their faith in Jesus Christ because of Christ's Calvary or the Cross or to be crucified that He died, near the place of Golgotha; Matthew 27:33, Mark 15:22, John 19:17, Luke 23:33, **Matthew 10:38—Red Print By Jesus, Matthew 16:24,** Matthew 27:32, 40, 42, **Mark 8:34, Mark 10:21,** Mark 15:21, 30, 32, **Luke 9:23, Luke 14:27,** Luke 23:26, John 19:19, 25, 31, I Corinthians 1:17, 18, Galatians 6:12, 14, Ephesians 2:16, Philippians 2:8, Philippians 3:18, Colossians 1:20, Colossians 2:14, Hebrews 12:2, Acts 2:23, 36, Acts 4:10, Acts 10:36, Philippians 2:11, I Corinthians 2:2, 8, Galatians 2:20, Revelation 11:8
10. Blessed are the poor in spirit to those who believe that Pentecost first returned on April 9, 1906 in Los Angeles, California pastored by Bishop William J. Seymour following in the book of Act of the Pattern Faith since on the Day of Pentecost. Acts 2:1, Acts 20:16 and I Corinthians 16:8, where Apostle Peter preached the Pentecostal Message that 3, 000 souls was saved that day. Acts 2:41-47 verse 41
11. Blessed are the poor in spirit to those who believe that the God, the Father, in the founder of this old age of the earth. I Corinthians 10:26
12. Blessed are the poor in spirit to those who want to love Christ is to know Christ. Philippians 3:10

Part DLXXXIII

Blessed Are The Poor In Spirit. Matthew 5:3

Blessed Means Happy

Poor means meek in spirit. Poor means humble in spirit. Poor means lowly in spirit. Poor means quiet in spirit. Read Matthew 5:3-12, Read also Mark 1:15

Jesus did not say "*rich*" in spirit. Jesus said "*poor*" in spirit.

1. Blessed are the poor in spirit to those who believe that Salvation mean Jesus. Acts 4:12
2. Blessed are the poor in spirit to those who believe that Salvation mean the Savior. Luke 2:11, John 14:42, I John 4:9, 14
3. Blessed are the poor in spirit to those who trust the Lord as their personal Savior and Lord. Psalm 2:12, Psalm 4:5, Psalm 7:1, Psalm 11:1, Psalm 16:1, Psalm 18:2, Psalm 18:30, Proverbs 3:5, Psalm 118:8-9, Psalm 115:11, Psalm 56:4, 11, Psalm 62:8, Psalm 64:20, Psalm 71:1, 5, Psalm 73:28, Psalm 91:2, 4, Isaiah 26:4, Matthew 12:21, Romans 15:12
4. Blessed are the poor in spirit to those who believe in the rapture of the Church at Christ Coming. I Thessalonians 4:13-17 verse 14, 15, **16, 17**
5. Blessed are the poor in spirit to those who believe and are able to say, **"Only Believe."** Mark 5:36
6. Blessed are the poor in spirit to those who believe and are able to say with sincerely tears: "Lord, I believe: help Thou mine unbelief." Mark 9:24
7. Blessed are the poor in spirit to those who believe that to know **Jesus** is to love **Him** because **He** is **God** and that the whole world need to know who **Jesus really is. John 14:7-9, Hebrews 13:8**, Genesis 1:1, John 1:1-18, **Philippians 3:10**, I Timothy 3:16, Acts 9:3-5, Acts 22:7, Acts 26:14, I John 5:20, Isaiah 52:6, John 4:25-26, John 9:36-38 verse 37, Matthew 3:15, Matthew 28:18-20, I Peter 2:21, John 13:15, Acts 17:29, Romans 1:20, Colossians 1:2, 9, II Corinthians 13:14
8. Blessed are the poor in spirit to those who want to believe that we did not hear from God, we did not hear from Christ and we did not hear from the Holy Spirit, but the Holy Bible speak true to us, that God hear us all, therefore we cry, "A'bba Father." Romans 8:15, Galatians 4:6, Genesis 1:1, Romans 10:17,

John 1:1-14, II Timothy 3:16, Romans 8:16, I Corinthians 2:7-13 verse 9, Isaiah 64:4

9. Blessed are the poor in spirit to those who believe that Jesus is **not a lesser man** because **Jesus is God Himself**. John 14:7, 8, 9, Hebrews 13:8
10. Blessed are the poor in spirit to those who believe that Jesus Christ is the Son of God. Acts 9:20, Acts 8:37, I John 5:9-13, I John 5:1-21 verse 1, 4, 5, 7, 8, 9-13, I John 4:10, 14, 15, Luke 1:35, Matthew 3:17, Psalm 2:7, Isaiah 42:1, Matthew 12:17, Mark 1:11, Mark 9:7, John 17:4, Matthew 17:5, Acts 13:33, Hebrews 1:5, Hebrews 5:5, Matthew 12:18, Luke 3:22, Luke 9:35, Revelation 2:18
11. Blessed are the poor in spirit to those who believe that Christ lives, we will also live with Him. John 14:19
12. Blessed are the poor in spirit to those who believe that Revelation represent the Revealing of Christ. Revelation 1:1-2, 5, Isaiah 9:6

Part DLXXXIV

Blessed Are The Poor In Spirit. Matthew 5:3

Blessed Means Happy

Poor means meek in spirit. Poor means humble in spirit. Poor means lowly in spirit. Poor means quiet in spirit. Read Matthew 5:3-12, Read also Mark 1:15

Jesus did not say "*rich*" in spirit. Jesus said "*poor*" in spirit.

1. Blessed are the poor in spirit to those who believe in **Eternal Salvation** *rather than loosing Eternal Salvation* (once saved always saved). Matthew 25:46, Mark 10:26-30 verse 30, John 3:15, John 4:36, John 6:54, 68, John 10:28, John 12:25-33 verse 25, John 17:2, 3, Acts 13:14-48 verse 48, Romans 2:7, Romans 5:1-21 verse 21, Romans 6:23, Romans 6:1-23 verse 23, Ephesians 3:11-12, I Timothy 1:11-17 verse 17, I Timothy 6:12, 19, II Timothy 2:10, **Titus 1:2, Titus 3:7, Hebrews 5:9**
2. Blessed are the poor in spirit to those who believe that *loosing Eternal Salvation* is a *dangerous belief.* Philippians 2:12, Hebrews 10:29-39 verse 31, 38, 39, Galatians 5:4
3. Blessed are the poor in spirit to those who believe that our word to God is not yea or yes, or nay or no, or maybe or maybe not, but our word to God is, "*Yes Lord*" to **His will** *according to His promise is Amen.* II Corinthians 1:17-20 verse 19-20, I John 5:14, Mark 11:22 (John 1:6), Matthew 6:8, Matthew 7:7-11, Matthew 8:19-20, Matthew 20:22, 23, Mark 10:38-40, Luke 11:9-13, John 14:13-14, John 15:7, 16, John 16:23-24, 26, John 18:20-21, Ephesians 3:20-21, James 1:5, 6, I John 3:22, I John 5:15, 16, II Peter 3:9-10, I Corinthians 2:14
4. Blessed are the poor in spirit to those who believe that the Bible is alive; that the Bible speak our language to us, that the Bible has feet to walk near us; that the Bible run after us; that the Bible has hands; that the Bible lay hold of us; that the Bible, which is of God; that the Bible, which is of Jesus Christ; that the Bible, which is of the Holy Spirit to grasp us. Genesis 1:1-2, John 1:1-18, II Timothy 3:16-17, II Corinthians 13:14, Ephesians 3:9-21, Deuteronomy 8:3, Luke 4:3, Matthew 4:4, Psalm 119:6, Hebrews 4:12, I Peter 1:22-23, I Timothy 3:16, Acts 1:9-11, Mark 16:9, Exodus 3:6-15, Isaiah 52:6, John 4:23-26, John

9:36-37, John 8:56-58, John 10:33, John 19:7, Luke 23:2, Matthew 28:18-20, John 14:1-12 verse 6-9, John 5:22-27, John 14:6, Revelation 3:20, Matthew 11:28-30, Mark 1:15, Matthew 3:2, II Peter 3:9, II Corinthians 7:10, I Timothy 2:4, Matthew 4:17, Matthew 17:5, Mark 9:7, Luke 9:35, Psalm 51:11, Isaiah 63:10-11, Acts 17:29, Romans 1:20, Colossians 2:9, Matthew 3:6-9, Luke 3:7-8, Matthew 23:33-39, Psalm 104:33, Acts 17:27-30, Philippians 3:10, Hebrews 2:1-18

5. Blessed are the poor in spirit to those who believe that the joy of the Lord Jesus is my strength. Nehemiah 8:10
6. Blessed are the poor in spirit to those who believe that the **Bold Word** stand **For The Gospel**; That The **Bold World** stand **For God**; That The **Bold Word** stand **For Jesus**; That The **Bold Word** stand **For The Holy Spirit** and That The **Bold Word** stand **For Surely** and That The **Bold Word** stand **Forever.** That The **Bold Word** stand **For Promise.** Genesis 1:1, John 1:1, II Timothy 4:2, I John 5:20, Hebrews 13:8, Revelation 22:20, Acts 12:11, Hebrews 7:22, II Peter 1:19, Romans 2:2, Acts 13:34, John 16:30, John 6:69, II Timothy 2:19, Psalm 19:7, Isaiah 28:16, Isaiah 32:18, Isaiah 55:3, Daniel 2:45, Genesis 15:1, 4, Numbers 22:35, 38, Numbers 23:5, 16, Deuteronomy 8:3, Deuteronomy 9:5, Deuteronomy 18:20, 21, Deuteronomy 30:14 (Romans 10:8), Deuteronomy 34:1-12 verse 4-5, I Samuel 3:1-18 verse 4, 6, 7, 8, 10-14, 21 (Himself), I Samuel 9:27, I Samuel 15:10-11, 23, 26, II Samuel 7:4-17, II Samuel 21:1, II Samuel 23:1-4, II Samuel 23:31, II Samuel 23:2, II Samuel 24:11-12, 16, I Kings 2:4, 42, I Kings 1:11-14, I Kings 8:15-20, 25-26, **56,** I kings 12:22-24
7. Blessed are the poor in spirit to those who believe that the **Word** speak to us. Genesis 15:1, 4, Number 22:35, 38, Numbers 23:5, 16, Deuteronomy 8:3, Deuteronomy 9:5, Deuteronomy 18:20, 21, Deuteronomy 30:14 (Romans 10:8), Deuteronomy 34:1-12 verse 4-5, I Samuel 8:1-18 verse 4, 6, 7, 8, 10-14, 21 (Himself), I Samuel 9:27, I Samuel 15:10-11, 23, 26, II Samuel 7:4-17, II Samuel 21:1, II Samuel 23:1-4, II Samuel 22:31, II Samuel 23:2, II Samuel 24:11-12, 16, I Kings 2:4, 42, I Kings 6:11-14, I Kings 8:15-20, 25-26, **56**, I Kings 12:22-24
8. Blessed are the poor in spirit to those who believe that **"Christ"** stand For **"Son Of God"—Luke 1:35, Acts 8:37,** John 1:49, Isaiah 7:10, Isaiah 9:6, Matthew 1:23, Jude 1:25, John 19:7, John 20:28, **Acts 9:4-5, 20, 22, Acts 18:5, 28,** I John 5:20, Hebrews 13:8, II Peter 3:2, 18, II Peter 1:1, 11, II Peter 2:20, Titus

1:3, 4, Titus 2:10, 13, Titus 3:4, 6, II Timothy 1:10, Philippians 3:20, Acts 13:23, Acts 5:31, John 4:42, Luke 2:11, Luke 1:47, Isaiah 43:3, Isaiah 49:26, Isaiah 60:16, Isaiah 63:8, **Matthew 26:63,** Matthew 27:43, 54, Matthew 28:19, Mark 1:11, Mark 3:11, Mark 10:47, Mark 10:48, Mark 12:35-37, Mark 14:61, Mark 15:39, Luke 1:32, **35**, Luke 4:3, 9, Luke 4:22, 41, Luke 8:28, Luke 18:38-39, Luke 20:41, Luke 22:70, **John 1:34,** 45, **49,** Luke 6:69, John 9:35, 36, **John 11:4, 27, John 19:7, John 20:31, Acts 9:20, Romans 1:4, II Corinthians 1:19, Galatians 2:20, Ephesians 4:13, Hebrews 4:14, Hebrews 7:3, Hebrews 10:29,** I John 1:7, I John 2:22, 23, 24, **I John 3:8,** I John 4:15, I John 5:5, 10, 11, **12, 13, 20, II John 1:9—Christ, Revelation 2:18,** Revelation 14:14

9. Blessed are the poor in spirit to those who believe that when **Jesus spoke the Word;** when **Jesus** *knew* too much, when Jesus *knew* so much; when **Jesus prophesied exactly;** when **Jesus performed some miracles;** when **Jesus** need no one else to tell Him what to do; what to believe; what to suggest; **we had no doubt** at all that **Jesus is, was and has always been existed in the past that He is indeed God Himself the Father, Almighty; the One True God; the One and Only, the One and the Same, Jesus is God always, always, always** that there is **no beginnings, no ending. He has always been existence. Some glorious day** we as God's children will **see Him as He is.** John 17:3, Romans 3:4, II Corinthians 1:18, I Thessalonians 1:9, I John 5:20, Revelation 19:9, 11, Revelation 21:5, Revelation 22:6-7, Revelation 22:20-21, Isaiah 52:6, John 4:26, John 9:37, Acts 17:29, Romans 1:20, Colossians 2:9, Genesis 1:1, John 1:1, John 1:1-18, II Timothy 3:16, John 14:6-12, John 14:7-9, Romans 8:21, Luke 23:8, John 6:14, Hebrews 13:8, John 10:41, John 12:18, Revelation 1:7, 8, 17-18, Revelation 4:9, Revelation 16:15, Revelation 3:11, John 8:56-58, Exodus 3:6, 14-15, Matthew 22:32, Mark 12:26-27, Luke 20:37, Mark 12:32, John 10:30, Revelation 1:11, Colossians 3:4, Hebrews 9:28, I Peter 5:4, I John 2:28, I John 3:2, Isaiah 53:4-5, Isaiah 7:14, Isaiah 9:6, Matthew 1:21, 23, 25, Luke 2:10-11, 22, Mark 3:21, **(Luke 23:2—Himself), (John 5:18—Himself), (John 21:14—Himself), (Acts 1:3—Himself), (John 10:33—Claim Himself) (John 19:7—They said He made Himself), (John 19:7, 12—Himself), John 19:12, (John 21:1—Himself),** Acts 9:4-5, 22, Acts 18:5, 25, **(II Corinthians 5:18, 19—Himself By Jesus Christ), (II Corinthians 5:19—God was in Christ Himself), (Galatians 1:2-4 verse 4—Himself), (Galatians 2:20—Faith of the Son of God, Christ Himself), (Ephesians 1:5, 9—Jesus Christ**

to Himself), (Ephesians 2:20—Himself), (Ephesians 5:2, 25, 27—Himself, Christ Himself), (Hebrews 2:18—Himself), (Philippians 2:8—Himself), (Philippians 3:21—Himself), (Colossians 1:20—Himself), (I Thessalonians 3:11—Himself God), (I Thessalonians 4:16—Himself Lord), (Acts 9:5 Jesus Same Lord), (II Thessalonians 2:16-17—Himself), (II Thessalonians 3:16—Himself), (I Timothy 2:6—Himself), (II Timothy 2:13—Himself), (Titus 2:14—Himself), (Hebrews 1:3—Himself), (Hebrews 2:14, 18—Himself), (Hebrews 5:5-14 verse 5—Himself), (Hebrews 7:27—Himself), (Hebrews 9:14, 25, 26—Himself), (Hebrews 12:1-3—Himself), (Revelation 19:12—Himself), (Revelation 11:3—Himself God)

10. Blessed are the poor in spirit to those who believe that when all else fail, try reading the Holy Bible's instruction, God's Holy instruction, Christ's instruction, the Holy Spirit's instruction. II Timothy 3:16, Genesis 1:1, John 1:1, John 1:1-8, Exodus 3:6-15, Psalm 51:11, Isaiah 63:10-11, Isaiah 52:6, John 4:26, John 5:18, Luke 23:2, John 10:30, 33, John 19:7, Hebrews 13:8, John 14:6-12, John 14:6, I John 5:20, Acts 1:11, Hebrews 9:28, I Timothy 3:16, I Thessalonians 4:13-18, Revelation 1:7-8, 11, 17-18, Revelation 2:8, Revelation 3:11, Revelation 16:15, Revelation 22:7, 12-13, 16, 20-21, Acts 17:24, Acts 17:29, Romans 1:20, Colossians 2:9, Exodus 33:20, Matthew 22:32, Mark 12:26-27, Luke 20:37-38, John 14:1-4, II Peter 1:20-21, Philippians 3:10, Mark 16:19-20, Acts 1:9, I Corinthians 15:4, Daniel 7:13, Zechariah 12: 10, Amos 4:12, Isaiah 44:2, 6, Isaiah 48:12, Isaiah 40:10, Isaiah 11:1, Matthew 1:1, Philippians 2:11, Acts 10:36, Romans 9:15, Exodus 37:19, I John 4:12, I Corinthians 2:9, Hosea 6:2, Luke 24:46, Matthew 24:30, Matthew 26:64, 65, Mark 13:36, Mark 14:62, 64, John 19:37, Isaiah 55:6, Isaiah 45:22, Isaiah 64:6-9, Mark 14:53-64, Leviticus 24:16, II Corinthians 13:14 *Notice* **this "He"** *is from* **Genesis to Revelation:** Read *Hebrews 13:8*
11. Blessed are the poor in spirit to those who believe that our future scholar kids get a chance to enter any universities or colleges for their future jobs or professional or on the job sites. Galatians 3:23-25, I Chronicles 25:7-8, Acts 19:9, James 1:17, John 15:5, Mark 9:29, John 5:19-20, 30, John 6:63, John 8:28-36 verse 28 *God said to me recently* that I would get a doctorate degree. I laughed. I will soon get my degree from Bible Institutes and Seminary in Houston, Texas. It is getting close I will be getting a doctorate degree for hard work through the years. *For Forty-five years* is a long time. *I got serious forty-two years ago* when I entered the

Tennessee Temple University and continue to study for more further education after I had graduated from the *37 years ago* on the doctrine of the Holy Spirit and other interest topic and Christians books and their testimonies concerning the Baptizing in the Holy Spirit seven years ago. My goal would to get a doctorate degree. It is almost coming true. It is my dream to get a doctorate degree. God answered my prayer when I do not know how it work. I *only knew through hard work*. It stated to be *15 years to 20 years of experience*. When I was in my forty, my mother explained to me that if I'd pastor my father's church, I would be the next Bishop of his church. My dream did come true but I decline. I just want to do God's will by continuing my Christian education for further studies. See Psalm 143:10, Psalm 40:8, Hebrews 10:7. So I stay in God's Will for 45 years.

12. Blessed are the poor in spirit to those who believe that **Only Man** should die for the people; only **One Man; That Man is Jesus Christ**. John 11:50, 51

Part DLXXXV

Blessed Are The Poor In Spirit. Matthew 5:3

Blessed Means Happy

Poor means meek in spirit. Poor means humble in spirit. Poor means lowly in spirit. Poor means quiet in spirit. Read Matthew 5:3-12, Read also Mark 1:15

Jesus did not say "*rich*" in spirit. Jesus said "*poor*" in spirit.

1. Blessed are the poor in spirit to those who believe that our Lord Jesus Christ is our advocate. I John 2:1-2, John 8:32, 36
2. Blessed are the poor in spirit to those who believe that our Lord Jesus Christ is our lawyer. I John 2:1-2, John 8:32, 36
3. Blessed are the poor in spirit to those who believe that our Lord Jesus Christ is our attorney. I John 2:1-2, John 8:32, 36
4. Blessed are the poor in spirit to those who believe that our Lord Jesus Christ is our procurator. I John 2:1-2, John 8:32, 36
5. Blessed are the poor in spirit to those who believe that our Lord Jesus Christ is our Chief Executive. I John 2:1-2, John 8:32, 36
6. Blessed are the poor in spirit to those who believe that our Lord Jesus Christ is our Chief Justice. I John 2:1-2, John 8:32, 36
7. Blessed are the poor in spirit to those who believe that our Lord Jesus Christ is our Agent. I John 2:1-2
8. Blessed are the poor in spirit to those who believe that our Lord Jesus Christ is our power of attorney. I John 2:1-2, John 8:32, 36
9. Blessed are the poor in spirit to those who believe that only God can turn a **Mess** into a **Mess***age*. I John 3:11, I John 1:5
10. Blessed are the poor in spirit to those who believe that only God can turn a **Test** into a **Test***imony*. Luke 21:10-17 verse 13
11. Blessed are the poor in spirit to those who believe that only God can turn a **Tri** into a **Tri***umph*. II Corinthians 2:14

Part DLXXXVI

Blessed Are The Poor In Spirit. Matthew 5:3

Blessed Means Happy

Poor means meek in spirit. Poor means humble in spirit. Poor means lowly in spirit. Poor means quiet in spirit. Read Matthew 5:3-12, Read also Mark 1:15

Jesus did not say "*rich*" in spirit. Jesus said "*poor*" in spirit.

1. Blessed are the poor in spirit to those who believe that God is good all the time because His mercy is endure for ever. Psalm 34:8, I Peter 2:3, Psalm 86:56, Psalm 100:5, Psalm 106:1, Psalm 107:1, Psalm 118:1, 29, Psalm 135:3, Psalm 136:1, Psalm 145:9, Psalm 136:15, 16, 26, Psalm 138:8, Jeremiah 33:11, John 6:27, I Peter 1:25
2. Blessed are the poor in spirit to those who believe that Christian stand for Jesus Christ. I Peter 2:21
3. Blessed are the poor in spirit to those who believe that the Flag of the United States of America stand for peace, love and trust. Psalm 33:12, Psalm 43:1, Psalm 83:4, Psalm 105:13, Psalm 106:5
4. Blessed are the poor in spirit to those who believe that to stand for justice, truth and freedom. Psalm 33:12, Psalm 43:1, Psalm 83:4, Psalm 105:13, Psalm 106:5 God bless our America as well as other nations.
5. Blessed are the poor in spirit to those who believe that Flag of the United State of America pledge one nation, indivisible under God with liberty and justice for all. Psalm 83:4, Psalm 105:13, Psalm 106:5, God bless our America as well as other nations. Psalm 33:12
6. Blessed are the poor in spirit to those who believe that the **Finished Work On Calvary is salvation.** John 19:30, I Peter 2:24, Isaiah 53:5
7. Blessed are the poor in spirit to those who believe that **sanctification** is **salvation** in Jesus Christ through grace and faith. I Corinthians 1:30, Acts 26:18, Romans 6:23, Ephesians 2:5, 8, John 17:16-18 verse 17, 19, 20, I Thessalonians 5:23, Jude 1:1, Hebrews 2:11, Hebrews 13:12, Romans 15:16, I Corinthians 6:4, I Corinthians 1:2, Hebrews 10:10, 14, II Thessalonians 2:13, I Peter 1:2, I Thessalonians 4:3-4, I Timothy 4:1-5

8. Blessed are the poor in spirit to those who believe that **Justification** is **salvation. Romans 1:17, Romans 4:25, Hebrews 4:2,** Galatians 3:11, I Corinthians 6:11, Galatians 2:16, Romans 5:11, 16, 18, Hebrews 10:38
9. Blessed are the poor in spirit to those who believe that **repentance** toward God and faith toward Jesus Christ our Lord is **salvation. Acts 11:18, Acts 20:21,** Acts 26:20, II Corinthians 7:10, Hebrews 6:6, II Peter 3:9, I Peter 1:5
10. Blessed are the poor in spirit to those who believe that **confession** with our mouth from **our heart** is **salvation.** Romans 10:10, I Peter 1:5, II Timothy 3:15
11. Blessed are the poor in spirit to those who believe that **salvation and faith** is through **Jesus Christ. Isaiah 45:22**, Acts 4:12, John 14:6, I Peter 1:5
12. Blessed are the poor in spirit to those who believe that **being born again** must go through Jesus Christ. John 3:3-7, I Peter 1:23, I Peter 1:3-4

Part DLXXXVII

Blessed Are The Poor In Spirit. Matthew 5:3

Blessed Means Happy

Poor means meek in spirit. Poor means humble in spirit. Poor means lowly in spirit. Poor means quiet in spirit. Read Matthew 5:3-12, Read also Mark 1:15

Jesus did not say "*rich*" in spirit. Jesus said "*poor*" in spirit.

1. Blessed are the poor in spirit to those who believe that we become the children of God; the sons of God; the daughters of God and the adoptions of God as His own children, and born of the Spirit. John 1:12, Romans 8:14-15, 19, Ephesians 3:15, I John 3:1-2, II Corinthians 6:18, Acts 2:17, Joel 2:28, Ephesians 1:5, I John 5:2, Matthew 5:9, 45, Luke 20:36, John 11:52, Romans 8:15-17, Galatians 4:5, 6 Acts 2:17, Philippians 2:15, Hebrews 2:10, Hebrews 12:7, John 3:8
2. Blessed are the poor in spirit to those who believe that **righteousness** in Jesus Christ is salvation. I Corinthians 1:30, I Peter 2:24, Romans 4:3
3. Blessed are the poor in spirit to those who believe that **redemption** through Jesus Christ is salvation. I Corinthians 1:30, Hebrews 9:12, Colossians 1:14, Ephesians 1:7, 14, Ephesians 4:30, Romans 3:24, Luke 2:38
4. Blessed are the poor in spirit to those who believe that **faith** in Jesus Christ is salvation. Romans 10:17
5. Blessed are the poor in spirit to those who believe that **grace** through Jesus Christ is salvation. Ephesians 2:5, 8, II Peter 3:18
6. Blessed are the poor in spirit to those who believe that **peace** come through Jesus Christ. I Peter 1:2, Romans 5:1, **Romans 14:17,** Galatians 5:22
7. Blessed are the poor in spirit to those who believe that **sanctification** mean to set apart for God's service. Romans 12:1-2, II Timothy 2:21
8. Blessed are the poor in spirit to those who believe that **regeneration** of the Holy Spirit is salvation. Titus 3:4-7, Matthew 19:28
9. Blessed are the poor in spirit to those who believe that **grace and peace** mean salvation through the knowledge of God and of Jesus our Lord. II Peter 1:2-4
10. Blessed are the poor in spirit to those who believe that **sanctification** mean holiness, becoming holy set apart for holy use or separation from the world

consecration, completely, vessel, sacred, special purpose for work and service, God's purpose according to Romans 8:28, special use, of God, serving God's for good works created in Jesus Christ, to walk in them, God's workmanship. Ephesians 2:10, Romans 12:1, John 17:17, 19, Hebrews 10:10, I Corinthians 1:30, I Peter 1:15-16, Hebrews 12:14, John 10:36, I Thessalonians 5:23, I Peter 2:9, Ephesians 1:4

11. Blessed are the poor in spirit to those who believe that **Hope** in Jesus Christ is salvation. I John 3:3, **Romans 15:13,** I Peter 1:3-4
12. Blessed are the poor in spirit to those who believe that **Joy in Jesus Christ** is salvation. Galatians 5:22-23, Matthew 25:21, 23, Luke 1:14, Luke 2:10, Luke 6:23, Luke 8:13, Luke 15:7, 10, Luke 24:41, 52, John 3:29, John 15:11, John 16:20, 22, 24, **John 17:13,** Acts 8:8, Acts 13:52, Acts 20:24, **Romans 5:11, Romans 14:17,** Romans 15:13, Galatians 5:22, Philippians 4:1, I Thessalonians 1:6, Philemon 1:20, Hebrews 12:2, Hebrews 13:17, James 1:2, I Peter1:8, I Peter 4:13, I John 1:1-4, Jude 1:24

Part DLXXXVIII

Blessed Are The Poor In Spirit. Matthew 5:3

Blessed Means Happy

Poor means meek in spirit. Poor means humble in spirit. Poor means lowly in spirit. Poor means quiet in spirit. Read Matthew 5:3-12, Read also Mark 1:15

Jesus did not say "*rich*" in spirit. Jesus said "*poor*" in spirit.

1. Blessed are the poor in spirit to those who believe in the atonement of Joy in God through our Lord Jesus Christ. Romans 5:11
2. Blessed are the poor in spirit to those who believe that **"Power"** is the **Baptism of the Holy Spirit through witnessing of Jesus Christ.** Acts 1:8 **Beginning The Old Testament Period:**
3. Blessed are the poor in spirit to those who believe that **"Genesis"** mean a beginning of God's Creation; God's Original Written Word. Genesis 1:1, John 1:1-2, II Timothy 3:16
4. Blessed are the poor in spirit to those who believe that **"Genesis"** could also mean God's Creation". Genesis 1:31 to Genesis 3:1-24
5. Blessed are the poor in spirit to those who believe in Moses' Time that **"Exodus"** means to leave the country; to exist; to go out, to leave; to move; to exile, to depart from Egypt unto the Promise Land. Exodus Chapters 1:22 through Chapters 40:1-38
6. Blessed are the poor in spirit to those who believe that **"Leviticus"** mean belong to the Israelite priests who were Levities and the ministry of these priests is discussed Leviticus also mean making law to live by, rule to settle the debate and marriage etc. Leviticus 1:1-17 through Leviticus 27:1-34
7. Blessed are the poor in spirit to those who believe that **"Numbers"** mean to count. It is stated the Numbers get it's name from two censuses of the nations. Numbers as it's count also knowing how many go to war to fight for their nation of Israel. Numbers 1:1-54 through Numbers 36:1-13
8. Blessed are the poor in spirit to those who believe that **"Deuteronomy"** mean second law giving. Deuteronomy 1:1-46 through Deuteronomy 34:1-12

9. Blessed are the poor in spirit to those who believe that **"Joshua"** is the life of his story as the chief character and a second command or general of the army with the nation of Israel. Read his life story. Joshua 1:1-18 through Joshua 24:1-33
10. Blessed are the poor in spirit to those who believe that **"Judges"** mean the judges of Israel when there war no central government at that time. Judges 1:1-36 through Judges 21:1-25
11. Blessed are the poor in spirit to those who believe that **"Ruth"** mean her character and her biographical life and love story of Ruth with her loving husband Boaz. Read her love story!!! Ruth 1:1-22 through Ruth 4:1-22
12. Blessed are the poor in spirit to those who believe **"I Samuel and II Samuel"** was the same character and life, and story of Samuel. Two books were named after him, who anointed the chief character of then King Saul and later King David as God's own man. Read I Samuel 1:1-28 through I Samuel 31:1-3 and II Samuel 1:1-27 through II Samuel 24:1-25

PART DLXXXIX

Blessed Are The Poor In Spirit. Matthew 5:3

Blessed Means Happy

Poor means meek in spirit. Poor means humble in spirit. Poor means lowly in spirit. Poor means quiet in spirit. Read Matthew 5:3-12, Read also Mark 1:15

Jesus did not say "*rich*" in spirit. Jesus said "*poor*" in spirit.

1. Blessed are the poor in spirit to those who believe that **"I Kings and II Kings"** was the same historical story concerning the history of different kings who ruled Israel and Judah. I Kings 1:1-53 through I Kings 22:1-53 and II Kings 1:1-16 through II Kings 25:1-30
2. Blessed are the poor in spirit to those who believe that **"I Chronicles and II Chronicles"** was the same name that wrote the entire history of God's people from Genesis through Kings. I Chronicles and II Chronicles mean "Newspaper" of the life and story of God's people. God's people were accounts for. I Chronicles 1:1-54 through I Chronicles 29:1-30 and II Chronicles 1:1-17 through II Chronicles 36:1-22
3. Blessed are the poor in spirit to those who believe that **"Ezra"** mean he was one of the books' Chief characters in his lifetime. It is stated that Ezra continued from exact place between I Chronicles and II Chronicles as it's ends. Read Ezra's short story and life. Ezra 1:1-11 through Ezra 10:1-44
4. Blessed are the poor in spirit to those who believe that **"Nehemiah"** mean that he was one of the books' chief character. It is stated that after twelve years the book of Ezra end with Ezra's return in the capital city of Jerusalem that Nehemiah's life began with receiving word about Jerusalem which was it's people in shambles both physically and spiritually and that Nehemiah's heart was broken as he went for many days and was granted permission to return to Jerusalem on a mission restoration. Read Nehemiah's short life and story. Nehemiah 1:1-11 through Nehemiah 13:1-31
5. Blessed are the poor in spirit to those who believe that **"Esther"** mean she was one of the books' chief character. With the help of her cousin, Mordeca, to help King Ahasuerus made a decision on selection as a queen to replace Queen Vashti,

as a result, Esther became Queen. Read the rest of Queen Esther's short story and life of her character. Esther 1:1-22 through Esther 9:1-32

6. Blessed are the poor in spirit to those who believe that **"Job"** mean he was one of the books chief character. Job had a wealthy and prosperous life on his farmland. He was upright with God. Satan came to destroy Job's life that made Job's life miserable. But God came and blessed Job. How great is our God!!! Read Job 1:1-22 through Job 42:1-17.
7. Blessed are the poor in spirit to those who believe that **"Psalms"** mean praise. **Psalms** mean hymn. **Psalms** mean to sing God's praises. Read from Psalm 1:1-6 throguh Psalm 150:1-6
8. Blessed are the poor in spirit to those who believe that **"Proverbs"** mean wisdom. **Proverbs** mean to get an understanding. **Proverbs** mean to apply to our life with wisdom and understandings. Read Proverbs 1:1-19 through Proverbs 31:1-31
9. Blessed are the poor in spirit to those who believe that **"Ecclesiastes"** mean a preacher of the gospel. Solomon looked back as a wasteful life as a preacher. It was past failures and apostasy in his life. He said, "Vanity of vanities; all is vanity (Ecclesiastes 1:2). Read Ecclesiastes 1:1-18 through Ecclesiastes 12:1-14
10. Blessed are the poor in spirit to those who believe that **"Song of Solomon"** is about love song. It mean the supreme song. Love song is about marriage, God's love for His people, the nation of Israel as its mission; and Christ's Love for His church. Read Song of Solomon 1:1-17 through Song of Solomon 8:1-14
11. Blessed are the poor in spirit to those who believe that **"Isaiah"** is name in his honor. He is the author and he is one of the prophets. It was about **Christ's Suffering** coming to Jerusalem. (Isaiah 53:1-12 verse 3-5, 8). Read Isaiah 1:1-31 through Isaiah 66:1-24
12. Blessed are the poor in spirit to those who believe that **"Jeremiah"** is name in his honor. He is the author and one of the prophets. It is the story about weeping for Jerusalem. Since Jeremiah wept, we believe that God also wept for the nation of Israel in the capital city of Jerusalem. Read Jeremiah 1:1-19 through Jeremiah 52:1-34

Part DXC

Blessed Are The Poor In Spirit. Matthew 5:3

Blessed Means Happy

Poor means meek in spirit. Poor means humble in spirit. Poor means lowly in spirit. Poor means quiet in spirit. Read Matthew 5:3-12, Read also Mark 1:15

Jesus did not say "*rich*" in spirit. Jesus said "*poor*" in spirit.

1. Blessed are the poor in spirit to those who believe that **"Lamentation"** takes it's name because of weeping; it's poetic lament about the destruction of Jerusalem. Lamentation is about Jeremiah who wept for the people of Jerusalem just as God wept for His. Read Lamentation short story. Lamentation 1:1-15 through Lamentation 5:1-22
2. Blessed are the poor in spirit to those who believe that **"Ezekiel"** is name in his honor. He is the author. He is one of the prophets. Ezekiel mean God's strengthen. God told Ezekiel to prophecy **these dry bones.** And he did as the Lord commanded him. (Ezekiel 37:1-14). Read Ezekiel 1:1-28 through Ezekiel 48:1-35
3. Blessed are the poor in spirit to those who believe that **"Daniel"** is one of the books' chief characters. He is the author. His book was name in his honor. Daniel mean "God is my judge." Daniel prophesied that he saw one like the Son of Man came with clouds of heaven, and came to the Ancient of days and they brought Him near before Him. One like the *Son of Man* represented **Jesus Christ.** (Daniel 7:13). Read Daniel 1:1-21 through Daniel 12:1-13
4. Blessed are the poor in spirit to those who believe that **"Hosea"** is name in his honor. He is the author. He is one of the prophets. He is one of the chief characters. He was a prophet with a broken heart. It is stated that Hosea married to Gomer. Read Hosea 1:1-11 through Hosea 14:1-9
5. Blessed are the poor in spirit to those who believe that **"Joel"** is name in his honor. He is the author. He is one of the prophets. Joel mean "Jehovah is God." It is states that Joel had been called the prophet because he prophesied about the coming of the Holy Spirit on the Day of Pentecost in the capital city of Jerusalem. (Joel 2:26-32). Read Joel 1:1-20 through Joel 3:1-21

6. Blessed are the poor in spirit to those who believe that **"Amos"** is name in his honor. He is the author. It is stated that Amos is often referred to as the "sycamore" grower from the south or "the herdsman of Tekoa. My favorite text to look at for years is *Amos 3:3* that read: "Can two walk together, except they be agreed?" Read Amos 1:1-15 through Amos 9:1-15
7. Blessed are the poor in spirit to those who believe that **"Obadiah"** is name in his honor. He is the author. Obadiah mean "servant of the Lord." Obadiah has 21 verses short. Read Obadiah 1:1-21
8. Blessed are the poor in spirit to those who believe that **"Jonah"** is name in his honor. He is the author. He is one of the chief character. Jonah was called of God to preach in Nineveh. Read his short life and story. Jonah 1:1-17 through Jonah 4:1-11
9. Blessed are the poor in spirit to those who believe that **"Micah"** is name in his honor. He is the author. Micah mean "Who is like Jehovah" He is one of the prophets. Read Micah 1:1-16 through Micah 7:1-20
10. Blessed are the poor in spirit to those who believe that **"Nahum"** is name in his honor. He is the author. Nahum mean "Comforter." He is one of the prophets. Read his short life story. Nahum 1:1-15 through Nahum 3:1-19
11. Blessed are the poor in spirit to those who believe that **"Habakkuk"** is name in his honor. He is the author. He is one of the prophets by God to warn the people of Judah of their Coming judgment. Habakkuk was told by God to write down the vision and make it plain upon the tables, that he may run that read it. Read his short story and his life. Habakkuk 1:1-17 through Habakkuk 3:1-19
12. Blessed are the poor in spirit to those who believe that **"Zephaniah"** is name in his honor. He is one of the prophets. It is stated that King Josiah was under the influence of the prophet Zephaniah when King Josiah began to be a very good king and institutes sweeping reforms. Read about Zephaniah's short story and his life. Zephaniah 1:1-18 through Zephaniah 3:1-20

Part DXCI

Blessed Are The Poor In Spirit. Matthew 5:3

Blessed Means Happy

Poor means meek in spirit. Poor means humble in spirit. Poor means lowly in spirit. Poor means quiet in spirit. Read Matthew 5:3-12, Read also Mark 1:15

Jesus did not say "*rich*" in spirit. Jesus said "*poor*" in spirit.

1. Blessed are the poor in spirit to those who believe that **"Haggai"** is name in his honor. He is the author. He is one of the prophets by the Spirit of the Lord coming upon prophet Haggai and prompt prophet Haggai to stir the people to rescue building the temple. Prophet Haggai was an old man at the time. Read his short story and his life. Haggai 1:1-15 through Haggai 2:1-23
2. Blessed are the poor in spirit to those who believe that **"Zechariah"** is name in his honor. He is the author. Zechariah mean "God Remember." Read Zechariah 1:1-21 through Zechariah 14:1-21. **"Holiness Unto The Lord."** Zechariah 14:20
3. Blessed are the poor in spirit to those who believe that **"Malachi"** is name in his honor. He is the author. Malachi mean "my messenger." That mean that John the Baptist who was the messenger to prepare the way of the Lord Jesus Christ's first coming to earth. Read Malachi 1:1-14 through Malachi 4:1-6.

End of the Old Testament Period!!!

Beginning Of The New Testament Period:

4. Blessed are the poor in spirit to those who believe that **"Matthew"** is name in his honor. He is the author. He is one of Jesus' original disciples. It is stated that 400 years later, the author of Matthew began to write the history of Jesus Christ because Matthew was the eye witnessed. Read the entire story of Matthew 1:1-25 to 25 through Matthew 28:1-20
5. Blessed are the poor in spirit to those who believe that **"Mark"** is name in his honor. He is the author. He write about Christ's deeds on earth. Mark was a

friend of Apostle Paul as a companion. Mark was an helper of Apostle Paul in Christ's ministry. Read about Jesus' deed upon earth. Mark 1:1-45 to Mark 16:1-20

6. Blessed are the poor in spirit to those who believe that **"Luke"** is name in his honor. He is the author. He also is the author of the book of Acts (will talk about it later). He is a friend and missionary companion of Apostle Paul. He was not a Jew, but he was a Gentile Christian. Luke's historical account for it about Jesus' life on earth and presenting Jesus' humanity more than any of the other Gospel. Read Luke 1:1-80 through Luke 24:1-53.
7. Blessed are the poor in spirit to those who believe that **"John"** is name in his honor. He is the author. John and his brother James were in the companion with John the Baptist as it's original disciples until they met Jesus who called John and James to be His disciples. John also was the author of four books: I John, II John, III John and Revelation. John was on e of Jesus close and beloved disciples. Read John 1:1-51 through John 21:1-25
8. Blessed are the poor in spirit to those who believe that **"Acts"** was written by Luke, who was one of the eyewitnesses of the miracles events happened during the Pentecostal Era that took place including in the companion of Apostle Paul. Luke witnessed the Holy Spirit in the life of the believers, the unbelievers now turned to believers of Jesus Christ, and the baptism of the Holy Spirit. He was also a physician that had became a doctor given by his Christian friend named Theophilus. Read Acts 1:1-26 through Acts 28:1-31
9. Blessed are the poor in spirit to those who believe that the book of **"Romans"** was written by Apostle Paul under the guide of the Holy Spirit. This letter was addressing to the church at Romans. Apostle Paul came to introduce himself to the people of Rome including the Gentiles called by God to preach the gospel that was at Rome. Apostle Paul in Rome was not ashamed of the gospel for it is the power of God unto salvation to everyone that believe; **to the Jew first**, and also (**second**) **to the Greek** (Gentiles). See Romans 1:16. Read Romans 1:1-20 through Romans 16:1-27, Romans 1:16, I Corinthians 1:18
10. Blessed are the poor in spirit to those who believe that **"both I Corinthians and II Corinthians"** were written again by Apostle Paul, his first and second recorded letters to the church in the city of Corinth. Read what happened; I Corinthians 1:1-31 through I Corinthians 16:1-24 and II Corinthians 1:1-24 through II Corinthians 13:1-14

11. Blessed are the poor in spirit to those who believe that **"Galatians"** was written by Apostle Paul. The address of this letter by Apostle Paul were in the city of Galatia to solve the problem between the Jews and the Gentiles that salvation is a gift of grace and faith in Jesus Christ. Read Galatians 1:1-24 through Galatians 6:1-10
12. Blessed are the poor in spirit to those who believe that **"Ephesians"** was written by Apostle Paul. This letter was addressed in the city of Ephesus who were faithful in Christ Jesus and passed along to other Rome cities as well. Paul came to aid the Jewish converted and Gentiles converted as a unity because of their separating themselves trying to excluding their Gentile brothers in Christ. Paul came to stress the unity of the believers of Jesus Christ to both the Jewish Christians and the Gentile Christians alike under the guidance of the Holy Spirit unity as one. See Ephesians 4:1-16, Read Ephesians 1:1-23 through Ephesians 6:1-24

Part DXCII

Blessed Are The Poor In Spirit. Matthew 5:3

Blessed Means Happy

Poor means meek in spirit. Poor means humble in spirit. Poor means lowly in spirit. Poor means quiet in spirit. Read Matthew 5:3-12, Read also Mark 1:15

Jesus did not say "*rich*" in spirit. Jesus said "*poor*" in spirit.

1. Blessed are the poor in spirit to those who believe that **"Philippians"** was written by Apostle Paul. This letter was address to the church in the city of Philippi. Paul came to aid his brothers and sisters in Christ with the Jews and the Gentiles alike. Read Philippians 1:1-30 through Philippians 4:1-23
2. Blessed are the poor in spirit to those who believe that **"Colossians"** was written by Apostle Paul. This letter was address to the church in the city of Colosse. Paul sent letters to Tychicus and the converted slave Onesimus to the church in the city of Colosse for Paul to help solve these false teaching and to those who claims secret knowledge and powers and denies Christ's true humanity. Paul was in prison at the time. Read Colossians 1:1-29 through Colossians 4:1-18.
3. Blessed are the poor in spirit to those who believe that both **"I Thessalonians and II Thessalonians"** were written by Apostle Paul, who had recorded letters to the church in the city of Thessalonica. Paul brought faith in Jesus Christ to the city of Thessalonica, but riot become a problem. Paul, the Thessalonian church became a confusion concerning the second coming of Christ. While the confusion was going on through misinterpretation in Paul's first letter, it was stated that they do nothing more than wait for the Lord return. See I Thessalonians 4:13-18. Read I Thessalonians 1:1-10 through I Thessalonians 5:1-28 and II Thessalonians 1:1-12 through II Thessalonians 3:1-18
4. Blessed are the poor in spirit to those who believe that both **"I Timothy and II Timothy"** were written by Apostle Paul to a young man by the name of Timothy, Paul's associate, his helper, his partner, his friend, his companion and his co-labor in the gospel. He recorded his first and second letters to Timothy. Timothy was born in Lystra. He was the son of a devote Jewish woman named Eunice. Timothy's grandmother's name was Lois. Timothy was a "beloved son"

and was given encouragement and advisement by Apostle Paul on spiritual leadership and development of a godly church. Timothy became the Bishop of that church. Paul and Timothy became like spiritual father and spiritual son in order to bring the gospel of Jesus Christ to the world. It was an honor to see Timothy's name. Read I Timothy 1:1-20 through I Timothy 6:1-21 and II Timothy 1:1-18 through II Timothy 4:1-22

5. Blessed are the poor in spirit to those who believe that **"Titus"** is written by Apostle Paul. It was an honor to see Titus' name. This letter was address to Titus on behalf of his companion with Apostle Paul. Titus is a Greek Gentile convert. He was from Antioch. He ministered along with Paul for a number of years. Read Titus 1:1-16 through Titus 3:1-15
6. Blessed are the poor in spirit to those who believe that **"Philemon"** was written by Apostle Paul. This letter was recorded to Philemon. Philemon was a Christian from Colosse who own slavery. One of his slavery by the name of Onesimus. Paul wrote to Philemon to give him pardon for the mistake that Onesimus made since Onesimus became a Christian and went back to Philemon. Philemon became a Christian. All things work together to them that loved God according to His purpose; His will. Romans 8:28 Read Philemon 1:1-25
7. Blessed are the poor in spirit to those who believe that **"Hebrews"** is uncertain who wrote this to address the letter to a congregation of Hebrews believers which may have been in Rome. And beside Paul, I had heard the names of Apollos, Barnabas, Clement, Luke, Phillip, Priscilla or Silas. Nevertheless, it is said that the writer of the Hebrews is heard around the world to declare of the gospel of Jesus Christ to the Hebrews believers at Rome. The Gospel is for all believers in the freedom of Christ. Read Hebrews 1:1-14 through Hebrews 13:1-25
8. Blessed are the poor in spirit to those who believe that **"James"** is name in his honor. He was the son of Mary and Joseph. He was the half brother of Jesus. James is the author. It was stated as I heard that James did not become a believer until after the resurrection of Jesus Christ. Later James became the leader of the church in Jerusalem. In Jerusalem James was among these who awaited on the day of Pentecost. James' lesson was the teaching of good works in the life of the believers. Read James 1:1-27 through James 5:1-20
9. Blessed are the poor in spirit to those who believe that both **"I Peter and II Peter"** was written by the same author. He was one of Jesus' disciples. He was one of Jesus close in the beloved. Peter preached the Pentecostal Messages and 3,

000 souls saved under the power of Jesus Christ. Peter was filled with the Holy Spirit. He was an apostle. His name was honor. In addressing the two letters in Asia, Minor, Apostle Peter comforted the believers and urge them to remain strong despite their sufferings. He also exposed that the false teaching had greatly contributed to the apostasy of the Christians and to encourage the believers to mature in the truth of God's Word. These letters were written to encourage the believers to stand strong for the Lord through their sufferings and persecution. Apostle Peter encouraged them to grow in grace and in the knowledge of Jesus Christ our Lord and Savior Jesus Christ to Him be glory the life of Jesus Christ our Lord and Savior Jesus Christ to Him be glory both now and for ever. Amen. II Peter 3:18. Read I Peter 1:1-10 through I Peter 5:1-14 and II Peter 1:1-21 through II Peter 3:1-18

10. Blessed are the poor in spirit to those who believe that the three books were written by the same author **"John."** His name was honor. He also was the author of the fourth Gospel and the book of Revelation. He was one of Jesus close and beloved disciples. This letter was addressed to Christian congregation found in truth and faith but realized of receiving serious challenges from false teachers. He also had some problems associated with these erroneous teachers. He wanted the Christians to withdraw all fellowship from these false teachers. It was stated that Apostle John was a leader of the Church at Ephesus for many years. Read I John 1:1-10 to I John 5:1-21, II John 1:1-3 and III John 1:1-14
11. Blessed are the poor in spirit to those who believe that **"Jude"** who is the brother of James and half brother of Jesus. Jude's name is in his honor. He is the author. This letter was address to false teachers in the church. False teachers in these days was the Gnosticism. The Gnosticism still exist to this day. Because of false teaching, Jude encouraged the believers to keep yourselves in the love of God looking of the mercy of our Lord Jesus Christ unto eternal life. See Jude 1:21. Read Jude 1:1-25
12. Blessed are the poor in spirit to those who believe that the last Book of the ending is **"Revelation"** was written Apostle John. It was stated that Apostle John was the long run in life for many years. And it was so. This Book of Revelation is about Jesus Christ as given to the Apostle John. It was revealed to him to tell of the **"Revelation"** that is to be revealed. In the Book of Revelation, Apostle John's name is in his honor to speak about Jesus and that Jesus will come again soon. The Roman government put Apostle John to exile at Patmos, a small island off

the coast of Greece, for preaching the gospel of Jesus Christ, the Word of God. While in Patmos, an angel came to help Apostle John to understand the vision. In that vision was told to Apostle John of sin's end and Satan's defeat; a special blessing promise to all who read, hear and obey which God wrote in the book of Revelation. And a promise warning of those who add to or take away from God's Words. Most of all Jesus said, "Surely I come quickly." Revelation 22:20. Read Revelation 1:1-20 through Revelation 22:1-21.

End of New Testament Period!!!

Part DXCIII

Blessed Are The Poor In Spirit. Matthew 5:3

Blessed Means Happy

Poor means meek in spirit. Poor means humble in spirit. Poor means lowly in spirit. Poor means quiet in spirit. Read Matthew 5:3-12, Read also Mark 1:15

Jesus did not say "*rich*" in spirit. Jesus said "*poor*" in spirit.

1. Blessed are the poor in spirit to those who believe: "Do unto others as you would have them do unto you" Luke 6:31, Matthew 7:12
2. Blessed are the poor in spirit to those who believe that the Bible teaches us about Love: Not Hate. John 4:19-21 verse 20, John 3:18, I John 3:14-16 verse 15, John 3:16
3. Blessed are the poor in spirit to those who believe that there are **match** couple in God's will concern you. I Thessalonians 5:18, Amos 3:3, Malachi 2:10, 14-16
4. Blessed are the poor in spirit to those who believe in following Christ. I Peter 2:21, John 13:15
5. Blessed are the poor in spirit to those who believe that our Lord Jesus Christ is our prosecutor. I John 2:1-2, John 8:32, 36
6. Blessed are the poor in spirit to those who believe that as a man of God, as a man of faith and as a Family Man, we talk the talk and we walk the walk. We live by faith. This is God's faith that He ask us to do. John 1:1-51 verse 6-7 verse 6, Romans 10:17, Habakkuk 2:4, Romans 1:17, Galatians 3:11, Ephesians 3:15, John 4:23-24, Hebrews 11:6, **Mark 11:22,** I Corinthians 4:1-5 verse 4, II Corinthians 5:7, I Peter 2:21, John 14:30-31—(do mean talk; do mean action; Talk mean action). Deuteronomy 5:24, Psalm 71:1-24 verse 24, Psalm 77:1-20 verse 12, Proverbs 6:22
7. Blessed are the poor in spirit to those who believe that **Enoch** walked with God. Genesis 5:24, Hebrews 11:5, Habakkuk 2:4, Romans 1:17, Galatians 3:11, Hebrews 10:38-39 verse 38,
8. Blessed are the poor in spirit to those who believe that the Lord is with you wherever you go. Joshua 1:9

9. Blessed are the poor in spirit to those who believe that the Gift of Tongues speak represent in Acts 2:1-47 verse 1-4 verse 4, verse 5-11, I Corinthians 12:1-11 verse 10, I Corinthians 14:1-40 verse 18, 21, verse 33
10. Blessed are the poor in spirit to those who believe in the imminent millennium. Revelation 20:1-15 verse 3-5, Revelation 1:7, Revelation 3:11, Revelation 16:15, Revelation 22:7, 12, 16, 20, Amos 4:12
11. Blessed are the poor in spirit to those who believe in the imminent rapture of the church at the Second Coming of Christ: I Thessalonians 4:13-18 verse 16-17, Revelation 1:7, Hebrews 9:28, Daniel 7:13, Matthew 24:30, Matthew 26:64, Mark 13:26, Mark 14:62, Acts 1:11, Revelation 3:11, Revelation 16:15, Revelation 22:7, 12-13, 16, 20
12. Blessed are the poor in spirit to those who believe that **imminent rapture** of the church at **the Second Coming of Christ**, would take place before **the Millennium**, which is the thousand years of peace predicted in the book of Revelation. 20:1-15 verse 3-5

Part DXCIV

Blessed Are The Poor In Spirit. Matthew 5:3

Blessed Means Happy

Poor means meek in spirit. Poor means humble in spirit. Poor means lowly in spirit. Poor means quiet in spirit. Read Matthew 5:3-12, Read also Mark 1:15

Jesus did not say "*rich*" in spirit. Jesus said "*poor*" in spirit.

1. Blessed are the poor in spirit to those who believe in the Blessed Book of the Bible called God's Inspiration. Genesis 1:1, John 1:1, II Timothy 3:16
2. Blessed are the poor in spirit to those who believe that they were baptized in the Holy Spirit the **"moment"** they **"received"** Jesus Christ as their personal Savior. Matthew 3:11, Matthew 28:19, Mark 1:8, Luke 3:16, John 1:26, 33, John 22:20, Acts 1:4-8, Acts 2:4—(**a**), Acts 11:16, Romans 6:1-14 verse 3-6, Colossians 2:12, Galatians 3:26-28, John 13:15, I Peter 2:21, I Corinthians 10:1-4 verse 3
3. Blessed are the poor in spirit to those who believe that they were baptized in the Holy Spirit **"moment"** they **"accepted"** Jesus Christ as their personal Savior. Matthew 3:11, Matthew 28:19, Mark 1:8, Luke 3:16, John 1:26, 33, John 22:20, Acts 1:4-8, Acts 2:4—(**a**), Acts 11:16, Romans 6:1-14 verse 3-6, Colossians 2:12, Galatians 3:26-28, John 13:15, I Peter 2:21, I Corinthians 10:1-4 verse 3
4. Blessed are the poor in spirit to those who believe in the **pre-Millennium Second Coming of Christ before** He return at any time than we ever believe so soon—He which testifieth these things saith, Surely I come quickly. Amen. Even so, come, Lord Jesus Revelation 22:20
5. Blessed are the poor in spirit to those who believe that the Lord is right. Psalm 33:4
6. Blessed are the poor in spirit to those who believe that they were baptized in the Holy Spirit the **"moment"** they **"received"** Jesus Christ as their personal Savior. Matthew 3:11, Matthew 28:19, Mark 1:8, Luke 3:16, John 1:26, 33, John 22:20, Acts 1:4-8, Acts 2:4—(**a**), Acts 11:16, Romans 6:1-14 verse 3-6, Colossians 2:12, Galatians 3:26-28, John 13:15, I Peter 2:21, I Corinthians 10:1-4 verse 2

7. Blessed are the poor in spirit to those who believe that they were baptized in the Holy Spirit **"moment"** they **"accepted"** Jesus Christ as their personal Savior. Matthew 3:11, Matthew 28:19, Mark 1:8, Luke 3:16, John 1:26, 33, John 22:20, Acts 1:4-8, Acts 2:4—(**a**), Acts 11:16, Romans 6:1-14 verse 3-6, Colossians 2:12, Galatians 3:26-28, John 13:15, I Peter 2:21, I Corinthians 10:1-4 verse 2
8. Blessed are the poor in spirit to those who believe the Word of God teaches that the **enemy and death** shall be **destroyed last** (to an end). I Corinthians 15:26
9. Blessed are the poor in spirit to those who believe that the Word of God teaches that the God of peace will soon **crush Satan** under your feet. Romans 16:20
10. Blessed are the poor in spirit to those who believe the Word of God teaches that the God of peace will soon **bruise Satan** under your feet. Romans 16:20
11. Blessed are the poor in spirit to those who believe the Word of God teaches that God will put the **Seed of the Woman**, which is **Jesus Christ to bruise the old serpent's** head over His feet. Genesis 3:15, Romans 16:20
12. Blessed are the poor in spirit to those who believe and saw that when Jesus was praying, there was **His sweat** was as it was **great drops of blood** falling down to the ground. Luke 22:44. So how much it cost to see that My Savior paid an high cost upon Calvary for our sins? How much did it cost? How much???

Part DXCV

Blessed Are The Poor In Spirit. Matthew 5:3

Blessed Means Happy

Poor means meek in spirit. Poor means humble in spirit. Poor means lowly in spirit. Poor means quiet in spirit. Read Matthew 5:3-12, Read also Mark 1:15

Jesus did not say "*rich*" in spirit. Jesus said "*poor*" in spirit.

1. Blessed are the poor in spirit to those who believe that the Bible itself can never go wrong because the Bible itself speak straight to the Truth. John 14:6
2. Blessed are the poor in spirit to those who believe that **Love** has no color. John 3:16, I John 4:19
3. Blessed are the poor in spirit to those who believe in "rejoicing in hope; patient in tribulation; continuing instant in prayer." Romans 12:12
4. Blessed are the poor in spirit to those who believe that God is our God even to (through) death. Psalm 48:14
5. Blessed are the poor in spirit to those who believe that Family is a happy home start with a happy family. Ephesians 3:15, John 19:27, John 20:10, Acts 21:6, I Corinthians 11:34, I Corinthians 14:35, II Corinthians 5:6, I Timothy 5:4, Titus 2:5, Luke 15:6, Luke 9:61, Mark 5:19, Matthew 8:5-7, 13-15, Deuteronomy 21:12, Deuteronomy 24:5, Judges 19:9, Ruth 1:21, I Samuel 2:20, I Kings 13:15, Luke 14:20
6. Blessed are the poor in spirit to those who believe are able to say, "I am too blessed not to be too stressful. Revelation 2:10, Ephesians 1:3, James 1:12-25
7. Blessed are the poor in spirit to those who believe this scripture: "Saying, *touch not mine anointed, and do my prophets no harm.*" I Chronicles 16:22
8. Blessed are the poor in spirit to those who believe this scripture: "Sing unto the Lord, all the earth; shew forth from day to day his salvation." I Chronicles 16:23
9. Blessed are the poor in spirit to those who believe this scripture: "Declare his glory among the heathen; his marvelous works among all nations." I Chronicles 16:24
10. Blessed are the poor in spirit to those who believe this scripture: "For great is the Lord, and greatly to be praised: he also is to be feared above all gods." I Chronicles 16:25

11. Blessed are the poor in spirit to those who believe this scripture: "For all the gods of the people are idols: but the Lord made the heavens." I Chronicles 16:26
12. Blessed are the poor in spirit to those who believe this scripture: "Glory and honour are in his presence; strength and gladness are in his place. I Chronicles 16:27

Part DXCVI

Blessed Are The Poor In Spirit. Matthew 5:3

Blessed Means Happy

Poor means meek in spirit. Poor means humble in spirit. Poor means lowly in spirit. Poor means quiet in spirit. Read Matthew 5:3-12, Read also Mark 1:15

Jesus did not say "*rich*" in spirit. Jesus said "*poor*" in spirit.

1. Blessed are the poor in spirit to those who believe this scripture: "Give unto the Lord, ye kindreds of the people, give unto the Lord glory and strength." I Chronicles 16:28
2. Blessed are the poor in spirit to those who believe this scripture: "Give unto the Lord the glory due unto his name: bring an offering, and come before him: worship the Lord in the beauty of holiness." I Chronicles 16:29
3. Blessed are the poor in spirit to those who believe this scripture: "Fear before him, all the earth: the world also shall be stable, that it be not moved." I Chronicles 16:30
4. Blessed are the poor in spirit to those who believe this scripture: "Let the heavens be glad, and let the earth rejoice: and let men say among the nations, The Lord reigneth." I Chronicles 16:31
5. Blessed are the poor in spirit to those who believe this scripture: "Let the sea roar, and the fulness thereof: let the fields rejoice, and all that is therein." I Chronicles 16:32
6. Blessed are the poor in spirit to those who believe this scripture: "Then shall the trees of the wood sing out at the presence of the Lord, because he cometh to judge the earth." I Chronicles 16:33
7. Blessed are the poor in spirit to those who believe this scripture: "O give thanks unto the lord; for he is good; for his mercy endureth for ever." I Chronicles 16:34
8. Blessed are the poor in spirit to those who believe this scripture: "And say ye, Save us, O God of our salvation, and gather us together, and deliver us from the heathen, that we may give thanks to thy holy name, and glory in thy praise." I Chronicles 16:35

9. Blessed are the poor in spirit to those who believe this scripture: "Blessed be the Lord God of Israel for ever and ever. And all the people said, Amen, and praised the Lord. I Chronicles 16:36
10. Blessed are the poor in spirit to those who believe that Christian stand for Daily Life with Christ. Palm 61:8, Psalm 68:19, Psalm 86:3, Psalm 88:9, Isaiah 58:2, Matthew 6:11, Matthew 26:55, Mark 14:49, Luke 9:23, Luke 11:3, Acts 2:46, 47, Acts 5:42, Acts 11:12-26 verse 26, I Peter 4:13-19 verse 16
11. Blessed are the poor in spirit to those who believe that **Christ** mean **Jesus.** Luke 23:28, 35-39
12. Blessed are the poor in spirit to those who believe that **Christ** mean the **Chosen One Of God.** Luke 23:35

Part DXCVII

Blessed Are The Poor In Spirit. Matthew 5:3

Blessed Means Happy

Poor means meek in spirit. Poor means humble in spirit. Poor means lowly in spirit. Poor means quiet in spirit. Read Matthew 5:3-12, Read also Mark 1:15

Jesus did not say "*rich*" in spirit. Jesus said "*poor*" in spirit.

1. Blessed are the poor in spirit to those who believe that Christ mean The Word. John 1:1, Colossians 1:14-20 verse 17, Hebrews 1:2
2. Blessed are the poor in spirit to those who believe that Christ mean the First Begotten. Hebrews 1:6
3. Blessed are the poor in spirit to those who believe that Christ mean the First Born. Colossians 1:15, 18
4. Blessed are the poor in spirit to those who believe that Christ mean the image of the "invisible' God. Colossians 1:15, Romans 1:20
5. Blessed are the poor in spirit to those who believe that Christ is the founder of the church; the foundation of the church. Isaiah 28:16, Matthew 21:42, Romans 9:33, I Peter 2:6, Matthew 16:18, Matthew 26:61 (Christ's Body), Mark 14:58-59 verse 58
6. Blessed are the poor in spirit to those who believe that Christ mean (as) God. John 1:1-5, Philippians 2:6, 9-10
7. Blessed are the poor in spirit to those who believe that Christ mean the Beginning. Genesis 1:1, John 1:1
8. Blessed are the poor in spirit to those who believe that Christ is the Incarnation, the Word and the Flesh. John 1:14, I Timothy 3:16 (Acts 1:11), Acts 1:9, Mark 16:19
9. Blessed are the poor in spirit to those who believe that Christ is the Judge. Ecclesiastes 12:14, II Corinthians 5:10, II Timothy 4:1-9 verse 1, Romans 2:16, Romans 14:10
10. Blessed are the poor in spirit to those who believe that Christ is the Son of Man. Matthew 8:20, Matthew 12:8, Matthew 16:28, Matthew 17:9, Matthew 17:12, 22, Matthew 18:11, Matthew 19:28, Matthew 20:18, 28, Matthew 24:27, 30,

37, 39, 44, Matthew 25:13, 31, Matthew 26:2, 24, 45, 63, 64, Mark 2:10, 28, Mark 3:7-12 verse 11, Mark 8:31, 38, Mark 9:12, 31, Mark 10:33, 45, Mark 13:26, Mark 14:21, 41

11. Blessed are the poor in spirit to those who believe that Christ is Lord of lords and King of kings. Revelation 17:14, Revelation 19:16, I Timothy 6:15
12. Blessed are the poor in spirit to those who believe that Christ is the Potentate (Ruler). I Timothy 6:15

Part DXCVIII

Blessed Are The Poor In Spirit. Matthew 5:3

Blessed Means Happy

Poor means meek in spirit. Poor means humble in spirit. Poor means lowly in spirit. Poor means quiet in spirit. Read Matthew 5:3-12, Read also Mark 1:15

Jesus did not say "*rich*" in spirit. Jesus said "*poor*" in spirit.

1. Blessed are the poor in spirit to those who believe that **Christ** is the King Eternal, Immortal, Invisible, the only wise God. I Timothy 1:17, Romans 1:20, Luke 23:2
2. Blessed are the poor in spirit to those who believe that **Christ** is called namely Jesus Christ is the **"Same" as yesterday, today and for ever.** Hebrews 13:8, Psalm 102:27
3. Blessed are the poor in spirit to those who believe that **Christ** is **Lord.** Acts 10:36, Philippians 2:11, Philippians 3:10, Acts 9:3-5, Acts 9:20, 22, Acts 18:5, 28, Mark 12:35-37
4. Blessed are the poor in spirit to those who believe that **Christ** is the Son of God. Matthew 26:63, Matthew 27:40, 43, 54, Matthew 28:19, **Luke 1:35,** Mark 1:1, Mark 15:39, John 19:7, Mark 14:61-62, I John 5:20
5. Blessed are the poor in spirit to those who believe that **Christ** is the **Godhead.** Acts 17:29, Romans 1:20, Colossians 2:9
6. Blessed are the poor in spirit to those who believe that **Christ** is the **threefold, the three, or the Trinity.** Matthew 28:19, II Corinthians 13:14, I John 5:6, 7, 8, Psalm 51:11, Isaiah 63:10-11, Ephesians 4:30
7. Blessed are the poor in spirit to those who believe that **Christ** is the Savior. Isaiah 63:8, John 4:42, I John 4:14, II Timothy 1:10, Titus 1:4, Titus 2:13, I Peter 1:1, 11, II Peter 2:20, Luke 2:11, II Peter 3:2, 18
8. Blessed are the poor in spirit to those who believe that **Christ** is the Son of the Blessed. Mark 14:61-62
9. Blessed are the poor in spirit to those who believe that **Christ** is the "I Am." Mark 14:62

10. Blessed are the poor in spirit to those who believe that **Christ** is the Lord and the Savior; that Christ is God, the Holy One of Israel. Isaiah 43:3, Luke 1:47, Titus 2:10
11. Blessed are the poor in spirit to those who believe that **Christ** is the Lord. Isaiah 49:26, Isaiah 60:16, Isaiah 63:8, Acts 5:31, Acts 13:23, Philippians 3:20, I Timothy 1:1, I Timothy 2:3, I Timothy 4:10, Titus 1:3, Philippians 3:20, I Timothy 4:10, Titus 1:3, Titus 3:4, Jude 1:25
12. Blessed are the poor in spirit to those who believe that **Christ**, the **Lord Jesus** our **Savior.** Titus 1:4

Part DXCIX

Blessed Are The Poor In Spirit. Matthew 5:3

Blessed Means Happy

Poor means meek in spirit. Poor means humble in spirit. Poor means lowly in spirit. Poor means quiet in spirit. Read Matthew 5:3-12, Read also Mark 1:15

Jesus did not say "*rich*" in spirit. Jesus said "*poor*" in spirit.

1. Blessed are the poor in spirit to those who believe that Christ Jesus is our Savior. Titus 2:13, II Peter 1:1, 11, II Peter 2:20, II Peter 3:2, 18
2. Blessed are the poor in spirit to those who believe that Christ is it's self the Title, but the Title is an "He" not an "it." Matthew 5:18, Matthew 23:9, II Peter 1:20, Matthew 12:30, Luke 16:17, John 5:22
3. Blessed are the poor in spirit to those who believe that Christ is He. Isaiah 52:6, John 4:26, John 9:36
4. Blessed are the poor in spirit to those who believe that Christ is God who said: "I am He that doth speak; behold it (this) is (am) I." Isaiah 52:6
5. Blessed are the poor in spirit to those who believe that Christ is the "I Am." Exodus 3:6-22 verse 6, 14, 15, Revelation 1:8, Matthew 22:32, Mark 12:26-27 verse 26, Luke 20:37-38 verse 37, Mark 14:62
6. Blessed are the poor in spirit to those who believe that Christ (Jesus) claim to be God. Luke 23:2, John 5:18, John 10:30, 33, Mark 14:61-62 verse 62, Philippians 2:6-11, I John 5:20
7. Blessed are the poor in spirit to those who believe that Christ is the mediator between God and men, the Christ Jesus. I Timothy 2:5, Hebrews 8:6, Jeremiah 31:31, II Corinthians 3:6
8. Blessed are the poor in spirit to those who believe that Christ is the Shepherd. Isaiah 40:10-11, John 10:11, 14, Ezekiel 34:12, Hebrews 13:20, I Peter 2:25, I Peter 5:4
9. Blessed are the poor in spirit to those who believe that Christ is the True Light. Luke 1:78-79, John 1:4, 9, I John 1:5
10. Blessed are the poor in spirit to those who believe that Christ is that Truth. I John 5:20, Philippians 3:10, Hebrews 13:8, John 14:6, Revelation 3:7, Revelation 1:8, Revelation 1:18

11. Blessed are the poor in spirit to those who believe that Christ is the Way. John 14:6, Hebrews 10:19-20, I Timothy 3:16, Acts 1:11
12. Blessed are the poor in spirit to those who believe that Christ is celebrated by The Redeemer. Revelation 7:9-12, Revelation 5:8-14, John 1:29, 36, Revelation 21:9, 27, Leviticus 23:40

Part DC

Blessed Are The Poor In Spirit. Matthew 5:3

Blessed Means Happy

Poor means meek in spirit. Poor means humble in spirit. Poor means lowly in spirit. Poor means quiet in spirit. Read Matthew 5:3-12, Read also Mark 1:15

Jesus did not say "*rich*" in spirit. Jesus said "*poor*" in spirit.

1. Blessed are the poor in spirit to those who believe that Christ is That Lamb. Isaiah 11:6, Isaiah 53:7, Isaiah 62:25, Hosea 4:16, John 1:29, 36, Acts 8:32, I Peter 1:19, Revelation 5:6, 8, 12-13, Revelation 6:1, 16, Revelation 7:9-10, 14, 17, Revelation 12:11, Revelation 13:8, Revelation 14:1, 4, 10, Revelation 15:3, Revelation 17:14, Revelation 19:9, Revelation 21:9, 14, 23, 27, Revelation 22:1, 3
2. Blessed are the poor in spirit to those who believe that Christ is the Almighty. Revelation 21:22, Revelation 1:8
3. Blessed are the poor in spirit to those who believe that Christ is Jesus (Jesus Christ speak in Red Print). Revelation 1:8, 11, 17-20 (Isaiah 44:2), Revelation 2:1-29 verse 7 (Genesis 2:9), verse 8 (Isaiah 44:6, Revelation 22:2), verse 14 (Numbers 31:16), verse 17 (Isaiah 62:2), verse 23 (Isaiah 62:12, Jeremiah 17:10, Romans 2:6-16, Ecclesiastes 12:14), verse 27 (Psalm 2:9, Revelation 3:1-22), verse 5 (Exodus 32:32, Luke 10:20), verse 7 (Isaiah 22:22, Revelation 1:18), verse 9 (Isaiah 60:14), verse 12 (Isaiah 62:2, Revelation 2:17), verse 17 (Hosea 12:8), verse 19 (Proverbs 3:12), Revelation 16:15, Revelation 22:7, verse 12 (Isaiah 40:10), verse 13 (Isaiah 44:6, Isaiah 48:12, Revelation 2:8), verse 16 (Isaiah 11:1), verse 20
4. Blessed are the poor in spirit to those who believe that Christ is imparted to saints (Christians), Acts 11:26; believers in Christ Jesus, children of God, God's children, family of God. Ephesians 3:15, Revelation 21:1-3 verse 3, Hosea 1:9, 10, Hosea 2:23, Romans 9:25, 26, Romans 11:2, 27, Romans 15:9-10, 12, II Corinthians 6:15-18, Titus 2:14-15 verse 14, Hebrews 2:17, Hebrews 4:9, Hebrews 8:10, Hebrews 13:12-25 verse 12, I Peter 2:5, 9, 10, Revelation 5:9, Revelation 7:9, Revelation 11:9, Romans 8:15, 16, 23, John 1:12-13 verse 12,

Romans 9:4-5, Galatians 4:5-7 verse 5, Ephesians 1:5-6 verse 5, Romans 9:17, 22-27, verse 25, 26, II Corinthians 6:18, I Peter 4:16, Hosea 1:10, Exodus 9:16, Proverbs 16:4, Psalm 94:14, Isaiah 41:17, I Kings 19:10, Deuteronomy 32:43, Psalm 117:11, Leviticus 26:12, Ezekiel 37:27, Jeremiah 31:31-34, II Corinthians 3:6, Hebrews 8:6, 10, Deuteronomy 10:15, Exodus 19:5, Leviticus 23:40, I Samuel 12:22, Romans 11:1-3, Revelation 19:1-2 verse 1, Romans 15:9, 10, 11, Hebrews 10:16, II Peter 2:5, 9, Isaiah 41:17, Psalm 18:49, Genesis 8:18

5. **Blessed are the poor in spirit to those who believe that** Christ's job, Christ's mission, Christ's purpose, Christ's life, Christ's responsibility, Christ's goal, Christ's aim, Christ's decision, Christ's determination, and Christ's precious people **that** He *created* **in** His *image* **since** *Adam***, was to return in the calling of the Gentiles as second but as well as His First Jewish's** *mission* **as well and His action for Israel. Psalm 72:17, John 12:21, 23**
6. Blessed are the poor in spirit to those who believe that Christ mean Grace and Truth. John 1:14
7. Blessed are the poor in spirit to those who believe that Christ is Exaltation. Acts 7:55-56, Matthew 28:18, Luke 9:43, John 10:18, John 19:11, Acts 1:7, Acts 26:18, Ephesians 1:19-23 verse 21
8. Blessed are the poor in spirit to those who believe that Christ is Sinless Perfect. Hebrews 7:26-28
9. Blessed are the poor in spirit to those who believe that Christ has power. John 12:18, Matthew 9:6, Luke 4:14, 32, John 10:10
10. Blessed are the poor in spirit to those who believe that Christ's transfiguration before Peter, James and John was that His face did shine like the sun, and His white robe was like the light. Matthew 17:2
11. Blessed are the poor in spirit to those who believe that Christ's triumph over Satan at His crucifixion and His Resurrection were inspired to victory. Christ was called Faithful and True and in righteousness. He doth judge and make war. Christ's Name was written, KING OF KINGS AND LORD OF LORDS. Revelation 19:11, 16, Psalm 96:13, Deuteronomy 10:17, Romans 2:11, Philippians 3:10
12. Blessed are the poor in spirit to those who believe Christ's Words. Luke 4:22, John 7:46

Part DCI

Blessed Are The Poor In Spirit. Matthew 5:3

Blessed Means Happy

Poor means meek in spirit. Poor means humble in spirit. Poor means lowly in spirit. Poor means quiet in spirit. Read Matthew 5:3-12, Read also Mark 1:15

Jesus did not say "*rich*" in spirit. Jesus said "*poor*" in spirit.

1. Blessed are the poor in spirit to those who believe Christ's Work. Matthew 13:54-58 verse 54, verse 57 (I Samuel 10:11), John 2:11 (Exodus 14:31)
2. Blessed are the poor in spirit to those who believe that Christ is incomparable. Song of Solomon 5:10, Philippians 2:9, 5-11 verse 9
3. Blessed are the poor in spirit to those who believe that Christ is unchangeable. Hebrews 1:10-12 verse 10 (Psalm 102:25), verse 11 (Psalm 102:26), verse 12 (Psalm 102:27), Hebrews 13:8
4. Blessed are the poor in spirit to those who believe that Christ, which is of God, the Father, God the Son and God the Holy Spirit is of Old and that Christ is indeed the Same Christ has always remain the Same. Hebrews 1:11, 12, Hebrews 13:8, Genesis 1:1, John 1:1-14 verse 1, II Timothy 3:16, Psalm 102:27
5. Blessed are the poor in spirit to those who believe that Christ is revealed in the Gospel by the Holy Spirit by the Bible, by the Word, by the Scripture, by the holy prophets, by the children of God and as Himself that wrote His Words for us to discover the Truth of who He really is. Isaiah 40:1-8 verse 4, verse 3 (Matthew 3:3, Matthew 11:10, Mark 1:2, Luke 7:27, Luke 1:76, Malachi 3:1, Luke 3:4, John 1:23), verse 6 (I Peter 1:24), verse 7 (James 1:6, II Timothy 2:19), I Samuel 3:21, Isaiah 22:14, Isaiah 40:5, Isaiah 53:1, I Samuel 3:1-21 verse 4-14, 21, Isaiah 40:1-8 verse 5, Isaiah 53:1 (Romans 1:16, John 12:38), Isaiah 56:1, Luke 2:26, Luke 17:30, John 12:38, Habakkuk 2:4, Romans 1:17, Galatians 3:11, Hebrews 10:38-39 verse 38, I Corinthians 2:10, Galatians 3:23-29 verse 23, Ephesians 3:5-6 verse 5, II Thessalonians 1:1-12 verse 7, 8 (Isaiah 1:28), I Peter 1:5, 12, I Peter 4:13, I Peter 5:1-11 verse 1, verse 8 (Job 1:1-22 verse 7, 8, 12, 22 (James 5:11), Job 2:1-13 verse 2-3, 6 (II Corinthians 12:7), verse 7 (Hebrews 5:5, Psalm 2:7), Matthew 3:17 (Isaiah 42:17), Matthew 17:5 (Psalm 2:7), Acts 13:33 (Psalm 2:7), Hebrews 1:5) (Psalm 2:7), Psalm 2:6 (Revelation 14:1)

6. Blessed are the poor in spirit to those who believe that the saints shall behold (see) Christ and His Glory from heaven. John 17:1-26 verse 24, 25, 26, verse 4 (Isaiah 42:1-2, Matthew 3:17, Mark 1:11, Matthew 12:17-18, Psalm 2:7), verse 12 (Psalm 41:9), verse 17 (Psalm 119:142)
7. Blessed are the poor in spirit to those who believe that the saints shall rejoice at the Revelation of Christ. I Peter 4:16-19 verse 17, verse 18 (Proverbs 11:31)
8. Blessed are the poor in spirit to those who believe in Christ at the Book of Revelation. Read Revelation Chapters 1 through Revelation 22:1-21 verse 7, 12-13, 16, 20
9. Blessed are the poor in spirit to those who believe that Thomas' Acknowledged and the Acknowledge by Christ's disciple. John 20:1-31 verse 24-31 verse 27-29 verse 28
10. Blessed are the poor in spirit to those who believe that Christ is the Creator of all things. Isaiah 40:28, John 1:3, Genesis 1:1, John 1:1, John 1:1-20 verse 1-18, II Timothy 3:16, I John 5:20, Hebrews 1:1-14 verse 2, verse 5 (Psalm 2:7, II Samuel 7:14), verse 7 (Psalm 104:4-5), verse 8 (Psalm 45:6), verse 9 (Psalm 45:7), verse 10 (Psalm 102:25), verse 11 (Psalm 102:26), verse 12 (Psalm 102:27, Hebrews 13:8)
11. Blessed are the poor in spirit to those who believe that Christ is not a robbery as we have believed or as we have *thought* as this led us to believe, but being in the *form of God*, Christ is indeed to be equal with God because Christ is God Himself. Christ is Lord. Christ is Jesus. Hebrews 13:8, Luke 23:2, John 10:30, 33, Revelation 1:8, 18, Revelation 3:7, Acts 9:5, Acts 22:8, Acts 26:15, Acts 9:22, Acts 18:5, 28, Mark 14:61-62, Acts 10:36. Is Christ, *A Robber for being equal with God*? John 8:56, 58, Philippians 2:6, John 5:18, John 10:33, My answer is NO. Christ is not claiming to be a robber, but claim to be God Himself who Christ said He *really is*. Read John 8:56, 58 and John 14:7-9
12. Blessed are the poor in spirit to those who believe that Christ has the power discerning the thoughts of the heart. Ezekiel 11:1-25 verse 5, Luke 5:17-39 verse 22, John 2:12-25 verse 24-25, verse 17 (Psalm 69:9, Romans 15:3)

Part DCII

Blessed Are The Poor In Spirit. Matthew 5:3

Blessed Means Happy

Poor means meek in spirit. Poor means humble in spirit. Poor means lowly in spirit. Poor means quiet in spirit. Read Matthew 5:3-12, Read also Mark 1:15

Jesus did not say "*rich*" in spirit. Jesus said "*poor*" in spirit.

1. Blessed are the poor in spirit to those who believe that Christ, which is Jesus, is entitled to equal honor with the Father because Christ is God Himself. Micah 5:2 (Matthew 2:6, John 7:42, Isaiah 9:6, John 5:23, John 1:1, Colossians 1:1)—(Proverbs 8:22), Hebrews 1:8-10, verse 8 (Psalm 45:6), verse 9 (Psalm 45:7), verse 10 (Psalm 102:25), Revelation 1:8, John 10:30, John 10:33, Luke 23:2, John 19:7, John 5:18, John 5:35-38 verse 37, John 4:26, John 11:25, Hebrews 13:8, John 14:7-9, II Timothy 3:16, I John 5:20
2. Blessed are the poor in spirit to those who believe that Christ is the Eternal God and Creator of The Universe, Creator of the World; Creator of the Earth. Micah 5:2 (Matthew 2:6, John 7:42, Isaiah 9:6, John 5:23, John 1:1, Colossians 1:1)—(Proverbs 8:22), Hebrews 1:8-10, verse 8 (Psalm 45:6), verse 9 (Psalm 45:7), verse 10 (Psalm 102:25), Revelation 1:8, John 10:30, John 10:33, Luke 23:2, John 19:7, John 5:18, John 5:35-38 verse 37, John 4:26, John 11:25, Hebrews 13:8, John 14:7-9, II Timothy 3:16, I John 5:20
3. Blessed are the poor in spirit to those who believe that Christ presents the church to Himself. Ephesians 5:27, Song of Solomon 4:7, Leviticus 1:3, I Corinthians 14:33
4. Blessed are the poor in spirit to those who believe that Christ redeem and that Christ purified, the church unto Himself (Christ Jesus). Revelation 5:1-14 verse 9, verse 1 (Ezekiel 2:9-10 verse 9, 10 (Revelation 1:6, Exodus 19:6), verse 11 (Daniel 7:10, Revelation 20:12-15 verse 12, Titus 2:14-15 verse 14, Psalm 21:11, Psalm 44:1-26 verse 22, Romans 1:1-20, Acts 21:32, Psalm 49:15, Psalm 72:14, Psalm 130:1-8 verse 8, Psalm 44:1-26 verse 22, Psalm 49:1-20
5. Blessed are the poor in spirit to those who believe that Christ which is God, is over all of us. God blessed for ever. Amen. Psalm 45:6-7 verse 6 (Hebrews 1:8), verse 7 (Hebrews 1:9), Romans 9:5

6. Blessed are the poor in spirit to those who believe that Christ is God which is that Word. John 1:1, Genesis 1:1, II Timothy 3:16
7. Blessed are the poor in spirit to those who believe that Christ which is Jesus is having the power to forgive sins. Colossians 3:13 (Luke 23:34), Mark 2:1-28 verse 7, 28, verse 23 (Deuteronomy 23:25), verse 27 (Exodus 23:12)
8. Blessed are the poor in spirit to those who believe that Christ Himself or (God/ Jesus) is the husband of the church. Isaiah 54:1-17, verse 5, verse 1 (Galatians 4:27), verse 13 (John 6:45), Ephesians 5:25-32, verse 27 (Song of Solomon 4:7, Leviticus 1:3), verse 31 (Genesis 2:24, Mark 10:8, I Corinthians 6:16, Ephesians 5:31, Revelation 21:2, 9
9. Blessed are the poor in spirit to those who believe that Christ is the King of kings and Lord of lords. Revelation 17:14, Revelation 19:16, I Timothy 6:14-15, Deuteronomy 10:17
10. Blessed are the poor in spirit to those who believe that Christ, which is God) is the Lord from heaven. I Corinthians 15:47-58 verse 47, verse 54 (Isaiah 25:8, Revelation 21:4, I Corinthians 15:54), verse 55 (Hosea 13:14), (I Corinthians 15:55)
11. Blessed are the poor in spirit to those who believe that Christ is Lord of all. Acts 10:36, Romans 10:11-13, Philippians 2:11
12. Blessed are the poor in spirit to those who believe that Christ is *Lord of the Sabbath.* Genesis 2:1-3 verse 2, 3 (John 5:17, Hebrews 4:10), Matthew 12:8—For the Son of Man is Lord even of the Sabbath day.

Part DCIII

Blessed Are The Poor In Spirit. Matthew 5:3

Blessed Means Happy

Poor means meek in spirit. Poor means humble in spirit. Poor means lowly in spirit. Poor means quiet in spirit. Read Matthew 5:3-12, Read also Mark 1:15

Jesus did not say "*rich*" in spirit. Jesus said "*poor*" in spirit.

1. Blessed are the poor in spirit to those who believe that Christ is the Son of Man is Lord even of the Sabbath Day. Matthew 12:8, Genesis 2:1-3 verse 2, 3 (John 5:17, Hebrews 4:10)
2. Blessed are the poor in spirit to those who believe that Christ is God; even Lord of the Sabbath or that Christ is Jesus even Lord of the Sabbath. Philippians 3:10, John 14:6-9, Revelation 1:8, 18, Revelation 3:7, Acts 9:5, Acts 22:8, Acts 26:15, Acts 18:5, 28, Acts 9:22, Hebrews 13:8, Philippians 2:10-11, Acts 10:36
3. Blessed are the poor in spirit to those who believe that Christ is the Divine. Hebrews 13:8, John 14:7-9, Philippians 2:6, Philippians 3:10, Genesis 1:1, John 1:1, II Timothy 3:16, I Timothy 3:16
4. Blessed are the poor in spirit to those who believe that Christ is the Deity. Hebrews 13:8, John 14:7-9, Philippians 2:6, Philippians 3:10, John 1:1, Genesis 1:1, I Timothy 3:16, II Timothy 3:16
5. Blessed are the poor in spirit to those who believe that Christ which is God spake and say "Let us." Genesis 1:26, Genesis 3:22, Exodus 3:6, 14, 15, Matthew 22:32, Mark 12:26-27, Luke 20:37-38, Acts 3:13, Acts 7:32
6. Blessed are the poor in spirit to those who believe that Christ which is the Lord God (Jesus) may rest upon us. II Corinthians 12:8-9, Hebrews 1:1-17 verse 6, 2, 3 (God express image of His person Jesus Christ) verse 10, 12 (Hebrews 13:8)
7. Blessed are the poor in spirit to those who believe That Christ is That Lamb: "Worthy is the Lamb that was *slain* to receive power, and riches and wisdom and strength and honor and glory and blessing: Jesus Christ as a Sacrifice Lambs. Revelation 5:12, John 1:29, 36-51, Revelation 13:8, Revelation 15:3, Revelation 17:14, Revelation 19:7, 9, I Peter 1:19, Acts 8:32, Isaiah 53:7, Matthew 27:12

8. Blessed are the poor in spirit to those who believe that Christ is the object of faith. We believe Christ. We believe in God (Christ) we also believe in Jesus (Christ). John 4:1-12 verse 1, 7-9
9. Blessed are the poor in spirit to those who believe that Christ which is Jesus, *claim* to be God (Christ). Philippians 2:6, Luke 23:2, John 10:33, John 5:18 (John 8:56, 58, John 10:30), John 14:7-9, John 8:56, 58
10. Blessed are the poor in spirit to those who believe that Christ Himself which is Jesus Himself is the Chief Corner Stone. I Peter 2:1-25 verse 6, 7, Matthew 21:24, Mark 12:10, Luke 20:17, Acts 4:11, Acts 26:26, Ephesians 2:20, Psalm 118:22-23 (Mark 12:11), Isaiah 28:16, Romans 9:33, Jeremiah 17:7
11. Blessed are the poor in spirit to those who believe that Christ is *Omnipotent*; that He has the *power*, and the *authority*. Psalm 45:3, Philippians 3:21, Revelation 1:8 (Genesis 3:14), Revelation 1:11, 17, 18, Revelation 3:7, 11, Revelation 16:15, Revelation 22:7, 12-13, 16, 20
12. Blessed are the poor in spirit to those who believe that Christ is *Omnipresent*; that He is indeed *presence everywhere every day 24 hours, 7 days a week*. There is no *sleep for* Christ's sake. God may see us. God may watch us. Genesis 16:13, Matthew 18:20, Matthew 28:20, John 3:13, Acts 18:9-10, 16

Part DCIV

Blessed Are The Poor In Spirit. Matthew 5:3

Blessed Means Happy

Poor means meek in spirit. Poor means humble in spirit. Poor means lowly in spirit. Poor means quiet in spirit. Read Matthew 5:3-12, Read also Mark 1:15

Jesus did not say "*rich*" in spirit. Jesus said "*poor*" in spirit.

1. Blessed are the poor in spirit to those who believe that Christ is *Omniscient*; that He is *all known*. John 16:30, John 21:14-25 verse 15-17, verse 17, Genesis 16:13
2. Blessed are the poor in spirit to those who believe that Christ is the One with the Father, but still Christ is God Himself in the *flesh of Jesus*. John 10:30, 38, See I Timothy 3:16, **Acts 1:11,** I John 4:2, 3, **II John 1:7, Read** John 14:7-9
3. Blessed are the poor in spirit to those who believe that Christ is the One with the Father, but still Christ is the Lord thy God. Acts 9:22, Acts 18:5, 28, John 10:30, 38, See II Corinthians 12:2-3 (Twice), See II Corinthians 12:8-9 (thrice or three times. The Power of Christ may rest upon me verse 9) thrice as may mean *Father, Son* and *Holy Ghost*. Matthew 28:19, II Corinthians 13:14, I John 5:6-8
4. Blessed are the poor in spirit to those who believe that Christ is God that is the Lord thy God in the Old Testament Period because there is none else like God beside Him during Israel's time. Isaiah 45:5-6, 14 (I Corinthians 14:25, 26, verse 25, 33), 17, 18, 19, 21, 22, Isaiah 46:9, Isaiah 47:8 (Revelation 18:7)
5. Blessed are the poor in spirit to those who believe that the **Christ**, that is **God**, is **Jesus** in the New Testament Period because **Christ** is the **Lord thy God** in the flesh of **Jesus** as the **Christ**. **I Timothy 3:16,** See **John 14:6-12 verse 7-9, John 4:25-26, 29, John 10:30, 38**
6. Blessed are the poor in spirit to those who believe that **Christ** is the **Savior.** Isaiah 45:21, John 4:42, I John 4:14, Jude 1:25, Isaiah 49:26, Isaiah 60:16, **63:8,** Luke 1:47, Luke 2:11, Acts 5:31, Isaiah 9:6, Isaiah 7:14, Matthew 1:21, 23, Acts 13:23, Philippians 3:20, I Timothy 1:1, I Timothy 2:3, I Timothy 4:10, II Timothy 1:10, Titus 1:3, 4, Titus 2:10, 13, Titus 3:6, II Peter 1:1, 11, II Peter 2:20, II Peter 3:2, **II Peter 3:18, Luke 1:-8,** Luke 1:77-80

7. Blessed are the poor in spirit to those who believe that **Christ** is God. Isaiah 7:14, (Matthew 1:23), Isaiah 9:6 (Luke 2:11)
8. Blessed are the poor in spirit to those who believe that **Christ** is Jesus. Mark 14:61-62 verse 62
9. Blessed are the poor in spirit to those who believe that **Christ** is the Lord. Acts 9:4-5, Acts 22:7-10, Acts 26:14-18
10. Blessed are the poor in spirit to those who believe that **Christ** is the Son of God which is Jesus, His Only Begotten Son; Father's **Full** of **Grace** and **Truth** (John 1:4); I Timothy 3:16, John 14:7-9, I John 4:9, Acts 1:11, Philippians 2:10-11, Philippians 3:10, Matthew 3:17, Matthew 4:3, 6, Matthew 8:29, Matthew 14:33, Matthew 26:63, Matthew 27:40, 43, 54, Luke 11:30, Luke 22:70, **Matthew 28:19,** Mark 1:1, 11, Mark 3:11, Mark 9:7, Mark 15:39, **Luke 1:35,** Luke 4:3, 9, 41, **Luke 5:24,** Luke 8:28, Luke 9:35, 44, 56, **58**, **Luke 12:8,** 40, Luke 17:22, 24, 26, 30, Luke 18:8, 31, Luke 19:10, Luke 22:20, **John 1:18,** 34, John 9:35, 36, John 11:4, **John 11:27,** John 19:7, John 20:31, **Acts 8:37,** Acts 9:20, Romans 1:3, 4, I Corinthians 1:19, Galatians 2:20, II Corinthians 1:19, Ephesians 4:13, Hebrews 3:6, Hebrews 4:14, Hebrews 7:3, Hebrews 10:29, II Peter 1:17, I John 1:3, 7, I John 3:8, I John 5:5, 10, 12, 13, I John 5:20, **II John 1:9,** Revelation 2:18
11. Blessed are the poor in spirit to those who believe that God spoke to Adam, Eve and Lucifer. Genesis 3:9-19, 22
12. Blessed are the poor in spirit to those who believe that God spoke to Cain. Genesis 4:6-7, 9-12, 15

Part DCV

Blessed Are The Poor In Spirit. Matthew 5:3

Blessed Means Happy

Poor means meek in spirit. Poor means humble in spirit. Poor means lowly in spirit. Poor means quiet in spirit. Read Matthew 5:3-12, Read also Mark 1:15

Jesus did not say "*rich*" in spirit. Jesus said "*poor*" in spirit.

1. Blessed are the poor in spirit to those who believe that God spoke to Noah. Genesis 7:1-4, Genesis 8:15, Genesis 9:1, 9, 17
2. Blessed are the poor in spirit to those who believe that God spoke to Abram. Genesis 12:1-3, 7, Genesis 13:14-17, Genesis 15:1, 4-5, 7, 13-16, 18-21, Genesis 17:1-16, Genesis 21:12-13
3. Blessed are the poor in spirit to those who believe that God spoke to Sarah's maid, Haggar. Genesis 6:8-12, Genesis 21:17-18
4. Blessed are the poor in spirit to those who believe that God spoke to Lot. Genesis 19:17, 21
5. Blessed are the poor in spirit to those who believe that God spoke to Abimelech. Genesis 20:3, 6-7
6. Blessed are the poor in spirit to those who believe that God spoke to Abraham. Genesis 22:1-2, 15-18
7. Blessed are the poor in spirit to those who believe that God spoke to Jacob. Genesis 32:9, 12 and became Israel 26–29, Genesis 35:1, 10-12, Genesis 46:2-4
8. Blessed are the poor in spirit to those who believe that God spoke to Moses and Aaron. Numbers 19:1
9. Blessed are the poor in spirit to those who believe that God spoke to Rebekah, Isaac's wife. Genesis 25:20, 23
10. Blessed are the poor in spirit to those who believe that God spoke to Isaac. Genesis 26:2-5, 24
11. Blessed are the poor in spirit to those who believe that God spoke to Jacob. Genesis 28:13-15, Genesis 31:3, 11-13
12. Blessed are the poor in spirit to those who believe that God spoke to Laban. Genesis 31:24, 29

PART DCVI

Blessed Are The Poor In Spirit. Matthew 5:3

Blessed Means Happy

Poor means meek in spirit. Poor means humble in spirit. Poor means lowly in spirit. Poor means quiet in spirit. Read Matthew 5:3-12, Read also Mark 1:15

Jesus did not say "*rich*" in spirit. Jesus said "*poor*" in spirit.

1. Blessed are the poor in spirit to those who believe that God spoke to Moses. Exodus 3:4-10, 12, 14-22, Exodus 6:1-8, 11, Genesis 6:1-2, 29, Genesis 7:1, 14, 19, Genesis 8:1, 5, 16, 20, Genesis 9:1, 8, 13, 22, Genesis 10:1, 3, 12, 21, Genesis 11:19, Genesis 12:43, Genesis 13:1
2. Blessed are the poor in spirit to those who believe that God spoke to Aaron. Exodus 4:27, Numbers 18:1, 8, 20
3. Blessed are the poor in spirit to those who believe that God spoke to Pharaoh through Moses and Aaron. Genesis 5:1
4. Blessed are the poor in spirit to those who believe that God spoke to Aaron and Moses. Exodus 6:26, Exodus 10:3, Exodus 12:1, Numbers 19:1, Numbers 18:1, 8, 20
5. Blessed are the poor in spirit to those who believe that God spoke to Balaam. Numbers 22:9, 12, 32-33, 35
6. Blessed are the poor in spirit to those who believe that God spoke to Balak through Balaam. Numbers 23:5, 7, 8, 11, 12, 13, 15, 16, 17, 18, 19, 25-30
7. Blessed are the poor in spirit to those who believe that God spoke to Joshua. Joshua Chapters 1through 9, See Deuteronomy 34:9, Joshua 7:10, Joshua 8:1, 18, Joshua 10:8, Joshua 11:6, Joshua 13:1-7, Joshua 20:1-6, Joshua 24:1-13
8. Blessed are the poor in spirit to those who believe that God spoke to Judah. Judges 1:2, Judges 20:18 and the people of God, God sent a prophet, to speak to Israel. Judges 6:8-10
9. Blessed are the poor in spirit to those who believe that God spoke to Gideon. Judge 6:12-13 verse 16, 18, 23, Judges 7:2-5, 9-11, Judges 10:11-14
10. Blessed are the poor in spirit to those who believe that God spoke to Jephthah. God worked through Jephthah. Judges 11:1

11. Blessed are the poor in spirit to those who believe that God spoke to Samson. God moved in through Samson. Judges 13:24-25, See Judges 14:4
12. Blessed are the poor in spirit to those who believe that God spoke to Phinehas. He permitted him to go to war. Judges 20:28

Part DCVII

Blessed Are The Poor In Spirit. Matthew 5:3

Blessed Means Happy

Poor means meek in spirit. Poor means humble in spirit. Poor means lowly in spirit. Poor means quiet in spirit. Read Matthew 5:3-12, Read also Mark 1:15

Jesus did not say "*rich*" in spirit. Jesus said "*poor*" in spirit.

1. Blessed are the poor in spirit to those who believe that God spoke to children of Israel as led by God for help for war. Judges 20:23
2. Blessed are the poor in spirit to those who believe that God spoke to Samuel. I Samuel 2:18, 26 and God called Samuel. I Samuel 3:4, 6, 8, 10-13, I Samuel 3:1-21, I Samuel 8:7, 22, I Samuel 9:15-17, There was no open vision - I Samuel 3:1, I Samuel 16:1-3, 7
3. Blessed are the poor in spirit to those who believe that God spoke to Eli—a man of God was sent to Eli by God. I Samuel 2:27
4. Blessed are the poor in spirit to those who believe that God spoke to Saul through Samuel. I Samuel 15:1-3—Samuel anointed Saul as King for Israel. Read I Samuel 15:1-35
5. Blessed are the poor in spirit to those who believe that God spoke to Samuel. God anointed David. I Samuel 16:12, Read I Samuel 6:1-23, II Samuel 5:3-4
6. Blessed are the poor in spirit to those who believe that God spoke to David. I Samuel 23:2, 4, I Samuel 30:8, II Samuel 2:1, II Samuel 5:2, 19, 23-24
7. Blessed are the poor in spirit to those who believe that God spoke to Nathan. II Samuel 7:5-16, 17
8. Blessed are the poor in spirit to those who believe that God spoke to Solomon. I Kings 3:5, 11-14, Solomon become King. He became the Third King. I Kings 5:1, I Kings 6:12-13, I Kings 9:2-9, I Kings 11:9-13
9. Blessed are the poor in spirit to those who believe that God spoke to A-hijah's Prophecy by the Lord God—I Kings 14:5, 7-15, I Kings 11:29-31 and gave to Jeroboam
10. Blessed are the poor in spirit to those who believe that God spoke to Shemaich. I Kings 12:22, I Kings 12:23-24, I Kings 13:2, 9, 17, 21

11. Blessed are the poor in spirit to those who believe that God spoke to Jehu. I Kings 16:1, II Kings 9:36-37
12. Blessed are the poor in spirit to those who believe that God spoke to Elijah. I Kings 17:1, I Kings 18:1, 31, I Kings 21:17-19, 21-24, 29

Part DCVIII

Blessed Are The Poor In Spirit. Matthew 5:3

Blessed Means Happy

Poor means meek in spirit. Poor means humble in spirit. Poor means lowly in spirit. Poor means quiet in spirit. Read Matthew 5:3-12, Read also Mark 1:15

Jesus did not say "*rich*" in spirit. Jesus said "*poor*" in spirit.

1. Blessed are the poor in spirit to those who believe that God spoke to Ahab. A Prophet from God came to Ahab. I Kings 20:13-14, 28, 42
2. Blessed are the poor in spirit to those who believe that God spoke to Naaman. God was with Naaman. II Kings 5:1, 5, 9, 17, 1-27
3. Blessed are the poor in spirit to those who believe that God spoke to Elisha. God was with Elisha. II Kings 5:8, 10, 25, II Kings 6:1-33, II Kings 7:1
4. Blessed are the poor in spirit to those who believe that God spoke to King Jehu. II Kings 10:30, II Kings 15:12
5. Blessed are the poor in spirit to those who believe that God spoke to Satan. Job 1:7-8, 12, Job 2:2, 3, 6
6. Blessed are the poor in spirit to those who believe that God spoke to Job. Job 1:1
7. Blessed are the poor in spirit to those who believe that God spoke to Isaiah. Isaiah 6:5-13. He witnessed the Lord and the Lord spoke to Isaiah 7:3
8. Blessed are the poor in spirit to those who believe that God spoke to Jeremiah 1:1. God spoke to Jeremiah 1:5, 7-19, Jeremiah 2:1-3, 5-37, Jeremiah 33:1, 19, 23
9. Blessed are the poor in spirit to those who believe that God spoke to Ezekiel. God came to Ezekiel. Ezekiel 1:28, Ezekiel 2:1-3, Ezekiel 3:1-10
10. Blessed are the poor in spirit to those who believe that God spoke to Daniel. Daniel 4:31-32
11. Blessed are the poor in spirit to those who believe that God spoke to Hosea. Hosea 1:1-2
12. Blessed are the poor in spirit to those who believe that God spoke to Joel. Joel 1:1

PART DCIX

Blessed Are The Poor In Spirit. Matthew 5:3

Blessed Means Happy

Poor means meek in spirit. Poor means humble in spirit. Poor means lowly in spirit. Poor means quiet in spirit. Read Matthew 5:3-12, Read also Mark 1:15

Jesus did not say "*rich*" in spirit. Jesus said "*poor*" in spirit.

1. Blessed are the poor in spirit to those who believe that God spoke to Amos. God used Amos to speak for Him to the people of Israel. Amos 1:1-15 through Amos 9:1-15
2. Blessed are the poor in spirit to those who believe that God spoke to Obadiah for Him to speak to the people. Obadiah 1:1
3. Blessed are the poor in spirit to those who believe that God spoke to Jonah. Jonah 1:2, Jonah 3:2, Jonah 4:9-11
4. Blessed are the poor in spirit to those who believe that God spoke to Micah. God came to Micah. Micah 1:1
5. Blessed are the poor in spirit to those who believe that God spoke to Nahum. God used Nahum to speak for Him to the people. Nahum 1:1
6. Blessed are the poor in spirit to those who believe that God spoke to Habakkuk. God used Habakkuk to speak for Him to the people. Habakkuk 1:1
7. Blessed are the poor in spirit to those who believe that God spoke to Zephaniah. God came and spoke to Zephaniah. Zephaniah 1:1
8. Blessed are the poor in spirit to those who believe that God spoke to Haggai. God used Haggai to speak for God to the people. Haggai 1:1
9. Blessed are the poor in spirit to those who believe that God spoke to Zechariah. God used Zechariah to speak for Him to the people. Zechariah 1:1
10. Blessed are the poor in spirit to those who believe that God spoke to Malachi. God used Malachi to speak for Him to the people. Malachi 1:1
11. Blessed are the poor in spirit to those who believe that God spoke to Paul through Jesus what he (Paul) must do. Acts 9:1-6
12. Blessed are the poor in spirit to those who believe that God spoke to Cornelius through an angel of God concerning Cornelius' prayers. Acts 10:1-4

PART DCX

Blessed Are The Poor In Spirit. Matthew 5:3

Blessed Means Happy

Poor means meek in spirit. Poor means humble in spirit. Poor means lowly in spirit. Poor means quiet in spirit. Read Matthew 5:3-12, Read also Mark 1:15

Jesus did not say "*rich*" in spirit. Jesus said "*poor*" in spirit.

1. Blessed are the poor in spirit to those who believe that only God can turn a **Vict** into a **Vict***ory*. I Corinthians 15:57, I John 5:4-15 verse 4
2. Blessed are the poor in spirit to those who believe that God is our God even to (through) death. Psalm 48:14
3. Blessed are the poor in spirit to those who believe this scripture: "Paul, and Silvanus, and Timotheus, unto the the church of the Thessalonians in God our Father and the Lord Jesus Christ:" II Thessalonians 1:1
4. Blessed are the poor in spirit to those who believe this scripture: "Grace unto you, and peace, from God our Father and the Lord Jesus Christ." II Thessalonians 1:2
5. Blessed are the poor in spirit to those who believe this scripture: "We are bound to thank God always for you, brethren, as it is meet, because that your faith groweth exceedingly, and the charity of every one of you all toward each other aboundeth;" II Thessalonians 1:3
6. Blessed are the poor in spirit to those who believe this scripture: "So that we ourselves glory in you in the churches of God for your patience and faith in all your persectutions and tribulations that ye endure:" II Thessalonians 1:4
7. Blessed are the poor in spirit to those who believe this scripture: "Which is a manifest token of the righteous judgment of God, that ye may be counted worthy of the kingdom of God, for which ye also suffer:" II Thessalonians 1:5
8. Blessed are the poor in spirit to those who believe this scripture: "Seeing it is a righteous thing with God to recompense tribulation to them that trouble you;" II Thessalonians 1:6
9. Blessed are the poor in spirit to those who believe this scripture: "And to you who are troubled rest with us, when the Lord Jesus shall be revealed from heaven with his mighty angels," II Thessalonians 1:7

10. Blessed are the poor in spirit to those who believe this scripture: "In flaming fire taking vengeance on them that know not God, and that obey not the gospel of our Lord Jesus Christ:" II Thessalonians 1:8
11. Blessed are the poor in spirit to those who believe this scripture: "Who shall be punished with everlasting destruction from the presence of the Lord, and from the glory of his power; II Thessalonians 1:9
12. Blessed are the poor in spirit to those who believe this scripture: "When he shall come to be glorified in his saints, and to be admired in all them that believe (because our testimony among you was believed) in that day." II Thessalonians 1:10

Part DCXI

Blessed Are The Poor In Spirit. Matthew 5:3

Blessed Means Happy

Poor means meek in spirit. Poor means humble in spirit. Poor means lowly in spirit. Poor means quiet in spirit. Read Matthew 5:3-12, Read also Mark 1:15

Jesus did not say "*rich*" in spirit. Jesus said "*poor*" in spirit.

1. Blessed are the poor in spirit to those who believe this scripture: "Wherefore also we pray always for you, that our God would count you worthy of this calling, and fulfill all the good pleasure of his goodness, and the work of faith with power:" II Thessalonians 1:11
2. Blessed are the poor in spirit to those who believe this scripture: "That the name of our Lord Jesus Christ may be glorified in you, and ye in him, according to the grace of our God and the Lord Jesus Christ." II Thessalonians 1:12
3. Blessed are the poor in spirit to those who believe that salvation is free to all that believe in Jesus. Matthew 11:28-30
4. Blessed are the poor in spirit to those who believe that salvation is free to all that believe in Jesus. John 3:8
5. Blessed are the poor in spirit to those who believe that salvation is free to all that believe in Jesus. John 7:37-38
6. Blessed are the poor in spirit to those who believe that salvation is free to all that believe in Jesus. John 8:32, 36
7. Blessed are the poor in spirit to those who believe that salvation is free to all that believe in Jesus. John 14:6
8. Blessed are the poor in spirit to those who believe that salvation is free to all that believe in Jesus. Acts 16:30-31
9. Blessed are the poor in spirit to those who believe that salvation is free to all that believe in Jesus. Romans 10:9
10. Blessed are the poor in spirit to those who believe that salvation is free to all that believe in Jesus. Romans 10:10

11. Blessed are the poor in spirit to those who believe that salvation is free to all that believe in Jesus. Romans 10:11
12. Blessed are the poor in spirit to those who believe that salvation is free to all that believe in Jesus. Romans 10:12

Part DCXII

Blessed Are The Poor In Spirit. Matthew 5:3

Blessed Means Happy

Poor means meek in spirit. Poor means humble in spirit. Poor means lowly in spirit. Poor means quiet in spirit. Read Matthew 5:3-12, Read also Mark 1:15

Jesus did not say "*rich*" in spirit. Jesus said "*poor*" in spirit.

1. Blessed are the poor in spirit to those who believe that salvation is free to all that believe in Jesus. Romans 10:13
2. Blessed are the poor in spirit to those who believe that salvation is free to all that believe in Jesus. Romans 6:23
3. Blessed are the poor in spirit to those who believe that salvation is free to all that believe in Jesus. II Corinthians 6:2
4. Blessed are the poor in spirit to those who believe that salvation is free to all that believe in Jesus. Isaiah 49:8
5. Blessed are the poor in spirit to those who believe that salvation is free to all that believe in Jesus. John 3:16
6. Blessed are the poor in spirit to those who believe that salvation is free to all that believe in Jesus. John 6:37-40
7. Blessed are the poor in spirit to those who believe that salvation is free to all that believe in Jesus. Ephesians 2:5
8. Blessed are the poor in spirit to those who believe that salvation is free to all that believe in Jesus. Ephesians 2:8
9. Blessed are the poor in spirit to those who believe that salvation is free to all that believe in Jesus. Romans 3:20
10. Blessed are the poor in spirit to those who believe that salvation is free to all that believe in Jesus. II Peter 3:9
11. Blessed are the poor in spirit to those who believe that salvation is free to all that believe in Jesus. Acts 4:12
12. Blessed are the poor in spirit to those who believe that salvation is free to all that believe in Jesus. Matthew 3:2

Part DCXIII

Blessed Are The Poor In Spirit. Matthew 5:3

Blessed Means Happy

Poor means meek in spirit. Poor means humble in spirit. Poor means lowly in spirit. Poor means quiet in spirit. Read Matthew 5:3-12, Read also Mark 1:15

Jesus did not say "*rich*" in spirit. Jesus said "*poor*" in spirit.

1. Blessed are the poor in spirit to those who believe that salvation is free to all that believe in Jesus. Matthew 4:17
2. Blessed are the poor in spirit to those who believe that salvation is free to all that believe in Jesus. Mark 1:15
3. Blessed are the poor in spirit to those who believe that salvation is free to all that believe in Jesus. Joel 2:32
4. Blessed are the poor in spirit to those who believe that salvation is free to all that believe in Jesus. Acts 2:21
5. Blessed are the poor in spirit to those who believe that salvation is free to all that believe in Jesus. John 1:12
6. Blessed are the poor in spirit to those who believe that salvation is free to all that believe in Jesus. Romans 8:14
7. Blessed are the poor in spirit to those who believe that salvation is free to all that believe in Jesus. Romans 8:15
8. Blessed are the poor in spirit to those who believe that salvation is free to all that believe in Jesus. Romans 8:16
9. Blessed are the poor in spirit to those who believe that salvation is free to all that believe in Jesus. Galatians 4:5
10. Blessed are the poor in spirit to those who believe that salvation is free to all that believe in Jesus. Ephesians 1:5
11. Blessed are the poor in spirit to those who believe that salvation is free to all that believe in Jesus. John 11:25-27
12. Blessed are the poor in spirit to those who believe that salvation is free to all that believe in Jesus. John 4:42

Part DCXIV

Blessed Are The Poor In Spirit. Matthew 5:3

Blessed Means Happy

Poor means meek in spirit. Poor means humble in spirit. Poor means lowly in spirit. Poor means quiet in spirit. Read Matthew 5:3-12, Read also Mark 1:15

Jesus did not say "*rich*" in spirit. Jesus said "*poor*" in spirit.

1. Blessed are the poor in spirit to those who believe that salvation is free to all that believe in Jesus. I John 4:14
2. Blessed are the poor in spirit to those who believe that salvation is free to all that believe in Jesus. I John 4:15
3. Blessed are the poor in spirit to those who believe that salvation is free to all that believe in Jesus. I John 5:11
4. Blessed are the poor in spirit to those who believe that salvation is free to all that believe in Jesus. I John 5:13
5. Blessed are the poor in spirit to those who believe that salvation is free to all that believe in Jesus. I John 5:7
6. Blessed are the poor in spirit to those who believe that salvation is free to all that believe in Jesus. Acts 8:37
7. Blessed are the poor in spirit to those who believe that salvation is free to all that believe in Jesus. Luke 1:35
8. Blessed are the poor in spirit to those who believe that salvation is free to all that believe in Jesus. Luke 2:10-14
9. Blessed are the poor in spirit to those who believe that salvation is free to all that believe in Jesus. Matthew 1:21
10. Blessed are the poor in spirit to those who believe that salvation is free to all that believe in Jesus. Matthew 1:25
11. Blessed are the poor in spirit to those who believe that salvation is free to all that believe in Jesus. Luke 1:31
12. Blessed are the poor in spirit to those who believe that salvation is free to all that believe in Jesus. Luke 2:21

Part DCXV

Blessed Are The Poor In Spirit. Matthew 5:3

Blessed Means Happy

Poor means meek in spirit. Poor means humble in spirit. Poor means lowly in spirit. Poor means quiet in spirit. Read Matthew 5:3-12, Read also Mark 1:15

Jesus did not say "*rich*" in spirit. Jesus said "*poor*" in spirit.

1. Blessed are the poor in spirit to those who believe that salvation is free to all that believe in Jesus. Matthew 28:18
2. Blessed are the poor in spirit to those who believe that salvation is free to all that believe in Jesus. Habakkuk 2:4
3. Blessed are the poor in spirit to those who believe that salvation is free to all that believe in Jesus. Romans 1:17
4. Blessed are the poor in spirit to those who believe that salvation is free to all that believe in Jesus. Galatians 3:10
5. Blessed are the poor in spirit to those who believe that salvation is free to all that believe in Jesus. Hebrews 10:38-39
6. Blessed are the poor in spirit to those who believe that salvation is free to all that believe in Jesus. John 5:22-27
7. Blessed are the poor in spirit to those who believe that salvation is free to all that believe in Jesus. Hebrews 5:9
8. Blessed are the poor in spirit to those who believe that salvation is free to all that believe in Jesus. Hebrews 5:12
9. Blessed are the poor in spirit to those who believe that salvation is free to all that believe in Jesus. Matthew 3:17
10. Blessed are the poor in spirit to those who believe that salvation is free to all that believe in Jesus. Matthew 12:8
11. Blessed are the poor in spirit to those who believe that salvation is free to all that believe in Jesus. Matthew 17:5
12. Blessed are the poor in spirit to those who believe that salvation is free to all that believe in Jesus. Mark 1:11

PART DCXVI

Blessed Are The Poor In Spirit. Matthew 5:3

Blessed Means Happy

Poor means meek in spirit. Poor means humble in spirit. Poor means lowly in spirit. Poor means quiet in spirit. Read Matthew 5:3-12, Read also Mark 1:15

Jesus did not say "*rich*" in spirit. Jesus said "*poor*" in spirit.

1. Blessed are the poor in spirit to those who believe that salvation is free to all that believe in Jesus. Mark 9:7
2. Blessed are the poor in spirit to those who believe that salvation is free to all that believe in Jesus. Luke 3:22
3. Blessed are the poor in spirit to those who believe that salvation is free to all that believe in Jesus. Luke 9:35
4. Blessed are the poor in spirit to those who believe that salvation belong to the Lord. Psalm 3:8
5. Blessed are the poor in spirit to those who believe that salvation is free to all that believe in Jesus. Romans 1:7
6. Blessed are the poor in spirit to those who believe that salvation is free to all that believe in Jesus. II Peter 1:17
7. Blessed are the poor in spirit to those who believe that salvation is free to all that believe in Jesus. I John 3:2
8. Blessed are the poor in spirit to those who believe that salvation is free to all that believe in Jesus. I Corinthians 10:4
9. Blessed are the poor in spirit to those who believe that salvation is free to all that believe in Jesus. Jonah 2:9
10. Blessed are the poor in spirit to those who believe that salvation is free to all that believe in Jesus. Zechariah 9:9
11. Blessed are the poor in spirit to those who believe that salvation is free to all that believe in Jesus. John 19:30
12. Blessed are the poor in spirit to those who believe that salvation is free to all that believe in Jesus. Isaiah 62:11

Part DCXVII

Blessed Are The Poor In Spirit. Matthew 5:3

Blessed Means Happy

Poor means meek in spirit. Poor means humble in spirit. Poor means lowly in spirit. Poor means quiet in spirit. Read Matthew 5:3-12, Read also Mark 1:15

Jesus did not say "*rich*" in spirit. Jesus said "*poor*" in spirit.

1. Blessed are the poor in spirit to those who believe that salvation is free to all that believe in Jesus. Matthew 21:4-5
2. Blessed are the poor in spirit to those who believe that salvation is free to all that believe in Jesus. John 12:15
3. Blessed are the poor in spirit to those who believe that salvation is free to all that believe in Jesus. I Thessalonians 5:8
4. Blessed are the poor in spirit to those who believe that salvation is free to all that believe in Jesus. Ephesians 1:13
5. Blessed are the poor in spirit to those who believe that salvation is free to all that believe in Jesus. Ephesians 6:17
6. Blessed are the poor in spirit to those who believe that salvation is free to all that believe in Jesus. Philippians 1:28
7. Blessed are the poor in spirit to those who believe that salvation is free to all that believe in Jesus. I Thessalonians 5:9
8. Blessed are the poor in spirit to those who believe that salvation is free to all that believe in Jesus. II Timothy 2:10
9. Blessed are the poor in spirit to those who believe that salvation is free to all that believe in Jesus. II Timothy 3:15
10. Blessed are the poor in spirit to those who believe that salvation is free to all that believe in Jesus. Titus 2:11
11. Blessed are the poor in spirit to those who believe that salvation is free to all that believe in Jesus. Hebrews 2:10
12. Blessed are the poor in spirit to those who believe that salvation is free to all that believe in Jesus. Hebrews 9:28

Part DCXVIII

Blessed Are The Poor In Spirit. Matthew 5:3

Blessed Means Happy

Poor means meek in spirit. Poor means humble in spirit. Poor means lowly in spirit. Poor means quiet in spirit. Read Matthew 5:3-12, Read also Mark 1:15

Jesus did not say "*rich*" in spirit. Jesus said "*poor*" in spirit.

1. Blessed are the poor in spirit to those who believe that salvation is free to all that believe in Jesus. I Peter 1:9
2. Blessed are the poor in spirit to those who believe that salvation is free to all that believe in Jesus. I Peter 1:10
3. Blessed are the poor in spirit to those who believe that salvation is free to all that believe in Jesus. II Peter 3:15
4. Blessed are the poor in spirit to those who believe that salvation is free to all that believe in Jesus. Jude 1:3
5. Blessed are the poor in spirit to those who believe that salvation is free to all that believe in Jesus. Revelation 7:10
6. Blessed are the poor in spirit to those who believe that salvation is free to all that believe in Jesus. Revelation 12:10
7. Blessed are the poor in spirit to those who believe that salvation is free to all that believe in Jesus. Revelation 19:1
8. Blessed are the poor in spirit to those who believe that salvation is free to all that believe in Jesus. Isaiah 55:1-2
9. Blessed are the poor in spirit to those who believe that salvation is free to all that believe in Jesus. Revelation 22:17
10. Blessed are the poor in spirit to those who believe that salvation is free to all that believe in Jesus. Matthew 5:6
11. Blessed are the poor in spirit to those who believe that salvation is free to all that believe in Jesus. John 6:27
12. Blessed are the poor in spirit to those who believe that salvation is free to all that believe in Jesus. John 4:6-14

Part DCXIX

Blessed Are The Poor In Spirit. Matthew 5:3

Blessed Means Happy

Poor means meek in spirit. Poor means humble in spirit. Poor means lowly in spirit. Poor means quiet in spirit. Read Matthew 5:3-12, Read also Mark 1:15

Jesus did not say "*rich*" in spirit. Jesus said "*poor*" in spirit.

1. Blessed are the poor in spirit to those who believe that salvation is free to all that believe in Jesus. Revelation 22:1-2
2. Blessed are the poor in spirit to those who believe in "Rejoicing in hope; patient in tribulation; continuing instant in prayer." I Corinthians 13:12, 13, Romans 12:12
3. Blessed are the poor in spirit to those who believe that Christ lives, we will also live with Him. John 14:19
4. Blessed are the poor in spirit to those who believe and become more grounded in the Truth, and strongly devote to the faith. I Timothy 3:14-16 verse 15, Ephesians 3:1-21 verse 17, Colossians 1:1-29 verse 23
5. Blessed are the poor in spirit to those who believe that God's Grace is enough. Ephesians 2:5, 8, II Corinthians 12:9
6. Blessed are the poor in spirit to those who believe to remember of God's people. Luke 23:42-43
7. Blessed are the poor in spirit to those who believe to rest upon Jesus' faith like a dew in the morning. Matthew 11:28, II Corinthians 12:9, II Thessalonians 1:7, Hebrews 4:1, 3, 4, 8, 9, 10, 11
8. Blessed are the poor in spirit to those who believe to manifest the Lord's name because He reign. Luke 1:46, Acts 10:46, Revelation 11:15
9. Blessed are the poor in spirit to those who believe Jesus Christ. Hebrews 13:8
10. Blessed are the poor in spirit to those who are able to say: "I believe Jesus Christ." Hebrews 13:8
11. Blessed are the poor in spirit to those who believe that the cross free us from sin. Romans 5:1, Romans 6:7
12. Blessed are the poor in spirit to those who believe the blood of Christ's cross. Colossians 1:20

Part DCXX

Blessed Are The Poor In Spirit. Matthew 5:3

Blessed Means Happy

Poor means meek in spirit. Poor means humble in spirit. Poor means lowly in spirit. Poor means quiet in spirit. Read Matthew 5:3-12, Read also Mark 1:15

Jesus did not say "*rich*" in spirit. Jesus said "*poor*" in spirit.

1. Blessed are the poor in spirit to those who believe this Psalm: "When I remember these things, I pour out my soul in me: for I had gone with the multitude, I went with them to the house of God, with the voice of joy and praise, with a multitude that kept holyday." Psalm 42:4
2. Blessed are the poor in spirit to those who believe this Psalm: "I will lift up mine eyes unto the hills, from whence cometh my help." Psalm 121:1
3. Blessed are the poor in spirit to those who believe this Psalm: "My help cometh from the Lord, which made heaven and earth." Psalm 121:2
4. Blessed are the poor in spirit to those who believe this Psalm: "He will not suffer thy foot to be moved: he that keepeth thee will not slumber." Psalm 121:3
5. Blessed are the poor in spirit to those who believe this Psalm: "Behold, he that keepeth Israel shall neither slumber nor sleep." Psalm 121:4
6. Blessed are the poor in spirit to those who believe this Psalm: "The Lord is thy keeper: the Lord is thy shade upon they right hand." Psalm 121:5
7. Blessed are the poor in spirit to those who believe this Psalm: "The sun shall not smite thee by day, nor the moon by night." Psalm 121:6
8. Blessed are the poor in spirit to those who believe this Psalm: "The Lord shall preserve thee from all evil: he shall preserve thy soul." Psalm 121:7
9. Blessed are the poor in spirit to those who believe this Psalm: "The Lord shall preserve thy going out and thy coming in from this time forth, and even for evermore." Psalm 121:8
10. Blessed are the poor in spirit to those who believe this scripture: "For therein is the righteousness of God revealed from faith to faith: as it is written, The just shall live by faith." Romans 1:17

11. Blessed are the poor in spirit to those who believe this scripture: "But when Peter was come to Antioch, I withstood him to the face, because he was to be blamed." Galatians 3:11
12. Blessed are the poor in spirit to those who believe this scripture: "*Behold, his soul which is lifted up is not upright in him: but the just shall live by his faith.*" Habakkuk 2:4

Part DCXXI

Blessed Are The Poor In Spirit. Matthew 5:3

Blessed Means Happy

Poor means meek in spirit. Poor means humble in spirit. Poor means lowly in spirit. Poor means quiet in spirit. Read Matthew 5:3-12, Read also Mark 1:15

Jesus did not say "*rich*" in spirit. Jesus said "*poor*" in spirit.

1. Blessed are the poor in spirit to those who believe this scripture: "But what saith it? The word is nigh thee, even in thy mouth, and in thy heart: that is, the word of faith, which we preach;" Romans 10:8
2. Blessed are the poor in spirit to those who believe this scripture: "That if thou shalt confess with thy mouth the Lord Jesus, and shalt believe in thine heart that God hath raised him from the dead, thou shalt be saved." Romans 10:9
3. Blessed are the poor in spirit to those who believe this scripture: "For with the heart man believeth unto righteousness; and with the mouth confession is made unto salvation." Romans 10:10
4. Blessed are the poor in spirit to those who believe this scripture: "For the scripture saith, Whosoever believeth on him shall not be ashamed." Romans 10:11
5. Blessed are the poor in spirit to those who believe this scripture: "For there is no difference between the Jew and the Greek: for the same Lord over all is rich unto all that call upon him." Romans 10:12
6. Blessed are the poor in spirit to those who believe this scripture: "For whosoever shall call upon the name of the Lord shall be saved." Romans 10:13
7. Blessed are the poor in spirit to those who believe this scripture: "So then faith cometh by hearing, and hearing by the word of God." Romans 10:17
8. Blessed are the poor in spirit to those who believe this Psalm: "Praise ye the Lord. Praise the Lord, O my soul." Psalm146:1
9. Blessed are the poor in spirit to those who believe this Psalm: "While I live will I praise the Lord: I will sing praises unto my God while I have any being." Psalm 146:2
10. Blessed are the poor in spirit to those who believe this Psalm: "Put not your trust in princes, nor in the son of man, in whom there is no help." Psalm 146:3

11. Blessed are the poor in spirit to those who believe this Psalm: "His breath goeth forth, he returneth to his earth; in that very day his thoughts perish." Psalm 146:4
12. Blessed are the poor in spirit to those who believe this Psalm: "Happy is he that hath the God of Jacob for his help, whose hope is in the Lord his God:" Psalm 146:5

Part DCXXII

Blessed Are The Poor In Spirit. Matthew 5:3

Blessed Means Happy

Poor means meek in spirit. Poor means humble in spirit. Poor means lowly in spirit. Poor means quiet in spirit. Read Matthew 5:3-12, Read also Mark 1:15

Jesus did not say "*rich*" in spirit. Jesus said "*poor*" in spirit.

1. Blessed are the poor in spirit to those who believe this Psalm: "Which made heaven, and earth, the sea, and all that therein is: which keepeth truth for ever: Psalm 146:6
2. Blessed are the poor in spirit to those who believe this Psalm: "Which executeth judgment for the oppressed: which giveth food to the hungry. The Lord looseth the prisoners:" Psalm 146:7
3. Blessed are the poor in spirit to those who believe this Psalm: "The Lord openeth the eyes of the blind: the Lord raiseth them that are bowed down: the Lord loveth the righteous:" Psalm 146:8
4. Blessed are the poor in spirit to those who believe this Psalm: "The Lord preserveth the strangers; he relieveth the fatherless and widow: but the way of the wicked he turneth upside down." Psalm 146:9
5. Blessed are the poor in spirit to those who believe this Psalm: "The Lord shall reign for ever, even thy God. O Zion, unto all generations. Praise ye the Lord." Psalm 146:10
6. Blessed are the poor in spirit to those who believe to the saving of our souls through Jesus Christ. Hebrews 10:39
7. Blessed are the poor in spirit to those who believe in keeping of the souls through Jesus Christ except one of Jesus' disciples who was the son of perdition; that the scripture might be fulfilled. Psalm 41:9, John 17:12
8. Blessed are the poor in spirit to those who believe in **life after death.** John 11:25
9. Blessed are the poor in spirit to those who believe in Jesus' Promised Words: "In Three Days I will rise again." And He did!!! And He will come back to take us home to Glory with Him to live for ever more!!! Matthew 27:63, Mark 8:31, Mark 9:31, Mark 10:34, Luke 18:33, Luke 24:7, 46, John 11:25, John

20:9, Acts 26:23, Matthew 17:9, Matthew 26:32, Matthew 28:6-20, Mark 9:9, Mark 14:28, Mark 16:6, 9, Luke 24:6-8, 9-53 verse 34, John 21:14, Acts 17:3, Romans 8:34, I Corinthians 15:13-14, 20, Colossians 2:12, Colossians 3:1

10. Blessed are the poor in spirit to those who believe that Faith is to have Faith in God. Mark 10:22, John 4:24, Hebrews 11:6, Romans 10:11
11. Blessed are the poor in spirit to those who believe this Psalmist: "For a day in thy courts is better than a thousand. I had rather be a doorkeeper in the house of my God, than to dwell in the tents of wickedness." Psalm 84:10
12. Blessed are the poor in spirit to those who believe this Psalmist: "Thy testimonies are very sure: holiness becometh thine house, O Lord, for ever." Psalm 93:5

Part DCXXIII

Blessed Are The Poor In Spirit. Matthew 5:3

Blessed Means Happy

Poor means meek in spirit. Poor means humble in spirit. Poor means lowly in spirit. Poor means quiet in spirit. Read Matthew 5:3-12, Read also Mark 1:15

Jesus did not say "*rich*" in spirit. Jesus said "*poor*" in spirit.

1. Blessed are the poor in spirit to those who believe this Psalmist: "Behold, how good and how pleasant it is for brethren to dwell together in unity!" Psalm 133:1
2. Blessed are the poor in spirit to those who believe this Psalmist: "Praise ye the Lord. Praise ye the name of the Lord; praise him, O ye servants of the Lord." Psalm 135:1
3. Blessed are the poor in spirit to those who believe this Psalmist: "Ye that stand in the house of the Lord, in the courts of the house of our God," Psalm 135:2
4. Blessed are the poor in spirit to those who believe this Psalmist: "Praise the Lord; for the Lord is good: sing praises unto his name; for it is pleasant." Psalm 135:3
5. Blessed are the poor in spirit to those who believe this Psalmist: "Praise ye the Lord: for it is good to sing praises unto our God; for it is pleasant; and praise is comely." Psalm 147:1
6. Blessed are the poor in spirit to those who believe that God know our own names because He is mine and we are His. Isaiah 43:1
7. Blessed are the poor in spirit to those who believe that we are amazed that God think of us everyday. Psalm 139:17
8. Blessed are the poor in spirit to those who believe that God will fight for us. Exodus 14:14
9. Blessed are the poor in spirit to those who believe that **God** is our **Rock.** Psalm 62:6. See I Corinthians 10:4 (Exodus 17:6)
10. Blessed are the poor in spirit to those who believe that **God** is our **Salvation**. Psalm 62:6
11. Blessed are the poor in spirit to those who believe that **God** is our **Defence.** Psalm 62:6
12. Blessed are the poor in spirit to those who believe that *my refuge* is **in God.** Psalm 62:7

Part DCXXIV

Blessed Are The Poor In Spirit. Matthew 5:3

Blessed Means Happy

Poor means meek in spirit. Poor means humble in spirit. Poor means lowly in spirit. Poor means quiet in spirit. Read Matthew 5:3-12, Read also Mark 1:15

Jesus did not say "*rich*" in spirit. Jesus said "*poor*" in spirit.

1. Blessed are the poor in spirit to those who believe that **God** is our **Refuge.** He is our **Salvation.** Psalm 62:7
2. Blessed are the poor in spirit to those who believe that **In God** is my *salvation.* Psalm 62:7
3. Blessed are the poor in spirit to those who believe that **In God** is my *glory.* Psalm 62:7
4. Blessed are the poor in spirit to those who believe that **In God** is the **Rock** of my *strength.* Psalm 62:7
5. Blessed are the poor in spirit to those who believe that when God forgives all of our past, He forget and **faithful** and **just to forgive.** I John 1:9
6. Blessed are the poor in spirit to those who believe that when God forgive all of our past, He forget by remembering no more. Hebrews 12:8, Isaiah 54:4
7. Blessed are the poor in spirit to those who believe that when God forgive, He forget when we are faithful to Him **daily until death**. Revelation 2:10, I Corinthians 15:31
8. Blessed are the poor in spirit to those who believe that when God forgive He forget, but others will forgive but won't forget. Philippians 3:13, Deuteronomy 9:7, Luke 17:32, Genesis 19:26
9. Blessed are the poor in spirit to those who that when God forgive, He forget. God expect of us as children of God to do the same. II Corinthians 2:7, 10, II Corinthians 12:13
10. Blessed are the poor in spirit to those who believe that when God forgive, He forget by having us to sin no more. John 5:14, John 8:11
11. Blessed are the poor in spirit to those who believe that when God forgives, He forget all of our past when we are **faithful** to Him in **His works**, in **His Love** and in **His ministry**. Hebrews 6:10

12. Blessed are the poor in spirit to those who believe that when God forgive, He forget as far as the east is from the west, so far has He **removed our transgressions from us**; like as a father pitieth his children, so the Lord pitieth them that **fear Him** because He *knows* our *frame*; He *remember* that we are *dust.* Psalm 103:12-14

PART DCXXV

Blessed Are The Poor In Spirit. Matthew 5:3

Blessed Means Happy

Poor means meek in spirit. Poor means humble in spirit. Poor means lowly in spirit. Poor means quiet in spirit. Read Matthew 5:3-12, Read also Mark 1:15

Jesus did not say "*rich*" in spirit. Jesus said "*poor*" in spirit.

1. Blessed are the poor in spirit to those who believe that Jesus told the Father to forgive them: "Then said Jesus, Father, forgive them; for they know not what they do. And they parted his raiment, and cast lots." Luke 23:34
2. Blessed are the poor in spirit to those who believe to apply God's Word in our life daily. Psalm 90:12, Proverbs 2:2, Proverbs 22:17, Proverbs 23:12
3. Blessed are the poor in spirit to those who believe that Jesus has thousand of famous speeches inspire us to be saved, to be filled with the Holy Spirit, to be baptized in the Holy Spirit to win souls, to declare of His Second Coming and to bring us home to Glory to live with Him for ever more. Proverbs 11:30, II Timothy 3:16, Matthew 11:28, Mark 16:17 (c), John 7:37-38, John 20:22, Luke 24:49, Acts 1:5, Acts 1:4-8, Revelation 22:20, Colossians 3:4, Acts 2:1-4, John 17:17-19, Joel 2:26-32, Acts 11:16, Acts 2:16-21 verse 19, Acts 10:44-47, Acts 2:1-47, Acts 11:1-6, Acts 8:14-17, Matthew 3:11 (b), Mark 1:8, Luke 3:16 (b), John 1:33, Matthew 5:6, Acts 4:8, 31, Acts 13:9, Ephesians 5:18, Amos 4:12, Revelation 3:11, Romans 16:15, Revelation 22:7, 12, 16, 20-21, Revelation 1:7, I Thessalonians 4:13-17, I John 3:2-3, Hebrews 12:10, Hebrews 12:14, Exodus 28:36, Exodus 39:30, Zechariah 14:20, II Corinthians 5:6-10, Revelation 2:10, Psalm 127:3, I Peter 2:21, Hebrews 9:28, I Peter 5:4, I John 2:28, John 14:16-21, John 15:26-27, John 14:1-4, John 16:1-16 verse 7, Ecclesiastes 12:13, I Thessalonians 4:11-12, II Timothy 2:15, II Timothy 3:14-17, II Timothy 4:6-8, Matthew 25:21, 23, I Thessalonians 3:13, John 17:17, 19, Micah 6:8

Conclusion:

Be Faithful To Christ:

Bible Scripture Readings:

1. II Timothy 4:6

2. II Timothy 4:7
3. II Timothy 4:8

Read Revelation 2:10

4. Blessed are the poor in spirit to those who believe that Jesus did not just come to make us live as salvation experience only but He came to fulfill the promise of the Father, the promise of the Holy Spirit, the promise of being filled with the Holy Spirit, the promise of winning souls and the promise of His Second Coming. Proverbs 11:30, II Timothy 3:16, Matthew 11:28, Mark 16:17 (c), John 7:37-38, John 20:22, Luke 24:49, Acts 1:5, Acts 1:4-8, Revelation 22:20, Colossians 3:4, Acts 2:1-4, John 17:17-19, Joel 2:26-32, Acts 11:16, Acts 2:16-21 verse 19, Acts 10:44-47, Acts 2:1-47, Acts 11:1-6, Acts 8:14-17, Matthew 3:11 (b), Mark 1:8, Luke 3:16 (b), John 1:33, Matthew 5:6, Acts 4:8, 31, Acts 13:9, Ephesians 5:18, Amos 4:12, Revelation 3:11, Romans 16:15, Revelation 22:7, 12, 16, 20-21, Revelation 1:7, I Thessalonians 4:13-17, I John 3:2-3, Hebrews 12:10, Hebrews 12:14, Exodus 28:36, Exodus 39:30, Zechariah 14:20, II Corinthians 5:6-10, Revelation 2:10, Psalm 127:3, I Peter 2:21, Hebrews 9:28, I Peter 5:4, I John 2:28, John 14:16-21, John 15:26-27, John 14:1-4, John 16:1-16 verse 7, Ecclesiastes 12:13, I Thessalonians 4:11-12, II Timothy 2:15, II Timothy 3:14-17, II Timothy 4:6-8, Matthew 25:21, 23, I Thessalonians 3:13, John 17:17, 19, Micah 6:8
5. Blessed are the poor in spirit to those who believe that the Baptism of the Holy Spirit is so **"precious"** and **"famous"** because they have talked about and have been mentioning of the Spirit Baptism for centuries according through the Spirit and belief of the truth. II Thessalonians 2:13, Matthew 3:11 (b), Mark 1:8, Luke 3:16, John 1:33, Acts 1:5 (b), Acts 11:16 (b)
6. Blessed are the poor in spirit to those who believe that if Jesus has given us "*an* **example"** to follow as He *led* us **"in His Steps,"** but **"lacking" the baptism of the Holy Spirit "except"** to the **Holy Bible** *literal* as simple as it is **"without Biblical Pattern** and just as it was **"taught,"** would be so **"unavailable"** in our life **"before" the coming of Christ:** I Peter 2:21, John 13:15, I Timothy 4:12, Hebrews 4:11, Hebrews 8:5, James 5:10, Jude 1:7, Amos 4:12. But thank you Jesus for telling us to receive the Holy Spirit and being baptized in the Holy Spirit. John 20:22, Acts 2:38, Acts 8:14-17 verse 15, Acts 11:16, Acts 1:4-8, Luke 24:49, I Corinthians 15:57-58, Matthew 3:11 (b), Mark 1:8, Mark 16:17 (c), Luke 3:16, John 1:33, Acts 2:1-47, Acts 2:1-4, So the baptism of the Holy

Spirit is so **"precious"** and **"famous."** We need Christ's Spirit Baptism instead of **lacking.** Christ expect us to take **"Action;" "Not Lacking"** the Bible. "*Act*" mean **"Action;" Not Lacking.**

7. Blessed are the poor in spirit to those who are able to say, "Fill my soul up, Lord. Fill me up, Jesus. Make a less of me. I want more of You, Jesus." Job 8:21, Psalm 81:10, Jeremiah 23:24, Ezekiel 3:3, Haggai 2:7, Romans 15:13, Ephesians 4:10
8. Blessed are the poor in spirit to those who believe to *kneel down* or *kneel*, at the **Master's** (Jesus) **Feet** and *adore* **Him** *worship* **Him** and *love* **Him** and *praise* **Him** and *thank* **Him** at all time. Psalm 95:6, Philippians 2:10-11, Psalm 119:29, Psalm 138:1-5, John 16:23-33 verse 27, **I John 4:19**, John 21:15-17, John 3:16, John 13:1, 23, 34, John 14:28, John 15:9, 12, John 16:27, John 17:23, 26, John 19:26, II Thessalonians 2:16, I John 4:10, 11, **19**, **Revelation 1:5,** Revelation 3:9, Revelation 12:11, John 20:2, John 21:7, 20, Romans 8:37, **Galatians 2:20, Ephesians 2:4, Ephesians 5:2, 25**
9. Blessed are the poor in spirit to those who believe that God is great and greatly to be praised. **Psalm 48:1,** Psalm 47:1-2, Psalm 77:1-13, **Psalm 96:4,** Psalm 99:3, **Psalm 145:3, 8**
10. Blessed are the poor in spirit to those who believe that God's lovingkindness is loving us. Psalm 26:1-3, Psalm 36:7, 10, Psalm 40:11, Psalm 42:8, Psalm 48:8-10, Psalm 51:1-15 verse 1, Psalm 63:1-4 verse 3, Psalm 69:16-17, Psalm 107:43, Psalm 119:88-90, Psalm 143:8, Jeremiah 9:24, **Jeremiah 31:1-3 verse 3, Jeremiah 32:18,** Hosea 2:18-19 verse 19, Psalm 25:1-22 verse 6, Isaiah 63:7-9 verse 7
11. Blessed are the poor in spirit to those who believe Palm Sunday which is salvation where Jesus as King came to town riding on colt: Blessed is He that come in the name of the Lord which is salvation. Matthew 21:4-11 verse 4-5, See Psalm 118:29, Matthew 23:39, Mark 11:9-10, Luke 13:35, Isaiah 62:11 and Zechariah 9:9, John 12:15
12. Blessed are the poor in spirit to those who believe that the Baptism of the Holy Spirit is *not* to *neglect the gift* that **God** has given in to you as believer, a child of God. I Timothy 4:14

Part DCXXVI

Blessed Are The Poor In Spirit. Matthew 5:3

Blessed Means Happy

Poor means meek in spirit. Poor means humble in spirit. Poor means lowly in spirit. Poor means quiet in spirit. Read Matthew 5:3-12, Read also Mark 1:15

Jesus did not say "*rich*" in spirit. Jesus said "*poor*" in spirit.

1. Blessed are the poor in spirit to those who believe that John the Baptist **"first" mentioned four times** that Jesus would baptize His children with His Spirit Baptism; John the Baptist mentioned: "He shall baptize you with the Holy Spirit." Matthew 3:11 (b), Mark 1:8, Luke 3:16, John 1:33 (b). John the Baptist never knew what Jesus meant. He died before Pentecostal event led by Apostle Peter. Matthew 14:5-13, Acts 2:1-47 verse 1-4
2. Blessed are the poor in spirit to those who believe that Jesus **"first"** mentioned to His disciples only once that "they shall speak with new tongues." However, His disciples never knew what Jesus meant (see my topic on "They did not understand what Jesus meant." Mark 16:17 (c)
3. Blessed are the poor in spirit to those who believe that Jesus told His disciples that the Father would send the promise of the Holy Spirit but to tarry beginning at Jerusalem. Luke 24:49
4. Blessed are the poor in spirit to those who believe that Jesus did say, "Receive ye the Holy Spirit." But did His disciples understand Him? John 20:22
5. Blessed are the poor in spirit to those who believe that Jesus reminded His disciples that the Father would send the promise of the Holy Spirit. Acts 1:5 (b)
6. Blessed are the poor in spirit to those who believe that Jesus would baptize His children with His Spirit Baptism not many days from now Acts 1:4-8 but His disciples still did not understand what Jesus meant at the time (See my topic: They Did Not Understand What Jesus Meant)
7. Blessed are the poor in spirit to those who believe that God's children were filled with the Holy Spirit. Acts 2:4 (a)
8. Blessed are the poor in spirit to those who believe that God's children discovered the meaning of Christ's Spirit Baptism; and they began to speak in tongues as the

Spirit gave them utterance (Final Jesus' disciples understood what Jesus meant, "They shall speak with new tongues. Mark 16:17 (c); and "but He shall baptize you with the Holy Spirit, not many days from now. Acts 1:4

9. Blessed are the poor in spirit to those who believe when Peter remembered the Word of the Lord how that He said, "John indeed baptized you with water; but you shall be baptized with the Holy Spirit." Acts 11:16
10. Blessed are the poor in spirit to those who believe that the Baptism of the Holy Spirit is a connection with Prophet Joel 2:26-32.
11. Blessed are the poor in spirit to those who believe that the Baptism of the Holy Spirit is speaking in tongues as the Spirit gave them utterance. Acts 2:4
12. Blessed are the poor in spirit to those who believe that the Baptism of the Holy Spirit is being filled with the Spirit, such as Peter, Paul and others. Acts 2:4, Acts 4:8, 31, Acts 9:17, Acts 13:9

Part DCXXVII

Blessed Are The Poor In Spirit. Matthew 5:3

Blessed Means Happy

Poor means meek in spirit. Poor means humble in spirit. Poor means lowly in spirit. Poor means quiet in spirit. Read Matthew 5:3-12, Read also Mark 1:15

Jesus did not say "*rich*" in spirit. Jesus said "*poor*" in spirit.

1. Blessed are the poor in spirit to those who believe that the Baptism of the Holy Spirit was that the 120 disciples or the 120 gathering believers came to be filled with the Holy Spirit and began to speak with other tongues as the Spirit gave them utterance. Acts 1:13-15, Acts 2:1-4
2. Blessed are the poor in spirit to those who believe that the Baptism of the Holy Spirit is through spiritual blessings. Ephesians 1:3
3. Blessed are the poor in spirit to those who believe that the Baptism of the Holy Spirit was that Cornelius and his band heard the Word and spoke with tongues and magnify (exalting) God. Acts 10:44-47 verse 46
4. Blessed are the poor in spirit to those who believe that the Baptism of the Holy Spirit was that there were ten men who spoke with tongues and prophesied (Acts 19:1-7 verse 6)
5. Blessed are the poor in spirit to those who believe that the Baptism of the Holy Spirit was that they laid hands on them to receive the Holy Spirit. Acts 8:17, (See I Timothy 4:14)
6. Blessed are the poor in spirit to those who believe that the Baptism of the Holy Spirit was that of being filled with the Spirit. Ephesians 5:18
7. Blessed are the poor in spirit to those who believe that the Baptism of the Holy Spirit is that of being sanctified by the Holy Spirit through Jesus Christ. Acts 26:18
8. Blessed are the poor in spirit to those who believe that the Baptism of the Holy Spirit is from I Corinthians 14:1-40
9. Blessed are the poor in spirit to those who believe that the Baptism of the Holy Spirit was when Apostle Paul spoke with tongues. I Corinthians 14:18

10. Blessed are the poor in spirit to those who believe that the Baptism of the Holy Spirit is of peace as in all churches of the saints where God is not the author of confusion. I Corinthians 14:33
11. Blessed are the poor in spirit to those who believe that the Baptism of the Holy Spirit is for all believers in Christ Jesus. Acts 1:12-15, Acts 2:4, Acts 2:1-4, Acts 2:47
12. Blessed are the poor in spirit to those who believe that the Baptism of the Holy Spirit is in Mark 16:17 (c)

Part DCXXVIII

Blessed Are The Poor In Spirit. Matthew 5:3

Blessed Means Happy

Poor means meek in spirit. Poor means humble in spirit. Poor means lowly in spirit. Poor means quiet in spirit. Read Matthew 5:3-12, Read also Mark 1:15

Jesus did not say "*rich*" in spirit. Jesus said "*poor*" in spirit.

1. Blessed are the poor in spirit to those who believe that the Baptism of the Holy Spirit is in Isaiah 28:11
2. Blessed are the poor in spirit to those who believe that the Baptism of the Holy Spirit is in I Corinthians 14:18-21
3. Blessed are the poor in spirit to those who believe that the Baptism of the Holy Spirit is in Matthew 5:6
4. Blessed are the poor in spirit to those who believe that the Baptism of the Holy Spirit is in Matthew 3:11 (b)
5. Blessed are the poor in spirit to those who believe that the Baptism of the Holy Spirit is in Mark 1:8
6. Blessed are the poor in spirit to those who believe that the Baptism of the Holy Spirit is in Luke 3:16
7. Blessed are the poor in spirit to those who believe that the Baptism of the Holy Spirit is in Luke 24:49
8. Blessed are the poor in spirit to those who believe that the Baptism of the Holy Spirit is in John 7:38
9. Blessed are the poor in spirit to those who believe that the Baptism of the Holy Spirit is in John 20:22
10. Blessed are the poor in spirit to those who believe that the Baptism of the Holy Spirit is in Acts 1:4
11. Blessed are the poor in spirit to those who believe that the Baptism of the Holy Spirit is in Acts 1:5
12. Blessed are the poor in spirit to those who believe that the Baptism of the Holy Spirit is in Acts 1:8

Part DCXXIX

Blessed Are The Poor In Spirit. Matthew 5:3

Blessed Means Happy

Poor means meek in spirit. Poor means humble in spirit. Poor means lowly in spirit. Poor means quiet in spirit. Read Matthew 5:3-12, Read also Mark 1:15

Jesus did not say "*rich*" in spirit. Jesus said "*poor*" in spirit.

1. Blessed are the poor in spirit to those who believe that the Baptism of the Holy Spirit is in Acts 2:4
2. Blessed are the poor in spirit to those who believe that the Baptism of the Holy Spirit is in Acts 11:16
3. Blessed are the poor in spirit to those who believe that the Baptism of the Holy Spirit is in Joel 2:28
4. Blessed are the poor in spirit to those who believe that the Baptism of the Holy Spirit is in Acts 2:16-18
5. Blessed are the poor in spirit to those who believe that the Baptism of the Holy Spirit is in Isaiah 44:3
6. Blessed are the poor in spirit to those who believe that the Baptism of the Holy Spirit is in John 4:14
7. Blessed are the poor in spirit to those who believe that the Baptism of the Holy Spirit is in I Timothy 4:14
8. Blessed are the poor in spirit to those who believe that the Baptism of the Holy Spirit is getting us prepare to meet God. Amos 4:12
9. Blessed are the poor in spirit to those who believe that the Baptism of the Holy Spirit is winning souls for Christ. Proverbs 11:30
10. Blessed are the poor in spirit to those who believe that the Baptism of the Holy Spirit is getting us ready for Christ's Return. Revelation 22:20
11. Blessed are the poor in spirit to those who believe that the Baptism of the Holy Spirit is getting us ready for Christ's Return. Revelation 1:7
12. Blessed are the poor in spirit to those who believe that the Baptism of the Holy Spirit is getting us ready for Christ coming. II Timothy 4:6-7 verse 7

PART DCXXX

Blessed Are The Poor In Spirit. Matthew 5:3

Blessed Means Happy

Poor means meek in spirit. Poor means humble in spirit. Poor means lowly in spirit. Poor means quiet in spirit. Read Matthew 5:3-12, Read also Mark 1:15

Jesus did not say "*rich*" in spirit. Jesus said "*poor*" in spirit.

1. Blessed are the poor in spirit to those who believe that the Baptism of the Holy Spirit is in Revelation 21:6
2. Blessed are the poor in spirit to those who believe that the Baptism of the Holy Spirit is in John 15:7
3. Blessed are the poor in spirit to those who believe that the Baptism of the Holy Spirit is in Revelation 22:17
4. Blessed are the poor in spirit to those who believe that the Baptism of the Holy Spirit is in Mark 11:22
5. Blessed are the poor in spirit to those who believe that the Baptism of the Holy Spirit is to have confidence in Christ Jesus. I John 5:14-15
6. Blessed are the poor in spirit to those who believe that the Baptism of the Holy Spirit is to ask the Father, our God in faith. Luke 11:9-13 verse 10, Matthew 7:8-11 verse 8
7. Blessed are the poor in spirit to those who believe that the Baptism of the Holy Spirit is to ask "*Without* (nothing) *wavering*." James 1:6
8. Blessed are the poor in spirit to those who believe that the Baptism of the Holy Spirit is that all that Christ ask is that *you* **"only believe"** and **"not be afraid"** through faith. Luke 8:50
9. Blessed are the poor in spirit to those who believe that the Baptism of the Holy Spirit is that all that Christ ask is that **not to dare to doubt Him.** Luke 8:50, **Matthew 14:31, Matthew 21:21**, Mark 11:23, Luke 11:20, **John 10:24, Acts 2:12, Matthew 28:17**, Acts 10:17, 20, **Acts 11:12 verse 22, 24**, Mark 11:22-26, **Mark 11:22**, Acts 2:12-47 verse 12, **I Timothy 2:8**
10. Blessed are the poor in spirit to those who believe that the Baptism of the Holy Spirit is to *receive*. Mark 11:24, John 20:22

11. Blessed are the poor in spirit to those who believe that the Baptism of the Holy Spirit is to *believe*. Mark 11:22-26 verse 22, 23, 24, John 4:23-24, Hebrews 11:1, 6
12. Blessed are the poor in spirit to those who believe that Baptism of the Holy Spirit is to *believe by faith*. Romans 10:17

Part DCXXXI

Blessed Are The Poor In Spirit. Matthew 5:3

Blessed Means Happy

Poor means meek in spirit. Poor means humble in spirit. Poor means lowly in spirit. Poor means quiet in spirit. Read Matthew 5:3-12, Read also Mark 1:15

Jesus did not say "*rich*" in spirit. Jesus said "*poor*" in spirit.

1. Blessed are the poor in spirit to those who believe that Baptism of the Holy Spirit is **yours** to *ask* to those who *ask* for the Baptism of the Holy Spirit or Spirit Baptism or Christ's Baptism in faith. John 16:23-28 verse 23-24
2. Blessed are the poor in spirit to those who believe that the Baptism of the Holy Spirit is to those who are *focus* on the Baptism of the Holy Spirit and Christ's Return for centuries to this day on forward until Christ come again. Mark 16:19, Luke 24:51, Acts 1:9, 11, Matthew 3:11 (b), Mark 1:8, Luke 3:16, John 1:33 (b), John 20:22, Acts 1:13-15, Acts 2:1-47, Acts 2:1-4, Acts 2:4, Acts 10:44-46, Amos 4:12, Revelation 3:11, Revelation 16:15, Revelation 22:7, 12, 16, 20-21, Genesis 11:1-9, Revelation 5:8-14 verse 9-10, 14, Revelation 7:9-17 verse 9, Revelation 1:7, 18, I Thessalonians 4:13-18, II Timothy 4:6-8, Hebrews 9:28, Romans 14:10, II Corinthians 5:10, Colossians 3:4, I Peter 5:4, I John 2:28, John 3:2-3
3. Blessed are the poor in spirit to those who believe that the Baptism of the Holy Spirit is **yours** to ask the Fathers in faith. John 14:13-21 verse 13-14, John 15:7, John 15:16, John 16:23-28 verse 23-24
4. Blessed are the poor in spirit to those who believe that the Baptism of the Holy Spirit is in Isaiah 51:1
5. Blessed are the poor in spirit to those who believe that the Baptism of the Holy Spirit is in Isaiah 55:6-12
6. Blessed are the poor in spirit to those who believe this Psalmist: "Have mercy upon me, O God, according to thy lovingkindness: according unto the multitude of thy tender mercies blot out my transgressions." Psalm 51:1
7. Blessed are the poor in spirit to those who believe this Psalmist: "Wash me thoroughly from mine iniquity, and cleanse me from my sin." Psalm 51:2

8. Blessed are the poor in spirit to those who believe this Psalmist: "For I acknowledge my transgressions: and my sin is ever before me." Psalm 51:3
9. Blessed are the poor in spirit to those who believe this Psalmist: "Against thee, thee only, have I sinned, and done this evil in thy sight: that thou mightest be justified when thou speakest, and be clear when thou judgest." Psalm 51:4
10. Blessed are the poor in spirit to those who believe this Psalmist: "Behold, I was shapen in iniquity; and in sin did my mother conceive me." Psalm 51:5
11. Blessed are the poor in spirit to those who believe this Psalmist: "Behold, thou desirest truth in the inward parts: and in the hidden part thou shalt make me to know wisdom." Psalm 51:6
12. Blessed are the poor in spirit to those who believe this Psalmist: "Purge me with hyssop, and I shall be clean: wash me, and I shall be whiter than snow." Psalm 51:7

Part DCXXXII

Blessed Are The Poor In Spirit. Matthew 5:3

Blessed Means Happy

Poor means meek in spirit. Poor means humble in spirit. Poor means lowly in spirit. Poor means quiet in spirit. Read Matthew 5:3-12, Read also Mark 1:15

Jesus did not say "*rich*" in spirit. Jesus said "*poor*" in spirit.

1. Blessed are the poor in spirit to those who believe this Psalmist: "Make me to hear joy and gladness; that the bones which thou hast broken may rejoice." Psalm 51:8
2. Blessed are the poor in spirit to those who believe this Psalmist: "Hide thy face from my sins, and blot out all mine iniquities." Psalm 51:9
3. Blessed are the poor in spirit to those who believe this Psalmist: "Create in me a clean heart, O God; and renew a right spirit within me." Psalm 51:10
4. Blessed are the poor in spirit to those who believe this Psalmist: "Cast me not away from thy presence; and take not thy holy spirit from me." Psalm 51:11
5. Blessed are the poor in spirit to those who believe this Psalmist: "Restore unto me the joy of thy salvation; and uphold me with thy free spirit." Psalm 51:12
6. Blessed are the poor in spirit to those who believe this Psalmist: "Then will I teach transgressors thy ways; and sinners shall be converted unto thee." Psalm 51:13
7. Blessed are the poor in spirit to those who believe this Psalmist: "Delver me from bloodguiltiness, O God, thou God of my salvation: and my tongue shall sing aloud of thy righteousness." Psalm 51:14
8. Blessed are the poor in spirit to those who believe this Psalmist: "O Lord, open thou my lips; and my mouth shall shew forth thy praise." Psalm 51:15
9. Blessed are the poor in spirit to those who believe this Psalmist: "The law of the Lord is perfect, converting the soul: the testimony of the Lord is sure, making wise the simple." Psalm 19:7
10. Blessed are the poor in spirit to those who believe this Old Testament Prophecy: "Make the heart of this people fat, and make their ears heavy, and shut their eyes; lest they see with their eyes, and hear with their ears, and understand with their heart, and convert, and be healed." Isaiah 6:10

11. Blessed are the poor in spirit to those who believe this New Testament Prophecy: Brethren, if any of you do err from the truth, and one convert him; Let him know, that he which converteth the sinner from the error of his way shall save a soul from death, and shall hide a multitude of sins." James 5:19-20
12. Blessed are the poor in spirit to those who believe where we go to church to where we believe in prayer. **Matthew 17:21**, Matthew 21:13, Matthew 21:22, **Mark 9:29**, Mark 11:17, Luke 6:12, Luke 19:46, Luke 22:45, Acts 1:14, Acts 3:1, Acts 6:4, Acts 10:31, Acts 12:5, Acts 16:13, 16, **Romans 10:1, Romans 12:12, I Corinthians 7:5, II Corinthians 1:11**, II Corinthians 9:14, **Ephesians 6:18,** Philippians 1:4, **Philippians 1:19**, Philippians 4:6, **Colossians 4:2, 5**, James 5:15, 16, I Peter 4:7

Part DCXXXIII

Blessed Are The Poor In Spirit. Matthew 5:3

Blessed Means Happy

Poor means meek in spirit. Poor means humble in spirit. Poor means lowly in spirit. Poor means quiet in spirit. Read Matthew 5:3-12, Read also Mark 1:15

Jesus did not say "*rich*" in spirit. Jesus said "*poor*" in spirit.

1. Blessed are the poor in spirit to those who believe Jesus' statement for salvation: "For this people's heart is waxed gross, and their ears are dull of hearing, and their eyes they have closed; lest at any time they should see with their eyes, and hear with their ears, and should understand with their heart, and should be converted, and I should heal them." Matthew 13:15
2. Blessed are the poor in spirit to those who believe Jesus' statement for salvation: "And said, Verily I say unto you, Except ye be converted, and become as little children, ye shall not enter into the kingdom of heaven." Matthew 18:3
3. Blessed are the poor in spirit to those who believe Jesus' statement for salvation: "That seeing they may see, and not perceive; and hearing they may hear, and not understand; lest at any time they should be converted, and their sins should be forgiven them." Mark 4:12
4. Blessed are the poor in spirit to those who believe Jesus' statement for salvation: "But I have prayed for thee, that thy faith fail not: and when thou art converted, strengthen thy brethren." Luke 22:32
5. Blessed are the poor in spirit to those who believe the Book of John 12:40: "He hath blinded their eyes, and hardened their heart; that they should not see with their eyes, nor understand with their heart, and be converted, and I should heal them." John 12:40
6. Blessed are the poor in spirit to those who believe the Book of Acts 3:19: "Repent ye therefore, and be converted, that your sins may be blotted out, when the times of refreshing shall come from the presence of the Lord;" Acts 3:19
7. Blessed are the poor in spirit to those who believe the Book of Acts 28:27-28: "For the heart of this people is waxed gross, and their ears are dull of hearing, and their eyes have; they closed; lest they should see with their eyes, and hear

with their ears, and understand with their heart, and should be converted, and I should heal them. Be it known therefore unto you, that the salvation of God is sent unto the Gentiles, and that they will hear it." Acts 28:27-28

8. Blessed are the poor in spirit to those who believe that Palm mean salvation; that Palm mean blessed be the name of the Lord. Matthew 21:4-11 verse 4-5, See Psalm 118:29, Matthew 23:39, Mark 11:9-10, Luke 13:35, Isaiah 62:11 and Zechariah 9:9, John 12:15
9. Blessed are the poor in spirit to those who believe this Psalmist: "Behold, bless ye the Lord, all ye servants of the Lord, which by night stand in the house of the Lord." Psalm 134:1
10. Blessed are the poor in spirit to those who believe this Psalmist: "Lift up your hands in the sanctuary, and bless the Lord." Psalm 134:2
11. Blessed are the poor in spirit to those who believe this Psalmist: "The Lord that made heaven and earth bless thee out of Zion." Psalm 134:3
    Blessed are the poor in spirit to those who believe that holiness is the right way to practice daily in our life and to live holiness before the Lord; and His Returning. Without holiness, God is not pleased because no man will see the Lord. Matthew 5:8, Luke 1:75, Romans 1:4, Romans 6:19, 22, 23, II Corinthians 7:1, Ephesians 4:24, I Thessalonians 3:13, **I Thessalonians 4:7**, I Timothy 2:15, **Titus 2:3**, Hebrews 12:10, **Hebrews 12:14**, See Exodus 28:36, Exodus 39:30, **Zechariah 14:20**, See also: I Corinthians 1:30, I Thessalonians 4:3, 4, II Thessalonians 2:13, I Peter 1:2, John 10:36, John 17:17, John 17:19, Acts 20:32, **Acts 26:18**, Romans 15:16, **I Corinthians 1:2, I Corinthians 6:11**, **I Timothy 4:5, II Timothy 2:21**, Hebrews 2:11, Hebrews 10:10, 14, 29, Jude 1:1, I Peter 1:15-16, Leviticus 11:44:45

Holiness Unto The Lord:
Zechariah 14:20

1. I Thessalonians 4:7
2. Titus 2:3
3. Hebrews 12:14

Read II Timothy 2:21

Holiness Mean Sanctification; To Set Apart From The World. Holiness Mean To Make Holy. (II Timothy 2:21, I Timothy 4:5, I Corinthians 6:11, I Corinthians 6:1)
This Is Christ's Commendation: (II Corinthians 3:1-6)

1. Hebrews 10:10
2. Hebrews 10:14
3. Hebrews 10:29

Read Hebrews 2:11

Sanctified Mean To Set Apart For The Master's Use:
John 17:17

1. John 17:19
2. Acts 20:32
3. Acts 26:18

Read II Timothy 2:21

Sanctified Mean To Set Apart For The Master's Use:
John 17:17

1. I Corinthians 1:2
2. I Corinthians 6:11
3. I Timothy 4:5 Read II Timothy 2:21

Part DCXXXIV

Blessed Are The Poor In Spirit. Matthew 5:3

Blessed Means Happy

Poor means meek in spirit. Poor means humble in spirit. Poor means lowly in spirit. Poor means quiet in spirit. Read Matthew 5:3-12, Read also Mark 1:15

Jesus did not say "*rich*" in spirit. Jesus said "*poor*" in spirit.

1. Blessed are the poor in spirit to those who believe the Glory of the Lord will come. I Thessalonians 4:16-17, Revelation 1:7, I John 3:2, Revelation 3:11, Revelation 16:15, Revelation 22:7, 12, 20-21, Hebrews 9:28, Matthew 24:36-51, Matthew 25:13, I Corinthians 11:23-26, Mark 13:35-37, Mark 13:26, Daniel 7:13, **Revelation 2:5, Revelation 2:16, 25, Revelation 3:3, I John 2:28,** II Peter 3:4, **II Peter 1:16, James 5:7, 8,** II Thessalonians 2:1, I Thessalonians 2:19, I Thessalonians 3:13, I Thessalonians 4:15, I Thessalonians 5:23, I Corinthians 15:23, I Corinthians 1:7, Luke 21:27, Mark 14:62, Matthew 26:64, Matthew 24:39, Matthew 24:30, Matthew 24:27, Matthew 16:28
2. Blessed are the poor in spirit to those who believe Christ is Immanuel; that Christ is Emmanuel. Isaiah 7:14, Matthew 1:23, Luke 2:11, Isaiah 9:6
3. Blessed are the poor in spirit to those who believe to have the communion and the fellowship with the Lord until He comes. I Corinthians 11:23-26
4. Blessed are the poor in spirit to those who believe in celebrating the Risen Christ who live and reign. Matthew 17:9, Matthew 26:32, Matthew 27:64, Matthew 28:6, 7, Mark 9:9, **Mark 14:28, Mark 16:6, 9, 14, Luke 24:6, 34,** John 21:14, **Acts 17:3,** Romans 8:34, I Corinthians 15:20, Colossians 2:12, Colossians 3:1, I Corinthians 15:57
5. Blessed are the poor in spirit to those who believe *in the sunset* of our Dying Savior and Lord. Luke 23:46, John 19:30
6. Blessed are the poor in spirit to those who believe *in the sunrise* of our Living Savior and Lord. Revelation 1:7, Revelation 1:18, Revelation 2:8, Luke 24:6, 34, Mark 16:6, 9, 14, John 20:19-31 verse 22, Matthew 28:1-20 verse 1, 6, Mark 16:1-20 verse 1-2, 6, 11, 14, Luke 1:1-53 verse 17, 25, 36, 38-39, 44, 46-49, Luke 24:1, 6, 34, John 20:1, 9, 11-18, 19-20, 21-31 verse 15, 17, 19, 21, 22, 23,

26-27, 29, John 21:1, 5-6, 10, 12, 15-19, 22, Acts 1:4-5, 7-8, Acts 9:4-6, 11-12, 15-16, Acts 11:16, Acts 20:35, Acts 22:7-8, 10, 18, 21, Acts 23:11

7. Blessed are the poor in spirit to those who believe Christ's Word: "In three days, I shall rise again. Matthew 12:40, **John 2:19**
8. Blessed are the poor in spirit to those who believe in Christ's Victorious the First Morning of the Sunrise; He is the Bright and Morning Star. Revelation 22:16
9. Blessed are the poor in spirit to those who believe that Christ Jesus is the Same Lord from the Beginning of the Creation. Hebrews 13:8, Genesis 1:1, John 1:1-2
10. Blessed are the poor in spirit to those who believe that Christ is the "I Am That I Am." Exodus 3:14, Revelation 1:8, Mark 14:62
11. Blessed are the poor in spirit to those who believe in Christ's True and His Promise: Behold, I come quickly (very soon; The Soon Coming King, God Almighty). Revelation 22:20-21, So come Lord, Jesus. Amen. See Revelation 16:15, Revelation 3:11, Revelation 1:8
12. Blessed are the poor in spirit to those who believe in Palm Sunday, Easter Sunday, The Resurrection Sunday and His Imminent Return. John 2:19, Revelation 22:20

Part DCXXXV

Blessed Are The Poor In Spirit. Matthew 5:3

Blessed Means Happy

Poor means meek in spirit. Poor means humble in spirit. Poor means lowly in spirit. Poor means quiet in spirit. Read Matthew 5:3-12, Read also Mark 1:15

Jesus did not say "*rich*" in spirit. Jesus said "*poor*" in spirit.

1. Blessed are the poor in spirit to those who believe that the **Day of Pentecost had fully come**. Acts 2:1
2. Blessed are the poor in spirit to those who believe that **Pentecost** means **"a New Day" on the Day of Pentecost.** Acts 2:1
3. Blessed are the poor in spirit to those who believe that Apostle Paul was in a hurry to be at Jerusalem **the day of Pentecost.** Acts 20:16
4. Blessed are the poor in spirit to those who believe that Apostle Paul had tarried at Ephesus until **Pentecost.** I Corinthians 16:8
5. Blessed are the poor in spirit to those who believe that the 120 disciples were believers of Jesus; that they were "*already saved*" therefore the 120 disciples of Jesus came for to receive the Holy Spirit (John 20:22, Acts 19:6) called the baptism of the Holy Spirit or filled with the Holy Spirit (Ephesians 5:18) **"before" the day of Pentecost.** Acts 2:1, Acts 1:1-26, verse 4-5, 8, 12-15, Luke 24:49
6. Blessed are the poor in spirit to those who believe that **Pentecost** was related in according to Mark 16:17 (c) **by Jesus Christ:** "*And they shall speak with new tongues*." Read Again Mark 16:17 (c), Acts 2:1-4 verse 4, Acts 2:1
7. Blessed are the poor in spirit to those who believe that **on the day of Pentecost, had fully come**, the 120 disciples of Jesus were all with one according in one place. Acts 1:1
8. Blessed are the poor in spirit to those who believe that **on the day of Pentecost,** the 120 disciples of Jesus felt (believed) and suddenly there came a sound from heaven as of a rushing mighty wind. Acts 2:1, 2 (a)
9. Blessed are the poor in spirit to those who **on the day of Pentecost** that the 120 disciples of Jesus felt (believed) and it filled all the house where the 120 disciples of Jesus were sitting. Acts 2:1, 2 (b)

10. Blessed are the poor in spirit to those who believed that **on the day of Pentecost,** the 120 disciples of Jesus felt (believed) and there appeared unto the 120 disciples of Jesus cloven tongues like as of fire. Acts 2:1, 3 (a)
11. Blessed are the poor in spirit to those who believe that **on the day of Pentecost,** the 120 disciples of Jesus felt (believed); and it (like as fire; what looked fire) sat (rested) upon the 120 disciples of Jesus. Acts 2:1, 3 (b)
12. Blessed are the poor in spirit to those who believe that **on the day of Pentecost,** the 120 disciples of Jesus felt (believed); and it (cloven tongues like as of fire) sat (rested) upon each of the 120 disciples of Jesus. Acts 1:3 (c)

Part DCXXXVI

Blessed Are The Poor In Spirit. Matthew 5:3

Blessed Means Happy

Poor means meek in spirit. Poor means humble in spirit. Poor means lowly in spirit. Poor means quiet in spirit. Read Matthew 5:3-12, Read also Mark 1:15

Jesus did not say "*rich*" in spirit. Jesus said "*poor*" in spirit.

1. Blessed are the poor in spirit to those who believe that **on the day of Pentecost,** the 120 disciples of Jesus felt (believed); and the 120 disciples of Jesus were all filled with the Holy Spirit. Acts 2:1, 4 (a)
2. Blessed are the poor in spirit to those who believe that **on the day of Pentecost,** the 120 disciples of Jesus felt (believed); and began to speak with other tongues (languages; different languages, other languages). Acts 2:1, 4 (b)
3. Blessed are the poor in spirit to those who believe that **on the day of Pentecost,** the 120 disciples of Jesus felt (believed) as the Spirit gave the 120 disciples of Jesus utterance (speak in tongues) See again Mark 16:17 (c): "And they shall speak with new tongues." Acts 2:1, 4 (d)
4. Blessed are the poor in spirit to those who believe that **on the day of Pentecost,** the 120 disciples of Jesus felt (believed); there were dwelling at Jerusalem Jews devout men, out of every nation under heaven. Acts 2:1, 5
5. Blessed are the poor in spirit to those who believe that **on the day of Pentecost,** the 120 disciples of Jesus witnessed (saw evident) and now when this was **noised** (heard languages spoken; other languages spoken: as the Spirit gave the 120 disciples of Jesus the ability to speak for the gospel of Jesus Christ. See Acts 1:8: "But ye shall receive power, after that the Holy Spirit is come upon you (the 120 disciples of Jesus): and ye (you); (the 120 disciples of Jesus) shall be witnessed unto **Me** (Jesus Christ) both in Jerusalem, and in all Judaea, and in Samaria, and unto the uttermost (farthest as the Spirit of Christ carried them to part of the earth) abroad, the multitude came together, and were confounded (amazed), because that every man heard the 120 disciples of Jesus speak in his own language. Acts 2:1, 6

6. Blessed are the poor in spirit to those who believe that **on the day of Pentecost,** the 120 disciples of Jesus witnessed (heard evident) that: and they were all amazed and marveled, saying one to another, Behold, are not all there (the 120 disciples of Jesus) which (again the 120 disciples of Jesus) speak Galileans? Acts 2:1, 7
7. Blessed are the poor in spirit to those who believe that **on the day of Pentecost,** the 120 disciples of Jesus witnessed (heard evident) that Apostle Peter preached the Pentecostal Message of Jesus Christ to various visitors that day in Jerusalem. Acts 2:1, Acts 2:1-47 verse 41, Luke 24:49, Acts 2:8
8. Blessed are the poor in spirit to those who believe that **on the day of Pentecost,** the 120 disciples of Jesus spoke out the Word of God to various visitors to come to Jesus and 3, 000 souls were saved that day. Acts 2:1, Acts 2:11, 41
9. Blessed are the poor in spirit to those who believe that **on the day of Pentecost,** the 120 disciples of Jesus witnessed (heard evident) that: "And how hear we every man in our own tongue (language), wherein we were born?" Acts 2:1, 8
10. Blessed are the poor in spirit to those who believe that **on the day of Pentecost,** the 120 disciples of Jesus witnessed (saw evident) that: "Par'thi-ans, and Medes, and E'lam-ites, and the dwellers in Mes-o-po-ta-mi-a, and in Ju-dae'a, and Cap-pa-do'ci-a, in Pon'tus, and A'sia." Acts 2:1, 9
11. Blessed are the poor in spirit to those who believe that **on the day of Pentecost,** the 120 disciples of Jesus witnessed (saw evident) that: "Phryg'I-a, and Pam-phyl'I-a, in E'gypt, and in the parts of Lib'y-a about Cy-ra'ne, and strangers of Rome, Jews and proselytes (followers)." Acts 2:1, 10
12. Blessed are the poor in spirit to those who believe that **on the day of Pentecost,** the 120 disciples of Jesus witnessed (saw evident) that: "Cretes and A-ra'biains, we do hear them (the 120 disciples of Jesus) speak in our tongues (languages—See Acts 2:4) the wonderful works (deeds) of God." Acts 2:1, 11

Part DCXXXVII

Blessed Are The Poor In Spirit. Matthew 5:3

Blessed Means Happy

Poor means meek in spirit. Poor means humble in spirit. Poor means lowly in spirit. Poor means quiet in spirit. Read Matthew 5:3-12, Read also Mark 1:15

Jesus did not say "*rich*" in spirit. Jesus said "*poor*" in spirit.

1. Blessed are the poor in spirit to those who believe that **on the day of Pentecost,** the 120 disciples of Jesus witnessed (heard and saw evident) that: "And they were all amazed, and were *in doubt,* saying one to another, *What meanth this*?" Acts 2:1, 12
2. Blessed are the poor in spirit to those who believe that **on the day of Pentecost,** the 120 disciples of Jesus witnessed (heard evident) that: "Others mocking (it's ridiculing) said, These men (the 120 disciples of Jesus) are full of new wine." (See Ephesians 5:18; see also Acts 2:15-21, Joel 2:28, 29, 32). Acts 2:1, 13
3. Blessed are the poor in spirit to those who believe that **on the day of Pentecost,** the 120 disciples of Jesus witnessed (heard evident) and (But) Peter, standing up with the eleven (one of Jesus' twelve original disciples from 3 years early with experience upon Jesus' teaching and that Jesus chosen Peter to lead the way of the disciples of Jesus Christ's Message. See Isaiah 42:16, **Luke 22:31-32,** John 21:15-18, Acts 8:14-25 verse 14, 20, Acts 9:34, 38-40, Acts 10:5-48, Acts 11:1-18, Acts 12:1-19, I Peter 1:1 through I Peter 5:1-14, II Peter 1:1 through II Peter 3:1-18, I Peter 2:9) lifted up his voice; and said unto them (those others that mocking), Ye men of Judaea, and all ye men of Judaea, and all ye that dwell (live) at Jerusalem, be this known unto you, and hearken (listen, heed), to my words:" Acts 2:1, 14
4. Blessed are the poor in spirit to those who believe that **on the day of Pentecost,** the 120 disciples and one of the original eleven, Apostle Peter began to preach the **Pentecostal Good News of Jesus Christ** to various visitors: "These men (disciples of Jesus) are full of new wine). See Acts 2:13, but are not drunken, as ye suppose (imagine), seeing it is but the third hour (9:00 am) of the day." Acts 2:1, 15

5. Blessed are the poor in spirit to those who believe that **on the day of Pentecost,** the 120 disciples and one of the original eleven, Apostle Peter began to preach the **Pentecostal Good News of Jesus Christ;** But this is that which was spoken by the Prophet Joel;" (See Joel 2:28)—Acts 2:1, 16
6. Blessed are the poor in spirit to those who believe that **on the day of Pentecost,** the 120 disciples and one of the original eleven, Apostle Peter began to preach the **Pentecostal Good News of Jesus Christ:** "*And it shall come to pass in the last days, saith God, I will pour out of My Spirit upon all flesh: and your sons and your daughters shall prophesy (speak up), and your young men shall see visions, and your old men shall dream dreams.*" Acts 2:1, 17
7. Blessed are the poor in spirit to those who believe that **on the day of Pentecost,** the 120 disciples and one of the original eleven, Apostle Peter began to preach the **Pentecostal Good News of Jesus Christ:** "And on **My** *servants* and on **My** *handmaidens* **I** (God) will pour out in those days of **My Spirit;** and they shall prophesy (speak up)." See Joel 2:29, Acts 2:1, 18.
8. Blessed are the poor in spirit to those who believe that **on the day of Pentecost,** the 120 disciples and one of the original eleven, Apostle Peter began to preach the **Pentecostal Good News:** "And **I** (God) will show wonders in heaven above, and signs in the earth beneath; blood, and fire, and vapor of smoke:" (See Joel 2:30). Acts 2:1, 19
9. Blessed are the poor in spirit to those who believe that **on the day of Pentecost,** the 120 disciples and one of the original eleven, Apostle Peter began to preach the **Pentecostal Good News of Jesus Christ:** "The sun shall be turned into darkness, and the moon into blood, believe that great and profitable of the Lord come:" (See Joel 2:30, 31) Acts 2:1, 20
10. Blessed are the poor in spirit to those who believe that **on the day of Pentecost,** the 120 disciples and one of the original eleven, Apostle Peter began to preach the **Pentecostal Good News of Jesus Christ:** "And it shall come to pass, that whosoever shall call on the name of the Lord (Jesus) shall be saved." (See Joel 2:32. Note: Romans 10:13). Acts 2:1, 21
11. Blessed are the poor in spirit to those who believe that **on the day of Pentecost,** the 120 disciples and one of the original eleven, Apostle Peter began to preach the **Pentecostal Good News of Jesus Christ:** [Apostle Peter's preaching] "Ye men of Israel, hear those words: "Jesus of Naz'a-reth, a man approved of God among you by miracles and wonders and signs, which God did by Him (Jesus)

in the midst of you, as ye yourselves also know:" (See Deuteronomy 18:15). Acts 2:1, 22

12. Blessed are the poor in spirit to those who believe that **on the day of Pentecost,** the 120 disciples and one of the original eleven, preached the **Pentecostal Good News of Jesus Christ:** [Apostle Preaching] "Him (Jesus), being delivered by the determinate counsel and foreknowledge of God, ye have taken, and by wicked hands have crucified and slain." Acts 2:1, 23

Part DCXXXVIII

Blessed Are The Poor In Spirit. Matthew 5:3

Blessed Means Happy

Poor means meek in spirit. Poor means humble in spirit. Poor means lowly in spirit. Poor means quiet in spirit. Read Matthew 5:3-12, Read also Mark 1:15

Jesus did not say "*rich*" in spirit. Jesus said "*poor*" in spirit.

1. Blessed are the poor in spirit to those who believe that **on the day of Pentecost,** the 120 disciples and one of the original eleven, Apostle Peter began to preach the **Pentecostal Good News of Jesus Christ:** [Apostle Preaching]: "Whom (Jesus) God hath raised up, having loosed the pains of death: because it was not possible that He (Jesus) holden (held) of it (death)." Acts 2:1, 24
2. Blessed are the poor in spirit to those who believe that **on the day of Pentecost,** the 120 disciples and one of the original eleven, Apostle Peter began to preach the **Pentecostal Good News of Jesus Christ:** [Apostle Preaching]: "For David speaketh concerning Him (Jesus), I (David) foresaw the Lord always before my face, for He is on my right hand, that I should not be **moved** (shaken):" (see Psalm 16:8), Acts 2:1, 25
3. Blessed are the poor in spirit to those who believe that **on the day of Pentecost,** the 120 disciples and one of the original eleven, Apostle Peter began to preach the **Pentecostal Good News of Jesus Christ:** [Apostle Preaching]: "Therefore did my heart rejoice, and my tongue was glad; moreover also my flesh shall rest in hope:" Acts 2:1, 26
4. Blessed are the poor in spirit to those who believe that **on the day of Pentecost,** the 120 disciples and one of the original eleven, Apostle Peter began to preach the **Pentecostal Good News of Jesus Christ:** [Apostle Preaching]: "Because Thou wilt not leave (abandon) my soul in hell, neither wilt Thou saith Thine Holy One (Jesus) to see corruption." Acts 2:1, 27
5. Blessed are the poor in spirit to those who believe that **on the day of Pentecost,** the 120 disciples and one of the original eleven, Apostle Peter began to preach the **Pentecostal Good News of Jesus Christ:** [Apostle Preaching]: "Thou hast made known to me the ways of life; Thou shalt make me full of joy with Thy countenance (presence)." Acts 2:1, 28

6. Blessed are the poor in spirit to those who believe that **on the day of Pentecost,** the 120 disciples and one of the original eleven, Apostle Peter began to preach the **Pentecostal Good News of Jesus Christ:** [Apostle Preaching]: "Men and brethren, let me freely speak unto you of the patriarch David, (Apostle Peter's preaching) that he (David) is both dead and buried, and his sepulcher (grave) is with us unto (to) this day." Acts 2:1, 29
7. Blessed are the poor in spirit to those who believe that **on the day of Pentecost,** the 120 disciples and one of the original eleven, Apostle Peter began to preach the **Pentecostal Good News of Jesus Christ:** [Apostle Preaching]: "Therefore being a prophet (God's spoken man) and knowing that God had sworn with an oath to Him, that of the fruit of His lions, according to the flesh, He would raise up Christ to sit on His throne;" (See I Chronicles 17:14, Psalm 132:11) Acts 2:1, 30
8. Blessed are the poor in spirit to those who believe that **on the day of Pentecost,** the 120 disciples and one of the original eleven, Apostle Peter began to preach the **Pentecostal Good News of Jesus Christ:** [Apostle Preaching]: "**He** (David) seeing this before spake of the resurrection of Christ; that His soul was not left in hell, neither His flesh did see corruption." (See Psalm 49:15, Psalm 16:10, See Acts 13:35), Acts 2:1, 31
9. Blessed are the poor in spirit to those who believe that **on the day of Pentecost,** the 120 disciples and one of the original eleven, Apostle Peter began to preach the **Pentecostal Good News of Jesus Christ:** [Apostle Preaching]: "This Jesus hath God raised up, whereof we all witnesses." Acts 2:1, 32
10. Blessed are the poor in spirit to those who believe that **on the day of Pentecost,** the 120 disciples and one of the original eleven, Apostle Peter began to preach the **Pentecostal Good News of Jesus Christ:** [Apostle Preaching]: "Therefore being by the right hand of God, exalted, and having received of the Father the promise of the Holy Spirit, He hath shed forth this, which ye now see and hear." Acts 2:1, 33
11. Blessed are the poor in spirit to those who believe that **on the day of Pentecost,** the 120 disciples and one of the original eleven, Apostle Peter began to preach the **Pentecostal Good News of Jesus Christ:** [Apostle Preaching]: "For David is not ascended into heavens: but he saith himself, The Lord said unto my Lord, sit Thou on My right hand," (Psalm 110:1), Acts 2:1, 34
12. Blessed are the poor in spirit to those who believe that **on the day of Pentecost,** the 120 disciples and one of the original eleven, Apostle Peter began to preach the **Pentecostal Good News of Jesus Christ:** [Apostle Preaching]: "Until I make Thy foes (enemies) Thy footstool." Acts 2:1, 35

Part DCXXXIX

Blessed Are The Poor In Spirit. Matthew 5:3

Blessed Means Happy

Poor means meek in spirit. Poor means humble in spirit. Poor means lowly in spirit. Poor means quiet in spirit. Read Matthew 5:3-12, Read also Mark 1:15

Jesus did not say "*rich*" in spirit. Jesus said "*poor*" in spirit.

1. Blessed are the poor in spirit to those who believe that **on the day of Pentecost,** the 120 disciples and one of the original eleven, Apostle Peter began to end his preaching the **Pentecostal Good News of Jesus Christ:** "Therefore let all the house of Israel know assuredly (for certain), that God hath made that same, Jesus, whom ye have [Peter ended the Pentecostal Good News of Jesus Christ] crucified both Lord and Christ (Messiah)." Acts 2:1, 36
2. Blessed are the poor in spirit to those who believe that **on the day of Pentecost,** the 120 disciples and one of the original eleven, Apostle Peter began to end his preaching the **Pentecostal Good News of Jesus Christ:** "Now when they (Acts 2: 5-13), heard this (Peter's Pentecostal Good News of Jesus Christ Acts 2:14-36, verse 36) they were pricked in their heart, and said, unto Peter and the rest of the apostles, men and brethren, what shall we do? [The 120 disciples of Jesus witnessed—saw and heard evident] Acts 2:1, 37
3. Blessed are the poor in spirit to those who believe that **on the day of Pentecost,** the 120 disciples and one of the original eleven, Apostle Peter began to end his preaching the **Pentecostal Good News of Jesus Christ:** [With Pentecostal Good News of Jesus Christ's conclusion] "Then Peter said unto them (Acts 2:5-13), Repent, and be baptized every one of you in the *name* (authority) of Jesus Christ for the remission of sins, and ye shall receive the gift of the Holy Spirit." (See John 20:22) Acts 2:1, 38
4. Blessed are the poor in spirit to those who believe that **on the day of Pentecost,** the 120 disciples and one of the original eleven, Apostle Peter began to end his preaching the **Pentecostal Good News of Jesus Christ:** "For the promise is unto you and to your children, and to all that afar off, even as many as the Lord our God shall call (example of salvation)." See Isaiah 57:19, Ephesians 2:1, 9, Psalm 100:3, Romans 10:13, Acts 2:1, 39

5. Blessed are the poor in spirit to those who believe that **on the day of Pentecost,** the 120 disciples and one of the original eleven, Apostle Peter began to end his preaching the **Pentecostal Good News of Jesus Christ:** "And with many other word did he testify and exhort, saying, Save yourselves from the untoward (perverse) generation." Acts 2:1, 40
6. Blessed are the poor in spirit to those who believe that **on the day of Pentecost,** the 120 disciples and one of the original eleven, Apostle Peter began to end his preaching the **Pentecostal Good News of Jesus Christ:** "Then they (Acts 2:5-13) that gladly received his word were baptized: and the same day (on the day of Pentecost—See Acts 2:1) there were added unto them (Acts 2:5-13) about three thousand souls (that came to accept Jesus Christ as Lord and Savior)." Acts 2:1, 41
7. Blessed are the poor in spirit to those who believe that **on the day of Pentecost,** the 120 disciples and one of the original eleven, Apostle Peter began to end his preaching the **Pentecostal Good News of Jesus Christ:** "And they (Acts 2:5-11) continued steadfastly in the apostles' doctrine (teaching) and fellowship and breaking of bread, and in prayers:" (See Hebrews 10:25, I Corinthians 11:23-26) Acts 2:1, 42
8. Blessed are the poor in spirit to those who believe that **on the day of Pentecost,** the 120 disciples and one of the original eleven, Apostle Peter began to end his preaching the **Pentecostal Good News of Jesus Christ:** "And fear came upon every soul: and many wonders and signs were done by the apostles" (twelve of Jesus' original disciples, except Judas was placed by Mathias—See Acts 1:26) Acts 2:1, 43
9. Blessed are the poor in spirit to those who believe that **on the day of Pentecost,** the 120 disciples and one of the original eleven, Apostle Peter began to finish his preaching the **Pentecostal Good News of Jesus Christ:** "And all that believed were together, and had all things common;" Acts 2:1, 44
10. Blessed are the poor in spirit to those who believe that **on the day of Pentecost,** the 120 disciples and one of the original eleven, Apostle Peter began to finish his preaching the **Pentecostal Good News of Jesus Christ:** "And sold their possessions and goods; and parted (divided) them to all men, as every man had need." Acts 2:1, 45
11. Blessed are the poor in spirit to those who believe that **on the day of Pentecost,** the 120 disciples and one of the original eleven, Apostle Peter began to finish his preaching the **Pentecostal Good News of Jesus Christ:** "And they, continuing

daily with one according in the temple, and breaking bread from house to house, did eat their meat (food) with gladness and singleness of heart." See Colossians 3:16-17, Ephesians 5:7-21 verse 16-18, verse 18, 20. Acts 2:1, 46

12. Blessed are the poor in spirit to those who believe that **on the day of Pentecost,** the 120 disciples and one of the original eleven, Apostle Peter began to finish his preaching the **Pentecostal Good News of Jesus Christ:** "Praising God, and having favor with all the people. And the Lord added to the church daily such us should be saved. See Acts 16:30-31, Acts 4:12, John 3:16, Acts 2:21, Romans 10:13, Revelation 21:24, Joel 2:32, Acts 20:21, Acts 26:20, II Peter 3:9, Hebrews 10:39, Acts 17:30, Mark 1:15, Matthew 3:2, Matthew 4:17, Mark 6:12, I Timothy 2:4, II Timothy 1:9, Titus 3:5, Acts 2:1, 47

Part DCXL

Blessed Are The Poor In Spirit. Matthew 5:3

Blessed Means Happy

Poor means meek in spirit. Poor means humble in spirit. Poor means lowly in spirit. Poor means quiet in spirit. Read Matthew 5:3-12, Read also Mark 1:15

Jesus did not say "*rich*" in spirit. Jesus said "*poor*" in spirit.

1. Blessed are the poor in spirit to those who believe that the Bible is like psychology. It help me to understand the people around me. Proverbs 3:5-6, **Romans 12:2, II Timothy 3:16, Psalm 119:89,** Isaiah 55:8, I Thessalonians 5:21, Philippians 4:8, **II Corinthians 5:17, John 6:26-58, Hebrews 4:12,** Romans 1:28-31, Luke 4:19-21, I John 2:15-17, II Timothy 3:17, **I Thessalonians 5:23,** Ephesians 5:11, **John 14:17, Matthew 5:1-10,** II Thessalonians 3:15, Isaiah 33:18, Isaiah 29:14, Isaiah 61:1-2, Psalm 37:11, Isaiah 55:1-2, II Samuel 22:26, **Hebrews 12:14,** II Corinthians 10:5, **Ecclesiastes 12:13, II Corinthians 6:14-18, I Corinthians 6:14-18, I Corinthians 13:1-13** (See John 15:5), Genesis 1:26-28, Romans 10:17, **II Corinthians 11:3,** I Corinthians 1:18-31, John 3:16, Matthew 4:4, Proverbs 23:7, Psalm 1:1-6, Genesis 3:1-7, Hebrews 9:22, **Psalm 119:169, James 4:8, Deuteronomy 31:6, Joshua 1:9, Matthew 28:20,** Proverb 14:12, Proverbs 16:25
2. Blessed are the poor in spirit to those who believe that we, as Gentiles by nature, are not only sinners, but of the Gentiles. Galatians 2:15
3. Blessed are the poor in spirit to those who believe that we, as Gentiles, are not justified by the works of the law, but that we as Gentiles are **justified by the faith of Jesus Christ.** Galatians 2:16 (a)
4. Blessed are the poor in spirit to those who believe that we as Gentiles, might be justified by the faith of Christ, and not by the works of the law. Galatians 2:16 (b)
5. Blessed are the poor in spirit to those who believe that we as Gentiles wherefore by the works of the law **shall no flesh** (man, human being, poor sinner, poor lost soul) be justified. See Psalm 143:2, Galatians 2:16 (c)

6. Blessed are the poor in spirit to those who believe that our life in Christ is not in vain. I Corinthians 15:58, I Corinthians 15:10, Matthew 6:4-15, Matthew 25:21, 23
7. Blessed are the poor in spirit to those who believe that our living for Christ is not in vain. We sing: "*Is Our Living Is In Vain*?" **James 4:5-10,** I Peter 5:5-6, Proverbs 3:34, I Thessalonians 2:1, Philippians 2:16, II Corinthians 6:1, I Corinthians 15:58, I Corinthians 15:10, Matthew 6:4-16, Matthew 25:21, 23
8. Blessed are the poor in spirit to those who believe that our life for Christ does not go to waste. I Corinthians 15:10, 58, II Timothy 4:8, Revelation 2:10, Matthew 25:21, 23, Matthew 26:6-13, Mark 14:1-9
9. Blessed are the poor in spirit to those who believe and think that our life is not waste for Christ. I Corinthians 15:10, 58, II Timothy 4:8, Revelation 2:10, Matthew 25:21, 23, Matthew 26:6-13, Mark 14:1-9
10. Blessed are the poor in spirit to those who believe that give me understanding: "Let my cry come near before thee, O Lord: give me understanding according to thy word." Psalm 119:169
11. Blessed are the poor in spirit to those who are believing **all** of the Bible Teaching on holiness. II Timothy 3:16, Hebrews 12:14
12. Blessed are the poor in spirit to those who believe this Psalmist: "Blessed (Fortunate) is the man that walketh not in the counsel of the ungodly, nor standeth in the way of sinners, nor sitteth in the seat of the scornful." Psalm 1:1 (Romans 7:22)

Part DCXLI

Blessed Are The Poor In Spirit. Matthew 5:3

Blessed Means Happy

Poor means meek in spirit. Poor means humble in spirit. Poor means lowly in spirit. Poor means quiet in spirit. Read Matthew 5:3-12, Read also Mark 1:15

Jesus did not say "*rich*" in spirit. Jesus said "*poor*" in spirit.

1. Blessed are the poor in spirit to those who believe this Psalmist: "But his delight is in the law of the Lord; and in his law doeth he meditate day and night." Psalm 1:2
2. Blessed are the poor in spirit to those who believe this Psalmist: "And he shall be like a tree planted by the rivers of water, that bringeth forth his fruit in his season; his leaf also shall not wither; and whatsoever (whatever) he doeth shall prosper. Psalm 1:3
3. Blessed are the poor in spirit to those who believe this Psalmist: "The ungodly are not so: but are like the shaff which the wind driveth away." Psalm 1:4
4. Blessed are the poor in spirit to those who believe this Psalmist: "Therefore the ungodly shall not stand (rise) in the judgment, nor sinners in the congregation (assembly) of the righteous." Psalm 1:5
5. Blessed are the poor in spirit to those who believe this Psalmist: "For the Lord knoweth the way of the righteous: but the way of the ungodly shall perish." Psalm 1:6
6. Blessed are the poor in spirit to those who believe that the Baptism in the Holy Sprit is the purpose to win souls for Christ. Proverbs 11:30, Acts 1:4-5, 8, Acts 2:41
7. Blessed are the poor in spirit to those who believe that the Baptism in the Holy Spirit to the purpose to see that a lost soul is being saved through Jesus Christ. Acts 2:41, Acts 4:12, Acts 16:30-31
8. Blessed are the poor in spirit to those who believe that the Baptism in the Holy Spirit is being filled with the Holy Spirit. Acts 2:4
9. Blessed are the poor in spirit to those who believe that the baptism in the Holy Spirit is being full of the Spirit and of power and of faith after the day of Pen-

tecost. Acts 4:8, Acts 4:31, Acts 6:3, 5, 8, Acts 7:55, Acts 8:5, 15-17, 35, Acts 10:36, 44-48, Acts 11:24, Acts 19:17, Acts 13:9, Acts 13:52

10. Blessed are the poor in spirit to those who believe that the Baptism in the Holy Spirit is a wake up call, realizing that Jesus Christ is coming anytime soon, any of these days. Revelation 3:11, Revelation 16:15, Revelation 22:7, 12, 20
11. Blessed are the poor in spirit to those who believe that baptism in the Holy Spirit is being baptized in the Holy Spirit. Luke 24:49, Acts 1:4-5, 8, John 20:22, Acts 11:1-6 (b)
12. Blessed are the poor in spirit to those who believe that the baptism in the Holy Spirit is Mark 16:17 (c)

Part DCXLII

Blessed Are The Poor In Spirit. Matthew 5:3

Blessed Means Happy

Poor means meek in spirit. Poor means humble in spirit. Poor means lowly in spirit. Poor means quiet in spirit. Read Matthew 5:3-12, Read also Mark 1:15

Jesus did not say "*rich*" in spirit. Jesus said "*poor*" in spirit.

1. Blessed are the poor in spirit to those who believe that the baptism in the Holy Spirit is I Corinthians 14:18
2. Blessed are the poor in spirit to those who believe that the Baptism in the Holy Spirit is being filled with the Spirit. Ephesians 5:18, Colossians 3:16
3. Blessed are the poor in spirit to those who believe that the Baptism in the Holy Spirit is being with all spiritual blessings. Ephesians 1:3-23 verse 3-6
4. Blessed are the poor in spirit to those who believe that the Baptism in the Holy Spirit is to be filled after righteousness. Matthew 5:6
5. Blessed are the poor in spirit to those who believe that the Baptism in the Holy Spirit is: "Blessed are ye that hunger now: for ye shall be filled. Blessed are ye that weep now: for ye shall laugh. Luke 6:21
6. Blessed are the poor in spirit to those who believe in the Baptism of the Holy Spirit is for a thirsty and floods upon the dry land (mean people of God). Isaiah 4:43, John 7:38
7. Blessed are the poor in spirit to those who believe in spreading the Good News of Jesus Christ, the Gospel call. Luke 2:10-11
8. Blessed are the poor in spirit to those who believe in walking on foot. Isaiah 52:7, Romans 10:15
9. Blessed are the poor in spirit to those who believe that the Bible will make us smart. Proverbs 22:6, Matthew 18:1-5, Mark 9:36-37, Mark 10:13-16, Luke 9:46-48, Luke 18:15-17
10. Blessed are the poor in spirit to those who believe that the Bible is full of the Holy Spirit. John 20:22, Acts 1:8, Acts 11:16
11. Blessed are the poor in spirit to those who believe that **Jesus** is **Fully God;** That **God** is **Fully Man** through **Jesus Christ** because **God** is **Christ. He** is still **Lord.** (See Acts 9:5-6, 22, Acts 18:5, 28, **John 14:7-9 verse 9**

12. Blessed are the poor in spirit to those who believe is seeing is believing by faith and not by sight. II Corinthians 5:7

Part DCXLIII

Blessed Are The Poor In Spirit. Matthew 5:3

Blessed Means Happy

Poor means meek in spirit. Poor means humble in spirit. Poor means lowly in spirit. Poor means quiet in spirit. Read Matthew 5:3-12, Read also Mark 1:15

Jesus did not say "*rich*" in spirit. Jesus said "*poor*" in spirit.

1. Blessed are the poor in spirit to those who believe that the Holy Spirit was coming to Jerusalem on the day of Pentecost. Genesis 11:1-9
2. Blessed are the poor in spirit to those who believe that **"A New Day Was Coming"** to Jerusalem on the day of Pentecost. Acts 2:1
3. Blessed are the poor in spirit to those who believe that **"A New Day,"** which was the Holy Spirit was coming to Jerusalem on the day of the Pentecost. Acts 2:1, John 14:16-17, 26, John 15:26-27, John 16:7-13, Mark 16:17 (c), John 20:22, Acts 1:4-5, Acts 1:8
4. Blessed are the poor in spirit to those who believe that the Holy Spirit was coming to Jerusalem to prepare us to enter the city of New Jerusalem when Christ come back to earth. Revelation 1:7-8, Revelation 3:11, Revelation 16:15, Revelation 22:7, 12, 13, 16, 20-21, Amos 4:12, Revelation 21:1-2, 10, Revelation 21:1-7, (Acts 2:1)
5. Blessed are the poor in spirit to those who believe that the Holy Spirit was coming to Jerusalem on the day of Pentecost where the multitude **heard noise** by hearing them speak in their own languages in Jerusalem. Acts 2:5-6
6. Blessed are the poor in spirit to those who believe that the Holy Spirit was coming to Jerusalem on the day of Pentecost. Isaiah 28:11-12, I Corinthians 14:21
7. Blessed are the poor in spirit to those who believe that the Holy Spirit was coming to Jerusalem on the day of Pentecost. Joel 2:27
8. Blessed are the poor in spirit to those who believe that the Holy Spirit was coming to Jerusalem on the day of Pentecost. Joel 2:28
9. Blessed are the poor in spirit to those who believe that the Holy Spirit was coming to Jerusalem on the day of Pentecost. Joel 2:29

10. Blessed are the poor in spirit to those who believe that the Holy Spirit was coming to Jerusalem on the day of Pentecost. Joel 2:31
11. Blessed are the poor in spirit to those who believe that the Holy Spirit was coming to Jerusalem on the day of Pentecost. Joel 2:32
12. Blessed are the poor in spirit to those who believe that the Holy Spirit was coming to Jerusalem on the day of Pentecost. Acts 2:16

Part DCXLIV

Blessed Are The Poor In Spirit. Matthew 5:3

Blessed Means Happy

Poor means meek in spirit. Poor means humble in spirit. Poor means lowly in spirit. Poor means quiet in spirit. Read Matthew 5:3-12, Read also Mark 1:15

Jesus did not say "*rich*" in spirit. Jesus said "*poor*" in spirit.

1. Blessed are the poor in spirit to those who believe that the Holy Spirit was coming to Jerusalem on the day of Pentecost. Acts 2:17
2. Blessed are the poor in spirit to those who believe that the Holy Spirit was coming to Jerusalem on the day of Pentecost. Acts 2:18
3. Blessed are the poor in spirit to those who believe that the Holy Spirit was coming to Jerusalem on the day of Pentecost. Acts 2:19
4. Blessed are the poor in spirit to those who believe that the Holy Spirit was coming to Jerusalem on the day of Pentecost. Acts 2:20
5. Blessed are the poor in spirit to those who believe that the Holy Spirit was coming to Jerusalem on the day of Pentecost. Acts 2:21
6. Blessed are the poor in spirit to those who believe that the Holy Spirit was coming to Jerusalem on the day of Pentecost. Matthew 3:11 (b)
7. Blessed are the poor in spirit to those who believe that the Holy Spirit was coming to Jerusalem on the day of Pentecost. Mark 1:8 (b)
8. Blessed are the poor in spirit to those who believe that the Holy Spirit was coming to Jerusalem on the day of Pentecost. Luke 3:16 (c)
9. Blessed are the poor in spirit to those who believe that the Holy Spirit was coming to Jerusalem on the day of Pentecost. Mark 16:17 (c)
10. Blessed are the poor in spirit to those who believe that the Holy Spirit was coming to Jerusalem on the day of Pentecost. John 1:33 (b)
11. Blessed are the poor in spirit to those who believe that the Holy Spirit was coming to Jerusalem on the day of Pentecost. John 20:22
12. Blessed are the poor in spirit to those who believe that the Holy Spirit was coming to Jerusalem on the day of Pentecost. Luke 24:49

PART DCXLV

Blessed Are The Poor In Spirit. Matthew 5:3

Blessed Means Happy

Poor means meek in spirit. Poor means humble in spirit. Poor means lowly in spirit. Poor means quiet in spirit. Read Matthew 5:3-12, Read also Mark 1:15

Jesus did not say "*rich*" in spirit. Jesus said "*poor*" in spirit.

1. Blessed are the poor in spirit to those who believe that the Holy Spirit was coming to Jerusalem on the day of Pentecost. John 7:39
2. Blessed are the poor in spirit to those who believe that the Holy Spirit was coming to Jerusalem on the day of Pentecost. Acts 1:4
3. Blessed are the poor in spirit to those who believe that the Holy Spirit was coming to Jerusalem on the day of Pentecost. Acts 1:5
4. Blessed are the poor in spirit to those who believe that the Holy Spirit was coming to Jerusalem on the day of Pentecost. Acts 1:8
5. Blessed are the poor in spirit to those who believe that the Holy Spirit was coming to Jerusalem on the day of Pentecost. Acts 2:1
6. Blessed are the poor in spirit to those who believe that the Holy Spirit was coming to Jerusalem on the day of Pentecost. Acts 2:2
7. Blessed are the poor in spirit to those who believe that the Holy Spirit was coming to Jerusalem on the day of Pentecost. Acts 2:3
8. Blessed are the poor in spirit to those who believe that the Holy Spirit was coming to Jerusalem on the day of Pentecost. Acts 2:4
9. Blessed are the poor in spirit to those who believe that the Holy Spirit was coming to Jerusalem on the day of Pentecost. Acts 8:15
10. Blessed are the poor in spirit to those who believe that the Holy Spirit was coming to Jerusalem on the day of Pentecost. Acts 8:16
11. Blessed are the poor in spirit to those who believe that the Holy Spirit was coming to Jerusalem on the day of Pentecost. Acts 8:17
12. Blessed are the poor in spirit to those who believe that the Holy Spirit was coming to Jerusalem on the day of Pentecost. Acts 8:18

Part DCXLVI

Blessed Are The Poor In Spirit. Matthew 5:3

Blessed Means Happy

Poor means meek in spirit. Poor means humble in spirit. Poor means lowly in spirit. Poor means quiet in spirit. Read Matthew 5:3-12, Read also Mark 1:15

Jesus did not say "*rich*" in spirit. Jesus said "*poor*" in spirit.

1. Blessed are the poor in spirit to those who believe that the Holy Spirit was coming to Jerusalem on the day of Pentecost. Acts 8:19
2. Blessed are the poor in spirit to those who believe that the Holy Spirit was coming to Jerusalem on the day of Pentecost. Acts 8:20
3. Blessed are the poor in spirit to those who believe that the Holy Spirit was coming to Jerusalem on the day of Pentecost. Acts 8:21
4. Blessed are the poor in spirit to those who believe that the Holy Spirit was coming to Jerusalem on the day of Pentecost. Acts 8:22
5. Blessed are the poor in spirit to those who believe that the Holy Spirit was coming to Jerusalem on the day of Pentecost. Acts 8:23
6. Blessed are the poor in spirit to those who believe that the Holy Spirit was coming to Jerusalem on the day of Pentecost. Acts 8:24
7. Blessed are the poor in spirit to those who believe that the Holy Spirit was coming to Jerusalem on the day of Pentecost. Acts 8:25
8. Blessed are the poor in spirit to those who believe that the Holy Spirit was coming to Jerusalem on the day of Pentecost. Acts 8:26
9. Blessed are the poor in spirit to those who believe that the Holy Spirit was coming to Jerusalem on the day of Pentecost. Acts 8:27
10. Blessed are the poor in spirit to those who believe that the Holy Spirit was coming to Jerusalem on the day of Pentecost. Acts 8:28
11. Blessed are the poor in spirit to those who believe that the Holy Spirit was coming to Jerusalem on the day of Pentecost. Acts 8:29
12. Blessed are the poor in spirit to those who believe that the Holy Spirit was coming to Jerusalem on the day of Pentecost. Acts 8:30

Part DCXLVII

Blessed Are The Poor In Spirit. Matthew 5:3

Blessed Means Happy

Poor means meek in spirit. Poor means humble in spirit. Poor means lowly in spirit. Poor means quiet in spirit. Read Matthew 5:3-12, Read also Mark 1:15

Jesus did not say "*rich*" in spirit. Jesus said "*poor*" in spirit.

1. Blessed are the poor in spirit to those who believe that the Holy Spirit was coming to Jerusalem on the day of Pentecost. Acts 8:31
2. Blessed are the poor in spirit to those who believe that the Holy Spirit was coming to Jerusalem on the day of Pentecost. Acts 8:32
3. Blessed are the poor in spirit to those who believe that the Holy Spirit was coming to Jerusalem on the day of Pentecost. Acts 8:33
4. Blessed are the poor in spirit to those who believe that the Holy Spirit was coming to Jerusalem on the day of Pentecost. Acts 8:34
5. Blessed are the poor in spirit to those who believe that the Holy Spirit was coming to Jerusalem on the day of Pentecost. Acts 8:35
6. Blessed are the poor in spirit to those who believe that the Holy Spirit was coming to Jerusalem on the day of Pentecost. Acts 8:36
7. Blessed are the poor in spirit to those who believe that the Holy Spirit was coming to Jerusalem on the day of Pentecost. Acts 8:37
8. Blessed are the poor in spirit to those who believe that the Holy Spirit was coming to Jerusalem on the day of Pentecost. Acts 8:38
9. Blessed are the poor in spirit to those who believe that the Holy Spirit was coming to Jerusalem on the day of Pentecost. Acts 8:39
10. Blessed are the poor in spirit to those who believe that the Holy Spirit was coming to Jerusalem on the day of Pentecost. Acts 8:40
11. Blessed are the poor in spirit to those who believe that the Holy Spirit was coming to Jerusalem on the day of Pentecost. Acts 10:1
12. Blessed are the poor in spirit to those who believe that the Holy Spirit was coming to Jerusalem on the day of Pentecost. Acts 10:2

Part DCXLVIII

Blessed Are The Poor In Spirit. Matthew 5:3

Blessed Means Happy

Poor means meek in spirit. Poor means humble in spirit. Poor means lowly in spirit. Poor means quiet in spirit. Read Matthew 5:3-12, Read also Mark 1:15

Jesus did not say "*rich*" in spirit. Jesus said "*poor*" in spirit.

1. Blessed are the poor in spirit to those who believe that the Holy Spirit was coming to Jerusalem on the day of Pentecost. Acts 10:3
2. Blessed are the poor in spirit to those who believe that the Holy Spirit was coming to Jerusalem on the day of Pentecost. Acts 10:4
3. Blessed are the poor in spirit to those who believe that the Holy Spirit was coming to Jerusalem on the day of Pentecost. Acts 10:5
4. Blessed are the poor in spirit to those who believe that the Holy Spirit was coming to Jerusalem on the day of Pentecost. Acts 10:6
5. Blessed are the poor in spirit to those who believe that the Holy Spirit was coming to Jerusalem on the day of Pentecost. Acts 10:7
6. Blessed are the poor in spirit to those who believe that the Holy Spirit was coming to Jerusalem on the day of Pentecost. Acts 10:8
7. Blessed are the poor in spirit to those who believe that the Holy Spirit was coming to Jerusalem on the day of Pentecost. Acts 10:9
8. Blessed are the poor in spirit to those who believe that the Holy Spirit was coming to Jerusalem on the day of Pentecost. Acts 10:10
9. Blessed are the poor in spirit to those who believe that the Holy Spirit was coming to Jerusalem on the day of Pentecost. Acts 10:11
10. Blessed are the poor in spirit to those who believe that the Holy Spirit was coming to Jerusalem on the day of Pentecost. Acts 10:12
11. Blessed are the poor in spirit to those who believe that the Holy Spirit was coming to Jerusalem on the day of Pentecost. Acts 10:13
12. Blessed are the poor in spirit to those who believe that the Holy Spirit was coming to Jerusalem on the day of Pentecost. Acts 10:14

Part DCXLIX

Blessed Are The Poor In Spirit. Matthew 5:3

Blessed Means Happy

Poor means meek in spirit. Poor means humble in spirit. Poor means lowly in spirit. Poor means quiet in spirit. Read Matthew 5:3-12, Read also Mark 1:15

Jesus did not say "*rich*" in spirit. Jesus said "*poor*" in spirit.

1. Blessed are the poor in spirit to those who believe that the Holy Spirit was coming to Jerusalem on the day of Pentecost. Acts 10:15
2. Blessed are the poor in spirit to those who believe that the Holy Spirit was coming to Jerusalem on the day of Pentecost. Acts 10:16
3. Blessed are the poor in spirit to those who believe that the Holy Spirit was coming to Jerusalem on the day of Pentecost. Acts 10:17
4. Blessed are the poor in spirit to those who believe that the Holy Spirit was coming to Jerusalem on the day of Pentecost. Acts 10:18
5. Blessed are the poor in spirit to those who believe that the Holy Spirit was coming to Jerusalem on the day of Pentecost. Acts 10:19
6. Blessed are the poor in spirit to those who believe that the Holy Spirit was coming to Jerusalem on the day of Pentecost. Acts 10:20
7. Blessed are the poor in spirit to those who believe that the Holy Spirit was coming to Jerusalem on the day of Pentecost. Acts 10:21
8. Blessed are the poor in spirit to those who believe that the Holy Spirit was coming to Jerusalem on the day of Pentecost. Acts 10:22
9. Blessed are the poor in spirit to those who believe that the Holy Spirit was coming to Jerusalem on the day of Pentecost. Acts 10:23
10. Blessed are the poor in spirit to those who believe that the Holy Spirit was coming to Jerusalem on the day of Pentecost. Acts 10:24
11. Blessed are the poor in spirit to those who believe that the Holy Spirit was coming to Jerusalem on the day of Pentecost. Acts 10:25
12. Blessed are the poor in spirit to those who believe that the Holy Spirit was coming to Jerusalem on the day of Pentecost. Acts 10:26

PART DCL

Blessed Are The Poor In Spirit. Matthew 5:3

Blessed Means Happy

Poor means meek in spirit. Poor means humble in spirit. Poor means lowly in spirit. Poor means quiet in spirit. Read Matthew 5:3-12, Read also Mark 1:15

Jesus did not say "*rich*" in spirit. Jesus said "*poor*" in spirit.

1. Blessed are the poor in spirit to those who believe that the Holy Spirit was coming to Jerusalem on the day of Pentecost. Acts 10:27
2. Blessed are the poor in spirit to those who believe that the Holy Spirit was coming to Jerusalem on the day of Pentecost. Acts 10:28
3. Blessed are the poor in spirit to those who believe that the Holy Spirit was coming to Jerusalem on the day of Pentecost. Acts 10:29
4. Blessed are the poor in spirit to those who believe that the Holy Spirit was coming to Jerusalem on the day of Pentecost. Acts 10:30
5. Blessed are the poor in spirit to those who believe that the Holy Spirit was coming to Jerusalem on the day of Pentecost. Acts 10:31
6. Blessed are the poor in spirit to those who believe that the Holy Spirit was coming to Jerusalem on the day of Pentecost. Acts 10:32
7. Blessed are the poor in spirit to those who believe that the Holy Spirit was coming to Jerusalem on the day of Pentecost. Acts 10:33
8. Blessed are the poor in spirit to those who believe that the Holy Spirit was coming to Jerusalem on the day of Pentecost. Acts 10:34
9. Blessed are the poor in spirit to those who believe that the Holy Spirit was coming to Jerusalem on the day of Pentecost. Acts 10:35
10. Blessed are the poor in spirit to those who believe that the Holy Spirit was coming to Jerusalem on the day of Pentecost. Acts 10:36
11. Blessed are the poor in spirit to those who believe that the Holy Spirit was coming to Jerusalem on the day of Pentecost. Acts 10:37
12. Blessed are the poor in spirit to those who believe that the Holy Spirit was coming to Jerusalem on the day of Pentecost. Acts 10:38

Part DCLI

Blessed Are The Poor In Spirit. Matthew 5:3

Blessed Means Happy

Poor means meek in spirit. Poor means humble in spirit. Poor means lowly in spirit. Poor means quiet in spirit. Read Matthew 5:3-12, Read also Mark 1:15

Jesus did not say "*rich*" in spirit. Jesus said "*poor*" in spirit.

1. Blessed are the poor in spirit to those who believe that the Holy Spirit was coming to Jerusalem on the day of Pentecost. Acts 10:39
2. Blessed are the poor in spirit to those who believe that the Holy Spirit was coming to Jerusalem on the day of Pentecost. Acts 10:40
3. Blessed are the poor in spirit to those who believe that the Holy Spirit was coming to Jerusalem on the day of Pentecost. Acts 10:41
4. Blessed are the poor in spirit to those who believe that the Holy Spirit was coming to Jerusalem on the day of Pentecost. Acts 10:42
5. Blessed are the poor in spirit to those who believe that the Holy Spirit was coming to Jerusalem on the day of Pentecost. Acts 10:43
6. Blessed are the poor in spirit to those who believe that the Holy Spirit was coming to Jerusalem on the day of Pentecost. Acts 10:44
7. Blessed are the poor in spirit to those who believe that the Holy Spirit was coming to Jerusalem on the day of Pentecost. Acts 10:45
8. Blessed are the poor in spirit to those who believe that the Holy Spirit was coming to Jerusalem on the day of Pentecost. Acts 10:46
9. Blessed are the poor in spirit to those who believe that the Holy Spirit was coming to Jerusalem on the day of Pentecost. Acts 10:47
10. Blessed are the poor in spirit to those who believe that the Holy Spirit was coming to Jerusalem on the day of Pentecost. Acts 10:48
11. Blessed are the poor in spirit to those who believe that the Holy Spirit was coming to Jerusalem on the day of Pentecost. Acts 11:1
12. Blessed are the poor in spirit to those who believe that the Holy Spirit was coming to Jerusalem on the day of Pentecost. Acts 11:2

Part DCLII

Blessed Are The Poor In Spirit. Matthew 5:3

Blessed Means Happy

Poor means meek in spirit. Poor means humble in spirit. Poor means lowly in spirit. Poor means quiet in spirit. Read Matthew 5:3-12, Read also Mark 1:15

Jesus did not say "*rich*" in spirit. Jesus said "*poor*" in spirit.

1. Blessed are the poor in spirit to those who believe that the Holy Spirit was coming to Jerusalem on the day of Pentecost. Acts 11:3
2. Blessed are the poor in spirit to those who believe that the Holy Spirit was coming to Jerusalem on the day of Pentecost. Acts 11:4
3. Blessed are the poor in spirit to those who believe that the Holy Spirit was coming to Jerusalem on the day of Pentecost. Acts 11:5
4. Blessed are the poor in spirit to those who believe that the Holy Spirit was coming to Jerusalem on the day of Pentecost. Acts 11:6
5. Blessed are the poor in spirit to those who believe that the Holy Spirit was coming to Jerusalem on the day of Pentecost. Acts 11:7
6. Blessed are the poor in spirit to those who believe that the Holy Spirit was coming to Jerusalem on the day of Pentecost. Acts 11:8
7. Blessed are the poor in spirit to those who believe that the Holy Spirit was coming to Jerusalem on the day of Pentecost. Acts 11:9
8. Blessed are the poor in spirit to those who believe that the Holy Spirit was coming to Jerusalem on the day of Pentecost. Acts 11:10
9. Blessed are the poor in spirit to those who believe that the Holy Spirit was coming to Jerusalem on the day of Pentecost. Acts 11:11
10. Blessed are the poor in spirit to those who believe that the Holy Spirit was coming to Jerusalem on the day of Pentecost. Acts 11:12
11. Blessed are the poor in spirit to those who believe that the Holy Spirit was coming to Jerusalem on the day of Pentecost. Acts 11:13
12. Blessed are the poor in spirit to those who believe that the Holy Spirit was coming to Jerusalem on the day of Pentecost. Acts 11:14

Part DCLIII

Blessed Are The Poor In Spirit. Matthew 5:3

Blessed Means Happy

Poor means meek in spirit. Poor means humble in spirit. Poor means lowly in spirit. Poor means quiet in spirit. Read Matthew 5:3-12, Read also Mark 1:15

Jesus did not say "*rich*" in spirit. Jesus said "*poor*" in spirit.

1. Blessed are the poor in spirit to those who believe that the Holy Spirit was coming to Jerusalem on the day of Pentecost. Acts 11:15
2. Blessed are the poor in spirit to those who believe that the Holy Spirit was coming to Jerusalem on the day of Pentecost. Acts 11:16
3. Blessed are the poor in spirit to those who believe that the Holy Spirit was coming to Jerusalem on the day of Pentecost. Acts 11:17
4. Blessed are the poor in spirit to those who believe that the Holy Spirit was coming to Jerusalem on the day of Pentecost. Acts 11:18
5. Blessed are the poor in spirit to those who believe that the Holy Spirit was coming to Jerusalem on the day of Pentecost. Acts 19:1
6. Blessed are the poor in spirit to those who believe that the Holy Spirit was coming to Jerusalem on the day of Pentecost. Acts 19:2
7. Blessed are the poor in spirit to those who believe that the Holy Spirit was coming to Jerusalem on the day of Pentecost. Acts 19:3
8. Blessed are the poor in spirit to those who believe that the Holy Spirit was coming to Jerusalem on the day of Pentecost. Acts 19:4
9. Blessed are the poor in spirit to those who believe that the Holy Spirit was coming to Jerusalem on the day of Pentecost. Acts 19:5
10. Blessed are the poor in spirit to those who believe that the Holy Spirit was coming to Jerusalem on the day of Pentecost. Acts 19:6
11. Blessed are the poor in spirit to those who believe that the Holy Spirit was coming to Jerusalem on the day of Pentecost. Acts 1-4
12. Blessed are the poor in spirit to those who believe that the Holy Spirit was coming on His Way to Jerusalem on the day of Pentecost. Acts 2:1–4

Part DCLIV

Blessed Are The Poor In Spirit. Matthew 5:3

Blessed Means Happy

Poor means meek in spirit. Poor means humble in spirit. Poor means lowly in spirit. Poor means quiet in spirit. Read Matthew 5:3-12, Read also Mark 1:15

Jesus did not say "*rich*" in spirit. Jesus said "*poor*" in spirit.

1. Blessed are the poor in spirit to those who believe that the Holy Spirit was coming to Jerusalem on the day of Pentecost so that the 120 disciples of Jesus could receive the Holy Spirit to witness the multitude in Jerusalem. Acts 2:1-41
2. Blessed are the poor in spirit to those who believe that the Holy Spirit was coming to Jerusalem on the day of Pentecost in order for the multitude as well as for us to this day to get saved. Acts 2:47
3. Blessed are the poor in spirit to those who believe that the Holy Spirit was coming to Jerusalem on the day of Pentecost in order for the multitude as well as for us to this day to get sanctified. Acts 26:18
4. Blessed are the poor in spirit to those who believe that the Holy Spirit was coming to Jerusalem on the day of Pentecost in order for the multitude as well as for us to this day to be filled with Holy Spirit promised by God to us. Acts 2:4, 39
5. Blessed are the poor in spirit to those who believe that the Holy Spirit was coming to Jerusalem on the day of Pentecost in order for the multitude as well as for us to this day for us to abide in the Holy Spirit for ever. John 14:16
6. Blessed are the poor in spirit to those who believe that the Holy Spirit was coming to Jerusalem on the day of Pentecost in order for the multitude as well as for us to this day is the purpose to get us ready when He come. Revelation 3:11, Revelation 16:15, Revelation 22:3, 7, 12, 16, 20, 21
7. Blessed are the poor in spirit to those who believe that the Holy Spirit was coming to Jerusalem on the day of Pentecost in order for the multitude as well as for us is the purpose to get us **ready** so that we may go back with Him when He come. I Thessalonians 4:16-17, Revelation 1:7, Hebrews 9:28
8. Blessed are the poor in spirit to those who believe that the Holy Spirit was coming to Jerusalem on the day of Pentecost in order for the multitude as well as for

us to this day to be saved, to be sanctified, to be baptized in the Holy Spirit, to witness for Christ and **His Imminent Return**, and to win souls for Christ. Acts 2:1, Acts 1:4-5, Acts 11:16, Acts 26:18, Acts 10:30-31, Proverbs 11:30, Luke 24:49, John 20:22, Acts 2:38-47 verse 41, 42, 46. 47

9. Blessed are the poor in spirit to those who believe that the Holy Spirit was coming to Jerusalem on the day of Pentecost because **Jesus Christ is coming soon. Get Ready**. Revelation 3:11, Revelation 15:16, Revelation 22:7, 12, 16, 20-21
10. Blessed are the poor in spirit to those who believe that the Holy Spirit was coming to Jerusalem on the day of Pentecost to fill us with the Holy Spirit or to receive the Baptism of the Holy Spirit. Acts 2:1-4 verse 4
11. Blessed are the poor in spirit to those who believe that the Holy Spirit was coming to Jerusalem on the day of Pentecost. Acts 2:41
12. Blessed are the poor in spirit to those who believe that the Holy Spirit was coming to Jerusalem on the day of Pentecost. Joel 2:25-32

Part DCLV

Blessed Are The Poor In Spirit. Matthew 5:3

Blessed Means Happy

Poor means meek in spirit. Poor means humble in spirit. Poor means lowly in spirit. Poor means quiet in spirit. Read Matthew 5:3-12, Read also Mark 1:15

Jesus did not say "*rich*" in spirit. Jesus said "*poor*" in spirit.

1. Blessed are the poor in spirit to those who believe that Macedonia was called for help, the Gospel Call Light, The Gospel Call, The Gospel Light. Acts 16:9-10, II Corinthians 4:5-6, Luke 1:76-79, Isaiah 9:2
2. Blessed are the poor in spirit to those who believe in spreading the Gospel Call. Mark 16:15
3. Blessed are the poor in spirit to those who believe in Evangelical's work, spreading the Gospel Call. Mark 16:15
4. Blessed are the poor in spirit to those who believe in elder's duty, spreading the Gospel Call. Mark 16:15
5. Blessed are the poor in spirit to those who believe in bishop's duty spreading the Gospel Call. I Timothy 3:1-2, Titus 1:7, Philippians 1:1
6. Blessed are the poor in spirit to those who believe in the apostle's duty, spreading the Gospel Call. Mark 16:15, Ephesians 4:11
7. Blessed are the poor in spirit to those who believe in the prophet's duty, spreading the Gospel Call. Mark 16:15, Ephesians 4:11
8. Blessed are the poor in spirit to those who believe in the Imminent Return of Christ. Revelation 3:11, Revelation 16:15, Revelation 22:7, 12, 20-21
9. Blessed are the poor in spirit to those who believe in Deacon's duty, spreading the Gospel Call, Philippians 1:1, I Timothy 3:8, 10, 12-13
10. Blessed are the poor in spirit to those who believe in mothering the church, spreading the Gospel Call. Mark 16:15, I Timothy 1:5-11 verse 5
11. Blessed are the poor in spirit to those who believe the Brother in Christ's duty, spreading the Gospel Call. Mark 16:15, II Corinthians 6:18, Joel 2:28-29, Acts 2:16-18 verse 17

12. Blessed are the poor in spirit to those who believe in the Sister in Christ's duty, spreading the Gospel Call. Luke 18:15-17, Luke 9:47-48, Galatians 3:26-28, II Corinthians 6:18, Acts 21:9, Joel 2:28-29, Acts 2:16-18 verse 17

Part DCLVI

Blessed Are The Poor In Spirit. Matthew 5:3

Blessed Means Happy

Poor means meek in spirit. Poor means humble in spirit. Poor means lowly in spirit. Poor means quiet in spirit. Read Matthew 5:3-12, Read also Mark 1:15

Jesus did not say "*rich*" in spirit. Jesus said "*poor*" in spirit.

1. Blessed are the poor in spirit to those who believe in children's ministry, spreading the Gospel Call. Mark 16:15, Matthew 18:1-6, Mark 9:36-37, Mark 10:13-16
2. Blessed are the poor in spirit to those who believe in the pastor's duty, spreading the Gospel Call. Mark 16:15, Ephesians 4:11, Jeremiah 17:16, Jeremiah 3:15
3. Blessed are the poor in spirit to those who believe in the church ministry, spreading the Gospel Call, Mark 16:15, Acts 11:26
4. Blessed are the poor in spirit to those who believe in the staff church administration, spreading the Gospel Call. Mark 16:15, Acts 11:26
5. Blessed are the poor in spirit to those who believe in gospel hymn, spreading the Gospel Call. Psalm 145:1, Psalm 150:1-6, Psalm 103:3, Psalm 95:6, Psalm 149:1, Psalm100:1, Psalm 47:1, I Chronicles 16:26, I Chronicles 29:30, Nehemiah 9:5, Isaiah 6:1, Exodus 40:34, 35, John 12:41
6. Blessed are the poor in spirit to those who believe in Gospel Mission, spreading the Gospel Call. Mark 16:15, Acts 11:26
7. Blessed are the poor in spirit to those who believe in the male's ministry, spreading the Gospel Call. Mark 16:15, II Corinthians 6:18, Joel 2:28-29, Acts 2:16-18 verse 17
8. Blessed are the poor in spirit to those who believe in the female's ministry, spreading the Gospel Call. Mark 16:15, Galatians 3:26-28, Luke 24:10, John 20:1-2, Mark 16:1-11, Matthew 28:5-10, Acts 2:16-18 verse 17, II Corinthians 6:18, Acts 21:9, Joel 2:28-29, Luke 18:15-17
9. Blessed are the poor in spirit to those who believe in the Gospel Chorus Ministry, spreading the Gospel Call. Mark 16:15, II Samuel 19:35, I Chronicles 6:32, II Chronicles 35:25, Ezra 2:65, Nehemiah 7:67, Psalm 126:2

10. Blessed are the poor in spirit to those who believe in the minister's call, spreading the Gospel Call. Mark 16:15, Ephesians 4:11, Jeremiah 3:15
11. Blessed are the poor in spirit to those who believe in the Bus Ministry, spreading the Gospel Call. Mark 16:15, Acts 13:49
12. Blessed are the poor in spirit to those who believe in the Van Ministry, spreading the Gospel Call. Mark 16:15, Acts 13:49

Part DCLVII

Blessed Are The Poor In Spirit. Matthew 5:3

Blessed Means Happy

Poor means meek in spirit. Poor means humble in spirit. Poor means lowly in spirit. Poor means quiet in spirit. Read Matthew 5:3-12, Read also Mark 1:15

Jesus did not say "*rich*" in spirit. Jesus said "*poor*" in spirit.

1. Blessed are the poor in spirit to those who believe in the Christian Ministry, spreading the Gospel Call. Matthew 16:20, Acts 11:26, Romans 8:28
2. Blessed are the poor in spirit to those who believe that the Light was sent to light the Gospel Call. John 1:4-9
3. Blessed are the poor in spirit to those who believe in Deaf Ministry. Isaiah 29:18, Mark 16:15, Romans 8:28
4. Blessed are the poor in spirit to those who believe in Deaf Ministry Team. Isaiah 29:18, Mark 16:15, Romans 8:28
5. Blessed are the poor in spirit to those who believe in Deaf Female Ministry. Isaiah 29:18, Mark 16:15, Romans 8:28, 31, Psalm 118:6, II Kings 6:16, Galatians 3:26-28, Luke 24:10, John 20:1-2, Mark 16:1-11, Matthew 28:5-10
6. Blessed are the poor in spirit to those who believe in Deaf Male Ministry. Mark 16:15, Matthew 10:7, 27, Luke 9:1-5, Mark 6:8-12, Acts 5:42, Acts 10:42
7. Blessed are the poor in spirit to those who in Deaf And Blind Ministry. Isaiah 42:16, Isaiah 29:18, Romans 8:28, Exodus 4:11, Leviticus 19:14, Leviticus 21:18
8. Blessed are the poor in spirit to those who believe that the Holy Bible has a license to preach to us. II Timothy 3:16
9. Blessed are the poor in spirit to those who believe that the Holy Bible has a license to preach to us from God. II Timothy 3:16
10. Blessed are the poor in spirit to those who that the Holy Bible has a license to preach to us is a gift from God. II Timothy 3:16
11. Blessed are the poor in spirit to those who believe that the Holy Bible has a right to have license "*toward*" us. II Timothy 3:16
12. Blessed are the poor in spirit to those who believe that the Holy Bible has a right to have license "*against*" us. II Timothy 3:16

Part DCLVIII

Blessed Are The Poor In Spirit. Matthew 5:3

Blessed Means Happy

Poor means meek in spirit. Poor means humble in spirit. Poor means lowly in spirit. Poor means quiet in spirit. Read Matthew 5:3-12, Read also Mark 1:15

Jesus did not say "*rich*" in spirit. Jesus said "*poor*" in spirit.

1. Blessed are the poor in spirit to those who believe that Happiness is praying in the Holy Spirit. Jude 1:20
2. Blessed are the poor in spirit to those who believe in the Festival Of Pentecost. Acts 2:1-47 verse 1, 4, 41, 47
3. Blessed are the poor in spirit to those who believe that praying in the languages of the Holy Spirit. Acts 2:1-41 verse 4-11
4. Blessed are the poor in spirit to those who believe that is unspeakable joy—I Peter 1:8
5. Blessed are the poor in spirit to those who believe that is unspeakable gift—I Peter 1:8
6. Blessed are the poor in spirit to those who believe that we may have Christ's joy. I John 1:4
7. Blessed are the poor in spirit to those who believe that is when we enter into the joy of the Lord. Matthew 25:21, 23
8. Blessed are the poor in spirit to those who believe that is to rejoice in that day, and leap for joy because our reward is great in heaven. Luke 6:23
9. Blessed are the poor in spirit to those who believe that the baptism in the Holy Spirit is when they that hear the Gospel; then come the devil, and take away the Word of the Gospel out of their hearts, lest they should believe and be saved. Luke 8:12
10. Blessed are the poor in spirit to those who believe is when they on the rock (solid foundation) are they, which, when they hear, receive the Word of the Gospel with joy; and these have not root, which for a while believe, and in time of temptation (testing) fall away. Luke 8:13

11. Blessed are the poor in spirit to those who believe is that on the good ground are they which in an honest and good heart, having heard the Word of the Gospel, keep it (salvation in Jesus Christ) and bring forth first with patience (after a time). Luke 8:15
12. Blessed are the poor in spirit to those who believe is when He (Christ) has the bride, is the bridegroom: but the friend of the bridegroom, which stand and hear Him (Christ; He is the bridegroom), rejoice greatly became of the bridegroom's voice (Christ's voice): this my (and mine is too) therefore is fulfilled. John 3:29

Part DCLXIX

Blessed Are The Poor In Spirit. Matthew 5:3

Blessed Means Happy

Poor means meek in spirit. Poor means humble in spirit. Poor means lowly in spirit. Poor means quiet in spirit. Read Matthew 5:3-12, Read also Mark 1:15

Jesus did not say "*rich*" in spirit. Jesus said "*poor*" in spirit.

1. Blessed are the poor in spirit to those who believe that speaking in tongues, a practice associated with Pentecostal and Charismatic churches according to Acts 2:4
2. Blessed are the poor in spirit to those who believe that speaking in tongues is an ancient Christian practice recorded in the New Testament in which people pray in a language they do not know; that they do not understand; and that they do not control in a prayer language according to Acts 2:4. See I Corinthians 14:13-19, 33, Romans 8:26-28, 31, Isaiah 28:11, I Corinthians 14:21
3. Blessed are the poor in spirit to those who believe that Pentecost of the Holy Spirit is found in I Corinthians 12:1-11, with one of the many "gifts" of the Holy Spirit with healing and the possibility (ability) to prophesy.
4. Blessed are the poor in spirit to those who believe that the speaking in tongues is need to the growing strength of the Pentecostal movement according to Acts 1:8 and Acts 2:4, and for Acts 2:41, and Acts 2:47
5. Blessed are the poor in spirit to those who believe that speaking in tongues is the Charismatic experiences are normative; something we do not always know or understand the Holy Spirit language speaking, but is of God who is not the author of confusion, but of peace in all churches. I Corinthians 14:33, See I Corinthians 14:13-19, Romans 8:26-28, 31, Isaiah 28:11, I Corinthians 14:21
6. Blessed are the poor in spirit to those who believe to *find* or to *discover* that the fast growing Pentecostal Christianity which now has an estimated 300 million followers worldwide, **since on the day of Pentecost** and the second of the early 20th century found. Acts 1:1-4 verse 1, Acts 2:4, Acts 20:16, I Corinthians 16:8, Acts 26:28, Acts 11:26, I Peter 4:16

7. Blessed are the poor in spirit to those who believe that all Christians should seek a post conversion religious experience called the Baptism of the Holy Spirit. Acts 2:4, Acts 19:1-6, Acts 10:44-46, acts 8:14-17, See Mark 16:17 (c)
8. Blessed are the poor in spirit to those who believe that speaking in tongues is spiritual languages call glossolalia, and interpret tongues. Acts 2:1-11, I Corinthians 14:1-19 verse 2, 4, 5, 6, 12, 13, 14-15, **18**, Ephesians 5:18-20, Colossians 3:16-17, Acts 2:11-18, 21, Joel 2:26-29, 32, I Corinthians 14:33
9. Blessed are the poor in spirit to those who believe are able to thank *the Religion News Service*, writing about the Southern Baptist to open their ranks to missionaries who believe to speak in tongues according to Acts 2:4. See Mark 16:17 (c)
10. Blessed are the poor in spirit to those who believe are able to thank *the Christianity Today* who wrote to tell us that International Mission Board drops ban on speaking in tongues and that the Bible indeed speak of speaking in Mark 16:17 (c) and Acts 2:4, I Corinthians 14:1-19 verse 18, Isaiah 28:11-12, I Corinthians 14:21
11. Blessed are the poor in spirit to those who believe are able to thank *the End Time Headlines* tell of us in the news that Southern Baptist change policy on speaking in tongues. Of course the Bible speak about speaking tongues according to Mark 16:17 (c), Acts 2:4, Acts 10:44-48, Acts 8:14-17, Acts 19:1-6
12. Blessed are the poor in spirit to those who believe that speaking in tongues is base upon the Bible, God's Spoken Word: Mark 16:17 (c), Acts 2:4, Acts 8:14-17, Acts 19:1-6, Acts 10:44-46, I Corinthians 14:1-19 verse 2, 4, 5, 6, 13, 14, 15, **18**, 21, 22, 23, 26, 27, 28, **33**. See *Isaiah 28:11-12, Genesis 11:1-9, Genesis 11:6-7, 9*

    a. Religion News Service (RNS)
    b. Christianity Today (CT)
    c. End Times Headlines (ETH)

Read Acts 2:4

Bible Scripture Readings:

1. Mark 16:17 (c)
2. Acts 2:4
3. Acts 2:41

Read Acts 2:1-47

Part DCLXX

Blessed Are The Poor In Spirit. Matthew 5:3

Blessed Means Happy

Poor means meek in spirit. Poor means humble in spirit. Poor means lowly in spirit. Poor means quiet in spirit. Read Matthew 5:3-12, Read also Mark 1:15

Jesus did not say "*rich*" in spirit. Jesus said "*poor*" in spirit.

1. Blessed are the poor in spirit to those who would read the contending of my writing call "The Holy Spirit Carried Pentecostal Spirit Baptism." Acts 2:1-4, Isaiah 28:11, Joel 2:28-32, Acts 2:16-21, Acts 1:8
2. Blessed are the poor in spirit to those who believe and read Genesis 11:1-9
3. Blessed are the poor in spirit to those who believe and read Isaiah 28:11-12
4. Blessed are the poor in spirit to those who believe and read Mark 16:17 (c)
5. Blessed are the poor in spirit to those who believe and read Acts 2:4
6. Blessed are the poor in spirit to those who believe and read Acts 10:44-46 verse 46
7. Blessed are the poor in spirit to those who believe and read Acts 19:1-6 verse 6
8. Blessed are the poor in spirit to those who believe and read I Corinthians 12:1-11 verse 10
9. Blessed are the poor in spirit to those who believe and read I Corinthians 14:5
10. Blessed are the poor in spirit to those who believe and read I Corinthians 14:18
11. Blessed are the poor in spirit to those who believe and read I Corinthians 14:21-22
12. Blessed are the poor in spirit to those who believe and read Revelation 7:9-17

Bible Scripture Readings:
Concerning Spirit Baptism—Acts 1:8 Genesis 11:7

1. Acts 2:4
2. Acts 10:46
3. Acts 19:6 Read Mark 16:17 (c)

Bible Scripture Readings:
Concerning Spirit Baptism—Acts 1:8 Mark 16:17 (c)

1. Psalm 51:11

2. Isaiah 63:10-11
3. Ephesians 4:30 Read II Peter 3:4

Bible Scripture Readings:
Concerning Spirit Baptism—Acts 1:8

1. Matthew 3:11 (b)
2. Mark 1:8
3. Luke 3:16 (b)

Read Acts 1:4-8
Bible Scripture Readings:
Concerning Spirit Baptism—Acts 1:8

1. John 1:33
2. Acts 1:5
3. Acts 11:16 (b)

Read Acts 1:4-8

"For Sinner's Prayer To Receive Salvation"

The Sinner's Prayer

Oh God, I am a sinner. I am sorry for my sins. I thank you that Jesus died for my sins. Please forgive all my sins. Come into my heart. I will live for you.

In Jesus' name I pray, Amen

Jesus says, "You Are Saved (Already)!!!"

Ephesians 2:8-9
Romans 10:9-13, 17
Acts 2:21, 4:12
John 3:6-7
II Corinthians 5:17
II Timothy 1:12-14
II Corinthians 6:2
Romans 8:1, 16
I John 1:9

God's Spirit say we are the children of God.

Be Blessed!!!
Evangelist John H. Manigo
I Corinthians 6:19-20

www.ingramcontent.com/pod-product-compliance
Lightning Source LLC
Chambersburg PA
CBHW080942120626
46546CB00010B/2811

* 9 7 8 1 9 6 4 4 9 4 2 7 2 *